History of the Norwegian Settlements:

*A translated and expanded version of the
1908 De Norske Settlementers Historie and the
1930 Den Siste Folkevandring Sagastubber fra Nybyggerlivet i Amerika*

Written by Hjalmar Rued Holand
Translated by Malcolm Rosholt and Helmer M. Blegen

• • • • •

*Chapter supplements, layout and graphic design,
32-page colored map insert and 3,800-name index
by Deb Nelson Gourley*

Edited by Jo Ann B. Winistorfer

Pre-production coordination by Lorna Anderson

Astri My Astri Publishing

History of the Norwegian Settlements: *A translated and expanded version of the 1908 De Norske Settlementers Historie and the 1930 Den Siste Folkevandring Sagastubber fra Nybyggerlivet i Amerika.* Copyright © 2006 by Deb Nelson Gourley, Astri My Astri Publishing. Printed in the United States of America. All rights reserved. No part of this book may be reproduced in any form or by any electronic or mechanical means including information storage and retrieval systems without permission in writing from the publisher, except by a reviewer, who may quote brief passages in a review.

Library of Congress Control Number: 2006902937

ISBN 0-9760541-1-6

Published and marketed by:
Astri My Astri Publishing
Deb Nelson Gourley
602 3rd Ave SW
Waukon, IA 52172 USA
Phone: 563-568-6229
Fax: 563-568-5377
deb@astrimyastri.com
http://www.astrimyastri.com

Printed by:
Anundsen Publishing Company, Decorah, Iowa

Cover design and colored section layout by Chris Shelton

First printing
2006
Made in Iowa. Made in USA.

FOREWORD

By Hjalmar Rued Holand

(From Halmar Rued Holand's book, *Norwegians in America: The Last Migration, 1930*)

In the course of less than a hundred years, so many Norwegians came to America that the combined numbers of those still alive and their descendants amount to millions.

This amazing mass movement of people from Norway to America will be studied with increasing interest as time separates us more and more from the events connected with it.

The most remarkable feature of this great popular migration is the enduring capability displayed by these Norwegian men and women in domesticating a wilderness in a strange hemisphere. There is no finer proof of the Norwegian people's viability than the way they—with very limited finances and absolutely no state aid—were able to transform a wilderness into a smiling garden and a temporary New Norway. In this experience and expenditure of energy, they found expression to the fullest extent for every human feeling and impulse that they possessed.

The history of their migration is a saga of distress and need, but not one of despair. It is a saga of toil without surrender and a saga of struggle without defeat. Their motivating force was not a lust for power to dominate others, nor was it the passionate pursuit of personal glory or revenge. It was, rather, the love they felt for family and kin, combined with a joy in peaceful pursuits, that moved and sustained these Norwegian pioneers.

Through all the vicissitudes of change there gleams, like the gentle glow of a sunset, a love for the old fatherland and the home community.

The purpose of the following account is an attempt to throw some light upon this migration and to preserve the memory of a few of the typical experiences encountered by the Norwegian pioneers as they strove to tame a wilderness.

CONTENTS

History of the Norwegian Settlements contains chapters from the following sources and page numbers coded as red and white:

• <u>Red</u> – *De Norske Settlementers Historie*, by Hjalmar Rued Holand, 1908, published by Trykt paa Forfatterens Forlag, Ephraim, Wisconsin (with corrections from 1912 reprint published by John Anderson Publishing Company, Chicago, Illinois), translated by Malcolm Rosholt

• <u>White</u> – *Den Siste Folkevandring Sagastubber fra Nybyggerlivet i Amerika*, by Hjalmar Rued Holand, 1930; *Norwegians in America: The Last Migration – Bits of Saga from Pioneer Life*, published by The Center for Western Studies Augustana College, Sioux Falls, South Dakota, 1978, translated by Helmer M. Blegen

Chapter 1 1–8
The Vinland Expeditions (Red 8–22)

Chapter 2 9–14
The Norwegian Pioneer (White 1–5)

Chapter 3 15–26
Cleng Peerson, Father of Norwegian-American Immigration (White 13–23)

Chapter 4 27–30
From New York to the West (Red 65–74)

Chapter 5 31–38
Fox River Settlement, northern Illinois (Red 84–94)

Chapter 6 39–44
Chicago, northeastern Illinois (Red 100–110)

Chapter 7 45–52
Muskego Settlement, Milwaukee County, southeastern Wisconsin (Red 111–122)

Chapter 8 53–56
Jefferson Prairie Settlement, Rock County, Wisconsin, and Long Prairie Settlement, Boone County, Illinois (Red 123–127)

Chapter 9 57–64
Rock Prairie (Luther Valley) Settlement, Rock County, Wisconsin (Red 128–141)

Chapter 10 65–74
Koshkonong Settlement, eastern Dane and western Jefferson Counties, Wisconsin (Red 142–157)

Chapter 11 75–78
Norway Grove Settlement, Dane County, Wisconsin, and Columbia County, Wisconsin (Red 158–165)

Chapter 12 79–84
Ashippun, Rock River, and Pine Lake Settlements, southeastern Wisconsin (Red 166–175)

Chapter 13 85–88
Wiota Settlement and the Lead Miners, Lafayette County, Wisconsin (Red 176–183)

Chapter 14 .... **89–94**
Blue Mounds Settlement (Dodgeville, Otter Creek and Castle Rock), Iowa, and Grant Counties, Wisconsin (Red 184–195)

Chapter 15 .... **95–96**
Winchester Settlement, Racine County, southeastern Wisconsin (Red 196–198)

Chapter 16 .... **97–102**
The Indian Land, western Waupaca and northeast Portage Counties, Wisconsin (Red 199–207)

Chapter 17 .... **103–106**
Mt. Morris Settlement, Waupaca County, Wisconsin (Red 208–214)

Chapter 18 .... **107–114**
Oldest Valdres Colony in America, Manitowoc County, Wisconsin (Red 215–228)

Chapter 19 .... **115–124**
Ephraim, Door County, northeastern Wisconsin (Red 229–249)

Chapter 20 .... **125–128**
Southern Door County (Sturgeon Bay, Hainesville and Clay Banks), Wisconsin (Red 250–255)

Chapter 21 .... **129–132**
Roch-a-Cree (Roche-a-Cri) Colony, Adams County, central Wisconsin (Red 256–260)

Chapter 22 .... **133–134**
Lemonweir Settlement, Juneau County, central Wisconsin (Red 261–264)

Chapter 23 .... **135–142**
Crawford and Vernon Counties, southwestern Wisconsin (Red 265–276)

Chapter 24 .... **143–146**
Rush River Settlement, between St. Croix and Pierce Counties, western Wisconsin (Red 277–283)

Chapter 25 .... **147–148**
Most heavily populated Norwegian area in U.S., western Wisconsin (Red 284–285)

Chapter 26 .... **149–150**
La Crosse County, western Wisconsin (Red 286–289)

Chapter 27 .... **151–152**
Black River Falls, Jackson County, western Wisconsin (Red 290–292)

Chapter 28 .... **153–156**
Trempealeau Valley and surroundings, Trempealeau County, western Wisconsin (Red 293–297)

Chapter 29 .... **157–160**
Lyster Colony in Buffalo County, western Wisconsin (Red 298–302)

Chapter 30 .... **161–164**
Chippewa Valley, northern Eau Claire and southern Chippewa Counties, western Wisconsin (Red 303–306)

Chapter 31 165–170
First Norwegians in Iowa and Minnesota (Red 320–329)

Chapter 32 171–176
Clayton and Allamakee Counties, northeastern Iowa (Red 330–336)

Chapter 33 177–192
Winneshiek County, northeastern Iowa (Red 337–357)

Chapter 34 193–224
Houston County and eastern Fillmore County, southeastern Minnesota (Red 358–378)

Chapter 35 225–226
Setesdal, western Fillmore County, southeastern Minnesota (Red 379–382)

Chapter 36 227–230
Bloomfield Settlement, Fillmore and Mower Counties, southeastern Minnesota (Red 383–386)

Chapter 37 231-238
Bear Creek Settlement, Mower County, southeastern Minnesota (Red 387–389)

Chapter 38 239-242
Little Turkey and Crane Creek Settlements, Chickasaw County, northeastern Iowa (Red 390–394)

Chapter 39 243-246
Clausen's Big Colony, Iowa and Minnesota border (Red 395–401)

Chapter 40 247-252
St. Ansgar and surroundings, Mitchell County, northern Iowa (Red 402–411)

Chapter 41 253-256
Six Mile Grove and Adams, Mower County, southern Minnesota (Red 412–417)

Chapter 42 257-262
Worth and Winnebago Counties, northern Iowa (Red 418–429)

Chapter 43 263-270
Freeborn and Waseca Counties, southern Minnesota (Red 430–441)

Chapter 44 271-272
Faribault County, southern Minnesota (Red 446–450)

Chapter 45 273-278
McGregor, Clayton County, northeastern Iowa (Red 451–457)

Chapter 46 279-284
Stavanger and Hordaland colony, Story, Hamilton and Hardin Counties, central Iowa (Red 458–467)

Chapter 47 285-286
Norway Settlement, Benton County, and Calamus Settlement, Clinton County, eastern Iowa (Red 468–469)

Chapter 48 287-290
Lykkensborg Village, Hennepin County, Minnesota (Red 470–476)

Chapter 49 291-294
St. Peter area and Nicollet County, Minnesota (Red 477–480)

Chapter 50 295-296
Christiania Settlement, Dakota, Scott and Rice Counties, Minnesota (Red 481–482)

Chapter 51 297-308
Big Goodhue County colony, Minnesota (Red 483–497)

Chapter 52 309-312
East and West St. Olaf colonies, Olmsted County, Minnesota (Red 498–501)

Chapter 53 313-320
Main community of Gudbrandsdøler in America, Brown and Watonwan Counties, southwestern Minnesota (Red 507–518)

Chapter 54 321-338
Jackson County and the 24 August 1862 Belmont Massacre, southwestern Minnesota (Red 519–521)

Chapter 55 339-340
Largest Norwegian Settlement in America, central Minnesota (Red 532–537)

Chapter 56 341-356
Norway Lake and surroundings, Kandiyohi County, central Minnesota (Red 538–565)

Chapter 57 357-368
The Indian war of 1862-65 (Red 566-583 and White 167–176)

Chapter 58 369-380
The first large prairie settlement (White 177–186)

Chapter 59 381-384
The grasshopper plague (White 187–190)

Chapter 60 385-392
The Land of a Thousand Lakes (White 191–196)

Chapter 61 393-396
When law and order came to Grant County, Minnesota (White 197–200)

Chapter 62 397-414
When Dakota was settled (White 201–214)

Chapter 63 415-422
The Red River Valley, western Minnesota (White 215–222)

DEDICATION

This book is dedicated to the hardy Norwegian immigrants who, despite hardships and peril, conquered the wilderness to create a new life in the American Midwest. An ocean away from their fatherland, they marched slowly but steadily onward, toward the setting sun—into Illinois, Wisconsin, Iowa, Minnesota, the Dakotas. They planted deep roots in the places they settled. Many generations later, their American descendants—outnumbering by far those in the Old Country with Norwegian roots—still proudly proclaim Norway as their country of origin.

PREFACE

History of the Norwegian Settlements is a combination of two books written by Hjalmar Rued Holand. In select chapters, Holand's material has been supplemented by information from historians and genealogists and/or from local, regional and church histories. These supplements and other items include:
• Chapter 1: Translation by Edna Rude
• Chapter 33: Supplement to Big Canoe, Winneshiek County, Iowa
• Chapter 34: Supplements to Houston and Fillmore counties, Minnesota
• Chapter 37: Supplement to Bear Creek, Mower County, Minnesota
• Chapter 54: Supplement to Jackson County, Minnesota
• Chapter 60: Supplement to Pope County, Minnesota
• 32-page full-color map section

Our purpose in publishing this book in English is to make Holand's research on Norwegian settlements in America, previously printed in Dano-Norwegian Gothic text, available to modern-day historians, genealogists, students of Norwegian studies in both Norway and America, and descendants of the thousands of immigrants listed in the book.

Translating and editing notes

For the most part, this is not a word-for-word translation. As editor Evelyn Ostraat Wierenga wrote in Blegen's translation, *Norwegians in America: The Last Migration*: "It was necessary in some instances to be primarily concerned with the concept of Holand's meaning as he related anecdotes and incidents from pioneer life."

In some cases, fluent readers of both Norwegian and English have pointed out errors in Rosholt's translation. We have tried to correct these instances during the editing process.

Readability was a big consideration in editing. While Rosholt's translation is basically as you find it in the text of this book, in some cases, long paragraphs have been broken up, word order transformed, repetitive text omitted, and some items deleted or rearranged where necessary. In all such instances, the goal was to clarify Holand's original message without confusing the reader.

Spelling inconsistencies, name changes

In editing, lots of time was spent going through the 1912 book, name by name, to restore the original Norwegian letters "æ," "ø" and "å" (or "aa") as per Holand's original text. These letters were omitted from the original translation, as Rosholt used a typewriter that lacked Norwegian letter keys. Holand and Rosholt both used "aa" for "å," which has been left intact.

Although we used Holand's third edition (1912) as our guide, Holand himself misspelled names of the immigrants. Examples: Hans Vædle in one spot, Hans Vælde in all other instances; Guttorm Gutterson (should have been Guttorm Guttormson, according to church records); Ole Næs in one place, Ole Næss in others. A name ending in *-son* in one paragraph might be listed as ending in *-sen* in the next, even though referring to the same person. Where a name was obviously misspelled (as in Vaedle and Naes), we changed it to the most frequently used spelling. When one of our reader-proofers and/or historians pointed out an incorrect spelling of a name, we corrected it. In instances where the name of an individual was spelled both as *-son* and *-sen*, we left it as is, not knowing which version was correct. Anyone searching for a *-son* or *-sen* name should be able to find it in the book under one or the other spelling in the index.

Individuals and families may have used a variety of surnames between the years they first came to this country and the date (around 1900) that a new U.S. law required everyone to adopt a standardized surname. Up to that time, many Norwegian immigrants Anglicized their names, dropped their farm or patronymic names, and/or continued to switch surnames every generation, as they did in the Old Country. It was not uncommon that members of one family may have gone by different surnames from that of other family members!

At the time the Norwegians immigrated to the United States, Norway used the *patronymic naming system*. This system involved three names: *the given name* (such as Ole or Knut), the *surname* (using the patronymic name, based on the father's first name—such as Olson or Larsdatter, meaning "son of Ole" or "daughter of Lars"), and *the farm name*. The farm name was really an "address name," listing the person's residence (farm) in Norway. Example: Lars Svensen Rud would mean Lars, son of Sven, living on a farm called Rud. The surname of Lars's children would then be Larson or Larsdatter.

Thus, there were lots of variations in the way one Norwegian immigrant's name might have been spelled over a span of time. For research purposes, every effort has been made to refer to the Norwegian immigrants by their original name, as well as names they adopted in America (if known).

We have also edited Norwegian place names to conform to those listed in Holand's 1912 book. However, if old place names were given, we added the most recent name to aid researchers in finding the location in modern Norway. Examples: Bratsberg *amt* changed to Telemark *fylke*; Tinn, Norway, change to Tinn in Telemark *fylke*; modern *kommune* name Seljord added after old name Siljord. At the time of settlement covered in the book, each district in Norway was called an *amt* rather than the modern Norwegian term *fylke*. The names of these districts underwent a change in 1918 (see colored map section for pre- and post-1918 *amt* and *fylke* names).

Index considerations

At the end of this book, you'll find a 3,800-count, first-name index. We chose to use a first-name index, since surnames included a mixture of patronymic (names ending in *-son* or *-datter*) and farm names (referring to places of origin in Norway). Rather than include an overwhelming list of all such names, we chose instead to include them on ***http://www.astrimyastri.com***, searchable by any portion of a person's name found in this book.

Part of the editing involved adapting the text so it could be indexed via computer. Thus, names such as "Herbrand and Haakon Pederson" have been expanded to include the whole name of each person: "Herbrand Pederson" and "Haakon Pederson." For indexing purposes, we had to omit hyphens within names as well as quotes surrounding names. Example: "Iver-Breaker," indexed as Iver Breaker.

The Norwegian letters "æ," "ø" and "å" (or "aa") are normally found at the end of Norwegian alphabetical listings. However, our computer-generated index lists "aa" and "æ" with "a" and "ø" with "o."

Illustrations and maps

Lithographs used in the book come from the following sources:

- *Hjem vi Forlod og de Hjem vi Fandt* (1892); one of the books Hjalmar Holand sold to Norwegian-American settlers in the Upper Midwest during his travels
- *Solskin i Hjemmet: Ung og Gammel* (1890)
- Three individual lithographs from a private collection

The cover illustration and 12 other watercolors sprinkled throughout the book are the work of artist Elsie Hotvedt Thorson. They appeared originally in Blegen's translation, *Norwegians in America: The Last Migration*.

To aid in locating early places of settlement, we have added antique maps showing the old U.S. locations or parishes, including once-thriving towns that are now sleepy villages or ghost towns. Also included in this book is a 32-page color section of Norway maps showing major administrative *fylker* (districts) and *kommuner* (municipalities).

Some editorial issues

Holand has at times been criticized for basing his research on 13 years of interviews with hundreds of first-generation settlers versus only on primary sources, original documents and materials. Rosholt writes, "If Holand is not entirely accurate in every respect, he probably comes as close to the truth as possible without a major investigation to retrace his steps and research related church records, town tax rolls, census returns, etc." However, records at the time the first settlers arrived—often moving into uninhabited territories or wilderness—were often scarce to nonexistent.

The reader should keep in mind that any account such as this is a secondary rather than a primary source. Thus, information found here should be verified with original and other records.

Some Norwegian emigrants had unpleasant encounters with Native Americans whose former lands they settled. Their attitudes and reactions are reflected in Holand's writings. This, too, is a part of the history and thus has been left in the text, largely unedited. Included in some cases are derogatory references to Native Americans. The reader needs to understand the times covered in Holand's books, and that this in no way represents the attitude of the contributors to this book in 2006. In other instances, the Indians are treated sympathetically by Holand, especially when it comes to the taking of their land and their treatment regarding broken treaties, etc.

An especially controversial portion of this book (found in Chapter 1) deals with the Kensington Rune Stone. Holand devoted more than 50 years of his life to exploring and writing about the Viking explorations of America. Although scholars on both sides of the Atlantic have debated the stone's authenticity for years, we chose to leave this section of the book intact. We offer no opinion about the stone's genuineness, other than to invite readers to keep an open mind and to explore the issue on their own.

• • • • •

It has been a privilege to prepare this long-awaited English translation and to contribute to what we trust will be an invaluable resource for anyone seeking information on Norwegian settlement in America in the future. Through his books, Holand has made a major contribution to recording Norwegian immigration and early Norwegian-American heritage and culture. We hope you enjoy this saga of these early pioneers.

—Deb Nelson Gourley, *author and publisher*
—Jo Ann B. Winistorfer, *editor*

1
The Vinland Expeditions
(Source: De Norske Settlementers Historie, by Hjalmar Rued Holand, translated by Edna Rude, 1908, pp. 8–22)

The ordinary view of America's discovery by Norwegians around the year 1000 is simply that Leif Erikson, a Norse explorer from Iceland, was the hero of an enormously lucky hit. They believe he found a portion of the world that was of no value for colonizing and thus was soon forgotten by all people. Such opinions show only a superficial acquaintance with historical documents.

Closer inspection will show that Norwegians not only discovered America but also made persistent attempts to colonize it, and for several hundred years made it the goal of numerous expeditions.

In these colonization attempts, the Norse discoverers placed a much higher view of America's importance than did the later Spaniards. Long after Columbus had discovered America, this was considered by the Spanish to be a fictional place where no one would think of settling. For them it was an Eldorado, where men could grab as much gold as possible and sail back to Castile.

The Norsemen, however, did not see it with thieves' eyes. They saw it as a place rich with forests and a good climate, with luscious wine grapes that grew wild—an ideal place to raise grain. That was their reason for beginning at once to colonize.

It must have been the intent of the first Vinland visitor, Leif Erikson, to return. In 1003, when Torfinn Karlsevne (a fellow Icelander and sea captain) wanted to journey to Vinland, Leif was willing to loan—not sell—the houses he had built on his first visit seven years earlier.

There is no doubt Torfinn Karlsevne intended to settle in Vinland. The sagas clearly explain, "He brought all kinds of cattle, as it was his intention to settle there." He also had many people along—about 160 persons, including women and children.

Torfinn Karlsevne thus had the honor of being America's first colonist. However, the land at that time was already populated, and after struggling for three years with the less-than-friendly natives, America's first pioneer and his company left.

Sagas mention Vinland voyages

The books *Hauksbok* and *Flatøybok* contain bits of sagas about these early-America travelers, but they mostly tell about Erik the Red's (Leif's father) family lines and are certainly not a history of all the expeditions to America.

Most of the expeditions mentioned in the sagas were successful. Returning to Greenland with valuable freight of hides and timber, they were recorded as "honorable and profitable journeys."

It is unfathomable to assume that the Norse Greenlanders, ambitious and eager for travel while existing in the cramped conditions of Greenland and Iceland, would not attempt to visit this rich land, generally called Vinland the Good. In fact, Vinland is mentioned and discussed in the sagas more often than is Greenland.

Papal letters documented events

We know from other sources that Greenland in the 14th century was a well-built colony with around 1,000 families, 15 churches and its own bishop. Yet the sagas do not mention that. They tell only about the earliest discovery and colonizing of Greenland.

Neither do they reveal anything about the later tragic history of Greenland. In 1409, Greenland was attacked by wild men from the shores of America who ruined and burned the villages, making slaves of the Norse farmers. Only nine of the churches far inland survived.

Thirty years later, the Greenlanders were able to return and build again what they could of their churches. They asked Pope Nicholas V to send them a bishop and priests to take care of their souls. The pope took much interest in these people and ordered the bishops in Iceland to restore the religion in Greenland. For unknown reasons, however, this was not carried out.

Another 40 years went by. The Greenlanders renewed their request to Pope Innocent VIII for help. Their condition was most pitiful. Left to themselves nearly 100 years without bishops or priests, they had mostly forgotten their faith. The only visible reminder they had for keeping their faith was the place where their last priest had consecrated the sacrament of the altar. This was exhibited once a year, and the people gathered here to send up their prayers for help.

Pope Alexander VI sympathized with the people and sent a Benedictine, Matthias, to be their bishop—in the Old Norwegian Diocese of Greenland, on the American side of the Atlantic. It is recorded that he was full of zeal for his work of bringing the message of salvation to a neglected people.

This happened in that remarkable year of our Lord that amazed the whole world with the discovery of America by Christopher Columbus: 1492. *[This information comes from the Papal Letters and is cited in The Northmen, Columbus and Cabot. –Rude]*

As mentioned, these interesting events are not to be found in the sagas and would be quite forgotten had they not been recorded in the Papal Letters of their time. Consequently, even though the sagas do not record any continued connection with America, this does not mean it didn't exist.

Other early records add credibility

We believe that connection can be proven. We shall not at this time refer to the stone at Dighton, Massachusetts, or the stone tower at Newport, Rhode Island, which was standing when the first settlers arrived there. There are enough other statements about America in sagas and other places showing that America was a place whose existence was well known.

The following list shows the most important references to America:

• The earliest known mention of America is not in the Icelandic literature. It is to be found on the Hønen stone in Ringerike, Norway. The historian Sophus Bugge (Norwegian philologist from Laurvik, Norway, 1833-1907) believed it was inscribed circa 1050. This (runic) inscription was read in 1904 and translated thus: "They came out (in the ocean) and on the ice over a great distance toward Vinland. They needed food and clothes. Evil can take away the joy, so man dies early."

• The next mention of Vinland is in German literature, circa 1070. Master Adam from Bremen visited the Danish palace to gather information about the Nordic lands, about which he planned to write a book. He did write the book and called it Descripteo Insularum Aquilania *[Description of the Islands in the Oceans –Rude]*.

After Adam had described the ocean around Norway and Iceland, he wrote: "Besides, he (the informer) mentioned another land, which had been discovered by many, in this ocean. It is called Vinland because vines containing very good grapes grow there by themselves. Also, *korn* (grain) grows in abundance without being planted."

• In Icelandic literature, Vinland is mentioned for the first time when described by Priest Ari the Learned (1067-1148) in *The Book of the Icelanders*, which he wrote circa 1134.

In Chapter 6, Ari writes: "The land which is called Greenland was discovered and built from Iceland. Erik the Red, who first went there from here, found both houses, remains of boats and stone tools and from this we have to believe the same kind of people had traveled here as those who lived in Vinland, and which the Greenlanders called Skrælings (Indians)."

• In *Landnammabok*, a second book by Ari the Priest, he tells about another man named Ari. Chapter 22, part 2, reads: "He was driven off his course to the 'White Man Land,' which some called Greater Island. It lies west in the ocean, near Vinland the Good."

• Abbott Nikolaus from Tingeyre was a well-traveled man who had journeyed widely in other lands. He died in 1159. Among his records we find: "…south of Greenland is Helluland, then Markland, and from there it is not far to Vinland the Good, which some say reaches clear from Africa. And if that is true, there is open ocean between Vinland and Markland."

• *Krisnisaga* deals with the coming of Christianity to Iceland, beginning with Styrmer the Learned, who died in 1245. It says: "That summer when King Olaf left the country going south to Wendland, he sent Leif Erikson to Greenland to bring the true faith to them. There Leif found Vinland the Good; he also found some people on a wreck in the ocean, and after that he was called 'Leif the Lucky.' "

• In *Konungabok (Kings' book)*, which was likely written early in the 11th century, we find: "…Leif sailed that summer to Greenland. He found people on a (ship's) wreck in the ocean and rescued them. Then (on that journey) he also found Vinland the Good, and came that fall to Greenland. He brought along a priest and other spiritual teachers, and they all went to Brattahlid to stay with his father, Erik the Red. After that time he was called 'Leif the Lucky.' "

But his father (being a pagan) said the one weighed against the other (or, six of one and half-dozen of the other); that Leif had "rescued the ship's crew but brought into Greenland a swindler," meaning the priest!

• The oldest records from Skalholt (Iceland), which were written circa 1362, adds this from 1347: "Then came also from Greenland a ship, smaller than the Icelandic traders. It came to outer Strømfjord, and had no anchor. Seventeen men were on board. They had aimed toward Markland, but were driven here (Iceland) by storms.

• *Flatøybok* from 1347 says: "A ship from Greenland came here (to Iceland), which had sailed for Markland. They had 18 men on board."

• Arthur M. Reeves (author of *The Norse Discovery of America*, 1906) adds this to the above annals: "Those travelers were obviously aiming for their home in Iceland directly from Markland. If they had not been driven off course and landed in Greenland, their journey would not have been recorded in Icelandic annals. All knowledge of this group would have disappeared as completely as the colony in Markland to which they belonged!"

• Finally, we have reference to another important Vinland expedition in which Greenland's bishop participated. In an annual record, written from 1280-1394, we find under Anno 1121: "Erik Upsi, Greenland's bishop, went to look for Vinland."

That same information, under the same title, is given in four other annuals. Catholic teachers believed the bishop went to live among his congregation in Vinland so he could evangelize the Skrælings.

The above information proves that those who insist Vinland was forgotten were (and are) entirely wrong. True, Icelandic literature (which is preserved to our time) is only a small part of what was originally recorded. In fact, we find America mentioned in 16 different sagas and documents, a basis for our historical understanding.

Three of the documents mentioned specify new and varied Vinland expeditions (during the years 1050, 1127 and 1347). All these documents tell us that Vinland was as well known a place as Ireland, Iceland and Greenland.

Vinland's existence was once common knowledge

These sober records of Vinland have their greatest value in what is NOT said. If the writers had believed their references to Vinland and its inhabitants would not be understood by their readers, they would certainly not have used them, as they did, to throw further light on Greenland and other lands.

In the geographical notes, one land does not get any more attention that another. The historical notes mention Leif's discovery of Vinland in the same way they tell about his rescue of a ship's sailors.

Since it is known that for several hundred years the existence and location of Vinland the Good were common knowledge, it is easy to see why the Norsemen visited and colonized it. They were much too daring and adventurous to be content with only hearing about the fabled descriptions of a rich, pleasant and wonderful land.

More evidence chiseled on Kensington Rune Stone

To complete the list of proofs that Norsemen visited America for several hundred years, we now turn to the last known of Vinland expeditions, the one which is the most interesting. Here we come to one of America's first historical documents—although this document is neither in sagas nor in Europe, but etched as runes on a stone in America.

In August 1898, a rune stone was found three miles northeast of Kensington, Minnesota, in a hilly but beautiful meadow. It lay under the root of a large aspen tree on a knoll encircled by bogs that had earlier been full of water.

Naturally, this find created a stir of attention. Both learned and unlearned people discussed the authenticity of it. Due partly to incorrect copying of the runes and partly to shallow judgments, the stone was cast aside as a clumsy example of "American humbug"—a hoax.

Angry over being fooled by a lying stone, its owner placed it in front of his granary as a doorstep—a good place for straightening nails and a backdrop for pounding in harness nails.

This stone is now (1908) owned by this book's author (Holand). The stone is granite, 28 inches tall, 16 inches wide and 6 inches thick. It is covered on two sides with nicely carved runes.

Rune Stone photos courtesy of *The Kensington Rune Stone: Compelling New Evidence*, **by Richard Nielsen and Scott F. Wolter, 2006.**

Translated into our modern speech, it reads: "8 Goths and 22 Norsemen on journey of discovery from Vinland westward. We had camp by 2 skerries one day's journey from this stone. We were out and fished. One day after we came home we found 10 men red with blood and dead. Ave Maria. Deliver us from evil."

The runes on the side read: "We have 10 men by the sea to look after our ship 14 (or 24) days' journey from this island. Anno 1362."

This author has in another article shown how clearly the language in this runic writing agrees or harmonizes with the Danish or Gothic dialects of the 14th century and brings out a number of arguments in favor of the stone's authenticity.

- *Location where the stone was found.* The stone was found under an aspen whose rings were counted, the tree proving to be at least 25 years old. The stone was squeezed between the two largest of the tree's roots.

Due to many years of growing (wrapped around the stone), the roots were entirely flat on the inside. A cross-section showed the roots grown to a "D" shape. One of those roots was preserved for many years but is now rotted. The names of at least 12 reliable men are available who insist the stone had

been there at least as long as the tree.

The stone was found in 1898, and the tree age, 25, brings us back to 1873. At that time, this area was in its earliest stages of pioneering. The first white man came into Douglas County (where the town of Kensington is located) in 1865, and there were only a few people here. The men who did live in the immediate area were all well known to each other, and not a single one of them had any idea how to carve runes nor any inclination to learn it.

The Swede on whose land the stone was found (who without any grounds was accused of "making the stone") had not arrived at the settlement until 1891 and in America in 1881.

If the stone is "false" (since it could not possibly have been carved on its location), it must have been brought here by strangers. But that was also not possible: The location was—at that time and for many years later—25 miles from the nearest railroad station and far from any road. That the stone (which is so heavy only a super-strong man might lift it, let alone carry it) may have been brought in through a large forest and across a wet bog is clearly unthinkable.

• *Weathered condition of the runes.* Further proof of the stone's great age is the weathered condition of its surface. The deep marks of the runes show clearly how the strong tooth of time has gnawed and rounded them so they are similar to the original surface.

With a strong magnifying glass, we can see how the deep marks of the carving show the same exposure as on the higher face of the stone, a slow and gradual decay. It would have been impossible for an imposter to achieve the same results by such means as rubbing or filing, which would be seen under a magnifying glass.

Neither could such have taken place over a few years. When the stone was found 10 years ago (from the date of this writing, 1908), some of the runes on the stone's edge were scraped by a sharp tool. These runes, after 10 years of exposure to the ground, show clearly the fresh marks of change.

• *The length of the inscription.* Had the stone been a fake, it would have been natural for its carver to make a brief sketch, as, for example: "Thor carved these runes." He would have realized that each little cut and each word left him in a position of being criticized. A brief inscription would have been as good a proof of the Norsemen's circumstances as a lengthy one, and would have saved him much intense labor and many headaches.

Yet the rune-cutter did not think of that. He was obviously an experienced rune master who had a lengthy report to give. Not only was the whole front of

the stone bedecked with small, graceful runes, but the carver turned the stone and cut further along its edge—62 words in all, one of the longest runic inscriptions. Its beauty has not been surpassed by anyone.

• *New date in runic literature, new runes.* On the Kensington stone, we find runes that differ from the prevailing runes of the 11th century but closely resemble those of the 13th century *[see the runic-written Laws of Skaane (from southern Sweden)]*.

Copies of the runes in Swedish law were not available in America until the last 10 to 15 years. An American rune writer before those years must therefore have used models from thin air, which is, of course, impossible.

While there is a close relationship between the Kensington Rune Stone and Swedish law, the writers were entirely different. In 1904, historian Sophus Bugge sent out his interpretation of the Hønen stone from Ringerike (just north of Oslo), and here we find the same model with only one insignificant difference.

As mentioned before, a Swede did the carving on our Kensington Rune Stone. Had he been one of the 22 Norsemen (as the first line of the carving shows), he would NOT have placed "8 Goths" first. A Norseman would also have used the common word "Svear" rather than the local designation "Goths." He would also have used "stein" and "monnum" instead of "sten" and "man." In the same way, the runes (on the Kensington Rune Stone) approach complete accord with those in Swedish law.

The Kensington Rune Stone is one of the most interesting and meaningful in all of runic literature. Not only is it the only (known) rune stone in America and one of our longest runic inscriptions, but it is from a period that is quite bare of inscriptions and throws new light on runic development. It is also one of the oldest documents in America.

Aiming a searchlight into the heretofore-unenlightened period of our country's history, it also adds a new chapter to the history of Vinland expeditions. And finally, it is of great interest in itself, as it tells of great plans, begun in courage and ending in tragedy.

It has been said that it is quite unbelievable how 30 men could make their way through a land populated by warring tribes. To that we can answer that it is more unbelievable how the Spaniard De Vaca, a couple of hundred years later and alone, could make his way through all of America from Florida to California, surrounded and pursued by vengeful Indians.

Near Elbow Lake, Minnesota, about 35 miles northwest of where the Kensington Rune Stone was discovered, another rune stone was also found that could possibly throw further light on these Norse travelers. It is clearly obvious that this stone, too (part of a larger stone lying just below the ground's surface), was there when the first white pioneers settled there. This stone has a somewhat lengthy message cut in a circular pattern (like a clock face), but as it is extremely weathered, it has not been possible to read the runes.

A few years ago, about four miles from this stone (on the old shoreline of Lake Agassiz, a large lake that many centuries ago filled the Red River Valley and surrounding area), someone found a small piece of petrified wood from a fir tree. The wood clearly showed the marks of three iron spikes. The Indians did not use iron, so this is more evidence, besides the rune stone, that tells of our Norsemen being in the immediate area.

Although it is merely a guess, it is easy to surmise this piece of wood as part of the boat used by our brave relatives 500 or so years ago. And while they were out fishing on Minnesota's lakes, their companions on the shore were attacked by a large group and fought in vain for their lives.

The above account, in which we

have tried to gather all the documents and references to the Vinland expeditions in one article, should be sufficient to ascertain that the Norsemen's discovery of America was not some disconnected fairy tale without results.

Instead, it introduced a connection that resulted in the colonizing of America that did not stop until around the time the Black Plague decimated Norway and Iceland. Rampaging Eskimos, meanwhile, eradicated Greenland, of its set-tlers. These three lands were so weakened that they were in no condition to be occupied with colonization.

[The actual date of the Black Plague that decimated Norway occurred during the years 1349 and 1350—12 or 13 years before the rune stone expedition. This chapter was written prior to Holand's extensive research and his more than 50 years of study to prove the authenticity of the Kensington Rune Stone. –Rude]

Vikingskibet

2
The Norwegian Pioneer

(Source: Den Siste Folkevandring Sagastubber fra Nybyggerlivet i Amerika, by Hjalmar Rued Holand, 1930; Norwegians in America: The Last Migration, by Hjalmar Rued Holand, translated by Helmer M. Blegen, 1978, pp. 1–5)

A thousand years ago, there took place a great migration out from Norway. In the course of only one human generation, more than 100,000 streamed out of the country and settled on all the islands of the western sea. They created a new population in Normandy and a new nation in Iceland.

This migration has always been interesting to historians, primarily perhaps because the descendants of these emigrants gave to the world a magnificent literature.

There is a general impression that Norwegian migration to America did not begin until 1825. This is not correct. Of course, the Sloopers, who came over on the sail ship *Restauration* in 1825, played an important part in this mass movement of people, but if we forget the Norwegian emigration that took place long before 1825, we leave out some of the most interesting events of the history of our immigration.

The Norsemen have always been a people on the move. They founded enduring colonies in England, Ireland, Russia, France, Spain and Italy. In the narrow valleys of Norway, they could not find sufficient outlet for their dynamic vitality and their indomitable love of battle. The result was that they were compelled to seek expression by venturing far out from the confines of their valleys to remote lands. They knew that they would encounter hardships, struggle and strife. This did not deter them. Perhaps it attracted them.

This was true of America, too. Norway sent a greater number of farmers to America than any other country in proportion to its own population, but this is not all: They were also the first to cultivate the soil of the United States. Erik Torvaldson, who was the leader of a large company of emigrants from Iceland to Greenland in 986, is famous as one of the world's great explorers, and he was also the first of America's colonizers. Greenland is certainly as much a part of America as the islands of the West Indies.

Never has a pioneer project been undertaken under less propitious circumstances. In a frigid, barren, treeless land, where many of the necessities of life were absolutely lacking, these Norsemen were able to create for themselves an independent society that endured for more than 400 years. This is a brilliant example of the rare talent possessed by the Norsemen that enabled them to overcome and control the most inhospitable of environments.

Not long after Greenland was settled, we find the Norsemen as pioneers on the mainland of America. Leif Erikson erected the first pioneer cabin in Vinland about the year 1000. Apparently, he planned to make this his permanent residence, for he always refused to sell it to subsequent Vinland voyagers who wanted to buy it—although he was quite willing to grant them the privilege of using it. His duties in Greenland, however, kept him from ever returning to Vinland the Good.

On the other hand, we have accounts of hundreds of others who, under the leadership of Thorfin Karlsevni and other commanders, went to Vinland to establish residence there.

What were their feelings as they tore themselves loose from their old homes? What were their trials and experiences in the new lands?

We know that they quickly rose to positions of power and authority and became rulers, even in long-inhabited countries such as Ireland and France. But we know almost nothing about their experiences as pioneers during the periods of transition.

Unprecedented migration

In our own day, we, too, have witnessed a similar great migration. It took place in the same short space of time: one human generation. It began to pick up speed in 1836, but did not assume any sizable proportions until after the Civil War. Then every section of Norway saw a mighty emigration that was greater than any previous movement of people out of such a small country.

Every summer a steady procession of sailing vessels crossed the ocean with a full load of emigrants. Often, there were several sailings in the same week. Later, the big steamships carried thousands of emigrants across the Atlantic every week.

A continuous movement across the ocean of Norwegians, Germans, Irish and other nationalities, who arrived daily by the thousands, made a steady stream through the narrow gates of New York's Castle Gardens (and, beginning in 1892, Ellis Island), where they were inspected, registered and then allowed to go on to their destinations.

The following table shows how many Norwegians arrived during five successive decades:

From 1866 to 1875	119,545
1876 to 1885	144,368
1886 to 1895	141,462
1896 to 1905	130,809
1906 to 1915	134,967

(The figures for 1906-15 do not include the Norwegian immigrants to Canada.)

During this period of 50 years, around 700,000 Norwegians came to the United States of America. If, at any time in all of Norway's history, an equal number of the nation's population had been terminated by war or by pestilence, the historians would surely have had much to say about such a catastrophe; but strange as it may seem, the older Norwegian historians have passed over this greatest of popular migrations with barely a mention. This peculiar silence may perhaps be explained by the fact that these historians were too contemporary with the events to see them in the proper perspective. However, this would indicate a woeful lack of acuity on their part that would be difficult to accept.

A more reasonable theory may be that, in their great contempt for those who left their fatherland, they superciliously preferred to kill the saga of the emigrants with silence. For a long time, there were many who looked upon emigration as one form of treason. There is, of course, no more treachery involved in leaving one's fatherland than there is in abandoning the beloved house in which one was born in order to seek a new home elsewhere.

When the farms have been divided and subdivided among several heirs too many times, the result will eventually become poverty for all concerned. Then it would be advantageous if some of them were to leave. It would benefit not only the one who departs, but also those who remain.

The poet may very well utter the sigh:
*"Would that I would own
And be master over a piece of this earth,
Were it no larger than a lot extending
Fifty feet from a fjord!"*

But any man forced to wrest a living from such a tiny lot would be doomed to an existence so limited and so wretched that his only way to avoid despair would be to build for himself castles in the air and in the New Jerusalem. A country must have an outlet for its superfluous population if it is to survive.

It is, therefore, not cowardice and treason to abandon a hopeless position devoid of any promise. It is, rather, a courageous and praiseworthy action. That is how we look upon the expeditions and migrations of the Vikings. Our historians are proud to call our attention to their initiative and enterprise, to the great men they produced, and to the great influence they exerted on the west-European history.

The great migration to America is still too recent for us to point out significant cultural results and great men. But the Norwegians certainly do not occupy positions of inferiority as the nation's hewers of wood and drawers of water. Quite the contrary.

Even in the political life of our country, where competition is so very keen, the Norwegian-Americans have, in proportion to their number, an inordinate number of creditable representatives. It required just as much ability, boldness and tenacity of purpose for a Knute Nelson, a Shipstead or a Norbeck to achieve a seat in the U.S. Senate as it did for an Olav Hvite or Sigtryg Jarl to rise to the positions of power they attained in Old Norway.

It is not, however, in the number of prominent men that the Norwegian immigrants in America have made their most important contribution. What is especially praiseworthy among them is their energetic industriousness. A traveler who has his eyes open can usually tell when he enters a Norwegian settlement by the high quality of the farm buildings and the manner in which the farms are operated.

Another noteworthy characteristic is their rugged honesty. Even though one can find an occasional Norwegian lawbreaker in an American penal institution, it is amazingly rare. Percentagewise, there are fewer Norwegians in American prisons than any other nationality.

Finally, the Norwegians are characterized by a tolerant consideration in their social relationships. When a Norwegian-American, especially one of the older generation, requests a service or expresses hospitality, he does it with a courtesy and decorum that calls to mind the communication of saga-day chieftains when they met. This quiet dignity makes it easy and peaceful to associate with them. *[It is necessary to interject here, however, that this toleration is not sufficiently broad to include their discussions on matters of politics or religion. –Blegen.]* These qualities make the best soil to yield a future culture, sure to arise.

Transforming the wilderness

In the earlier migrations, the sword was a determining factor. Vast hordes of alien peoples penetrated into new environments and drove out the inhabitants by force. This is how the Israelites took over Canaan, and this is how the Nordic hordes treated the Celts, the Franks and the Romans.

But this last migration was quite different. These modern invaders had exchanged their battle-axes for plowshares and lumberjack axes. They were not out to assault humans, but to conquer nature.

It was as if we were transported back to remotest antiquity, when man heard the first divine command to replenish the earth and subdue it. The greatest contribution the Norwegians have made to America is their obedience to this ancient command.

All great projects need workers of tested ability and tenacity of purpose, and these were precisely the qualities possessed by the Norwegian pioneers who first broke the prairie sod. They arrived early enough to have a free choice among the many regions of our vast land. They chose for themselves the best, the fertile area of the north central district. They transformed it to become the breadbasket of America, and they were (among) the leading components of the populations that added this province to the nation.

It is impossible to evaluate the huge expanse that the Norwegian pioneer's plow has domesticated. Here are some figures (from 1908):

• Wisconsin has approximately 35,000 Norwegian farmers, each owning an average of 100 acres—a total of 3,500,000 acres in the hands of Norwegians.

• On the billowing plains of Iowa, about 16,000 Norwegian farmers reside, owning an average of 140 acres each—totaling 2,240,000 acres.

• In Minnesota, 60,000 Norwegian farmers each own an average of 160 acres. This amounts to 9,600,000 acres.

• On the prairies of North and South Dakota live about 30,000 Norwegians, each owning, on the average, 240 acres—7,200,000 acres in all.

Figures from Canada are not available, but it may be safely assumed that there, together with Illinois, Nebraska and other states, the Norwegians own at least 10 million acres. All this amounts to a total of 32,540,000 acres.

Assuming that perhaps one-third of this land consists of forests, swamps or other uncultivated land, there still remains approximately 22,000,000 acres of land that have been cleared, cultivated and built up by Norwegians in America.

As a comparison, it may be stated that in all of Norway there are only 2,200,000 acres of land under cultivation. This means that the Norwegian pioneers in America have acquired possession of about 10 times as much cultivated land as there exists in the entire nation of Norway. What an eloquent proof of industry and perseverance these statistics reveal!

With indomitable will and energy, the pioneer set about to clear this land and subdue it by attacking the primeval forest and the virgin prairie with axe and plow. He struggled and strove with stumps and stones, he contended with the tough turf and sod, and he defied all of nature's harshest whims.

He had very few means for construction, and his tools of the trade were primitive or nonexistent. But he built a cabin of logs or a hut with the sod of the prairie, and with milk from his cow and the grain from his soil, he made a plain but nourishing food supply. Where shoes and clothing could not be bought, he made his own out of birch bark, skins and hides.

Norse among first frontiersmen

The Norwegians were usually among the first to venture out on trackless expanses of the West, and it was from their hearths that the first columns of smoke rose skyward and waved like a banner of triumphant victory over the wilderness.

Norwegians plowed the first furrows in the virgin Western plains. They built the first churches and schoolhouses. They left to others the crowded security of cities, and they allowed those who so desired to be content with the restraints of factories. They preferred to go out—out in the wide-open wilderness, where they could create for themselves a home upon the fertile soil. To this they felt themselves drawn. They were not afraid to confront Nature in all her power upon the prairie and in the deep woods:

"Break out a clearing in darkest of forests!
Room for a cabin and some loam for the plow.
Hew away all that is gloomy, depressing;
Hew out a hall for the youthful and fair.
Build your own home where before was bare mountain,
Build it yourself! Build it yourself!"

All honor to the old pioneer! By his courage and labor, the desert was transformed into a garden that now lies fertile and fair as the Promised Land. Now the Norwegian settlements extend from horizon to horizon. Norwegian speech is heard in society and in church. Here the inherited Norwegian characteristics flourish in propitious circumstance.

The thunder of heavy freight trains breaks the night's silence, carrying his produce to a hungry world. By night and day, mighty mills keep grinding his grain to furnish bread for a million mouths. Thousands of busy cities with noisy factories have arisen to process the fruits of his labor. His work, like a tiny, planted seed, has resulted in the growth of so tall a tree that it can now shelter hosts of humans in its shade. His struggles are now over; having become old, tired and sated with years, he has gone to rest in an American grave.

To his sons and daughters, he bequeathed a fine heritage of uprightness, perseverance and material welfare. They will nurture this inheritance. Some day it will flourish and bear fruit that will bring honor to him as well as to his fatherland over the sea.

ELSIE THORSON

Rjukanfos

3

Cleng Peerson, Father of Norwegian-American Immigration

(Source: Den Siste Folkevandring Sagastubber fra Nybyggerlivet i Amerika, by Hjalmar Rued Holand, 1930; Norwegians in America: The Last Migration, by Hjalmar Rued Holand, translated by Helmer M. Blegen, 1978, pp. 13–23)

The most important name in the saga of Norwegian emigration is Cleng Peerson. He was not only the guide who pointed the way for the last great Norwegian popular migration, but he made frequent trips back and forth over the ocean in order to expedite and direct it.

When he made his first trip to this country, the Norwegian people knew practically nothing about America. Thirty years later, when he finished his work, the name *America* was the tempting symbol of hope that occupied their minds more than anything else. Thanks to him, the stream of immigrants was also steered to the best part of the entire country.

Although the chief impulse for the great emigration of people from Norway in the 19th century was economic, there was, in the very beginning, a contributing religious factor. In the war of 1808 to 1814, the English took many Norwegian sailors prisoners. Most of these prisoners were visited by English Quakers, and not a few of them were converted and accepted the tenets and practices of Quakerism. When they were released and went back to Norway, they were subjected to annoyance and persecution of various kinds by the authorities.

Stavanger was the most important center for the Quakers of Norway, even though they represented no more than a score of families. Quaker missionaries from England who had been in America visited these families and told them about the freedom of the U.S. constitution and the great opportunities to be found in the New World.

The Quakers in Stavanger began to discuss the pros and cons of moving to America. Finally, they resolved, in typical Quaker manner, to send out two men to explore the situation there. The two men selected were Cleng Peerson and Knut Olsen Eide (Knud Olsen Eie).

First Norse exodus to America

Cleng Peerson (Kleng Pedersen) was born 17 May 1782 at Lervik in Tysvær, Rogaland fylke, later moving to the farm Hesthammer. Not much is known about his early years, outside the fact that he had been in England, Germany and France, where he acquired some facility for the languages of these lands. He himself was not a Quaker, but he was related to several of them and respected them highly.

A sum of money was collected to cover the traveling expenses of the two men. To ensure against possible fraud, this sum was deposited with a Stavanger merchant, who was to send a remittance from time to time. In the summer of 1821 they set out.

Several years went by before the Quakers saw their agents again. The first letter they received from the homeland informed them that the merchant to whom they had entrusted the funds had gone bankrupt and that, because of the difficult times, the Quakers did not see their way clear to raise any more money. Thus the two found themselves stranded in a foreign land, broke and far from home.

As if this were not enough, shortly thereafter, Knut Olsen Eide fell ill. And now we receive the first proof of Cleng Peerson's noble character: In the daytime he worked as a carpenter on the site of what is now Broadway in New York. At night he kept watch at his ill friend's bedside. *[Here, Holand states that Knut Eide died. According to Blaine Hedberg, Vesterheim Genealogical Center in Madison, Wisconsin, some accounts suggest Eide recovered, returned to Norway and then immigrated to the U.S. in 1837 with his second wife, Martha Jonsdatter, and four children.]*

Even though he received no money from his Quaker friends in Stavanger, he remained as steadfastly loyal to them as ever. In fact, he set out to explore several states in search of a suitable location for the proposed Norwegian colony. He finally decided on a place in Orleans County in northwestern New York, on the shores of Lake Ontario. An American Quaker owned some land there that he was willing to sell for a reasonable price. In 1824, Peerson returned to his home community.

Although it is not mentioned in any of the thick tomes of Norway's history, this homecoming of Cleng Peerson from his trip to America is one of the most significant events in that country's history.

Before Peerson, there had been no thought of emigration; the name *America* had been scarcely known. But the appearance of his clear and factual report of the land across the sea seemed to light a lamp whose gleam increased in intensity until it illuminated the entire nation.

The exodus begins

Now began Norway's great popular exodus that seriously drained every community and town of its best blood.

Cleng Peerson's stay in Norway was brief. He conferred with his friends, and they agreed that they would buy a sloop and go to America the following year, 1825.

Late in the autumn of 1824, Cleng returned to New York with a companion named Anders Stangeland (Andrew Stangeland) from Tysvær, Stavanger. Here, he proceeded to purchase six parcels of land on the site selected as the future location of a colony for his friends, in whose behalf he was acting as advance agent. After he had made the deal, he began the construction of dwellings for the colonists.

When the time for departure arrived, only a few Quakers prepared to emigrate—three or four families. The entire passenger list totaled 52 persons, 22 of whom were adult males. About one-half of the company were people from Cleng Peerson's home community, Tysvær.

On his advice, they bought a small sloop and loaded it with a cargo of iron. On the 4th of July, the sloop *Restauration*, with its pioneers aboard, started out from Stavanger:

"The pioneers of nations yet to be—
The first low wash of waves where soon
Shall roll a human sea."

The following, from Holand's *De Norske Settlementers Historie*, pp. 35-37, is a list of the passengers and, if known, their places of residence in Norway:

- Lars Larson with wife and daughter, from Stavanger
- Cornelius Nilson Hersdal, wife and four children, from Tysvær, Stavanger (Hersdal's wife was Cleng Peerson's sister)
- Johannes Stene, wife and two children, from Tysvær, Stavanger
- Oyen Thompson, wife and three children, from Jæderen
- Daniel Stenson Rossadal, wife and five children, from Tysvær, Stavanger
- Thomas Madland, wife and three children, from Stavanger
- Simon Lima, wife and three children, from Jæderen

- Nils Nilson Hersdal and wife, from Tysvær, Stavanger
- Jacob Anderson Slogvig, from Tysvær, Stavanger
- Knud Anderson Slogvig, from Tysvær, Stavanger
- Sara Larson, from Stavanger
- Henrik Christopherson Harwick (Henrik Christopherson Hervig) and wife, from Tysvær, Stavanger
- Ole Johnson
- Gudmund Haugaas
- Thorstein Olson Bjaadland, pastor, from Jæderen
- Georg Johnson
- Endre Dahl
- Halvor Iverson
- Nils Thompson, from Jæderen
- Ole Olson Hetletvedt, from Ombø, Stavanger
- Lars Olson Helland, captain
- Erikson Styrmand, from Bergen

The *Restauration* was one of the smallest vessels that ever crossed the ocean with emigrants as passengers. It was only 54 feet in length and its tonnage was approximately 38. Even an experienced Viking of old would certainly have declined to attempt a crossing of the ocean in such a wretched little sloop.

Besides, there were so many passengers that there was scarcely space enough for all of them to sit down on the deck at one time. The skipper of the sloop was Lars Olsen Helland from Stavanger, and six of the emigrants were listed as members of the ship's crew.

They also had a very long and difficult voyage. For a variety of reasons, they strayed far from their course. And after a month's tossing about, they found themselves far down into the tropics.

Here they discovered, floating in the water, a barrel of old wine and hauled it on board. This magnificent beverage was highly welcome, for they had little else to eat but a daily fare of boiled groats, and a little juice of the grape would certainly improve the taste of this hasty pudding.

Apparently they had sampled it at other times of the day, too, for several days later, when they came drifting into the harbor of Funchal in the Madeira Islands, they were all lying asleep.

The commander of the fort peered in vain through his spyglass. He saw no sign of a flag above nor any human moving below on deck, and the sail was flapping at will. He accordingly assumed that it was a pestilence-ridden ship and began preparations to sink it to the bottom of the sea.

Fortunately, a Norwegian captain on a Bremen ship anchored in the harbor recognized the Norwegian costumes. He hailed them and shouted that they had better hoist their flag if they did not want to be shot at and sunk. Then one of the women recovered sufficient presence of mind to make all possible haste to hoist a piece of cloth aloft.

When an inspection proved that there was no infectious pestilence among them, the passengers were given a very friendly welcome. They were given fresh provisions of better quality, and after enjoying three good days of rest, they set sail once more. But they still were to endure 10 more weeks of seafaring before they arrived at New York.

Not until 9 October did they drop anchor in New York's harbor. By then, they had spent almost 14 weeks at sea.

The Kendall settlement

Their arrival in New York caused tremendous excitement and amazement over the fact that these emigrants had dared to cross the ocean in such a small vessel. Several of the city's newspapers expressed their admiration for the boldness of the captain and the daring courage of the passengers.

They ran into difficulties with the port's customs authorities, for they had broken the law of the land by carrying too many passengers for the size of the ship. The captain was arrested, and the authorities confiscated both ship and cargo.

Had it not been for Cleng Peerson's

aid, it would be difficult to say what might have happened. He was in the city to receive them on their arrival. Peerson was a capable interpreter. Furthermore, he succeeded in getting several influential Quakers of the city interested in the case. With their help, the authorities were persuaded to overlook the infraction, and the immigrants got their property back without any punishment or fine. Then Cleng Peerson guided them about 300 miles up to their new home on Lake Ontario.

This district, later known as the Kendall settlement, was at the time heavily wooded and on the very edge of the wilderness. Cleng Peerson had erected two houses, one for himself and the other for his brother-in-law. These two small houses, only 12 by 12 feet, now had to serve as shelter for 40 people for several weeks. The others found lodgings in New York and Rochester. Before long, they had several more houses built, and they survived the winter with no serious damage.

But conditions in the new land proved to offer many unexpected difficulties, and for many years these pioneers suffered great want. It was a continuous hand-to-mouth struggle for them. Everything was new and strange.

They wrote few letters to people back home, partly because they felt so depressed, and partly because many of them could not very well afford to pay the high postage, two *kroner*. Consequently, there were only about half a score of new immigrants during the next decade. If it had not been for Cleng Peerson, there apparently might have been no emigration to speak of for many years, as was the situation in Sweden and Denmark.

In search of new land

For many years Cleng Peerson shared the hard struggle of pioneer life with the rest of them, and it was just as new and difficult for him as it was for them. He finally realized that the everlasting labor that was necessary in order to transform a wilderness to cultivated fields and meadows offered no advantages over the restricted but comfortable conditions in the Old Country.

But he still believed that America had better things to offer. So he made up his mind to take a long, exploratory trip into the interior of the country to see what he could discover there. He was one of those strong and tireless explorers who felt duty-bound to heed the call of Nature to pursue untrodden paths, and all his activity in America was inspired by the thought of finding better living conditions for his hard-pressed countrymen.

In the spring of 1833, he and two companions started out on foot through Pennsylvania, Ohio, Indiana and Michigan. His companions soon tired of the wearisome wandering and hired out to work for American pioneers. Peerson, however, would not give up so easily. He kept dauntlessly on the trail, built a fire at night, and sometimes fell asleep with the howling of wolves ringing in his ears. At last, he reached Chicago.

Chicago in 1833! Although the first house had been built almost 60 years previously, the village had not made the least progress. In 1830 there was still no post office, school, church, harbor, road or bridge. The next year they finally had mail connection with the East, twice a month. But for several years, a letter required 20 days to reach New York from Chicago.

It was therefore a very quiet place Cleng Peerson found when he arrived in Chicago on a fine summer's day. The village consisted of about 20 modest log cabins—not all of them occupied, for the Asiatic cholera and the warlike Black Hawk Indians had recently visited the village.

Most of the houses were located at the junction of the north-and-south branch of the river, where today (1908) we find the beginning of Milwaukee Avenue. The entire north side was covered with fine oak woods. The south side, in contrast, was an open, sandy prairie with billowing grass and a multitude of wild flowers. There was not a house to be seen on the entire broad plain. Along the north boundary of this plain, the river slowly meandered between banks of rushes and low shrubs, with an occasional solitary fisherman dozing with his pole and pipe on the bank.

Only a couple of times a month did this little outpost on the outer edge of the wilderness spring to life and activity. That was when the driver of the postal wagon at long last came clattering into town with the U.S. mail. He did not bring much—10 to 15 letters and a half a

dozen old newspapers. But when these belated communications from the outside arrived, there was great rejoicing. Then one or another of the village fathers stepped up on a stool or box and read the latest news of the world to the assembled members of the pioneer settlement.

Afterward, there was dancing, drinking and general merriment, for whiskey was very cheap and the village harbored ambitious dreams of future glory and power, when its population would perhaps rise to a total of 50,000 inhabitants.

For the sake of comparison, it can be stated that today (1908) more than 3,000 passenger trains arrive in Chicago every day. There are people living who can recall the time when not a single road led out of the town.

Cleng Peerson used to say that he was the first Norwegian and the first Scandinavian in Chicago. But he was mistaken in this. On his way to Chicago, he stopped to rest for a while in the shade of some luxuriant aspen trees a couple of miles south of the village. On one of these aspens was nailed a board, painted white, on which at one time one could have read the following inscription: *Sacred to the memory of the fallen soldiers of Fort Dearborn, 1812, the first martyrs of the West*

But the inscription had become illegible after years of erosion by wind and weather, so that Cleng Peerson would not have been able to decipher it.

As a matter of fact, a Norwegian had been there 21 years before, and he was one of the first of a long series of men who bought with their blood those broad plains from its redskinned sons.

His name was Frederik Peterson, and he enlisted on 1 June 1808. On the fateful day of 15 August 1812, he was one of the members of the small garrison who, on their way back from Fort Dearborn, at Chicago, were attacked by a band of 500 Potawatomi Indians. Two-thirds of the whites were killed and the rest taken prisoner. Frederik Peterson was one of those killed.

We have no information regarding what part of Norway Peterson came from or how he happened to be in this outpost of civilization. His name is all that is found in the official records.

Descendants of the surviving soldiers can faintly recall hearing their sires talk about a Norwegian fiddler who was one of the soldiers. It is an interesting thought that, already 120 years ago, a Norwegian fiddler had sat here in the future metropolis of the Midwest, playing his old folk-melodies, and that he later, like so many of his countrymen, gave his life for his new fatherland.

While Cleng Peerson was sitting here taking a rest in the shade of the aspens, a bare-footed French half-breed came padding by, and the two strolled into town together. On their way north, the man pointed out an 80-acre plot that he owned, approximately where the mighty Chicago post office building now majestically towers. He urged Cleng Peerson to buy this land. His asking price was extremely reasonable: All he asked for was Cleng's meerschaum pipe, and that they swap clothes.

Peerson, however, was disinclined to make the deal. He was afraid that the Frenchie's tattered costume might be shelter for an assortment of livestock not mentioned in the transaction. He also had some doubts as to whether the seller would be able to furnish a clear warranty deed to said property.

From Wisconsin to Illinois

Cleng Peerson did not linger long in Chicago. He found nothing to attract him, either in the village or in its swampy surroundings. But as an old sailor, he found much to attract him in the restless surface of Lake Michigan's waters, and he decided to walk for a while along its shore.

Late one evening he arrived in Milwaukee, but it did not take him very long to inspect the whole town. It consisted of three small cabins, one of which was empty. A brisk northeast wind was blowing off the lake. It was a cold night, and Peerson relates that, chilled and hungry, he crept into this hut and tried in vain to keep warm until daylight.

Solomon Juneau and his brother-in-law occupied the other cabins. At this time, this comprised the entire population of the future metropolis. Juneau was a man of extraordinary fortitude. He carried on a small barter trade with the Indians, who came to him—some from a hundred miles away—with their beaver furs and bearskins in exchange for sugar, syrup and whiskey, the necessities of life.

Even though he (Juneau) was all alone most of the time, he was never molested. If, as occasionally happened, some jovial buck got too fresh with the merchandise, Juneau grabbed him by the belt and, lifting him at arm's length over his head, heaved him out through the door. The Indian would always come back, very meekly, and would beg permission to present him a set of deer antlers, or some such service.

In the morning, Cleng Peerson went to the vigorous Frenchman to inquire about the nature of the landscape to the west and to the north.

"Woods, nothing but woods," was the answer. "Many days' journey north of here, there is a small settlement called Green Bay, on a fjord bearing the same name. But the forest is so dense that I always go there by water and use a rowboat to fetch my wares from there. Otherwise, there is nothing but trackless woods to the end of the world."

Disappointed with his visit to southern Wisconsin, Peerson turned his steps toward the south again, and then westward toward the broad plains of Illinois.

Several counties to the west of Chicago are flat lowlands, which at that time were overgrown with coarse grass as tall as a man. There were no roads anywhere, which made it hard work to make progress. The tall grass twined

Skandinavisk Skovparti

itself around his legs and beat against his face. Day after day he walked and saw no sign of human habitation, not even an Indian wigwam. He was ready to succumb to hunger and exhaustion in the intolerable heat.

Cleng Peerson has said that this trip was the most exhausting journey he had ever in his life undertaken. He would frequently lie in a daze, overcome by hunger and thirst and plagued by mosquitoes. Occasionally, as he lay there only partly conscious, he seemed to see, floating before his eyes, a dream vision of a cozy cabin in a cool valley with a glimpse of the sea in the distance. But he resolutely shook off these visions and dragged himself onward. He felt himself to be a responsible messenger, a scout called to penetrate into new territory to find a home for a people oppressed, and this feeling would not allow him to rest or relax.

Fox River settlement

After several weeks of roaming about, late one evening he came to a place where the terrain was a little hillier. He had had no supper and was hungry and tired. Bone-weary, he lay down under a tree and immediately dropped off into profound sleep.

As he slept, he saw in his dreams that he was lying in the midst of a great community with beautiful large mansions and huge red barns on all sides. Wherever he turned his gaze, he saw rich fields of golden grain. Near the spot where he was lying, he saw a stately church, and he seemed to hear the powerful singing of familiar old Norwegian hymns mingled with angelic music from on high.

In ecstasy as he awakened from his dream, he sprang to his feet. In the clear gleam of the sunrise, his eyes discovered a scene that was scarcely less beautiful than the one he had beheld in his dream. The dreary monotony of the flat plain was now relieved by a delightful rolling landscape, with here and there a little clump of trees.

In the depressions were many small brooks, and toward the west he glimpsed a fairly large river that flowed between wooded hills. Never had he beheld a fairer landscape than this. It made him recall Moses as he stood on Mt. Nebo, looking out over the Promised Land.

The spot on which he was standing was about a quarter of a mile to the southwest of the present village of Norway, in LaSalle County, Illinois, and he had good reason to be enthusiastic. There are few places in America where one can find a more attractive place, where hill and dale, woods and streams are so harmoniously mingled to produce a scene of peace and beauty. Nor are there many places where the soil is more fertile than here.

Profoundly satisfied that he had at last found a place that far exceeded the expectations of his fondest dreams, and also amazed to discover that this ideal area was still open and available for settlement, he made all possible haste to return to his friends in the Kendall colony and inform them of his discovery.

When Cleng Peerson shortly thereafter passed through Chicago again, he could scarcely recognize that village. It happened that his arrival, late in September of 1833, coincided with the meeting at which a very important treaty with the Indians was being signed. Under the terms of this treaty, the Indians gave up all of the magnificent territory through which he had traveled. There were 7,000 Indians encamped near the village.

In addition to the Indians, this event had attracted a host of agents, spectators, horse-traders, gamblers, thieves and scoundrels of all kinds and colors. They were trading, bargaining, swearing, cursing, drinking whiskey and running around like crazy. On the outskirts lay the Indian camp, where the redskins howled, sang, cried and danced all through the night.

In the midst of all this chaos, Cleng

caught sight of his old acquaintance, the French half-breed, gaudily decked out in all the garish frippery that he had been able to find in the village. He had sold his 80 acres for $400 and, in his delirious jubilation, had immediately bought an Indian squaw, with whom he was now staggering about, urging everyone he knew to drink to his new-found prosperity. This came to an end at last, when his dusky spouse pushed him out into the darkness, while he lay drunk on a wheelbarrow.

When Cleng Peerson came back to the New York settlement late in the fall following his long journey of exploration, there was great rejoicing. He had walked more than 2,500 miles. But he also had something in return: He now could report that he had found a location for a Norwegian settlement that could not be surpassed anywhere in America in fertility, attractiveness and climate.

Almost every member of the colony decided to move, and with Cleng Peerson as their guide, they started out for Illinois the following spring. For himself, he bought 80 acres of the land where he had had his dream. And on this land, he built the first house erected by a Norwegian west of the Great Lakes. As a curious coincidence, a Norwegian church stood for many years on the spot where he had envisioned a church in his dream.

This journey is of supreme significance in the history of Norwegian immigration. Many have wondered why these Norwegians chose to settle here so far into the interior of the country. But this is the answer to that question: It was Cleng Peerson's visit that brought knowledge about the great Midwest, where the finest and most fertile prairie land could be had at a price of five *kroner* per acre, and this land was ready to plow.

This wonderful opportunity was the cause of the great folk-migration that followed. The rocky, forest-covered and relatively infertile tracts in Pennsylvania and other eastern states were not of a nature to attract any great mass movement of people.

Even though Cleng Peerson had now found a distinguished location that perfectly satisfied all his demands, he nevertheless did not settle down. As soon as the news of the wonderful Fox River lands reached Norway, it set off such a great migration that in a short time all the desirable acres were taken up. Then Cleng Peerson resumed his travels of exploration in order to discover suitable locations for still more new settlements.

These journeys took him to remote areas. He found, for example, a very fine district in the northern part of Missouri (Shelby County) 400 miles from Fox River. In 1837 he led a large company to this area, where he had high hopes of establishing a great Norwegian colony. But this was so far removed from all other Norwegian settlements that the immigrants did not thrive here, and the settlement did not last very long.

Immediately thereafter, he started the first Norwegian colony in Iowa, in the southeast corner of the state. But the Mormons settled in the neighborhood and won many converts among the Norwegians. Ten years later, when the Mormons moved to Utah, these converts went with them.

Cleng Peerson also took several trips to Norway in order to encourage emigration.

Encounter with communist colony

In 1847 he sold his land in Missouri and planned to retire peacefully near his relatives at Fox River. On the way to Fox River, he had an experience that made a profound impression upon him.

Far out on the naked prairie, he came upon a circle of many mud huts arranged in the form of a village. These were dugouts in hillsides, and each had a door and a small window. In the center of the circle was a large tent, which at that moment held a crowd of about 500 people.

They were gathered for noon religious services, and when Peerson arrived, they were closing the services with the strong notes of a hymn issuing harmoniously from the tent.

The congregation then came out and scattered to resume their various tasks. Some were excavating new dugouts. Others went to work in the fields. There was a mill on the banks of a stream that ran through the village, but at this time the brook was dry. However, this did not prevent the mill from operating, for inside the huge millwheel stood a dozen men who, by concerted treading, made the wheel turn.

Since all this was many miles removed from the nearest human habitation, it was a remarkable sight to see. Peerson made inquiries and found out this was the later-so-famous Swedish Bishop Hill communistic colony, founded by Erik Janson and his 500 pietistic disciples the year before.

The 12 men who were treading the millwheel were the 12 future apostles of the colony, who were in this manner getting a little recreation from their regular business of searching the Scriptures. The reason for haste in constructing additional dugout residences was that they were preparing to receive 500 new members from Sweden and Norway, who would arrive shortly.

The more knowledge he gained concerning this colony, the more Peerson felt attracted to its communal society. The main elements in his religious beliefs were a love of humanity and the virtues of cooperation among human individuals.

Still immature in experience, Peerson thought this young, communistic experiment was a perfect manifestation of brotherly love. Like his Quaker friends, these people, too, had left their native land because of religious persecution, and he sympathized with them.

Peerson applied for permission to become a member of the colony and turned over to it all his money, unconditionally. He did not retain for himself even enough money to buy a new hat for his wedding, which took place a few days later—when he took as wife one of the female members of the colony. However, an accommodating countryman lent him a suitable headpiece for the solemn ceremony.

Few events in Cleng Peerson's career gave him greater hope and expectation than membership in this communal enterprise, but he was quickly disillusioned. He soon found that it was not a society of equality and brotherhood that he had joined; on the contrary, he had been enticed into an irresponsible and narrow-minded autocracy.

The 500 new recruits arrived on schedule, but they brought with them cholera. Since no medical aid was provided, a terrible epidemic broke out and took the lives of many. Cleng Peerson was himself smitten with the plague, but the only treatment he was given was a series of long lectures admonishing him to shun sinful thoughts.

After some time, he recovered sufficient strength to leave the place. He was, to quote his own words, "sick in body and soul, and completely stripped of everything I possessed." The final phrase included his wife, for no women were allowed to leave the colony.

Texas becomes final home

Cleng Peerson was now an old and disappointed man, and all he wanted was to find a suitable place where he might spend his remaining days in peace and quiet. For several months he did simple farm work in order to earn a few dollars for travel expenses, and then he went a thousand miles south to Texas, where he planned to build a pioneer home in a mild climate. He had already visited Texas, even prior to the year 1843; for when Johan Reiersen in that year came to Fox River, Peerson was able to tell him a great deal about his travels there.

Reiersen was the editor of the Norwegian newspaper *Kristiansandsposten* and an eager proponent of emigration. His friends subscribed a total of 200 *kroner* to enable him to investigate conditions in America. On Cleng Peerson's recommendation, Reiersen established a settlement of Norwegians in Texas in 1845.

Four years later, Peerson visited this settlement, but he did not like the location. He made extensive exploratory trips farther west, and in Bosque County he found a landscape that appealed to him very much. He settled down here in 1854 and gave up his wanderings.

The majority of the Norwegian pioneers in Texas also moved to Bosque County. It is now an important community comprising three parishes. Most of the people here are from Hedmark fylke. In all, Peerson made three trips from Fox River to Texas and seven voyages across the Atlantic Ocean.

Two years later, Cleng Peerson was given a very honorable recognition. The State of Texas had become aware of the disinterested contribution this industrious man was making by bringing desirable immigrants to the state. On 13 August 1856, the Texas legislature passed a special resolution whereby Cleng Peerson was given a 320-acre farm as a token of appreciation for his services.

Neither he nor any of his friends had the slightest knowledge of this act before the governor had signed the resolution. He is the only Norwegian who has ever been shown such an honor in the United States of America. He died 16 December 1865.

Cleng Peerson was the moving spirit in the first emigration from Norway, and he opened ways and visions so effectively that a mighty mass movement of people was initiated.

Several writers, especially Professor George Flom, have criticized him severely for not taking advantage of an opportunity to become a wealthy man who could have owned much livestock, both large and small. He calls him a Peer Gynt (a shiftless character in a play by Norwegian playwright Henrik Ibsen), a vagabond, a tramp and an impractical fellow, who died a pauper! Roald Amundsen (noted Norwegian polar explorer, whose expedition was the first to reach the South Pole, in 1911) might just as well be chided for not having remained at home to plant potatoes.

Cleng Peerson was inspired with a great idea that had nothing whatever to do with personal enrichment: to find homes for people living in poverty and want, who had no opportunity to find expression for their talents and abilities. He was motivated by that love for discovery that has always been a characteristic of the Norwegian people.

Beyond every horizon that he encountered, there lay undiscovered territory. What did this unknown region have to offer? With matchless discrimination, he boldly advanced and examined the new lands to find out what they had to offer. He has been the guide that has led thousands from penury to prosperity. Never did he do this for a wage or salary.

It would be hard to find a more unselfish and interesting character in all history than Cleng Peerson. He did not lack opportunities to reap a profit from speculative land agents on one hand and naive newcomers on the other. But, up to now, no one has dared to maintain that he exploited an opportunity to enrich himself.

The chief purpose of his life was to find homes for his countrymen, and for him that was enough. The pioneers he helped sought gain for themselves. Not so with Cleng Peerson. He sought it for the generations yet unborn.

The old pioneers who knew him personally understood this very well, and they have erected a fine monument in honor of his memory over his grave in Texas.

Romsdal

4
From New York to the West
(Source: De Norske Settlementers Historie, by Hjalmar Rued Holand, translated by Malcolm Rosholt, 1908, pp. 65–74)

For the majority of Scandinavian immigrants to the United States in the first six-plus decades of the 19th century, the sea voyage lasted from four weeks to four months. Although it seemed an eternity, it still had an end, and the immigrant could finally put his feet down on solid ground.

Very few of the immigrants had any concept of the vastness of length and breadth of America. When they reached New York harbor, many thought they were near their destination. Had they known they still had several weeks of less-than-desirable living conditions ahead before they reached the West, no doubt many of them would have completely despaired.

For after New York, there still remained the steamship ride up to Albany on the Hudson River, and from there a journey by canal boat west to Buffalo on the Erie Canal, where the traveler had to cross the Great Lakes before reaching Milwaukee or Chicago. Then followed several hundred more miles on foot or by ox team over newly built roads before they reached that little settlement in some corner of the Midwest, where some would spend the rest of their lives.

Although their arrival in New York did not create the sensation that the immigrants had expected, there was one class of Americans happy to see them— namely, the agents of the transportation companies. These agents crowded around the newcomers and, with unintelligible eloquence mixed with Norwegian and German phrases, offered to make fast arrangements and comfortable conveyances to the west at unbelievably low prices.

But with these low prices came many a hitch. Either the ticket the immigrant held was not valid for farther than Albany or Buffalo (although the contract was made out for the entire trip to Milwaukee or Chicago), or there were "mistakes" in the ticket that forced the immigrant to pay excessive surcharges.

That the entire agent-runner system was so worm-eaten with deceit and fraud seems incomprehensible in the light of present-day travel agents so well known for their integrity. *[At this point, Holand quotes a letter in a footnote written by J. R. Reierson to Hans Gassman, dated 12 December 1843, which purports to describe the abuses rampant in the passenger business at the time. –Rosholt]*

Presumably, the Norwegian government had a consul in New York, whose immediate duty should have been to protect the many thousands of confused countrymen, unfamiliar with the English language, from the unscrupulous practices of the travel agents. But if any of these consular representatives ever did anything whatsoever to help their fellow countrymen, none of the immigrants ever mentioned it.

On the other hand, there were in New York and Milwaukee several Norwegians who made a sort of living fleecing their countrymen like sharks. J. R. Reierson mentions several of them by name in his book published for would-be immigrants in 1844.

Finally, the immigrant and his wooden chest were loaded on board the steamer that was to transfer them to Albany. The vessel glided smoothly up the Hudson River's mighty current.

As the ship sailed among the hills along the banks, the passenger may well have felt something heavy weighing on him, an uneasiness that he had never known before. The salty sea, which he had now left behind, held warm memories of things past as it washed ashore on the other side of the ocean against the fatherland's lovely beaches. He recalled the little ship that had been his home for so many weeks on the Atlantic, like an arm reaching out from the fatherland. But now he was moving among complete strangers bound for that legendary land called America.

Arriving in Albany, the immigrant learned for the first time how unreliable the transportation agents were. According to agreement, all luggage and things were to be carried free, but the newcomers were not permitted to leave ship before the purser's extortions were paid. It was no use to either protest or argue.

Inflexibly and disgracefully, the purser yelled out his fee: "One dollar! Two dollars! Three dollars!" as one piece of luggage after the other was brought out on deck to be unloaded. Angry and impoverished, the passengers had all they could do to reach the canal boat for the balance of the journey.

This canal, whose muddy waters several hundred thousand immigrants of all nations sailed over, was more than 360 miles long. It connected Albany on the Hudson River with Buffalo on Lake Erie. Before the railroad came this way, the canal was the only means of communication between the Northwest Territory and the Atlantic seaboard.

The canal boats were actually big lighters (or barges) with a deck—dark, floating boxes without windows, beds, cooking stoves or anything else that might be considered necessary for passengers.

On the trip from Buffalo east to Albany, the lighter was loaded with grain, furs and all the products of the West. From Albany west to Buffalo, the cargo consisted of immigrants and their baggage, in addition to tools and products from Eastern factories.

This "Noah's Ark" was pulled by one or two mules at a speed of up to three miles per hour. If there were no unnecessary delays en route, the trip from Albany to Buffalo took about 12 days—a trial of patience and forbearance seldom surpassed.

Even if the accommodations on board had not been so miserable, it was still not possible to sleep. The entire trip

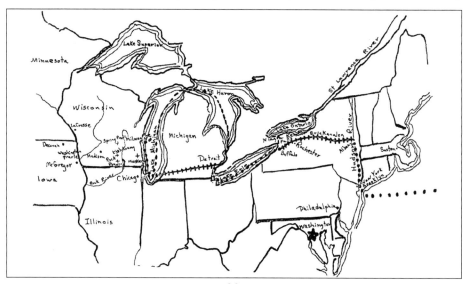

was one continuous and maddening bustle to negotiate the many canal locks, of which there were no fewer than 83. Added to this was the commotion of discharging cargo at the frequent stops, the banging together with other boats, the coarse language heard between the barge captains, and the uproar that followed when the barge now and then became stranded on a sandbar.

The Great Lakes

There were other canal boats, quite cozy and ingeniously arranged for passenger traffic, which made up to six miles per hour. But mighty few of the immigrants had the means or opportunity to avail themselves of these. *[My great-grandfather, Jacob Tollefsen Rosholt, arrived in New York in 1845; he had no other route to follow to Wisconsin but over the Erie Canal. –Rosholt]*

Ahead now lay the thousand-mile trip across America's sea-like Great Lakes, from Buffalo to Milwaukee or Chicago. The immigrant had sailed and drifted across the ocean; now he would be riding in a steam-driven craft.

These ships were much larger than the common sailing ships of the Atlantic and carried up to 1,000 passengers and considerable cargo. The accommodations were not much better than on the canal boats, but a person made much better time than on the earlier stages of the journey. These large lake steamers with their speed and reliability carried all sorts and classes of people, each taking care of his own.

Once aboard, the immigrant saw a pattern of a busy, varied world that was now to become his home. The trusted company of his countrymen and friends who had accompanied him several months from Stavanger or Skien were now, through death or other reasons, spread out or reduced to a few neighbors. Instead, he found himself surrounded by Yankees, Englishmen, Irishmen, Germans, Indians and others.

More than on any part of the long journey, the immigrant on these lake steamers was faced with the greatest disregard for human life. The arrogance and carelessness of those in command often caused great misfortunes. The lack of good harbors in the lakes caused many ships every year in times of bad storms to become stranded or to sink. From time to time people in those days heard the most heart-rending reports about the lake steamers—reports about ships blowing up with hundreds of passengers on board.

A deadly collision

The worst disaster to overtake Norwegian immigrants occurred in August 1852, when another steamer in the middle of the night intentionally rammed a steamer with more than 800 immigrants. More than 300 immigrants drowned. Details of the incident defy description.

It probably happened this way: The steamer *Atlantic*, commanded by Captain Petty, left Buffalo around 11 p.m. one night in mid-August, bound for Chicago. The ship was carrying 830 immigrants in addition to a big cargo. All cabins were filled, while other passengers lay huddled on deck surrounded by their bundles of clothing, barrels of preserved fish and farm implements.

During the night the captain of the *Atlantic* spied the steamer *Ogdensburg*, owned by a rival shipping line. Between the two skippers and the ship owners there existed a deadly feud, and their thoughts, words and deeds could only end in mutual destruction.

"What about giving that hated *Ogdensburg* a whack in the side?"

Captain Petty had many hundred passengers on board the *Atlantic* who, under normal circumstances, should be protected. But why bother about such people? To him they were only dirty and ignorant immigrants, the dregs of foreign lands and America's ruin.

Along the deck he saw them lying, gaping and snoring, wrapped in their rags. Down below where the oil lamps burned, a pungent odor rose, accompanied by children crying and the jabbering of all sorts of languages.

A glance at the brilliantly lit *Ogdensburg* was enough. The captain ordered all lights out and set his course for the *Ogdensburg*. It was only by a mighty fast maneuver that the *Ogdensburg* avoided a collision.

Embittered by such a foul attempt in the dark of night, the *Ogdensburg* captain turned and with a powerful thrust sent his own ship amidships of the *Atlantic*.

The poor immigrants were suddenly torn from their sleep, water pouring in on them like a waterfall. Crazed and screaming, they ran for the stairway to escape this death trap. But it was hopeless, because above stood members of the crew with clubs and handspikes, hitting anyone who tried to come up. The people fell backward with bruised skulls and smashed hands.

When this failed, the crew took the stairway and overturned it, with women and children flying off. There was no further attempt to escape by those below, as the ship sank shortly after. Among the immigrants in this disaster were 130 people from Valdres bound for the Valdres settlement near Manitowoc, Wisconsin. About half of them drowned.

To Chicago, Milwaukee and the West

Fortunately, not all steamers met such a gruesome fate. The lack of information among the immigrants concerning the many accidents that had happened gave them confidence to board these ships. For the most part, this portion of their journey was the least of their worries; indeed, for the patient ones it was, with all its diverse scenery, still a pleasure.

From Buffalo the immigrants traveled through Lake Erie's entire length to Detroit, and from there through Lake St. Clair's beautiful surroundings. Then came the storm-filled Lake Huron, until the approach was made to Mackinaw's romantic island of rock. Then the direction was south, through Lake Michigan's majestic 300 miles to Milwaukee or Chicago.

On the starboard side the immigrants finally saw Wisconsin's primeval forests, with now and then a foaming river issuing forth. Yonder, the eye could be captivated by a meadow never grazed by other than creatures of the wild. The coastline now and then rose in steep sand hills, some of them covered with trees and brush, which gave a uniform connection with the shoreline, while others towered in perpendicular walls of sand 300 feet over the water.

And then again, a person could see how the restless waves, working together with the sand hills, had hollowed out a gulf where finally the overhanging bank with its centuries-old pines and cedars had tumbled down in chaotic confusion.

Out there lay the West, that mysterious land, with the waves breaking against a shoreline that the immigrant had traveled halfway around the earth to reach. There lay the land where he had left father and mother, birthplace and his forefathers' graves to build a new home.

What did this land have in store for him? Would he find honor, a decent life in the future for his children and a quiet old age? Or was his journey a folly, his hopes a mirage and his future just a bad joke? Would he be like Abraham, who went west into a foreign land to find fortune in life and peace in death? Or would he, like the Israelites in Egypt, only harvest a weeping and gnashing of teeth? Only Providence could answer that.

Finally, after the seventh day from Buffalo and about 120 days after leaving Norway, the immigrant arrived in Milwaukee or Chicago, the entry ports to the Promised Land. The wandering through the wilderness was at an end, the ordeal through which one had to pass on the way to Paradise realized.

5

Fox River Settlement, northern Illinois

(Source: De Norske Settlementers Historie, by Hjalmar Rued Holand, translated by Malcolm Rosholt, 1908, pp. 84–94)

The main stream of emigrants from Norway in the 1830s consisted of people from the mountain communities north of Stavanger. It was from here that the widely known Sloopers *[the first party of Norwegian emigrants to arrive in New York on the sloop Restauration —Rosholt]* departed in July 1825 and paved the way for others to follow.

It was from Stavanger that another group left under the leadership of Knud Slogvig in 1836. This was also Cleng Peerson's native place, which he visited three times after being in America and interesting thousands of people in the American dream.

Many of these first pioneers did very well in America and after a few years began to write to their friends and relatives around Stavanger about conditions in America. These letters awakened such a desire among people to leave Norway that the movement blazed into flames, and people lived for the day when they, too, might leave for America. It was a secular revival, sweeping through Stavanger and southern Hordaland—more gripping than any religious upheaval that had once had such a strong appeal in this region.

America at this time seemed a distant and strange land, more mysterious than the interior of China. It was like calling it the planet Mars. This was before trade and the telegraph had knit together the far ends of the earth. To most Norwegians, America was a never-never land nearly impossible to imagine, and about which the local schoolteacher related obscure events concerning Cortez's conquest and Pizarro's hunt for the treasures of the Incas. But now people were hearing from reliable neighbors that over there lay a blessed nation with vast expanses of rich land that could be had for the asking. The climate was excellent, living conditions good and opportunities beyond comparison.

The farmers who had already immigrated to America were heroic figures, and people were proud to consider them distant relatives. Their letters home were looked upon as inspired gospels, copied without end and finally pasted in the back of the Apostle John's *Revelation* as a holy tiding to be preserved alongside the family Bible.

It was not only the more adventuresome who were gripped by their ancestors' lust to travel and to try their luck. Most of the people by now had been awakened, and among these the "America fever" raged as strongly with them as the others. These gentle pietists, their thoughts attuned to the future, reflected in their humility on their lack of progress from generation to generation. With soul-rending voices and dull eyes they had moved about, stopping and sighing, thinking that life was only a preparation for death. But now the dawn of a new era was at hand for these forgotten mountaineers, and they were awakened to a new interest in life.

Over there lay America, tempting them like an earthly paradise, and no angel with a flaming sword to guard the entrance. How delightful it would be to take a little of this good earth and those rich pastures! Had not the Lord directed that man should inherit the earth? What was that scripture reading, anyway? "Get thee out of thy country and from thy kindred, and from thy father's house, unto a land that I shall show thee, and I will make of thee a great nation..." This was surely a prophecy about America. If only one could share in this prosperity!

The weekly religious meetings were gradually becoming merely pretence for people to talk over the latest news about those who had gone to America or were thinking of leaving.

Fox River colony in northern Illinois was the Mecca for these first pioneers. There, all poverty and slavery ceased, while ahead lay the good life and happy days. For a time, probably the most important wish in Stavanger, both temporal and eternal, was: "If I only could get to Fox River!"

And people worked and struggled, saved and pinched, patched on patches, and after a few years scraped enough money together to be among the lucky ones in the community who had also fought and won and were now en route to Stavanger to board a ship for America.

Every family had its representative and every valley its following. The communities of Etne, Skonevik, Fjeldberg, Tysvær, Skudenæs and Skjold, all sent their hundreds—yes, even thousands—until it resembled a terrible epidemic, devastating the villages in certain parts of Norway.

For a period of five years everyone was headed for Fox River, and from there they spread north to Wisconsin and west to Iowa. Nearly all of these first ones were from Stavanger, Hardanger and Hordaland.

Among the first Norwegians to settle on Fox River in Illinois were members of the group who, under the leadership of Cleng Peerson, moved from the first Norwegian colony in America called Kendall in upstate New York. Those who came in 1834 to Illinois were Jacob Slogvig, Knud A. Slogvig, Tosten Olson Bjaadland, Endre Dahl, Thomas Barland, Nils Thompson, Ole Olson Hetletvedt, Gudmund Haukaas, Hans Bøe, Buer Bøe and Halvor Knudson. Nearly all settled in Mission Township, LaSalle County, Illinois.

In 1836 came Gjert G. Hovland, Gudmund Sandsberg, Nils Nilsen Hersdal, Kari Nilsen (who was Cleng Peerson's sister), Daniel Rosdal with sons Ove Danielson Rosdal and Johannes Danielson Rosdal, Thomas Madland, Jørgen Johnson and Einer Aasen. Most of them were one-time passengers on the sloop *Restauration* that landed in New York in 1825.

The movement of immigrants to Fox River continued every year until all land near wood and water was taken. Among the many who came in the years 1837-40 were Knut Pederson, later to become a Mormon bishop; Hans Valder (originally Hans Vælde), later the first Norwegian Baptist preacher in the world; Knud Person, better known under the name of "Old Knut" and a well-known lay preacher; Elling Eielsen; and Johan Nordbo, the first to leave from Gudrandsdal. Nordbo was the first Norwegian doctor in America and in 1838 became the first Norwegian in Texas.

In addition, there were Lars Brimsø, Hans Barlien, Thomas Erikson, John Hattle, Nils Frøland, Henrik Sæbbe, Christian Olson, Knud Williamson and Nils Nilsen Jr., nearly all from Stavanger.

The Fox River settlement, which originally was confined to both banks of the Fox, now takes in a much larger territory and runs from Ottawa north and east through Sheridan, Seneca, Morris, Norway, Leland, Lisbon, Newark and Millington. There are now (1908) about 7,500 Norwegians in the area.

Anders Anderson, Ole T. Olson, Halvor Nilsen and Hans Valder, all from Stavanger, were the first to settle at Leland, also known as Indian Creek. Ole Olson Hetletvedt was the first at Lisbon in 1837, which later became the site of the largest Norwegian Lutheran congregation. He also was the first Norwegian preacher in America. *[Holand here uses the word prædikant, which does not necessarily mean that the man was an ordained pastor. –Rosholt]*

The first to chop down some trees and build a house was Cleng Peerson, who in 1834 built a house for his sister, the widow Kari Nilsen, on a piece of land described as the West of the SW 1/4, Section 33, Township 35, Range 5 East. A part of this house still stands (1908) and is used by her grandson, Cornelius Nilsen, who has the old farm. This is the first farm and first house owned and developed by Norwegians in the Midwest. Only a few steps away is the tree under which Cleng Peerson had a prophetic dream.

Peerson lived here for many years, honored and respected by Americans and Norwegians alike. An elderly American tells how he learned to read with the help of an old copy of the book *Pilgrims Progress*, which his parents had borrowed from Peerson.

For many years there were neither newspapers nor books in the settlement, with the exception of some Bibles, huspostils and that one copy of *Pilgrims Progress* with its horror-filled illustrations. That book was passed back and forth, like a traveling library, read and discussed by Americans and Norwegians alike.

A large spring was located on Peerson's land and for many years people came here for water. Here the girls assembled with their washing, and later in the day the boys arrived to help them carry it home. Many a respected couple in the neighborhood trace memories of their early love to this spring of gurgling waters.

Death visits Fox River

But among the older pioneers there are more memories of tears than of laughter. This place, which they had once looked forward to as a paradise, actually caused them an agonizing appraisal never anticipated, and to escape they would gladly have exchanged their big farms for the most modest mountain nook in Norway.

Malaria, which struck first, never missed a home. The illness lasted about three months, and its symptoms were burning fever alternating with trembling chills. Quinine was not yet in common use, and people doctored with bees' wax and *Wauhoo*, that simple name for a heroic remedy, the mere recollection of which is enough to make

Brudefærd i Hardanger

old settlers shudder.

But malaria was not fatal, and people managed to survive this torture. However, in 1849 and onward, cholera broke out, and for this they had no cure. It spread through all the old settlements like the Spirit of Death, especially on Fox River and in Muskego, Wisconsin, where thousands of young and old were thrown wantonly into their graves.

Lars Brimsø, that powerful carpenter on Fox River, for a time had all he could do to nail together simple boxes to contain the sacrificial remains. In order that he might not become infected himself, people shoved boards into his shop through a window. In return, through the same opening, they received a rough, unpainted coffin box for mother or father.

Of the hundreds of these first Norwegians who died on Fox River in 1849, it can only be reported that they were mostly cholera victims.

Religious diversity

Although this is the oldest permanent settlement of Norwegians in America, no permanent church organization was realized here. Pastor J. C. W. Dietrichson, on his first visit to America in 1844-45, organized congregations elsewhere, but found no disposition among the people here for church order.

This did not mean these early settlers were lacking a sense of spiritual values. On the contrary, it was their extraordinary interest in religious matters, driving them irresistibly into the first religious current that came along, that made J. C. W. Dietrichson's visit in 1845 fruitless.

He found the greatest religious confusion possible. "There were," he says, "Presbyterians, Methodists, Baptists and Ellingianers *[followers of Elling Eielsen –Rosholt].*" Quakers and Mormons were also members. The last-named were quite numerous and not only had a church, but a pastor, bishop, and, yes, even high priest—namely, Gudmund Haukaas, one of the original Sloopers, who allegedly possessed the gift of speaking in tongues.

Dietrichson says that when the spirit overcame Gudmund, he "grimaced terribly and with trembling lips uttered sounds of which only two words could be made out: 'Schavi! Schava!' When Gudmund had relieved himself of these words, a prayer to God was offered by one of the interpreters, who commonly explained that the spirit working through Gudmund had recognized the Mormon Church to be God's true church."

Gudmund's full title was "high priest after the order of Melchizedek in Jesus Christ of the Latter Day Saints," and it is possible that he was the first ordained Norwegian pastor in the United States. He was a thorn in the flesh to Dietrichson.

Several other Mormon pastors left the settlement about the same time—among them, Erik Midtbø (Erik Midtbøen) and Ole Olson Heier, two of the first to emigrate from Tinn in Telemark. Heier was an extremely eloquent man with a winning personality, which made him a power among the Mormons. He also was said to have the gift of healing, and he was soon made a bishop. He later left the Mormons and thereafter preached for the Baptists.

The biggest man among these Norwegian-Mormons was Knud Peterson from Eidsfjord in Hardanger. He came to Fox River, Illinois, in 1837 and was soon chosen one of the church's 70 disciples. In this capacity he very early on served as a preacher in Fox River, Koshkonong (Wisconsin) and other settlements. Eventually he was sent to Norway to explain the Mormon teachings, which he did, with great success.

In 1856 he returned to America with 600 proselytes who marched all the way to the Great Salt Valley in Utah. *[Actually, the majority of these converts were Danes. –Rosholt]*

In Utah, Peterson became a bishop and one of Brigham Young's chief advisors. In this enormous effort, which the

Mormons made in the following years, the Utah desert was transformed into one of the most productive pioneer states in America, and Bishop Peterson was one of its leaders and its most capable men.

In addition to the Mormon pastors, who always managed to keep people on their toes concerning the doctrine of baptism by immersion, laying on of hands, speaking in tongues and other spiritual aberrations, there was a pair of headstrong Methodists or Baptist pastors and an overflow of unctuous lay preachers of all classes and beliefs.

In Fox River, these far-out preachers gradually assembled an important share of the West's highest and most ambitious laymen. First and foremost was Ole Olson Hetletvedt, a zealous and talented man who must be remembered as the first to preach the gospel among the Norwegian people of America. One of the Sloopers, he had conducted religious worship on board ship.

His son, Porter Olson, distinguished himself in the Civil War. A brigadier-general, he fell at the head of his regiment in the battle of Franklin, Tennessee. Only one other Norwegian rose to the rank of brigadier—namely, Hans Heg.

There was also Jørgen Pederson, who as early as 1838 administered the sacraments in the Fox River settlement. He had thought of becoming a Lutheran pastor but joined the Mormons instead. Among others may be mentioned the stern Aslak Aae, Endre Arakerbø, Herman Arakerbø, Per Asbjørnson Mehus and Kamme Knud (Knud Peerson).

B. L. Wick writes of Kamme Knud in *Skandinaven* under date of 1 May 1907: "It is said of Kamme Knud that, as a young man, he became an itinerant lay preacher in western Norway, and when he left for America, people urged their children to settle near such an exemplary man. He was already an elderly man in the 1850s, weak in body and mind. But when he heard his native place in Norway mentioned, a smile played on his face and perhaps a word 'yes' came from his lips and then the visit was at an end."

Finally there was Elling Eielsen, always defiant and ready to do battle. In Fox River he attracted most of his early followers and built a house in 1843, the second floor being used to hold worship services. Eielsen had many staunch friends here, but he also drove conservatives away from him by his obstinacy and willingness to condemn everything. It seems he could not harmonize the elements.

Congregations organize

A stronger man than any of these was needed, and he came in 1850—namely, Pastor P. A. Rasmussen. With a steady and capable hand, he took over the leadership of Lutheran church work and insisted on a sense of church order in this religious chaos. This settlement, where that bold champion of the church, Dietrichson, was unable to organize a congregation, now has a whole string of congregations. Their contributions, missionary zeal and good works stand higher than all other congregations in the Norske Synod.

The congregation at Lisbon on Fox River has been especially noted for its keen interest in church work. It alone gives more each year to missions, the synod treasury and associated endeavors than the entire circuit farther west. When big things need doing, then a person turns to the Lisbon congregation.

Among the old pioneers, a high value is still placed on old-fashioned church-going and patriarchal acceptance of life's responsibilities. Many of them handle their property as God's stewards and each year make an accounting of their balance sheet with their Lord. Without haggling, they give their entire surplus to the work of the church.

While often pinched and tight with themselves, they nevertheless, as sure as day follows night, send $100 to $200 to the mission treasury in Stavanger.

The first attempt to establish a Norwegian Lutheran high school was

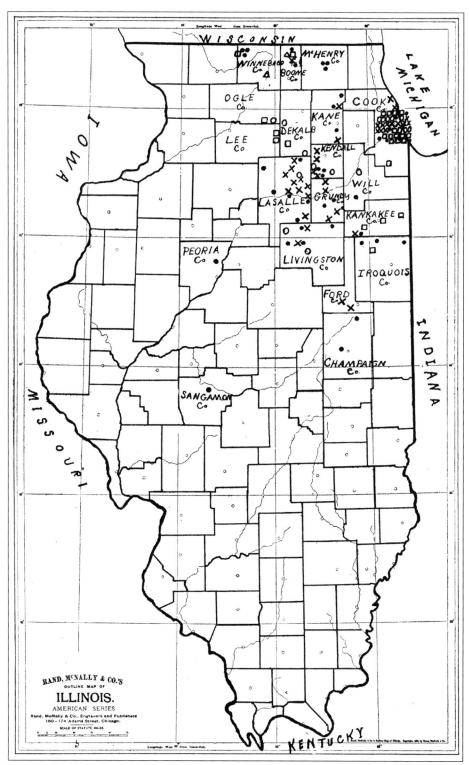

made on Fox River. In a history of Red Wing Seminary written in 1904, N. N. Ronning has the following to say on this:

"Owing to the shortage of ministers required in the administration of the church, Elling Eielsen, president of the Hauge Lutheran Synod, made a motion at the annual meeting held in 1854 to establish a seminary in order to train and educate young and gifted men for the ministry. The motion was seconded by Pastor P. A. Rasmussen and adopted unanimously. A man of whom it is said lacked vision for schools and seminary-trained pastors proposed it."

A motion also was adopted at this meeting to buy a quarter section of land in the neighborhood of Lisbon, on which stood a large building sufficient to serve for school purposes. The deal was made before the synod meeting at a price of $1,800.

The next annual meeting of the Hauge Synod, held in 1855, was concerned mostly with matters relating to the school. It was agreed to open the doors to students in October, with P. A. Rasmussen serving as principal and teacher.

On the basis of information furnished by Bjørn Holland of Hollandale, Wisconsin, the school opened in the fall of 1855 in the aforesaid building with one teacher and three students in attendance. The teacher was Rasmussen and the students his two brothers-in-law, Bjørn Holland and Syver Holland, and Olaus Landsværk. The last named was a son of John Landsværk, who for many years served as a parochial school-teacher and choir leader in Rasmussen's and Eielsen's congregations. No more than the three students mentioned attended the school that continued to operate for one school year up to May 1, 1856. As well as Bjørn Holland can recall, classes were conducted in grammar, diction and church history. The Augsburg Confession was also studied.

"This was, as far as known, the first high school operated by Norwegians in America." *[Holand, in a footnote, says Nils Otto Tank, a Norwegian of the Moravian faith, opened a school at Green Bay, Wisconsin, in 1850, which continued for a year with five students attending.]*

The reason for the brief existence of the school on Fox River was not because the Hauge people lacked vision for higher education. It fell by the way because of differences between Rasmussen and Eielsen. The result was a split in church affairs between the two men. This ended the history of the school for the training seminarians at Lisbon.

Although the Fox River settlement is now (1908) 75 years old, not only the children of this colony but the parents and grandparents of these children were born in this country. Yet it is still as Norwegian as ever. The Norwegian language is heard daily, both at home and in church. A Norwegian high school in this area is well attended, and a local Norwegian newspaper is published at Ottawa.

Lee County, Illinois

Some miles northwest of the Fox River colony is a settlement known as Lee County *[today, probably Lee Center –Rosholt]*. It was one of the first offshoots of the Fox River settlement.

Omman Hilleson (Amund Helgeson Maakestad) from Sørfjorden in Hardanger came to Fox River in 1843, but remained only a short time before moving about 40 miles to the northwest to Lee County, where he found unclaimed land. As a result of his encouraging letters, a host of people from around Hardanger came to this settlement, and it is now entirely made up of these people, numbering some 400.

The first group arrived in 1847 and included the following: Lars L. Risetter, Lars Hilleson, Helge Hilleson, Lars Olson Espe, Sjur Arneson Bly and Torkel Knudson Maakestad. Omman Hilleson, who accompanied them to Lee County, met them all in Chicago. He was a generous and well-liked man, highly respected by his neighbors. No congregation was organized here until 1858.

Flaadal

6
Chicago, northeastern Illinois
(Source: De Norske Settlementers Historie, by Hjalmar Rued Holand, translated by Malcolm Rosholt, 1908, pp. 100–110)

This book's purpose is to tell the story of Norwegian settlements in the 19th century. While a record of our towns and cities might be desirable, it lies outside the range of this work.

Chicago, however, with a Norwegian population of 75,000, has been the port of entry through which several hundred thousand emigrants have found their way to new homes—many staying here a year or more. Thus it becomes almost a necessity to provide an insight into the pioneer Norsemen of this city.

The first Norwegian to arrive in Chicago was David Johnson, a young seaman who came to New York in 1832 and first found work in a printing office. Two years later the owner of the *Chicago Democrat*, the first newspaper to be published in that city, came to New York, where he became acquainted with Johnson and took him back to Chicago to work as a typesetter. Johnson thus became the first Norwegian typographer in America.

Two years later, in 1836, more Norwegians arrived in Chicago—namely, Halstein Torrison from Fjeldberg in Sør-Hordaland, Johan Larson from Kobbervig *[probably Kobberdal off the west coast of Nordland. –Rosholt]*, Nils Røthe from Voss, and Svein Lothe from Hardanger. As Torrison did not arrive until 16 October 1836, it seems fairly safe to assume that the others arrived earlier. Torrison worked for a gardener by the name of Newberry in whose memory that splendid Newberry Library was built. As Torrison was a very competent person, he early on built himself a nice house and at the time was considered a leading man among his countrymen. His house stood on the riverbank where the Chicago and Northwestern station is presently (1908) located.

Nils Røthe was the first to leave from Voss in Hordaland, getting many of his neighbors to join him later in Chicago. This was the beginning of an entire colony of Voss people (which was referred to as the "Voss district") in the future city. Among the first to come were Baard Johnson, who arrived in 1837; and Anders Nilsen Hjelland, Anders Larson Flage, Erik Endreson Rude, Asle Endreson Rude and Endre Endreson Rude, who came in 1839.

The Endreson brothers were born in Valdres but the family moved to Voss. Erik Endreson Rude was later the founder of the famed Winneshiek County settlement near Decorah, Iowa. Iver Larsen (Iver Lawson) and Knut Larsen (Knut Lawson), Endre Iverson Røthe and Ole Gilbertson, all from Voss, came in 1840. Iver Lawson grew rich as a speculator in city lots. His son, Victor Lawson, is the owner of the *Chicago Daily News* (1908), the world's largest newspaper.

Thousands of Norsemen came to Chicago in the 1840s and 1850s but did not remain long. The overwhelming number of the city's Norwegians actually settled there in the years to come.

Among the older Norwegians in Chicago, special mention should be made of Jens Olsen Kaasa, who was in the first emigrant group to leave from Skien on the southern coast of Norway. He and a number of his relatives came first to Boone County, Illinois, where they founded the Long Prairie settlement near Belvedere. *[My grandfather, Henry Aul Anderson, came from Skien. –Rosholt]*

Jens Olsen moved to Chicago in 1853. He was a mason by trade and in the 1880s got the contract to build Our Saviors church at the corner of Erie and May streets. He and Pastor Jens Krohn were mainly responsible for getting this splendid church built.

In addition to his commission, which he donated to the church, Olsen continued to give of his time and money to see his dream of a new church edifice realized. He was for many years a council member of the Norwegian Synod church. His home on Erie Street was an open house to everyone. Pastors and other travelers always found it a haven of friendliness and generosity.

Those were the days of glory in Jens Olsen's life, and when his memory began to fail and his limbs grew weak, this old man could always tell about the visitors to his house, and anecdotes about such noted names in church history as Muus, Bjørn, Schmidt, Koren and others. Before his retirement he had become a much-sought-after mason contractor, and in the course of a career had built a great number of the city schools in Chicago.

John Anderson, later the publisher of *Skandinaven*, arrived in Chicago in 1846, accompanied by his parents from Voss. Among pioneer Norwegians in the city, he has left the greatest imprint on his times. He began his association with the newspaper world as a newsboy for the *Commercial Advertiser*. Two newsboys, of whom Anderson was one, handled the entire circulation at this time. He well recalls that he had one subscriber as far west as Halsted and Randolph streets.

Early Chicago churches

For many years Norwegians in the city had no other cultural association except through the church. Pastor Claus Lauritz Clausen organized a congregation here as early as 1844 but found few occasions to serve it. A Swedish preacher called J. G. Smith was thereupon called as pastor. This Smith appeared to be an adventurer who, under a cloak of piety, created a big scandal in the congregation. He was the first self-installed pastor to administer the sacraments among the Scandinavians in America, as he had in 1841 already organized some sort of a congregation at Koshkonong in Wisconsin. *[Gustaf Smith—more correctly, Gustaf Schmidt, a Swede and allegedly a druggist, came to America in 1843, but it is true that he had organized "some sort of a congregation" at Koshkonong before J. C. W. Dietrichson came in 1844. –Rosholt]*

Gustav Unonius, a well-educated Swedish Episcopal pastor who lived in Wisconsin at the time and knew Smith well, says of him that it was uncertain which country, Sweden or Norway, could take the credit for being Smith's fatherland. After some time in Sweden, he allegedly was thrown into jail for thievery. After his release, he went to America. Here he represented himself as having been a pastor at the court of Stockholm, who for political reasons was forced to leave his fatherland. As a former court pastor, he was accepted as pastor by a group at Koshkonong.

When J. C. W. Dietrichson came to Wisconsin Territory in 1844, he and Clausen were fortunate enough in removing the mask of this impostor. J. G. Smith left these parts and turned up in Chicago. Here he did not claim to be a court pastor, but upheld his churchly authority on the basis of a certificate he had been granted by some unidentified Lutheran synod. When the time came for him to be ordained, Dietrichson sent a strong protest to the congregation. But the letter arrived a day too late, and Smith was installed as pastor for the Norwegian-Swedish congregation in Chicago. This man became the first Norwegian "pastor" in Chicago and was along in the building of the first

Norwegian church in the city. With substantial help from the Presbyterians, a church was raised in 1847 and later sold to a Swedish group.

Smith's activities led to a split in the church that finally forced his ouster. A news story appearing in *Nordlyset* on 18 May 1848 has this to say of the affair: "I want to summarize for our esteemed countrymen living round about, that the brave Norwegians in Chicago today (13 May 1848) celebrated the departure of J. G. Smith. They marched through the streets, following him to the steamboat, with yelling and shouting and the worst condemnations for his outrageous conduct against the Norwegians. More about Smith I do not wish to discuss, nor is there room here in *Nordlyset's* columns. I will say that there is now hope for the future peace and unity of Norwegians in Chicago since St. Anna (Smith) with his false cloaks and six-shooter has retreated in the face of Norwegian valor." *[The reference to St. Anna is no doubt to the Mexican general Santa Anna and the recent war with Mexico. –Rosholt]*

The next Norwegian pastor in Chicago was Paul Anderson, who took over the congregation in 1848. He belonged to the Franckean Synod of Lutherans, which eschewed confirmation. This displeased many of the Norwegians, who withdrew to join the Swedish church under Gustav Unonius.

The latter was an Episcopalian and a very popular pastor. The noted concert artist, Jenny Lind, donated $2,000 toward a church building fund, and as a result, this congregation was to have a beautiful church building. It was to be owned in common between the Norwegians and Swedes, but this arrangement later proved to be a sad mistake.

In those days, people in Chicago had little interest in the Norwegian language, and Paul Anderson often apologized for now and then having to preach in Norwegian for the benefit of the many newcomers. He taught his own children English only, a fact that came to light some years later when he visited Bergen and his children were unable to converse in their mother tongue.

[A footnote in Holand's third edition of De Norske Settlementer's Historie (p. 604) has this to say: "John Anderson, publisher of Skandinaven, who knew Pastor Paul Anderson well, does not agree with the content of this paragraph. He says that Anderson always preached in Norwegian for the main morning service." –Rosholt]

The most important congregation or association of church people was at Our Saviors, organized in Chicago in 1857, which has always been the center of Norwegian affairs in the city. This congregation built a church that soon became too small. In 1871, the year of the great Chicago fire, the congregation constructed an edifice that is still the largest and most architecturally attractive Norwegian church in America.

Owing to the fire, all sorts of building contracts were broken, and costs of construction rose sky-high. The church was finally completed at a cost double the original estimate, or $42,000 *[Norsk Lutherske Menigheter i Amerika (1843-1916) gives a figure of $63,000 –Rosholt]*.

In those days people were overly generous, as the following list of biggest contributors may suggest. Jens Olsen Kaasa donated $3,230; Pastor Jens Krohn, $2,370; Sivert Lund, $799; K. O. Boldstad, $704; H. Halvorsen, $650; Ole Larson, $500; Halvor Mikkelson, $500; John Anderson, $500; G. Gabrielsen, $450; Ole Fosse, $350; Lars Larsen, $300; P. Olsen Skaaden, $250; Arne Hansen, $200; Nils Olai Nilsen, $200; Peter Holst, $150; Bjørn Holland, $150; Knud Karlsen, $150; Peter Thompson, $150; John Halvorsen, $129; George Olsen, $116; and Jacob Wulff, $108.

Norwegians in Chicago now own nearly 30 splendid churches, some of which, when completed, will surpass Our Saviors, but none of which will raise the spirits of as many people as happened on 5 October 1872, when Our Saviors was dedicated.

Charity work

Norwegian business affairs have had a steady growth in Chicago, especially insurance companies. Cultural life is noteworthy for the many glee clubs and choral groups—chiefly under the National Society. With wise management of Norwegian festivities, the society has raised the esteem and dignity of Norwegians to a level previously unknown. The society has also operated an employment bureau where hundreds of people annually find work.

While these civic associations have seen a constant growth and participation in public concerts and other events whose profits will be used for charitable purposes, the churches' own benevolences are carried on by charitable organizations that have had a thorny path to travel.

The work began slowly, as there was no charitable work of any importance before 1885. In the fall of that year, Pastor A. Mortenson from Oslo gave a sermon on the importance of deaconess work, and this made a big impression on the congregation. As a result, on 3 November that same year, the Norwegian Lutheran Tabitha Society was organized and a campaign launched to raise funds for a deaconess building.

But a violent difference of opinion arose over the purposes of the society. As a result, the society split into two factions, each working for its own ends—the one seeking to build a hospital, the other a deaconess institution. After extended arguments and jealousies, an agreement was finally reached in 1892. Enthusiasm ran high: A big sum of money was collected and used for the construction of that grand Tabitha Hospital.

But permanent peace was not to be. The same cantankerous elements that earlier had banded together were still predominant, and a new split in the organization developed in 1895. The Tabitha Society then consisted of 12 clubs, seven of which withdrew on the grounds that the deaconess work and other important functions were being overlooked. These seven clubs met separately—five deciding they would work toward founding a home for the aged, one group opting for an orphan's home, and only a few members of the last of the seven clubs holding out for the original aim, deaconess work.

But "the last shall be first," and this also held true for the friends of the deaconess project. Although they now agreed to support the original aims, it was done with great misgivings. Reservations gave way to a change of heart when it was learned that the United Lutheran Church Synod was becoming more and more interested in this type of work.

In 1892 a large deaconess home and hospital was built, and in 1906 the entire property of the Tabitha Society, which was now considerable, was taken over legally by the United Lutheran Church. The synod has now decided to build a new and larger hospital and deaconess home costing nearly $100,000, the plans for which have already been approved. The deaconess home has for many years now been sending out nurses to hospitals in other cities and to the mission fields.

Meanwhile, the five clubs that were chiefly interested in a home for the aged have purchased a big piece of property in Norwood Park, where many elderly people have since found a home. At present there are 50 members in the home.

It was old Elling Eielsen who first proposed the building of an orphan's home, and when he died in 1882 he left $1,500 in his will for this purpose. But it was not before 1897, chiefly owing to Mrs. Sophie Michaelsen and one of the seven Tabitha clubs, that any interest was taken in the care for orphans. The following year a building was purchased, and here an orphan's home has found its place. It now gives a home to 70 children. As it is already crowded, thought is being given to a larger home to be built in Edison Park.

The rise of respectability

It is particularly in the last 30 years that the great Norwegian population of Chicago became a factor in the growth of the city. It was in the 1880s, when up to 30,000 emigrants came to America from Norway annually, that the great migration from the cities and towns of Norway got under way. For the most part, these city people settled in Chicago as laborers, eager businessmen and respectable medical students—people who had failed to find enough room for their talents in the crowded conditions of the homeland. But in Chicago, there was action and work for everyone.

To Chicago also came the no-goods who thought the city streets were paved with gold, unlucky businessmen, and "black sheep" who wanted to begin life anew, rejected sons of the rich, and drunken students anxious to shut out the past. Yes, Chicago was the labyrinth big enough to hide everything and everyone.

Out of this many-colored hodgepodge of mankind's extremes, there has gradually developed a respectable colony of progressive and law-abiding citizens. A ticket to America has been a lifesaver for more than one man, and Chicago today prides itself on the large number of prominent Norwegian businessmen, lawyers, doctors and enterprising workmen.

Among the many Norsemen who in later years—especially after the Civil War—have made Chicago their home, four men stand out who for enterprise and public esteem have won recognition among all people of Norwegian descent in America. These are Helge A. Haugen, banker; Andrew P. Johnson, a chair manufacturer; Dr. Anders Daae; and Nicolay Andreas Grevstad, a publisher.

Helge A. Haugen was from eastern Norway, the others from the western fylker. This proportion of one eastern Norway man to three western Norway men among our leading men holds more or less true as far as the entire American Midwest is concerned, especially in business and politics.

Andrew P. Johnson, who was from Voss, belongs to the early period, as he was already in Chicago by 1861 and comes from that unusual place in Norway that has sent more enterprising men to America than any other. He opened his first chair factory in 1868. Under his management, it developed into the largest of its kind in the world. The gigantic complex of a seven-story building has floor space covering nearly four acres, and the factory gives steady employment to 700 men. Andrew P. Johnson had great business acumen even by American standards.

Helge A. Haugen was from Oslo and came to Chicago in 1863. For 30 years he has been Chicago's leading Norse banker and is noted as a reliable and levelheaded manager of other people's money. He is president of the State Bank of Chicago, one of the city's largest financial institutions with a capital of $1 million and $17 million in deposits.

Dr. Anders Daae, who came to Chicago in 1880, is neither businessman nor politician but must be considered one of the city's most prominent men. Despite his warm heart, he is best known as a witty satirist and critic of Norwegian-American life, a position he holds without peer. But a satirist, be he ever so witty, cannot maintain his popularity indefinitely. Therefore, there must be other reasons for Dr. Daae's popularity, as he is always first to be asked to national holiday celebrations among his countrymen. As an extemporaneous and entertaining speaker, he has a gift seldom found among Norwegians.

Nicolay Andreas Grevstad came to

Chicago in 1883 and has now been lecturing to Norwegians for 25 years as editor of different Norwegian and English publications. Since 1892, he has been editor-in-chief of *Skandinaven*, the world's largest Norwegian paper. The most enlightened and progressive Norsemen across the entire West read *Skandinaven*, first and last, and the paper holds a position of influence unmatched by any other. The credit for this goes first and foremost to Editor Grevstad, who has the right word and right viewpoint at the right time.

Skandinaven has always desired to represent and lead Norwegian-Americans and is first to refute or correct any false impressions or information that often appears in the American press about Norway and the Norwegian people. To an even greater degree, it has been in the forefront of all noble aims, such as taking up collections for the needy people in the homeland.

Although born in a renter's cottage on Søndmøre (Sunnmøre), Editor Grevstad possesses a world outlook so necessary for the direction of a powerful newspaper of the people. He writes as well in English as in Norse.

7
Muskego Settlement, Milwaukee County, southeastern Wisconsin
(Source: De Norske Settlementers Historie, by Hjalmar Rued Holand, translated by Malcolm Rosholt, 1908, pp. 111–122)

Nearly all the Norwegians who settled in northern Illinois were from Stavanger and the west country of Norway. The people from eastern Norway went farther north and settled in Wisconsin, where the oldest of the settlements was Muskego, made up largely of people from Telemark fylke in southern Norway.

Telemark is represented in America by great numbers of people: Tinn in Øvre-Telemark has sent out more immigrants to America than any other community in Norway, with the possible exception of Lyster (Luster) in Sogn.

In several settlements of the American Midwest, one will find only those people from Tinn. These settlements include Muskego in Racine County (Wisconsin), Winchester in Winnebago County (Wisconsin), Trempealeau Valley in Trempealeau County (Wisconsin), and Harmony and Bloomfield in Fillmore County (Minnesota).

From the Telemark mountain district below Gausdal came the first large influx of pioneers from eastern Norway. In March 1837, while the snow still covered the ground, the trailblazers who left from the east country for America were Ole Nattestad, Ansten Nattestad and Halstein Halvorsen Fløse from Veggli in Numedal.

Norwegian churchmen opposed this emigration from Norway, and the Nattestads used skis to cross the mountains (their destination, Stavanger), stopping overnight on Rue estate, a big farm lying nearest to Tinn. The people here became quite excited over this proposed trip to America and got the *Numedøler* to promise to write them as soon as they reached their destination. This they did, and their letters were full of praise.

The result was that, as early as the summer of 1837, a group of *Tinndøler* prepared to follow the Nattestads, including Gro Jonsdatter Einungbrekke Håkaland, the widow of Torstein Olsson Gollo Rue, and her sons Torstein Torsteinson Rue and Jon Torsteinsson Rue *[Jon later became known as John A. Thompson or Snowshoe Thompson –Gourley].* Also included were Erik Gauteson Midtbø (Erik Gauteson Midtbøen), Nils Johnson Rue and Thov Kittilson Svimbil, all married, plus Gaute Gauteson, a bachelor. They all settled on Fox River (Illinois).

The Rue family was along with the group under Cleng Peerson who in 1838 went to Shelby County, Missouri, and founded a colony there. A couple of years later they moved to Sugar Creek, Lee County, around Keokuk, Iowa, on the Mississippi River, where they founded the first Norwegian settlement in Iowa. Gro Jonsdatter remained in Iowa until 1846, when her son Torstein Rue, together with other *Tinndøler*, went north into Wisconsin and founded

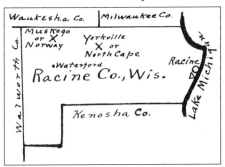

the now widespread settlement at Blue Mound in western Dane County. Gro's son Jon (Snowshoe Thompson) carried the mail on skis across the California mountains for 20 years.

During the period the Rue families lived on Fox River, letters sent to friends in Norway influenced others to join them—one of them being John Nilson Luraas, a respected farmer and man of good insight. Under his leadership, 40 other *Tinndøler* prepared to leave for America in the summer of 1839.

The other heads of families included Knut Nilson Luraas, Torger Østenson Luraas, Halvor Østenson Luraas, Helge Mathieson, Halvor T. Lyngflaat (Wind Lake), Halvor Nelson Lohner, Ole Hellikson Krokan and Østen Møllerflaten, all from Tinn; and Nils Johnson Kaasa from Hitterdal, all with their families. In addition, there were four bachelors—John Evenson Molee (Møly), Nils Tollefsjorden, Ole Tollefsjorden and John Tollefsjorden. A number of these men were highly regarded in their home communities.

In Goteborg (Sweden) they joined a party of 20 people from Stavanger, Gitle Danielson among them. The two groups were bound for Boston and were the first Norwegians to arrive in this city. They crossed the Great Lakes on a miserable ship loaded with ammunition. There was not as much danger of an explosion as of drowning, because the ship leaked like a sieve and twice nearly sank. But the passengers finally reached the ship's destination—Milwaukee.

Immigrants diverted to Muskego

While the newcomers laid over waiting for accommodations to Chicago, where they were to go on to Fox River, some clever Americans became aware of these strong, accustomed-to-work immigrants. They would be splendid people for the development of Milwaukee's outland. It certainly would not do to let them continue to Illinois.

A committee was organized to explain to the immigrants what great opportunities awaited them here and how unwise it would be to go on to Illinois, where the sun burned up the crops and malaria attacked people like flies. Wisconsin had great forests to burn for kitchen wood, building materials and navigable inland waters.

As the Americans had no interpreters, most of this talk went over the heads of the newcomers. However, a pale and emaciated chap named John W. Pixley, a recent arrival from Illinois, was brought forward as an example of the fate that awaited those who went there. Pixley had a hollow cough, and those who heard him were visibly impressed, in a sense confirming everything that had been said.

The committee chairman, George H. Walker, a heavy-set man with a quick tongue and a resident of Milwaukee for several years, pointed to himself as an outstanding example of the region's productivity and healthy climate. Another man present at the meeting was the city's first settler, Salomon Juneau, a man who without straining himself could throw a grown man over his head—further evidence of Milwaukee's bracing climate.

It was more than enough for the trusting country people, and some of them forgave in their own mind the captain of the ammunition ship, since they had been lucky enough to have landed in such a wonderful place as Milwaukee.

A committee from the city and from among the newcomers was then sent out to find a suitable place for a colony. The nearest location where the land had not yet been taken up was in the neighborhood of Lake Muskego in Waukesha County about 15 miles southwest of Milwaukee. Of course, the region was marshy with many towering oaks, which earlier American pioneers had declined with thanks. But the American guides thought these raw-boned mountaineers would be just the kind of people to clear the forests and drain the swamps.

The marshes in summer heat were dry and covered with high grass, and the *Tinndøler* thought this looked very promising. They returned to Milwaukee and all entered claims, happy in the thought that, after four months of travel, they had found a home at last.

But this bright outlook was short-lived. When the autumn rains began, the waving grassland was soon under water, and the newcomers had to take to the forest if they were to find any productive land.

In addition, it was an extremely unhealthy place, where endemic fever prevailed many months of the year. The terrible scourge of malaria, which they had been warned against, did not fail to come, as there is probably no place in Wisconsin more conducive to malaria than the region around Muskego.

There were also many rattlesnakes, but the settlers, after killing four or five a day, became accustomed to them, crushing the head of the snake beneath their heel without batting an eye. Worse were all the toads and worms that had to be removed from the drinking water before one could quench his thirst.

But the endurance of these old pioneers was unbelievable. Clearing the land of trees, plus dealing with sickness and tribulation, could well check their progress—but not their courage. They sweated and slaved against the wilderness and against disease with a patience that would not accept defeat.

Although some of them buckled under and went to an unconsecrated grave in a foreign land or went away to a less hardy place, most of them stayed at the same time new settlers were constantly arriving, mainly *Telemarkinger*.

At home in an Indian mound

At this time there lived in Drammen, Norway, an enlightened merchant who needs to be remembered—namely, Tollef O. Bakke. Bakke was deeply interested in America's freedom and had given considerable thought to the new era for mankind in that country. His son, Søren Tollefson Bakke, was an impractical dreamer, full of all sorts of whims and conceits, and many people were convinced there was something wrong with his head.

In 1839 his father decided to send him to America in the hope that it would do something for him. He provided his son with ample funds and sent a companion with him, an agreeable and trusted office friend by the name of Johannes Johannesen from Ledsager.

These two young men came to Fox River settlement in the fall of 1839, but here all the woodland along the river had been claimed, and Johannesen was very suspicious of the naked prairie.

That same year the two men accompanied Elling Eielsen to the north and came to Wind Lake south of Muskego where the *Telemarkinger* had already settled. This location suited them fine, and the two men shoveled out a sod dugout on the west side of a big Indian mound where Muskego church presently stands (1908). The dugout was later boarded on the inside, and here the two men lived in comfort. The Indian mound later came to be the central point of the settlement known as Muskego.

Since Johannes Johannesen and Søren Tollefson Bakke were highly pleased with their circumstances in America, they wrote to their acquaintances in Norway, and a number of them prepared to leave. In the fall of 1840 a big group from Drammen and Lier arrived, including Even H. Heg, Johannes Skofstad, Ole Anderson, Helge Thompson and Syvert Ingebretsen. Arriving at the same time were the families of Knut Aslakson Svalestuen, the first to leave from Vinje in Telemark, and Ole Hogensen, the first from Eggedal.

Even H. Heg was a well-to-do yet generous man whose first house in Muskego became a Mecca for the newcomers. Later, when he built a large barn, it, too, was often filled with new arrivals, especially in the summer months when most people chose to travel to America. At the Hegs, people knew beforehand that there was free lodging and hospitality. Thousands of old pioneers slept in this barn. And when the immigrants were ready to continue on to Koshkonong and other places in the West, one of Heg's sons was always willing to act as a guide.

In recognition of Heg's great contribution to the Muskego settlement, it was often referred to as "Heg." Noblest among all pioneers was this kindly disposed man.

His son, Hans Christian Heg, has won a name most honored in Norwegian-American history. When the Civil War began, he took the lead in recruiting the 15th Regiment, Wisconsin Volunteers, which was mostly made up of officers and men of Norse descent. Under his command, this regiment took heavy casualties but won fame for its bravery. This also marked the end of the Heg saga when, as brevet brigadier general, he was fatally wounded in the battle of Chickamauga in Georgia.

West of the Indian mound, or on the site of the present (1908) Muskego settlement, there lies a big marsh several miles in length. To the west of this marsh lies a beautiful prairie with spotted woodlands, now known as North Cape. *[Actually, North Cape lies south of Muskego in Racine County. –Rosholt]*

This part of the settlement traces its

beginning to 1840, when Mons Adland from Samnanger in Bergen settled here. He was the last man to leave the unlucky Beaver Creek settlement south of Chicago. One of his brothers was the well-known leader and later editor, Knud Langeland, who came to Muskego in 1843. Langeland contributed much to the welfare of the settlement and was a leader among Scandinavians in Wisconsin—not only as a journalist, but also as a man who interested himself in politics. A school in Chicago is named after him.

Accompanying Mons Adland to Wisconsin was Nils Johnson, the first man to leave from Hitterdal *[the modern Heddal in northeast Telemark –Rosholt]*. A man of many talents and by nature a born leader, he came to America in the same group that included the Luraas clan, working a year in Milwaukee. Ten years later he led a group of newcomers to Winneshiek County, Iowa, where he founded the well-known Washington Prairie settlement.

Nils Johnson's nearest neighbor in Iowa was Halvor Larson Lysenstøen or, as he was more often called, Halvor Modum, the first to emigrate from Hadeland in 1842. In 1846 he revisited his home in Norway and created a sensation when he appeared unannounced one Sunday morning on the church hill at Brandbu.

"Look at that man, will you!" people said. "He has been all the way to America and returned home alive! Think of all the sea monsters, rattlesnakes and scalp-hunting Indians he has escaped."

People were stunned at the sight of him, and old women approached him devoutly, while everyone listened to his slightest remarks as if they were the inspired word of God.

Hermond Nilsen Tufte, the first to leave from Hallingdal and a fine old pioneer, also went to the Winneshiek settlement. He became the father-in-law to three other well-known pioneers—namely, Elling Eielsen, O. B. Dahle and Mons Adland. His son was known as one of the most kindly disposed persons in Racine County (Wisconsin). Now there are twice as many *Hallinger* in America as in Hallingdal, Norway (1908).

To North Cape, or Yorkville Prairie as it was also known, came the first people from Nord-Trøndelag fylke in northern Norway. Elling Hendrikson Spillum from Overhalden *[today Overhalla –Rosholt]* came to America in 1844 and quickly took a liking to his new environment. He returned to Overhalden, gathered together some of his old neighbors and left for Yorkville Prairie in 1845. This group included Elling Spillum, Ole J. Homstad, Matthias L. Heimo and Mads Rynningen, all with families, and the first people to leave from Trøndelag.

The most widely known man in Muskego for many years was James Denoon Reymert, a lawyer from Farsund who, as a result of his training, took a lead in many undertakings in America. He first operated a sawmill at Reymert's Lake *[today, Silver Lake in Waukesha County, Wisconsin –Rosholt]*, which was a great help to the new settlers. Later he won a contract to build a plank road between Muskego and Waterford. Many of his countrymen were given employment on this project, and it became a boon to the two communities.

Reymert was the first Norwegian to win a seat in the state legislature, where he played an important role in Wisconsin politics. Later he removed to Polk County, Wisconsin—the first Norwegian in that county, where he owned considerable property around St. Croix Falls and did a thriving business in real estate. From there he moved to New York City, where he returned to law practice. He finally ended up as a federal judge in Arizona Territory, an appointment made by President Cleveland.

Meanwhile, Søren Tollefson Bakke

and Johannes Johannesen were doing a brisk business in real estate from their "office" in the Indian mound. This mound was an old burial ground, where hundreds of Indians had been buried. This did not bother these two cave dwellers, even when a leg bone now and then protruded through the walls.

As Svein Nilson writes: "Here was the main office for intelligence information and culture, a depot for luxury and good living, and here were handled all banking and money matters."

Unfortunately, the activities of Bakke-Johannesen did not last very long. One day, when Søren Bakke had been out with his gun roving through the woods, he returned with Pastor Clausen to the house of a newcomer named Ole G. Storlie, originally from Kviteseid in Telemark. As Bakke sat and toyed with his gun, a bullet discharged, striking and killing Storlie's wife.

Bakke was almost beside himself with grief and did all he could to assuage the husband's loss. He offered either to bring up all the Storlie children and provide for their education, or to give Storlie several pieces of land as well as money, which he accepted.

Søren Bakke never got over this accident, and his old friend Johannes Johannesen died shortly thereafter. Later, Bakke returned to Norway. *[Later historians believe that it was not Søren Bakke's grief but the illness of his father that brought him back to Norway. From the extensive diary kept by Bakke and recently translated, it is difficult to believe that this certified gossip took anything very seriously for long. –Rosholt]*

Churches, schools, newspapers take root

Muskego is a community that boasts many great men and holds many memories. In this Telemark settlement, despite low ground and unhealthy living conditions, the foundations were laid for several important institutions. Here, Scandinavians first began to participate in American politics and directions.

From here went the call to arms for Norwegian participation in the Civil War, in which the immigrants willingly and staunchly were ready to defend their adopted land. Here began the first Norwegian parochial school, which is now continued in the many important institutions of higher learning.

Here was organized the first Norwegian Lutheran congregation to which the first Norwegian pastor was called. *[Holand is referring to C. L. Clausen, who was ordained in Wisconsin, rather than Elling Eielsen, founder of the Hauge Synod. – Rosholt]*

Here, the first Norwegian church was built. *[Construction on a church was begun at Muskego in 1844 but not completed until the spring of 1845, several months after East Koshkonong church was completed and dedicated in December 1844 and West Koshkonong in January 1845. –Rosholt]*

Here, *Nordlyset*, the first Norwegian newspaper in America, was published.

Norwegian church history in America actually begins with Claus Lauritz Clausen, born in Denmark, but who spent most of his early life working in Norway. In 1843 he was urged by Tollef Bakke, referred to earlier, to go to America to serve as a pastor or parochial schoolteacher among his countrymen.

He arrived in Muskego on 8 August 1843, and soon realized that what the people really needed was a pastor and not a schoolteacher. A letter of call dated 19 September 1843, with 69 signatures, was sent him. On 18 October he was ordained by a German pastor, and a month later it was decided to build a church the following year.

Here, Tollef Bakke expressed his concern for his countrymen in America by sending $420 for the proposed building—apparently the only instance of any significant sum of money ever sent from Norway to America.

Meanwhile, Clausen was using

Even Heg's big barn to hold worship services. On the second Sunday after Easter (1844), the first Norwegian confirmands renewed their baptismal vows. Also in this barn, the first Norwegian couples to be married by a Norwegian pastor in America included John Evenson Mølee to Anne Jacobsdatter Einong, and Hans Tveito to Aslaug Jacobsdatter Einong, all *Tinndøler*. The double wedding was a memorable occasion for everyone.

Pastor Clausen was a highly gifted, zealous and patient man. In his unassuming and folksy manner, he was able to win over the hearts of everyone. *[This is rather doubtful in view of the split that occurred in his church a year later. –Rosholt]*

Clausen's wife also is remembered with great esteem. While he was out in the woods competing with experienced loggers cutting big oak trees to be used in the new church, his wife remained at home instructing, without pay, the children of the community.

The first Muskego church was an impressive building made entirely of logs, the very best timber, and carpentered with a skill unmatched by any Norwegian log church built later. It was "a noble heritage … venerable in its simple beauty, most holy in its antiquity, the proudest of our days." *[Holand gives no source for this quotation. –Rosholt]*

The head carpenter was Halvor Nilsen Lohner from Hjartdal in Telemark fylke. Ole Hogenson shingled the roof while Kari, his wife, carried the shingles up the ladder.

[A footnote by Holand relates that when he went to see what the old Muskego church looked like in 1897, he found that it was being used as a pig house. He wrote a letter to Skandinaven expressing his indignation and shame at seeing the once-famous building reduced to such ignominy. As a result, Pastor Germund Høyme, president of the United Lutheran Synod based at Eau Claire, Wisconsin, and Gerhard Rasmussen took the lead in a movement to rescue and restore the building. It has since been moved to St. Anthony Park in St. Paul, Minnesota, on the grounds of the Luther Seminary, where it is preserved as a museum.]

Even as sin and dissension entered the world after the fall of man, Muskego did not escape its consequences. At the same time that Clausen was being ordained, so also was Elling Eielsen. He had no new gospel to proclaim but was most anxious to be considered the founder of the Norske Synod in America.

Eielsen therefore refused to concede an inch to Clausen, a regularly ordained pastor, and bent every effort toward organizing an opposing congregation at Muskego. *[Holand was unaware of documentary evidence since brought to light, which suggests that Eielsen was also a "regularly" ordained pastor. –Rosholt]*

When Dietrichson, this domineering representative of Norway's state church, arrived in Muskego the year following (1844), the camps really came to life.

It is said that Eielsen at one point grabbed Dietrichson by the whiskers and melodramatically quoted: "Hear me, you pope, I'll be your plague as long as I live."

[There is more than one version of this alleged incident and the wording used. It paraphrases an older exclamation, but after translating Dietrichson's own version of his meeting with Eielsen, I have reason to believe it did not happen in this manner. The two men, Eielsen and Dietrichson, argued hotly, and Dietrichson walked out of one confrontation rather than accept further abuse. But a year later when the two men met by chance on a roadside, their meeting was cordial. –Rosholt]

Here in Muskego, the first Norwegian newspaper, *Nordlyset*, came out in 1847 under the sponsorship and editorial direction of Even Heg and James Reymert. It was a newspaper of four pages, with four columns to the page. Subscriptions ran fairly well the first year, with about 200 names on the list. But money was scarce and when the day came to pay up, there were not many renewals. *Nordlyset* lasted only two years or so. Now (1908) our Norwegian papers in America have a combined subscription list of nearly 300,000.

Epidemics claim many lives

One of the reasons for the failure of *Nordlyset* was the pestilential diseases that took thousands of Norwegian immigrants in the years 1849 to 1852. Nearly all settlements were affected, but Muskego was probably the hardest hit. The place was unhealthy to begin with. Pastor Clausen said that when he came here in 1843, malaria and endemic fever were rampant and scarcely a house in the settlement escaped. Nearly every day someone died. Poverty increased the misery, as those who came from Norway in the fall, who had no means of support further than their destination,

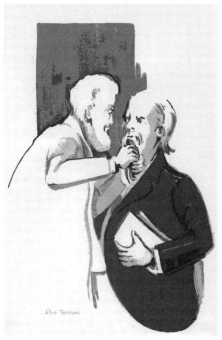

remained in the settlement because it was the closest to Milwaukee.

The poverty and need among them was so great that Clausen at last turned to the Americans for help. *[Township records on Waukesha County for this period confirm Clausen's statement about assistance given the Norwegians at Muskego by the town board. –Rosholt]*

The worst year at Muskego was 1849, when cholera broke out and ravaged the entire settlement. Like the angel of death in the land of Egypt, it passed scarcely a house. There was not even time for funeral services, as people died so fast that the living were absolutely bewildered. Healthy people who went to bed at night lay stiff in the morning.

The powerfully built Hans Tveito and his brother-in-law, John Mølee, had all they could do to carry out the dead. Other men worked day and night to make coffins from rough, unpainted boards. Here the dead were laid out without washing and lowered into graves without ceremony. The next day it was perhaps the turn of the pallbearer to be carried away. People became panic-stricken, and those who could get away left this pestilential community.

There is hardly a place among Norwegian settlements in America where so many tears have been shed, nor hardly a community that has lived through so many hardships and disappointments. Nor has there been a place more frequently marked by internal dissension, illness and misery.

But for others it means much more. It signifies great accomplishments conceived in prayer, and far-reaching undertakings born of struggle. Here, many of our greatest and best men have dreamed of the future, and here was the port of entry through which many thousands of our upright but hard-pressed countrymen went on to long and useful lives and pleasant old age.

Long live Muskego!

8
Jefferson Prairie Settlement, Rock County, Wisconsin, and Long Prairie Settlement, Boone County, Illinois

(Source: *De Norske Settlementers Historie*, by Hjalmar Rued Holand, translated by Malcolm Rosholt, 1908, pp. 123–127)

When the remaining members of the Beaver Creek colony moved away from this unlucky spot, some went to Chicago, but the majority went to the Fox River settlement (west of Chicago). Ole Nattestad, however, went north into Wisconsin Territory and on 1 July 1838, became the first Norwegian to settle in the future state.

The spot he chose as his future home, and for that of the others who were to follow, was a couple of miles south of the present city of Clinton in Rock County on what was then known as Jefferson Prairie. The Wisconsin-Illinois line runs fairly through the middle, east to west.

Meanwhile, Ansten Nattestad, a brother of Ole Nattestad, had some business affairs to clear up in Norway and had returned home, where he also oversaw the publication of a booklet written by Ole Rynning on conditions in America.

As to his visit home, he had this to say: "While I did not wish to exaggerate the excellent opportunities in America, I did explain in simple terms to those I talked to of my own experiences in the New World. Nevertheless, reports of my homecoming spread throughout the countryside like a forest fire, and during the winter people kept coming from far and near to hear about America. Letters of inquiry arrived from all directions. Some men came 20 Norwegian miles *[140 English miles –Rosholt]* just to talk with me. By the spring of 1839 there were so many emigrants ready to leave from Rollag alone, that Captain Anderson's ship, anchored in Drammen —which had accommodations for 100 passengers—could not find room for them all, and many had to go to Goteborg in Sweden to board another ship."

When Ansten Nattestad arrived in Chicago, he heard that his brother, Ole Nattestad, had taken land in Wisconsin. He therefore went on to Wisconsin, accompanied by the immigrants who had joined him. Most of them settled on Jefferson Prairie and round about.

Until Ansten Nattestad's return to Norway, there had been only an insignificant movement of emigrants from eastern Norway, but with his visit many people began to leave. Among those who returned to America with him were Erik G. Skavlem, Kittel Nyhus (Kittel Newhouse), Christopher Nyhus (Christopher Newhouse), Thore Helgeson Kirkejord and Thorstein Helgeson Kirkejord, all from Numedal. They sailed on the *Emilia*, the first ship to carry emigrants from eastern Norway.

Jens Gulbrandsen Myhre and Gulbrand Gulbrandsen Myhre from Numedal, two men who later became well-known pioneers, also arrived in Jefferson Prairie in 1839. The settlement is made up mainly of *Numedøler*, who are now united in one big church congregation. The farmers here do not go in for tobacco-growing, so common in other Norwegian settlements of southern Wisconsin. Nevertheless, they are well-to-do farmers.

Klemet Stabæk, a wealthy man, came to America in the same group under Ansten Nattestad in 1839. However, he took a claim at Rock Run across the state line in Stephenson County (Illinois), where he founded a settlement once considered important but now practically nonexistent.

Long Prairie

A few miles south of Jefferson Prairie and nearly running together with it is a smaller settlement called Long

Bedstemoders Brudekrone

Prairie in Illinois. This is the original home of the people from Sogn. Although there are not more than 400 Norwegians, many large groups from Sogn had temporarily located here and later spread into the Midwest, especially to Freeborn County, Minnesota, and Worth County, Iowa.

The name "Long Prairie" is a misnomer, as it is not a prairie but a heavily wooded district. A small opening in the forest a few miles to the west gave its name to the settlement.

The people from Sogn are, without doubt, the most numerous among Norwegian settlements in America. There are thousands of them in Dane, Crawford and Buffalo counties of Wisconsin, and Fillmore, Freeborn, Faribault and Goodhue counties in Minnesota. Lyster (Luster) in Sogn alone is represented by nearly 10,000 sons and daughters who on the whole are quite well-to-do. There are many successful businessmen among them.

The first to arrive among all these 50,000 or so *Sogninger* was a man known as Per Unde from Vik. He saw a copy of Ole Rynning's *True Account of America* and, though a man in good circumstances, was carried away by the traditional Viking lust for freedom of movement.

In 1839 he sailed to America and came to Chicago, together with some people from Voss who were en route to Hamilton Diggings (now Wiota, Wisconsin) to dig for lead. Per Unde, who went along with them, soon took a piece of land in the same neighborhood and built a shanty on the slope of a hill.

It was his letters home that caused the great emigration from Sogn. So great was his enthusiasm for conditions in America that in 1844 two shiploads of people from Vik left to join him—actually, the first two ships to sail with emigrants from Sogn. The names of the ships have been forgotten, but the captains were Brock and Vingaard. People therefore refer to these ships as *Brock-ship* and *Vingaard-ship*.

Fortunately, the names of nearly all the passengers are preserved. Among those on *Brock-ship* were Lars Johnson Haave, Ole Berdahl, Ole Aavri, Iver Ingebretson Hove, Ingebret Vange, Ole Vange, Iver Risløv, Endre Stadheim, Ole Stadheim, John Hove, Per Hove, and Little John Hove.

Among those on *Vingaard-ship* were John Fylie (John Following), Ole Tistel, Andreas Hermundson Numedal, Ole Orvedahl, Ansin Seim, Iver Fylie, Lars Olson Hove, Ole P. Tenold, and Lars Jenson Hove. Most of these men were married, self-supporting farmers in Norway, and as a result some of them had working capital when they came to the U.S. Among the latter were John Fylie and Lars Johnson Hove, who both purchased tickets for a number of younger men and women so they could leave with them.

The weather was bad on the day these pioneers were ready to sail. Sognefjord's waves rolled darkly under the narrow mountain outlet to the sea. Captain Vingaard decided to wait a day before sailing, but Brock weighed anchor despite the weather and got a head start. But self-congratulations were premature, because early one morning a few days later *Brock-ship* saw a sail on the horizon to the east. This was *Vingaard-ship* which, with a good wind, was approaching the other with loud hurrahs and by noon had passed *Brock-ship*. By nightfall it had passed out of sight, and Vingaard arrived in New York three weeks ahead of the other.

[Holand appears to have confused his ships. Brock-ship, actually the Albion, was commanded by Jacob Thode Brock. It arrived in New York from Bergen on 10 July 1844, with 62 passengers on board. But the passengers listed by Holand as sailing on Vingaard-ship were actually on the Juno, commanded by Niels Bendixen, which reached New York on 24 June 1844, with 110 passengers. Captain Uldrich Wilhelm Vingaard is listed in Norsk

Biografisk Leksikon, p. 355, as a skipper out of Bergen in 1845. It is still possible that the race referred to by Holand actually took place between Vingaard and Brock at another time, but from the evidence of the ships' manifests, obviously not in the summer of 1844. The race referred to here apparently involved the Albion and Juno, which would have made this Brock-ship and Bendixen-ship. –Rosholt]

All these passengers were en route to Wiota to join Per Unde. After getting through the Erie Canal, where they experienced many difficulties, they finally arrived in Belvidere (Illinois). Here they met a *Telemarking*, Thore Olsen Kaasa, who strongly advised them against the move to Wiota.

He had traveled widely in Wisconsin and said it was impossible to live on the hills in Lafayette County where Wiota is located. Furthermore, the place was 200 miles from market. He suggested they go with him to his home near Capron in Boone County (Illinois), about 12 miles southwest of the Jefferson Prairie colony, where the land is flat and rich and moreover only 70 miles from Chicago.

Thore Olsen Kaasa was so persuasive that the entire group decided to accompany him, leaving behind a few in Belvidere to advise the incoming group from *Brock-ship* of their new destination. When the second group finally reached Belvidere, it, too, decided to join the colony near Capron, and Wiota's hills were, therefore, never populated with *Sogninger*.

Thore Olsen Kaasa and his brothers, Jørgen Olsen Kaasa and Jens Olsen Kaasa, later a mason contractor and leader among Chicago Norsemen, had come to Boone County in 1843, the first to arrive there. Thov Knutsen Traim, Bjørn Bakketo (Bjørn Brekketo), Johannes Kleiva, and Ole T. Kaasa, all from Seljord in Telemark, joined the colony in 1844. Later arrivals were all *Sogninger.*

At the same time he organized a congregation on Jefferson Prairie, Pastor Dietrichson organized a congregation of Lutherans here in 1844. The area had always been plagued by church dissension, and this harmed the colony's growth. There were four different Lutheran congregations in the area.

Re

9
Rock Prairie (Luther Valley) Settlement, Rock County, Wisconsin

(Source: De Norske Settlementers Historie, by Hjalmar Rued Holand, translated by Malcolm Rosholt, 1908, pp. 128–141)

Four of Ansten Nattestad's comrades did not like it on Jefferson Prairie. The disenchanted ones were Gullik Olson Gravdahl, Gisle Halland and Eno Bjøno, from Numedal, and Lars Røste, the first man to leave from Land in Oppland fylke and the Lake Mjøsa region about 65 miles north of Oslo.

These men went farther west and by nightfall came to a stretch of rolling prairie, well provided with woodlots and water resources. They liked it here and all took out claims. Eno Bjøno also bought enough for Gunhild Ødegaarden, a well-to-do widow from Numedal, who had paid for the tickets to America of several people less well situated. Her house was therefore the first to be built, and this marked the beginning of Rock Prairie settlement (Luther Valley), one of the most noted in Norwegian-American history.

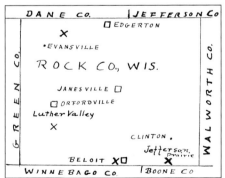

It should be added that Pastor Dietrichson, who visited the settlement in 1844, says that Gullik Halvorson Skavlem from Numedal was the first to settle here in 1839.

Gullik Knudsen Laugen and Halvor Pederson Haugen, two later well-known pioneers, also came from Numedal accompanied by Ansten Nattestad. In 1841 Laugen and Haugen removed to Rock Prairie, as did others, including Lars Skavlem, Hellik Glaim, Nils Olson Vegli, Hellik B. Brekke, Paul Skavlem and Ole Halvorson Valle, the last named being the first to found a settlement of Norwegians in Iowa.

Gullik Laugen settled on Rock Prairie near a spring and thereafter was always known to his neighbors as Gullik Springen. Here he built a shanty of wattle brush and covered it with straw. Gunnel Stordock, who arrived in May that same year, lived three months in a haystack.

The first winter, Gullik Springen and Hellik Glaim went on skis across the prairie to Beloit to purchase flour. The Americans along the way saw these phantoms moving across the snow and could not imagine what sort of animals these were that left such strange tracks. The sight of them caused all kinds of talk, and people went out into the snow to lock their gates.

Luther Valley (Rock Prairie) menighet.

Orfordville (4½ mil sydøst), Rock Co., Wis.
Utenom, 1844–51; Norske synode, 1851–68.
Organisert 1844. Splittet 1868, paa grund av slaveristriden (Luther Valley—Fk, Luther Valley—Ns). 250 sjæle i 1844, 355 i 1868. Prester: C. L. Clausen, 1844–51; G. F. Dietrichson, 1851–59; C. F. Magelssen, 1859–69.

The community's leading naturalist explained that out here in the forests of the West there was bound to be one or another previously unidentified monster whose organs of locomotion produced these tracks. But whether this creature could travel in summer, and whether it would attack in force and eat humans, he was unable to say.

One of the most highly regarded old-timers on Rock Prairie is Hellik Olson Holtan, who came from Flesberg in Numedal in 1843, where he was considered an enlightened man. Because of his unimpeachable character and fairness, the farmers of Numedal went to him to settle their disputes and legal affairs that neither town officials nor sheriffs could handle. Nor was there ever an appeal made by either party in a dispute.

Among other noted *Numedøler* must be mentioned the Haugen clan. J. C. Johnson, writing in *America* in 1907, has this to say:

"The family ancestor in this country, old Halvor P. Haugen, came from Numedal with Ansten Nattestad in 1839. With him were his wife, three sons—Peter Halvorson Haugen, Halvor Halvorson Haugen and Andreas Halvorson Haugen—and daughters Bergit Halvorsdatter Haugen and Sigrid Halvorsdatter Haugen. He borrowed funds from Erik Skavlem to defray the cost of the journey to America. With these advantages, the family foundation was laid.

"He was a type of backwoods philosopher with a remarkable memory and powers of observation, possessed with such profound knowledge of the wind and weather that it could have made monkeys of our scientific forecasters of today. Had he had a background in science, he undoubtedly would have earned a name for himself. He was also endowed with an even temperament and a liberal outlook on life.

"His oldest son, Peter Halvorson Haugen, resembles his father the most, both outwardly and inwardly. A helpful person, he thought nothing of staying up night after night, caring for the sick in times of stress. He had a boundless thirst for good reading."

Halvor P. Haugen was one of the first men to visit Minnesota. This occurred in 1850 when he, together with five other youths from Rock Prairie, journeyed to the site of the present city of Red Wing. Here, Haugen and an American started a business in lime-burning. This continued for about a year, when the partnership failed owing to the inability to make collections.

This was before any white man began to plow the ground in the later well-known county of Goodhue. Haugen and his companions then returned to Rock Prairie.

Pioneer counterfeiters

Hellik Glaim was a local hero of big dimensions. There are many stories in circulation about him; his strength, coolness and zest for life would be hard to match. His heroic deeds were expressed mostly in playing tricks.

In those days the monetary system was far from sound. Chicago and other cities passed their own laws according to local conditions. Small slips of paper or notes printed by every Tom, Dick and Harry, with words such as "Good for a shave," "Good for a nickel drink," or "Good for a cord of wood," were used as money. These passed from one hand to another until finally, after wide circulation, they were worn out and valueless to the source of issue and could no longer be redeemed for the original goods or service.

Some of our pioneers, and especially Hellik Glaim, began to wonder about this and decided that if everybody could issue notes, then so could they. In order that this currency would last longer and not lose its value, Glaim decided to make it of metal. A mint was started on Glaim's farm located about a quarter of a mile west of the parsonage on Rock Prairie.

Operations were mainly carried on in the quiet hours of the night. One can still find here and there on this farm 25-cent pieces dated 1840, which are exactly like real coins except that there is not a trace of silver in them.

Some of Glaim's assistants moved to Koshkonong where they went into the same business but were later arrested. Later, Hellik Glaim was among the pioneers of Fillmore and Yellow Medicine counties in Minnesota.

Pioneers from Hallingdal

Rock Prairie (Luther Valley) is patently a settlement of *Numedøler*, but it also is the oldest and most important settlement of people from Hallingdal. Many prominent men of the Midwest of Halling descent first stubbed their toes on Rock Prairie.

In the first wave of Halling pioneers were Knud Ellingsen Solem and John Ellingsen Solem, who came in 1842 from Flaa, about 60 miles northwest of Oslo. Another prominent Halling leader, Kleofas Halvorson from Hansemoen in Næs, came to Rock Prairie in 1843. Encouraged by his letters home, many people prepared to leave, and by 1846 there were as many as 300 *Hallinger* who had left to join the settlement on Rock Prairie.

Among the more well-known were Hans Husemoen, Erik Kolsrud, Ole Sande, Ole Hei, Tollef Tollefsrud and sons, Ole Rime, Henrik Rime, Timan Burtness, Johan Burtness, Asle Hesla, Nils Haugen, Halvor Næs, Guttorm Roen, Ole Roen, Knut Trøstem and Henrik Trøstem.

In 1848 two sailing ships arrived in the U.S. carrying only *Hallinger*, among them the big Kvarve clan, today probably the most widely spread people of Halling descent in America. The *Hallinger* have, since the beginning, been the most numerous on Rock Prairie, and thousands of others have paused here before going elsewhere and founding the big settlements in Clayton, Allamakee and Mitchell counties in Iowa, and Spring Grove, New Richland, Kenyon and Blooming Prairie in Minnesota. The largest of all is in Richland County, North Dakota, south of Fargo. Now (1908) there are around 25,000 *Hallinger* in America.

Many of the above-mentioned pioneers were prosperous farmers in Norway and assisted their less-fortunate neighbors in buying tickets to America.

People from Land, Oppland also found a Mecca on Rock Prairie. Lars Røste, as already mentioned, came here as early as 1839, accompanied by Gullik Gravdahl. Røste was the first to leave from Land, where he was highly regarded. In 1843 his neighbors decided to leave their fishing industry and join him—a man so stupid and rash as to leave a good farm in Land and take off for this pagan America.

Among others who left Land that year (1843) were:
- Peter Gaarder
- Harold Ommelstad
- Peter Lundesæther
- Søren Olson Sørum (The first Norwegian to visit St. Paul, Minnesota)

Peter Gaarder paid the expenses of Søren Olson, who as compensation agreed to work three years for him without wages. This is about the only instance of a man accepting Norwegian money in exchange for indentured labor in America.

Hans C. Tollefsrude left Hallingdal in 1844. The progenitor of a large family in America, he was known as a man of nervous energy who never lost his sense of balance, was capable and trustworthy but unmovable once he had made up his mind. The Tollefsrude Family Association now (1908) has a membership of nearly 300.

Old Tollefsrude kept a diary of his first years in America in which he wrote down the names of each person who arrived from Land. His son, C. H. Tollefsrude, has turned over this list to Pastor P. O. Langseth, who permitted its publication in *Amerika* (8 March 1907).

Here are some of the entries:
- 1839: Lars Røste has also arrived.
- 1842: Hans Smedsrud and wife arrived.
- 1843: Harold Ommelstad (five in family); Peder Gaarder (five in family); Anders Lundsæteren (five in family); Søren Sørum and Anne Mari Nilsdatter
- 1844: Lars Nord-Fossum with family of six; Andreas Erstad and wife; Hans C. Tollefsrude with wife; Anders Midtbøn (Anders Midtbøen) with wife and one child; Syver Johnson Smed; Gudbrand Gaarder; Helene Gaarder; Anders Engen; Inger Gaarder; and Helene Klevmoen. Erstad went to Rock Run and Syver Smed to Wiota.
- 1845: Two families arrived, each with six members—namely, Askild Ullensager and Tarald Jørandlien.
- 1846: Mari Engen with a son and daughter arrived, in addition to Erik Nederhaugen.
- 1847: Svend Nørstelien with family of seven; Ole Nørstelien; Christine Nørstelien; Hans Sveum with family of seven; and Kari Lillebæk with family of seven arrived. The first and last-named families went to Wiota.

1848 saw a big expansion. Ole Gaarder and wife; Andreas Sørum; Christian Lunde (later migrated to Zumbrota, Minnesota); Hovel Tollefsrud and family of seven; Ingebrigt Fossum and family of six; Halvor Ruud with family of seven; Johannes Nederhaugen with family of four; Johan Frankrige with family of five; and Hovel Jensvold. H. Tollefsrud went to Wiota as well as the following four families: Johan Smed with family of four; Johannes Brenom with five; John Smedsand with four; Hans Brenden with five; Hovel Smeby; and Bertha Lybæk, who married S. Midtbøn—a total of 53 souls.

In 1849, also a good year, saw a total of 48 arrivals, including Johans Lybæk; Johannes Ommelstadsæteren; Ingeborg Ommelstadsæteren; Marthea Brendingen; Bertha Frøslie; Marit Frøslie; Nils Aasen and Ole Monsen Tollefsrud with family of five, who went on to Wiota; Hans Engen Frøslieit with family of five; Ole Stadsvolden with family of five; Hans Stadsvolden and wife (these last two families went to Rock Run); Syver Gaarder and family totaling 13, who settled at Albany; Torkild Husværet and family of five, who went to Wiota; and Jonas Gjerdet and family of five.

1850 is the last year reported, when the following arrived:
- Ole Smeby and family of five
- Østen Lundsæteren and family of five
- Sjugul Frankrige and family of six
- Helene Frøslie
- Bertha Sørum
- Hovel Fossum
- Ole Hovdelien
- Hans Værhaug

Syver G. Gaarder was another respected man who came from Land. When he left Norway, he provided tickets for 20 people. He arrived in 1849 and was the first to settle near Albany, Wisconsin, northeast of Monroe, where he became the progenitor of a large family and the grandfather of the noted Dr. J. S. Johnson of St. Paul.

In 1843 the first emigrants from Valdres arrived in America. In Norway there are about 17,000 people in Valdres, whereas in America there are already over 30,000. Guul Guttormsen from Ildjernstadhaugen in Sør-Aurdal was the first to leave from that locality, where he had worked in a paint factory at Modum. It was here that he heard of America for the first time.

When he arrived on Rock Prairie, he wrote long letters to his friends in Sør-Aurdal—letters that were widely circulated. When the people of Valdres, after considerable deliberation, decided to join the settlement at Rock Prairie, they found that all the land had been taken, and they had to go farther northwest, where they founded a large settlement around Blue Mounds in Dane County (Wisconsin).

An outstanding settlement

Old Rock Prairie is a praiseworthy settlement, less for its prosperity than for its meaning in history and its remarkable people. It is quite possible that more immigrants made Rock Prairie their destination than any other settlement in America, particularly people from Hallingdal, Numedal, Land, Biri, Ringerike and Hadeland.

In the latter 1840s, when Pastor C. L. Clausen served congregations on and around Rock Prairie, thousands of immigrants arrived annually—strong and courageous pioneers whose sons have founded many large communities throughout the Midwest.

When the gold rush to California began in 1849, there were many Norwegians from this area who struck out across the continent to dig for gold. The very first group included Knud Knudson from Drammen, who acted as leader; Torstein Stabek, Narve Stabek, Christopher Rostad, Torstein Knudsen, Nils Nilson, Halvor Kjørn and Halvor Gallog, all originally from Numedal; Halvor Hersgaard, Adne Engen, Ole T. Wi and Christen Evenson, all from Hallingdal; Ole Hanson and Frederik Gawog from Modum; Salve Nilsen from Stavanger; and Gunder Halvorsen from Telemark.

When the Civil War broke out, the men of Rock Prairie were not afraid to risk their lives for the Union. No less than 76 Norwegians volunteered—nearly every able-bodied man in the settlement.

Rock Prairie is also the cradle of Norwegian-American journalism. As mentioned earlier in the chapter on Muskego, *Nordlyset*, the first Norwegian newspaper in the U.S., was founded there, and after two years of hand-to-mouth existence, the paper folded.

Pastor Clausen, who was then serving Rock Prairie congregations in the late 1840s, began to edit a monthly paper from his own office under the auspices of the Norwegian Synod. This publication is still alive (1908) under the name of the *Norsk Luthersk Kirketidende*.

Under his leadership, an appeal was made to sell stock in a Norwegian newspaper. A meeting was held in the church *[presumably at Luther Valley –Rosholt]* on 15 November 1851, for this purpose, and 73 shares were sold at $10 each.

A publishing company was organized, with James Reymert as president of the corporation, and the first issue of *Emigranten*, with Clausen as editor, came out on 12 January 1852. This paper still carries on under a different name.

[Holand's information in the foregoing paragraph is misleading. Pastor O. J. Hatlestad is recognized as the first editor of Kirketidende, which began publishing in Racine County in 1852. Also, Norsk-Amerikanernes Festskrift, 1914, gives 23 January 1852, as the date of the first number of Emigranten. –Rosholt]

In the same year (1852), the publishing company came out with a number of books, such as Lindrot's *Huspostil*, the *Forklaring*, *Katekismus*, *Læsebog*, *Historisk Læsning* and others.

The old stone church

The pioneers on Rock Prairie were especially foresighted in church affairs. In February 1844, a letter of call representing the congregations of Rock Prairie, Jefferson Prairie, Rock Run and Wiota was sent to Bishop Sørenson requesting that a competent pastor be sent. They offered a salary of $300 per year plus extras for ministerial acts, and a parsonage with 80 acres of land. About 200 members signed the letter.

This letter of call, written by Knut Knutson of Wiota, was the first of its kind sent to Norway from America. Earlier, the Muskego congregation had called Clausen, but he was not yet an ordained pastor.

Clausen was called to Rock Prairie shortly thereafter, and an impressive stone church was built there in 1845. The first bell to ring in a Norwegian church in America was hung in the tower at this church on 14 July 1857. A rather large bell costing $250, it gave new meaning to people's lives. For many, the sound of a church bell had not been heard for years. To make up for this inner longing, the bell was rung the first time from 3 o'clock in the afternoon until dark, while people sat around on their haystacks and enjoyed the music.

Dr. J. S. Johnson, writing in *Valdris Helsing*, has given an interesting account of this church with its deservedly literary background. As this is of interest to others, it will be repeated here:

"As far as I know, this is the second oldest Norwegian church in America and was built in 1845. Pastor C. L. Clausen, the first Norwegian pastor to preach here, had earlier held worship services in a log schoolhouse that stood near the spot where the church was later built, and held confirmation service in his own house.

"As indicated, the new church was built of stone, which was plentiful around here. There were no building contracts or blueprints. People donated labor according to what they could best do. Those who could do mason work laid the stone; others burned lime for mortar, dug sand, uprooted stones or worked with a shovel. Engebret Thorson served as general foreman and Peder Helgeson as head carpenter.

"The church stood on top of a small hill near the old parsonage once occupied by Clausen, somewhat in the center of the community. By modern standards it was small but proportionally high with a small frame bell tower, three high windows on each main wall and two in the front. At the back was a gallery resting on pillars that were shaved and planed out of native oak. These pillars were 'marbleized,' which means that they were painted with a blue grain to resemble Italian marble. The many obvious axe marks crosswise and the long, deep cracks lengthwise betrayed the illusion of reality, except to us kids.

"To tell the truth, it was a humble and unadorned temple, cold or hot according to the season, but always filled for worship services. It was definitely the only common meeting place for the entire settlement, and in those good old days everyone went to church.

"If a member could not attend divine services, then it was for business reasons—such as to trade a horse or to answer a summons to work on a public road, or dickering about threshing crews and exchange of labor, listening to the news of the day, etc. *[Here Dr. Johnson seems to suggest that the men may have brought their families to church but remained outside to discuss their personal affairs with their neighbors, to feed their horses and probably to keep the family dogs from running into the church door. –Rosholt]*

"In summer, especially as time for church service neared, people could be seen approaching from all directions. The men came in pairs, walking with long, labored steps—carrying their suit jackets, pants cuffs upturned; white Sunday shirts shining under the black vest worn on holy days; red handkerchiefs either tied around the neck or hanging out of a back pocket or even worn on the crown of the hat according to whatever age, custom or cultural period one wished to follow.

"Barely visible through the dust the horses raised could be glimpsed a red or yellow painted wagon, and along the road near the church, children could be seen on the ground putting on their shoes and stockings, which they had been carrying up to this point.

"That handsome young lady who trudges undaunted through the heat of the sun over yonder in a new calico dress, straw hat, parasol and veil over her face, but barefooted, is our own hired girl recently arrived from Norway.

"Peer, in a cloud of tobacco smoke, came quite regularly to church, driving a team of stallions hitched to a red, two-wheeled sulky. But if people seldom saw him, it was because he had wormed his way into the crowded gallery. Here the seats were arranged in the manner of a circus tent, one row higher than the next, open at the back. Here the young folks gathered with all kinds of goings-on.

"The stairs to the gallery were so cleverly arranged that when a person came up the narrow steps, he came directly under the back row of the highest seats and got an outer and inner view that one seldom has the opportunity to see: red and white stockings, ringed and striped stockings, long and short, old and new; undershirts and overshirts, trousers of both sexes of all possible colors and style. Under or between the audience, a man could stand unseen by the pastor yet watch him in the pulpit or glance down below where his wife stood in the queue with the other mothers who had children to be baptized.

"Back of the stadium-like seats in the gallery was an opening where a ladder ran up to the bell tower. On this ladder the boys teetered and tottered, trading jackknives, pictures and pets, playing the game of finger pulling, which often led to silent fights between the antagonists. If things got out of hand, the church warden quietly approached and looked around—everything all quiet, the boys staring intently into their hymn books.

"In the corner of the churchyard stood an old flagpole erected when the Civil War began, and the flag continued to be raised for divine services. When the stars and stripes waved from the top of this high pole on a beautiful summer morning, it gave a festive air to the occasion and helped imbue a spirit of patriotism in the rising generation of young people.

"After the church bell had ceased ringing, and after the old pioneer land-breaker had found his accustomed place, he glanced around piously and sat down with his hat on. *[Most churches in pioneer times were not heated until late autumn and after that very badly if at all. –Rosholt]*

"Then the presenter raised his august person from the seat below the pulpit and stepped solemnly forward. Having assured himself that all was in order, he carefully removed a red handkerchief from a back pocket, turned away and blew his nose—a blast that could be heard all over the church. This was a formality I have never seen duplicated since, and it set the mood for the beginning of holy worship services with the reading of the indgangs prayer. *[This is a reference to indgangskone, the ceremony of readmitting a woman who had recently given birth back into the congregation, usually followed by the baptismal service. This ceremony was discontinued in most Lutheran churches before the turn of the 20th century. – Rosholt].*

Gravesites reflected status

"Across the road from the church lay the cemetery, adorned in front with a high stone wall. Here, under the trees and around the grass-covered graves, there was usually a group of people who remained outside when the weather was nice. Women with children found it a convenient place to answer the needs of their offspring, and linens of different kinds were spread over the graves and decked with milk bottles, apples and cakes.

"Primitive as these graves were, there was, nevertheless, a certain pecking order established for the dead. It was not easy, even for unknown people, to claim the right to be buried among the graves of the more well-to-do farmers' wives who lay in the vicinity of the pastor's wife, surrounded by picket fences and cypress trees. And there, too, was the grave of a newcomer's child, lying back in the corner with a small, simple wooden cross, where the tall weeds grew instead of lilies and forget-me-nots. Here now rest a great part of the courageous Norwegian men and women who cleared the wilderness of the Wisconsin frontier.

"North of the cemetery there was a big apple grove that Pastor Clausen planted, and behind the grove was the old, somewhat gloomy stone parsonage. Here there was a well, where in warm weather an amazing amount of water was consumed as a refreshing beverage.

"The road to the parsonage ran through a garden where red apples hung heavily over the fence. And no doubt it could happen that, while the pastor was in church thundering against sin and admonishing his flock to remain steadfast against temptations of the flesh, old Clausen's apple orchard was the occasion for more than one small fall from grace.

A chance to socialize

"After the conclusion of divine services, a social gathering was held out in the churchyard. There were at this time no women's societies or sewing circles, and it was good manners and common courtesy for the womenfolk to greet all the other women they knew, to ask about the children while making their own quiet calculations about the probability of future prospects, etc., etc.

"Those who lived a long distance away and who did not have an invitation to take lunch at some nearby home, departed first in their newest, highly-polished lumber wagons, on which there were several spring seats and cross-boards for the members of the family and neighbors to sit. Farthest back in the box, either sitting or standing by an empty nail keg, was the newcomer hired man in his homespun clothes and heavy shoes. Halvor Haugen was the last to leave the churchyard, as he had to attend to a great deal of business.

"Small and plain-looking as it was, this old stone church preserved many cherished memories. Here the Norwegian Lutheran Synod was organized, and here it was that the famous 'slavery synod' meeting was held in which slavery and the question of the Sabbath were first brought up for public discussion. Here, many of the great predecessors in the work of the Lutheran church in this country raised their voices on behalf of the Lord—men such as Clausen, Dietrichson, Magelsen and Muller-Eggen, not to mention many nonresident pastors.

"In this church there were many men and women who participated in the American pioneer saga, not only in spiritual but also in material matters. Many were baptized, confirmed and married here, and here they were eventually buried. There are few among them of whom the old stone church had reason to be ashamed.

"The bell in the tower is the oldest Norse church bell in America. From this tower its silver tones have echoed across the land on so many sunny Sabbath mornings, calling God's congregation together, proclaiming the very words found in the inscription of the bell: 'With my voice I shout to the Lord!'

"The old church (at Luther Valley) finally became obsolete and in 1871 was razed to make way for a larger, more attractive building situated on the same site and even incorporating the old stones. But it is not just that the new building rests on the same foundation. It is the witness that it attests to, still alive and being heard, while the spirit it has helped to shape will never die as long as Norsemen abide in this land, and so long as the Norwegian language is heard and Lutheranism is proclaimed to the faithful." [*End of quote by Johnson –Rosholt*]

Rock Prairie, which lies northwest of Beloit, now has a Norwegian population of 3,500. Rock Prairie and Koshkonong have been the two most important entry and transient centers for Norse immigrants to America.

10

Koshkonong Settlement, eastern Dane and western Jefferson Counties, Wisconsin

(Source: De Norske Settlementers Historie, by Hjalmar Rued Holand, translated by Malcolm Rosholt, 1908, pp. 142–157)

Koshkonong is the best-known of all Norwegian colonies in America. Located in the eastern part of Dane County, Wisconsin, it shines forth like a jewel for all to see and admire.

Here is a community of some 9,000 of our countrymen, and here may be found the real Norwegian heritage, adapted to the changes of American life while achieving its own highest development.

Here is a colony where people have long finished with the struggles of pioneer life and are already making important contributions to the cultural life of America, a progressive people with strong memories and old traditions.

One of the reasons for the fame of Koshkonong is that the pioneers here found in abundance all those conditions deemed necessary for a future home—wood, water and good farming land.

Koshkonong was the home of many Norwegian immigrant farmers in the 1840s and 1850s. When the movement of emigrants from Norway began in earnest, Koshkonong became the "stopping place" for those thousands and still more thousands of newcomers who came here first and later spread out across the Midwest of America to establish new colonies of their own.

Another reason for the fame of this colony is that more illustrious men have gone out from here to make their community known than from any other place in the U.S. Yet another reason is that in the past 50 years it has become known as the wealthiest Scandinavian colony in America.

The old-timers refer it to as "Kaskeland." If a small change in the spelling were made so that the word reads "Kakseland," it would be more to

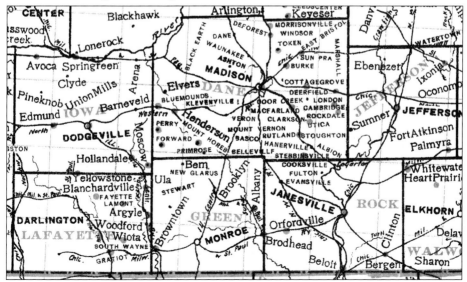

the point, as there is an oversupply of money-laden bigwigs and rich farmers. *["Kakseland" can be translated as "land of the big-shot farmers," after the word kakse, a rural bigwig. –Rosholt.]*

In the newer colonies of northern Wisconsin, most farms are only 40 acres. Around Koshkonong, no one is considered much of a farmer unless he has five times that. There are numerous instances of farms as big as 400 to 500 acres. As land here commonly sells for $125 per acre (1908), it is obvious that this is no longer a place for peasants.

The terrain features high, rolling fields covered by a rich, black earth. Small, uneven forests and marshlands separate these fields. It was here, on the less rich ground around the edges of the marshes and in the woodlots, that the first pioneers chose to settle. They looked with suspicion on the open prairie or treeless land.

The Koshkonong settlement dates from 1840, a year when three different groups of Norwegians took land here. Of these three, the following information is the most important to bear in mind.

Arrivals from Voss and Numedal

In the fall of 1839, three young men from Voss—Nils Larsen Bolstad, Nils Syverson Gilderhus and Magne B. Bystolen—decided to quit the Fox River colony in Illinois and look for cheaper land. They hired another Voss emigrant, Odd J. Himle, who had been in the United States for some years, to accompany them and help make a choice of location. At the last moment, Bystolen became ill and was prevented from joining the group, but followed a year later.

The other three roamed about on foot for a couple of weeks until they came to Dane County, Wisconsin, close to the present village of Cambridge. Here they saw beautiful stretches of unclaimed land, of which they had their pick. They did not occupy the much richer fields but chose instead 40 acres each of some wooded hills, today regarded as of little value. They then returned to Fox River to pick up their things, their discovery of new land having created a sensation.

Meanwhile, the three men had made entry on their claims at the federal land office in Milwaukee on 6 May 1840.

Two weeks later, Gunnul Olson Vindeg and Gjermund Sunde, who were temporarily located on Jefferson Prairie, came to Koshkonong. According to an old story that very few of the pioneers have heard anything about (but which the family of Vindeg believes to be accurate), these two *Numedøler* came by way of Beloit, where they got possession of an Indian canoe and paddled upriver 70 miles to their destination.

Although this story cannot be denied, it seems unreasonable that a couple of poor newcomers—strangers to the land—could have borrowed or purchased a boat in Beloit and then paddled against the river current in spring flood, with a couple of waterfalls thrown in for good measure. Farther up Koshkonong Creek, the stream is so narrow, crooked and filled with waterfalls that no one since has ever even considered it a feasible route to follow.

The fact is that old Vindeg was some kind of a joker who liked to spice his stories with a few embellishments. He wrote, for example, to his people in Norway that he liked life in America; he had a big farm with a three-storied house and livestock, of which his 20 pigs and 100 chickens were ample evidence of his newfound prosperity. The *Numedøler* in Norway were proud to hear that one of their sons had made out so well in such a short time, and many packed up and left to share in this pot of gold.

With great expectations, they took the road across the rolling hills of Koshkonong to visit their rich acquaintance on his mighty farm. What they found instead was a miserable shanty, one end of which served for a stable. The newcomers were quite disappointed.

"You wrote that you had a three-story house, Gunnul."

"Ja, can't you see? Cellar, living room and loft. That makes three!"

"Humm. Where are the 20 pigs, then?"

"Well, take a look at these two sows. Would it be too much to expect a litter of nine from each sow if I had them bred?"

"Maybe. And where are all the chickens? There are only three here."

"I've got lots of eggs, and if I only had a rooster, there would certainly be chicks around here aplenty."

"Yeah. And one sparrow doesn't make a summer, either."

Nevertheless, many newcomers found a temporary shelter in this shanty, since Gunnul Vindeg was a hospitable man.

For many years Vindeg was a celebrity because he was the only one in the neighborhood who owned a horse—a worn-out old nag but nevertheless in a class by itself. People getting married were forever borrowing the horse for the drive to and from the church.

Stavanger, Voss, Sogn and Telemark settlements

A third group of men to visit Koshkonong in that year of 1840 were six from Stavanger who came up from Fox River. One or more had heard about Koshkonong through Odd Himle and, anxious to try their luck, arrived in June 1840. This group included Bjørn Anderson Kvelve, Torsten Olson Bjaadland, Lars Dugstad, Amund Anderson Hornefjeld, Amund Rosseland and Lars Scheie.

Among the three groups, the first had the biggest influence on the future of the colony. Encouraged by letters from these *Vossinger*, their countrymen in Norway began to immigrate until this became the largest colony of *Vossinger* in America. One of these early pioneers, Lars Davidsen Reque (the eldest), purchased land in December 1840. He is widely known as a most generous and helpful person. Every year he has provided travel money for one young man who wished to come to the U.S.

There are also quite a number of people on Koshkonong from Sogn fylke north of Bergen. The first of these was Iver Larson Hove from Vik, who was in the first group of emigrants from Sogn, although not all settled on Koshkonong. Hove himself went first to Long Prairie near Capron, Illinois, in 1844. When he wrote to his friends that he raised 35 bushels of wheat to the acre and in one day could easily cut enough hay to feed one cow for an entire winter, he convinced many to emigrate from Sogn.

But among all the communities in Norway, the most numerous on Koshkonong as well as in other places are the emigrants from Telemark. The leader of this movement was Ole Knudson Trovatten, the first klokker (church sexton) and parochial schoolteacher on Koshkonong. He left Laurdal around 1840 and came to Dane County in 1843. Regarded as a man of wisdom, he could silence both preacher and judge according to circumstances. Thousands of prosperous *Telemarkinger* throughout the Midwest owed their good fortune to Ole Knudson Trovatten's straight-forward and well-written letters.

John Nilson Luraas, another pioneer leader among *Telemarkinger*, was one of the founders of the Muskego colony in 1839. In 1843 he was first to settle west of Koshkonong in the town of Dunkirk. Accompanying him to Dane County was Knud Helliksen Roe, the first white man in Pleasant Springs Township. *[Holand obviously suggests that he was the first to settle there, as others had presumably surveyed the section lines before Roe arrived. –Rosholt]*

Among other trailblazers from Telemark may be mentioned Aslak

Olsnes (Alexander O. Norman), who came from Vinje in Telemark in 1842; Ole Knudson Dyrland, who arrived in the first group from Seljord in 1843; and Jacob Wetleson, the first from Kviteseid. The latter joined the California gold rush, traveling by way of Montana, where he actually went into cattle ranching and did very well—the first Norwegian to enter this business. He later returned to Stoughton, Wisconsin.

Amund Drotning, another *Telemarking*, settled in Madison in 1843, the first Norwegian in the future city. In addition, there was Gunder T. Mandt, who came with the first group to leave from Moe in Telemark. Further names to this pioneer list of settlers on Koshkonong would include Halvor Kravik from Numedal, who sailed in 1843; Lars Johanson Holo, the first to leave from Hedmark in 1839; and Anders Johanson Tømmerstigen, a brother of Holo, the first to leave from Vardal in 1846.

The Dietrichson-Funkelien feud

The first to leave from Kongsberg in eastern Norway was Halvor Funkelien, who came to Koshkonong in 1842. He is best known for his famous victory over Pastor Dietrichson. This is a priceless story, demonstrating that the pioneer pastors had other things to endure besides small salaries and long journeys.

Funkelien was a drunk and a subtle squabbler of the worst kind. The pastor had several times warned him about his shortcoming but without effect. Finally, Funkelien was expelled from the congregation. But he was not to be frightened. The next Sunday, which was Pentecost, he was in church and took a seat directly in front of the pulpit. He also had a pocket flask, and sure enough if he did not take a sip right under the nose of the pastor. This was slightly irritating to Dietrichson, but he refrained from saying anything.

When the flask was brought out again and still again, Dietrichson could restrain himself no longer, shouting, "I cannot preach any longer with this abominably filthy sinner in front of me, drinking whiskey in church! Throw him out!"

Several strong men got up at once and escorted Funkelien outside.

When they got out in the yard, Funkelien said, "Tell me, what are you throwing me out for?"

"Because you are a pig and you drink whiskey in church."

"Would I drink whiskey in church! Here, Ola, you know whiskey as well as I do. Take my flask and tell me what kind of whiskey this is. I am an old man who gets dry in the throat when I sit still and therefore have to quench myself with a drink of water."

And sure enough, after Ola and the others had tasted of the bottle, they had to admit that it was without a doubt nothing but warm creek water that, for once, Funkelien was carrying. After this affair there was something else to gossip about around Koshkonong besides the price of wheat.

Funkelien felt he had to do something to preserve his good name and reputation and swore out a complaint against the congregation. Bjørn Anderson Kvelve, or Tøndebjørn (Thundering Bear), as he was called (father of Rasmus B. Anderson), liked to tweak the pastor's nose. He acted as some sort of a lawyer in the case, and Funkelien got something better than water to put in his flask for a long time to come.

[The Dietrichson-Funkelien confrontation becomes more embellished and absurd with each telling in the latter half of the 19th century. In a footnote to this incident, Holand says Dietrichson, in his own account of it, stated that Funkelien was escorted out of the church and makes no mention of the flask, which might suggest that Holand had read the original Dietrichson account in Reise Blandt de Norski Emigranter, published in Norway in 1845. Holand adds that the Dietrichson account must have lacked some of the

facts in the case when it was known that Dietrichson had to pay a fine of $100. Holand was either writing from memory or on the basis of oral tradition. If he had read the Dietrichson book, he would have known that Dietrichson was not fined $100. Instead, he and two deacons of the church were fined around $12 or $13, including costs, and that Dietrichson appealed the case to Dane County Court, where through a technicality, the appeal was dismissed and the original fine imposed by a Justice of the Peace waived. Dietrichson would not have made up this story because it surely could have been checked in the court records of Dane County at the time. –Rosholt.]

Pastor J. W. C. Dietrichson came to America and made Koshkonong his principal field of work until his return to Norway in 1850. He was sent to Wisconsin originally in 1844 to organize church affairs under a government subsidy of $200 and private gifts of $425 for travel expenses.

[Actually, Dietrichson volunteered for the assignment to America. On his first residence at Koshkonong from 1844-45, he was entirely subsidized by a philanthropic businessman in Oslo, as the Norwegian government and the state church saw no need to serve the spiritual needs of people who had left their native land to go to America. The subsidy mentioned by Holand probably refers to Dietrichson's second journey to America in 1846, when he returned to the Koshkonong congregations and remained there until 1850. –Rosholt]

Dietrichson was a big person with a commanding presence and also a quick temper, which often left him quarreling with those with whom he came in contact. He did everything possible to reinforce his dignity as a pastor and went to the absurd length of wearing his church vestments and ruffed collar when driving a stone-boat for hauling water to his house.

Meanwhile, Dietrichson organized a number of congregations: The first two were at east and west Koshkonong in October 1844. The same fall, two churches were built, the first to be dedicated by the Norwegian church in America—the east church on 19 December 1844, and the west church on 31 January 1845. *[These dates correspond to Dietrichson's own information in his Reise. –Rosholt]*

From bears to Ole Bull

Henrik Henrikson Fadnes was one of the best-known emigrants from Voss on Koshkonong in the 1850s, especially known as a man of great strength. One year too many bears in the cornfields were plaguing the settlement. The neighbors got together to eliminate the thieves, and Fadnes decided to join in the hunt but had no gun. He walked along one bank of a river while one of the other men followed the opposite bank carrying a gun.

Sure enough, Fadnes was first to run smack into a big bear and grabbed it in the back feet while yelling to the neighbor, "Shoot now while I hold him!" And he did not let go until the bear dropped dead.

Among the well-known professional men on Koshkonong may be mentioned Dr. J. C. Dundas, a descendant of northern Norway's poet, Peter Dass. Dr. Dundas saw an entire generation born and buried on Koshkonong. He was a gifted physician who was considered by both Americans and Norwegians as a real miracle worker.

But the doctor was more proud of the poetry he composed than of his healing arts and sent these poems to all the newspapers. These poems were not received with the enthusiasm the doctor thought they deserved, and this caused him great disappointment. He was a cozy person with a warm disposition but outwardly capricious. Bjørnstjerne Bjørnson said of him that he was the most singular character he had ever met. *[Bjørnson, the poet and writer of Norway, probably met Dundas when he came to America on a lecture tour. –Rosholt]*

Dundas and Ole Bull were good friends. *[Ole Bornemann Bull was born in Bergen, Norway, on 5 February 1810. In Norway, his violin-playing aroused attention before he was 10 years old. By the time he reached his middle 20s, he had won European recognition as a virtuoso. In 1852, he purchased land in Pennsylvania for a Norwegian settlement he called Oleana. His second wife, Sara, was a daughter of Wisconsin lumberman and state senator, Joseph Thorp. The United States became Ole Bull's second country. In the latter part of his life he spent his winters here and the rest of the year at his beautiful Norwegian estate. Ole Bull died in Norway 17 August 1880. –Rosholt]*

The lutefisk capital

It was not before 1848 or so that Norwegians began to settle in Stoughton, Wisconsin. One of the first (and one of Stoughton's greatest) was Hans Andreas Hoverson from Flekkefjord in Vest-Agder fylke. As a boy in Lunde, in Norway, he was apprenticed to a shoemaker and for five years of work was awarded one *krone*. This did not appear to have much of a future in it. As a result, he became the first emigrant from Flekkefjord. Today the population of Stoughton is more than 3,000, most of them from Norway (1908).

Stoughton is best known for its wagon factories operated by Norwegians. The city is also the *lutefisk* capital of Wisconsin.

In the early period of the city's history, there were two large Lutheran congregations here. Later a split occurred in one, and the dissenters organized their own congregation. The older congregation was still quite large and active, and one fine day decided to serve a real festive *lutefisk* supper for the benefit of the stomach and soul's encouragement. People from far and near came and ate *lutefisk*, to the tune of $260 in total ticket sales. The customers went home stuffed, and the ladies of the church were pleased with the income realized. This event hurt the smaller congregation, and a couple of truckloads of *lutefisk* were prepared. People fasted, went to the dinner, loosened their belts and ate *lutefisk* for $290, which was considered amazing.

Strangely, there are not many people from Valdres on Koshkonong. Above Blooming Grove there is a settlement made up of Valdres people with a Valdres pastor. Nils Hanson Fjeld, founder of this peripheral colony in Dane County, was one of the first to leave from Aurdal in Valdres in 1847. He was a well-to-do landowner, taking with him to America $1,000 in silver. He sailed on a ship that nearly fell to pieces, and many times during the voyage he wished he were back in Aurdal. He finally reached the Promised Land after 14 weeks at sea.

Life in a sod hut

Although the soil around Koshkonong is uncommonly rich and the farmers of today are exceptionally well situated, it was not always so in the beginning. There were many years when the people here found it difficult to manage. It was not only because of depressed prices on farm products but also because of the long distance to either flour mill or market.

Construction materials for floors and roofing were nearly impossible to get, and this explains why the first dwellings of the pioneers were extremely primitive. For many years there was not a decent house to be found in the settlement, nearly everyone living in small sod huts. These were carved out of the hillsides and covered with a layer of sod several feet deep with timberwork in front, divided by a door and a couple of windows covered with paper or sometimes with glass. Although there was no board flooring, the sod huts were warm, and it was great fun for the kids to carve play cellars in the sides of the earthen walls.

As might be expected, it was often over-crowded in these sod huts as newcomers and relatives came pouring in and arrangements had to be made for them somehow. When they arrived, bug-eyed and bashful in their queer mountain clothes, there was interminable talk over the coffee cups concerning the latest news from back home, interspersed with ambitious hopes and plans for the new life in America, whereupon the newcomers were put to work driving a yoke of oxen or splitting rails at 25 cents a hundred.

Hidden in their sod huts surrounded by trees and far from the main roads, it was often difficult for a stranger on an errand to find a particular family. The story is told of a man sent out by the state in 1847 to take a census. Finding it troublesome to locate the Norwegians, a smart Yankee acquainted in the area told the enumerator to get up early in the morning, climb to the highest hilltop, count the chimney fires, multiply by 10, and he would come within a score of all the inhabitants! So said, so done, and the result was quite satisfactory.

Life in the sod huts and on the farms was fairly comfortable. The real burden of pioneering was felt when a man had to leave home with a load of wheat for market or to have flour ground. For many years the nearest marketplace was Milwaukee, 75 to 100 miles away. The road was miserable, and as a man had to bump over stones and logs, he often got stuck in a mud hole. Then it became necessary to unload, shout and curse at the oxen and finally, after some hours of shifting and shoving, to get free of the hellhole.

Often it took a week to reach Milwaukee, and on arrival, the pioneer's troubles were still not over. At the gristmill he might hear that his turn to have wheat ground would not come up for another week! The man then had to go out on the streets and find work to live while he waited. When his turn at the mill came, he had to sift his own flour or meal, as there was no sifting machine.

Finally the job was accomplished.

"Get along!" was shouted at the oxen like a victory won, and after another week of hardship, the traveler returned home. This was costly flour.

There were Indians around, but they did not harm anyone. On the other hand, they did scare the cattle, which fled to the woods and remained away for two and three weeks at a time. Wolves were the worst threat. They were spotted occasionally, and it was a long time before it was possible to raise sheep.

Time seemed to move at a slow pace. Without newspapers to read and stories to follow about wild trips to the local saloons, it did not appear to the pioneers that they were making much progress. Some old-timers say now that they did not believe there would be much to look forward to in less than 500 years.

But in 1854 the railroad came to Madison, and then changes came fast and furious. Prices went up overnight, both on farms and produce. People bought and sold, plowed new ground and enlarged both barn and farm. Then the Civil War came on, sending prices still higher, bringing increased well-being as well as splits in church synods. But, by damn, it was fun to be alive.

Lawsuits involve church matters

Among all the many lawsuits heard on Koshkonong, most of which were concerned with church matters, none created a greater stir than the case naming Pastor J. A. Ottesen as defendant in "State of Wisconsin vs. J. A. Ottesen for assault and battery with intent to do great bodily harm." The lawyers who took the case were the later well-known senators William Vilas and John C. Spooner, who made a painstaking examination of it. The story, as reported in *Skandinaven*, goes as follows:

"In Ottesen's congregation there was a man with a reputation for uncommon meanness and cantankerousness who apparently resented his mother-in-law more than anyone else in the world. Although he was a man of means himself, he took his mother-in-law one cold morning in winter and drove her 18 miles to a poor house, where she shortly died. The incident aroused everyone, and after many long discussions in the congregation, the man was dismissed.

"Late one evening he came to the parsonage and requested an interview with the pastor. Ottesen was apprehensive and told the people in his house to remain in the next room.

"Sure enough, the man asked to see the documentary evidence of his dismissal. Ottesen laid the papers on the table while holding his hand on one corner for security, but the man grabbed them and stuck them in his coat pocket.

" 'It will not be right to take those papers,' said Ottesen.

" 'I'm not taking them. You gave them to me,' he replied and walked around to Ottesen who had, meanwhile, got up from his chair.

"As the man hovered over him, Ottesen thought it was his opportunity to snatch the papers from the pocket. This was just what the troublemaker wanted, for in the same moment he grabbed Ottesen's hand with both of his own, threw himself over backward across the floor with Ottesen on top of him, yelling 'Help! Murder!' At this instant the pastor's wife and the people of the house ran in to find the man on his back with Ottesen on top.

"The man now swore out a complaint, and the sheriff came to arrest Ottesen during holy worship services. A long and costly court case followed, with the congregation paying for Ottesen's defense. The prosecution subpoenaed nearly 50 witnesses who all declared that they would never believe the charges against the pastor, and he was finally acquitted."

But the most important lawsuits were the series, mutually associated, that erupted over the doctrine of predestination in the Lutheran church in the 1880s. Essentially, these cases hinged on the right of a congregation to fire its own pastor when the members felt it was for the good of the congregation.

The majority of members in two congregations and a minority in a third left the old Norwegian Synod and affiliated with the anti-Missourians and helped to organize the United Lutheran Church Synod in 1890, while Pastor Ottesen and the minority swore allegiance to the traditional confessions of the Norwegian Synod.

In order to preserve peace in the congregations, Pastor Ottesen offered to resign. He later withdrew this offer and refused to give up the parsonage when the new pastor arrived, on the grounds that he had been installed for life and could not be forced to resign except for immoral conduct, false teachings or by mutual consent.

Ottesen and his party were successful in the lower courts but lost in appeals to the high court, which upheld the right of the majority in a congregation to decide the ownership of property. The court decreed that the pastor had to resign whenever the congregation decided, and that decisions reached by a majority of members were binding on the entire congregation.

The intent of the law and its interpretation in these several cases involving the Koshkonong congregations makes interesting reading, which ought to be published in pamphlet form and distributed to help prevent judicial church strife in the future.

Great men grow in Koshkonong

The most important farm crop on Koshkonong is tobacco, and the Norwegians living across these hills have long been considered among the best tobacco-growers in America. The town of Christiania, the most heavily populated by Norwegians, also has the most acreage devoted to tobacco of any in the country. In the year 1900, when tobacco-growing reached its peak in Wisconsin, around 15,000 acres of Dane County were under cultivation, and the total production jumped to

22,500,000 pounds. Since that time, there has been less tobacco growing, as the farmers are not as keen on it as they once were.

But the most important crop on Koshkonong is great men. From here more noted Norwegian-Americans have come than from any other settlement in America.

- O. Aasen, Synod pastor
- N. C. Amundson, Stavanger, teacher
- Able Anderson, Stavanger, Synod pastor
- J. J. Anderson, Skien, professor
- R. B. Anderson, Stavanger, editor
- Nils B. Berge, Sogn, Synod pastor
- K. E. Bergh, Voss, Synod professor
- Knut Bjørgo, Voss, chairman, Minnesota Synod
- Fred P. Brown, Koppervig, Minnesota state secretary
- Gullik M. Erdall, Hardanger, Synod pastor
- John L. Erdall, Hardanger, corporation trade union
- Nelson A. Falk, Sogn, sawmill operator
- O. G. Felland, Telemark, professor, United Church
- T. L. Flom, Sogn, Iowa University professor
- N. A. Giere, Hallingdal, United Church pastor
- N. O. Giere, Hallingdal, Synod pastor
- Erik S. Gjellum, Sogn, Editor
- Knut Henderson, Voss, author
- Peter Hendrickson, Telemark, editor
- Chas. N. Herreid, Hardanger, South Dakota governor
- J. J. Holman, sawmill operator
- Nels Holman, editor
- Andreas Holo, Ringsaker, teacher
- L. L. Hulsæther, sawmill operator
- Halvor B. Hustvedt, Telemark, Synod pastor
- Bendix Ingebretson, Sogn, Methodist pastor
- Christopher Jerdee, Sogn, sawmill operator
- Andrew O. Johnson, Kristiansand, Adventist professor
- J. H. Johnson, Voss, Methodist pastor
- G. M. Johnson, Sogn, teacher
- Henry Johnson, Kristiansand, Adventist pastor
- J. A. Johnson, Telemark, manufacturing
- J. L. Johnson, Ringsaker, judge
- Albert Kittelson, Numedal, teacher
- Levi Kittelson, Numedal, tobacco business
- O. O. Klevjord, Valdres, Synod pastor
- N. A. Ladd, Sogn, sawmill operator
- G. A. Larson, Numedal, pastor
- A. J. Lee, Sogn, Synod pastor
- Ole T. Lee, Telemark, Synod pastor
- Andrew Lee, Stril, South Dakota governor
- G. M. Johnson Lee, Sogn, teacher
- A. E. Lien, Hallingdal, Synod pastor
- Olaf Mandt, Telemark, Synod pastor
- T. G. Mandt, Telemark, manufacturing wagons
- C. R. Mattson, Voss, sheriff in Chicago
- John M. Nelson, congressman
- Knute Nelson, Voss, senator, Minnesota governor
- William Nelson, Voss, sawmill operator
- O. A. Norman, Telemark, Synod pastor
- Christian K. Næseth, Nedre-Telemark, Synod professor
- E. J. Ohnstad, Sogn, administrator
- J. E. Olson, Drøbak, Wisconsin University professor
- Albert Olson, Kristiansand, Adventist pastor
- Alfred B. Olson, Kristiansand, teacher
- Edvard Olson, Kristiansand, Adventist pastor
- Andrew Olson, Kristiansand, Adventist pastor
- Martin Olson, Kristiansand, Adventist pastor
- Ole A. Olson, Kristiansand, Adventist president
- Otto Ottesen, Nedre-Romerike, Synod pastor
- N. A. Qvammen, Hardanger, Synod pastor
- Knute Reindahl, Telemark, violin specialist

- Lars S. Reque, Voss, Synod professor
- Peter Reque, Voss, Synod pastor
- S. S. Reque, Voss, Synod pastor
- Per Røthe, Voss, editor
- A. K. Sagen, Telemark, Synod pastor
- N. O. Stark, Voss, inventor
- Halvor Stenerson, Telemark, congressman
- A. M. Teigen, Sogn, teacher
- Aslak Teisberg, Telemark, editor
- T. K. Thorvildson, Telemark, pastor
- A. Trovatten, Telemark, editor
- Ole K. Vangsness, Sogn, Ellingean pastor

Udskaaret Ramstnkke, Trækrus og Stabur

11

Norway Grove Settlement, Dane County, Wisconsin, and Columbia County, Wisconsin

(Source: De Norske Settlementers Historie, by Hjalmar Rued Holand, translated by Malcolm Rosholt, 1908, pp. 158–165)

There are many who believed that Dane County took its name from its heavy Scandinavian population. Actually, the county got its name in 1836, before any Scandinavians reached the area. It honors Nathaniel Dane, in memory of the *Northwest Ordinance* of 1787, which he helped to frame.

Dane County has a rural Norwegian population of about 16,000. This includes some 10,000 in the Lake Koshkonong district and the city of Madison, several thousand located south of Blue Mounds in the west end of the county, and a settlement of about 1,000 *Sogninger* in the northern part of the county (usually referred to as the Norway Grove settlement).

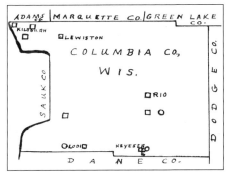

This colony and the adjacent colony across the line in Columbia County are actually extensions of the Koshkonong settlement. It is populated mostly by people who came to Koshkonong after all the good land had been claimed by Yankee and German settlers and therefore had to travel farther north.

But they lost little in the bargain. The same beautiful landscape and productive soil extends nearly all the way to the city of Rio and the Wisconsin River, where one comes into sandy soil and stretches of wild marshland. The Norwegian immigrants avoided this sand country and sought land around Coon Prairie, or went farther west into Minnesota.

The first Norwegian to settle in northern Dane County was Svennung Dahle from Flatdal in Øvre-Telemark, who came in 1843 and took land by the present Norway Grove. Several others came to inspect the land; among them, Halvor Bjoin, later one of the best-known pioneers on Koshkonong.

These Norwegians were not overly pleased with what they found, because it was considered entirely too wild up there on the high and open prairie country—the nearest white man 13 miles to the south and perhaps even farther away toward the north. They picked up their things and went back to Koshkonong. Dahle was then the only man around Norway Grove.

In 1846 three men arrived who became the actual founders of the Norway Grove colony—namely, Erik Engesæth, John Rendalen and Engebrigt Larson. Although, oddly enough, none was called Ole, they were all real *Sogninger*. Erik Engesæth, moreover, was widely known in Sogn and wrote frequent letters urging his people to come to America. The following year, the *Sogninger* answered his letters in person and continued to arrive until all the land was taken, forcing the latecomers to settle around Spring Prairie and Bonnet Prairie.

Sjur Grinde was another pioneer who urged his people in Sogn to come to America. It is said that he was considered an honorable man in his home community, but when he wrote that in America the pumpkins grew to the size of half a bushel basket, people began to wonder whether he was all there.

When he further wrote that the farmers in America drove oxen and cut two or three acres of wheat in a single day with a gimmick called a "cradle" (which the teacher of English in the local school defined as a rocking cradle for children), things really got out of hand. The local pastor went so far as to charge that immigration to America was having an adverse effect on the minds of the immigrants.

But the people left just the same, and while the landscape in Wisconsin was not quite the same as in Sogn, the people nevertheless liked it out on the prairie. Soon there was a settlement of around 1,000 *Sogninger* in northern Dane County. These pioneers, who are now well situated, have founded large families. Among them may be mentioned the names Farness, Eggum, Røisum, Holum, Grinde, Linde, Slinde, Engesæth and others.

Today the capable *Sogninger* have built one of the finest rural churches among Norwegians in America, costing $20,000 and cheap at that.

Spring Prairie and Bonnet Prairie

From Norway Grove the settlement reaches out in two directions—one to the northwest past Lodi, where it finally breaks off in some miserable marsh holes approaching the Wisconsin River, and the other northwest to Spring Prairie and Bonnet Prairie. These last two are the most important and both lie in Columbia County.

The founder of Spring Prairie is no less than Knud Langeland, who originated in Samnanger near Bergen, served for many years as editor of *Skandinaven*, and was one of the most gifted men of Scandinavian ancestry America has had. He came to the U.S. in 1843. Being less than enthusiastic about Muskego, where he first settled, he went farther west. Concerning this journey and its results, he has this to say in his book *Nordmændene i Amerika* (1889):

"It was in the summer of 1845 that I raised my first shanty in the present county of Columbia, which gave me the opportunity to live near that glorious territory called Spring Grove and Bonnet Prairie, Lodi and surroundings—soon to be occupied by the Norwegians before the Yankee-American stream of migration began spreading to the north with powerful strides.

"It was this way: When I arrived at Yorkville Prairie in Racine County (Wisconsin) in 1843, the best land was already taken. The 80 acres that I bought seemed to be mostly lowland, and I was not satisfied with it. I and another young man, Niels Torstensen, whose ticket I had paid for to America, decided therefore to go farther west.

"Driving a yoke of powerful oxen hitched to a wagon provided with a small stove, provisions, blankets and other necessities needed for camp life, we took off in August 1845, guided by a compass and a map of Wisconsin Territory. We drove straight to Koshkonong, where we had been a couple of times before, and it was from here that the actual quest for land would begin.

"I was under the impression that the same rolling prairies of Koshkonong continued farther to the north. We took the beaten track to Madison, which was then no place for a prairie farmer, as it had nothing to offer but its natural beauty and the big territorial capitol building, which stood out in contrast to the small log huts (but which would now seem puny in comparison to the splendid new dome of the present).

"We drove a mile from the city, but frightened by the steep hills where the state university is presently located, we turned west where we joined the old road from Madison to Fort Winnebago.

I had heard that a fellow Norwegian, Amund Rosseland, with whom I was acquainted in Norway and who had immigrated in 1837, had come to this part of Wisconsin, and so I was anxious to locate him. It was said that he had settled near the Dells on the Wisconsin River a few miles from the old fort. The land around the fort *[near the present city of Portage –Rosholt]* for several miles was low, swampy and rather depressing. After a lot of trouble and tiresome meandering, we finally began to approach his place shortly after noon one day.

"Before we got there, we met a Norwegian raking hay who was so talkative that we scarcely could learn more from him other than Amund had gone away and would not be back for several days. This news, together with the poor quality of land hereabouts, made us turn around. But as both the oxen and we were tired, we made camp near some water. It was like home to us in our wagon, and the same could be said for the oxen that stood knee-deep in grass. We baked our cakes, fried our meat, cooked coffee and ate with an appetite that a prince might envy.

"We took the same road back for about 20 miles to a place where an intelligent American by the name of Young was at work building a house. He told us if we turned a few miles east, we would find what we were looking for, prairie land near woodlots.

"We followed his advice and soon came to a stretch of land alternating with wood and prairie. Here we met a couple of Americans who also were building a house. One of them, an old pioneer by the name of Gilbert, offered to sell us his claim. But when we learned that we could make our own choice of claims and on just as good land as his, we drove a couple miles to the north, where our biggest difficulty was in making a choice among many excellent pieces of land. We finally made a choice, began to build our log house, and soon we could sing as the poet. ... *[Here follows a poem that need not be included. –Rosholt]*

"It was now approaching late September, and our first concern was to cut hay and build a stall for the oxen against the winter cold. In this manner, the beginnings were made in those rich and flourishing Norwegian settlements on Spring Prairie, Bonnet Prairie, Lodi and those other beautiful stretches of prairie in this part of Wisconsin.

"No other Norwegians arrived that fall. Up to the first of November, we were busy with this and that in preparation for the winter months. Meanwhile, we heard that a Norwegian by the name of Kleppen had taken land somewhat south of our place but we never saw him, as he was some sort of a recluse. He sold his claim early the following year, I heard.

"When I later went to Milwaukee to make a pre-emption claim on my land, I told people on Koshkonong about my place. I knew from experience that with so many newcomers arriving from Norway, it would be easy to predict that by next season they would fill up all the Norwegian settlements in Dane County. I therefore wrote to friends in LaSalle County (Illinois), which resulted in two of them moving early the next year.

"The following summer was a time of trouble in our new settlement. While I was in Milwaukee, I had acquired some needed implements such as a plow, a harrow and such. Early in the year a personal friend of mine, Peder Frøland (Per Frøland), arrived from LaSalle County, where he had been since he immigrated in 1837. He brought with him a yoke of oxen, a wagon and other implements. The two of us then joined hands in helping each other. In June the newcomers began to arrive in flocks around Koshkonong.

"One group had asked Ole Trovatten, a well-known figure on Koshkonong, to accompany them in their search for land. I was already acquainted with this man and when he learned that I, too, could pick out good land, he was soon fed up with tramping all over hell's half acre with no more remuneration than a 'thank you' for his efforts. So he returned to Koshkonong, leaving me with the burden. All the land that was worth taking in the area was soon in the hands of the newcomers. I and Per Frøland now had a team of four yoke of oxen, and that summer we plowed about 100 acres of prairie land for the newcomers."

Anders Langeteig from Sogn and Odd J. Himle from Voss were among other early settlers to Spring Prairie. Himle, one of the most highly respected among *Vossinger*, came to America in 1837 and in 1844 returned to Norway on a visit. His personal encouragements resulted in a big wave of emigration from Voss. The following year he returned to Spring Prairie, where he has lived for nearly 50 years.

At Bonnet Prairie, an extension of Spring Prairie, Hans Hansen Tangen from Saude in Telemark, was one of the first settlers. A capable and progressive man, he was active in bringing most of the *Telemarkinger* to settle in this area.

Per Frøland remained only two years at Spring Prairie and in 1847 moved west to Lodi and founded a colony of people from Hardanger, where he also originated. Ole Jone, who came the same year to Spring Prairie, was also a *Haring* from Hardanger.

The soil in this settlement, similar to Koshkonong, was originally rich, but the many years of tobacco-growing, which takes all the fertilizer available, had seriously affected its productivity. Farmers who originally got 30 to 40 bushels of wheat to the acre now get only a tenth of that, and 30 bushels of oats to the acre is considered good.

These four or five widespread stretches of land, all related colonies, have five parishes supported by one pastor, with a total Norwegian population of a little more than 3,000. For a long time, this district was served by Pastor Herman Amberg Preus, one of the patriarchs in the Lutheran church among Scandinavians. *[Preus was actually the first pastor here. –Rosholt]* In addition, he served congregations scattered over central Wisconsin and was forced to make many long journeys by horse or on foot.

Kilbourn (Wisconsin Dells)

Kilbourn, or Moe, or Portage settlement, as it was commonly called in pioneer times, is a small colony of about 400 people in the northwestern tip of Columbia County in the neighborhood of the Dells. This colony was essentially made up of people from Jæren in southwestern Norway. It got its name from Per Olson Moe from Sandsvær in Telemark, who came here in 1843 or 1844. Amund A. Rosseland and Lars Scheie, two of the very first to reach Fox River in Illinois and also Koshkonong, settled at Kilbourn the same year.

It is difficult to understand what drove some of these first newcomers to flit around like a flock of crows. These men, for instance, could have had their choice of the best farmland on Koshkonong or Jefferson Prairie. Not a single Norwegian had yet settled in the later richly endowed colonies at Norway Grove and Spring Prairie. Columbia County and most of the rest of the territory of Wisconsin lay open to them, and after seven years of travel with ample time for thought and consideration, they finally settled on some of the poorest land in the territory.

The settlement is situated for the most part on yellow sand, stony hills and bottomless swamps and is absolutely one of the poorest Norwegian settlements in quality of its soil of any in America. *[Holand overlooks the fact that one of the reasons early pioneers may have been attracted to Kilbourn was the availability of seasonal employment in the great rafting days on the Wisconsin and Wolf rivers. –Rosholt]*

12

Ashippun, Rock River, and Pine Lake Settlements, southeastern Wisconsin

(Source: De Norske Settlementers Historie, by Hjalmar Rued Holand, translated by Malcolm Rosholt, 1908, pp. 166-175)

In 1841 a young man in Sweden, filled with ambition and seeing little prospect for advancement in his own country, decided to immigrate to America. His name was Gustaf Unonius. A one-time student at Uppsala University, Unonius was destined to become one of the first to leave Sweden and the very first Swede to try farming in the Midwest of the United States.

Late in the fall of 1841, Unonius got a log hut built in the northwest corner of Waukesha County, about 30 miles from Milwaukee. *[The three settlements in this chapter roughly take in the northwest corner of Waukesha County in Wisconsin and extend a bit into Dodge and Jefferson counties north and west. –Rosholt]*

Here, in the enchanting surroundings around Oconomowoc, Nashotah and Pine Lake, today a favorite resort area, he founded a Scandinavian settlement, which in some respects became one of the most noteworthy in America.

Unonius is one of the most interesting figures to step across the pioneer stage. He was an educated, pleasant and understanding person who had many colorful and varied experiences. These he has described in an intelligent manner in his book called *A Pioneer in Northwest America 1841-58: The Memoirs of Gustaf Unonius*, which is no doubt the best description we have from the pioneer period. His picturesque descriptions of his journey to America, his at times deep feeling for

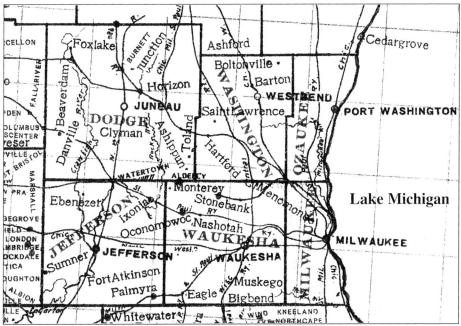

others and at other times his humorous portraitures of the early days, and his delicate references to his wife's participation in all his undertakings, are all both meaningful and captivating.

A large number of Scandinavians have lived in this section of Waukesha County. As it is not far from Milwaukee, where most of the immigrants landed, many came here first to look for land. It was also one of the first sections in America to have a resident Norwegian pastor—Nils O. Brandt.

But the land was covered with forests that were hard to clear, and most of the newcomers remained only a short time and moved on. Most of them were originally from Skien, Gausdal and Setesdal. Many large settlements were founded later by these people, such as the Indian Land of Waupaca County and eastern Portage County in central Wisconsin, the Rush River community in Pierce County and other places. Many an old tiller of the soil got his first experience in America on old Ashippun Creek, Rock River and Pine Lake. Now (1908), there are only three small congregations left, with a total membership of about 500.

The aristocrats of Pine Lake

The Swedes, of which there are only a couple of families remaining, were the first to populate the area around Pine Lake. Shortly after Unonius settled here, he wrote a report of his new home and of conditions in America to a newspaper in Sweden, a correspondence that caused quite a sensation. A charming and youthful enthusiasm for the beautiful scenery and the vast expanses of productive land, practically free for the asking and awaiting the land-poor workers in overpopulated European countries, gave to his descriptions a more rosy hue than they actually deserved. The result was that a highly extraordinary class of people was persuaded to emigrate.

Instead of workers or peasants, a group of representatives from the Swedish aristocracy and military establishment arrived. They gradually assembled on Pine Lake, and around this settlement grew enough fairy tales to fill a couple of oriental kingdoms.

There were a couple of counts and one baron, several former gentlemen of the bedchamber in the Swedish court and a whole raft of gold-braided lieutenants.

They all came to this little settlement, poor in everything except dignity and pompous hopes for the future. Perhaps they thought that, out there in the Midwest's unsettled expanses, they could strike it lucky and make their kingly dreams come true, even if this did not quite measure up to the days of Cortez and Pizarro. Who knows what marvelous developments for the honor of the fatherland and, incidentally, for their own enrichment, lay concealed out there in the Midwest's mysterious wilderness?

With such romantic notions in mind, there arrived one "gentleman" after the other to join Unonius's great establishment. But the wilderness would not conceal its powerful reality, whether for counts or gentlemen-in-waiting. The noble sirs soon found that plans for their grand castles would have to wait, while they went with untested axes into the forest to cut down trees sufficient to build a shack. Their dreams of big estates turned out to be a patch of ground in a woods big enough to pasture a cow.

For a time these honorable gentlemen refused to admit the depths of their false hopes, but sought with ridiculous pomp to maintain their aristocratic dignity. On Sunday they brought out their gold-braided uniforms and resplendent silk dresses that once shone in the elegant dance salons. Then they visited each other in style, in home-made driving duds and wooden-wheeled wagons (*kubberuller*) pulled by steady oxen, with one or another Norwegian newcomer from Gudbrandsdal acting as coachman or lackey.

But pioneer life recognizes no aristocracy and requires the same strong accounting from a baron as from a peasant. And as the former did not have what it takes to stay alive in the wilderness frontier, the result was a foregone conclusion: poverty and misery. Little by little this pioneer nobility gave up its cherished dreams of empire-building. Some were ruined in their effort to clear the land; others made their way back to Sweden. And today, the royal households on Pine Lake are only a legend.

First Norse settlers arrive

The first Norwegians arrived on Pine Lake about the same time as the Swedes. Unonius writes of them as follows:

"Toward the end of the summer (1843) the settlement was increased by several more Swedish and more than 50 Norwegian families. Most of the latter were from the neighborhood of Skien and, with few exceptions, poor in worldly goods. They settled on canal land or took small parcels of land on pre-emption clearings, built their small cottages almost without financial means, and began by working for other farmers who had already gotten a start. The wives helped with laundry work and other occasional jobs; the daughters secured employment in Milwaukee, where they earned a dollar or two a week.

"In this way they soon improved their condition, so that in a couple of years their plowed fields and the cows and oxen grazing in their pastures testified to the fact that America can offer great opportunities to the poor immigrant. But he must be a workman, and he must work.

"The great problems he has to face besides his ignorance of the language are malaria and other diseases. If he succeeds in leaping these hurdles and if circumstances are not too much to cope with, he will be able, by industry and due care, to make a living and soon be more independent than he could ever have hoped for in his homeland. …

"Among the Norwegians there was a gentleman farmer, Hans Gasmann, a man with a big family and a considerable fortune as fortunes are reckoned among new settlers. He settled in the woods by a small river, the Ashippun, where at great cost he bought a couple of sections of land and built a sawmill. The soil was good, but the location was bad. With the means at his disposal, he would no doubt have done better to select more easily tilled land instead of forestland with a growth of timber.

"He was one of the many who came to America with a good deal of money but who, being unacquainted with the conditions in the countryside, are unable to use it properly. They are therefore after a few years on a par with an industrious and energetic working man who, when he drops the first tree on his claim, hasn't a cent in his pockets.

"Gasmann, with his many grown and growing children, became a valuable addition to our restricted social circle. We always enjoyed kindness and Nordic hospitality in his home, and we have many precious memories of him and his family."

[I have here used the English translation of Unonius's Memoirs, as translated by Jonas Oscar Backlund and Nils William Olson. –Rosholt]

Arriving at the same time as Hans Gasmann were Halvor Halvorson and Ellef Bjørnson from Saude in Telemark. Bjørnson soon had a well-developed farm and carries on as the most successful farmer around. Besides these, most of the old pioneers were from Gjerpen and Slembdal (Siljan), men such as Erik Helgeson, G. Løberg, Peter Næss, Jacob Rosholt, Halvor Rosholt, Peter Danielson, Hans Røe and Christen Puttekaasa.

[Jacob Tolefson Rosholt, my great-grandfather, settled on a quarter section in the southwest corner of Pine Lake before moving to Waupaca County in 1851. But mention of the name Halvor Rosholt in the same breath is probably an error. An immigrant who appears to

have settled near Oconomowoc later took the name Rosholt and may have come from near Lardal, where the Rosholt farm is still located, but there is no evidence that Jacob or Halvor were related. –Rosholt]*

Tollef Waller was also among the 1843 arrivals, the first man to leave from Eidanger. *[I located his headstone in the Episcopal Cemetery of Holy Innocents located off County Trunk C west of Pine Lake. –Rosholt]*

Aside from these communities in Norway, Gausdal and Gudbrandsdal were the best represented in this area. Johan Lie was the first to leave from Gausdal for America in 1843. He made a tour of the land in this part of Wisconsin and liked it so well that he returned to Norway for his family.

The common people of Norway at this time considered America almost a fairyland, and one can imagine the sensation created when Johan Lie sold his big farm to sail for this new land so far away and from which people felt there was no return.

Lie settled in the heavy forest country in the northeast corner of Jefferson County, not far from the junction of the Rock and Ashippun rivers, where he built a sawmill on the latter. For those *Gausdøler* who dared to leave in the next few years, they naturally directed their steps to his place, and for a time there were quite a number here. But soon some went farther on, either to the Indian Land of Waupaca and Portage counties, or to Pierce County.

Johan Lie died a few years later, and his widow married a Swede by the name of Wetterhal. One of their children, a daughter, gained fame as a pianist.

This section of Wisconsin was also the first where people from Setesdal began to settle. Ole Nummeland and Tolleiv Røisland from Valle in Setesdal were already here in 1843, the first year that anyone left for America from that area. The following year two fellow villagers, Gunnar Bjørgusson Homme and Knut B. Rystad (father of Pastor J. K. Rystad) arrived, and for a time quite a few more came. Later emigrants from Setesdal mostly came to Fargo, North Dakota, and the Red River Valley of Minnesota. Christopher Aamodt and Hans Uhlen, both of Modum and the first to leave from there, came to Rock River in 1843.

Although Unonius was a loyal Swede, he found more friendliness and tolerance among his Norwegian neighbors than among his own people, and he is full of praise for them. Among other things, he has this to say:

"The Norwegian farmer folk that settled here were, as I have already suggested, generally a vigorous and industrious people who made speedy progress, while the Swedes—belonging as a rule to a social class that had hardly fitted them for the life of farmers and laboring men—were far behind them in enterprise and industry. Norwegian pride and independence therefore became more obvious, since there was here no Swedish superiority that must be acknowledged and that might nourish the natural tendency toward small-minded envy. …"

Meanwhile, in 1845, Unonius organized the first Norwegian congregation (St. Olaf Episcopal) in this section and, after a couple of years at the Episcopal seminary in Nashotah, he was ordained. In this capacity he served not only this and other congregations nearby, but for a time carried on an extensive missionary work among the scattered Norwegian settlers.

Many old pioneers remember him as a highly gifted and energetic preacher whose company they considered it a pleasure to share, but they could not find sufficient grounds to join the Episcopal Church as he had done. Unonius returned to Sweden in 1858. *[Earlier, Unonius left Pine Lake and moved to Chicago, where he served a mixed congregation of Scandinavians for several years and then returned to Sweden in 1858. –Rosholt]*

Memories of a Norse burial

Unonius's memoirs of his ministerial duties around Ashippun are not numerous, but he tells about a Norwegian burial service at which he officiated. This is a humorous story that all those who lived around there will remember. It also is described by Ingebret Tveitan of Scandinavia (Wisconsin), one of the participants, in an interview with O. A. Buslett, which appeared in *Vor Tid (Our Times)* for November 1906. Although the two versions were described 50 years apart, they agree and form the basis for the following:

"As I have said," began Ingebret, "I have been along in many parties in America and in the Old Country. But in that settlement where I first lived, I was along in a funeral service that I have never in the world seen the like of before or since.

"At this time there lived in the settlement a rather comical man called Kristen Puttekaasa from Slembdal—a good man who wouldn't hurt a flea, good to work and good to drink. One could say about him the same as the man said of his good-for-nothing old mare: 'She pulled pretty good, but she ate good, too.'

"This Kristen had it figured this way, that whiskey was good for everything, and he was not alone, that I can tell you. He had a cousin named Ola, and it was this one who became ill and died. As there was no other relative closer than Puttekaasa, it was up to him to take charge of the burial rites.

"Well, the day of the funeral came, the funeral whiskey also came, the pastor arrived, and the whole neighborhood came with their fine horn-horses (oxen) because there were no other horses around at this time.

"The pastor was telling us that the Canal Land would soon be on the market. A company had received a land grant from the government to build a canal—I think it was between Rock River and Fox Lake, if I'm not mistaken. Many Norwegian and Swedish families had settled on this land, which they always referred to as the Canal Land. Nothing came of the canal, and the land came on the market for sale.

"Immediately after the funeral, the Swedish pastor was to make a trip to Milwaukee. Unonius had promised those people who had built their shanties on the Canal Land that he would go to the land office and learn how soon the land could be purchased.

"While the Swedish pastor and the other Swedes and Norwegians stood around talking about the Canal Land, Puttekaasa had been mixing a reasonable drink, with which he wanted to treat the crowd.

"He went over to Unonius and said: 'Herr Pastor! We Norwegians have a custom of having a little round of drinks before we begin services.'

" 'Well, you will have to follow custom then,' said the Episcopalian.

" 'Skaal, Herr Pastor!' said Puttekaasa and drank to him.

" 'Thank you so much, but I don't drink,' said Unonius.

"Then they sang a hymn, and the Episcopalian gave a short talk, which was not too bad. Jacob Rosholt was to haul the coffin because he had the best oxen and the best long-sleigh in the neighborhood. *[Grandfather was between 30 and 35 years of age. –Rosholt]*

"The Episcopalian and Puttekaasa took their places on one of the sleighs farthest back. The funeral procession was about to start when Puttekaasa yelled out at the top of his voice: 'Ho, now! Stop, Jacob! There is no great rush. We must, so help me *(søren tute mig)*, have one for the road.'

"And he turned to the Episcopalian and said: 'Herr Pastor! We Norwegians have a custom of having a good drink of whiskey before starting off on a funeral march!'

" 'Well, you will have to follow

custom, then,' said Unonius.

"Puttekaasa went up to Jacob Rosholt, who was in the lead, and poured one for him, then worked his way back through the others. Of course, the procession was not that all-fired long. There could have been six or seven ox teams or so.

"Well, finally the procession got under way again. When we had come about half way, we saw Puttekaasa running up ahead so the snow flew in all directions.

He got up to Jacob and yelled, 'Ho, now! Stop! We have to have a shot for the road, no matter what!'

"Then he ran back to where the pastor waited and said: 'Herr Pastor! We Norwegians have a custom that we have to have a little slurp on the road, too.'

" 'Well, you will have to follow custom,' said the pastor again.

"When everyone had taken his drink, the procession went on and finally arrived at the graveyard. But the end was not yet here, because Puttekaasa's jug was not quite empty.

"He went to the Episcopalian and said: 'Herr Pastor! We Norwegians have a custom of taking us a snort before beginning the service.'

" 'Well, you will have to follow custom,' said the pastor.

"After we drained the last drop from the jug, we were about to lower the coffin, when two of the most polluted in the crowd nearly fell into the hole ahead of the coffin. But the coffin got into the hole ahead of them and for a moment was standing on one end. We had to haul it up again, and when we finally got it lowered properly, the pastor performed the graveside rites and gave a short prayer.

"The choir leader and Puttekaasa, who stood nearest the pastor, began singing at the top of their voices the hymn, 'Who Knows How Near My End May Be.' When they reached about halfway through the first verse, Puttekaasa said, 'Herr Pastor! You must not forget to ask about the Canal Land,' and he continued to sing the rest of the verse with the others. The pastor merely nodded.

"It appeared by now that the Swedish pastor had become weary of this Norwegian funeral and asked to excuse himself, saying he had to leave. The others would have to finish the burial rites as well as they could, he said, and he left.

"He had not gone far when the choir leader started to run after him, hymn book in hand, as he also wanted to remind him about the Canal Land. But Puttekaasa, who wanted to do things in an orderly manner, considered this interruption an abuse of holy matters. He grabbed the choir leader by the neck and drove him back to the graveside with the words, 'You take care of your business. Is it a Christian custom to run off in the middle of a service?'

"Later on, when the Swedish pastor met some Norwegians, he stopped to ask whether it was customary for Norwegians to 'drink so shockingly' at a funeral. They told him that Norwegian custom called for a few stiff ones on such occasions.

" 'Then I will never attend another Norwegian funeral, no, never,' said the Swedish pastor."

Nils O. Brandt, the first Lutheran pastor at Ashippun, was called in 1851. As there was no Lutheran pastor working west of the Mississippi River, the other pastors hoped he would not accept the Rock River call. But at a meeting of the congregation held after services one day, the members refused to release him. He conducted the church liturgy with so much consecration, it was said, that there was no parting with him. Moreover, he was a small person, quick and light on his feet, and Brandt stayed.

[The "Rock River church" refers to St. Luke's, located in Jefferson County a few miles northwest of Oconomowoc. But Dietrichson, C. L. Clausen and H. S. Stub preceded Brandt here. –Rosholt]

13

Wiota Settlement and the Lead Miners, Lafayette County, Wisconsin

(Source: De Norske Settlementers Historie, by Hjalmar Rued Holand, translated by Malcolm Rosholt, 1908, pp. 176–183)

Wisconsin was first known as a mining state. As far back as the 1700s, restless Frenchmen had discovered that the southwest corner of Wisconsin was rich in lead ore. But it was not before 1820 or so, when Eastern capital became interested, that the mines were operated on any systematic basis and people began to stream in to find work.

Galena, Mineral Point, Dubuque and Wiota, Shullsburg, Mifflin and other places were lively towns before anyone had even heard of Chicago. Many of these places were larger than they are now, and Galena was, for a long time, the heart of the West, with its own newspaper—long before any newspaper appeared in Chicago.

Lead-mining was at its height in the 1840s, and there were hundreds of Norwegian newcomers who worked here. In Galena there was an entire colony that cut wood and worked in the mines. Although there is not much information on this group, suffice it to say that it was the first step on the ladder of their newfound economic independence. They earned a dollar a day and patiently drank their black coffee and ate rye bread and syrup, meal after meal, day after day.

Around Wiota, lying in the southeast corner of Lafayette County, there were big lead mines, and here in particular many newcomers got their start in America. In 1843, Norwegians—most originally from Voss—conducted all of the mine operations around Wiota. After working a few months or years, these people spread out and established additional colonies.

The first Norwegians to find work in the Wiota mines were the brothers Andreas O. Week and John O. Week, who arrived at Wiota in the spring of 1840. They were from Eidfjord in Hardanger. In 1844 John Week moved to Dodgeville where he, together with John Lee from Numedal, opened the first shoemaker shop outside of Milwaukee. A few years later, Andrew Week moved north to Marathon County, where he became the first Scandinavian in that county. Here he built a sawmill and began a lumber camp 25 miles or so northwest of Stevens Point (Wisconsin).

[Olaf Druetzer, the Swede, was probably the first Scandinavian in Marathon County. There is reason to believe it was he who selected the site for the later well-known "Week Mill" on the Big Eau Pleine River, and took in Andrew Week as a partner. This partnership lasted only a couple of years when Dreutzer moved to Waupaca and Andrew sold out to his brother John and left to join the gold rush to California. –Rosholt]

In 1841 three men arrived in Wiota via Chicago—namely, Per Davidson Skervheim from Hardanger, Arne Arneson Vinje from Voss, and Per J. Unde, the first to emigrate from Sogn. After working in the lead mines a short time, they bought land three or four miles southeast of Wiota and established the foundations for one of the biggest Norwegian colonies in Wisconsin. This colony stretches from Gratiot in Lafayette County to Black Earth in Dane County, a distance of more than 40 miles long, 18 miles wide, and settled entirely by Norwegians.

The terrain is hilly, containing narrow valleys and ridges. It is fertile and well-watered, with springs and creeks on nearly every farm.

Blue Mounds, Wisconsin's highest mountain, lies on the northern boundary of the colony. From its top on a clear day, a person can see most of the 21 large Norwegian churches that lie behind the ridges and that serve about 8,500 parishioners.

The people who live in these valleys are especially hospitable and preserve real Norwegian ideals and manners of speech. Their farms and church work are likewise praiseworthy.

Everything is fine except the roads. These are about as miserable as possible, especially in the southern sections. This results from an old custom of laying roads along the section lines, no matter what the terrain might be. There is scarcely a house to be found near the main road, and homes are built along the floor of the valleys, not on the section lines. Nor has any thought been given to the fact that a road that goes up and down over a hill is twice as long and 10 times as difficult to drive over. Section lines were meant for road construction, these brave New World immigrants say, so that's the way it is. And furthermore, they've got money enough to buy new horses when the old ones wear out.

These two settlements were originally surveyed for two different influxes of newcomers, who eventually met in the middle to form a single community. The southern part takes in Wiota and the Yellowstone Valley in Lafayette County, where there are around 2,500 people from Land and Hadeland in Oppland fylke. People who came up from Rock Prairie on the Illinois-Wisconsin line settled this stretch.

The northern part of the settlement (to be described in the next chapter) is generally known under the joint name, Blue Mounds, and includes Mt. Horeb, Black Earth, Spring Dale, Perry, Primrose, York and Adams. Here there are about 6,000 Norwegians, mostly from Valdres.

It was at Wiota, at the southernmost point of the settlement, where the first three pioneers already alluded to came to settle. Quite a few people from Voss arrived but later moved away.

A deadly voyage

One of the leaders among these first settlers was Per Davidson, a man whose life ended in tragedy. In 1852 he learned that a relative of his family was coming from Norway to join him at Wiota. He drove his wagon to Chicago to meet them. Cholera had broken out in the city, and when his relatives arrived they found Per bedridden with the plague. The newcomers were also infected, and a short time later all, save two boys, were dead.

Meanwhile, Davidson's young wife was at home waiting for him and the relatives. Every day she went out to a hill to catch a glimpse of the party. But one week passed another without any sign of them. She had baked and scrubbed and, still thinking they would come shortly, baked anew in order to provide a fitting welcome for the relatives of her husband.

Finally, one day she caught sight of the horses, so familiar to her, approaching the valley. But her happiness was short-lived, for instead of her husband and his relatives, she saw only two boys. The others had found nameless graves at the expense of the city of Chicago.

One could write an entire chapter on the criminal negligence that was shown the newcomers to Chicago. Many of my countrymen told me of their coming to Chicago and how they were huddled together in a single room where several people already lay ill with cholera. In this room they had to part with many dear relatives and fellow travelers, because by dawn the following morning many of them would be dead. An attack of cholera was deaf to all prayers, and the killing poison was inexorable.

The northern part of the settlement near Wiota is best known as the largest colony of people from Land in Oppland fylke. Up to 1847, newcomers from Voss had the place for themselves, but in that year the *Landinger* began to pour in until every ridge and slope were occupied. The first of these people was Syver Johnson Smed, followed by Sven Nørslien, Ole Monson, John Smedsrud, Johannes Brennum, Martin Bonli and Frederik Torkelson. Most of them worked in the mines around Wiota for a time.

California Knudsen

Among the Norwegians in Wiota was a man from Drammen, well remembered by hundreds of the pioneers—namely, Knud Knudsen, who started a blacksmith shop in Wiota in 1843 or earlier, as he was already doing well in business by that time. He left Drammen in 1838, the first to leave from there. He was the person who took the lead in organizing a congregation among the several small colonies around Wiota, on Rock Prairie and Jefferson Prairie, which agreed to pay $300 in salary plus further increments to bring a resident pastor from Norway.

A letter of call was drawn up in February 1844, and the answer to this was the arrival of Dietrichson, as mentioned earlier. Wiota therefore did not get a pastor before 1855 when the later, well-known, Johan Storm Munch accepted.

Knudsen was an uncommonly bold and far-sighted man in material matters. In 1849 he was among the first to leave for the California gold fields. He returned in a couple of years and organized a big party that went overland to California—in fact, the largest party of Norwegians to join the gold rush. California Knudsen, as he was later called, is also known in La Crosse County, where he owned hundreds of acres of land in Bostwick Valley and Halfway Creek. He eventually retired to San Francisco.

The dream versus reality

Nearly all the land in Lafayette County is covered with oak timber, which is not easy to cut down or saw. Here and there lay a small meadow, but despite the backbreaking labor, it seemed that this area had everything the pioneers from Land were looking for—wood, water and meadow.

Directly south of this settlement lies the Warren Prairie, a wide stretch with hay growing in abundance, no stumps and no stones as far as the eye can see. It could happen, of course, that now and then one of these newcomers from Land got tired of fighting with the oak trees (white oak) covering the hills. Then he might stroll across the uninhabited prairie and ruminate how easy it would be to build a farm here, where all that was needed was to plow up the ground. He could easily visualize the waving wheat and sleek-looking cows knee-deep in clover, while up on the higher ground stood an impressive farm with big barns stocked with big horses, small pigs, cackling hens and noisy geese! Wow! It would be better than any big shot had it back in the Old Country.

But old Sven Nørslien quickly brought the dreamer to his senses.

"What are you standing there gaping at? Do you think for a moment that wild prairie is suitable for farming? Where would you get water for the livestock or rails for the fences? And think how the wind blows around there! If your shanty doesn't blow away before Christmas, you'll freeze to death before the New Year."

With this blast, our foolish, crestfallen newcomer had to retreat, convinced that the Warren Prairie would never be settled to the end of time.

North of the Land people, up among the Yellowstone Valley ravines and secret nooks, lies a large settlement of folks from Hadeland—actually the largest offspring of Hadeland people in

America, who arrived at the same time as the *Landinger*. The Klinkenberg brothers were the first in 1847, and shortly after came Erik Tanberg, Anders Gaarsrud, Brede Holt, Syver Talla, Ole F. Ringen (now 100 years old) and Frederik Goli. In 1867 an entire ship, the *Dagmar*, commanded by Captain Svend Foyn, arrived in the U.S. with 300 passengers from Hadeland, most of whom settled around the present Blanchardville.

The first white man to settle in this area, however, was Thore Thompson Røisland, a noted son of Norway who originated not in Hadeland but Tinn in Telemark. He came in 1844 and settled two miles west of the present city of Argyle.

He also was among the first to strike out for California in 1849. In this venture he did something unparalleled: He drove a whole herd of milk cows through hostile Indian country, across the deserts and snow-covered mountains, to California, where he sold milk at outrageous prices. Later, his luck turned against him and he was forced to take a job as a teamster hauling freight.

Once, while driving through the mountains, a gang of desperadoes held him up and took everything he had, valued around $1,200. Røisland continued for a year with the freight company and on the anniversary of the holdup, he returned to the district where the water runs so free and easy.

Unarmed, he made his way to the bandit leader and coolly shouted: "You remember quite well you borrowed $1,200 from me a year ago. As I thought you had forgotten my address, I've come to collect my money."

The leader of the gang stared at him in disbelief, but Røisland stood there without batting an eye, whereupon the leader grabbed a heavy sack of gold dust and threw it at him, saying, "You're a cool one, all right. Take that!" There was about $1,500 worth of gold dust in the sack.

When Røisland later returned to his own farm near Argyle, he discovered a rich lead vein only a few feet below the surface of his land and became a wealthy man. He was a half-brother of the widely known Snowshoe Thompson.

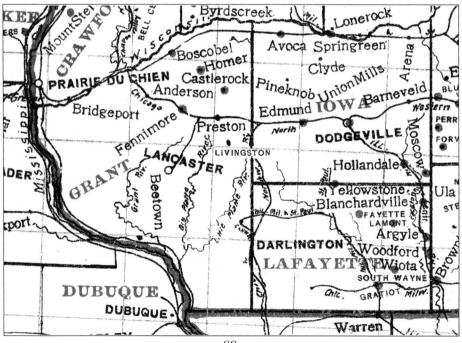

14

Blue Mounds Settlement (Dodgeville, Otter Creek and Castle Rock), Iowa, and Grant Counties, Wisconsin

(Source: De Norske Settlementers Historie, by Hjalmar Rued Holand, translated by Malcolm Rosholt, 1908, pp. 184–195)

Among other scenic wonders, Wisconsin also has some real mountain peaks. Blue Mounds, about 25 miles west of Madison, has the highest peak among these. Majestic and blue and nearly 2,000 feet above sea level, it towers over the valleys below. Deep gorges and narrow ravines hide shady nooks on all sides, and fresh springs gush forth from stones that begin rivers running in all directions. *[Wisconsin's 1968 Blue Book, p. 560, lists Blue Mounds as the highest point in the southern part of the state. –Rosholt]*

A view from the top of this peak is a picture of natural beauty without equal in Wisconsin. On all sides lie fruitful acres with deep, tree-decked valleys, sun-flecked meadows and winding ridges. Somewhat directly east and west runs a broad ridge, which divides the waters between this part of Wisconsin and the Mississippi Valley.

Along this treeless ridge the first road in the Upper Midwest was laid—the famed Military Road between Fort Winnebago at Portage and Fort Crawford at Prairie du Chien. The first U.S. mail was carried over this route, linking Lake Michigan and the Mississippi. These stagecoaches were huge affairs seating 10 passengers inside and still more outside. With four horses at the gallop, the stages went one each way during the day, horns blowing, echoing and re-echoing across the Blue Mounds hills.

Not everyone, however, went through Blue Mounds. Several thousand Norwegians stopped here and established a widespread and famous settlement, the largest assembly of people from Valdres in America.

Of all places in America, the name of Blue Mounds is probably the best known in Valdres as a place where the longings of the Valdres people have been realized for the past 60 years. They had heard that it was the name of a mountain peak; therefore, it was not strange that they associated it with some sort of Mt. Nebo, where a man could see clear across the Promised Land. *[Mt. Nebo in Israel is reported to be the burial place of Moses. –Rosholt]*

Most of these people came from Sør-Aurdal and Nord-Aurdal in Valdres. They took entire possession of Spring Dale Township's beautiful park-like areas; Vermont's many hills and bottoms are full of *Valdriser*. They built up Mt. Horeb, that widow's refuge and retired farmer's paradise. Their farms dot the landscape along Blue Mounds and Perry townships.

The first Norwegian in Blue Mounds was not from Valdres. He was Iver Thorson Aase from Sogn, who arrived in 1844 after working in the Wiota lead mines a year. He is usually called Iver Breaker because he used to plow for his neighbors as soon as they had found a piece of land and got settled. A message was sent to Iver Breaker and in time he would appear with his long breaking plow pulled by six oxen. Where there were stones and small grub, three or four men clung to the plow while it turned a furrow two to three feet wide.

Iver was the only settler here for two years, and his name is remembered only in connection with the breaking of the land. He had no influence on later emigration.

With the arrival of a party of 15 people in 1846, the real beginning of the settlement got under way. Thore Thoreson Spaanem, the leader of this group, is considered the father of the settlement. Others in the group included John Ingebretson Berge, Tosten Thompson, Nils Halverson Græsdalen, Halvor Halverson Græsdalen, Ole Sørenson Kvisterud and Knut Sørenson Kvisterud, all capable and enterprising men and all originally from Tinn in Telemark fylke, by way of Muskego.

Only Spaanem had a wagon with oxen; the others walked behind. They all settled in a valley a couple of miles west of Mt. Horeb—except for Spaanem, who took a piece of land in a long valley a couple of miles farther south, where Syver Brustuen lives.

Tosten Thompson was a brother of Snowshoe Thompson, who later won national recognition for carrying the mail on skis across the Sierra Mountains during several winters. Tosten's house was the first one occupied by a Norwegian west of Madison on the old Military Road, and here hundreds of tired land-seekers were welcomed without charge.

In 1847 Thore Spaanem wrote a piece for *Nordlyset* about the Blue Mounds region, and it was this article that brought the people from Valdres. Among the first to arrive were Ole Lee, Aslak Lee, Ole Olson Bakken and Gudbrand Elseberg from Nord-Aurdal. Aslak Lee was a former sergeant in the Norwegian Army and an intelligent and progressive man. His inspiring letters to acquaintances in Valdres were the most important factor in the growth of the settlement.

Aslak Lee was also a first-class carpenter, and his old house, which still stands at Klevenville, reveals more than a common beauty for a house of log construction. It became a popular stopping place for strangers, and many a pastor and professor slept here in the old days. A. O. Throndrud from Nord-Aurdal lives there now. His brother Gundbrand Throndrud came here in 1849, and his letters home also hastened emigration.

The same year (1849), Arne Hoff arrived from Sør-Aurdal, together with Levor Anderson Marelien, Thomas Lie, Ole Hjelle, Iver Lund, Gulbrand Wold and Knut Olson Syverud. The last named, accompanied by his family, covered the 100 miles from Milwaukee on foot. He was a well-liked man, always ready to help the newcomers in word and deed (i raad og daad).

[A footnote by Holand: "Among the first to arrive at Blue Mounds were also Sæbjørn Pederson Dysterud and Gullik Svendsrud, both from Numedal, who came in 1847. Dysterud had worked in St. Louis for a time as early as 1841." –Rosholt]

Ole Olson Bakken was the first Norwegian in Perry Township. A native of Nord-Aurdal, he arrived in August 1848. Arriving that same fall were Lars Halverson Langemyr from Tørdal, Hans Johnson from Drangedal, and T. Thompson and Torge Johnson Tvedt from Amli in Nedenæs *[the modern Nedenesengene on the coast of Norway –Rosholt]*.

But the best-known man in Perry Township was O. B. Dahle from Nissedal in Telemark. He first went to California where he experienced many hardships but did manage to find some gold. He arrived in Perry Township in 1853, where he went into the real estate business and gradually amassed a fortune. He was an enterprising man and is still remembered with great respect.

The first Norwegian church in west Dane County—an unpretentious log house 20 feet square—was erected in Perry in 1851.

Vermont and Primrose settlements

Vermont is rough and hilly and as a result was not settled as early as the other townships. But here, too, the Valdres people were nearly everywhere. One of the first was Mikkel Halsteinson Blekkelien from Sor-Aurdal, who came by way of Manitowoc County, where he thought the forest was too heavy to tackle. He made himself a sort of Laplander's sledge on which he loaded his tools and necessities (weighing some 300 pounds) and proceeded to pull his baggage over hills some 200 miles across the state to Mt. Horeb.

Among other prominent men, mention must be made of Sam Thompson, or Svien in Lien, as he was known among the Valdres people. He is considered a cornerstone of Mt. Horeb and one of the Valdres people's main supporters. His father, Thrond, was a noted gun-maker and bear-hunter in Valdres.

Michael Johnson is one of the few people from Sogn to be found at Mt. Horeb. Among the first pioneers to Norway Grove, where most of his relatives lived, he arrived at Blue Mounds in 1856 and has taken an important role in local politics and in church affairs. He served six years on the Norwegian Synod's council during the debate over predestination in the 1880s.

Neri Dalen was already in Blue Mounds by 1849, but did not settle here until 1854. In the meantime, he was in California with six other Norwegian gold-seekers, and was quite lucky. He returned to Norway via Panama and in Tinn recruited a big party of emigrants to accompany him back to Dane County.

Arne Røste came from Etnedal in 1850, accompanied by a big family. His sons are influential men who go by the name of Arneson as well as Røste.

[A footnote by Holand: "Arne Røste died shortly after his arrival and his widow was married in 1857 to Anders Mikkelson. The couple celebrated their golden wedding in 1907. It was then 80 years since old Mother Røste, as she is still called, married her first husband, and she was still quite lively. She had 11 children by her first husband and nearly as many by the second. The family now runs into the hundreds."–Rosholt]

Down in Primrose Township, the tide of immigration began simultaneously with the arrival of Thore Spaanem and party to Spring Dale. The first Norwegian to settle in Primrose was Christian Hendrickson from Lier. Like so many other pioneers mentioned above, he first worked in the lead mines around Wiota (1842). He had accumulated sufficient funds to buy a yoke of oxen and a wagon, with 75 cents left in change. He moved to his present home in Primrose in 1846. Milwaukee, 100 miles away, was the nearest marketplace. A person would think that the lead-mining district would have been a better place to sell goods, but here meat sold for only 2 cents per pound.

Two years after Hendrickson reached Primrose, the real movement of immigrants to the township began, many arriving from Hendrickson's home community in Norway. Among the first were Nils Einarson, Salve Jørgenson, Nils N. Skogen, and Kittil Kittilson Moland from Førrisdal.

[In my personal copy of Holand's, De Norske Settlementers Historie, an anonymous hand has penciled in the information that Nils Einarson was from Næsherred, Sande Kittilson Moland and Kittil Kittilson Moland from Bøherrad. –Rosholt]

The most widely known among the old pioneers to Primrose was Gunolf Tollefson from Setesdal, a member of the first party of emigrants to leave from that district. Others in the party included Tollef Gunolfson, father of Gunolf, Kjøgei Harstad, and Hage Olson and families. With $180 among them, the party left Bygland on foot and walked to the port. After crossing the ocean, they arrived in New York with one dollar.

Aboard ship, young Tollefson had picked up several English phrases. On his arrival in New York he was not the only one who felt out of place in his bottomless Setesdal trousers. But he had a desire to be the first to display his newfound proficiency in the English language. He went into a tailor shop and bought a simple pair of trousers. When he asked how much, the storekeeper replied, "Two and six (62 cents)."

The reply came so fast he failed to catch on, and to this he shouted, "I will give you three shilling (75 cents)," and the deal was made.

In an article about his pioneer days, which Tollefson later wrote for an English paper, he says that a man by the name of Bakke gave the party free tickets from New York to Wisconsin. This was no doubt Søren Bachke of Muskego. The party remained in Muskego for a time, and in 1844 Tollefson went on to Primrose.

Concerning his arrival here, he says: "As I wanted to own my own land as soon as possible, I went to Primrose in 1849. Here I met Nils Einarson. There was plenty of land, but where to find the description of a given tract was the big question. After considerable searching we found a big oak tree quite a distance from the place where Norman Randal now lives. This tree was clearly marked with the following letters and numbers: NW 1/4, S. 23, T. 5, N. R. 6 E.

"There was neither pencil nor paper to be had without going many miles to purchase it, and something had to be done fast. I borrowed an axe from Einarson, cut down a small aspen, and after smoothing out two sides so that it was quite narrow, I took my pocketknife and carved the letters and numbers just as I found them on the oak tree.

"With this piece of aspen under my arm, I went to the land office and laid the aspen and my money on the counter, to the amusement of the officials in charge. They understood the inscription, and I got my land."

Shortly after Tollefson settled here, he cut a trail north to a military road near Blue Mounds and set up a sign on which he wrote in good Norwegian: "Anyone wishing to meet Norwegians, follow this path." Many accepted the invitation. It also is one reason why so many different communities in Norway are represented in Primrose.

Club Law

Primrose was the first community where people organized themselves into what later became known as the Club Law. *[Holand probably means first community in Dane County. –Rosholt]* This Club Law was an association of neighbors created to defend themselves against strangers conniving to take their land away from them.

As most of the pioneers in the beginning did not have money to buy their land immediately, they took up "squatter's" rights, which were recognized by others in the same position as a requisite right to ownership. Many strangers refused to recognize these rights and purchased the land from under the squatters on occasion. It was then that the unwritten Club Law was enforced, and life was made so uncomfortable for the stranger that he found it best to leave. In other places such as in Goodhue County (Minnesota), the Club Law in some instances degenerated into plain land piracy by the first arrivals.

Two *Numedøler*, Gunuld Haugen (Gunuld Jackson) and Gjermund Haugen (Gjermund Jackson) arrived in Primrose with Tollefson in 1849. Their father was the first Norwegian to die in Wisconsin in 1840.

In 1856, when Gunuld Jackson was out West searching for gold, some Irishman in Montrose thought this would be a good time to take some nice timber that grew on Jackson's land. The members of the Club Law heard of this and met early one morning to prevent the theft. Their captain was Nils Olson, a big bruiser from Lier. He suggested that they go secretly and take the

Irishmen, who usually held the unobtrusive Norwegians in contempt and of no account.

The leader of the Irish group was a formidable fellow who, without further ado, began cutting down a big oak tree that was not on his land. Nils Olson grabbed an axe, jumped before the Irishman and said, "If you take the stump, I'll take the tree," whereupon he began chopping furiously at the tree above the Irishman's head.

This was soon too much for the latter as the sharp axe whistled over his head. After considering Olson's strong, agile swings with the axe for a moment, he took his crestfallen troops out of the woods. Since that time, peace has reigned between the Norwegians and Irish.

Nils Olson died later in the Civil War. Many other Norse pioneers from Primrose also died in the war, as a large number of volunteers were raised here. The above-named Gjermund Jackson recruited an entire company from Primrose and surrounding area and was promoted to Captain, Company 1, 43rd Wisconsin Regiment. Not less than 56 Norwegians went off to the Civil War from Primrose alone.

This was for many years a remote area in Wisconsin. The nearest city was Milwaukee, 100 miles to the east. The roads were so bad it often took two weeks to make the trip one way. Across swamps and over bridges, a teamster often had to take planks from one end of a bridge and lay them down on the other end to get across.

Sometimes the price of wheat was down to 25 cents a bushel, and it could even happen that there was no sale for wheat at all. Then a man hauled his wheat all the way home again and west to the Mississippi River. If there was no sale for it here, there was nothing to do but dump the entire load in the river as something accursed.

When the road was too difficult for two oxen on a load, a man often had to borrow two more. If he had to pay 25 cents' rental for the oxen and 25 cents for the wagon, the wheat might not be worth hauling. There was little economic progress made by the pioneers these first years.

But the worst for the pioneers was to see their children grow up without being baptized. Instead of lawful branches upon the tree of life, it was like looking at weeds in a beautiful meadow. Several meetings were held to discuss the matter, and finally a man was sent off to Koshkonong to see whether Pastor Dietrichson could be persuaded to come. He agreed to come for $10. This amount was at length collected, whereupon, in 1850, Dietrichson conducted the first worship services, in the house of Thore Spaanem. Here, many children were baptized.

Confirmation services were held later in the woods, where logs served as benches. Later in this same woods, the annual synod meeting was held, a historic occasion because it was here that Elling Eielsen and Rasmussen parted company *[presumably P. A. Rasmussen –Rosholt]*.

For a time, both parties *[one representing the Norwegian Synod, the other the Eielsen or Hauge Synod –Rosholt]* held services in the same schoolhouse. One group waited outside until the other had finished.

Green County

South of Primrose and Perry townships lies Green County, where there are large numbers of Norwegians in York and Adams townships. On the west range line these townships border Lafayette County, where there is a large settlement of people from Land and Hadeland. There are also quite a few Valdres people in Green County, a settlement that stems directly from Blue Mounds. Amund Eidsmo, Christopher Eidsmo and Mikkel Eidsmo from Sør-Aurdal were the first ones here (to York Township), in 1854.

It was around 1852, after Stephen

Olson Helle's second visit to Valdres, that emigration from Valdres began to assume significant proportions. One of the best-known pioneers in those days, founder of the big Valdres community in York and Adams townships, was Amund O. Eidsmoe.

At the age of 88, Eidsmoe wrote an account of his trip to America. He was along in that terrible accident on Lake Erie, a tragedy about which there are legends still being told in all Valdres communities.

Dodgeville and Otter Creek

Approximately 20 miles west of Blue Mounds in a valley known as Otter Creek, there is also a Norwegian colony of about 1,300 people, mainly from Valdres. This settlement is a continuation, or offspring, of the Blue Mounds. When there was no more good land to be found in the latter, people went farther west to Otter Creek.

Strangely enough, the first settlers here came from Dodgeville and Mifflin, where there were once important lead mines and where many Norsemen worked. Among these early lead miners may be mentioned the real founders of the Norwegian communities later established in Iowa—namely, Ole Halvorson Valle and Ole Tollefson Kittilsland, both from Numedal.

Here, too, came Halstein Halvorson Fløse. Together with the Nattestad brothers, he was the first to leave for America from eastern Norway in 1837. Several things suggest that he was the first Norwegian to visit Iowa County and he must, therefore, be considered the founder of the settlement there.

He had two brothers, Erik Halvorson Fløse and Ole Halvorson Fløse, who settled nearby on the prairie west of Dodgeville, in addition to some other *Numedøler* such as Knut Olson Hoff, Knut Bromdalen, Herbrand Pederson, Haakon Pederson, Hellik Haugen Stevens and John Lee. The last named became the best-known, as he still lives on his original place and has reached an old age. Nearly all the others have moved away. Lee also worked in the lead mines for a time, but in 1844, in company with John O. Week of Hardanger, he opened the first shoemaker shop in Wisconsin, or at least, west of Milwaukee. He was married to the sister of John Luraas, founder of the Muskego settlement, and a veritable mine of information on the early Norwegians of Wisconsin. *[John Lee was also an uncle of John Week. – Rosholt]*

After the *Numedøler*, people from Hadeland began to settle in Iowa County. Hans Jacobson Sollien was the first of these in 1851. Later, the Valdres people began to arrive but settled farther north on Otter Creek.

Castle Rock

In 1854 a Norwegian settlement was founded at Castle Rock in Grant County, 15 miles west of Otter Creek, which now includes two congregations with a membership of around 800. The men who arrived in 1854 were Sven Hanson from Numedal, Endre Johnson Lindelien and Guttorm Iverson from Valdres, Jørgen Gunderson Bostrok from Drangedal, John Peterson from Østerdal, and Lars Jenson.

The terrain around Castle Rock has many small valleys and somewhat sandy soil.

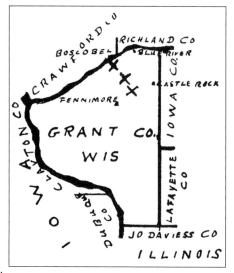

15

Winchester Settlement, Racine County, southeastern Wisconsin

(Source: De Norske Settlementers Historie, by Hjalmar Rued Holand, translated by Malcolm Rosholt, 1908, pp. 196–198)

About 10 miles west of Neenah, Wisconsin, lies Winchester settlement, marked by big marshes and meadows on all sides so that the high ground in the center appears to be a big island. On the top of this high point stands the church, where the view is magnificent.

Winchester is one of the first offshoots of Muskego. In the fall of 1846, three *Telemarkinger*, Søren Wilson, Andrew Thompson and John Rud, came to this region to look for land. They wanted wood, water and meadow and here all three were combined in plentitude. They returned in the fall of 1847 to settle here, and on this trip were accompanied by the brothers Christian Johnson Aalterud, Per Johnson Aalterud and Johannes Johnson Aalterud from Toten. Even Thompson and Knut Luraas also came that same year.

The Johnson brothers were the first to leave from Toten, Oppland fylke, in 1846. They were accompanied by Ole Larson, Ole Christianson and Per Rølstad. The last named was an uncommonly capable carpenter as well as enterprising man. He was the leader of this group, but his story in America was not destined to be long. A widower, he became infatuated with a girl on board ship. But his grown sons were against the lovely Helene for stepmother and, in his despair, Per Rølstad took his own life by swallowing poison a week after reaching Winchester.

Among other early pioneers were Helge Mathieson, Ole Klokkerengen and the Amundsen brothers, all from Telemark. It also was here that Peer Strømme was born, and Winchester settlement became the locale for Strømme's first-rate story (written in Norwegian), titled *How Halvor Became Pastor*, which is based on actual events and the lives of Winchester people.

The Amundson brothers were mechanically inclined. Peer Strømme remembers seeing all kinds of farm implements in their yard, some recently

patented by others, which they had made themselves. But the law governing patent rights was enforced, and this new implement company went out of business.

Helge Mathieson is best remembered among old settlers by the name Hølje Tavane, as he operated some sort of tavern or hotel. Mrs. Mathieson was a powerful woman who not only could carry on the business, but also directed passing strangers on their way. Often there were travelers who could not find their way across the flooded roads on the marshes nearby. But Mrs. Mathieson took a long pole, boldly wrapped her clothing around her head and waded into the water up to her hips. Steadily forward she went, thrusting the pole here and there and calling out, "Her er fast Grund!" *["Here is firm ground." –Rosholt]* This has since become a classic expression around Winchester.

A Lutheran congregation was organized here in 1850 and first served by A. C. Preus from Koshkonong. In a few years, a new congregation was organized and another church built next door to the first one. Hymn singing in the one could be heard through the open windows of the other, a grating dissonance if people in the opposite church were praying. As people from the two congregations left their churches they glared at each other across the green lot, daggers in their eyes. Instead of bringing people to charity, church attendance in those days was mainly an exercise in bitterness and set the tone for hateful comments heard in the community the rest of the week.

Finally, people realized the soul-corrupting influence in this order of things and tore down both churches as totems of pharisaic arrogance, and rebuilt a large and beautiful edifice which, with its harmonious architectural lines and lovely ornamental effects, shines far and wide across the entire settlement. The churchly battle-axe has been buried, and peace and understanding reign over the community.

Sæterpige ved sin Rok

16

The Indian Land, western Waupaca and northeast Portage Counties, Wisconsin

(Source: De Norske Settlementers Historie, by Hjalmar Rued Holand, translated by Malcolm Rosholt, 1908, pp. 199–207)

Central Wisconsin is not as fruitful as either the southern or northern part of the state. Nevertheless, it is a pleasant and poetic land to view. Instead of the big meadows of southern Wisconsin and the great forests of northern Wisconsin, small prairies surrounded by oak groves and many sparkling brooks and freshwater lakes characterize the terrain here. This is especially true of western Waupaca County and northeast Portage County.

This region was especially favored as a camping ground by the Indians, and it is still called *Indilandet*, or Indian Land. Nowhere was there a greater abundance of deer or so many black bear and beavers. The creeks were full of trout, and the silver lakes teemed with bass and pike. In addition, the land was sandy and easily cultivated for the little corn or potatoes the Indians needed. *[There is no evidence that the Indians in central Wisconsin planted potatoes until the latter part of the 19th century. –Rosholt]*

The coming of the white man

Only 50 years ago this was an Indian paradise, undisturbed by the foot or ambition of the white man. From the tall weeds and on shores of the lakes to the forest that covered the ridges, it was a land of peace and plenty. All this *Manitou* had given his red children, and life moved easily. They smoked their pipes in comfort and told stories of bygone days. They hunted or picked berries, or danced the lively buffalo dance. *[Holand does not explain the buffalo dance. –Rosholt]*

But one day the white man came to these parts—the energetic Yankee and the strong, serious Norseman. For him, life is not long and far from carefree, but short and filled with responsibility, and he knows from something he has read that mankind is damned. So now he seeks out a place where the curse is less awesome.

He digs himself a hole in the side hill for a house, to begin life anew. He chops and saws the hard oak trees and builds strong fences around his property, sows his corn, digs a well, drains and irrigates, plows and digs. Soon a small church appears where he can beseech a God he more fears than loves. For him, life is serious.

It is well that the pioneer is not alone in his fight to conquer the lonesomeness of the frontier. He has a wife along with him who is just as game as he. She has walked behind the wagon, her face burned and weather-beaten by wind and sun. She now begins to taste the full measure of the pioneer struggle. She must be up at dawn, milk her cows, carry water for cooking and washing from the nearest well a quarter of a mile away, chop wood and keep the fire going. Her complexion becomes coarse

and her movements difficult, but her heart is still light and with affection and prayer she raises her children.

The hardships of the pioneers are nearly forgotten, and where there were once the wigwams of the Indians, there is now a large Norwegian colony. It extends about 30 miles from the city of Waupaca to the village of Rosholt, and 25 miles wide between Amherst and Big Falls. The Green Bay and Western Railroad cuts across the southern part. All the big farms and potato acreages one sees on a drive from Ogdensburg to Amherst Junction belong to Norwegians. Other villages in this area include Iola, Scandinavia and Nelsonville.

First Norwegians arrive

In the late summer of 1850, the first Norsemen came to these parts and settled west of the present village of Scandinavia. This group included Hans Jacob Eliason, Christian Olson and Lars Larson Hasler; the two latter were grown boys for whom Eliason was a guardian. They were from Eidanger north of Brevig.

Also in the same group came Gunstein Tollefson Krostu from Setesdal, and Østen Flaten from Tinn in Telemark. Knut Luraas from Winchester, where Krostu and Flaten had stopped for a time, went along with the party to Waupaca County as a guide. Krostu was the first to sink a plow in the ground.

Although this first party had some influence on later immigration to the settlement, it was not as important in this respect as the party that followed the next year (1851). The following are listed on the ship: Jacob Rosholt, Jacob Listul, Torkel Listul, Ole Christianson Gunholt, Ingebret Erikson Tveitan, Andreas Waller, Bjørn Tollefson, John Hartvig and a couple of others, all from Gjerpen and Slembdal. *[Not all; Rosholt was from Laurdal. He and Jacob Listul actually walked from the Pine Lake settlement in Waukesha County to Waupaca County in the latter part of 1850 and established squatter's rights to two tracts of land in the northwest of the township. Listul appears to have returned the same year with his family shortly before Christmas; Rosholt moved his family up from Pine Lake in the spring of 1851. –Rosholt]*

The first Norwegians to settle in eastern Portage County were Aslak Moe, Ole Moe and Peder P. Kjær, all from Gjerpen, in addition to Peder K. Hiller—usually known as Per Muskego —from Laurdal, who came in 1853.

New arrivals on the Indian Land in 1853 included Jacob Bestul (Rasmus Bestul*)*, Harald Evenson Gulseth, Thomas Knopf, Stephen Jacobson Nygaard from Haugesund, Lars L. Løberg, Anders Steensrud, Nils Anderson Tholdness, Nils O. Walderdalen, Lars Gorden, Simon Løberg, Johan Løberg, and Simon Aamodt and his two sons Nils Simonson Aamodt and Simon Simonson Aamodt. All were from around Skien. *[Not all came in 1853. Knopf, at least, was in Scandinavia, Wisconsin, as early as 1852 to start the first store. –Rosholt]*

After these people, many others from the same place in Norway arrived. It is now the biggest colony of people from the Skien neighborhood in America. Among them one finds an unusual number of gifted men whose sons now hold influential positions in different parts of the country. Among the older pioneers, none were more honored than Ole Wrolstad and Ole Wogsland from Tørisdal in Norway.

All these men moved north to the Indian Land from Ashippun, Rock River and Pine Lake, which are merely names for three parts of the same settlement in Dodge, Jefferson and Waukesha counties, the mother colony, so to speak.

A steady stream of immigrants continued to move north to Waupaca and Portage counties. However, as most of these were people from Gudbrandsdal, especially *Gausdøler*, the largest settlement of *Gudbrandsdøler* in America was found here. *[Here Holand is refer-*

ring chiefly to New Hope Township in eastern Portage County, and Harrison and Iola townships in Waupaca County. –Rosholt]

Among the *Gausdøler* the following may be mentioned: Johan Hole, Amund Mortenson, Simon Iverson, Johan Iverson, Hans Kankrud, John Hagemoen, Hans Hagemoen, Johannes Aamodt, John Reiton, Simon Rustad and Ole Lien, who came in the years 1855 and 1856.

Mention also must be made of Anders Nyflødt, who contributed greatly to the expansion of the Gudbrandsdal settlement when he returned to Norway on a tour in 1857 and told people about the delightful Indian Land. As a result, a large body of emigrants from Ringebu returned with him.

Eventually, a significant colony of people from around Heddal settled in the north of Iola Township. Among the first, circa 1853, were Kittil Tubaas, Mathias Lia, Anders Siljord, Halvor Sutenje, and Gregor Holden [*more commonly written as Holla –Rosholt*]. Mention must also be made of Thrond Throndsen Hovde from Sigdal, a leading man among his countrymen.

Gunstein Tollefson Krostu was the only man from Setesdal on the Indian Land those first years, but he gradually attracted quite a few of his people to a colony south of Scandinavia, Wisconsin, in Farmington Township. His son, Tollef Gunsteinson Krostu, was the first Norwegian child born in the county.

[Scandinavia church records indicate that Helene, a daughter of Christian Olson, was born earlier. Entries were made after the fact, so it is possible that Tollef Krostu was first. –Rosholt]

"Krostu was known as the 'fastest rail splitter on the Indian Land.' He came with two empty hands and worked himself up to a prosperous retirement. There are few men who have achieved so much by hand labor. I heard his wife tell my mother one time that when her husband was out working for others, it often happened that she did not see a white man for several weeks. But the Indians saw her with a gun out hunting, accompanied by a dog. She felt so lonely and afraid that she actually cried and wished for her own security that she had her father's big hound dog with her (the famous *Næshunden* in Setesdal). From this we can see that the old mothers had to carry their share of pioneer life."
[Holand does not give any source for the above quotation. –Rosholt]

A couple of characters

Hans Jacob Eliason, the real founder of the settlement, was a terrible joker. He was a suspicious, selfish and conceited person who now and then revealed a deep understanding of nature. Despite his biblical name, he was far from crestfallen and liked much better to lose himself in a glass than in confession. He did not want to think of work. What in the world were his two boys for?

Christian Olson, now a lively old grave-digger approaching 80, is certain that his limbs still ache after all the heavy days of labor he had to perform for Hans Jacob. He recalls the time when he and Hans Jacob one spring had made a difficult journey to Winchester to bring back wheat seed. On the way home they came to the Little Wolf River, then a swollen stream (south of Scandinavia village).

Christian had to carry not only the wheat seed across on his head, but finally Hans Jacob, because, as usual, Hans had been tippling from a pocket flask and was only half conscious. Hans also had a crying jag and was singing, "How wonderful it is here in America" as the two men stumbled across the river.

After 50 years, Olson still regrets he did not let his guilty burden fall in the river and stay there.

Hans Jacob did not consider willow-grubbing suitable work for a man of his talents. *[A small creek runs through the one-time Eliason farm and the creek banks were probably marked by a heavy willow growth at the time Eliason came. –Rosholt]* He found greater pleasure in finding land for the newcomers, and he often did this. In this manner he liked to think of himself as a modern-day Leif Erikson, who had discovered a new continent for his countrymen.

But Hans Jacob's favorite pastime was hunting. And when things were not going smoothly at home, which was almost daily, he would take off rather than listen to Anne Kristine, a religious person who was forever warning him to consider his immortal soul rather than to be chasing around hitting the bottle. Often they fought like a cat and dog, and then Hans Jacob took off for the ridges, grumbling that people never would understand him.

Sometimes Anne Kristine was more agreeable and went along hunting, and then everything was rosy. She walked ahead ringing a cowbell while he sneaked behind, ready to shoot when a deer or bear might stick its nose out of the thicket. Once he shot a monster of a bear weighing over 500 pounds.

When a man so lucky returned home and recounted tales of the hunt over a cup of coffee, all was love and affection. "Yes, you are the woman for me just the same, Anne Kristine," he would exclaim. "Had it not been for you and the cowbell, we would never have got that big fellow. No, sirree."

But a greater nimrod than Hans Jacob was Johan Løberg, another old pioneer from Gjerpen. In those early days when deer and bears were plentiful, Løberg killed no end of them. One fall he said he shot 15 bears. Another time he shot five bears in a single cornfield. The following account is taken from a private letter he once wrote:

"Yes, if Hans Jacob has seen 200 deer in a herd, I believe him because I, too, have seen that many. But I think I have him beat when it comes to bears. One fall, word came to me of some bears that were destroying a cornfield owned by a German. I took a small boy along and let the dogs loose. It was not long before they scared up a bear, which climbed a tree. As it clung there so nicely, I let the boy shoot. And just as lucky, we got another one that same day.

"But then it got dark, so I sent the boy home with the dogs. It was soon pitch dark. When I stood up I couldn't see anything, but when I lay on the ground and gazed upward against the open sky, I got a glimpse of the animals. First I shot a cub and waited for the mother bear to come.

"While I lay there, an enormous beast moved out from the nearby woods, grabbed a corncob between its front paws and began to enjoy a meal of corn. I crawled forward on all fours, got sight of it and banged away. With a terrifying squeal it jumped several feet into the air and then all was still.

"I waited but heard nothing more and began to crawl forward again, which was like groping around in a coal cellar. I kept the gun barrel ahead of me so as not to stumble over bruin. These were long, anxious moments. There could be life in it and…

"Hold it! I had struck something bloody. I lit a match and there lay the bear, a huge male no doubt out on a mating expedition, stone dead. It was the largest bear I ever shot. The next day I got the mother bear and in all five bears from that one cornfield."

Another well-known pioneer, aging but still well preserved, is Jens J. Torgerson, who lives two miles north of Scandinavia *[my great-grandfather on my father's side –Rosholt]* He was born at Nes Iron Works in Holt in 1810 and is now 98 years old. *[As Torgerson died in 1911 at the age of 101, Holand's reference to "now" suggests that this chapter was written in 1907-08. –Rosholt]* He came to Scandinavia in 1853. Torger A. Torgerson, the late president of the Iowa district for the Lutheran Synod, was his son *[one of his sons –Rosholt].*

Other well-known men from this

colony are the sons of Jacob Rosholt *[Julius Rosholt, James Rosholt, Joachim Rosholt and John Rosholt –Rosholt]*; Pastor G. G. Krostu; Professor A. Mikkelson, superintendent of the synod-backed academy at Sioux Falls, South Dakota; and John A. Murat, Portage County judge at Stevens Point, Wisconsin. There are a score of young pastors, lawyers and doctors, etc., who spent their boyhood here.

Rafting down the river

Among the economic opportunities that brought in a few extra dollars for the pioneers on the Indian Land, none were more popular than the river drives. Thousands of boards and planks were bound together into rafts and floated down the Wisconsin River into the Mississippi River and on to St. Louis or up to Galena in Illinois. It took several weeks to make one trip, the man sleeping and eating on board the rafts.

As Galena lies a short distance upstream on a tributary of the Mississippi, the raftsmen had to push their rafts by hand-poles to reach the city. This was once called Fever River, which got its name because it was a place where people contracted malaria. *[The origin of the name "Fever River" is far from certain, but Holand accepts the common explanation. –Rosholt]*

Arriving at Galena, to save travel money, the raftsmen walked home to Stevens Point via Portage, and often as not turned around and went back on another lumber fleet, a rather tedious toboggan slide of life.

The Indian Land area with its 8,500 Scandinavians makes up a prosperous and especially fruitful settlement of honest-to-goodness Norwegians and ideals. Several types of Norwegian architecture may be noted, and buildings are generally sound.

South of Scandinavia Township lies Setesdal, where the bold and powerful *Sætersdøler* enjoy a good living. North and west of Iola and around Nelsonville there are old enclaves of enterprising and self-made sons from around Skien. North of Iola lies Hitterdal, with its moody but imaginative *Telemarkinger*. Farther north and west lies a big settlement of steady and thoughtful *Gudbrandsdøler*.

The terrain is pleasing—for the most part, meadows, shallow valleys and low-lying ridges. The soil in the meadows is rich in clay and loam, and the ridges with brush and boulders of granite. Stones are found nearly everywhere.

In the first years, the pioneers planted wheat, and old Torgerson says the farmers raised 30 to 40 bushels to the acre, but still there was poverty when wheat only sold for 25 to 50 cents a bushel. The last generation has been growing potatoes, which have proved more profitable. This is now one of the biggest potato-growing areas in Wisconsin. People of Norwegian descent harvest not less than a million bushels every year.

About a mile north of Scandinavia village in the center of the most beautiful stretch of land in the entire colony stands the old Scandinavia church, simple in its splendor. But this modest exterior holds many precious memories. It is the oldest church now in use among Norwegian people in America, as it was built in 1856 *[and finished in 1857 –Rosholt]*. Here the United Lutheran Church Synod was organized in 1889.

For a long time, this plain-looking frame structure was the house of worship for the largest Norwegian congregation in America, with nearly 2,000 souls. The membership included people from Iola, Amherst and St. Lawrence townships as well as Scandinavia Township. The congregation was organized in 1853 and got its first resident pastor, O. F. Duus from Norway, in 1854.

Now, new churches have been built in Iola and elsewhere, and the honor of having the largest Norwegian congregation goes to Eau Claire, Wisconsin.

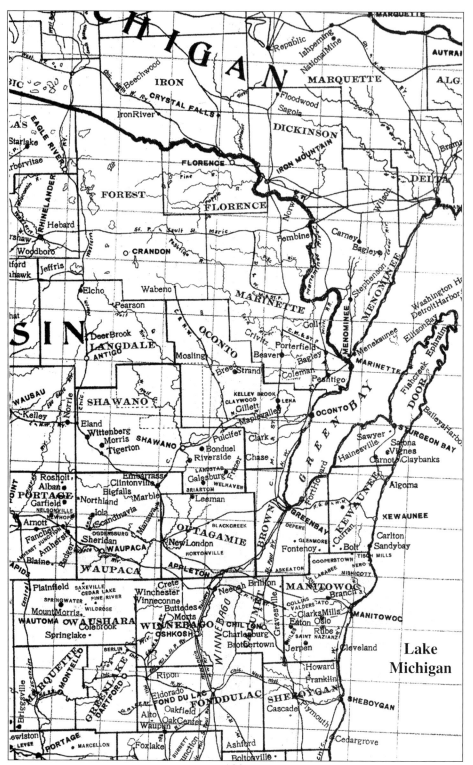

17
Mt. Morris Settlement, Waupaca County, Wisconsin

(Source: De Norske Settlementers Historie, by Hjalmar Rued Holand, translated by Malcolm Rosholt, 1908, pp. 208–214)

Twenty miles south of Scandinavia, Wisconsin, on the Indian Land lies a smaller Norse settlement that was also referred to as the Indian Land. Situated around the municipalities of Wautoma, Wild Rose and Mt. Morris, it features the same charming, game-filled land that made Waupaca County such an attraction to the Indians.

The founder of this settlement was a bold man from Holden in Sør-Telemark by the name of Nils Nilsen Haatvedt, who came here from Muskego in 1850 accompanied by his father-in-law, Ole Anderson Lunde, and a brother-in-law, Per Gunderson Feen, both from Holden. These three men were among the very first to journey northwest through Wisconsin, when it was still filled with Indians.

They set out with no particular goal in mind, but were anxious to explore the terrain. When they finally reached what later became Mt. Morris, they found a beautiful wilderness with tree-lined lakes, plunging rivers filled with trout and flower-covered meadows inhabited by big-eyed deer that stared at them more in wonder than in fright.

Although the quality of land was quite sandy, the explorers decided to make this their home, and they made entries on land covering the slope directly southwest of the present church *[now demolished, circa 1915 –Rosholt]*.

The following year, their little colony was increased by the arrival of Halvor Arveson and Gullik Arveson (William Arveson), who also were from Holden in Norway. In 1852 came Jacob Alfson of Skien, and Anders A. Potterud and Stener Olson of Sandsvær.

In 1853, quite a few more newcomers arrived. The reason for their coming can be attributed mostly to Marie Feen (now Mrs. Arveson), daughter of Per G. Feen. She had worked as a hired girl that summer in a small hotel at the ferry crossing where Berlin, Wisconsin, was later built. From this crossing on the Fox River, roads led north in several directions.

Among the travelers who happened to stop here was a wealthy Norwegian, Torger Kjøstulson Sveningen, from Holt parish in Nærheden, Tvedestrand. Together with his four sons, Kjøstul Torgerson, Ellev Torgerson, Lars Torgerson and Nils Torgerson (Nils Thompson), he intended to settle in Waupaca County, where he had friends who had recently settled there.

But Marie Feen talked so eloquently of the superior advantages to be found around Mt. Morris that Torger Sveningen changed his itinerary and went there instead. Here the old man bought land for all his sons on the shores of a beautiful lake, later called Norwegian Lake after him. As he was an influential man with many friends, it was not long before people from Holt parish and other places in Norway populated Mt. Morris. Among these were: Reier Olson and sons Ole Reierson, Gustav Reierson, and Lars Reierson; Lars Anderson Songe; and Ellev Kjøstulson, who took the name of Ellev Charleson, all from Holt. Other arrivals included Jens Hundere (James Jarvis), Johannes J. Thorstad, Ole P. Selsing, Erik Johanneson and Johannes Erikson, all from Sogndal in Sogn, and Christen Pederson, Ole Bendixen, Bendik Bendixen, Anders Stedje, Peter E. Lee and Andrew Larson from Hafslo.

So many people arrived that a congregation was organized in 1854 and served by Pastor O. F. Duus from Scandinavia, Wisconsin, to which the Mt. Morris congregation was, for quite a long time, considered an annex. The congregation's name, Holden, was proposed by Nils Nilsen, who took the others somewhat by surprise. Only the first three families to arrive here were from Holden, and the others did not know that this name was pronounced "Holla" with a thick 'l.'

On the other hand, there were many from Holt and from Sogn in the congregation. And when "Holden" was used according to the official Dano-Norwegian pronunciation, it reminded the people of Holt of their old home, and they accepted the name without realizing that the minority were actually honoring their own birthplace.

After the first wave of settlement of the early 1850s, only a few settlers came—until after the Civil War. One had to go all the way to Milwaukee to grind grain or sell anything, and the remoteness of the place was a factor that discouraged rapid growth. Among the few who came in the mid-1850s may be mentioned Erik Henningsen, Peter Jenson and Iver J. Klurdal (father of Pastor G. J. Klurdal), all from Trondheim.

In 1858 Amund Holt and sons, Anders Amundsen Holt, Ole Amundsen Holt, Knut Amundsen Holt and Lars Amundsen Holt arrived. They were all from Holt parish, and the family is now widespread as well as esteemed.

The Mt. Morris settlement, until a few years ago, was far removed from a railway, and keen memories recall the harsh 20-to-30-mile trip over sandy roads and steep hills to Berlin or to Waupaca with potatoes, which for a long time was the main cash crop. But with stubborn patience, people got ahead and were already on good footing when the railway came and lightened their burden.

The railroad runs directly through the settlement, which is now prosperous and well developed economically. With its natural beauty and hospitable people, it is a delightful place in which to live. Since it has always been spared any church strife, there is a harmony and coziness here seldom noted elsewhere.

There is only one thing for which one can fault the Norwegians here—namely, their lack of independence when it comes to family surnames. Practically all have added something to their names, and as many as possible have twisted their name to Thompson, which is clearly un-Norwegian. Thorson, Torgerson, Thorstenson, Tollefson—nearly all names beginning with 't' have been changed to Thompson, a name that is now used by a good half of the community.

Those who cannot find an opportunity to adopt this ideal name have, as a matter of course, made or permitted other changes. A man from Sogn who had the strong name of Jens Hundere when he went to work in the logging camps, quietly renamed himself James Jarvis; Ellev Kjøstulson became Ed Charleson; Gullik became William; Lars became Louis; Anfin, Andrew; Knut, Newton, etc. It would honor Mt. Morris if the people here would give up this ridiculous and demeaning custom of patching up their names for the benefit of Yankee ears and insist on the immutable dignity of their baptismal names.

Nils Nilsen was one of the few who was not led into any embellishments of his name. It was no doubt pointed out to him that it would be presumptuous to change his name because the high-faluting American tongue should be able to say Nils Nilsen, who obviously should be Nels Nelson. But Nilsen stood his ground and refused to change the spelling.

The Grange movement

Nilsen was, in most respects, considered one of the leading men in the settlement. He was a willing and helpful person. As he was also an enterprising man, he is remembered today with esteem by the entire settlement.

Now and then his lively interests led him to take a position that for a long time was unpopular. One of these was his interest in the Grange movement, which, in the 1870s, became powerful in the country. This was a secret society of farmers whose aim was to boost prices on all farm products while holding down the price of manufactured goods. Wheat and potatoes should sell at $1 per bushel, while the salary of the hired man should be fixed at $8 per month. Double income and reduce expenses to the bone—that was the political philosophy that recommended itself to these bucolic thinkers!

People sat far into the night while Nils Nilsen developed his theories—ideas that looked to good times ahead, when the world would bend its knee to the farmer's amiable face. The result was that both Yankee-Americans and Norwegians throughout the Mt. Morris district enrolled as Grange members and joined ranks to realize this great plan. But here and there fissures began to develop in this solid edifice. And now the memory of it all is a bitter one.

[Earlier in this chapter, Holand says the Holden congregation was free of church strife, which usually meant the struggle over the doctrine of predestination. But there was a split in 1873 when one faction left Holden over the question of its membership in the Grange and organized a rival church called Bethany. This group joined the United Lutheran Synod in 1890. –Rosholt]

Reluctant bridegroom

In this settlement, there is an amusing story about matrimonial troubles. Pastor Mikkelson, in his *Notes on a Pastor's Experiences*, describes a situation he faced, with the following story *[written in Norwegian by Pastor Amund Mikkelson, who served Scandinavia and Holden churches in the 1860s –Rosholt]*:

It was early one Sunday morning, raining heavily, when the lady of the house where Mikkelson was staying announced that there was a man outside who insisted on seeing the pastor. Poor man, she said, he looks so awful there must be something wrong with him.

The pastor got his clothes on in a hurry and asked the stranger in. The man was a sad-looking sight, soaking wet, hair hanging over his eyes and forehead, water running down a face filled with bewilderment.

The pastor looked at him with pity and asked, "What's wrong, Jeppe?"

But Jeppe only sniffled while the tears ran down his face, joined by rain dripping from a forelock.

Deeply impressed, Mikkelson asked, "Has something bad happened at home?"

"I . . . I don't know what to say," Jeppe replied.

"Is someone in the family dead?"

"No, not that. But I wish I were dead," he said, trying to wipe away a fresh stream of tears with his coat sleeves and leaving a streak of mud across his face.

"Tell me, how I can help you, Jeppe?"

"I want the pastor to marry me."

"What!" the pastor exclaimed, almost speechless. "What are you saying?"

"I want the pastor to marry me."

"This is a strange way of asking to be married. I thought something awful had happened to you, and now I learn to my amazement that you want to enter the bonds of holy matrimony. But why cry about it? Wouldn't it be better to raise your voice in joy?"

"But I don't feel that way. No sir."

"Why not?"

"Ah . . . I'm forced to."

"Forced to? Why are you forced to marry?"

"I'm in trouble with a widow."

"Can it be that you have chosen a life partner?"

"No, not that! She's chosen me."

"Don't you love her, then?"

"No, as God is my witness, I don't."

"Have you told the widow you don't?"

"You better believe it!"

"What does she say to that?"

"Well, you ought to know how crazy women are."

"Won't the widow leave you alone under any circumstance?"

"Of course, but that would cost too much."

"How much?"

"Three hundred bucks."

"And you haven't got that much?"

"Of course. I've got that and more, but I've worked so hard for the money that I do not feel like throwing it away."

"But wouldn't this be to your advantage?"

"I'm not sure. It remains to be seen."

But married he was to the widow, and if his sorrow was heavy then, his chagrin only increased when he found out there was no way to escape her. On closer investigation, he learned that her wedding riches consisted only of some rags and wraps that she, with womanly cunning, had decked herself out with to bring him into Hymen's fetters.

Can anyone blame Jeppe if he sought comfort in the bottle? People say he drinks, but no one will tell you why.

En Sæter i Norangsdalen

18
Oldest Valdres Colony in America, Manitowoc County, Wisconsin
(Source: De Norske Settlementers Historie, by Hjalmar Rued Holand, translated by Malcolm Rosholt, 1908, pp. 215–228)

Around 30,000 people from Valdres—a region in southwest Oppland fylke—now (1908) live in America. By comparison, in Norway there are only about 17,000 *Valdriser*.

Therefore, the Valdres-Americans are an important community that has taken a leading role both in the spiritual and material development of Norwegians in the United States.

The Valdres saga begins in 1843 when the first of these people emigrated—namely, Guul Guttormson from Hedalen in Sør-Aurdal, who left the well-known estate *Ildjernstadhaugen* to settle in Rock County, Wisconsin, in the neighborhood of Brodhead, where many of his descendants still live.

Up to 1846, however, few people immigrated to the U.S. In that year, Stephen Olson *Kubakke* Helle arrived, a man who did more to speed up emigration from Valdres than any other. Born in Øystre-Slidre in 1818, he lived for a time in Vang and left from there for Port Washington, Wisconsin, at age 28. As he was an expert carpenter, he followed his trade in the new village, which was then attracting many newcomers.

Further on in the summer of 1846, he struck out haphazardly into the forest to the north to find good farmland. He eventually reached a spot in Manitowoc County, home today of a large Norwegian settlement. Despite the surrounding forest filled with Indians and wolves, he purchased several tracts of land and decided to make this his future home.

Returning to Port Washington, Stephen Olson Helle worked a couple of years, and in 1848 went to Norway on a visit. He was the first *Valdris* to brave the dangers of the oceans twice and therefore could speak from experience about the wonders of the New World.

His visit to Norway was a turning point in Valdres history. Under his leadership, some 12 to 15 families were

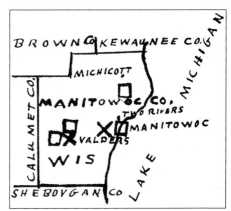

Manitowoc menighet.

Manitowoc, Manitowoc Co., Wis.
Utenom, 1850–53; Norske synode, 1853–97.
Organisert 1850 (en del av Gjerpen). Splittet 1897, paa grund av naadevalgstriden (First Norw. Ev. Luth. Church—Ns; St. Pauli ev. luth. mght.—Fk). 190 sjæle i 1868, 325 i 1885. Prester: H. A. Stub, 1849-52; J. A. Ottesen, 1852–60; L. M. Bjørn, 1861–79; A. O. Alfsen, 1873–80; C. F. Magelssen, 1880–93; J. O. Hougen, 1894–98. Embedsmand i 1897: b. Aug. Eriksmoen. Kirke, 1897, $7,000. (3503—373)

induced to leave, boarding a ship called the Drafna. *[A question mark follows the name Drafna in the original text. Perhaps Holand was uncertain about the name or its spelling. Theodore Blegen in his Norwegian Migration to America—the American Transition, Northfield, Minnesota, 1940, p. 14, mentions the ship. –Rosholt]*

Included in this first group (besides Helle himself) were:
• Thomas Olson Helle (Stephen Olson Helle's brother), Hurum, Vang
• Jul Olson Guldhaug, Vestre-Slidre (a father to the Juul family of pastors)
• Knut Syverson Aaberg, Nord-Aurdal
• Anders Olson Aabol, Skrautvaal
• Ole Olson Aabol, Skrautvaal
• Knut Arneson, Ulnes
• Ole Olson Oppen, Ulnes

Oppen, in particular, was an enterprising man and born leader. All settled in Manitowoc County.

Two others in the same group, who temporarily settled elsewhere before coming to Manitowoc, included:
• Haakon Knudsen Roble, Vestre-Slidre
• Haldor Anderson Veblen

Others in the group who remained in Port Washington and later moved to the Midwest included:
• Ole Tostenson Bunde, Hurum, Vang
• Ingrid Tostensdatter, Hurum, Vang
• Knut Ødegaard (Knut Kvedne), Skrautvaal
• Christopher Austreim, Vang
• Guldbrand Høyme, Vestre-Slidre
• Knut Høyme, Vestre-Slidre
• Ola i Rundtøp

[Holand does not identify Ola i Rundtøp, which is apparently a nickname. –Rosholt]

On a second ship of newcomers from Valdres, Gudmund Gudmundsen Brekken from Vang was the only one to settle in Manitowoc County. Three others on this ship were:
• Aslak Lie, Aurdal
• Knud from Skogen, Aurdal
• Kristian from Skogen, Aurdal

With the arrival of these people, the big movement of emigration from Valdres began.

The following four men left in 1847:
• Nils H. Fjeld, Sør-Aurdal
• Knud Olson Oppen, Ulnes
• Knut Thorson Døvre (a brother to the banker Harold Thorson)
• Thomas Anderson Veblen, Hurum (father to Professor Thorstein Veblen)

In 1851 Stephen Olson Helle (henceforth going by the name of Stephen Olson) made another trip to his birthplace in Valdres, and after that, still more people began to leave for the States.

Lake Erie collision

Considering the poor means of transportation 50 years ago, it is remarkable that there were not more accidents. But the last party of Valdres people who emigrated in 1852 under arrangements made by Stephen Olson became the fatal exception. Together with several hundred other European emigrants, their ship collided with another in the middle of the night on Lake Erie *[see Chapter 4, New York to the West –Rosholt]*.

Stephen Olson, who was home at the time, went to find his bride, who had been rescued from the water in the night. But his aged mother was among those who were trampled to death in the wreck of the *Atlantic*. In addition, there were about 70 Valdres people among the missing. Nearly all were destined for Manitowoc County.

According to Stephen Olson, the following lost their lives:
• Mrs. Marit O. Helle, Vang (Stephen Olson's mother)
• Ole Pederson Helle, Vang
• Anders Østenson Bøen, Vang
• Finkel Olsen Røvang, wife and two children, Slidre
• Barbo Olson Røvang, Slidre
• Ole Oleson Moen, Slidre
• Johannes Iverson Rudi, wife and four children, Slidre
• Anne Tostenson Ulve, Slidre
• Nils Helgeson Mørstad, wife and

three children, Slidre
- Knud Helgeson Jøten, Slidre
- Mrs. Anne Nilsen Oxhovd and child, Slidre
- Ole Nilsen (Anne Nilsen's brother), Slidre
- Knud Larson Feeres Eien, Slidre
- Ole Olson Brøthovd, wife and six children, Slidre
- Mrs. Sigrid Nilsen Majestad and two children, Slidre
- Knud Olson Fugelhaug, wife and three children, Aurdal
- Bjørn Olsen Bøen, wife and child, Aurdal
- Aslag Dølven, wife and two children, Aurdal
- Halsten Johnson Brakkehaugen, Aurdal
- Syver Bøle, wife and child (a girl), Aurdal
- Mrs. Anne Sæterbraaten and five children, Aurdal
- Ole Olson, wife and three children, Toten

There were 68 lost and 66 saved in Stephen Olson's party.

As a result of Stephen Olson's great efforts to better the standard of living among his people in America, Norwegians quickly populated Manitowoc County. On 4 October 1850, just two years after the first settlers arrived, Pastor H. A. Stub organized a congregation. A letter of call, signed by 113 people, was sent to Pastor J. A. Otteson in Norway.

On 16 June 1851, several more members joined the congregation. The names of these people (which follows) also reveal who had settled in the county by 1850:
- Michael Mathison
- Gunder Madsen
- Hans Madsen
- Peter Madsen
- Nils Gullikson
- Juul Olson Hoyme
- Johannes Knudsen
- Finkel Finkelson
- Ole Evenson
- Ole Larson Ballestad
- Chr. Larson Ballestad
- Knud O. Oppen
- Ole Aubol
- Ole Thoreson Dovre
- Johannes Svendson
- Stephen Olson
- Thos. O. Helle
- Guldbrand H. Sørum
- K. Lunde
- Chr. Anderson
- Nils Johnson Riis
- James Halvorson
- Mikæl Mikælson
- Lars Mathieson
- Nils Madsen
- Ole Madsen
- Jacob Madsen
- Ole Syverson
- Ole Thompson
- Boye Amundsen
- Anders Isaksen
- Even Jerruldsen
- Anders O. Øien
- Helge Guldbrandsen
- John Lasseson
- Anders Aubol
- Ole J. Rebne
- Knud Syverson
- Ole Jørgenson Flaten
- Hans G. Sørum
- Anders Amundsen
- Andreas Halvorsen
- Anders C. Qual
- Johan Christiansen
- Jacob Halversen
- Amund Salveson
- Lars Larsen Gulseth
- Lars Larsen Sannes
- Lars Larsen Ballestad
- Osuld Torrison
- Nils Larsen
- Anders T. Knudtsen
- Helge N. Mørstad
- Iver O. Berge
- Iver G. Berge
- Guldbrand O. Berge
- Ole O. Berge
- Gullik Iverson
- Ulrik J. Hovrud
- Nils A. Aas
- Peter J. Flaten

- Carl Solberg
- Ole Sigurdson
- Ole Anderson
- Michael Olson
- Østen Østenson
- Ole Rundberg
- H. M. Hansen
- Jens O. Boldstad – *[See Gothic text, p. 111]*
- Jens Gunderson
- Gunder Evensen
- Anders Johannesen
- Lars Knudsen
- Ole Halvorson
- Gudmund Brækken
- Isak Isaksen Sætre
- K. K. Snortum
- Johan Eriksen
- G. Christensen
- Isak Larsen
- Nils Salveson Kjær
- Christen Nilsen
- Rasmus Nilsen
- Anders Grini
- Gabriel Abrahamson
- Lars Isaksen
- Johan Christiansen
- Rasmus H. Leikaas
- Ole Andreasen
- Lars Salvesen
- Knut Arneson
- Gulbrand G. Haslebrek
- Isak Hansen Findall
- Haldor Olsen Viste
- Søren L. Ballestad
- Ole O. Oppen
- Torjus Abrahamsen
- Ole Christenson
- Jerruld Hansen
- Ole Torjussen
- Isak A. Pederson
- N. J. Nilsen
- Lars Simundsen Høn
- O. K. Gigstad
- Tosten K. Rogne
- Lasse Olsen
- Rasmus Bækaasen
- Knud Olson
- Gulbr. Gulbrandsen
- Gulbr. Vaarum
- Hans Hansen
- Hans Kjøstulsen
- Mads Olsen
- Elias Halvorson
- Ole Svendsen
- Ellert A. Langøen
- Chas. Gustaveson
- Oliver Thompson
- Gudmund O. Quale
- Michael Bekkelien
- Torjus Kjøstulsen
- Peder Jørgensen
- Knud K. Berge
- Lars Larsen *[possibly a duplicate – Rosholt]*

Today (1908), the settlement reaches all the way to the city of Manitowoc with its ungodly saloons and 20 miles west to St. Nazianz, with its holy monks and cloisters for nuns.

The small town of Valders on the Wisconsin Central Railroad is the center of the colony, lying about halfway between the above-named places, both geographically and morally. It is the oldest Valdres settlement, the largest and strongest. It has been the mother colony to numerous enclaves of Valdres people across the Midwest. Despite its antiquity, business of the day is carried on in real Valdres-style.

Stephen Olson was a friendly man, wise and helpful in word and deed, a zealous member of the church, a leader and a businessman in every respect. One hears in all Valdres communities about Stephen *Kubakke*. He was a master builder, and many buildings between Valders village and Manitowoc—among them, the county courthouse—stand as a witness to his creative energy. On one occasion he nearly froze to death, an incident long since forgotten. At Manitowoc, he built an iron foundry, which burned. He rebuilt a big mill on the same site, which was washed out in spring floods. He rebuilt another mill that still stands.

Despite his ups and downs, nothing ever fazed him. An American said of him: "That Stephen Olson beats everybody I ever saw; he was frozen out, burned out and drowned out, and yet he is on his feet."

Den ældste Valdriskoloni i Amerika.

[Sample page from De Norske Settlementers Historie p. 221 see p. 110 for English translation]

Jens O. Boldstad,
Jens Gunderson,
Gunder Evensen,
Anders Johannesen,
Lars Knudsen,
Ole Halvorson,
Gudmund Brækken,
Isak Isaksen Sætre,
K. K. Snortum,
Johan Eriksen,
G. Christensen,
Isak Larsen,
Nils Salveson Kjær,
Christen Nilsen,
Rasmus Nilsen,
Anders Grini,
Gabriel Abrahamson,
Lars Isaksen,
Johan Christiansen,
Rasmus H. Leikaas,
Ole Andreasen,
Lars Salvesen,
Knut Arneson,
Gulbrand G. Haslebrek,
Isak Hansen Findall,
Haldor Olsen Viste,
Søren L. Vallestad,
Ole O. Oppen,
Torjus Abrahamsen,
Ole Christenson,
Jerruld Hansen,
Ole Torjussen,
Isak A. Pederson,
N. J. Nilsen,
Lars Simundsen Høn,
O. K. Gigstad,
Tosten K. Rogne,
Lasse Olsen,
Rasmus Bækaasen,
Knud Olson,
Gulbr. Gulbrandsen,
Gulbr. Vaarum,
Hans Hansen,
Hans Kjøstulsen,
Mads Olsen,
Elias Halvorson,
Ole Svendsen,
Ellert A. Langøen,
Chas. Gustaveson,
Oliver Thompson,
Gudmund O. Quale,
Michael Bekkelien,
Torjus Kjøstulsen,
Peder Jørgensen,
Knud K. Berge,
Lars Larsen.

Nu strækker Settlementet sig fra Manitowoc med sine ugudelige Salooner, tyve Mil bestover til St. Nazianz, med sine hellige Munke- og Nonneklostre. Den lille By Valders paa Wisconsin Central Banen er Midtpunktet for Kolonien, og ligger omtrent Midtveis mellem de ovennævnte Yderpunkter, baade i geo-

Clearing the land

In the eastern part of the settlement there are quite a few people from Gjerpen. Many of these were also among the first settlers in Manitowoc County. Søren Larson Ballestad and Gunder Madsen were in the first party to leave from Gjerpen in 1843, working in the sawmills of Michigan for some years. They moved to this colony in Manitowoc County in 1849.

Although the settlement had a promising beginning, it did not become large. There are now about 3,000 Norwegians here, of which half reside in the city of Manitowoc. The forest in this area was heavy and difficult to clear. It demanded a courage and perseverance that few can muster.

When the first settlers came to the county, there were no pleasant homes, no open fields, no roads. On arriving, the newcomer bought an axe and took off through the wilderness for his 40 of land, which looked exactly like every other 40 in the woods. Here, he was told, was his future piece of ground, paid for at $1.25 per acre.

Here was clearing work to be done in earnest. The forest heaved and threatened with the great trees that stood back to back by the thousands, their bristling branches shutting out the sun, while at their feet lay the windfalls, overgrown with brush and bracken.

The first impression of it all was overwhelming. It seemed presumptuous to attack this majestic jungle. The north wind sighed disconsolately through the trees. It seemed to the new settler that the forest spirit was talking to him, saying, "Since creation, my roots have held this ground, and my crown will continue to cast its shadow over this land until the last flash of lightning is seen. The storms of a thousand years have whirled around my head, ancient thunders have boomed over my crown, and the earth has trembled under my feet, but I am still young! The heavy snows of winter have proudly shaken from my branches, and the summer rains I have absorbed into my roots for food. From the interstices of the earth have I fastened my feet, and my crown to the rims of the sky. Your red brothers have gathered healing herbs in my humid soil, the loping deer chew at my lower branches in unconcerned freedom, and the bear suckle their young undisturbed in my dark shadows. In fact, all Nature's children bow to my silent might. And think you, a midget with an axe in your hand, that you can do what time's teeth failed to accomplish?"

It was a challenge that not all had the strength to accept, and many newcomers left, despondent, seeking a place where they could build a home with less hardship. But the majority stayed on and, with real Valdres persistence, swung their axes. One by one the mighty trees began to tremble and plunge to the ground with a resounding crash. Then they were trimmed and sawed into logs and decked, while fires from the brush piles rose in the still of night like great victory dances in the sky.

The work went slowly, this clearing of a piece of ground from nature's chaos. The new farmer was reminded of the Hydra-headed trolls, because for each birch or beech or aspen cut down, there were many seedlings, which again have to be put down. But persistence was their motto, and the war continued year after year.

In winter the pioneer struggled with maple trees two feet on the stump; in summer, he laid siege to the stubborn stumps. Stubborn as rocks, they clung to the earth despite axes, dynamite and stump-pulling machines, and the new settler had to give up for this year in his battle with one or another of the older basswoods or pine stumps.

Meanwhile, the small clearings, ringed with brush and log piles, grew wider until they finally merged with a neighbor's clearing, and the forest receded farther and farther back.

Now, the fields stretch miles wide, divided here and there by a measured farm and handsome house, the wind blowing across the green meadows containing not a single stump.

Now, cars move across the smooth roads. But the old man sitting on the porch thinks of a time 50 years ago. Back then, the sleek road was a blazed trail through the wilderness, and he and his wife struggled to haul their cooking stove through the brush, around the stumps and windfalls, to their newly raised log house five miles from the nearest highway.

Norwegian author Bjørnstjerne Bjørnson has devoted much of his writings to his Aulestad farm in Norway. He has felled trees, grubbed stumps and cleaned the ground of stone and brush. Nothing gives him more satisfaction as this work of clearing the land.

His books, he says, have only a doubtful value, and the best of them will have served their purpose and be forgotten. But the ground he has made productive will continue for all time to contribute to the nation's breadbasket. In this manner, among these green acres, Bjørnson concludes, he will continue to be of benefit to future generations.

How much greater reason the Norwegian-American pioneer has to be satisfied with his life! Without help or praise, he has created a new culture from Nature's dour wilderness. The hunger in his children's eyes was his incentive, and his own strong arms his trust. Now there are 40,000 acres with rich humus soil in Manitowoc County as a witness to the work of our Valdres forefathers.

Trees provide cordwood, maple syrup

Second only to the task of clearing the land was the job of cutting stove wood. Many a cold trip was made 10 to 15 miles to Manitowoc, hauling a big load of wood for sale in the city. But the Valdres man is tough and not given to heroics. When he is ready to return home, he stops at a local store to get a little coffee and tobacco, and, of course, there is always a barrel of whiskey and tin cup chained to the barrel where he can fortify himself a little. A small pocket flask for the trip home is also on the house. If he had a jug along, it might cost 16 cents a gallon.

This woodcutting requires further explanation. Thousands of countrymen in northern Wisconsin are still engaged in this industry every winter. The author (Holand) met a man who alone had cut 15,000 cords of firewood. For 26 years he remained on a small island in Lake Michigan and chopped cordwood. Unbelievable as it may sound, the crosscut saw did not come into general use until after the Civil War.

Summer and winter, war and peace followed one another, but this man remained on his little piece of ground and chopped two cords of wood a day. Small boys were to grow up and explore new lands, which now feed millions. But for the woodchopper on the island, the chips continued to fly in the same small grove of trees.

The forest was not meant only for hauling wood. Toward spring, when the sun warmed up and the snow began to melt and there were hard frosts at night, then the settler was happy that he lived on a place where the proud sugar maple raised its crown. On a nice day, a hole was augered into the tree and a small wooden spout driven into the hole. Pails, cups, bottles and kettles of all sorts were placed underneath to catch the sap.

Then the neighbors were invited over to a "sugaring-off party." The man carried the sap and wood for the cooking; the womenfolk stood around, joking and laughing, while attending to the cooking. On a log nearby sat the old-timers with their pipes, exchanging stories, with now and then some good advice to the careless girls. When the sap was cooked down, the wooden tubs were filled with snow and the syrup poured in to cool for a taffy-like candy.

One or another artist might use the taffy to draw his sweetheart's name in the snow with great flourishes, or make a grotesque sketch of a local hero. After a cup of coffee or a shot of whiskey, the violin was brought out and everyone joins in a dance.

But spring was soon here, and there was clearing work to be done in earnest. Land that had been cleared of trees in winter was usually sowed to oats for several years until the stumps were somewhat rotten. There was always enough new land to plow.

For this as well as for other farm purposes in the early days, the pioneers used oxen, which were best adapted for this rough work. It was a surprise to the newcomers when they first arrived to learn that oxen were still used and that people in America could get a stupid beast of nature to actually work for them. It was something to write home about.

But the oxen became his best friends. Steady, strong and tough, there were few horse teams that could beat them. There was little that could break in the single chain that pulled either a plow or a log. No need for costly harnesses, no shoeing required, and no runaways. Furthermore, they were cheap to feed: In the morning and the evening, the farmer threw a little corn to them, and the oxen grazed at large in the woods at night. If one broke a leg and had to be destroyed, then a man swallowed his sorrow with a good steak.

It was quite difficult to break the oxen, and the Yankee-Americans, who were best at it, were usually called in to do the job. The Germans could not understand this. The man doing the breaking approached the ox with sweet words and first got the yoke around its neck. Then the animal was let out in the pasture to fight and struggle with this new burden around its neck.

After the ox cooled off a bit, the trainer approached it and made the ox pull something a short distance, but not far, because in the beginning the ox was still fighting this new burden. Everything had to be done with kindness; otherwise, it could take several years before an ox could be relied upon.

A progressive community

The Valdres colony has one of the prettiest landscapes in the Midwest. Here there is just the right mixture of rich ground and pleasant meadows, with here and there a grove of shade trees or winding river with iron bridges, which a city man likes to believe is the way it should be in the country. From the wide-sweeping hills, a person can see the big, well-built farms. It is unlikely that there is any place in the United States where one can find a Norwegian settlement marked by more substantial, not to mention modern, buildings. Good roads there are, too. Everything points to prosperity and abundance.

Here, too, many of our well-known countrymen were born. Of some 40 pastors of Valdres descent who are spreading the gospel in America, a sixth of them originate in this settlement. Professors Anders Veblen and Thorstein Veblen also came from here. In addition, there are a number of younger doctors, lawyers and prominent businessmen whose fathers came as pioneers to this land.

The rural community has done better in this respect than the Valdres people in the city of Manitowoc, although there is among the latter the gifted Torrison family. The father, Osuld Torrison, originally from Grimstad in Norway, was among the first to settle in the city when he arrived in 1849. He has a noble personality and has built up one of the largest business houses in Wisconsin.

These pioneers won an honorable name not only as physical workers on the land and spiritual trailblazers. To their crown of glory must be added the fact that when the nation was struggling for its existence in a Civil War, not less than 73 Norsemen volunteered for service.

Not all came back. Today, 36 old soldiers rest at the west church cemetery.

19

Ephraim, Door County, northeastern, Wisconsin

(Source: De Norske Settlementers Historie, by Hjalmar Rued Holand, translated by Malcolm Rosholt, 1908, pp. 229–249)

If a person will study a map of Wisconsin, he will note in the east a long tongue of land running northeasterly into Lake Michigan. This peninsula, which is nearly 100 miles long and averages 10 miles wide, is divided from the mainland by a big *fjord* called Green Bay. North of the tip of the peninsula lies Washington Island, which covers an area roughly the size of a township. This, together with the peninsula and countless small islands along the coast, makes up Door County.

The name for the county comes to us from the time when the Pottowatomi Indians congregated around here on their hunting forays and internecine wars. Between Washington Island and the peninsula runs a dangerous strait where all winds roar.

The story is told that there was once an Indian band of several hundred warriors who set out from the peninsula in their canoes to engage an enemy force on the island. They were met in the middle of the strait by an army from the island, and a terrible sea battle was fought in a storm, during which hundreds of men lost their lives.

After that, the strait came to be called "Death's Door," from which Door County took its name.

Many of the bodies from the battle washed up on the island, and when the first pioneers arrived here, they found bleached bones along the shorelines. Ever since, the Indians have avoided this part of the county.

As far as is known, this was the first place in Wisconsin or any other northern state to be visited by a white man. As far back as 1634, Jean Nicollet sailed along Door County's picturesque coastline, stopping here and there to admire its magnificent wilderness, finally arriving at the place where the city of Green Bay now lies.

At the time, this was a big Indian village. As Nicollet approached the village, he put on a colorful cape of damask material and, carrying a pistol

in each hand, marched in among the expectant warriors. Women and children fled, crying that *Manitou* had arrived, bringing with him lightning and thunder. But the chief received him with great hospitality, and 120 beavers were consumed at a single feast.

After Nicollet came many famous Frenchmen. Green Bay, the oldest city in the Midwest, was soon platted. There are about 1,200 Norwegians here now (1908).

In northern Door County, with which this chapter is concerned, there are about 2,000 Norwegians. The honor for the founding of this colony belongs chiefly to one of the most remarkable men to ever come to America, and probably the only member of the Norwegian aristocracy to do so.

In 1846 a member of the Moravian church named Olson from Farsund in Norway landed in Milwaukee. He was a well-known singer and energetic lay preacher. As there was little opportunity to hear one's own religion preached in the mother tongue at Milwaukee, there were many Norwegians who were attracted to Olson and the Moravian church.

In 1849, Olson wrote to the Moravian mission in Norway to send an ordained pastor. Andreas M. Iverson, a young student, answered this call. Born in Kristiansand in 1823, he came to Milwaukee in the spring of 1849 and was received with great joy. There was still no Norwegian congregation organized in Milwaukee, although Iverson had up to 400 people listening to his worship services, which indicates there already were many Norwegians in the city. The following year (1850), Iverson was ordained at Bethlehem, Pennsylvania, the main center of the Moravian church in America.

These were hard times in Milwaukee —little work and small wages. Furthermore, there were many temptations in the city that the Moravian elders sought to avoid for their children.

The people decided, therefore, to form a congregation and move elsewhere, to a place where they could make a living with more assurance of security, engaging in farming and at the same time escaping the temptations of the big city.

Nils Otto Tank: A remarkable man

Just about the same time there arrived in Milwaukee one of the most remarkable Norwegians ever to immigrate to America— Nils Otto Tank, a descendant of an old aristocratic family near Fredrikshald (Halden).

[The Tank family believes that it was raised to the nobility by King Frederik III of Denmark (1609-1670), but historians are not certain of this. –Rosholt]

Nils Otto Tank, born in 1800, was the only son of Carsten Tank, who in his time was one of the most powerful politicians in Norway and prime minister to King Christian Frederik.

When the latter was deposed, this ambitious politician began to make far-reaching plans. King Karl was old and without heirs, and someone would soon have to choose the new king. Why not the prime minister's promising young son? He came from royal stock, had a kingly aspect, possessed great gifts and knowledge, and had a father who stood at the helm of government.

In these unsettled times of intrigue and cabals, when kings were rapidly being deposed and parts of nations traded off like horses, the idea was not entirely far-fetched. The odds would be raised in his favor if a marriage pact could be arranged between one or another of the princesses of some royal line.

With this in mind, his father sent Nils Otto abroad to travel and study in Europe's best social circles. Everything went well. Nils Otto, after considerable time spent abroad studying at the universities and mixing with cultural leaders, had acquired the highest degree of polish and worldly refinement and was ready to return home to fulfill his role in the court intrigues.

Then it happened: High up in the mountains of Germany in a small Moravian village, he gazed into a pair of deep, soul-filled eyes belonging to a young maid of the pietistic brotherhood that dominated the population of this district. Forgotten were his father's mundane reminders, kingly dreams, pomp and circumstance, not to mention secular power and honor. It was love at first sight, and when she said "yes," he returned home with his bride.

But his father, the honorable old statesman, had long forgotten anything about romance and love. Now he saw his highest hopes and a dream of a lifetime at an end. With scorn and deprecation, he disowned his son. *[A footnote by Holand: "The above account was related to the author by old people who were once close to Tank and his wife."]*

Nils Otto, however, was more deeply affected by his wife than his father realized. Taking his bride away, he sailed for South America as a missionary. Instead of the dance salons where smiles and witticisms were bandied back and forth, we find him now among heathens, uncomplaining and modestly trying to advance the gospel of salvation.

When he returned to Norway in 1850 after several years in Surinam and the Netherlands East Indies, where he was remarried after the death of his first wife, he learned of the new congregation that was about to be organized among the Norwegians in America. He decided to help them. On his arrival in Milwaukee, he learned that the congregation was planning to leave the city. He then purchased 960 acres of unsurveyed forestland, which today takes in the southwest side of the city of Green Bay. He invited the entire congregation to move here, which it did in August of 1850.

He further promised that everyone would get land for farming for little or no money, as it was his aim to plat a village according to the precepts of the Moravian church. Twenty-six lots consisting of a third of an acre in size were hurriedly laid out on both sides of the main road between Fort Howard and DePere, now known as State Street. The project contained a park 112 feet wide and three times as long, running along the bank of the Fox River, where a church would be constructed. In addition, there were a number of three-acre lots, and members of the congregation purchased 10 of these.

As a symbol of the high hopes people set by this enterprise, the colony was called *Ephraim*, which means "fruitful." The entire colony was organized 17 November 1850, as one Moravian congregation, the first in the West. On 1 December, a room in Tank's cottage was dedicated for churchly use.

It was also Tank's wish to build an institution of higher learning for the new generation of Norwegian immigrants, unaffiliated with any religious denomination. Meanwhile, a two-story school was also built in 1851, which was attended the first year by five students—actually the first attempt to operate a Norwegian high school in America. This, then, was the origin of the big Norwegian colony in Green Bay and the many congregations round about.

Green Bay was at this time only a village in the wilderness, ringed by huge forests for hundreds of miles. As fairy-like as it may sound, this old man of the world, Nils Otto Tank, with his richly endowed life, settled down here and later became one of the city's and the Fox River Valley's most important figures. Even to this day (1908), the old settlers never cease to wonder about his princely deportment, excellent taste in clothes, and innate courtesy.

For his own use, he bought an estate belonging to a Frenchman, and here he lived until he died. The house is the oldest in Green Bay and one of its most remarkable monuments. *[A footnote by Holand: "Tank's old house has now been purchased by the city and moved to one of the city parks." It is located in Tank Park on the west side and is open to tourists in the summer months. –Rosholt]*

The Tank house was furnished and decorated with the taste of an artist, unmatched by any palace in the entire area. Elegant furniture chosen from rare French originals, faded portraits by Dutch masters, old silver plate with embossed figures and Wedgwood china all were imported. He had a library scarcely unmatched by any private library in the country. Part of this collection, consisting of 5,000 copies of old Dutch books, documents and manuscripts, was donated to the State Historical Society of Wisconsin in 1868. It was through information provided by this library, with the assistance of Norwegian-born James Hanson, who is now with the Library of Congress, that a quarrel between England and Venezuela was avoided over a boundary dispute in 1898.

Iverson's Eagle Island colony

Now back to the Norwegians of Green Bay. As there were many things to put in order in these pioneer times, it was some time before Tank could convey his hundreds of acres to the colonists. In the meantime, he asked that the people should work the land without a deed.

This appeared to the irascible Pastor Iverson as an attempt to restore power to the Norwegian gentry, and he spoke against what he called an importation of the Norwegian system of renters. Other disputes also arose, and as a result, Iverson convinced most of the colony to move away. For this purpose, he got a loan of $500, signed in his own name, from the Moravian church body at Bethlehem.

In the fall of 1852, with the $500 in hand, Iverson sailed across to Sturgeon Bay, where at the time there were only three fishing shacks. Here there was good land, but it was difficult to get clear title to the land. In addition, the mosquitoes were so thick that he got a bad impression of the place.

He returned to Green Bay the next day. Despite this adverse report, several of his followers decided to move to Sturgeon Bay—among them, Anton Thompson from Farsund, who is generally recognized as the first Norwegian in that area.

At the time Iverson returned to Green Bay from Sturgeon Bay, he met a man named Ole Larson, who came to him from a spot in Lake Michigan hitherto unknown. The meeting had important results.

Larson, who was from near Skien in Telemark, immigrated to Buffalo, New York, in the 1840s, where he operated a lodging house for a time. In 1850 he moved to Green Bay where he operated a bakery, which did not do well. He then learned from some sailors of the great opportunities for commercial fishing in Lake Michigan—an industry that later made Green Bay famous.

Larson heard there was a beautiful little island about 75 miles northeast with a fine harbor protected against all kinds of wind and weather. The island was called Eagle Island, but was also known as "Horseshoe Island" because of its shape. While traveling about in this land of ours, the author has met hundreds of old farmers who were originally sailors on Green Bay and who could relate how good it was to make port in this safe harbor.

Larson recruited some Indians to help him establish a home on the island, moving there in the spring of 1851. Here he carried on a successful fishing business for many years.

When he heard that Pastor Iverson and the Moravian colony had become dissatisfied with conditions in Green Bay village, he went to Iverson and gave him such a glowing account of the advantages to be found in his new surroundings that he convinced him to make his home here, too.

In February 1853, Iverson, accompanied by Dr. H. P. Jacobs, a Dane who served as guide, journeyed northeast across the bay ice. Larson *[who apparently met them on Eagle Island –Rosholt]* guided them around the peninsula opposite Eagle Island, and the visitors got a favorable impression of the location.

It was in the middle of winter, and the snow prevented an inspection of the quality of the soil. But Iverson had heard that there were maple, aspen and beech growing and good soil. Satisfied with what he had seen, Iverson returned to Green Bay village and not long after went to the government land office in Menasha, where he made entry on 424 acres. Most of the members of the Moravian congregation then moved to Eagle Island and lived with Larson temporarily.

Many of this pioneer party later moved away and all, with rare exception, are dead. It is therefore difficult to provide many of their names. The following men and their families can be confirmed:
• Tobias Morbæk, Listerlandet in Vest-Agder
• Abraham Oneson (Abraham Aanundson), Listerlandet
• Hans Peder Hanson, Listerlandet
• Gabriel Sakariason Vatne, Listerlandet
• Sakarias Sakariason Vatne, Listerlandet
• Thomas Davidson, Listerlandet
• Rasmus Hanson, Stavanger
• Dr. H. P. Jacobs (Denmark, married to a Norwegian)
• Henrik Johnson (Denmark, married to a Norwegian)

Tobias Morbæk went along merely to help Iverson, but a few years later returned, accompanied by his brother Sakarias. *[A footnote by Holand: "These two brothers were prominent men, Tobias as a gun-maker and Sakarias as a pharmacist. A daughter of Tobias married another pioneer, Emil Christenson, who had a homestead nearby. Christenson later studied theology and was the first Norwegian pastor in Dakota Territory, where he had many amazing adventures in the 1860s. A son is now a pastor on the Pacific Coast, another a doctor and postmaster at Lake Mills, Iowa, and a daughter is married to Pastor Søren Urberg, who served congregations in Trempealeau County."]*

All these people lived together six months on Eagle Island and engaged in commercial fishing. Meanwhile, there were several births and burials.

Late in the fall of 1853, more members who had been sent there by Tobias Morbæk augmented the colony. They included:
• Ingebret Torgerson, Larvik in Vestfold
• Hans Hanson Omli (together with his grown sons, Hans Hanson Omli and Anders Hanson Omli), Larvik in Vestfold
• Jørgen Amundson, Larvik in Vestfold
• Ingebret Johnson, Larvik in Vestfold

They also lived a few weeks on Eagle Island. *[A footnote by Holand: "This little island, which covers only 35 acres, was the home of more than 100 people for several months. Several houses were built, and holy worship services were held every Sunday. They had one horse and some cattle, lived on the proceeds of their fishing and boat work in the harbor and carried on a sociable life. All this has since returned to a state of nature, and no stranger coming to the island today would ever dream that it had ever been inhabited. The old huts have rotted away, the graves are forgotten, and the woods have closed in on the once-plowed garden spots stretching from shore to shore. The island lies a short mile straight out from the author's window."]*

But the island became too confining, and one day in November 1853 the people decided to move over to the peninsula to build their homes. Thomas Davidson took the lead. The forest along the shore was so thick that he had to use an axe to clear a spot on the beach big enough to tie up his boat.

The same fall (1853), John Thoreson from Larvik arrived and was the first to settle in the neighboring township of Liberty Grove. In 1854, the following came:
• Ole Sørenson, Larvik
• Søren Hanson Estey, Larvik
• Henrik Hanson Estey, Larvik
• Aslak Anderson, Ulevaag, Tvedestrand
• Halvor Anderson, Ulevaag, Tvedestrand

Aslak Anderson built the first pier north of Green Bay village. This proved to be a big help to the pioneers. In 1856, Carl Nilson and Peter Peterson arrived, also from Ulevaag.

Iverson's first task was to survey the land, and in this he copied Tank's plan. One piece was set off for a village, while the rest was platted into 10-acre farm lots. All lots and farms were thereupon estimated and a drawing held to decide who should have what. Iverson also adopted Tank's name for a village—Ephraim.

Although Ephraim and its surroundings possibly have not lived up to the name in a material sense, it nevertheless answers to it in a spiritual way. From here have gone many who have established Moravian congregations in all parts of the country. Several pastors also were trained here, and the colony in the past 50 years has been a mainstay for the many mission endeavors of the church.

From all this, it may be seen that the Ephraim colony holds a special place among our Norwegian pioneers. It is the only Norse colony that was organized almost entirely along religious lines and operated in part on communistic principles where men, separated from the attractions of the world, hoped to live holy lives.

There has never been any permanent church work on Washington Island. There are about 500 Norwegians and Icelanders there, but no Lutheran congregation. The Mormons once had a fairly large following here.

Pastor Iverson was the first and only Norwegian-Moravian ordained pastor in America. It was mainly under the leadership of this competent man that the colony made as much progress as it did. He took an active interest in everything concerning the welfare of his people.

In the early years of settlement, it was difficult to drive all the way to Green Bay village for supplies. Iverson got a sailing ship to take a cargo of fence posts down to the village in return for provisions, and he himself, despite his age and inexperience, cut 3,000 posts and carried them out on his back to the pier. With his own hands he built half of the parsonage, which is still in good condition. He built a sailboat that for many years was the best on the bay. Several excellent landscape paintings still exist that reveal his skill as an artist with the brush. In addition, he served a whole generation as the colony's doctor as well as pastor.

As his activities carried him into many counties, he endured many hardships in the execution of his duties, and many times hustled on foot through the snow on the ice between Ephraim and Sturgeon Bay *[about 30 miles one way –Rosholt]*. He was a pastor here for 38 years, and when nearly 70, he took a course in a medical school. He then practiced as a doctor in Sturgeon Bay and even at the age of 80 was as lively as in his youth. *[Holand told me on one occasion that Iverson was still active when he moved to his last call to Ephraim in 1900. –Rosholt]*

Although Pastor Iverson is the real founder of the Norwegian settlement in northern Door County, it would not have been possible without a couple of other Norsemen like Peter Wiborg and Ebbe Nilson. Wiborg was the first white man to cultivate a piece of ground in this part of Wisconsin, north and to the east of Green Bay.

No doubt it was some fisherman

who had set his nets around a point of an island waiting for that lively whitefish who was first, but Peter Wiborg was the first to clear the forest. He left from Lom in Gudbrandsdal in 1845, the first to immigrate to America from the entire Øvre-Gundrandsdal district. But it was not until 1852 that he actually reached Door County.

Ebbe Nilson accompanied him from Porsgrund, and the two men settled on the bay's shore two miles north of Fish Creek at the foot of a cliff called Blaasenberg. Here still stands an old but cozy house, and his cooper's shop, in northern Wisconsin. *[Holand refers to Door County as "northern" Wisconsin, but northeastern would probably be more correct. –Rosholt]*

For more than 50 years, old Wiborg's light has shone across the bay like a lighthouse. It was a happy sign for Pastor Iverson and those with him when they caught sight of Wiborg's window light after marching 30 miles across the snow and ice.

Ole Sørenson, from Larvik in Vestfold, built the hut lived in by Ole Klungeland. Sørenson arrived here shortly after Peter Wiborg and worked as a surveyor in the brush and stones when the country was being platted and mapped. Every now and then, Sørenson accompanies a neighbor out to find a pine stump, which serves as a "quarter post."

Sørenson is known for other reasons as well. Little as he is, he is one of the strongest men in the county. On one occasion he lifted a 160-pound barrel of meat on his back and carried it home on the ice from Petersen's shop in Ephraim, three miles away, without stopping to rest. Although now around 80 years old, he can still get to town and return with a 100-pound sack of meal on his back.

Blaasenberg—Blossomberg

Blaasenberg's name is a reminder of the early period of settlement when there was no road down the peninsula. Anyone in Ephraim who wanted to see Thorpe, the landbroker at Fish Creek, could only travel via the lake or on the ice in winter. It was so common that a strong breeze came up as soon as a boat got out into the bay, that the place got the name Blaasenberg *[probably translated as "sandy mountain" –Rosholt]*.

Another story holds that Ole Klungeland named it after a similar place in Stavanger, where he originated. Today both the name and its origin are nearly forgotten, and the thousands of tourists who frequent the place know it as "Blossomberg."

Here is an instance where the distortion is better than the original name, for though the winds still stir up the white caps at the foot of the mountain, people are no longer afraid of them. The mountain itself, with its delightful fragrance and flowers, is much better symbolized by its revised name.

Where in the whole Midwest can one find such a variety of trees as here? The small, deep-green sumac, with its clusters of scarlet red flowers, reminds one of a tropical sun and luxuriance. The mighty pines on Blossomberg's top could be a half brother to the sighing ancients covering Dovre Mountain's shadowy expanse *[a reference to the famed Dovre mountain range in Norway –Rosholt]*.

If the southwest wind is strong and the snow deep, people remember the peace of summer with its aromatic cedar trees and church-spired balsams that cling to the side of the mountain, always green and ever young. When the warmth of spring approaches, the entire side of the mountain breaks out with wild cherry blossoms, fragrant lilacs and lush mountain ash. Yes, even the pigpen of Simon Evenson is so filled with elderberry blossoms that it resembles a children's garden more than a dwelling for animals.

High on the top of the mountain lies a beautiful plateau from which a person can see more land and water than an old sea king's kingdom. Five light towers guard the difficult harbor entrances. Six villages speak of human communication and comfort. Seven tree-covered islands dot the horizon. Dark, romantic headlands extend into the water, giving ear to thousand-year-old songs of the waves.

Here a person can forget sickness and sorrow in favor of the good life and pleasant dreams. Here is wild nature, unspoiled, majestic but not forbidding. Most glorious of all is the daily scene when the sun sinks at dusk into the bay's blue waves, with a variety of colors so rich that even the Mediterranean can scarcely match it.

Fishing: A dangerous livelihood

It is only in the last few years that any attention has been paid to farming and tourism. For an entire generation, commercial fishing was the main source of income. Farm income is small but steady; fishing on the contrary is sometimes good but always uncertain.

Although the net proceeds from fishing are completely negligible, it still tempts men by its alluring possibilities, and this has also left its mark on character. Still an important trade, fishing has fallen off recently. It is certainly not an exaggeration to say that in Green Bay alone there is an annual fish harvest of more than 100 million pounds, mostly herring. Mostly Norwegians carry on this work.

The fishing season is divided between the spring and autumn seasons, when the weather is at its worst and the water in turmoil. It is a dog's life. At 3 in the morning, a fisherman leaves his warm bed and goes forth in big, clumsy sailboats to set out his nets. These nets are quite complicated affairs, which cost a fellow $400 to $500 and cause more trouble than a catch of fish.

If the water is quiet, the net is most likely empty of fish. If a brisk sea breeze comes up, something is apt to happen. With the boat fighting furiously with the sea and the rain pelting down or a snowstorm blowing and spray soaking everyone, the men wind up the heavy net with stiff fingers. Finally, they get the wiggling herring into the boat, sometimes not enough to pay for the breakfast of the crew. But it can also happen now and then that they pull in a hundred half-barrels of white fish that sell for $250.

After breakfast the fish are cleaned at a furious pace—just three slashes with the knife. If the chapped hands break open in the salt brine, take no notice. The herring are now salted down in half-barrels and exported to fish-hungry landlubbers across the Midwestern prairies.

Fishing is also done in winter, but with hook and line. People haul out a small canvas shelter equipped with bed and cook stove and set it up in the lea of one of the islands or even directly out in the open, chop a hole in the ice and wait for trout.

When a person drives across the ice on a winter's day, it resembles somewhat the Red River Valley (along the Minnesota-North Dakota border, known for its flat terrain) landscape. The bay is not more flat than this, and here and there a person sees a fishing hut, which could easily be imagined as a lonely pioneer home on the prairie.

There is also considerable traffic across the ice, especially between Sturgeon Bay and Marinette, a distance of some 25 miles. Four or five sleigh stages cross back and forth daily, filled with passengers, and there are many private sleighs and cargo haulers as well. An enterprising Yankee, or whatever he is, worried that some of the passengers would get thirsty on the trip across the ice, has come every winter to operate a "Midway Saloon." But the last winter the cold was too bitter and the north wind too strong for a lazy saloon-keeper to tempt anyone from the warmth of his furs, and he drives past without a look. With many complaints about the thanklessness of people, the peddler packed up his bottles and went home in mid-season.

Toward spring, ice fishing is the best, and people wait to the last before moving ashore. But this has also spelled doom to some. In one night the wind can change and suddenly begin to break up the ice, moving in great sheets out across the bay. If a person is not already safe on land, there is little hope for him out there, and many a man has seen his home on shore vanish before his eyes while he floats outward on a thin ice cake into the devouring waves of Lake Michigan.

Anton Olson and Anton Amundson, a couple of commercial fishermen living near Ephraim, had a trip like this, which they will not soon forget. They had left their fishing shack on Chambers Island and were yet some distance from land on their return to Ephraim when the ice suddenly broke up. To reach land now was out of the question, and there was nothing to do but push the ice pack across the bay with caution but boldly.

The dark night began to close in with its indescribable sense of loneliness, and both men thought they had seen the last of both light and life. Suddenly they struck something.

What was this? It was solid land—an island where they could survive for a while. Half dazed, they hurried to get ashore and keep from floating past the island. But they scarcely got foot on shore before the ice cake broke up, the black water engulfing them. They were then standing on a small reef without a single piece of brush on it.

The situation was desperate. The reef was just big enough for the two men to jump around on and keep warm in the wild wind. Heavy and dark, the heavens hung over them while the ice twisted and crunched passed them through the endless night.

Dawn finally broke but brought no hope. The men gazed hopelessly across the bay, waiting for signs of a sail, knowing full well that no ship would venture out on the bay for another couple of weeks. With the help of their fishing tackle, they caught some fish, which they ate raw. This quieted their hunger for a time, but the wind did not get warmer and brought on stomach pains.

Again night came on with its terrifying loneliness, cold and numbness of spirit. And now they had another enemy to fight. The fearful strain, bitter cold and lack of food and sleep had made them prone to drowsiness, and it was only with the greatest effort that they were able to stay awake.

Finally they began to wonder what difference it would make to anyone anymore if they could only lie down and sleep a bit. Memories of family, cozy homes and sun-streaked paths had already passed them by. Yes, cold, hunger and the horror of death were forgotten in the irresistible temptation to sleep. They staggered around, bumping into each other with only one thought in mind: sleep, even for an hour or so. Thus two nights and days passed.

They were too exhausted to notice for a time that the wind had changed. Finally, they became aware that the ice cakes were striking the reef on the opposite side. This brought them out of their trance, and they saw that the entire bay was in motion and the ice pounding in toward land. Now there was hope. If they could board an ice flow, they might be driven toward landfall and possible rescue.

For an entire day they waited in vain. Most of the ice cakes were being crushed and chewed up and were too small to ride. A few large ones came along but were too far from the reef to reach, and hour after hour passed insufferably. Finally a big ice flow seemed to be heading for the reef. To judge from appearances, it could well be the same unlucky piece of ice they first came on. It went three, four, five fathoms out in the water. The two men dove in and climbed over the edge. A few hours later they sat comfortably by a cook stove. They had been three days and four nights on the bay without food or sleep.

Owing to its isolated position, northern Door County had more than its share of difficulties for the first settlers. Anders Hanson, Ephraim's cozy old postmaster, can recall that, on more than one occasion, he and others had to follow the stony and crooked road along the shore of the bay all the way to Green Bay city and return home with provisions on their backs. It is 75 miles as the crow flies, but there was no direct road through the woods.

Usually people tried to stock up a winter's supply of foodstuffs by taking the last vessel in the fall to Green Bay and back. One time this ship became frozen in before it could return, and the entire colony in Door County was in danger of starvation. Flour soon gave out. Coffee, sugar and salt disappeared. In vain, the children pleaded for a slice of bread. Many a family existed that winter on cooked potatoes.

The terrible forest fires described in the next chapter also raged around Ephraim for several days, threatening the settlers with complete ruin.

In recent years, the importance of the fruit orchards has increased sharply and in time will become even more important. Owing to its peculiar and especially favorable climate, this county is suitable to the growing of all kinds of fruits, particularly winter apples. *[Holand could not have foreseen, of course, the real blessing-to-come in the cherry tree. –Rosholt]* Time and again, Door County has won first prize in national competitions.

But uppermost in Door County's manifold glories is its scenery. Here, according to Indian tradition, lay the original Garden of Eden. In 1669, Claude Dablon, a French writer who accompanied Father Claude Jean Allouez, the Jesuit missionary, on his first visit here, also called it an "Earthly Paradise," although unaware of the Indian legend.

Tourists who come here by the hundreds in summer declare enthusiastically that there is not a more charming place between the Atlantic Ocean and the Rocky Mountains. The entire peninsula is lovely in its ever-changing scene of land and water, rolling hills and islands, particularly the beautiful terrain around Ephraim itself. Here the land rises in perpendicular cliffs to a height of more than 200 feet over the bay, and here and there hides a cave, a clinging cedar tree or a spring.

From the top of the cliffs a person can see across the glistening bay of Lake Michigan with its silent, tree-covered tongues of land and cliff-studded islands. Beautiful lies the bay, with here and there a jumping fish, a gentle sail or a watchful eagle high in the sky. Far in the distance comes the rumbling sound of a steamship.

Kystparti fra Omegnen af Molde

20
Southern Door County (Sturgeon Bay, Hainesville and Clay Banks), Wisconsin
(Source: De Norske Settlementers Historie, by Hjalmar Rued Holand, translated by Malcolm Rosholt, 1908, pp. 250–255)

The saga of southern Door County is one of struggle against the forest. Pioneers waged a violent battle against a vast and dark wilderness, with millions of roots holding fast the ground below. Theirs was a long and costly fight against the big stumps that stood like soldiers, opposing the advent of the plowshare. Finally there ensued a smoke-filled battle against the brush, when whole forests burned to the roar of snapping trees—a sea of flames overwhelming in its horror yet irresistible as Judgment Day.

No stranger unacquainted with life in the woods and the power of the axe would have believed that, 50 years ago, this impassable forest ever would have been good land for agriculture. For there were no sun-flecked, grass-covered prairies here ready for the plow—only a vast chaos of basswood and maple, birch and pine, whose heavy foliage and underbrush the sun never penetrated.

But like the lonely prairies with their heroes who refused to retreat in the face of hunger and Indian attacks, so also has the deep forest its heroes who stubbornly hacked away against the most hopeless odds to recover, for the sake of humanity, the use of fruitful land.

For the real pioneer of the forest, this is not a thankless struggle in a miserable existence, but an exciting battle wherein each fall of a crashing tree giant becomes a roar of victory. He feels that every chop of the axe ringing in the forest's deep silence is a benediction, a gift to the creative process of the future previously unrealized. Those who have never tried it can never understand how refreshing such a battle with the forest can be, at least when it is not entirely too strenuous. *[Holand is speaking from experience here, as he and his sons cleared most of the land for a cherry orchard the family operated outside Ephraim. –Rosholt]*

Southern Door County's Norwegian population is divided into three colonies: Sturgeon Bay, Hainesville and Clay Banks. Together they form a contiguous community of some 2,000 Norsemen.

When Nils Otto Tank's Moravian colony at Green Bay broke up in 1851, some families went with Pastor Iverson to Ephraim, while others settled around Sturgeon Bay, where Iverson first had thought of settling. The early people here included, from Listerland:
• Anton Thompson
• Captain Louis Klinkenberg
• Nils Erikson
• Christian Knudson Aunevik
• Salve Salveson

In 1854, Anders Nilsen from Larvik arrived. More were added later, many going into fishing or Great Lakes sailing.

Tollef T. Haines (originally Tollef T. Heen) was the founder of Hainesville colony. He arrived here from Bamble in 1856 and was later followed by others from the same place in Norway.

The biggest and best part of the settlement is at Clay Banks. This also is the youngest in years, as it was not founded until 1868-70. It came to be populated almost entirely of Valdres people, now numbering around 600 souls, who support two churches and a resident pastor. As the colony takes in an area not larger than six sections of land, it is by far the most densely populated among Norwegian communities in America.

The great fires of Peshtigo

In the beginning, the pioneers of Door County made cash money shaving shakes or cutting cedar posts. As no one had a horse and only a few had oxen, it was customary for a man shaving shake shingles to live in a shanty in the woods while his wife, with the aid of a wheelbarrow or a yoke over her shoulders, brought the shingles over to the bay shore. Here, small sailing vessels picked up the shingles or fence posts.

The role of pioneer women is often overshadowed by the difficulties their men faced, but it should be emphasized that they not only had the responsibility of keeping house, but also had to share in the outside work. It was not entirely complimentary to the women that they had to do this, but the nature of the circumstances made it unavoidable.

The position of the women was especially heartbreaking during the years of the Civil War, when a man had to shoulder his gun and go off to fight. How many times didn't it happen here in Door County that a woman in search of her cattle lost her way in the woods and had to spend the night there? How many women haven't stood in the snow to their knees and searched for acorns or hay to feed their hungry cattle through the winter?

But much of this is now forgotten, and the mellowing process of old age has mitigated these early struggles. However, one experience of indescribable horror still lurks in the memory of everyone—namely, the great fires of Peshtigo in 1871.

This fire occurred in the same year and on the same days as the Chicago fire of October 1871, laying waste to several counties in northeastern Wisconsin. Several villages also were burned—among them, Peshtigo, with its many sawmills and several thousand people.

For several days a big part of north-

Parti af Romsdalen med Billede af en norsk Vei

eastern Wisconsin became a flaming hell in which both people and animals were consumed. Fleeing to the rivers and immersing themselves in the water saved many people. In many of these rivers, people fought one another for a place to stand in the dirty mud with howling wolves, frightened deer, bellowing cattle and slithering snakes.

Meanwhile, the great fires raged and roared as if the end of the world were at hand. The author is acquainted with several people who became insane on this terrible day, and others who have not grown an inch since that time.

This area was fast settled after the Civil War, but little land had been broken. The forest was still heavily wooded, although many settlers had built their shanties in its shadows.

The summer of 1871 was extremely dry, and what little crops came up stood shriveled and scorched. Week after week went by and still no rain fell. Small lakes dried up, and the marshes became ash heaps.

The fires began in September, creeping through the underbrush, destroying roots and trees and, here and there, a fence, a haystack or dwelling. It was impossible to stop it, but the settlers saved most of their property and thought they could still manage.

The worst of it was that the air in all directions became so filled with smoke that it became almost impossible to breathe. The scene at night was terrifying. The entire horizon glowed and the deep red hues of the fires, seen through the smoke-filled atmosphere, seemed like a prophesy of doom.

On Sunday, 8 October, the wind quieted down, and many people thought the worst was over. But there was something eerie about the stillness, which neither men nor animals could quite feel at ease about. Again and again, people went to their doors to look outside, while the cattle in their stalls moved restlessly.

Late in the night a strong wind came up, soon followed by a heavy roar. Toward the south and southwest, great flames arose. The fire was no longer confined to the ground, but all at once had kindled the entire forest of living but parched trees.

The roaring wind, together with the crashing of burned trees, was enough to make the most stouthearted tremble. Whistling birds flocked around, now here, now there. Burning branches and glowing ashes flew over all. Bellowing clouds of smoke and great tongues of flame rolled amok. People became panic-stricken and fled headlong into the night.

Some miles southwest of Sturgeon Bay, the Wilhelmsen brothers had laid out a small community where shaving shake shingles was the main occupation. It was called Williamsonville, and around 80 people were living there in a clearing of six or seven acres. All but 17 were burned to death.

A rescue party left from Sturgeon Bay the following day. The road out was a fearful sight, smelling of human corpses, dead game, birds and cattle, which mixed with the heavy smoke from the burned trees. It was almost unbearable. In some stretches, the road was buried under nine feet of burnt trees.

Finally, the rescue party reached the clearing—but what a scene! Dead bodies lay everywhere, for the most part burned beyond recognition. Around 35 people lay in one mound. Some had one or both legs burned off, others an arm, while still others had their heads missing. The bodies not actually burned were cooked through and, when touched, fell apart. Above it all raised the awful stench of decomposed flesh bloated by a heavy rain.

Ten feet from the big funeral pyre in the middle of the clearing sat Mrs. Wilhelmsen, staring with blank eyes at the rescue party. She had thrown a wet horse blanket over herself and was saved, but she had stared at death so long that her mind had snapped.

Søndag i Norge

21
Roch-a-Cree (Roche-a-Cri) Colony, Adams County, central Wisconsin
(Source: De Norske Settlementers Historie, by Hjalmar Rued Holand, translated by Malcolm Rosholt, 1908, pp. 256–260)

Adams County is generally considered the poorest in Wisconsin. It is the only county without a railroad, and it is often accepted as a fact that the horses walk on wooden bog shoes to keep from sinking into the sand. There are still 1,000 acres of homestead land left in the county, but no takers. Many people have assumed, with some justification, that only sand burrs and potato bugs can be raised in this forsaken country, plus here and there a starved-out Norwegian.

It is therefore a source of wonderment to find well-kept farms in the Roch-a-Cree colony near Arkdale, where there are around 1,000 Norwegians. To judge by their nicely furnished homes and well-kept farm buildings, they certainly must enjoy a good living.

But this holds true only as far as the Norwegian settlement extends. Among the Americans and other nationalities one finds, for the most part, lonely log huts among dreary sand hills, plus skinny dogs guarding the yards.

Our countrymen in Roch-a-Cree are an unusually hard-working and diligent people. The ground is suited to potato growing, and every effort is made to take advantage of this feature. In the fall, after the potatoes have been dug, it is quite a sight to see the hundreds of loads being hauled to Necedah and across Petenwell Bridge, where the din of wagons is so unceasing that the woman who collects the toll scarcely has time to cook herself a cup of coffee.

The first Norwegians to settle in Adams County were Peter Larson and

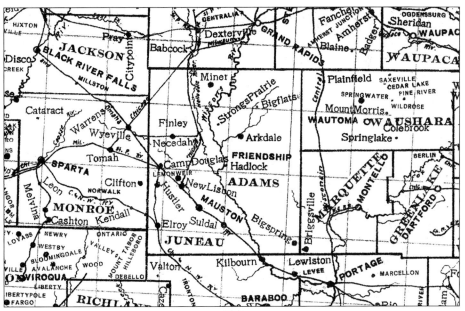

Ole Tollefson Stølen, who arrived from Stavanger in 1850 by way of Koshkonong, where they and some others had worked for a time.

As the terrain along Roch-a-Cree Creek had a surplus wood, water and meadow—the three elements considered indispensable by the pioneers, it was not many years before nearly all the land presently occupied by the Norwegians was taken.

The following is a list of the men who came here between 1850-55, which was provided by Martin M. Mikkelson, a leader in the community and able person in his own right:
- Kristen Rønning, Telemark
- Halvor Swenson, Telemark
- Tore Gullickson, Telemark
- Neri Asmundson, Telemark
- Arne Rustad, Telemark
- Hans Øien, Telemark
- Ole Stølen, Stavanger
- Anders Svartangen, Stavanger
- C. C. Lecy, Stavanger
- Per Ulric, Kristiansand
- Ole Olson, Kristiansand
- Even Mahl, Hardanger
- Hans S. Hilleboe, Hardanger
- Knut Berge, Hardanger
- Per Haug, Sogn
- Zakarias O. Eggum, Sogn
- Ole Karness (Ole Kjørnes), Sogn
- Ole Orvold, Sogn
- Elling Underdahl, Sogn
- Bretta Underdahl, Sogn
- Sylvester Orvold, Sogn
- Peter Skardrud, Solør
- Ole Skardrud, Solør
- Martin Skardrud, Solør
- Per Bredeson, Solør
- Kjel Bredeson, Solør
- Ingebret Bjørneby, Solør
- Gunerius Bjørneby, Solør
- Kristen Bjørneby, Solør
- Guro Bjørneby, Solør
- Marthias Mikkelson, Solør
- Ole Paasaas, Solør
- Berger Sagerud, Solør
- Iver Olson, Solør
- Isaac Rosgaard, Numedal
- Iver Rosgaard, Numedal
- Guri Rosgaard, Numedal
- Anders Himle, Voss
- Ole Kauserud, Toten
- Hans Kauserud, Toten
- Marthe Kauserud, Toten
- Lars Holm, Gjerpen
- Anders Holm, Gjerpen
- Isaac Holm, Gjerpen
- Ole Thompson, Sandsvær
- Thomas Warp, Sandsvær
- Halvor Warp, Sandsvær
- Halvor Ristveit, Sandsvær
- Halvor Nyhus, Sandsvær
- Torger Hanson, Sandsvær
- Kristoffer Jorandby, Valdres
- Olea Jorandby, Valdres
- Kristoffer Bøland, Valdres

The Solør region of Norway is the best represented in the settlement, and one of the first to arrive was Isaac Rosgaard of Numedal, who came in 1851, together with his family and one cow.

One night the cow failed to return home and, as she was the staff of life to the average pioneer family, Isaac took his axe and set out in search of her the following day.

Quite some distance away, he found the cow eating hay that was of a far superior quality to hay in his own pasture. Without a moment's hesitation, he began to fell some trees to build a cabin with the intention of raising a building the next morning. No one ever knew when some wandering tramp or unknown might stick his nose into the clearing and take possession.

Zakarias O. Eggum was one of the first people from Sogn to arrive here (1853). He, too, could tell you that it was important to be quick about it if you aimed to get good land.

He and another man had both taken a fancy to the same piece of land. Zakarias got up early in the morning and hurried on foot to the land office at Stevens Point, 80 miles to the north, to make an entry on this piece of land.

Later in the same day, the other

man learned that Zakarias had left for Stevens Point. Hurriedly, he rented a rig and followed. A few miles from Stevens Point he overtook Zakarias, tired and dispirited, making his way along the sandy road. Confident that he had things going his own way, he condescendingly invited Zakarias to ride, an invitation willingly accepted.

On their arrival in the village, they went to a hotel to find a place for the horses. At this point Zakarias used his native cunning, so common among the Sogn people, and in the confusion of getting the horses into the barn, he suddenly disappeared and took off for the land office before the other realized what had happened.

Zakarias demonstrated on other occasions, too, that a man had to get up pretty early in the morning to get the best of him. But one time he fooled himself.

Many of the new settlers had no watch or clock. This was Zakarias's downfall. He had never felt a watch was necessary, because the sun and one's appetite had never failed him before.

One day he decided to take a trip to Necedah, a distance of 10 miles or so, and as he wanted to get an early start in the morning, he went to bed early. After he had slept for a while, he woke up and looked out the window to see whether there was daylight. Over at a neighbor's house, there was a light in the window. Worried that he had overslept, Zakarias pulled on his trousers on the double, swallowed some lukewarm coffee and took off.

Then he found out how important a clock could be: He had to sit all night and early morning waiting for the 11 o'clock ferryboat to cross the Wisconsin River. The light he had seen at the neighbor's was the evening lamp, where people had still not gone to bed.

Money hard to come by

It was difficult to make any money in pioneer times, and nearly everything was bartered. A gold coin was therefore a treasure to be guarded. One of the old-timers had somehow or other gotten possession of a $10 gold piece, and he went on for some time wondering how he could hide it in a safe place.

Finally he hit upon the bright idea of boring a hole in the wall, inserting the coin and plugging it up with a wooden peg. No sooner said than done. And just to be on the safe side, he squirted some tobacco juice around the peg. Now he could feast his eyes on the precious spot without anyone else knowing.

But tax time came around all too soon, and there was no other way than to sacrifice the gold piece. Now the question arose: How was he to get it out? The peg was stuck fast.

He had to take the auger again, and then he had the bad luck to bore a hole in the gold piece, which he later had to dispose of for half its value.

It is really difficult to describe how incredibly hard it was to make money in those years. Splitting rails was the most common way to realize a few shillings, and these were split for 25 cents a hundred. What a person had to sell scarcely could find a buyer, while everything a man wanted to buy was sky-high.

Homespun clothes could be had, but shoes were the most difficult to come by. Those handy at making things fashioned their own shoes from hides with the hair on the outside. Those who could not make anything went barefoot, even to church, where they also used to appear in shirtsleeves. Overcoats and overshoes were unheard of.

The Norwegians could not overcome the difficulty of making decent shoes as easily as the Danes could. Over to the east of Roch-a-Cree is a big Danish settlement, where both young and old patiently walk around in wooden shoes, picking potato bugs in a bucket to feed to the pigs.

Pastor H. A. Preus organized a Lutheran congregation here in 1853.

Næreimsdalen

22
Lemonweir Settlement, Juneau County, central Wisconsin
(Source: De Norske Settlementers Historie, by Hjalmar Rued Holand, translated by Malcolm Rosholt, 1908, pp. 261–264)

About 25 miles southwest from Roch-a-Cree, in the southwestern part of Juneau County, Wisconsin, lies the Lemonweir settlement. For many years it was part of the Roch-a-Cree church parish.

While Roch-a-Cree is flat and swampy, Lemonweir lies high among inaccessible hills. All the blue-tinted hills visible to the south of Camp Douglas, New Lisbon and Mauston are crawling with Norwegians. The settlement includes some 500 people from Øvre-Telemark and 1,200 from around Suldal in Rogaland. In fact, it is the Suldal heath in America.

Ole Gjermundson Tvedt from Øvre-Telemark must be considered the actual founder of this colony, although he did not settle here before 1856. He worked at a sawmill nearby as early as 1850, and in his rambles around the countryside, he found an uncommonly beautiful valley a few miles west of Mauston.

Tvedt informed his acquaintances at Koshkonong of his discovery. As a result, four of them that same year came here to live. They were:
• Nils Bjørnson, Øvre-Telemark
• Ole Johnson, Øvre-Telemark
• Knut Ormson, Suldal in Rogaland
• Knut Mikkelson, Røldal *[a township in Hordaland fylke –Rosholt]*

Bjørnson left for Stevens Point on skis to get title to the land in the valley. As the valley was not large, it was soon completely occupied, and later arrivals had to move into the nearby hills. The *Telemarkinger* and the *Suldøler*, accustomed to hilly terrain, competed with one another for the uplands.

In 1854 there were 12 Norwegians here, including the four mentioned above. Among them they decided to organize a church congregation and call a pastor. Following is a reproduction of the original letter of call sent to Pastor Preus at Spring Prairie, north of Madison. This precious document casts an interesting sidelight on local conditions:

"To Herr Pastor Phrøis (sic)

"Inasmuch as we are living here in a small colony far removed from other Scandinavian settlements, and since our coming here we have not been visited by any Norwegian pastor, we honorable people hereby unite and beg from our hearts for the privilege of having a Norwegian pastor to visit our colony one or two times a year, and whenever at different times you might be visiting the Norwegian colony located north of Portage (village) that borders in part on the Wisconsin River, when a continuation of your journey via the Sand Prairie road would not be too far off your itinerary. From the bridge at the Dells to our colony is about 20 miles in a line running northwest through Adams County to the place we are at, which is called the township of Lisbon in Lemonweir. We, therefore, request and hope it is agreeable with you to make a trip here this summer to discuss the above-mentioned matter.

"We have begun building a schoolhouse and in addition have chosen a site for a cemetery that we wish to have dedicated. Thus, in order that our heartfelt desires may be realized, we wonder if you would write and tell us what time you plan to come and how much it will cost for each trip here. We are 12 settlers with about 43 people. Adams County, town of Lisbon, 22 May 1854.

"We hereby sign our names, all of whom were present when this letter was written. We send greetings to you from all of us and firmly hope to see you this summer. Farewell. Lemen Lemmonvier (sic), town of Lisbon, 22 May 1854. The address of our settlement is Seven Mile Creek, Adams County. (Signed) John Halvorsen, Knud Ormson, Ole Jhanson (Ole Johnson), Nils Bjørnsen, Gunder Johansen, Lauraus Augondsen, Anders Mikelsen."

At the foot of this letter, Pastor H. A. Preus has written in pencil these notations relative to the distances involved from Spring Prairie to Lemonweir: "12 miles from Kingsberry's Tavern—no road. 10 miles from Roggers (Rodgers) mill—have road."

The penciled notations on the itinerary are now 50 years old (in 1908) and nearly illegible, but nevertheless cast light on what a pioneer pastor had to reckon with. It reads as follows:
- Monday–Travel to …
- Tuesday–9 o'clock services at …
- Wednesday–Travel to …
- Thursday–Services at …
- Friday–Travel to and service at …

Of all the place names given above, only the name of Waupaca can be recognized.
- Saturday–Traveling.
- Sunday–Services at Roch-a-Cree
- Monday–Travel to Lemonweir
- Tuesday–Services at Lemonweir
- Wednesday–Travel to Moe settlement
- Thursday–Services at Moe settlement
- Friday–Travel to and services at Portage settlement at 11 o'clock
- Saturday–Return home

[The Scandinavia Lutheran Church records suggest that H. A. Preus was in Waupaca County on 18 and 19 July 1854. He probably left Spring Prairie and went first to Winchester, then to Holden congregation in Waushara County and from there to Scandinavia village. From there he turned southwest across the state into Juneau and Adams counties—quite a trip by horse and buggy in the middle of July. –Rosholt]

There was no significant movement of immigrants to Lemonweir before 1864. In that year, a party of 50 people from Suldal arrived, under the leadership of Lars Bakken, a former schoolteacher in Norway. He was an all-around man, good at composing verse and of easy disposition. Snatches of songs he wrote may still be heard in Suldal, his home in Norway.

Lars Larson Austeraa was an early arrival and a leader in the community. This also can be said about his son, Odd Larson Austeraa.

Gunder Johnson Braatvedt was the most influential man among the *Telemarkinger* and was called the Norwegian king, patriarch and philosopher. Genial and talkative, he also was a clever lawyer for the newcomers.

In those days it was common to set up a whiskey shop at election time where drinks were served free to several hundred voters. But Gunder Braatvedt and his people refused to be taken in by these blandishments.

Said he: "Yes, we will drink your whiskey and smoke your cigars, but we will vote as we please." This has become a favorite saying in the community.

The Norwegians here are now raising considerable tobacco. Messrs. Felland and Nevestvedt were the first to try tobacco-growing, and the crop has brought prosperity to the farmers the last years.

This is the home ground of the Suldal people in America. From one ridge to the next, one hears the peculiarly soft dialect of the *Suldøler*, which is unlike any other dialect in Norway.

Here is an example: *"Den Austmann veia Jasa saa de va ei fura aa sjaa,"* meaning, "This *Telemarkinger* was great at shooting rabbits."

Jonas Nilsen Ørekvam was the first to leave for America from Suldal. He went to Fox River settlement in Illinois in 1838 and later removed to Iowa.

23
Crawford and Vernon Counties, southwestern Wisconsin

(Source: De Norske Settlementers Historie, by Hjalmar Rued Holand, translated by Malcolm Rosholt, 1908, pp. 265–276)

At one time, the southwest part of Wisconsin was one vast plain, covered with the same rich topsoil as Iowa and southern Minnesota. But through the passage of time, the numerous rivers and great rainfalls have eroded the land, leaving behind sharp ridges and rolling prairies.

At Westby, in the north part of Vernon County, lies a prairie that reminds one of Minnesota. This high plain, encroached upon on all sides by uncertain river courses, is about the size of a township. It is the largest of its kind in the southwestern part of the state. Here, a big Norwegian settlement was founded.

In 1846, Even O. Gullord, born 15 January 1824, left for America. He was one of the first to emigrate from Biri in Oppland. He worked around Koshkonong and in the lead mines near Galena a couple of years before deciding to look for good land. He was a man of independence and energy who did not trust to luck, good advice or companions to accompany him on his mission.

Early in the spring of 1846 a steamship came up the Mississippi River. He decided to go along for the ride, not knowing where he was going, but confident that somewhere in that great Upper Midwest one could find land. After a few days, the steamer came to a place called Coon Slough, where it took on cordwood. This was just south of Stoddard, Wisconsin, at the mouth of Coon River.

The valley along the river looked inviting, and Even Gullord left the ship to look around a bit. Had he debarked on the other side of the Mississippi, he would have been the first Norwegian in Minnesota.

Gullord went up Coon Valley, but this region did not look as good on closer inspection as he first thought. He then continued up the entire length of the valley some 20 miles until he arrived at Coon Prairie, which lay high and wide over all stony slopes and gaps. The prairie reminded him of the best land he had seen around Koshkonong, and here he chose to begin farming.

The place lies on the east side of the prairie, straight north of Coon Prairie's big synod church *[a reference to the old Norwegian Synod organized in 1853 as opposed to the United Lutheran Synod organized in 1890 –Rosholt]*.

Well satisfied with his discovery, Gullord returned to the lead mines near Galena, where he continued to work with other newcomers from Biri.

The same fall, he and his compatriots left for Coon Prairie to take land for farming. They included:
- Even Gullord
- Hans O. Liebakken and family
- Syver Nilsen Galstad and family
- Hans N. Neperud and family
- A bachelor named Kristen

All settled immediately south of where the city of Westby was later platted.

Up to this time, Koshkonong had been the farthest point of penetration for the rather steady influx of immigrants. But now it was becoming crowded, and people were looking around for unclaimed lands. Even Gullord's "discovery" made a big stir. It was reported that the rolling prairie was just as rich as around Koshkonong, with big groves of trees, and creeks and valleys that looked a great deal like beautiful Norway. Of course, it was located in the wilderness 150 miles west of Koshkonong, but the Mississippi River lay not far away. And it was only a two-day journey north to Black River Falls, where there was work to be had at good wages in the logging woods and sawmills.

There was considerable interest in Coon Prairie. In the first five years, a couple of thousand Norwegians prepared to leave for this place. Coon Prairie was a name of redemption that comforted the disappointed newcomer to Koshkonong or Muskego who found that conditions in these two places were worse than in Norway. It represented the message of hope that drifted across the Atlantic and inspired thousands to try their luck in the New World. The settlement now (1908) numbers 13,000 Norwegians. *[Holand here uses the expression "Norske Folk," literally, Norwegian people. But he no doubt also means people of Norse descent, because when he wrote his book, so-called Norwegians on Coon Prairie were mostly children and grandchildren of the pioneers. –Rosholt]*

The settlement, which reaches from Sparta in the north to Ferryville and Soldiers Grove on the south, covers the southwest of Monroe County, most of Vernon County extending westerly, and the north part of Crawford County. As it is 50 miles long and about 20 miles wide, it is no surprise to learn that people are not acquainted with one another at the farthest ends of this area.

Divided into two principal parts, the north of the settlement includes Coon Prairie, Coon Valley in Vernon County, and the Hurdal and Holand communities in Monroe County. Here live the people from Biri, Gudbrandsdal, Flekkefjord, Hurdal and Høland. Coon Prairie itself is the main stomping ground of Biri emigrants to America, with a population of no less than 2,500. There are also many from Flekkefjord, in addition to the largest colony of people from Høland in America. However, there are scarcely 500 of them, because not many emigrants left this Norwegian community.

The southern part of the settlement includes Kickapoo, West Prairie and Utica. With the exception of a small colony of people from Nordfjord down in Utica, people from Sogn, Lyster (Luster) and Aardal populate all of these hills and ravines. There are fewer than 4,000 Sogn people divided into 13 congregations to be found here. Nowhere in America can one hear the sonorous Sogn dialect so pure and uncorrupted.

In 1849, Even Gullord's father, Ole Torstenson Gullord, arrived.

Accompanying him were:
• Henrik Gullord, Biri, Oppland
• Hans K. Larson, Biri, Oppland
• Even Peterson, Biri, Oppland
• Peter Unseth, Biri, Oppland
• Torsten Unseth, Biri, Oppland
• Even Swennestuen, Biri, Oppland
• Peder Heggestuen, Biri, Oppland
• Helge Gulbrandsen, Sigdal
• John Bergum, Sør-Land
• Ole Syverson, Gausdal
• Lars Christopherson, Ringerike

All settled around the area where Westby was later platted. Prairie du Chien and Black River Falls were the nearest towns and La Crosse only a village.

Ingebret Homstad from Trondheim arrived in 1850 and went a few miles north across the prairie, where he opened a hotel, which became very popular with both Norwegians and Americans. Ole Dalen, Kjøstil Øiom and Nils Rudi, the first to leave from Nord-Fron in Gudbrandsdal, arrived the same year and settled west of Westby.

Johannes Berg from Øier, one of the most hospitable men on the prairie, arrived at the same time and settled east of Westby, now known as "East Village." With the arrival of these men, the great trek of *Gudbrandsdøler* began, and it is these people who now make up the main ethnic group in Vernon County.

Helge Valley

North and west of Coon Prairie lies Coon Valley, narrow and irregular, stretching 25 miles from Stoddard to Cashton and populated entirely by Norwegians. The first person to settle here was Helge Gulbrandson. He toured the region all summer in 1849, looking for a good place, and that fall decided on a spot very near to where the upper Coon Valley church now stands *[probably Northwest Prairie congregation, 12 miles northeast of Viroqua –Rosholt]*. This valley was long known as "Helge

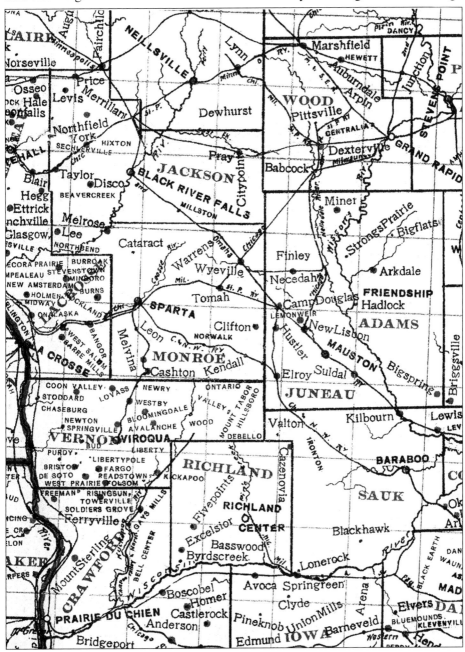

Valley" *[more correctly, Helgesenryggen or "Helgeson ridge" –Rosholt]*. H. N. Neperud now owns this farm.

The next year, the following arrived:
- Hans Nilsen, Biri, Oppland
- Ole Gullord, Biri, Oppland
- Tosten A. Klomsten, Biri, Oppland
- Mathias Lisbakken, Biri, Oppland
- Lars Swennungsen, Hardanger

A nice memorial marker honoring these old settlers now stands in front of the main church in Coon Valley.

Iver Øiom and Hans Dalen, who arrived in 1853, were the first people from Gudbrandsdal to reach the valley, and these people now make up 90 percent of the population.

It has been a source of amazement to many people that this valley was settled so early when so much good land lay unclaimed on the prairie nearby. But the prairie was windblown, and there was not enough wood and water.

In addition, many thought there was no future on the prairie for grain production when the market was so far away and prices down. It was therefore better, they thought, to find a sheltered area where a person could raise cattle and where they could find ample wood, water and game. All these were abundant in Helge Valley.

There were animals, and a man could shoot a bear every time he went hunting. Moreover, all these early settlers were crack shots. Hans Nilsen could sit in his yard and hit a fly on the barn door, and old Hans Dalen could hit a bull's-eye at 40 rods even after he was past 50.

Among other well-known pioneers in Coon Valley was a Halling by the name of Per O. Brye, who arrived here in 1853. He was a man whose talents were known far and wide. For many years he handled most of the town offices by himself, without any trouble. If anyone died without leaving a will (which was usual), Per Brye was named administrator and straightened out everything to the satisfaction of all concerned.

But thousands with a shrug of horror remember another pioneer in Coon Valley. He operated a saloon and "blind pig," where he filled his guests with rotgut whiskey and robbed them to boot. It is said that he served up, burned up and murdered, that he gave his wife and children arsenic, and set fire to a house in which eight persons had gathered. He also had an irresistible desire to cut down apple trees.

He was a big, red-haired fake who on Sunday, when the pastor drove by, positioned himself on the highway decked with a ruffed collar made of paper, a cowbell in hand, and preached, or made believe he was chanting the liturgy by reading from the newspaper *Skandinaven*.

Coon Valley is a remarkable place where Norwegian customs, both good and bad, have remained unchanged longer than any other place among Norwegians in America. A great many antiques from Norway may be found in the homes to this day. Up to a few years ago, the community exported considerable goat's cheese. Big herds of goats could be seen, with young goat-herders chasing them through the hills.

In the northern part of the settlement, in those hills and ravines sloping down toward Sparta, the Høland people have their homes. Magnus Swenson, a noble old patriarch, was the first among them to arrive, but the first to leave from Høland was old Heyerdahl at Rock Prairie, who came to the U.S. in 1853 *[probably an ancestor of Thor Heyerdahl who skippered the Kon-Tiki across the South Pacific without a man being lost – Rosholt]*.

In the northern part of Coon Prairie lies the oldest and most important settlement of people from Hurdal *[today, Hurdalsverk on modern maps –Rosholt]*. Thorsten Søgaarden, the first to emigrate from this area, came to Muskego in 1843.

Westby is one of the prettiest towns in America. It is named for Tosten Westby, Even Gullord's brother, the first to operate a trading post here. He was a good-natured old veteran of the Civil War.

Southwest of Westby is a rather important colony of people from around Flekkefjord. Mikkel Larson from Lunde parish, who came in 1851, was the first of these. His brother, Tønnes Larson Ekeren, was a boon among the old settlers and a man who took the lead in maintaining the church. He is still remembered with deep affection.

Coon Prairie has always been one of the most generous Norse communities in America, a leader in both religious and secular affairs. Some of the best congregations in the United Lutheran church are located here, as is the Norwegian Synod's largest congregation (1908).

In 1851, a man from Sogn by the name of Ingebret Ness came to Coon Prairie. As he could not find the kind of land he was looking for, he continued 25 miles southwest along the ridges until he came to a plain known as West Prairie. Here he began farming on a piece of land that is now used for the parsonage, on the boundary between Vernon and Crawford counties. He was from Lyster (Luster) in Sogn and was the founder of the first settlement of Sogn people in America.

Ness returned to Koshkonong a year or two later and worked until 1853, when he came back to Coon Prairie accompanied by a number of people from Lyster (Luster), including:
• Ole Rønnei (Ole Runnice)
• Søren Jerman
• Kristoffer Johnson (usually called California Johnson)
• Anders Thompson Sandvik
• Skak Thompson Sandvik
• Herman Larson Rønnei (Herman Larson Runnice)
• Lars Christenson
• Anders Kilen (Anders Call)
• Jens Kilen (Jens Call)
• Christian C. Olson

Many arrived that same year from Flekkefjord; among them:
• Ole O. Rosenwater from Hægebostad, Vest-Agder
• Didrik Olson Mjøvand (Didrich Olson White) from Fjotland

There was also a Halling by the name of Jørgen Buckcreek Lee who came with the first pioneers, a great one to carouse around and fight. Tall stories about him are still circulated by the Irish around the village of Rising Sun.

It was probably an overwhelming pride in his nationality that forced him to behave in the manner he did, because he seldom fought with his own people. One time in a saloon he engaged 11 Irishmen, but when it was over he was so beaten up himself he could scarcely walk home.

Over in Kickapoo, 10 miles east of West Prairie, other families from Lyster (Luster) and Aardal began to settle at this time. Arriving in 1853 was the large Fortney (originally Forthun) family that included several brothers, their wives and children. Accompanying them were Gunnerius Olson from Aasnæs in Solør, and Christian Hooverson Nundal from Sogn.

Arriving in 1854 were Anders Olson Hestehun and Anders Thompson Nundal, one of the strongest men in Aardal, in addition to Anders Bottolfson and Nils Peterson Bjørkum. The last named was an enterprising man and father to the well-known Utley Peterson in Soldiers Grove.

As early as 1855, a congregation was organized on Coon Prairie and in Kickapoo. *[Norsk Lutherske Menigheter i Amerika gives 1853 as the date of organization for Coon Prairie. The identity of the Kickapoo congregation is not clear. This was once a post office in Kickapoo Township, Vernon County, but has been discontinued, and the name itself is not included on modern maps of Wisconsin. –Rosholt]*

The indefatigable Pastor H. S. Stub found his way up to these hills of the Sogn people. After this visit, regular worship services were inaugurated. Nils Peterson's house was small but the best there was, and therefore used for worship services. When night came, the one room, which was also used for kitchen and sleeping quarters, was reserved for the visiting pastor, while Peterson and his family slept in the loft.

As the loft was seldom used, there was no need for a stairway. But on these special occasions, Peterson climbed up through the rafters and pulled his wife and children after him.

Pastor Nils O. Brandt was the first Norwegian pastor to visit Vernon County. He stayed with Even Gullord in 1852. After giving instructions to 12 confirmands in a five-day cram session, he confirmed them all at the house of H. A. Neperud. One of those confirmed was Bertha Bakkum, originally from Biri in Oppland fylke, who later married Jeremiah Rusk. Rusk rose to the rank of general in the Union Army, was elected governor of Wisconsin, and finally was made a member of the President's cabinet in Washington.

Although the terrain in this region was hilly and rough, it was nevertheless considered highly desirable by the people of Lyster (Luster) and Aardal. Soon the people from the Sogn district began moving in to such an extent that the various settlements are now welded into one.

Ingebret Ness and California Johnson were brothers-in-law and good friends. Both were also big men and strong. But one night, after they had been touring the saloons of Rising Sun, they began to argue about who was the stronger.

Ness said he could manage anyone in the community and a little beyond to boot. Furthermore, he was certainly the founder of the whole settlement, and a little respect should be shown him. But California Johnson thought this was plain tomfoolery for any housecat such as Ingebret to make anyone believe that he was a scrapper. How could he compare to one who had been all the way to California, fought with gold-diggers and Indians, and struggled the length and breadth of Mormon country? In addition, mountain lions and rattlesnakes were as thick as flies!

Finally, they agreed that the answer to this weighty problem could not be put off till morning. Despite the darkness and a light rain, they jumped off their wagons, tied up the horses in the brush and tore into each other. The following morning the battleground looked as though two elephants had been fighting there.

Ingebret's wife, a sister of California Johnson, was a woman of great humor who could entertain the whole neighborhood with her whims and conceits. It was she who got people to change their good old Norwegian names.

Her husband's name she got changed from Ingebret Ness to Albert Nash; Ronnei to Runnice; Kilen to Call; Mjøvand to White, etc.

Apparently to keep people's minds from completely stagnating, she managed to start all kinds of quarrels among them. She never gave her husband a moment's rest, either, and he finally went off to war and was killed in action. After that, she turned Methodist and toured the countryside, holding noisy revival meetings. There are still legends of her deeds and accomplishments.

1850s: Hard times in America

The 1850s in America saw hard times. The decade or so preceding the Civil War was a period of great unrest, and business in general was paralyzed. The effects of this monetary crisis were felt in the farthest corners of the land, and overall ran a spirit of despondency, shiftlessness and misery.

The newcomers who came to settle here during these trying times had therefore to contend with a very unfavorable climate in the national economy. This was especially true in the case of Coon Prairie and neighboring districts which, for a number of years, were considered the last outposts of civilization, north and west.

A man slaved and sweated in the most primitive manner in the hope of making enough to keep body and soul together for another day. No one dreamed that there could ever be a time when there would be prosperity again. But these were a patient people who refused to be overwhelmed by the odds against them in a foreign land.

It was a godsend for many in those days that Black River Falls was already an important logging and sawmill center. While the wife remained at home with the children and the cow, her husband went off to the "Pinery." And if the women were especially enterprising, they might even set up a shanty in the pine forest and spend the winter shaving shake shingles. These were shipped down river in spring and brought $3 per thousand.

Although there was considerable timber in Vernon County, no sawmill was built until years later. But this did not hinder people from sawing lumber for their own buildings. A log was rolled up to the top of two high sawhorses and, while one man stood above, another stood below, pushing and pulling on a whipsaw [called the up-and-down saw –Rosholt] to make boards or planks. Two men could saw 200 board feet in a day.

Grain was naturally harvested in the same manner as in biblical times, using scythe and sickle. The same thousand-year-old methods were used when threshing came around. The grain bundles were laid outside in a ring on a clean, hard, earthen floor, and six or eight head of oxen were used to tramp on the grain to separate the husks from the straw. One man had to follow around as a chambermaid to the oxen and catch any droppings, lest the grain be dunged.

Luckily, it was not necessary to use these cumbersome methods for long. After a few years, Even Gullord acquired the first threshing machine in the community, an amazing affair resembling a cylinder that lay on the ground. Grain and straw came out in the same pile, which then had to be tossed into the air for winnowing. Still, it was almost a miracle to see the cylinder cut up the grain bundles.

Tobacco-growing has for some years been the main cash crop. Wherever a person may travel, even into the most remote parts of the valley, he will see the big, dirty-looking tobacco sheds. Wisconsin now harvests more tobacco than any other state in the union (1908), and here it is almost entirely harvested by people of Norse descent.

Koshkonong is the oldest community for tobacco-growing, but Vernon and Crawford counties now are the largest and produce the best quality in the state. In 1906, a grower realized up to 17 cents per pound, slightly more than elsewhere in the state.

The average tobacco farm runs to five acres, on which a grower can average 1,275 pounds to the acre. Taking an average of 13 1/2 cents per pound, the gross income per acre in 1906 would have been $172.12. Reckoning expenses at $40 per acre, which is more than enough, the net profit would have come to $132 per acre, or a net income for Wisconsin's 40,000-acre tobacco crop of $5,280,000. Nearly all this went into Norwegian pockets, as they nearly monopolized the growing of tobacco in the state.

Gunnerius Olson on Kickapoo was the first to raise tobacco in this part of the state, beginning in 1876, and he has continued ever since. Now there are several large warehouses in all the small towns, in addition to a big industry in Sparta, where nearly 1,000 men and women from that Norwegian settlement are employed in the sorting of tobacco leaves.

Det Indre af et Telemarkshus for nærværende ved Bygdø i Nærheden af Kristiania

24
Rush River Settlement, between St. Croix and Pierce Counties, western Wisconsin
(Source: De Norske Settlementers Historie, by Hjalmar Rued Holand, translated by Malcolm Rosholt, 1908, pp. 277–283)

In 1849, the entire western part of Wisconsin was still a wilderness. With the exception of half a dozen Norwegian newcomers on Coon Prairie in Vernon County, scattered trappers, "town-site squatters" and small bands of Indians, the area between Prairie du Chien and Lake Superior was uninhabited.

Early in the spring of 1849, a man left Rock Prairie and traveled up the Mississippi River to look for a suitable place for a Norwegian settlement. He stopped at the mouth of many cozy, sunlit valleys framed by sharp ridges to see if any of these places would meet his requirements. He finally reached St. Paul, Minnesota.

At this time, St. Paul was considered the tag end of the world, because directly west lay the "Big Woods," which prevented, or at least hindered, encroachment in that direction.

There were only 30 houses, and Minneapolis was nothing but a name until several years later. In fact, the site where Minneapolis was platted attracted the stranger because of its "oak openings" and beautiful tree-lined lakes, but the prairie land here was limited and the soil too sandy for good farming.

While in St. Paul, this same man was informed by an Indian of a big prairie with forests around it that lay 20 to 40 miles east, in Wisconsin. The man went to see for himself and became enthusiastic about the charming landscape and rolling prairie country, not to mention unlimited possibilities for fishing. And finally, there were large forests lying still farther east of the prairie country. This was the most delightful place in western Wisconsin, excellently suited to a large Norwegian settlement.

The stranger was especially impressed by the area later known as the valley of New Centerville on the line between St. Croix and Pierce counties. Here he decided to lay out a place for his Norwegian colony. He then returned to Rock Prairie.

The man who made it possible for this fine stretch of land to come into Norwegian hands was Pastor C. L. Clausen. When he returned to Rock Prairie and told of the beautiful land he had discovered, five people from Biri decided to journey there, namely:
• Matthias Sletten
• Hans Iverson Haugen
• Hans Stumlie
• Per Granum
• Lars Dahle

All settled at the edge of the forest, between the present villages of Martell and New Centerville. Their little colony

then lay 200 miles beyond any other, and many counties between that were still unoccupied. In the beginning these few people were full of good cheer, because they were still expecting Pastor C. L. Clausen to follow up with a big party of more settlers.

But the Norwegian immigrants who continued to reach Rock Prairie were of one opinion—that northwestern Wisconsin was entirely too far away and separated by roadless forests and wild country to compensate for the doubtful glories of Pierce County. The newcomers were now inclined to follow the new stream of pioneers pouring into Iowa.

Clausen, in an effort to find an outlet for the persistent flood of immigrants reaching Rock Prairie, made a journey through northern Iowa and laid out St. Ansgar settlement in Mitchell County. Meanwhile, the five *Biringer* up in Pierce County lived by themselves for five years and felt quite let down by Clausen.

But in 1852, five Norwegians working in the lumber village of Menomonie paid them a visit. They had sailed down the Chippewa River on a lumber raft to the mouth of the Mississippi. From there, they walked north along the banks of the Mississippi to look for land. They liked everything about the region where the *Biringer* were located and moved there, with the addition of one more man, in 1853. The five of them, all from Modum, were:
• Nils Kristoffersen
• Per Hovde
• Guul Wahl
• Guttorm Anderson
• Anders Bakke
Many more arrived later from Modum.

Shortly thereafter, Nils Kristoffersen became a Methodist pastor and conducted big revival meetings among his old settler friends. As it was some time before any Lutheran pastor appeared here, it seemed for a time that the entire community would turn Methodist. Kristoffersen also went back to Modum in Norway to proclaim his own teachings.

In 1852, the first Norwegian came to Hudson, Wisconsin. He was Ingebret Svenson Grøthem from Grimstad, a cabinetmaker.

Arriving from Modum in 1854 were:
• Christian Gunvaldsen
• Christian Thomasrud
• Hans Thomasrud
• Laurits Thomasrud
• Knut Halvorson
• Jørgen Johnson
• Nils O. Hengsly
• August O. Hengsly
• Ole H. Thoen

All lived for a time on Rock Prairie in Jefferson County. Rock Prairie, in fact, was the mother colony for pioneers to Pierce and St. Croix counties, all of whom settled a few miles south of the present village of Baldwin. Ole Thoen, who settled at New Centerville, actually left Norway to join the gold rush to California before coming to Wisconsin.

The family of old Even Christianson and sons Matthias Evenson, Christian Evenson and Johan Evenson, from Vardal, arrived shortly after the above-named. They had lived at Koshkonong and now decided to settle at the edge of the forest on the north branch of Rush River. Accompanying them was Nils Kristenson from Biri.

New arrivals from Drangedal in 1855 included:
• Stener Thorson (a brother of Pastor Marcus Thorson)
• Elling Thygeson
• Halvor Peterson Berge
• Lars Olson

They had previously lived at Rock River and took land a short distance south of New Centerville *[not listed in the zip code index –Rosholt]*.

The same year and also arriving from Drangedal were old Halvor T. Herrum and sons Svennung Halvorsen Herrum, Halvor Halvorsen Herrum, Søren Halvorsen Herrum and Torbjørn Halvorsen Herrum. This family originated in Bamble in the vicinity of Skien. Accompanying the group was Tønnesen *[no first name provided –Rosholt]*, father of pastor T. H. Tønnesen.

There were further arrivals from Modum in 1855, including the following:
• Finbur Hanson
• Ole Hanson
• Elling Hanson
• Peder Nilsen Haugen

Peder Nilsen Haugen, father of the former congressman Nils P. Haugen, settled in Pierce County, and the Hanson brothers took claims in the forest region east of Baldwin *[Wisconsin –Rosholt]*.

The movement of emigrants from Østerdal *[Glomma River Valley down to Elverum and tributary districts –Rosholt]* began in 1855, and now people from this region make up a majority of the settlement at Rush River. The first to arrive from Tyldal, an annex of Tynset in Hedmark, were:
• Anders Baardsen
• Ole Moen
• Tore Svendsen
• Carl Olson
• Bersvend Iverson Riseggen
• Ole Thorud

These five men, who had spent several years around Muskego, bought all the land in Section 36 of Martell Township. These people from Østerdal had their doubts about the prairie for farming and preferred to clear the forest, where they considered the land more productive.

Ole Thorud, the first to leave from Tyldal, arrived in the U.S. in 1849, settling first at Little Elk Creek in Dunn County, where a small colony had been established.

There were quite a few *Haringer* (Hardanger) south of Baldwin, some of whom were among the very first. They included, from Eidfjord:
• Charley H. Geisness
• Knut Larson
• Hellik Larson
• Johannes Larson
• Thomas Larson
• Syver Nilsen
• Syver Thompson
• Syver Hoel
• Jo Amundson Herreid

All arrived in 1856. Hans Larson also accompanied them from Biri.

Most of the Norwegians, especially the people from the eastern valleys, had settled a short distance into the forest, surrounded by timber that today would be worth a fortune. But to the pioneers, the timber was of little value and a hindrance to cultivation. Many originally thought they could turn this timber into profit, but in this they were completely disappointed. The timber was cut and burned as fast as a man could pile it up.

Clearing bees were organized. Men from around the neighborhood, bringing their oxen, gathered at the home of a newcomer to help skid the great logs into piles for burning. One man shuffled around with a jug and a glass, and the coffee can was kept warm at all times. In the evenings, when these huge pyres went up in smoke, the young people gathered around to celebrate a victory ball over the forest's dark and ancient domain. The fires were a sign of the future, while the spring air around them was as soft and fragrant as it is today.

It was a great pity that these beautiful trees had to be sacrificed for no better purpose than to burn them. Many a man from eastern Norway, where the forests are a source of pride, scratched his head trying to think of something better to do than to go on with this waste.

Finally, someone made a trip all the way to Stillwater, 40 or 50 miles distant, just to find out whether the sawmills there had any use for the timber.

To be sure, the operators said, they could use it to make "logdowns"—thin pieces of wood about 15 inches long, an inch wide and an eighth of an inch thick, used in binding log rafts to be run down river. For these they would pay $2 per thousand. This was really something to be made from a giant tree three or four feet on the stump!

The settlers went ahead and chipped away with all their might to make logdowns. Something had to be done to pay the grocer. Flour was $14 a ton and syrup $2 a gallon.

[Holand is mistaken here. The word is "lockdown," not "logdown," and it does not refer to a piece of wood as described above. Agnes Larson, in The White Pine Industry in Minnesota, p. 93, explains how a log raft was held together with poles that were "fastened to each log by hickory, elm or birch branches bent over the pole like a staple with the ends stuck into holes bored in the log. This arrangement was called a lockdown. Plugs were driven in the holes in the logs in order to hold the lockdown in place..." What the farmers on Rush River were probably asked to make at home were the plugs, and these were obviously rounded and up to 18 inches long. –Rosholt]

In later years, people hauled firewood to River Falls, 15 miles away, and got $2.15 per cord.

From all this it may be deduced that conditions in this neighborhood were difficult for many years. There were days when bread was absent from the table. Coffee made from wheat was served instead of mocha, and cooked potatoes instead of cakes. A brown, unpleasant syrup called "nigger-sweat" was also part of the bargain.

Shortly after their first pastor arrived, a festive day offering was taken, and only two men in the main congregation, Halvor Herrum and Guul Wahl, made any offering. The others had nothing. One of them, now a prosperous farmer, describes the following about his plight in those days:

"In the beginning of spring, I went to a wealthy American who lived a few miles from my place to see about getting some provisions on credit. But the high prices on everything had forced him to sell out, and now he, too, could scarcely support himself. All he could offer me was some of last year's unpicked frozen potatoes and beets, which were being turned up by the plow. Following him in the furrow, I gathered as much as I could in one sack, because even frozen potatoes were more than I had at home.

"The load became too heavy in more than one respect: I realized it represented poverty, which I was still not sufficiently hardened to, and which so few know how to endure without quarrel. Both my inner and outer strength weakened under the weight, and for the first time in my life I broke down and cried over my bad luck in life." *[No source is given for this quote. –Rosholt]*

Pastor Nils O. Brandt was the first pastor to visit this settlement. So many from his congregation on Rock River had moved here that he wanted to see his people again. He remained from 6 July to 8 July 1855, reading with those who wished to be confirmed and holding worship services and confirmation in a log barn.

Lauritz Larson became the first resident pastor at Rush River. He had been called to Highland Prairie in Fillmore County (Minnesota), but there was no parsonage there, and he had a family. At the advice of the synod council, he went to Rush River, where a small house had been built. Here he began his career in 1857, at the age of 24.

In 1859 he was called to serve as a theology professor in St. Louis *[probably at the Missouri Synod's Concordia College and Seminary –Rosholt]*. When he was preparing to leave, Ole Thoen, a simple and well-meaning man, said: "In a way, you should be thankful that you were here. When you first came, you weren't much of a man, but now we like you very much." This free advice stung the future doctor of divinity deeply.

This settlement is close to St. Paul and stretches from Red Wing northward nearly to Glenwood City, and from River Falls east to Spring Valley. It has a population of 9,000, and people have prospered.

25

Most heavily populated Norwegian area in U.S., western Wisconsin

(Source: De Norske Settlementers Historie, by Hjalmar Rued Holand, translated by Malcolm Rosholt, 1908, pp. 284–285)

If a person wishes to get a good impression of the overwhelming number of Norwegians in the United States, he should take a trip through the jumbled hills and valleys in western Wisconsin lying between La Crosse, Eau Claire, Black River Falls and Menomonie.

Approximately 42,000 Norwegians occupy one township after the other. Of this number, there are 1,000 in Black River Falls, 4,000 in Menomonie, 6,000 in La Crosse and 7,500 in Eau Claire. The remaining 25,500 live on farms hidden in the hills and ravines all the way north through Chippewa County.

The terrain here with its high ridges and sheltered, church-still valleys, is reminiscent of Norway. The population is homogeneous: People from the same neighborhoods in Norway inhabit every encircling valley almost entirely. Unaffected by others, they speak their own dialect.

If a man journeys from Black River Falls to Mondovi, he must first travel through Little Norway, where most are from Ringebu. West from here lies a series of large valleys—Skutlidalen, Trompsdalen, Teppendalen and Salvedalen. Around the lake sloughs are where the sons of Solør thrive.

A stretch north of here lies a labyrinth of narrow valleys and high hills where the aroma of coffee never dies and tobacco smoke never quits. There live Øvre-Telemark mountain people in peace and tranquility. Farther west in Buffalo County, where the ridges are higher and valleys are narrower, we find *Sogninger* from Lyster (Luster) by the thousands. *Haringer,* *Biringer* and *Trønderne* we find in large quantities. There are entire congregations from Skiaker, Sør-Fron and Hallingdal. Norwegian speech and songs are used at church.

You also find people from Germany and Poland who forget their native speech, ignore English and adopt one or the other of the mountaineers' dialects. They may join the local congregation, confirm their children and join in complaints about how the community fund is being spent.

The story is told about a doctor who was called to aid a farmer near Blair. As he was not sure where the man came from in Norway, he asked if the patient was from Solør.

"No," he replied, "I'm not a *Solung.* I'm Bohemian."

In Black River Falls we have an old Negro barber who is very knowledgeable about Sør-Trons' personal and family history, even though he has never left the country. He speaks better English than his customers, who hold themselves to the old *bygde* (community) dialects. He speaks with all seriousness about the church controversies that Per Bakkens and other Missourians advocate.

Immigration into this hilly country began at several different points about the same time in the 1850s, but most of the good land was not claimed before the 1870s. The reason for this was that the Indians had for many years set fire to the grass and burned the forests so that most of the ridges, when the pioneers arrived, stood naked and treeless. This melancholy scene scared those looking for land.

Today, all the ridges are covered with big, beautiful groves of trees, and people sell considerable firewood, which previously a man had to travel miles to buy.

Hornindalsrokken

26
La Crosse County, western Wisconsin
(Source: De Norske Settlementers Historie, by Hjalmar Rued Holand, translated by Malcolm Rosholt, 1908, pp. 286–289)

The Norwegian settlement in La Crosse County is divided into three contiguous areas: La Crosse Valley, Lewis Valley and Halfway Creek. Here, there are about 2,000 Scandinavians, most of them from Hedmark fylke in eastern Norway. In addition, there are thousands of Norwegians in the city of La Crosse.

Anfin Anfinson, either a *Sogning* or native of Bergen, was the first Norseman in La Crosse County. He arrived in 1849 accompanied by his family, driving his cattle ahead of him across the ridges.

At this time there was only one man, an American, in the beautiful La Crosse Valley, and only one man in the future city of La Crosse. But Anfin Anfinson was apparently frightened by the Mississippi River and drove his ménage up into a side valley now known as Hulberg Valley, three miles northwest of West Salem.

There, he found an uncommonly well-situated piece of land, flat and productive, with running water and large forests. This farm was so superior to anything else that it sold for $2,000 in 1854, even though most of the land nearby still lay unclaimed. Anfin Anfinson then left for Steele County, Minnesota, where he founded a colony of Sogn people.

Meanwhile, more Norsemen arrived in 1850, including Simon Aanrud and his son Gunnerius Simonson, who settled in an adjoining valley known as "Englishman's Valley." People from Ringsaker, who came here as a result of the Aanruds, now populate all these small valleys.

Nearly all the Ringsaker people remained for a time in Koshkonong at the home of Lars Johansen Holo, the first to leave from Ringsaker and considered some sort of doorkeeper for everything concerning them.

In 1851 came Even Smith Evenson (Aren Evenson) with his son Audun Evenson, a strong supporter of the Norwegian Synod. Along with them came:
- Johannes Olson Sau, Ringsaker
- Christian Hulberg, Ringsaker
- Johannes J. Hønne, Biri
- Jørgen Georgeson, Ringsaker
- Christian Georgeson, Ringsaker
- Johannes Georgeson, Ringsaker

All were from Ringsaker with the exception of Hønne, who was from Biri.

Two years later (1853), new arrivals included Ole Hulberg and Nils Hulberg. In 1854, the following came:
- Torger Ingvaldson Haug, Ringsaker
- John Torgerson, Ringsaker
- Even Erikson, Ringsaker
- Ole Knudsen Hoiby, Ringsaker
- Thore Knudsen Hoiby, Ringsaker

These men settled near Anfin Anfinson in La Crosse Valley.

Meanwhile, the movement of immigrants into Lewis Valley and Halfway Creek was also under way. The first to arrive in Lewis Valley in 1850 were John Anderson Bækimellem and Christian Ekern, both from Biri. Shortly afterward, Syver Olson and Syver Anderson from Ringsaker arrived.

Halfway Creek is the main settlement, and Per Anderson Hogden led those who arrived first in 1850 from Vardal. He settled on a piece of land where the Lutheran parsonage is presently located.

The next year (1851) brought the following:
- Ole Olstad, Vardal
- Johan Stensveen, Vardal
- Andreas Skogen, Vardal
- Johannes Henriksen, Vardal
- Børre Hanson, Vardal
- Even Hanson, Vardal

Pastor H. A. Stub, who took in the entire area in addition to Bostwick Valley (at one time an important settlement), organized a congregation in 1856, but the land is now exhausted. Pastor Nils O. Brandt had earlier visited these pioneers a number of times. In 1862, the congregation called the Reverend (and later professor) Johannes B. Frick from Norway to serve as resident pastor.

The parsonage was already built at Halfway Creek and has an interesting history: It was here that the first successful attempt was made to operate a Norwegian school of higher learning in America. A campaign for funds was launched among the churches of the old Norwegian Synod to establish a Norwegian university or "college." This ingathering was well-supported and brought in around $20,000 in two years.

Temporary quarters, it was decided, were to be located in the parsonage at Halfway Creek, and school opened 1 September 1861, with 11 students and two instructors. The parsonage was small and crowding was unavoidable, but things went well for a year. The school was then moved to Decorah, Iowa, and is now known as Luther College.

Shortly after the Civil War, there was a big Baptist revival among the Norwegians of this settlement. A large church was built in West Salem, and a great number of second baptisms were performed by immersion in every creek. But times changed, and those second-time sheep strayed back to the Lutheran church. The Baptist preacher, who once enjoyed such a big following, now sits and ruminates atop a ridge. Bereft of his sheep, he now raises pigs for a living.

This is one of the most rugged stretches of ground in the U.S. upon which Norwegians have ever settled. The soil is good. With the exception of a few of the oldest farms, the roads through this area are so sharp and overhanging that a traveler sits in his carriage wondering whether everything isn't going to tumble headfirst. But here people take their time, sowing and plowing, using a stubborn plow that turns the furrow down with the slope, backward and forward.

With equal modesty it can be said that there is little interest in spiritual affairs here, and none of the young people have left to pursue higher studies. Their outlook on life is still confined to the milk pail and pigpen, and the contribution of the settlement to any spiritual development is zero.

In the city of La Crosse, the Norwegians have played an important role since the first country store was built. Two Norwegians came here as early as 1850—Ole Knudsen, a blacksmith from Drammen (and brother of Knud Knudsen of Wiota), and John Halverson, a wagon-maker from Ringsaker.

The most prominent pioneer in La Crosse, however, was Mons Anderson from Valdres, who settled here in 1851.

27

Black River Falls, Jackson County, western Wisconsin

(Source: De Norske Settlementers Historie, by Hjalmar Rued Holand, translated by Malcolm Rosholt, 1908, pp. 290–292)

Black River Falls is an old city, located at the site of an old sawmill built around 1840. Many newcomers learned to scale lumber here.

The first Norwegian known to have visited the Falls was Martin Madsen from Gausdal, who came here in 1848. He is also considered the first Norseman west of the blackish stream called Black River.

Madsen worked two years in a sawmill. There was not a bit of cultivated land for 50 miles around, and provisions for men and animals had to be hauled in. It occurred to him that he could make more money following a plow than pushing planks.

In 1850, Madsen left the mill and moved several miles southwest, where he began to clear a piece of ground among the scrub oaks and jack pines. Soon the sun began to shine into a small clearing. Although the land was sandy and stony and still covered with stumps, it was good enough to grow potatoes and hay.

This was before the machine age had advanced very far, and there was not a steel plow to be had. Madsen, however, used his wits and made a wooden plow, borrowed horses and barged through both stones and roots. It was not long before he had potatoes and hay to sell. And prices were so good that he scarcely dared mention the matter to others, for fear there would be a flood of immigrants to his new Eldorado.

But as time went on, other Norwegians came to find work at the mill and soon followed Madsen's lead.

The first among them to make a claim was Jacob Hanson Stiga from Ringebu, who came in 1854. He was a leader among old pioneers and, in fact, was the cause of the big movement of immigrants to this area from Ringebu in Norway.

Martin Madsen's brother, Torstein Madsen, together with his son-in-law, Ingebret Enerson Bøe, arrived in 1856. Others arriving at the same time included:
- Hans Gilbertson, Ringebu
- Anders Gilbertson, Ringebu
- Elan Peterson, Sør-Fron
- Andreas A. Prestemoen, Sør-Fron

Not long after these people arrived, they were favored by a visit from Pastor H. A. Stub in 1856—a festive occasion. Stub was at this time the pastor at Coon Prairie.

He had learned that some of his old acquaintances had moved into Trempealeau Valley. He left in August, following the Black River upstream to see whether he might find a road through the hills to Trempealeau Valley. A few miles south of Black River Falls, he had a runaway in which his buggy was damaged and one of his horses injured.

He saw a pioneer shanty a short distance ahead and was amazed to find Norwegians here—actually, he had found the home of Martin Madsen. The pastor decided to have holy worship services that same evening, and invitations were sent out to the other settlers busy cutting brush in the neighborhood. Fifty years later, Pastor Stub tells about this occasion that he calls "one of the most remarkable experiences in my life."

Said he: "On my first journey to

Trempealeau Valley, which was made on a hot summer day in 1856, I arrived at twilight at the little log house of Martin Madsen. An extraordinary event occurred, a blessing in disguise, in which an accident had brought me to those few Norwegian families living in the wilderness around Black River Falls.

"I conducted worship services with baptism and communion, and at midnight when we were finished, a terrible storm came up that prevented anyone from leaving. We all spent the night together, both pastor and congregation resting on straw spread over the floor—a delightful evening, but no sleep!"

This little group, for the first time in America given the means of grace that night, became the first fruits of that big congregation now (in 1908) celebrating its 50th anniversary. Martin Madsen's little log house has become the foundation of that fine church whose spires point to heaven. *[A footnote by Holand: "In a letter to Trempealeau congregation dated 18 April 1907, Pastor Stub twice states that this event occurred in May 1857."]*

It is not known whether any congregation was organized at the time Stub visited these people, but Professor J. A. Frich relates that he found an orderly congregation when he began to visit the settlement in 1862. But no records could be found until Pastor Ole Waldeland was called here in 1866.

During the period from 1856 to 1866, there were scarcely any immigrants. But after the Civil War a new wave of emigration from Norway began, made up almost entirely of *Gudbrandsdøler*. There are now in the city of Black River Falls and surrounding area about 2,000 of these people, about equally divided with former residents of Ringebu. Almost all of the Fron people live in the city.

Andreas Prestemoen was chiefly responsible for bringing the majority of Fron people to America. He could always spare some money and made arrangements with an agent of the steamship company to facilitate passage.

Rosy descriptions of America's opportunities were sent to all his former neighbors in Norway and tickets for those who wanted to come. If they did not have the money, Prestemoen would help out, although the interest on the loan was not exactly what one would call cheap. Nevertheless, Black River Falls was definitely the Mecca for Sør-Fron people.

28

Trempealeau Valley and surroundings, Trempealeau County, western Wisconsin

(Source: De Norske Settlementers Historie, by Hjalmar Rued Holand, translated by Malcolm Rosholt, 1908, pp. 293–297)

The people in Trempealeau Valley for whom Pastor Stub was looking when he accidentally ran into the *Gudbrandsdøler* south of Black River Falls in 1856 or 1857 were some *Telemarkinger* from Kviteseid, whom he had earlier known in Muskego. These people had made their way to the valley in July 1854 and included the following:
• Mrs. Hegge Anderson Lunden (a widow) and her four sons—Ole Heggeson, Knut Heggeson (the older), Gunder Heggeson and Knut Heggeson (the younger)
• Mrs. Turi Svinnungsen Tyttegraff (a widow) with sons Johannes Tyttegraff and Peter Tyttegraff
• Mrs. Gro Johnson Nichols (a widow) with three sons, Johannes Nichols, Ole Nichols and Gunder Nichols
• Gunleik Olson Storlie and his family
The sons of the widows were mostly teen-agers.

This group left Muskego in the spring of 1854 and traveled first to Bad Axe in Vernon County where Gunleik Olson and other former neighbors from Norway had settled. But the terrain around Bad Axe is not very inviting, and it failed to please the widows, who were looking for land. They decided to go on.

Gunleik Olson, who already had a small house on a hillside, was not impressed with his present situation, either. He asked the widows to wait for him three days, whereupon he went away and traded his 40 acres of land for 20 head of cattle, large and small.

After a long and tedious journey through wild and forbidding country, the party finally reached Trempealeau Valley, where the scenery was beautiful. All decided to settle here on land about three miles east of the present village of Blair. In making this decision, Gunleik Olson became the first white settler in Trempealeau County. The three widows settled a short distance to the east but across the range line in Jackson County.

Joining the community in 1855 were the following:
• Bjorgø Olson, Telemark
• Jacob Tønneson Lavold, Flekkefjord
• Peter Tønneson Lavold, Flekkefjord
• Salve Tønneson Lavold, Flekkefjord
• Nils Halverson from Hetland near Egersund

This neighborhood developed into the center of the community, stretching in all directions. For some years, thousands of Norwegians passed through here to settle in the surrounding valleys. However, there were not so many *Telemarkinger* among them, The most important group to settle here were the *Solunger*. This is now the biggest settlement of people from Solør in the U.S., with not fewer than 2,000 around the present village of Blair. Teppen Valley, Tromp Valley, Salve Valley, Vose Valley and the village of Blair are made up almost entirely of *Solunger*.

The first of the Solør people to arrive were Ole Olsen Teppen, Syver Iverson and Iver Iverson, originally from Vaaler. They had spent several years making a miserable living in Ole Bull's famous colony in Pennsylvania, which for the most part was supported by *Solunger*. They arrived in Trempealeau

Valley in 1858; Teppen Valley is named for Ole Olsen Teppen.

In 1859, Tosten Torrison Forkerud and Helge Opland, both *Solunger* who had also left Ole Bull's Oleana colony, arrived in Tromp Valley. Tjeran Thompson from Valestrand was the first to settle in this valley in 1858.

Pastor H. A. Stub organized the Trempealeau Valley congregation in May 1857. It is the oldest congregation for some distance north of Black River Falls, although a church was not built here before 1868.

To the south of the *Solunger* lies the charming Beaver Creek, with its 2,000 people from Hardanger. Iver Øriansen Torblaa and Iver Knudsen Syse came first. They had spent some time on Koshkonong and arrived in Beaver Creek in 1857. Letters were sent to friends and in 1858 many followed them, including from Hardanger:
• Knut Hallanger
• Amund Olson Haaheim
• Knud Rikoldsen
• Thomas Herreid
• Nils Herreid
• Ole Nilsen Skaar
• Simon Nilsen
• Tosten T. Ringøen
• Nils Haldorson (Nils Henderson)
• Lars Hanson
• Ole Ellingson
• Ørians Torblaa
• Ole Iverson Dale

In addition, there were Erik Gree from Voss and Nils Økland from Stavanger. These people took claims in the upper end of Beaver Creek Valley, as the lower end between Ettrick and Hegg, which is now the best land, was then too soft to work.

Pastor Nils O. Brandt organized a congregation in Beaver Creek in November 1858. He had been visiting in Trempealeau Valley, and Ørians Torblaa brought him to Beaver Creek across the high ridges. There was no road across the hills, but Torblaa drove quite unconcerned up and down the steep hills, while Brandt sat in the wagon box, begging his host to take it easy.

A church was built here in 1861, probably the first in the entire western part of the state. For a fee of $4, a Swede who owned an excellent stand of timber permitted the members of the congregation to cut all they needed for the church.

The entire congregation went into the forest, competing with one another to chop down the trees. The church, the dimensions of which were 24 by 30 by 12 feet, stood in the upper end of Beaver Creek, just inside the Jackson County line. Sjur Herreid now uses this historic building for a dwelling house.

Among other early arrivals to Beaver Creek Valley were the following:
• Henrik Svendsen
• Arne Arneson
• Torkel Gunderson Bergo with sons Haldor Torkelson and Iver Torkelson
• Torkel Haldorson and family

They came in 1859, most of them from the vicinity of Lodi, Wisconsin, where they had once formed part of an important settlement of people from Hardanger.

Joining the Beaver Creek settlement in 1860 was K. K. Hagestad, a member of the council of the old Norwegian Synod, and long considered the most distinguished and gifted man in the community.

Below Ettrick, two big valleys join the main valley of Beaver Creek. These are French Creek on the right and South Beaver Creek on the left. Mainly people from Biri and Land in Oppland fylke, of which there are more than 2,000 in Hardies Creek and Abrahams Valley, populate these two valleys.

The first to begin farming in these valleys was Per Anderson Hogden from Vardal, who settled here in 1850. The land he occupied is presently part of the Lutheran parsonage. He then moved to Trempealeau Valley, where he lived for three years. In 1859 he moved to French Creek. He finally left for Dakota

Territory in 1874, where he became one of the first settlers in Traill County (North Dakota).

In 1859, Hogden's brothers, Johannes Hogden and Andreas Hogden, arrived in French Creek. In 1860, Ole Gilbertson Glopstuen, the first man from Biri, arrived. Two others from Biri who came that year were Gulbrand Nilsen and Hans Smestuen. Both settled in South Beaver Creek.

Early pioneers to Hardies Creek included the following from Biri:
• Martinus Scarseth
• Ole Semb
• Martinus Grythe
• Kristian Hoff
• Gulbrand Ekern
• Andreas Ekern

Things were really wild these first years, deer mingling with the cattle and wolves all over the hills. But the ridges were treeless, and people went north into the "big forest" to steal kitchen wood. Valdres people later settled this forest area.

Today, all the ridges are tree-covered, and the valleys, especially French Creek, are extremely beautiful and pleasant. One is constantly reminded that this is a Norwegian community by the sonorous names painted on the mailboxes. In Hardies Creek, there is not one name that ends in "son." In French Creek, one finds names like Enghagen, Smedhaugen, Nilestuen, Ofsdahl, Hogden, etc.

Northern Trempealeau and western Jackson counties were not developed for many years, although there are many nice valleys here. Pigeon Valley is one of the largest and richest valleys in the county, but was not settled until around 1870. It was essentially the treeless ridges and impossible roads to market that held up settlement in this area. There are now nearly 1,000 *Landinger* in Pigeon Valley. Hans Tangen and Hans Anderson Fremstad were among the first to arrive, the former in 1868 and the latter in 1870.

Peter Ekeren from Biri, a well-informed person, was also among the first settlers in Pigeon Valley, where he built a sawmill at Pigeon Falls in the early 1870s. He also developed a dairy farm and managed a big land office business. Wisconsin's talented young speaker of the assembly at Madison is a son of Even Ekeren, a brother to Peter.

The seven-mile stretch of road that lies between Pigeon Falls and Whitehall is one of the most heavily traveled in the entire Midwest. At Pigeon Falls, one runs into a series of heavily populated valleys. Most of the people trade in Whitehall, the nearest railroad station. The traffic is nearly all Norwegian.

The Norwegians also began to settle the Beef River Valley south of Strum and Eleva around 1870. Østen Johnson Dalen from Tolgen (Tolga) in Hedmark was the first; he came in the spring of 1867 to Johnson Valley, two miles south of Strum. The same year, Ole Olson, Aslak Olson and Andrew Olson from Telemark settled in Elk Creek, four miles south of Johnson.

Hellik Kjøntvedt from Tinn was the first to settle around Chimney Rock, where many *Tinndøler* have since made their homes. He arrived in 1864, but as the valleys in north Trempealeau County are narrow, boggy and sandy, this area was not developed until much later.

The Sogn people passed through this region some 12 or 14 years earlier and went about 40 miles farther northwest to the adjoining Buffalo County, where they founded a big settlement.

Norsk Sneploug

Parti af Hardanger Fjord

29

Lyster Colony in Buffalo County, western Wisconsin

(Source: De Norske Settlementers Historie, by Hjalmar Rued Holand, translated by Malcolm Rosholt, 1908, pp. 298–302)

Buffalo County lies in the western part of Wisconsin, bounded on its west line by the Mississippi River. Narrow valleys and sharp ridges that rise as high as 500 feet over the valley floors mark the entire county. The farms here are situated snuggly along the wooded slopes. The soil is good, and though the land is hard to work, the farmers are well-to-do.

In the northern part of the county lies a settlement of more than 3,000 Norwegians, of whom 90 percent are from Lyster (Luster) in Sogn. Most of them live in the area between Mondovi and Nelson, while a minority live about 10 miles southeast of Mondovi. The origin of this colony may be described as follows:

In the 1850s, many from Lyster (Luster) immigrated to Spring Dale and Blue Mounds in Dane County. Good land in this area was already dear and hard to find. After numerous consultations among themselves, it was agreed by the newcomers to send a man to the northwest to find and buy land. They delegated Ole Hanson Lerum from Lyster (Luster) for the mission.

Hanson left on foot in the spring of 1856, traveling far and wide, even as far west as the Minnesota prairie and north into Dunn County's forests. A couple of times he thought he had found a place meeting his specifications, and he went to the land office to make entry.

But in each instance the land speculators thwarted him. These leeches had a secret understanding with the agents of the government, and they frequented the land office to keep in touch. When they saw a farmer coming in to buy a certain piece of land, they quickly informed him that it had already been purchased, although the very fact that he was asking for it had raised its value.

This racket was quite common and a source of great vexation and harm to the honest land-seeker. However, Hanson finally purchased a large tract in Buffalo County and returned to Dane County.

The news of Ole Hanson's tour of exploration created a big stir among the people of Spring Dale. Some of the men took a day off to listen to what Hanson had to say. Not wishing to play down his own heroic role in the affair, Hanson went into great detail about his long journey on foot. He described all the fine land he had seen, of his meeting the Indians, of his involvement with the speculators, and about the wind and weather, the big forests and wide plains.

The question now arose among the people as to what they should take with them. Finally, after several weeks of preparation, their wagon caravan was ready to make a new track in the stream of immigration. The party consisted of:
• Ole Hanson Lerum and family
• Jens J. Hovland and family
• Arne Ottesen Sørheim
• Erik Alme
• Skak Ormsen Hauge

There were 13 persons all told. Their caravan consisted of four good wagons heavily loaded, five yoke of oxen, milk cows, sheep, pigs and chickens.

The party moved westerly out of Dane County along the old Military Road between Madison and Prairie du

Chien, crossed the Wisconsin River on a ferry, and drove up the narrow Kickapoo Valley to Coon Prairie. From there they continued north to Sparta and Black River Falls. From this point, for nearly a week they passed through a wilderness with unknown and lonesome valleys seemingly without end. Norwegians today populate all these valleys in Trempealeau County.

For days on end, they saw no sign of a human being, but had all the necessities of life in their wagons. They baked bread and cooked coffee, milked their cows and had fresh eggs for breakfast. Here and there they had to build a bridge or cut through the forest to make a road. The children drove the pigs and sheep, plucking flowers and wild berries and having a big time. And there were all kinds of partridge to shoot, too.

After reaching the northern part of Eau Claire County, the party turned west to Maxwell *[no longer listed on modern maps –Rosholt]* and finally reached the Norwegian Valley, their future home. They had been five weeks on the journey.

[Holand's directions here appear confused. If they turned west from the northern part of Eau Claire County, they would have gone into Dunn County. As it was Buffalo County where this party landed, it must have turned west from Trempealeau County. –Rosholt]

On 6 July 1856, the smoke rose from the first Norwegian fireplaces in Buffalo County. For the next two years, these were the only people for many miles around, with the exception of a big Indian camp in the same valley. At first the womenfolk were concerned about their safety, never knowing whether or not the Indians would sweep down and scalp them.

It is said that Jens Hovland was out walking on the high ridges and, looking down into the camp of the Indians, noted that there was an unusual number of them engaged in a dance, singing in high-pitched voices. This could only mean that they were on the warpath.

With troubled eyes, he hurried home, gathered the oxen and cattle, wife and children into the log cabin and barricaded the door. Then he stared hard through the cracks in the wall, ready to sell his life as dearly as possible. Hovland maintained this defensive posture a couple of days. But when no Indians appeared, he carefully opened the door and began to breathe again.

The Indians were peaceful Chippewa. Often in the evenings, after one of their hunting forays in the hills, they returned home, passing by the new settlers with venison or other game. They were anxious to bargain with this wild game for tobacco or syrup. Considerable haggling went on in sign language. Unlike other Indian tribes, the Chippewa were quite good at bringing back anything they borrowed, and when an iron kettle was returned, it was always filled with meat.

A menace much worse than the Indians was the wolves. Even now it is not possible to let the sheep stray into the woods. There were also many bears in the early days of settlement, and often they were quite troublesome, too.

Halvor Svenson, who lived near Lookout, was bothered for a time by a milk thief. Just as sure as anything, whenever his wife went into the cellar in the morning, she found her precious milk and cream basins empty. And what made her even angrier was the manner in which the thief fouled everything up.

It was not enough that he wasted the milk so that everyone had to drink black coffee, but the thief loused up the place so that it resembled a pigsty. The wife protested to her husband about this and Halvor, a mild sort of person, convinced one of his neighbors, a hunter, to stand watch over the cellar and give the thief a crack in the wing bone the next time he paid a visit.

The great hunter came and watched, but nothing happened for several nights. Then one morning, just as daylight was breaking, the hunter, nodding half asleep, suddenly heard a rumbling in the cellar. He softly moved forward until he could see through the open cellar door.

At that moment he almost forgot to shoot when he saw a powerful bear with his head in a milk pail held between two front paws. Luckily, the hunter recovered his senses, and when the bear looked up, he got the full force of the buckshot right between the eyes.

The wife of Endre Johnson could tell of another frightening experience. One evening she saw two creatures jumping around in the corn. Thinking they were the calves that had broken loose, she ran at them with a broom, shouting, "Get the hell out of here, you young critters!"

Suddenly two big bears stood up, and the woman nearly fainted. She started to scream so loud in her terror that the bears became frightened and loped away.

Two years after the first settlers came here, Jens Syverson arrived. He was also from Lyster (Luster). After that, the *Sogninger* kept coming until now the valleys are full of them.

All these farms, now situated so luxuriantly and peacefully in the valleys, were once covered with brush and trees. But with such big guns as Ole Hanson to take the lead, it was not long before a man had land for plowing. In harvest time, for example, Hanson could cut five acres of wheat a day with the cradle scythe.

The first congregation was organized here in 1866 and a church built the following year. For many years the entire community was one congregation, but then came predestination. The people of West Norway take their religion seriously, and when the big debate over predestination began, their emotions were aroused to fever pitch and concomitant bitterness.

The church was decorated with a hangman's noose as a warning to the opposition party not to enter God's temple, but the zeal of the opposition party was so great that they made their way into the church with the help of a wrecking bar. Brotherly love such as this was common in many other settlements as well.

The culture of these people still does not accord complete freedom of choice in this matter. But people's hearts are as kind as anywhere, and hospitality is unbounded. Peer Strømme *[he wrote a minor classic in Norse called How Strømme Became a Pastor –Rosholt]* was the resident pastor here for a year and a half. He recalls that though he had neither a cow nor chicken, he never went to town without butter or eggs to sell.

When he left here, he got so many fine wool stockings from the womenfolk, that he sold 20 pairs in St. Paul and still had enough to keep himself and family in socks for the next 15 years.

Rosendal

Et Telemarkshus

30
Chippewa Valley, northern Eau Claire and southern Chippewa Counties, western Wisconsin
(Source: De Norske Settlementers Historie, by Hjalmar Rued Holand, translated by Malcolm Rosholt, 1908, pp. 303–306)

The Norwegian communities in Trempealeau and Buffalo counties continue quite a distance into Eau Claire County. But here the land becomes sterile and uninviting. As a result, settlement was delayed until after 1870.

A large number of *Hallinger* now live in Drammen Township, the first to arrive being Knut Knutson from Gulbrandspladsen near Næs (Nes) in Hallingdal.

Just a few miles north of Drammen's town line, the Chippewa Valley begins. Here there are other, and older, colonies of Norwegians. On the left there is a settlement around Meridian that reaches north to Menomonie; on the right lies Eau Claire with its 7,500 Norwegians.

The first Norseman known to have explored and then settled in the Chippewa Valley was August Dahl from Trondheim, an engineer by trade. He worked for a lumber company in the early 1850s, rafting lumber down the Chippewa River. He is one of the few who rafted lumber on this dangerous river before the drives were halted owing to the many difficulties that had

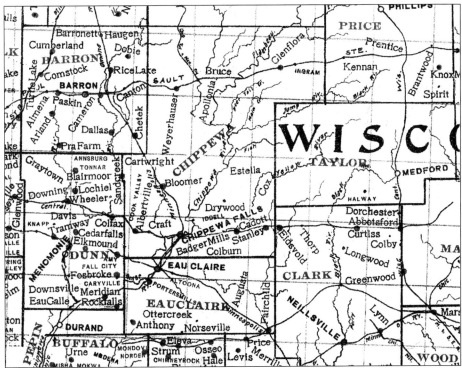

Gausta

to be overcome.

In 1854, Dahl took a claim on some land about 15 miles north of Chippewa Falls at Bloomer Prairie, where a Norwegian colony was later founded. For many years Dahl acted as a surveyor, and he is believed to have laid out the original plat of Chippewa Falls. Both he and his son, Anthony Dahl, were decorated for outstanding service in the Civil War.

In 1855, Dahl was on a lumber drive that took him down the Chippewa into the Mississippi and on to La Crosse.

Here he met some newcomers who were looking for advice on where to find land. Dahl told them about the wide bottomlands along the Chippewa River that were easy to cultivate and close to market by means of a steamboat that cruised up and down the river.

The leader among these land-seekers, Hans Torgerson Dahl, was from Nord-Fron. He and Torger Olson, also from Fron—together with Anders Fauske from Sør-Fron—went back up the Mississippi with their new guide, settling just east of the later village of Meridian *[actually a post office in east Dunn County on the Soo Line but now a ghost town – Rosholt]*. This was in the fall of 1855.

The following year, Ole Hanson Underdahl from Sør-Fron joined the new colony. These four men were all who came for many years.

In 1858, Ole Torgerson Dahl from Nord-Fron arrived with his sons Ole Torgerson, Amund Torgerson and Iver Torgerson. Ole and Amund settled in Little Elk Creek, where a Lutheran congregation was organized the same year.

Meridian is noted for the many people who came here from Skjaak, Oppland fylke. The first was probably Ole Lund, who had lived some years in Eau Claire and moved to Meridian during the Civil War. Ole Bruden was also one of the first in Meridian. He later visited Norway, and many from around Skjaak, Oppland fylke, returned with him to the U.S.—although Eau Claire was usually the first stop to find work before moving to Meridian. Peder Gilbertson Jevne came from Skiaker in 1870, just about the time that the colony at Meridian was getting started.

On the north side of the Chippewa River there are only Trøndelag people. Among the first of these was Martinius Olson from Inderøen *[the modern Inderøy, an island in Trondheimsfjorden –Rosholt]*. He arrived in 1868, and Jon J. Børseth from Trondheim came about the same time.

This settlement, with a population of some 1,500 *Trønderne*, stretches, with small intervals, all the way to Menomonie—an old assembly point for the people from Trondheim. A sawmill was built here in the early 1850s and many Norwegian emigrants, especially from Trøndelag, worked here.

It was from here that Abercrombie settlement, oldest and richest in North Dakota, drew its first and largest influx of settlers. *[Lieut. Col. John J. Abercrombie built the first military post in Dakota Territory in 1857, some distance south of the present city of Fargo. –Rosholt]*

There are still many old-timers shuffling around the mills in Menomonie who, as youngsters, helped to bring some of their friends and fellow workers in Menomonie to America— some of whom are now small kings in the Red River Valley.

Eau Claire

Eau Claire with its 7,500 Norwegians (1908) is the northernmost point of that widespread settlement described in the foregoing pages. Thousands of Scandinavians have worked in the city and later bought farms in the surrounding hills. The city was also for many years the main marketplace for these early settlers.

The first Norwegian to work in the city, if memories of older people can be trusted, was a Mrs. Rud, who was married to an American and operated a boarding house. She was already there in 1855 when Torger Olson of Meridian first visited the future city.

There were only three small huts at the time. The outlying hills, which are now all built up, were covered with blueberries, which Mrs. Rud picked for her hungry boarders. Small oak trees grew in abundance, and through these trees there went a crooked lane that served for a road. Lots on Barstow Street sold for $10.

It is difficult to reconstruct a history of the first Norwegians in Eau Claire, because most of them worked here for a few years and then moved on. Probably the first to arrive was Ole Lund from Skiaker, who came around 1860 and, in fact, still lives there (1908).

Pastor Amund Johnson, a quiet-spoken, folksy person who was always helpful, organized a Lutheran congregation. Whenever he returned from the city, he carried all kinds of packages for members of his congregation who lived 20 or 30 miles out.

Big-Paul settles down

One of the men who has lived longest in Eau Claire is without doubt Paul Brandstad from Fron in Gudbrandsdal, who came in 1868. He is one of the leading personalities in the city in more ways than one.

As someone has written: "Whenever we are traveling and the conversation turns to Eau Claire, one of the first questions asked by former residents is: 'Does Big-Paul still live?'

"The present generation in the city knows him as the trusted policeman, Mr. Brandstad, but for those who knew the city more than a score of years ago, he was 'Big-Paul'—a champion whose giant strength and deeds were known all over.

"When he came to the city in 1868, there were many small sawmills, and it was about this time that the Norwegians began to arrive. This was a rough-and-tumble period that continued well into the 1870s.

"Most of the early mill workers were Irishmen from Canada—the 'Canadian Irish.' Then the Norwegian lads moved in and began to squeeze the Irish out of the mills and logging camps, because the Norwegians were easier to get along with and were better liked. These youngsters made good money and, forgetting the cares of tomorrow, especially in spring when they came out of the woods, they frequently engaged the Irishmen in knock-down, drag-out fights.

"Brandstad was named policeman the first time in 1876, and there are many stories told about how he went into the saloons and threw out the troublemakers. Both Norwegians and Irish came to regard him as a common enemy, and it was lucky that he was a powerful man. There probably never was a more diligent policeman." *[Holand fails to give the source of this quotation. –Rosholt]*

The largest Norwegian Lutheran congregation in the U.S. is now (1908) located in Eau Claire, with nearly 2,000 souls. For a number of years, Pastor Gerhard Høyme, first president of the United Lutheran Synod, served it.

Fra Kristiania Omegn

31
First Norwegians in Iowa and Minnesota
(Source: De Norske Settlementers Historie, by Hjalmar Rued Holand, translated by Malcolm Rosholt, 1908, pp. 320–329)

No fewer than 400,000 Norwegians, a third of all Norwegians in America, live in Minnesota. It is therefore the most Norwegian state in the Union. Its large population is a direct result of Cleng Peerson's founding of the Fox River colony in northern Illinois in 1833.

The three principal needs of the pioneers were wood, water and hayland. When no more land was available that met their specifications around Fox River, the newcomers began to look elsewhere. As most of Illinois was without trees, the early Norwegians moved north into Wisconsin. From here the movement of migration went northwest from woodland to woodland, across the Mississippi River, through the northeast corner of Iowa and into southern Minnesota.

A number of colonies in Minnesota stemmed from Fox River, but most were founded by men from Rock Prairie (Luther Valley) *[in Rock County, Wisconsin –Rosholt]*, the first offshoot of Fox River settlement and, with the possible exception of Koshkonong, the mother colony of more Norwegian settlements than any other.

A small settlement was founded in 1840 in the southeast tip of Iowa near the present Keokuk. But these Norsemen were Mormon converts and left with Brigham Young's following to Utah in 1846. This colony had no influence on later immigration to Iowa and has long ceased to exist.

Aside from this beginning, the real tide of Norwegian immigration to Iowa got under way in 1849 and to Minnesota in 1852, although a few Norsemen had found their way to these states earlier. Here, as in Wisconsin, the people from Numedal were first—namely, Ole Halvorson Valle and Ole Tollefson Kittilsland. To the astonishment of the Indians, these men came gliding across the plains on skis in the early spring of 1843 en route to Fort Atkinson in Winneshiek County.

As a well-meaning Irishman who was a little confused in his geography put it: "The first two white men in Winneshiek County were two Norwegians who came clear from the Old Country on a pair of snow shoes."

From the first visit of Valle and Kittilsland may be traced the beginning of several of the largest Norwegian communities in Iowa. Both Valle (born 21 November 1821) and Kittilsland, who originated in Rollag, Numedal, came to Rock Prairie in 1841. There, they worked in the lead mines around Dodgeville for about a year.

They then learned that workmen were needed in Fort Atkinson, an Army base in the southern part of Winneshiek County, Iowa, activated by the government to handle Indian affairs. And it was to this Army post that our *Numedøler* traveled on skis in the early spring of 1843, finding work at $12 per month.

One of the reasons leading to the establishment of a fort in Winneshiek County was the federal government's intention to teach the Indians to become agriculturists, build homes and cease their nomadic life. Valle and Kittilsland were employed to plow the ground for the Indians. They recalled that they plowed many pieces of land through the rolling hills where the city of Decorah was later platted. In 1846, Ole Valle left his job at Fort Atkinson but got an acquaintance, Søren Olson Sørum from Sør-Land, to take his place.

Olson actually came to Rock Prairie in 1843. In order to get to the U.S., he made an agreement with Peter Gaarder, who was also leaving, to work three years for him at Rock Prairie to cover the cost of tickets. When this rather expensive passage money was redeemed, Valle left for Fort Atkinson, where he worked for four years. In 1847 he learned that a cousin, Ingeborg Nilsen, had arrived at the fort.

In 1848, the government gave up trying to civilize the Indians and decided to move the tribe 300 miles north into Minnesota, to a location near present-day Long Prairie in Todd County. *[Long Prairie lies about 50 air miles northwest of St. Cloud. The Indians were mostly of the Winnebago tribe, formerly located in southeastern Wisconsin. –Rosholt]* Ole Tollefson, his wife and Ingeborg Nilsen were hired as cooks for this migration of Indians.

Søren Olson, meanwhile, took time off to transport a pastor's family to St. Paul, where he remained until the head of the family returned from a trip to the East. As far as is known, these four Norwegians were the first to visit and live in Minnesota.

In the fall of 1848, after Søren Olson was released from his employment with the pastor's family in St. Paul, he went to Long Prairie. Here, all four of the above-named Norwegians lived for two years.

This would be a good time to bring up the romantic episode involving Søren Olson and Ingeborg Nilsen and their first love way out there on the Minnesota prairie, surrounded by melancholy Indians, nearly 400 miles from the nearest pioneer shanty. But we must pass over this tempting subject with a recommendation to a future novelist and only add that they were married as soon as they got back to the company of white men in 1850.

Meanwhile, in 1846, Ole Valle and his wife moved 35 miles southeast into Clayton County, Iowa, where they began to farm. They were the first to settle in the northern part of the state as agriculturists.

St. Paul named territorial capital

The next Scandinavian to visit Minnesota was Pastor C. L. Clausen. Although a Dane by birth, he was usually considered a Norwegian. He was, at the time, working in the interest of the Norwegians on a mission to find a suitable area for the hard-pressed members of his congregation on Rock Prairie. He arrived in St. Paul on the first steamboat to reach this far north in the spring of 1849.

This same boat brought the long-awaited news that Minnesota had been granted territorial status. At the time, the town scarcely had more than 4,000 inhabitants. Most of them were trappers and township squatters, with scarcely an honest-to-goodness farmer among them.

St. Paul had about 30 houses, inhabited mostly by French half-breeds who hoped to get rich by the sale of town lots in the event that St. Paul was named the state capital of the territory. There was therefore terrific excitement among the fortune hunters, who were anxious to learn what the outcome of the decision might be on the territorial issue.

Pastor Clausen relates that despite a dark night and bad weather, the entire population was down to meet the steamboat. The rain fell heavily and lightning flashed, but everyone who could walk or crawl swarmed over the boat, hungry for news. Shortly, the important news was released and a great shout went up, repeated on shore and back across the hills. Minnesota was now a territory and St. Paul its capital.

The immediate surroundings of St. Paul are not especially attractive to a discerning man of the soil, and Pastor C. L. Clausen found nothing here that pleased him. He liked the area where

Minneapolis is located much better, with its rolling prairies and beautiful tree-lined lakes.

But the prairie here was too small for a big settlement, and the land is quite sandy. Therefore, Clausen did not become the father of one of these two big cities. Instead, he went east into Wisconsin, as described earlier, where he founded a big settlement in Pierce and St. Croix counties.

Minnesota's first Norse settlers

That same year, 1849, Nils Nilsen reached St. Paul. He was destined to become the first Norwegian settler in Minnesota. Born on 2 January 1830, on Klægstad farm in Modum, he came to the U.S. in 1849. After spending some time in the lead mines around Galena, he found work with an American farmer in the neighborhood of Decorah, Iowa.

In the late summer of 1849, a man arrived from Prescott, Wisconsin, on an errand to buy some small pigs. Nils Nilsen accompanied the buyer back to Prescott as a teamster on one of the loads of pigs. From Prescott, he went by foot to St. Paul, where he found work as a hostler in the stable called "Moffett's Castle," a pioneer hotel that stood on the slope about where Union Station is located *[and farther east from the new capital –Rosholt]*.

Nilson recalls that the business of the hotel could not have been very profitable, as he could have bought the entire property, including a 40 of land, for $200. But he continued until the spring of 1850, at which time he went over to Stillwater and found work in McCusick's sawmill. Here he also served as a hostler for McCusick and somehow or other got to be known as "Nils McCusick." Old-timers still remember him best by this name.

While he worked for McCusick, he slept in the barn and on one occasion nearly lost his life as a result of a landslide. The land slipped from an overhanging hill and buried the barn with its two- and four-footed inmates under an avalanche of sand. The barn was heavily damaged, but luckily Nils McCusick escaped injury. He continued with various jobs around Stillwater until 1882, when he purchased a big farm near New York Mills (Minnesota).

Finally, the first Norwegian woman to find a home in Minnesota was also making her way here. Her name was Ingeborg Leversdatter Langeberg. She arrived in St. Paul in 1850, accompanied by her brother. They were originally from Hallingdal and had lived for a time on Rock Prairie.

Amund Langeberg remained in St. Paul only three months and later became one of Worth County's pioneers in Iowa. But his sister found work as a hired girl in the household of Territorial Governor Alexander Ramsey.

In 1851 she went to Fridley, a small village newly platted a short distance above St. Anthony Falls. In 1854 she married an American named Clark. Ten years later she was married a second time, to Mikkel Johnson, one of the founders in 1857 of the *Trønderne* settlement in Meeker County. In 1864, she moved to north Minneapolis, where her presence led to the founding of a big Selbu colony in this part of the city.

Late in the fall of 1850, we come to the next Norwegians to visit Minnesota. Also from Rock Prairie, they were Halvor H. Peterson Haugen and Østen Burtness, both *Numedøler*, who had worked in a copper mine at Mineral Point (Wisconsin) but decided to move closer to St. Paul. There were no towns between La Crosse and St. Paul, and the steamboat stopped only to take on provisions and cordwood.

At one of these stops, in the middle of the night a man named Snow, a licensed Indian trader who wanted to build a trading post, offered jobs to Peterson and Burtness. They accepted, and Peterson did the masonry for the foundation. The completed building became the first store in Red Wing, Minnesota.

The following year (1851), Burtness went to St. Paul, where he disappeared. Peterson, meanwhile, had gone into business with Snow and built a lime-burning factory. As the enterprise appeared to be doing well, Peterson returned to Rock Prairie to recruit more help. Those who went with him were his father, in addition to the following:
• Steiner Valle, Numedal
• Sven Hanson, Numedal
• Guul Guttormson, Valdres
• Johan Peterson Ringdahl, Faaberg
• Matthias Peterson Ringdahl, Faaberg

Guttormson, incidentally, was the first to leave from Valdres for America in 1843.

Through the summer and fall of 1851, these men continued to work in the lime factory. A firm in St. Paul took all they could make, but it was extremely slow about making payments. Although the business outlook still seemed favorable, it came as a big disappointment when the company went bankrupt in the late fall of 1851.

Luckily for Peterson and his associates from Rock Prairie, they still owned a yoke of oxen, and with these they drove to Stillwater. There, they sold the oxen and divided the proceeds. But this money did not go very far.

During the time that these men were working in what later became the city of Red Wing, they had an experience that nearly cost them their lives.

One night when they had been out having a good time around Red Wing's romantic hills, they came upon an Indian camp, located below the hill where the Lutheran Ladies Seminary now stands (1908). All was quiet at the camp, and not even one of the many dogs found in all Indian camps reported the presence of the strangers.

Close to the path they were following was a wigwam. Through an opening in the door, a soft light shimmered. One of them, filled with curiosity, had to peek through the opening. To his astonishment, he saw an Indian squaw lying flat on the ground, feet toward the fire, stark naked. As a joke, he could not resist the temptation of picking up a glowing coal and throwing it at her.

This is something he should never have done, because in a moment the entire camp was in a hubbub, people shouting and dogs barking. In the confusion and under cover of darkness, the other Norwegians escaped into the night, but the jokester found the entire pack of Indians on his heels and ran for a couple of miles farther than he had ever run before. Finally, dead tired and dazed, he fell on his head into a small creek but had sense enough to stay there until the dogs lost his tracks.

Had any of the whites been captured, there is no doubt that the Indians would have made short work of them.

In the spring of 1852, the government opened for settlement 11 million acres of land purchased from the Indians. This included Goodhue County (Minnesota) and offered a wonderful opportunity for anyone to begin farming in the best agricultural county in the state.

But the people in Red Wing more or less agreed that the land around them would never be cultivated for another hundred years. Deeply dejected over their lost time and money, our Norwegian charcoal-burners returned to Rock Prairie. *[Here Holand forgets that he had them driving to Stillwater with a yoke of oxen first. –Rosholt]*

Only one of the Norwegians in this group remained in Goodhue County— namely, Matthias Peterson Ringdahl, who after a time began farming near the present city of Zumbrota. By this move, he became the first Norwegian settler in the county. Halvor H. Peterson Haugen, a well-known pioneer, now lives in retirement at Alta, Iowa.

In the same year (1852), a Norwegian named Ole Bergesen made his way as far north as St. Cloud, where he became the first white settler in Stearns County. All that is known about him is that he followed the government surveyors through the woods and swamps until they reached the area of St. Cloud, which he liked, thus becoming the first settler in the future city. The following year he sold his property and disappeared.

[A footnote by Holand: "In the first number of Norske Selskabs Ovartalskrift, Earl Hanson describes a Norwegian who earlier in the 1850s is believed to have made a pre-emptive claim on the entire Nicollet Island (an island in the Mississippi River at Minneapolis). Later, Hanson states that he sold the island to a Mr. Eastman for $500. It has been impossible for me to find any grounds for this assertion. The city's earliest address books do not mention any Norwegians. Further, the records on Nicollet Island suggest that others have always owned it. It would be useful, however, if this matter could be cleared up once and for all."]

The first Norwegian farmer to settle in Minnesota in 1851 was Even Ellertsen Dahl, a man originally from Sandøkedal near Kragerø *[the modern Sannidal –Rosholt]*. He may have been the first man to leave these parts, as he had already reached Muskego in 1843 and was among the people who helped build old Muskego church. He also helped to haul lumber for Bøvre church on Koshkonong, where he lived for a time. *[Bøvre church, now discontinued, once stood about two miles west of Ithaca in Dane County. It never was a large congregation, and its dwindling members finally joined a church in Stoughton. –Rosholt]*

In the summer of 1851, Even Dahl came to Looking Glass Prairie, an unusually beautiful landscape in the northern part of Winneshiek County, Iowa. At this time there were no settlers north of Decorah, but Dahl took a claim at the north end of the prairie just across the state line in Minnesota's Fillmore County. Here he built a comfortable house where hundreds of poor land-seekers were hospitably received. Later, many of these settlers returned to buy flour and wheat seed, which he sold them for little or nothing as long as the supply lasted.

Although he had a farm as good as anyone could find in Minnesota, Dahl was not entirely satisfied. His neighbors were for the most part Americans, and it was also a long distance to a Norwegian church.

In 1856 he sold his place for $4,000 and moved to Highland Prairie, 15 miles farther north in the same county where his sons had found land the year before. In a few years, a country village was platted on his property, which at Dahl's suggestion got the name "Bratsberg," after the *amt* of the same name in Norway where most of the people in the neighborhood originated. *[Holand here uses the word "amt" for an administrative district, which was correct when he wrote. The designation was changed in 1918 to "fylke," and Bratsberg was changed to Telemark. –Rosholt]*

A man without ostentation, quiet, helpful and well-informed, Even Ellertson was an exemplary neighbor and the mainstay of work in the local church. There was great sadness when he died.

Paa Sæteren

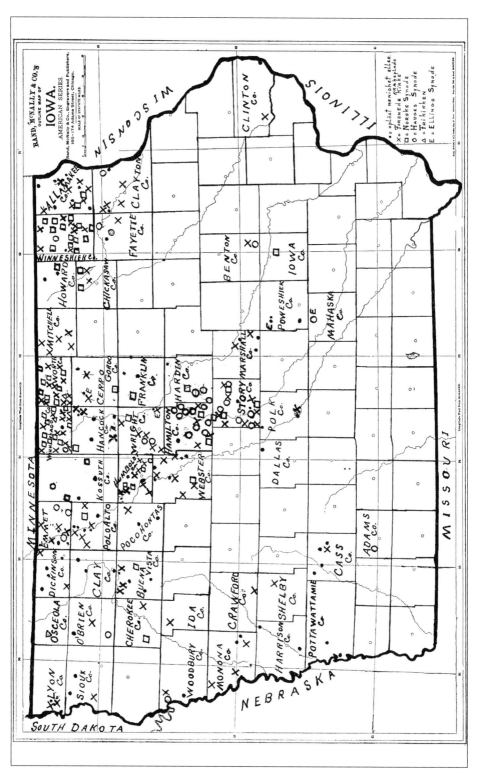

32

Clayton and Allamakee Counties, northeastern Iowa

(Source: De Norske Settlementers Historie, by Hjalmar Rued Holand, translated by Malcolm Rosholt, 1908, pp. 330–336)

As mentioned earlier, in 1846, Ole Halverson Valle went to Clayton County, Iowa, to begin farming. This date marks the beginning of Clayton County history as well as the history of Norwegians in Iowa.

Valle's farm lies about three miles southeast from St. Olaf on the south side of Bowman's Grove. A German named Bill Schmidt now owns the place. It was here that Jorund Halvorson was born, 20 September 1846, the first white child in Clayton County and the first Norwegian born in the northern part of Iowa. She now (1908) lives in the village of St. Olaf and is married to Lars Thovson from Gausdal.

The Valle farm was originally purchased as a partnership between Valle and Ole T. Kittilsland. When the latter, together with Søren Olson, came to Clayton County in 1850, Valle turned the farm over to Kittilsland and took another piece of land lying half a mile south of the village of St. Olaf. Both of these farm homes became stopping places for the many Norwegians from Wisconsin looking for land.

Meanwhile, other Norwegians were arriving in Clayton County. After Ole Valle was comfortably settled, he wrote to Ole Herbrandsen, an acquaintance on Koshkonong and a fellow *Numedøler*, about his new home. He explained that Clayton County was a better place to live than Koshkonong because it was not far from market (20 miles to McGregor, while in Koshkonong people had 75 miles to travel to Milwaukee). *[McGregor lies on the west bank of the Mississippi River opposite Prairie du Chien. –Rosholt].* There were also good mills in the area, and the soil and terrain could not be faulted.

Ole Herbrandsen visited Valle in 1848. Well satisfied with conditions, he returned to settle here, presumably in May 1849.

Before he left Koshkonong, he informed Tollev Helgeson, another *Numedøler* and future settler in Clayton County, about the land in Iowa. Helgeson then wrote his brother-in-law, Halvor Nilsen at Rock Prairie, about the prospects, and he, too, prepared to join up. With the arrival of Nilsen in Clayton County, the big migration of *Hallinger* to this county got under way.

Halvor Nilsen Espeseth was a man who enjoyed power and left a respectable legacy after him. He arrived in the U.S. from Hallingdal in 1846, accompanied by his parents and family of nine. On the family's arrival in Milwaukee, they had one dollar left,

and none could speak a word of English. But they were intent on reaching Rock Prairie. Leaving their baggage behind, they took off on foot, carrying a copper kettle and some coffee beans, still clad in their Halling mountain clothes. The youngest children had to be carried part of the way, but all reached their destination 85 miles away.

On 11 June 1849, Halvor Nilsen and family, together with Knut Hustad, Embret Skarshaug and Ole Søndo, reached the farm of Ole Valle, but were not particularly impressed with the land there. They continued 20 miles farther west, where they began farming in the neighborhood of Clermont *[Fayette County –Rosholt]*.

The departure of this party from Rock Prairie created quite a sensation and was soon followed by others.

The same summer, on 2 July, Abraham Olson Rustad with his large family joined the settlement, in addition to Jens Anderson Holt and Brede Anderson Holt. These people were the first to leave for the U.S. from Hadeland. The settlement now includes about 800 from Hallingdal, 600 from Numedal and 600 from Hadeland.

Tallak Gunderson and family, and Bertil Osuldson, both families from Ombli near Arendal in Norway, also arrived in 1849. Gunderson had a two-wheeled cart with oxen that he traded with an Irishman for his claim. These two families settled in the neighborhood of Clermont.

In 1850 many new settlers augmented the eastern part of the settlement. Among them were Ole Valle's brother, Lars Halverson, and the well-known pioneer from among Numedal people, Hellik Glaim. Others included Torkel Eiteklep and Ansten K. Blækkestad, all from Numedal. Another man, Helge Larson Ramstad from Sigdal, also came that year. He remained with Ole Valle over the winter before building his own place where Norway church now stands.

Ole Embrigtson Grønhovd, Lars Embrigtson Grønhovd and Peter Helgeson from Sigdal also came in 1850, as well as Knut Jæger and Ole Gunbjørnson (Ole Brownson) from Hallingdal.

Among other well-known pioneers who came later were Ole Olson Wold and the Grøth family, which included old Halstein Grøth and several sons, Kittil Halsteinson, Sever Halsteinson, Ole Halsteinson, Assor Halsteinson, Torkel Halsteinson, Svein Halsteinson and Johannes Halsteinson.

A few weeks after Halvor Nilsen settled near Clermont, he and his brothers, Torkel Nilsen and Haakon Nilsen, left to dig for gold in California. They drove with oxen straight across the continent.

Halvor was especially fortunate in this enterprise. After two years he returned to Clayton County, where he purchased around 700 acres of land. In 1867, he purchased 5,373 acres in Big Sioux Valley in the region of the present city of Beloit, Wisconsin *[in the extreme southern corner of the state –Rosholt]*.

The following year he personally led a party of 30 Norwegian families from Clayton County to the Big Sioux Valley for the purpose of selling them farm lands. When they reached their destination, they learned that a prairie fire had gone through here some time earlier, and Nilsen's entire tract lay scorched and covered with weeds that had grown since the fire.

The newcomers assumed that there must have been something unfavorable about the quality of this land and decided to cross the Big Sioux River into Dakota Territory, where they purchased land around the future city of Canton, South Dakota. This was the beginning of that big settlement in Lincoln County, South Dakota, originally intended for Lyon County, Iowa. For that reason, Halvor Nilsen could also be considered the founder of the first colony of Norwegians in South Dakota.

When the Orphans' Home was built in Beloit (Wisconsin), he donated a big tract of land to the institution. He and his brother Ole Nilsen built many of the first gristmills in neighboring villages.

Ole Nilsen's ferry

Ole Nilsen was also an enterprising man of whom we can well be proud. He operated the first ferry on the Mississippi River between McGregor and the south bank of the Wisconsin River *[below Prairie du Chien –Rosholt]* and made a small fortune. This was in 1851, and it was just about this time that the new settlers began to swarm into Iowa. Many thousands of them will remember this lively Halling who gave them their first greetings to the widely celebrated state of Iowa.

Nilsen's ferry first used mules to turn the sidewheels, but as business improved, Nilsen installed machinery run by steam. But his newfound prosperity was short-lived. When the railroad came to Prairie du Chien (from Milwaukee) in 1856, he was forced to sell the ferry to the railroad company.

When the railroad was being projected from North McGregor to St. Olaf village, Nilsen contracted to build it. He hired several hundred men with horses, who shoveled and dug, leveled the hills and filled in the ditches, cut ties and operated big camps along the route of the tracklayers.

But the company lacked sufficient capital. For example, in the beginning it installed wooden railway tracks. It later sold out to the Milwaukee railroad, still owing Nilsen thousands of dollars he never collected. He now lives in North McGregor, where he serves as postmaster and county surveyor.

Pastor Nils O. Brandt organized a congregation in Clayton County in the fall of 1852. This congregation was one of three that sent a letter of call to Pastor Ulrik Vilhelm Koren in Norway—the first letter of call in the Norwegian church sent from west of the Mississippi River. The letter to Koren, dated 11 October 1852, included the following names:
• Torkel Peterson Eiteklep
• Ole Engebretson Grønhovd
• Lars Engebretson Grønhovd
• Syvert H. Grøth
• Svend H. Grøth
• Ansten Knudson
• Halvor Halvorson
• Ole E. Sando
• Iver Olson
• Ole H. Tingelstad
• Helge L. Ramstad
• Ole Hanson
• Tallak Gunderson
• Bernt Hanson
• Sevat Sevatson
• Halstein H. Grøth
• Kittil H. Grøth
• Jacob Abrahamson
• Paul Jenson Brørby
• Jacob Paulson
• Hans Henrikson
• Knud Iverson
• Abraham Olson
• Abraham Hanson
• Engebret Gudbrandsen
• Paul Kittilson Galoger

This settlement has never had any serious differences among the members of the church. It is divided into two parishes, both of which now belong to the United Lutheran Synod. The landscape is charming, the people well-to-do, and the community as a whole is one of the most attractive to visit in America.

Indløbet til Kristianiafjorden

Paint Creek, Allamakee County, Iowa

Although this colony lies 30 miles north of the Clayton County community, its history runs parallel with that of Clayton County. Because of a coincidence, it became a distinct settlement.

Among those who had thought of leaving Rock Prairie for Clayton County in 1850 was a large party of *Hallinger*. A man originally from Numedal by the name of Nils Nilsen Arnesgaard was a sort of guide for this group.

The road to Clayton County went over the lower ferry at McGregor. Owing to a misunderstanding about their travel instructions, these *Hallinger* crossed the Mississippi on the upper ferry, which landed nearly five miles north of McGregor.

Knut Jæger, who was en route to St. Olaf village at the same time, knew the correct route, but was accused by Nils Nilsen of being a swindler and contemptible spy who wanted to misdirect his countrymen into an uninhabitable wilderness. Without taking Jæger's advice, the party crossed the river on the upper ferry.

A short distance above the ferry landing, one approaches Paint Creek. The party followed this river valley to where Waterville now lies. And on the prairie lying to the north, they found farmland—but not as good as in Clayton County.

Among the *Hallinger* in this party were:
- Sven Enderson Hesla
- Ole O. Storla
- Ole Grimsgaard
- Thomas Anderson Grønna
- Lars Knutson Jeglum
- Nils Tollefson Rue
- Ole Syverson Lekwold
- Bjørn Hermundson

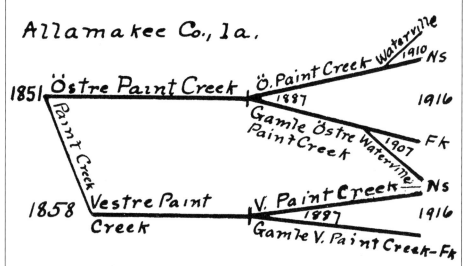

Paint Creek menighet.

(Painted Creek menighet.)
Waterville (5 mil syd-sydvest), Allamakee Co., Iowa.
Utenom (Ns), 1851–53; Norske synode, 1853–58.
Organisert 1851. Delt 1858 (Østre Paint Creek—Ns; Vestre Paint Creek—Ns). 250 sjæle i 1851. Prester: N. O. Brandt, 1851–54; C. L. Clausen, 1851–54; U. V. Koren, 1854–58. Embedsmænd i 1851: a. Svend Endresen; b. J. L. Møller; c. Engebrigt Knudsen; e. Ole Rotnem, Thomas Anderson, Syver O. Wold, Nils T. Roe. (4125—1103)

- Halvor Ellefson Turkop
- Ole Larson Rotnem

Nils Nilsen, their leader, later moved to Clayton County, where his son is now a successful businessman in the village of Gunder.

This group of *Hallinger* included several descendants of the most progressive families in Hallingdal. Others, therefore, followed them. As a result, this is now perhaps the largest Halling colony in America.

Later, many people from Land in Oppland fylke came and settled in the west side of the settlement. Among them can be mentioned Hans Smeby, who came in 1851, the father of Pastor O. H. Smeby. The Paint Creek community is about equal to the Clayton County community, with about 1,300 people from Hallingdal and 700 from Land.

In 1852, when Pastor Nils O. Brandt organized several congregations in this region that were to call Pastor U. V. Koren, he got the biggest response from the Paint Creek congregation. The letter of call to Koren, dated 22 September 1852, included not less than 45 members, or twice as many as from Winneshiek—even though there were more settlers in Winneshiek. The Paint Creek group also promised to build a parsonage. Signatures included:

- Østen Peterson
- Ole O. Storlag
- Svend Enderson Hesla
- Carl Larsen
- Ole Knutson
- Ole K. Gaarder
- Jacob Olson
- Peder Larson
- Engebret Larson
- Helge Olson
- Jacob Hanson
- Ole Olson
- Ole Olson
- Ole Olson
- Ole Larson
- Thos. Anderson
- Thrond Jacobson
- Ole Rude
- Bjørn Hermandson
- Helge Syverson
- Tollef Arneson
- Asle Svendson
- Helge Halvorson
- Syver Hermandson
- Helge H. Næs
- Østen Johanneson
- Hans Smeby
- Halvor O. Storlag
- Andreas Olson
- Lars Knudson
- Nils Bottolfson
- Arne Knudson
- Endre Endreson
- Dan. Johanneson
- Erik Kittelson
- Aslak Gulbrandson
- Henry Sølverson
- Aslak Sølverson
- Ole Hanson
- Ole Grimsgaard
- Iver Aslakson
- Halvor Ellefson Sr.
- Ole Ellefson
- Halvor Ellefson Jr.
- Chr. Halvorson
- Ole O. Tveten

Sæbø og Hjørend Fjord

33

Winneshiek County, northeastern Iowa

(Source: De Norske Settlementers Historie, by Hjalmar Rued Holand, translated by Malcolm Rosholt, 1908, pp. 337–357)

Wisconsin has its Koshkonong, Minnesota its Goodhue County and Iowa its Winneshiek. Among these, Winneshiek is by no means the least famous. It became the first big settlement of Norsemen west of the Mississippi River and from here the immigrants branched out and spread across the fertile lands of northern Iowa and into southern Minnesota.

This district was so well known in pioneer times that there are more immigrant chests painted on the side with "Dekora, Iova" than with any other place of destination except Milwaukee.

Another reason for Winneshiek's fame is that for nearly 50 years, the city of Decorah has shaped the cultural life of the Norwegian people. Thousands of farm boys from around the Midwest have looked up at this little city as a paradise.

The big circulation of *Decorah Posten*, a weekly newspaper printed in Norwegian, has also made the city widely known. It is no doubt the largest paper in the world to be published in such a small town.

The saga of Winneshiek County began in 1843, when Ole Halverson Valle and Ole Tollefson Kittilsland started working here for the federal government, as mentioned earlier. These men had no idea that this quiet, far-removed countryside would one day become the center of Norwegian-American cultural life.

When the Indians were removed to northern Minnesota in 1848, the two Norsemen went with them. They left Winneshiek County behind, silent and deserted even as it has been since time began, with only the forest's wild creatures and the birds of heaven to disturb the silence.

But the fullness of time was at hand, and in this distant country the footsteps of the daring pioneer were approaching, looking to the possession of this corner of the earth, and intending to force Winneshiek's fertile highlands and lowlands to support human society.

First Norwegian settlers

Some time in 1850, with unoccupied land in the older settlements becoming scarce, there was much talk in Koshkonong and Muskego about Coon Prairie and Kickapoo (Wisconsin). In the spring of 1850, a man by the name of Erik Endreson (Erik Anderson), and several others from Koshkonong, went to Kickapoo. Although not entirely satisfied with the outlook here, they nevertheless picked up some 40s of land and returned to Koshkonong to make ready for moving. *[In 1841, under an act passed in Congress, you were entitled to 80 acres if you made an improvement on the land. –Rosholt]*

Among the new settlers, Erik Anderson was well-known and respected. He was born on the Rude farm in Slidre in Valdres, but his father later moved to Voss. It was from here that the family left for the U.S. in 1839 and, after living temporarily in other places, became one of the first Norwegian families to settle in Chicago. Erik Anderson was also the first man to set Norwegian type in America, for a weekly called *Nordlyset (Northern Lights)*.

Meanwhile, the party leaving for Kickapoo had grown. It included, in addition to Anderson:
• Andrew O. Lomen, Valdres
• Ole A. Lomen, Valdres
• Halvor Halvorson Groven, Valdres
• Knud Anderson Bakke, Valdres
• Anders Hauge, Valdres
• Ole Gulliksen Jevne, Valdres
• Mikkel Omlie, Kviteseid in Telemark
• Ole Torstenson Haugen, Hægebostad near Flekkefjord
• Staale Torstenson Haugen, Heggebostad near Flekkefjord

As the party approached the vicinity of Prairie du Chien, two men from Muskego, Johannes Quale of Haugesund and John Brakstad of Voss, joined them. At this point in the journey, the migrants heard reports of the fertile plains west of the Mississippi River and decided to go there instead of continuing to Kickapoo.

Washington Prairie

On 20 June 1850, they arrived on Washington Prairie at a point a few miles southeast of the future city of Decorah. Here they pitched camp, while some of the men made a tour of the county in search of land. They first went north all the way to the Minnesota line but found nothing they liked. So they returned, coming directly back and taking land in the neighborhood of the present Norwegian Synod's Washington Prairie church.

About this same time, Tore Peterson Skotland, Ellef Land and Lars Land from Jefferson Prairie (Wisconsin) arrived in Iowa. All were originally from around Soknedal in Ringerike, Buskerud. They took land near Whisky Grove, just east of Calmar. Endre Peterson Sandager, brother to Skotland, settled here later in the summer.

On 2 July, 12 days after the main party from Koshkonong arrived, a third party of land-lookers approached from Muskego, namely:
• Nils Johnson Kaasa, Hitterdal
• Gjermund Johnson Kaasa, Hitterdal
• Jacob Abrahamsen, Tinn
• Aslak Simonson Aa, Kviteseid
• Iver Quale, Valdres
• Knud G. Opdahl, Valdres
• John Thun, Valdres
Tollef S. Aa came the same summer.

These people, too, had originally intended to go to Coon Prairie, where some of them had taken land the previous year. But at Prairie du Chien, they heard about Iowa. As a result, the party split, half going to Coon Prairie and the above-mentioned men to Winneshiek.

A little later in the summer, two more men—Halvor Modum and

Christopher Estrem—arrived from Muskego. Writing in *Decorah Posten* (1896), U. Kolkin had this to say about them:

"Halvor Modum had been a neighbor to Nils Johnson back in Muskego and now wanted very much to be his neighbor in Iowa as well. Jacob Abrahamson had some land next to Nils Johnson, and Halvor Modum asked whether he would sell his claim so that he could enjoy the same neighborly relations with Johnson as he had in Muskego.

"Abrahamson was willing to sell on condition that Halvor Modum arrange to get him a certain piece of land in its place. Ole Lomen and Andrew Lomen had more land than they could use, and Abrahamson said that if they would give up a 40, then Modum could have his.

"When the bargaining began, Andrew Lomen and Ole Lomen asked $8 for the 40. Money was scarce, but Halvor Modum, who had made a little money farming in Racine County (Wisconsin), was not quite as broke as they were.

"No, Modum thought this was too much and he offered $5 but no more. At this point it appeared that Modum, as much as he desired it, would have to sacrifice his wish to live as a neighbor to Johnson. But when the latter heard about this, he said he would make up the $3 difference. So Abrahamson traded."

The people on Washington Prairie were for the most part from Valdres, and many well-known *Valdriser* were brought up here—among them, the late Gerhardt Hoyme. As a grade schooler scarcely dry behind the ears, he drove his father's cattle cross-country through Wisconsin from Port Washington to Winneshiek County.

We do not have space here to mention all who came the first years, but will name Thrond Lomen and Knut Gudmundson Norsving, both *Valdriser*, who arrived in 1851. Lomen died early in life but was a leader among the first pioneers. He was the father of Professor Knut Throndson.

Goodhue County's famous mill

Knut Gudmundson, father to Gudmund Norsving, one of the first *Valdriser* in Goodhue County, Minnesota, was also a level-headed and farsighted man. His arrival in the community avoided a serious crisis because he had brought along two millstones for grinding flour. It was a two-day journey to any mill in the area, and the stones were therefore a boon to the community.

These millstones have a history in themselves. They came originally from around Trondheim but were taken from there to Lærdal in Sogn. Here they were used for a time before Gudmundson bought them and packed them over the mountains to Vang in Valdres. It is said that the packhorses became swaybacked under their heavy loads.

When Gudmundson prepared to leave for America, he thought it would be best to take the grindstones along, as he had heard there was a shortage of stones in America. The grindstones were carefully hauled to the ship, carried across the Atlantic and lugged on board canal boats and sailboats to Manitowoc County. From there they were taken across the sand hills, swamps, rivers and ridges till they found their rightful place on Washington Prairie. There, they ground grain for the hungry newcomers for many years—which, it may be added, old Gudmundson never took a dime for.

Today these grindstones, thin and worn, are preserved at the Decorah Museum (Vesterheim).

Among the pioneers on Washington Prairie, special mention must be made of Ingebret Nilsen Sølland from Sigdal, who came to the U.S. in 1843 and to Winneshiek County in 1851. He was a brother of Erik Nilsen, a most helpful man in Fox River settlement, and first to leave from Sigdal in 1839.

Like his brother, Ingebret was a first-rate man, honorable and understanding.

He was also the best man in the harvest field and was widely known for his "cradling" abilities.

One of his hobbies was collecting old Huspostiller *[books of sermons for laymen –Rosholt]*. He also paid for the printing of an edition of Tauler's Conversions, which he gave to people *[probably a book entitled Dr. Tauleri Omvendelses–Historie, written by Johannes Tauler, a Christian mystic during the 1300s; the story of his conversion was very popular among the Haugeans]*.

Whisky Grove (Calmar), Stavanger and Madison settlements

Meanwhile, many had also joined Tore Skotland's community at Whisky Grove (Calmar). These people, like Skotland, were mainly from Ringerike, coming in 1851:
• A. L. Kittilsby
• Thrond H. Engen
• Ole Shervin
• Erik Støveren

Tore Skotland must also be considered one of the founders of the Stavanger colony, which stretches southward from Ossion far into Fayette County, Iowa. A friend of his on Jefferson Prairie, John Anderson Aksdal, Avaldsnes, Rogaland fylke, was encouraged as early as the fall of 1850 to follow him. A progressive man, he took a farm where the Hauge Synod cemetery lies. Now he is almost forgotten, but his letters to friends on Jefferson Prairie and to Stavanger brought the following people to Iowa in the spring of 1854:
• Tosten Næsvig
• Tosten Kaasa
• Kolbein Sebbø
• Nils Evenson Ramsfjeld
• Lars Østerhus
• Halvor Paulson
• Halvard Hageli
• Lars Aasland
• John Kaasa
• Ellev Johnson Kaasa

All these pioneers who have been mentioned settled to the southeast and south of Decorah.

The actual founder of the Norwegian settlement lying to the west of Decorah was Johannes Evenson from Valdres, who migrated from Koshkonong in the fall of 1850, accompanied by Jørgen Lommen, Ole Larson Bergan and Knud Larson Bergan. The last named settled south of Decorah, while Evenson went to the northwest and became the first white man in Madison Township in Winneshiek County.

Most of the Norwegians in this part of Winneshiek County are from Sigdal and Eggedal. Engebret Haugen, who moved from Rock Prairie at the urging of Johannes Evenson, was the first. Haugen took a claim in the fall of 1850 three miles southwest of Decorah, where there had once been an Indian trading post. Earlier that summer, he had gone north to St. Paul, where he thought of settling. He had been in the U.S. quite a few years, made a little money and got many of his countrymen to move to Winneshiek County.

Among the first to join him may be mentioned:
• Iver Ringestad, Valdres
• Ole Asleson Myran, Eggedal
• Helge Asleson Myran, Eggedal
• Ole Kittlelson Holong, Numedal
• Herbrand Præstgaarden, Sigdal
• Hans Aakre, Hjartdal in Telemark
• Johannes Aakre, Hjartdal in Telemark

In 1851, Knut Alfson Veseth at Ridgeway came at the same time, but not in the party mentioned above. He was the first from Tinn in Telemark, and there is now a fairly important colony of these people from Tinn. Ole Paulson, a prominent pastor in the Lutheran Free Church Synod and founder of Augsburg Seminary located in St. Paul, Minnesota, accompanied Alfson.

Alfson relates that on the way to Winneshiek County, he and Paulson went barefoot while driving the cattle. One day a calf broke loose from the herd and started off across the prairie. Paulson took after it but suddenly jumped into the air with a sharp cry. A rattlesnake had bitten him.

The people in the caravan faced a crisis. All knew that a rattlesnake bite was fatal, but had heard that if the poisoned spot was scraped off, there was a chance of recovery.

After some searching in an old trunk, they found a barber's knife, but no one had the nerve to perform the operation. The affected spot was in the upper joint of the big toe and difficult to cut into. Ole Paulsen tried to do it himself but failed.

Then Alfson grabbed the knife, took a good grip with the other hand and made a powerful cut. Unfortunately, he also cut a blood vessel, and now the patient was in danger of bleeding to death.

The foot was bound, the blood stopped, and the patient taken to a quack doctor several miles away. This was a grim gentleman. Without further ado he tore off the bindings and packed the foot in "rattlesnake grass," which he picked on the prairie.

By the next morning, Paulson had lost half a bucket of blood and was nearly dead. Then the quack tried to cauterize the wound but without success, whereupon he took a pair of pincers owned by Alfson, who had once been a goldsmith, and attempted to pull the blood vessel forward in order to tie it. This did not work, either.

Finally, in a fit of temper, the quack departed, leaving the patient to the heavy-handed helpers who first attended

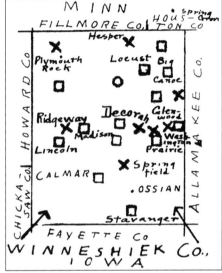

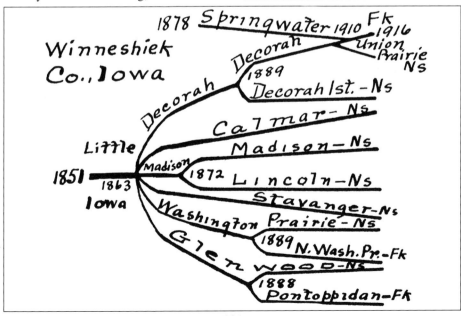

him and who finally got the bleeding stopped again.

Knut Alfson's wife, the first Norwegian woman in Decorah, came in 1851 and worked a couple of years.

Somewhat earlier, Peder Sampson from Voss established a shoemaker shop, the first Norwegian male in a town which, for its "Norse-ness," is the most well-known in the U.S.

Skjæggedalsfossen

Big Canoe named after Indian Chief One Eyed Decorah

North and east of Decorah, the terrain is hilly. As a result, this area was not occupied as soon as Washington Prairie and other places. Most of the early pioneers skirted this area and went farther north into Houston and Fillmore counties (Minnesota).

Some people believe that one Lars Iverson arrived here with the government surveyors and settled in Canoe Township in 1845. In this case, he would be the first white man in the county, but this suggestion probably has no basis in fact.

The first to arrive in these parts was undoubtedly Peder Larson Haugen, who settled six miles north of Decorah in the fall of 1850. He was the first to emigrate from Maanselven in Nordland (Bardø subparish).

The area immediately to the north is called Big Canoe. The landscape here is uneven, but it is densely populated by Norwegians from all different parts of Norway. Here, too, the first settlers were from Valdres. In 1851, Hover Evenson, Ole Magneson and Erik Erikson arrived from Koshkonong.

Erikson's unique house was an example of the true Valdres spirit of perseverance. The entire house was built from a single pine tree. The planks were six inches thick and so wide that only three were needed from the floor to the ceiling. The floors, doors, windows and shingles were also made from the same tree. Everything was sawed with a handsaw, as the tree was too large to move.

M. Langeland from Voss, the father of Rev. Magne Langeland, was also living here in 1852, when Rev. Nils O. Brandt, the first Norwegian pastor to visit this area, held worship services at his home.

Among the first to settle further north in Highland were Tollef Arneson Sanden, Jørgen Brunsvold and Halstein Støen.

The following information on Big Canoe, compiled by Deb Nelson Gourley, is from the book Big Canoe Lutheran Church 1853-1978, 125 Anniversary, *pp. 5-7:*

Big Canoe gets its name from an Indian chief named Big Canoe, who was also known as One Eyed Decorah. The region bearing his name included the northeast part of Winneshiek County and a part of northwest Allamakee County in Iowa, stretching into southern Fillmore County in Minnesota.

Norwegian Lutherans began immigrating to the Big Canoe region in 1851. Their numbers increased rapidly in succeeding years.

Like their fellow settlers who came from Norway to carve out homes on wilderness land formerly occupied by Indians, the Big Canoe pioneers experienced struggles and hardships. Dugouts and simple log huts served as their first homes.

During the summer of 1852, Pastor Nils O. Brandt from Rock River, Wisconsin, visited this early settlement. The year before, he had conducted services in communities in Allamakee, Clayton and southern Winneshiek counties, but hadn't gotten as far north as Big Canoe.

The first services in the Big Canoe settlement were held at the home of Peder Langeland, during which the following three children were baptized:
• Ingeborg, daughter of Mr. and Mrs. Ole Hovde, first white child born in Highland Township
• Barbro, daughter of Mr. and Mrs. Jørgen Brunsvold
• Ole, son of Mr. and Mrs. Tollef Sanden Arneson

In late August 1853, at the home of Torgeir Luraas, the congregation was formally organized, with Erik Ellefsen Sleen serving as chairman.

Unfortunately, the minutes of this meeting have been lost. But thanks to the memories of the participants, the names of those in attendance, as well as names of the charter members, have been recalled.

Names of those listed as being at the first meeting included:
- Erik Ellefsen Sleen
- Ole Magneson Sætre
- Erik Erikson Selland
- Bottolf Olson Øine
- Svend Olson Bidne
- Halsten H. Støen
- Ole H. Støen
- Harald H. Støen
- Ole Hovde
- Mikkel Solberg
- Knut K. Bjørgo
- Arne Arneson
- Tollef Sanden
- Amund Arneson
- Jørgen O. Brunsvold
- Torgeir Luraas
- Halvor Bergan
- Lars Dommerude
- Ingebrigt Grindeland
- Lars N. Garen
- Elling Foss
- Henrik Fadness
- Magne Langeland
- Halvor Førde
- Peder Ulrikson
- Paul Dagfinson
- Anders Bersei
- Ole Torson
- Jørgen Sande
- Erik Hatlestad
- Elling Ellingson
- Steinar Ellefson
- Lars Medaas
- Iver Hagen
- Siver Rishovd

Although this congregation was not among those who extended the call that brought Pastor Ulrik Vilhelm Koren to America in late 1853, he served as pastor of Big Canoe Lutheran Church from 1854 to 1857. Koren's parish included all of northeast Iowa and southeast Minnesota. Because of the size of his territory, services were held infrequently: At least 40 Lutheran pastors now serve congregations in territory once covered by Pastor Koren.

Glenwood settlement

East of Decorah in Glenwood Township of Winneshiek County, people from Toten—perhaps the first from that area to immigrate to the U.S.—founded a large colony. Nils Voldeng and Johannes Sivesind were the first of these to come in 1851.

The Norsemen in Glenwood have an extraordinary record, as their township sent more volunteers to the Civil War than did any other in the county. Old Thrond Steen's family deserves special mention, as six of his sons saw combat action in the service of their new fatherland. The seventh son also wanted to go but was not accepted when the recruiting officers learned how many the family had already contributed. This family was originally from Hadeland.

Northeast Iowa's early churches

Pastor Nils O. Brandt organized all these congregations in northeastern Iowa, such as Little Iowa, Paint Creek and Norway (Clayton County). The decision to take this step was made in the fall of 1852 at a meeting held in the house of Engebret Haugen near Decorah. It was decided to give the provisional church council in Wisconsin authority to call a pastor from Norway.

Several of the Valdres members present strongly urged that Mads Vefring, a lay preacher who later studied theology, be called. When the majority at the meeting refused to agree, the Valdres group became sullen and refused to sign the letter of call.

Those from Winneshiek County who signed this first letter of call under date of 14 October 1852, were as follows *[apparently this letter is the same signed 11 October by the congregation in Clayton County –Rosholt]*:
- Ole Asleson Myran
- Hans Olson
- Ole Kittelson Holong
- Lars Tovson
- Ole Pederson Ruen
- John Tovson

- Hans Anderson Blegen
- Tov Janson
- Torkild Hanson Holla
- Helge Nilsen
- Hans Larson Tinderholt
- Johannes Evenson
- Brede Bredeson Sander
- Johannes Simonson
- Hans Olson
- Kolbein Torrison
- Ole Herbrandsen
- Amund Pederson
- Hans Pederson
- John Knudson
- Herbrand Anstenson
- Anders Olson

Many of the older settlers were at this time zealous Methodists, who had been won over to that church by O. P. Fredrikson, the first Norwegian Methodist pastor in the world. Among them were Nils Johnson, the leader and founder of the settlement, who later became a Methodist pastor himself.

In addition, there was Peder Asbjørnson Mehus, a lay preacher and later pastor in the Augustana Synod of the Lutheran church. Mehus had quite a following and organized congregations.

Finally, Elling Eielsen had also attracted an important following. It was therefore a sharply divided community in church affairs that young Pastor Ulrik Vilhelm Koren (born in Bergen, Norway) came to in December 1853.

Pastor U. V. Koren's call covered an area that is today served by no less than 40 pastors. He was not only alone but also for several years separated from the nearest pastor of the church by 200 miles or so. He has provided an excellent account of his first years in Iowa in an article appearing in the Norwegian magazine *Symar*, 27 (1905). His account follows.

"When we came to Prairie du Chien, I heard that we could not cross the Mississippi River, as it was still ice-bound and no one had traveled over it. We therefore had to wait several days.

"Finally a man, hearing of our predicament, said he might be able to help us. Certainly no horse had crossed the river, but he thought that with my

Reverend and Mrs. Koren cross the Mississippi

En Lofoten Landsby i Fisketiden

wife in a light rig and the rest of us pulling or pushing, we could get across.

"The stranger said he was a doctor, a small person with big gold-rimmed glasses and high hat. This was really something to see; ahead went the little doctor with a big stick in his hand, testing the safety of the ice. I stood between the buggy shafts, wearing a big sou'wester and boots that reached to my knees.

"In the buggy (or one-horse wagon) sat my wife, wrapped in buffalo robes. There was also room for our luggage. Behind the wagon followed a young Norwegian boy the doctor had recruited to help us. It was his duty to push.

"After the doctor tested the ice a short distance ahead, he returned and threw a rope to me that was attached to both ends of the shafts, and with the rope around his neck and under his arms, he went forward. It was a big help that we had *terra firma* under us when we crossed the big islands in the river channel, and fortunately for everyone, we reached McGregor safe and sound.

"I have made many rather dangerous crossings over the Mississippi under various circumstances, which I cannot enumerate here, but the first one was no doubt the most incredible.

"We arrived at the Egge home after lunch the day before Christmas. This little log house, 14 by 16 feet, we divided into two rooms with calico curtains, the one for two beds which took up the one wall of the house and this in turn divided by another curtain. The other half of the house served as kitchen and quarters for the head of the house, his wife and two children—a place for parochial school and also the pastor's study. The following day, which was Christmas, invitations were sent out for worship services to as many people as possible.

"I now had to prepare my Christmas sermon. For books I had only the New Testament, the altar book, ritual and hymnal. My library was still in Milwaukee and was not unpacked until nearly six months later. Pen, ink and paper I had, but it was difficult to find decent light to write by, and I had no candles myself.

"But we made a lamp with a linen rag in a saucer filled with fat, turned the coffee can upside down and set the saucer on top of the can so the light was higher than my paper. In this manner I worked on my inaugural sermon nearly all night, because to discuss the word of God without all preparation possible has never occurred to me, nor have I changed my mind since.

"There I sat in the little Egge house about four days' journey from my nearest fellow pastor, without books and without experience, and now everything had to be made orderly. I said 'I sat.' No, there was not much 'sitting' here. I was traveling nearly all the time.

"It would amuse you to see my primitive travel gear. My first sleigh, consisting of runners and thills in one, was made of two long hickory poles. Over this was placed a small box with a board for a seat, all held together by wooden linchpins, with no springs under the wagon box. All the running parts of my first harness, including the reins, were made of clothesline.

"I well recall the searching stare with which I was greeted when I sometimes approached a 'tavern' in this rig, gave the 'hostler' the reins and asked him to grease the wheels. In his eyes I could see that he was wondering what kind of a 'tramp' this was, and whether it would not be more to the point if he told me to grease this sad-looking outfit myself!

"I did not own a heavy fur coat for traveling nor even buffalo robes, and freeze I did. But I was determined to make good, and with my youthful enthusiasm I managed to surmount most mundane problems."

In 1854 the first church was built in this community. District President Koren recalls that it was a shabby-looking affair, practically a shack with board walls, without floor or seating. When worship services were held, rails were brought in from the fence line and used for seats. In summer it was roasting hot and in winter freezing cold, but it was God's Temple just the same for the undemanding pioneers who built it.

Pastor Jacobson's recollections

Among all the inhabitants of Winneshiek, none is better able to tell its story than Pastor Abraham Jacobson, who himself arrived on Washington Prairie in 1850—the Year of the Pioneers. The narration that follows is from his pen:

"In the spring of 1850, my parents and several other families around Muskego in Racine County decided to move west. The leader of this party was Nils Johnson, whose son, M. N. Johnson, was then an infant but grew up to become a U.S. congressman from North Dakota.

"Nils Johnson had a big wagon that had earlier been used in government service and was so heavy it took three yoke of oxen to pull it. There was room for all kinds of household goods in the big box, with a roof made of white canvas. Sticking out of both sides were some stovepipes. From a distance, for one with imagination, it looked like a ship of war. It was no wonder such a wagon in its time was called a 'prairie schooner.'

"Other vehicles used for hauling goods varied widely, both in size and shape, including the *kubberuller* whose wheels were made by sawing a cross-section of an oak log resembling the wheels on our own carts in Norway.

"The trip overland was tedious. At Koshkonong we picked up a big addition to our party that altogether brought the total number to more than 100 souls, 200 head of cattle, some sheep and hogs, one mare and a colt. Madison, capital of Wisconsin, was just a small village and not the first capital. The capital building consisted merely of a two-story frame house built on the site where the great stone edifice stands today.

"The caravan was originally destined for Coon Prairie, but near Wingville we met a man by the name of William Painter, who had settled in Iowa on a site where Decorah is presently located. He gave a vivid description of the land west of the Mississippi River, especially of the area where he had settled.

"On reaching the Wisconsin River, our party decided to send out a deputation of men with the most experience in these matters to reconnoiter and report back to us. The result was that, when we reached Prairie du Chien, our party divided, one-half taking the road to Vernon County where Viroqua and Westby are now located, and the other going on to Iowa.

"To cross the Wisconsin River, we had to use a small ferry whose paddle wheel was driven by a horse in a treadmill. Only one yoke of oxen with a wagon could be freighted across at a time, while the other cattle had to swim across. The entire operation was fraught with danger but went without incident.

"Five mules drove the larger ferryboat on the Mississippi at Prairie du Chien on a treadmill, but the water level was high. As a result, the distance across was nearly two miles. Considerable time was consumed in getting the wagons and people to the west shore.

"Thirteen miles northwest of McGregor at Poverty Point, later called Monona, camp was pitched for a week. The men who had been on the scouting party had seen several different tracts of land, and this gave rise to a division among the people as to the best place for settlement. As a result, the party divided into three. We went along with the original leader, and on 3 July arrived in the neighborhood of Decorah that became our home. The journey, reckoning from the beginning, took five weeks *[presumably from Muskego –Rosholt]*. A few of the people had room enough to sleep in their wagons with canvas tops, but the rest had to sleep on the ground under the wagons.

"If time and ordinary living expenses were taken into account, this would be quite a costly journey, but to the pioneer, time was not a factor and the cost of living was held to a minimum.

"The tract of land we had selected was in all truth beautiful, what with rolling prairies and rich soil, groves of trees and bubbling brooks, all reasonably distributed for future use. For miles there were neither house nor road nor any other sign of civilization. The paths followed by the Indians, with some changes, were for a long time used by the pioneers until fields became established and the roads made to go around the fence lines.

"One of the first things to do was to plow some prairie land for cultivation, and the second thing was to cut hay for the cattle for the coming winter. This accomplished, the building of log houses was undertaken late in fall. Many of us had not been under a roof from the middle of May until September or October, although everyone was in good health.

"The Indians who had lived on the land we now occupied had been removed by the military authorities two years before we came. It was clear that the Indians were expecting to return here, as they had dug deep holes like cellars in which were stored supplies of corn and other articles carefully packed and covered with bark. These things were still in good condition when the first settlers dug them up.

"Quite a number of Indians were still wandering around our neighborhood, although their home was in Minnesota, and they did not molest us. The first year there was scarcely anyone living to the northwest of us, but people along the periphery became quite concerned when it was learned that there were traders selling whiskey to the Indians.

"There were many Indian graves along the shores of the upper Iowa River. The bodies of the dead were buried sitting up, just deep enough down so that the head protruded through the surface of the ground. A forked stick was driven down at the ends of the grave

Henningsvær

on which was laid some sort of small pole or beam, and from this hung a thin piece of hide which sloped down on both sides like a tent.

"The question of providing for the necessities of life, food and clothing was uppermost in our minds. The nearest market west of the Mississippi was 50 miles away, where a ton of wheat flour cost $12, a bushel of corn 55 cents and other provisions proportionally high. Whenever my father could spare time from work at home, he worked out at 50 cents per day, while all that my own time was worth for driving four yoke of oxen plowing the prairie was 25 cents a day. Hunting and fishing helped a great deal.

"The menfolk who could be away from home went up to the Wisconsin 'Pinery' to work in the logging camps or as wood cutters down along the Mississippi River. My father took me, then 14 years old, along on one such expedition to cut wood. It was in 1850, two weeks before Christmas, when a heavy snow came down just as we were preparing to leave.

"Walking 28 miles to the place we were to stop at overnight was another problem. The loft in the log house where we slept had only clapboards of oak for a roof. During the night a strong wind came up and the snow seeped through the cracks in the roof. When morning came, there must have been eight inches of snow on the bed and blankets we slept in.

"When we arrived on the following day at the place where we assumed there was work to be had, conditions were so bad we could not buy a job. This was on the Mississippi five miles above McGregor. Despite the late hour of the day, we thought that a walk at this distance along the shore of the river held no danger even if the night was dark.

"When we had come halfway— that is, to the site where North McGregor now lies, it was evident that we had made a serious error. A creek called Bloody Run opens into the Mississippi at this point, and it was so wide that we could not possibly get across without going way upstream.

"We finally decided to chop down a big tree and cross over on this. We then took a footpath over the ridge leading to McGregor rather than follow the banks of the Mississippi, but now we were in deep trouble. The sharp hills, covered with snow and burnt brush, made our progress difficult. As a result, we did not reach our destination until after midnight.

"Luckily for us, a group of young people was having a dance in a small hotel, which continued until early morning, and this gave us a chance to enjoy a warm room for the rest of the night. When I was called to breakfast the next morning, I had a terrific appetite, as I had not eaten since the morning of the day before. But my feet were so sore and stiff that I could hardly get to the table.

"We took a contract here to cut wood for 50 cents a square cord (6 feet long, 4 feet wide and 4 feet high), and furnish our own board and lodgings. There was no cheap place to stay, either. We therefore had to put up at the hotel, where the only thing of high quality was the price. The profit from this undertaking, after two weeks of hard labor, amounted to a saving sufficient to buy iron for two wedges and two mallet rings used in rail splitting, in addition to four pounds of coffee and a little sugar *[most likely brown sugar –Rosholt]*.

"The trip home became just as strenuous as the trip over. We left early in the morning in company with a neighbor who had come down with a yoke of oxen and wagon to pick up some supplies. This slow-paced affair did not suit me, and when we met a man of our acquaintance, I went ahead with him in the hope of reaching home the same day.

"My share of the little lunch we had

taken along was, in my haste, forgotten. Thus I made a trip on foot of nearly 50 miles over bad roads without a bite to eat, as I did not have a penny to buy anything and was both too proud and bashful to beg. Long after dark, after I had eaten something on reaching home, my limbs were so completely exhausted that I felt like I was going to fall into a faint. But I soon recovered after resting a bit.

"The situation in regard to clothing was just about as desperate as it was with food. I recall clearly that during the first two winters I did not have underclothing or overcoat for the simple reason that there was none to be had, while overshoes were something scarcely mentioned, much less seen. Nevertheless, everyone, both young and old, appeared to be in good health.

"The land where we first settled was not yet listed for sale by the government, but the neighbors agreed on a plan to prevent any stranger from taking it away from them. 'Club claim' is a word that accurately defines the movement, because it meant both that the men were all members of one club, and on the other hand, were ready to use clubs and sticks to protect their squatter's rights.

"When the government got ready to sell the land, the price was $200 in gold for each quarter section *[probably $1.25 per acre. –Rosholt]*. 'Land warrants' given to veterans of American wars could be bought and sold for less per acre than the government land, and were widely used by the pioneers to get title to their property.

"But to find the necessary funds to pay for their land was for many pioneers almost impossible. Those who had money would not loan it out for less than 3 to 4 percent per month against good security. Usually the man with the money to loan purchased the land in his name, but with the provision that he would deed it over to the buyer when the loan was satisfied. Fortunately for the poor, the land was not considered worth much, as there was so much of it, and it was generally assumed that it would not be settled for a long time to come.

"In the beginning, therefore, there were no difficulties with the land office at Dubuque, which our district came under. But this situation did not last long. People poured in much faster than expected, and the sharp rise in demand for land could scarcely be imagined. There was no blood shed over land in our neighborhood, but there were some ridiculous scenes elsewhere that gave the speculators something to laugh about, even though it was no laughing matter for those involved.

"In those days it was legal to buy as much land as a man wanted, if only he had the money to pay for it. This gave speculators the opportunity to buy up large tracts of land to the harm of the real settlers, and the bad effects of this policy are felt to this day.

"The pre-emption law, which gave a man a year in which to pay for land he cultivated and on which he built a house, was a big boon to the poor people. It made it possible for them to own their own homes. But it was the Homestead Act, passed in the 1860s, *[actually 1862 –Rosholt]* more than anything else that was responsible for the settlement of the great Midwest.

"For nearly 20 years, McGregor, about 50 miles away, was the nearest market for us. But in 1867 the railroad was built to Conover, on the boundary of the settlement, where it terminated for some years. Conover quickly became a lively trading town center, incorporated as a city, and at one time had no less than 32 saloons open for business. Now the corn grows tall where once ran busy streets."

Winneshiek County has a Norwegian population of about 10,000. This same settlement continues north across the state line into Houston and Fillmore counties, where no fewer than 17,000 Norwegians live.

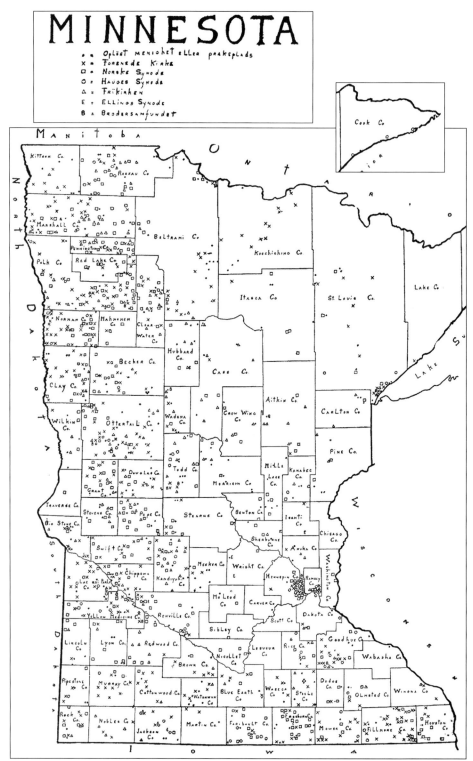

34
Houston County and eastern Fillmore County, southeastern Minnesota
(Source: De Norske Settlementers Historie, by Hjalmar Rued Holand, translated by Malcolm Rosholt, 1908, pp. 358–378)

Information from church and area history books and church records has been woven into this chapter to complement Holand's research. Historians who contributed to this project include Georgia Rosendahl, Spring Grove, Minnesota; Gordon Eddy, Cresco, Iowa; and Jim Skree, Caledonia, Minnesota.

Deb Nelson Gourley, Waukon, Iowa, provided additional information on the following: Garness, Scheie, Neutral Ground, Highland Prairie, Highland, Elstad, Greenfield, Strung-Out-Town (Stringtown or Amherst) and North Prairie.

Note that names and places of origin added to this chapter by these researchers may differ from those in Holand's account. We offer both versions and remind you that secondary sources (such as this book) should always be compared with primary sources (such as church records) to verify their accuracy.

• • • • •

Most Norwegian settlements have had a central core that attracted the first newcomers, and from that hub the colonies spread outward. This was not true of the Houston-Fillmore area of Minnesota.

The western half of Houston County and the eastern half of Fillmore County were settled about the same time

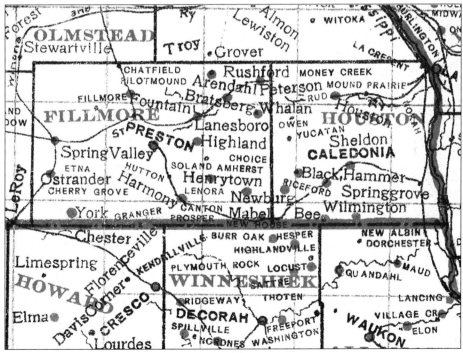

at several points by different parties, unknown to one another—including numerous Americans. Later, the Americans sold out to the Norwegians, and the different colonies merged into a large, homogeneous settlement, 20 miles wide and 30 miles long. It is therefore difficult to give a complete report of its development.

There is something grand about this part of Minnesota, leaving one in awe of its overwhelming vastness. One ridge after another towers on the horizon, tightly populated by Norwegians. Long valleys, a mile wide, rest cozily in the lap of the land, and innumerable smaller valleys hide behind forest-clad heights where wild game still abounds.

High above the murky hillsides and narrow gaps, there are wide prairies dotted with large farms. Here, too, is one church parish after another. The inhabitants of the region are almost entirely Norwegian. They govern eight villages, with almost a thousand people in each.

All told, the Norwegian population here numbers about 17,000 (1908), although the settlement is much larger, as these towns are but a continuation of the earlier settlement in Winneshiek County across the state line.

Houston County
Spring Grove and Wilmington
Supplemented by Georgia Rosendahl

In 1852, quite a number of Norwegians took land along the high ridges a short distance west, north and east of the present village of Spring Grove.

The ridge on which the best farms in Houston County are situated is a rather peculiar phenomenon. Between the Upper Iowa River and Root River, the valleys stretch into a wide and uneven plateau divided by gaps and slopes. Along the middle there rises a 12- to 15-mile-long, smooth, solid limestone outcropping a couple hundred feet above the plain. The top is flat and without a bush on it. The scraggly sides are forest-covered and watered by springs.

Up here the first Norwegians climbed and clung hard to the tree groves by a brook. Here there was good soil for plowing on the flat and plenty of wood and water nearby along the slopes. Therefore, these tracts of land were the first to be occupied.

High up on this broad ridge, with a view extending 15 to 20 miles on both sides, lies the village of Spring Grove, perhaps the most thoroughly Norwegian town in the U.S. The population of the village is about 800, of which only a couple of families are not Norse.

There are few towns in America with only one church and no saloons, but this is one of them. Pastor U. V. Koren organized the congregation, the oldest and largest in Minnesota, in 1855. Mons Fladager from Valdres, founder of the village and its first businessman, came here in 1858.

Among the first settlers in the community, special mention must be made of Peter Johnson Lommen, a highly respected man. Lommen was one of several brothers, all known as leading figures in the early period of settlement. One of the brothers is Gjermund Johnson Lommen, the first Norwegian in Wilmington east of Spring Grove. Another is Tosten Johnson, who has held many commissions of trust and is still one of the community's most distinguished men.

A third brother of Lommen's was the pioneer pastor, Thomas Johnson, whose home mission work among the pioneers covered a territory that is today (1908) served, it is said, by 50 pastors. Peter Lommen's son, J. P. Lommen, now a businessman in Caledonia, was the first Norwegian child born in Minnesota, 12 December 1852.

The people of Spring Grove and Wilmington are, for the most part, from Hallingdal, Sigdal, Valdres, Ringerike and Hadeland.

When the pioneers arrived here, they had considerable trouble with a big

American ruffian named Arthur Bow. He tried to make the newcomers believe that he had prior title to the land. As he was big and mean as a troll, as well as fast with a gun, it was not easy to deal with him.

Finally he met his superior in a good-natured Sigdal person called Ole Gudbrandsgutten *[literally, Gudbrand's-boy –Rosholt]*, who threw him, Halling-style, rolling him down the hillside. After that, the Yankee left for other parts.

Many of the early pioneers first settled in Wisconsin. The following list gives names of pioneers and their year of arrival to Spring Grove and Wilmington:

Spring Grove—1852
- Torger Johannesen Tendeland, Stavanger (the first man from Stavanger to settle in Minnesota, in July 1852)
- Haaken Narveson, Sigdal
- Knud Knudsen Kieland, Sigdal
- Fingal Aslesen Flaten, Sigdal
- Truls Haga, Sigdal
- Peter Johnsen Lommen, Valdres
- Tosten Johnsen Lommen, Valdres
- Knud Olsen Bergo, Valdres
- Even Høime, Valdres
- Ole Amundsen Berg, Hallingdal
- Tollef Amundsen Berg, Hallingdal
- Knud Olsen Wold, Hallingdal
- Ole Olsen Ulen, Hallingdal
- Hans Torgrimsen Tveito, Telemark

Spring Grove—1853
- Embrik H. Melbraaten (Engebret Hansen Melbraaten), Hallingdal
- Knud Gilbertson, Hallingdal
- Ole E. Stenerodden and wife, Hallingdal
- Levor Timansen Quarve, Hallingdal
- Jørgen Timansen Quarve, Hallingdal
- Knut Olsen Blexrud and wife, Soknedalen, Ringerike
- Nils Olsen Blexrud, Soknedalen, Ringerike
- Dr. Thore Jensen with his parents, Røraas (Røros)
- Anders Pedersen Kroshus, Hadeland
- Ole Kolberg, Solør
- Peter Halverson Torgenrud, Toten
- Ole Christophersen Sagedalen, Hallingdal
- Nils Gullicksen Ristey, Valdres
- Ole Knudsen Ristey, Valdres

Spring Grove—1854
- Timan Gilbertson, Hallingdal
- Gulbrand Nilsen Myhra, Hadeland
- Hans Nilsen Myhra, Hadeland
- Elling Knutsen Kieland, Sigdal
- Ole Olsen Lee, Hallingdal
- Engebret Knutsen Opheim, Hallingdal
- Gunder Guelsen Traaen, Numedal
- Bjørn Thorsen Kolsrud, Hallingdal
- Engebret Gundersen Benson Enderud, Sigdal
- Ole Olsen Gulbrandsgutten, Sigdal
- Gulbrand Michelsen Ruud, Land
- Paul Hansen Rosendahl, Hadeland
- Lars Reiersen Halstenrud, Sigdal
- Mikkel Larsen Dal (Walhus), Hadeland
- John Johnsen Lommen, Valdres
- Knud Christophersen Sagedalen, Hallingdal
- Anders Nilsen Kjos, Hadeland
- Dyre Halvorsen Lindaas, Sandsvær

Spring Grove—1855
- Even Olsen Haugen, Sigdal
- Goro Sanager (wife), Eggedal
- Ole Christiansen Stensrud, Krødsherrad
- Anders Christiansen Stensrud, Krødsherrad
- Helge Ellingsen Bergsrud, Soknedalen, Ringerike
- John Steingrimsen Bergrud, Sigdal
- Nels Christophersen Tveto (Tweito), Hadeland
- Hans Hansen Bakke, Gudbrandsdalen
- Ole Johnsen Svartebraaten, Eggedal
- Elling Erlandsen Snedkerpladsen, Krødsherrad
- Hans Erlandsen Snedkerpladsen, Krødsherrad

Spring Grove—1856
- Ole Paulsen Wolden, Nord-Land
- Knut Guttormsen Tyribakken, Hallingdal
- Elling Hendricksen Solberg, Soknedalen, Ringerike

- Steingrim Steingrimsen Bergrud, Sigdal

Wilmington—1853
- Gjermund Johnsen Lommen, Valdres
- Ole Bye, Røraas (Røros)
- Andrew Olsen Bye, Røraas (Røros)
- Haavel Pedersen Johnsrud, Hadeland

Wilmington—1854
- Thov Olsen Tveten (Thov Olsen Tweeten), Telemark
- Amund Gulbrandsen Lunde, Ringerike
- Gulbrand Andersen Guberud, Valdres
- Østen Andersen Guberud, Valdres
- Anders Østensen Guberud, Valdres
- Herman Pedersen Dustrud, Numedal
- Ole Thomasen Scotland, Soknedalen, Ringerike
- Baard Olsen Qualey, Sogndal
- Endre Knutsen Roble, Hallingdal
- Ingvald Throndsen Doely, Hakkedalen
- Ole Knutsen Myhre, Hallingdal
- Asbjørn Stenehjem, Sogndal

Wilmington—1855
- Christian Johannesen Glasrud, Toten
- Ole Olsen Qualey, Sogndal

Wilmington—1856
- Iver Pedersen Kinneberg, Hallingdal

Black Hammer, Houston County
Supplemented by Gordon Eddy

North of Spring Grove lies Black Hammer, furrowed and shaggy. For a township name, Black Hammer is unique. There is no other name like it in the United States.

Knud Olsen Bergo, who was living across the line to the south in Spring Grove Township, had gone out one morning in the early 1850s. He saw that a fire had swept across the prairie to the north of his place and had burnt the lone bluff in the middle of the prairie completely black.

The charred, blackened appearance of the bluff reminded him of a similar bluff in his home district of Vestre Slidre, Valdres, Norway, and he exclaimed in Norwegian, *"Sort Hammer,"* which in English translated to "Black Bluff." The word "hammer" in Norwegian was the same both for bluff and for the tool. It was only a coincidence that the bluff out on the prairie was also shaped like the tool.

When the county supervisors in 1859 had to discard the name "Clinton" because it had already been used elsewhere in the state, the next suggestion was "Black Hammer." And that has been its name ever since.

Black Hammer Township was originally split off from Spring Grove and Yucatan townships. The prairies and bluffs in the south-central part of the township are surrounded on three sides by creeks that run through numerous coulees and deep valleys. Spring Grove Township, with its Norwegian Ridge, borders Black Hammer in the south.

In 1852, an Englishman named Ed Stevens was here for a brief time but soon moved on. Torkel Aageson, originally from Stavanger, who came here via Rock County in Wisconsin, was the first Norseman to settle around Black Hammer.

Torkel was wandering around to the north one day in March 1853, carrying only an axe, a steel wedge on his back and a pair of rings for a relseklubbe *[apparently a homemade mallet for splitting wood –Rosholt]*. Down at the foot of the hill he found a spring, and there he shortly had a house of aspen logs and birch bark. Knut Olson Ike (Knut Olson Eik) came in June, but after that there were no more settlers from Stavanger.

Following is a list of Norwegian pioneers to the area and the years they arrived:

Black Hammer—1853
- Torkel Aageson Rosaaen, Haugenes, Hjelmeland, Stavanger
- Knud Olsen Eik (Knud Olsen Ike), Hjelmeland, Stavanger; wife Martha Knutsdatter, born at Eik
- Jens Ellingsen Vinjum (Jens Ellingsen Winjum), Aurland, Sogn; wife Anna Olsdatter Otternes
- Guttorm Olsen Otterness (Guttorm Olsen Otternes, Guttorm Olsen

Aaotnes), Aurland, Sogn; wife Brita Ivarsdatter Frondal
• Jens Olsen Otterness (Jens Olsen Otternes, Jens Olsen Aaotnes), Aurland, Sogn; wife Martha Larsdatter Ytre Lie
• Halvor Olsen (didn't stay long)
• Kristoffer Eriksen (didn't stay long)
• Peder Kristensen Onstad (Per Kristensen Onstad, Peder Kristensen Ohnstad, Per Kristensen Ohnstad), Aurland, Sogn; wife Randi Jensdatter Otternes

Black Hammer—1854
• Lars Ellendsen Skajem (Lars Ellendsen Skahjem, Lars Ellendsen Skaim), Aurland, Sogn. Family later used "Skime" for surname.
• Lars Ellingsen Vinjum (Lars Ellingsen Winjum), Aurland, Sogn; later married Martha Larsdatter Skajem (Martha Larsdatter Skime)
• Kari Jensdatter Dyrdal Vinjum
• Knud Aamundsen Lee (Knud Amundsen Lie, Knud Amundsen Ytre Lee), Aurland, Sogn; wife Barbro Marie Ellingsdatter, born at Vinjum
• Johannes Botolvsen Berkvam, the older of two brothers named Johannes (Johannes Botolvsen Berekvam), Flaam, Aurland, Sogn
• Johannes Botolvsen Berkvam, the younger of two brothers named Johannes (Johannes Botolvsen Berekvam), Flaam, Aurland, Sogn; married in 1853 to Mari Olsdatter Otternes
• Lars Findreng
• Knud G. Tyribakken (Knut Guttormson), later used Guttormson as family surname
• Ole Ingebrigtsen Bjergum (Ole Ingebrigtsen Bjørgum, Ole Ingebrigtsen Bjørgo), Aurland, Sogn; wife Johanna Jensdatter Otternes
• Valentin Valentinsen, Stavanger
• Ole Aagesen Rosaaen, brother to Torkel Aagesen Rosaaen, who came in 1853
• Elling Bjertnes, Krødsherrad
• Ole Eiene (Ole Eik). Brother to Knud Olsen Ike, who came in 1853
• Tosten Johnson Lommen, Valdres; wife Thora Ingebrigtsdatter Gjesme (Thora Ingebrigtsdatter Jesme)
• Johannes Aamundsen Lie (Johannes Aamundsen Indrelid), Flaam, Aurland, Sogn
• Torkel Aamundsen Lie (Torkel Aamundsen Indrelid), Flaam, Aurland, Sogn, brother to Johannes Lie
• Ole Olson Wendelbø (Ole Olson Gjerløv), Aurland, Sogn; wife Randi
• Ole S. Olson Gjerløv, Leikanger, Sogn
• Jens Jensen Gjesme (Jens Jensen Jesme), Aurland, Sogn. Later married to Martha Ivarsdatter Frondal (Martha Ivarsdatter Frandle)
• Lars Larsen Lie (Lars Larsen Ytre Lie), Aurland, Sogn

Black Hammer—1855
• Andreas Kristensen Onstad (Andreas Kristensen Ohnstad), Aurland, Sogn; wife Gunild Aamundsdatter Lunde
• Ole Aamundsen Lee (Ole Aamundsen Lie, Ole Aamundsen Ytre Lie), Aurland, Sogn
• Østen Helgesen Børtnes (Østen Helgesen Burtness), Nes, Hallingdal
• Kristian Lamen (Kristian Laamen), Trøndelag
• Ivar Botolvsen Berekvam, Flaam, Aurland, Sogn
• Ole Botolvsen Berekvam, Flaam, Aurland, Sogn
• Botolv Botolvsen Berquam (Botolv Botolvsen Berekvam), Flaam, Aurland, Sogn
• Ivar Jonsen Frandle (Ivar Jonsen Frondal), Aurland, Sogn.
• Andreas Bjørnsen Viig (Andreas Bjørnsen Vigh, Andreas Bjørnsen Vik), Stavanger. Family used Benson as surname.
• Borre A. Benson Viig (Borre A. Benson Vigh, Borre A. Benson Vik); family later used Borreson as family surname. Wife Ingeborg Ingebrigtsdatter Gjesme, Flaam, Aurland, Sogn
• Knut A. Benson Viig (Knut A. Benson Vigh, Knut A. Benson Vik),

Stavanger; wife Martha Marie Winjum
• Tørjus Kittilsen Eiken (Tørjus Kittilsen Eken), Telemark
• Ole Bjørnsen Vinge (Ole Bjørnsen Vinje), Voss
• Peter O. Vinge (Peter O. Vinje), Voss
• Helge O. Bjøre
• Rauk family
Black Hammer—1856
• Helge Ellingsen Solberg, Ringerike
• John Souter
• Lars Olsen Blexrud
• H. Arnston
• Truls Swenson
• Ole Jacobsen Myhre
• John Jacobsen Holm
Black Hammer—1857
• Aamund Eriksen, born at Vikesland, Holum; wife Anna Torsdatter, born at Holum; Flaam, Aurland, Sogn
Black Hammer—1858
• Lars Eriksen Svartaas, Krødsherrad
Black Hammer—1859
• Trond Olsen Hemri, Nærøyfjord,

Juleneget opreises

Aurland, Sogn
- Botolv Olsen Hemri, Nærøyfjord, Aurland, Sogn
- Ananias Olsen Hemri, born in Nordland
- Martha Botolvsdatter Berekvam Hemri (widow)

Black Hammer—1860
- Tollef Hoganson; wife Julia
- Johannes Eriksen Berdahl (Johannes Eriksen Berdal), Feios, Leikanger, Sogn
- Elling Torsen Holum (Elling Torsen Hauglum), Flaam, Aurland, Sogn
- Nils Nilsen Exe (Nils Nilsen Ekse), Evanger, Voss; wife Kari Hermundsdatter Nese, Vik, Sogn
[great-great-great-grandparents to Deb Nelson Gourley]
- Knut Nelsen Exe (Knut Nelsen Ekse), Evanger, Voss
- Lars Larsen Exe (Lars Larsen Ekse), Evanger, Voss; wife Anna Eriksdatter Berdahl, Feios, Leikanger, Sogn
- Elias Cooper; wife Trine Eriksdatter Berdahl
- Mikkel Christensen Onsgard
- Peder Christensen Onsgard

Black Hammer—1861
- Elling Andersen Karlsbraaten
- Nils Olsen Vinjum (widower), Aurland, Sogn

Houston and Badger Valley
Supplemented by Jim Skree

Below Black Hammer runs a narrow and rugged valley before one comes to Sheldon and Badger Valley and other valley areas around Houston, Minnesota. Here lies a large community of intelligent and prosperous *Telemarkinger*. Badger Valley in particular, a broad but short valley surrounded by high ridges, is a most pleasant place. Its large farms make it one of the most appealing areas in Minnesota. In this beautiful valley, immigration to the Root River Valley area began.

One day in the spring of 1853, high up on a hill on the east side of this valley, sat Mikkel M. Synnes (Mikkel M. Sinnes), picking out a site for his future farm. With him was his brother *[brother-in-law –Skree]*, Aamund M. Sanden, Amund Veum and Guttorm Gutterson—all four from Kviteseid, Øvre-Telemark. *[The men were Aanund M. Sanden, Øvre-Telemark; Aanund Veum from Fyresdal; and Guttorm Guttormson, who arrived separately from Gol, Hallingdal. –Skree]*

Steiner Knutson Meaas, father of Congressman Halvor Steenerson, came the same year and settled in another part of the valley *[actually Sheldon Valley –Skree]*, where he raised a family of more than common intelligence. Gulbrand Kassenborg and Ole Studlien, both originally from Valdres, arrived the following year (1854). This particular valley is the mother colony of the Telemark community in Clay County, Minnesota.

In 1854, the movement of immigrants into this part of Houston County began in earnest. It included the large family of Ole Krokenes (Ole Kragness) and Anne Krokenes (Anne Kragness), with their grown sons and daughters: Hans Dahle, Torger Kragness, Leiv Kragness, Olaf Sanden, Sigrid Sanden, Kari Revskil, Dagny Swan, Gunhild Folson and Tone Findreng, all from Kviteseid in Telemark.

Next year came John E. Homme, father to one of the Norwegian Lutheran Church's most prominent sons, Pastor Even Johnson Homme *[founder of charitable institutions for senior citizens, etc., in Wittenberg, Wisconsin –Rosholt]*.

Ole Knutson from Drammen in Norway, brother to the well-known California Knudsen of Wiota Wisconsin, himself a veteran of the gold rush, was the first man to settle in the village of Houston. In 1852, he and Mons Anderson from La Crosse rowed and poled up the Root River in a flat-bottomed boat and platted a village where "Old Town" now lies. When the railroad came through, the village was moved a mile west. Knutson, the first businessman here in 1854, also operated a ferry, and became one of the first three commissioners on the county board. He later moved farther west.

They can still tell stories about happenings from the earliest years. Olav Skrei (Olav Skree) and Olav Lie (Olav Lee) built themselves a house over toward the hill directly east of Væting. They wanted the level land east of here for their house. But there was an Irishman on the west side who also wanted this land.

Lie and Skrei were newcomers and could not speak English. When the Irishman jabbered at them that he would have it, they jabbered right back, just like he did. So the Irishman carved out a man on a large aspen tree and put a bullet hole right in his forehead. He thought that should tell it clearly enough. But when the two *Fyresdøler* saw that, they carved out another man on the aspen tree and gave him an axe chop in the neck, and that was equally clear. The Irishman decided it was best to give up his claim to the land.

Lie and Skrei both took up land for themselves, where their farms are now (1908), and Christian Brokke bought land where the Væting (Vathing) farm is. *[Olav Skrei was a great-great-grandfather to Jim Skree.]*

The following list was compiled from these sources: 1853 History of Houston Co., 1882 and 1982; Telesoga, No. 17, 13:

Badger Valley—1853
From Telemark
• Mikkel Mikkelson Sinnes; wife Hæge, Vraadal
• Aanund Mikkelson Sanden; wife Anne, Vraadal
• Aanund Gjermundson Veum; wife Hæge, Fyresdal
• Hans Olson Dahle, Vraadal
• Targe Olson Kragness, Vraadal
• Targe Larson Revskil; wife Kari, Vraadal
• Osmund Larson Juve (Osmund Larson Weom); wife Ingeborg, Laardal
• Stener Knudson Meaas; wife Bergit, Morgedal and Seljord

Badger Valley—1853
From other areas
• Sigurd Anderson Skar; wife Christine, Maridalen (1st in church records, 1855)
• Guttorm Guttormson (Øino); wife Liv, Gol, Hallingdal

Houston Lutheran Stone Church records
From Telemark—1854
• Halvor Olson Storaasli; wife Else, Skafsaa
• Ole Tarjeson Kragness; wife Anne, Vraadal
• Leif Olson Kragness, Vraadal
• Jorand Aanundsdatter Vraa (widow), Vraadal
• Leif Olson Vraa, Vraadal
• Lavrants Anderson Vraa; wife Turine, Vraadal
• Kjøstuf Knutson Storaasli; wife Tone, Skafsaa
• Ole Aslakson Graver (Ole Aslakson Grover), Fyresdal
• Kristi Olsdatter Graver (widow), Fyresdal
• Tallef Olson (Tallef Olson Storaasli?), Skafsaa
• Tone Olsdatter (Tone Olsdatter Storaasli?), (widow), Skafsaa
• Ole Halvorson Skree; wife Sigrid, Fyresdal
• Ole Johnson Lee; wife Gro, Fyresdal
• Tarje Gunnarson Findreng; wife Tone, Vraadal
• Ole Anundson Jore; wife Sigrid, Vraadal
• Ole Gjermundson Vraa, Vraadal

From other areas—1854
• Arian Tønneson and wife, Farsund
• Ole Knudson Omodt; wife Martha, Helleland, Egersund
• Ole Eivindson Dølhus, Gol, Hallingdal
• Gulbrand Gulbrandson Kassenborg; wife Astri, Land
• Knud Olson Sorum, Valdres
• Herman Olson Norjord; wife Kari
• Albert Olson (Albert Ousel?); wife Tone
• Bernt Jacobson; wife Ingeborg

- Ola Knudson; wife Anne
- Aune Toreson; wife Inger Dorotea
- John Olson
- Anders Pederson
- Maria Amundsdatter
- Kari Olsdatter
- John Monsen; wife Sigrid Torgersdatter
- Sigrid Eivindsdatter
- Kristi Eriksdatter (widow)
- Mari Pedersdatter
- Wilhelm Augusta Johanneson
- Anders Monson and wife
- Knud Anderson

From Telemark—1855
- John Torson Lee; wife Gro, Kviteseid
- Amund Torson Barskor; wife Margit, Skafsaa
- Tarje Aslakson Grover, Fyresdal
- Samund Thorson Sanden; wife Sigrid, Vraadal
- Ingebjør Kjøstufsdatter Storaasli, Skafsaa
- Anne Kjøstufsdatter Storaasli, Skafsaa
- Jorand Gjermundsdatter Storaasli, Skafsaa

From other areas—1855
- Ole Olson Stutlien (elder of two Olson brothers named Ole); wife Ingri, Land
- Ole Olson Studlien (younger of two Olson brothers named Ole); wife Birte, Land
- Abraham Christensen (widower), Lillesand
- Magnus Anderson (Skar), Maridalen
- Hans Hanson Loken; wife Mari
- Tobias Henderson, Farsund (?)
- Beate Larson (widow)
- Andrew Hendrikson; wife Kristine Gulbrandsdatter
- Hendrik Hendrikson
- Peder Olson; wife Anne Pedersdatter
- Knud Salveson; wife Berthe
- Jette Tobiasdatter
- Ole Larson; wife Petronelle Olesdatter
- Osmund Jorgenson
- Ole Jenson and wife
- Christian Jacobson and wife

From Telemark—1856
- John Mattiason Sannes; wife Anne, Vraadal
- Ole Johnson Juve; wife Gunhild, Vraadal
- Ole Anundson Kragnes; wife Kari, Vraadal
- John Evenson Homme; wife Kari, Skafsaa and Vraadal
- Ole Bjørgulfson Tvedten; wife Bergit, Skafsaa
- Knud Anundson Lønnegrav; wife Sigrid, Vraadal
- Svennung Larson Revskil, Vraadal
- Lars Asmundson Juve; wife Ingerid, Laardal
- Ole Olson Bergland (widower), Skafsaa
- Eivind Johnson; wife (Haugejord?)—Kviteseid
- Andrew Anderson; wife (Vraa?), Vraadal

From other areas—1856
- Martin Christianson; wife Randine, Christiania
- Bernt Christianson
- Malene Torgesdatter (widow of Bernt Christianson?)
- Carl Christianson
- Dortea Johnson
- Hans Isakson Mo; wife Lovise
- Peder Erikson
- Marie Reiersdatter
- Kari Halvorsdatter
- Aanund Aanundson
- Gellaug Svendson
- Peder Asbjørnson
- Kristi Evensdatter
- Bernt Swenson and wife
- John Iverson and wife
- Harald Olson and wife
- Anne Eivindsdatter

[Note that most of the information listed here is from local church records, which are a primary source. They do not record the year that an individual arrived in the area, but rather when that person first took communion or was involved in a baptism ceremony, so they could have been here earlier. Marriage and confirmation records do not begin until the late 1850s. –Skree]

Fillmore County
Mabel and Newburg

Ten miles west of Spring Grove lie Newburg and Stavanger Prairie. Even Ellertson came to this region in 1851, settling on the south line of Minnesota near the future village of Mabel. He was the first real farmer in Minnesota.

The next Norsemen to arrive, in June 1853, were the following:
• Lars Tollefson Haugen and family, Hallingdal
• Hans Arneson, Ringerike
• Lars Trulson Ask, Ringerike
• Thomas Trulson Ask, Ringerike
• Lars Johnson, Ringerike
All were from Rock Prairie, Wisconsin.

They remained with Even Ellertson three days while looking for land. Joining them later were:
• Anders Gulbrandsen Ellestad, Hallingdal
• Iver Gulbrandsen Ellestad, Hallingdal
• Gulbrand Gulbrandsen Ellestad, Hallingdal

A couple of weeks later, the first Stavanger people began to arrive. Today they make up the majority of inhabitants in Newburg and Preble townships. Included in this group from Stavanger, Rogaland fylke, were:
• Hans Vælde (Hans Valder)
• Thor Olson Faae
• Iver Thompson Botne
• Knut Ytrevold
• Nils Johnson Nessa
• Nils Nilsen Kinnestad
• Lars. C. Tarvestad, Stavanger

They came up from Fox River in Illinois but were originally from the islands north of Stavanger. *[A footnote by Holand: "Pastor C. L. Clausen had just reached St. Ansgar, Iowa, and wrote to Emigranten about the excellent land in the vicinity. It was this letter that inspired Hans Valder and party."]*

About 1,000 from Stavanger now (1908) live in the neighborhood of the old Scheie church and form a prosperous community.

In the 1870s, when the fever to move to the Red River Valley was at its height, the ridges of Preble were depopulated for a time. Old Pastor Scheie *[presumably A. A. Scheie –Rosholt]* and nearly his entire congregation moved to Norman County and founded a large Stavanger colony in the neighborhood of Hendrum *[50 miles north of Moorhead, Minnesota –Rosholt]*. One year, there were only nine men to pay the pastor's salary *[presumably in the First Evangelical Lutheran church at Newburg in Fillmore County –Rosholt]*.

Hans Valder, leader of the first group of Stavanger people, platted a small village on his land, which he called Newburg, in the southeast corner of Fillmore County. Here he became the first postmaster in 1854 and operated a hotel for many years.

As he was quite good in English and a person who took a lively interest in everyone, Hans naturally held a position of leadership in the early days. He was a former schoolteacher in Norway and came to Leland, Illinois, in 1837, where he was the first Norseman in the city. He joined the Baptists there, and in 1844 was ordained—the first Norwegian Baptist minister in America.

But the salary was not enough to live or die on, and he left the ministry to become a farmer and hotelkeeper. In 1871 he was a member of the Minnesota legislature. As he was not only non-Lutheran but also hot-headed and opinionated, people lost respect for him.

Peter Asbjørnson Mehus organized the congregation here in 1855. *[It is not certain which congregation Holand refers to here. Norsk Lutherske Menigheter, p. 440, gives Den lste Evangelisk Lutherske ved Newburg Menighet, organized 8 June 1857, apparently by Peter L. Asbjørnson of the Augustana Synod. –Rosholt]*

First Evangelical Lutheran Church, Newburg

The First Evangelical Lutheran Church at Newburg ws organized on 8

June 1857 at the home of Thore Olson Faae. At this meeting, Rev. Peder Asbjørnson acted as chairman, with Iver Thompson as secretary.

The following joined the congregation that day:
- Jacob Jacobson Haga
- Guri Jacobson Haga
- Thore Olson Faae
- Elizabeth Olson Faae
- Hans Arneson
- Hokina Arneson
- Christian Christopherson
- Thore Nelson Sunde
- Martha Nelson Sunde
- Isaac Isaacson
- Inge Isaacson
- Lars Iverson
- Anna Iverson
- Jacob Larson
- Sevrena Larson

At the second meeting held a week later, Thore Faae was elected chairman and Christian Christopherson, secretary. Two new members joined, including Christian Iverson and Bertha Iverson. A letter of call was sent to Rev. A. A. Scheie of Milwaukee, Wisconsin.

Garness Church,
located between Newburg and Mabel

The Norwegian settlers in southeast Minnesota's Fillmore County came from settlements such as Fox River near Chicago and Muskego and Koshkonong in Wisconsin, and others in the east. In their search for good land, they staked their claims in some of Fillmore's County's best land and most pleasant countryside.

The first of these pioneers began their push into the area in 1851. Twenty-five years later, Fillmore County was claimed to be the most populated county in the whole state!

One of the earliest settlements in the county was at Newburg. The first white settlers came in 1851, shortly after a treaty with the Indians opened up the territory. As the new Norwegian immigrants arrived in this locality, they formed and organized the early congregations.

Among the first group of immigrants to settle in the section south of what is now (1908) the village of Newburg were the following:

Lille Lerfos i Nærheden af Trondhjem

- Ole Viger (1851)
- Andreas Førde (1852)
- Thorkel Dengerud (1853)
- Mikkel T. Lunde (1853)
- Gullick Olson Haugen (1853)
- Nils Knudson (1854)
- Morten Kjelsberg (1854)
- Neri Syverson (1854)
- Ole O. Bagli, who came with his parents from Flesberg, in 1843 at the age of 3. They settled here in 1854.
- Bjørn Olson Garnaas (Bjørn Olson Garness, Bjørn Olson Sata), wife Sidsel Nilsdatter Nubgarden and seven children:
- Ole Bjørnson Garnaas (Ole Bjørnson Garness)
- Niels Bjørnson Garnaas (Niels Bjørnson Garness)
- Hans Jørgen Bjørnson Garnaas (Hans Jørgen Bjørnson Garness)
- Mari Bjørnsdatter Garnaas (Mari Bjørnsdatter Garness)
- Engebret Bjørnson Garnaas (Engebret Bjørnson Garness, Embrik Bearson)
- Guri Bjørnsdatter Garnaas (Guri Bjørnsdatter Garness)
- Kari Bjørnsdatter Garnaas (Kari Bjørnsdatter Garness)

The Garnaas/Garness family, together with Iver Gulbrand and Andreas Gulbrandson Ellestad, immigrated to America in 1853. They settled in Wisconsin, then came to Minnesota and homesteaded in Newburg Township, built log cabins and returned to Wisconsin to bring back their families to their new home. They arrived here in 1854.

Arriving in the next few years were the following:
- John P. Førde (1855)
- Gabriel Gabrielson (1855)
- Ole Leverson Berge (1856)
- John Erickson (1858)
- Botolf Olson (1859)

While land was a priority of the first Norwegian colonists to the area, their thoughts also turned to God. Lutheran by heritage, they used the Bible, hymnbook and catechism in their homes as a source of comfort and inspiration. This helped them cope with the hardships and struggles of pioneer life. Yet they missed worshipping in a church led by a pastor. So the call went out for men of God to move to their communities to serve their spiritual needs.

Many a pioneer pastor traveled many miles by foot or by horse to reach these remote outposts. Garness Trinity Church's second pastor, E. P. Jensen, wrote down his memories of several of these "traveling preachers." Jensen's message, placed in (and later recovered from) the cornerstone of Garness Trinity Church, reads:

"Pastor Ulrik Vilhelm Koren from Washington Prairie Church near Decorah, Iowa, a zealous leader in the early Norwegian Evangelical Lutheran Church and at Luther College, was evidently the first Lutheran pastor to preach to these new settlers south of Newburg. He held services in the home of Østen Golberg when he came, during the years of 1854-56, and by the end of 1856, there was a small group that gathered for his services.

"In 1857, Pastor C. L. Clausen came from Norway to Spring Grove and served a large territory, including these first pioneer families of Garness Trinity. As there was no church building yet, they still gathering in the homes, now usually that of Bjørn Olson Garnaas (Bjørn Olson Garness) *[great-great-great-grandfather to Deb Nelson Gourley]*, where the foot-traveling pastor would also stay overnight. Pastor Clausen preached his farewell sermon at Spring Grove on 2 July 1865, having served a large territory for eight years.

"Then, for three years, the folks south of Newburg worshipped at Hesper as part of the parish served by Pastor H. A. Stub, who lived at Big Canoe across the Iowa line. The Hesper folks encouraged the Newburg group to join them in building a church at Hesper. However, since the distance was considerable in those days (of primitive transportation), the Newburg group decided to build its own church."

The first church building plans were drawn up early in 1868. The congregation separately organized as the Norwegian Evangelical Lutheran Trinity Church of Newburg, most probably under the leadership of Pastor Kristian Magelssen of Highland Prairie.

The building, completed in 1869, was built on the southeast corner of land owned and donated by Bjørn Olson Garnaas (Bjørn Olson Garness) about one and a half miles south of Newburg village. Building costs were $1,023. It was commonly called the "Garness Church" after his name and land, and also "Newburg Church," although that was confusing because of the Newburg church to the north, later called "Scheie."

Stavanger Prairie and Scheie Church

By the early 1850s, new immigrants had already taken up all available land in Illinois. This, combined with poor wages, prompted a group from Stavanger, who had come to Fox River in La Salle County, Illinois, as early as 1849, to go farther west.

An article written by Pastor C. L. Clausen caught the attention of Hans Valder, who had come to Illinois in 1836. This glowing report, appearing in a spring 1853 issue of *Emigranten*, boasted of the beautiful golden prairies of Iowa. The author had led a large group of Stavangers to St. Ansgar, Iowa.

That summer, Valder himself led a party of land-seekers into Fillmore County. They included:
• Thore Olson Faae
• Nels Nessa
• Iver Thompson Bothne
• Knute Ytrevold
• Nils Nilson Kinnestad
• Lars Tarvestad

In staking a claim, three items were of major importance: "ve og vand og slaateland"—that is, wood, water and hay ground. Here they found plenty of each. They and their families soon settled in a valley later named "Chickentown." Along with them came three yoke of oxen, some other horned stock, two rickety lumber wagons and a few household goods.

Thore Faae and Nels Nessa built a two-room log cabin, each room 10 by 12 feet. Basswood formed the roof, which sheltered an earthen floor.

Times were hard, with no money to buy more than just the basic necessities. Mrs. Faae had told that only once a year could they have sugar, and that was one dollar's worth for Christmas. For lights, they burned a rag in a pan of grease. Later, they made tallow candles. Their clothing was made of homespun material.

In August 1854, a land office was established in Brownsville, Minnesota, so the settlers could go there to pre-empt their land. After building a hut and living in it four or five days, any man over 21 could go to Brownsville where he had to swear it was for his own use and that he had no more than 160 acres. If he could pay $1.25 per acre for the same, the farm was his.

Christian Faae, son of Thore Faae and Mrs. Faae, was the first white child born in Preble Township (1854). John N. Johnson, son of Nels and Mrs. Nessa, was also born that year. Mary Monroe, born in 1852, was the first white child born in Newburg Township.

In 1854, these first immigrants were joined by many more—most from Stavanger, Rogaland. They had come as early as 1849 to La Salle County, Illinois, to the Fox River settlement. So many from Stavanger and the small islands near there settled here, that this became known as "Stavanger Prarien."

Others who staked land claims were Nels Kinnestad and Iver Thompson.

Hans Valder was a big help to the pioneers. He was well educated and was an ordained Baptist minister. After staking his claim in Newburg Township, he founded the village of

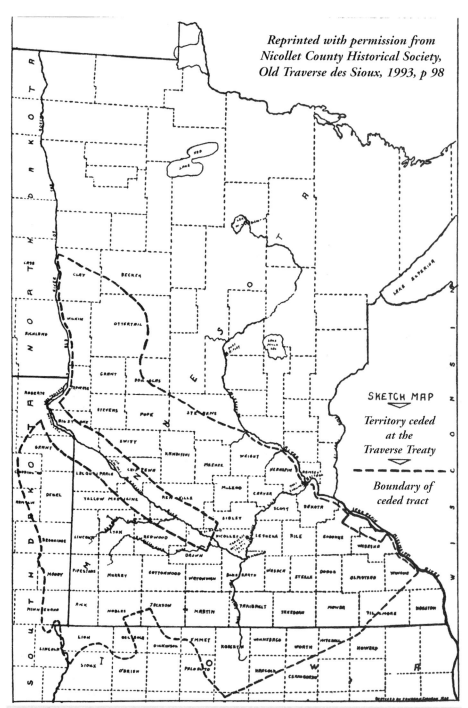

Map showing lands ceded by the Sioux Indians to the whites at the Doty Treaty and that of Traverse des Sioux, 23 July 1851; also showing the 10-mile-wide strip along the Minnesota River reserved for the Indians. The tract included some of the world's richest farming land. An empire of 24 million acres sold for $1,665,000.

Newburg. To accommodate the many travelers who went through on the Brownsville stagecoach, he opened a hotel called "Newburg House." Bjørn Spande built it in 1856, as well as the first store for Gabriel Gabrielson.

The records show that Ellef Tollefson and Kjerstine Tostensdatter were the first couple to be married in Newburg Township. They were married by Hans Valder. In 1856, he became Newburg's first postmaster and is said to have laid out the first roads in the area.

Others who settled in Preble Township included:
- Jacob Jacobson Haga (1854)
- Rasmus Spande (1854)
- Isaac Isackson (1854)
- Bartel Christopherson (1854)
- S. S. Hookland (1854)
- Clarence Iverson (1854)
- Peder Pederson (1854)
- Hans Arneson (1854)
- Ole Hendrickson (1854)
- Anders Halvorson (1856)
- Aslak Housker (1854)
- Jacob Elefson (1854)
- Christian Iverson
- Lars Iverson
- Jacob Larson Egrene
- Samson Anderson
- Anne Scheie
- Thore Nelson Sunde
- Bjørn Spande

Some of these families had Indians for neighbors, sometimes as many as 30, living in Chickentown. Had it not been for the kindness of the white men to the Indians, the early settlers would have fared much worse.

Neutral Ground

According to the book *History of Spring Grove*, 1852-1952, the Winnebago Indians, an outlying Siouan tribe, occupied part of Houston County in Minnesota between 1833 and 1848. In 1837, they signed a treaty in which they ceded all their lands east of the Mississippi to the U.S. government. The only land left for their occupation was in three townships of what is now Houston County: Spring Grove, Black Hammer and a corner of Yucatan.

For many years, the Sioux, Sacs and Fox Indian tribes had been in dispute about land in the Wisconsin-Iowa-Minnesota area. To put an end to the Indian wars, the government created a neutral zone. This zone was 40 miles wide from north to south and stretched from the Mississippi River, 100 miles to the west. The line started north of Clear Lake, Iowa, and went northeasterly to a point south of La Crosse, Wisconsin. All Indians were ordered to move out of this zone, and no more Indian wars were to be fought there.

The Sacs and Fox tribes agreed to cede to the United States the southern 20-mile strip of the zone and to move south into Iowa; the Sioux agreed to cede the northern 20 miles and retreat north into what is now Minnesota. The northern boundary of this "peace" zone runs through the area that comprises the Scheie congregation.

In 1832, the government hired Nathan Boone, youngest son of the famous Kentuckian and frontiersman, Daniel Boone, along with a crew of 10 men, to survey for this line. Boone's task was to record in writing every mile on this line, as well as to mark the boundary. If a tree grew along this line, it was carved on the south side with a large "U.S." to signify that side of the tree was United States territory. On the north side of the tree, a big "S" was carved to signify that the Sioux territory lay in that direction. If no trees were in the survey line, Boone planted a cylinder of charcoal and raised a mound over it.

Christ Austin, a pioneer from Newburg, used to tell of these high mounds. His father purchased Rev. Scheie's farm when he left; the family moved there when Christ was a young boy. The line fence between the Austin and Amdahl farms is part of the Boone survey line. Boone crossed into Minnesota near the Niagara Caves (and what is now Highway 52), in the Big

Bend south of the (1957) Sherman Haugerud farm *[from field notes of Boone]*. Austin said the pioneers found these mounds on the farms of Theo. Nesse, Jacob Larson and S. Hookland.

In June of 1848, the Winnebago were forcibly removed from the neutral ground. To aid in their removal, the government supplied 166 covered wagons with teams and drivers, and 500 tents for shelter. The cavalcade that left Houston County consisted of between 2,100 and 2,800 Indians, 1,600 ponies and 150 cattle. Military officers from Fort Atkinson, Fort Crawford, Prairie du Chein and Fort Snelling led the procession in their turn, accompanied by mounted soldiers and volunteers, mission and agency people, and even 60 northern Sioux. They followed the Fort Atkinson-Winona Indian trail from southeastern Minnesota to the Crow Wing River region in Minnesota.

Treaty of Traverse des Sioux (1851)

In July of 1851, at a crossing point along the Minnesota River just outside of St. Peter, Minnesota, a treaty was signed that a dozen years later would culminate in the bloody Minnesota Indian Uprising of 1862. The treaty bore the name of this crossing: "Traverse des Sioux" (or "crossing place of the Sioux").

At this peaceful spot, the U.S. government treated with the Dakota Indians of the Sisseton and Wahpeton bands. The 33 Indians signing the treaty ceded 24 million acres of prime land to the government—19.5 million in southern Minnesota, 3 million in northern Iowa, and 1.75 million in eastern South Dakota in exchange for cash (in the form of annuities).

Stipulations of a second "trader's paper," which they signed the same day, in effect made them pawns of the traders and caused much bitterness and hardship.

Many Norwegians were among the first to settle in this newly opened territory, whose ownership was still being contested by the Sioux. Meanwhile, the Indians were forced to move from this area, maintaining a narrow strip of land along the Minnesota River.

Highland Prairie

North of Stavanger Prairie lies Highland Prairie. Owing to the gaiety that prevailed here in former times, it is the best known of all these communities in southern Minnesota. It is populated almost entirely by *Telemarkinger*.

As early as 1853, Ole Johnson Øverland and Halvor Erikson had wandered about *Vaslausprærien*, as they called Highland Prairie *[vaslaus, suggesting "waterless" –Rosholt]*. When they did not find water here, they went back to Walworth County, wintering in a dugout near Calmar, Iowa. In March of 1854 they returned with a big party, riding in oxen-drawn wagons. This time they found water high up in a grove of trees.

Those who took land around this spring were the following, all from Kviteseid in Telemark:
• Johannes Olson Øverland, wife Tone, sons Steinar Johnson Øverland and Knud Johnson Øverland and daughters Guro Øverland, Anne Øverland and Bergit Øverland
• Ole Johnson Øverland (oldest son of Johannes Olson Øverland), wife Gunhild Franson Rue and two children
• Halvor Erickson and wife Kari Johnsdatter Øverland
• Kari Øverland Rue (sister of Johannes Olson Øverland), a widow, and her families
• Harold Olson Rue (Harald Olson Jordgrav), wife Bergit Fransdatter Rue and five children
• Hans Franson Rue (son of Kari Øverland) and sister Kari Fransdatter Rue
• Gunnuld Evenson, Kaasa

[Note: Lorna Anderson is a great-great-granddaughter of Johannes Olson Øverland through two lines, as well as descending from his sister, Kari Øverland Rue (a great-great-grandmother). Thus,

Lorna is related to most of the Telemark settlers at Highland Prairie.]

A letter was sent to friends in Walworth County, and another party came from Wisconsin, arriving in June 1854 and bringing their cattle and household goods. Members of this group, all from Kviteseid, included:
• Carl Franson Rue, wife Mari Olafsdatter Rue and six children (including Ole C. Rue)
• Kittel Olson Jordgrav (Kittel Olson Rue), wife Margit Øygaarden and four children
• Karl Olson Rue and children
• Eyvin G. Dølali (Even G. Dølalie) with sons Aslak Eyvinson and Østen Eyvinson
• Hans Gunderson Lia
• Ole Gunderson Lia
• Hans Paulson Blom
• Gunnar Paulson Blom
• Ole Jacobson
• Mikkel Mikkelson Jordgrav
• Saamund Thorbjørnson Nykus

Thus, all at once everything became quite folksy on *Vaslauspraerien*. Up to 100 people lived there that first summer and fall in their wagons, camping under the trees near the spring. And with all the cows, pigs, chickens and so on, things were quite lively.

That same fall of 1854, the following joined the community:
• Ellert Ellertson, Isak Ellertson, Nils Ellertson and Elling Ellertson (all sons of Even Ellertson)
• Ole Jørgenson Wold

From Highland Prairie northward runs a long and twisted ridge generally known as griserumpen *[the pig's tail –Rosholt]*. To this ridge in 1855 came another party of *Telemarkinger* via Walworth County in Wisconsin. Members of this party included, from Flaabygd:
• Ole Kittelson Stensrud
• Ole Mikkelson Rekaness
• Ole Solid
• Ole Kittelson Kaasa
• Halvor Kittelson Dumpendahl
• Tosten Gunderson Veungen
• Kittil Gunderson Veungen

Ole Kittelson Stensrud, the leader, settled farther north, where he had a bigger tract of land to rule over. Because of his large farm and his weakness for boasting about himself—not to mention an alleged cache of money he kept, people gave him the title of "King Busil," after Busil in Bø, where he grew up in Norway. The king's palace, however, was quite modest—a log house 10 by 12 feet.

There was also another "king" on Highland Prairie—"King" Haakon Olson—and amusing scenes were sure to follow whenever these two majesties met. Anecdotes about Olson, nicknamed "The Buffalo King-on-the-Pig's-Tail," added a touch of color to Highland Prairie's early history.

On Highland Prairie there is also an important colony of people from Nannestad in Øvre Romerike. The first of these to arrive in 1855 were John Larson Jahr and John Larson Stensgaard, who came via Koshkonong. Jahr was later a member of the state legislature in Minnesota *[from Fillmore County, elected in 1871 –Rosholt]*.

In 1857, a party of people originally from Øvre Romerike moved up from Lafayette County in Wisconsin. They included, from Nannestad:
• Lars Humble
• Martin Stensgaard
• Jens Hanson
• Ole Wensel
• Lars Sevig
• Lars H. Jahr
• Christoffer Haug
• John O. Gaarder

The most prominent citizen of Highland Prairie was Andreas S. Byholt, a former schoolteacher in Gjerestad, who arrived in the community in 1856. He was consulted on all sorts of legal matters.

One of the best-known men in Fillmore County is Thomas Kopperud, who came here with his father from Nannestad in 1861. A man of means when he came to the U.S., he has since added to his fortune.

Though a kind and helpful person, Kopperud is an independent thinker in religious affairs. As an example of this independence, he expressed dissatisfaction with the management of the local church. As there was no other in the vicinity that he wanted to join, he built his own church with a spire that can be seen across the prairie a long way. Here he should be contented, because he has both pastor and congregation.

To build a church is quite something for a Norwegian farmer to manage, but it was nothing to raise the eyebrows on a man like Kopperud. Take, for instance, the time that the congregation in Rushford built a new church and was willing to sell its old building for $1,200. A small "Free-Free" (Evangelical Free Church, not a Lutheran church) congregation wanted to buy it but could not raise more than $200. Kopperud heard about this, dug into his mattress for a thousand dollars and drove down the hill to Rushford, where he bought the church and gave it to the poor-in-pocket as well as in spirit.

Highland Prairie Lutheran Church

In the early 1850s, the first Norsemen, some of whom had lived for some time at Rock Prairie, Skoponong and Koshkonong, came to Fillmore County. By this time, most of the good land at these places was already settled. This, plus the fact that they had little or no money, prompted their move to Minnesota, where there was still free land available.

They had been warned that Minnesota was too cold for corn to ripen there, but that they could raise wheat. In 1853, Ole Johnson Øverland and Halvor Erickson (mentioned earlier in this chapter) immigrated to Fillmore County. Some of their friends and relatives joined them the following year.

From Koshkonong in 1855 came several families who were originally from Nannestad, Norway. The community where these people settled was well adapted to farming, the soil being very fertile.

There being only Norwegian settlers in the township, it was called Norway. The community in Norway from which many of the settlers came was called Bratsberg (older name for Telemark). Therefore, the name Bratsberg was chosen for the first post office. Due to the higher terrain compared to the surrounding territory, the community was called Highland Prairie.

In the first years, Indians would quite often come and beg for something to eat. They asked for pork, butter, flour and soap. During storms, the Indians would sometimes, without asking, walk into the home of the pioneer and simply stay until inclined to leave. If the pioneers had not been as friendly toward the Indians as they were, chances are that the settling of the pioneers would not have been such an easy task.

Han Lia, one of the first settlers, had staked out the land he wanted to claim. A large Indian came and pulled the stakes up and made Lia understand that the land belonged to him and that he did not want him there. This was probably true. Hans Lia put the stakes back in the ground again and let the Indian understand that he intended to stay there. The Indian left.

Following are the first settlers:
- A. Byholt
- G. Gaarder
- J. Stensgaard
- Even G. Dølalie
- O. Overland
- Halvor Eriksen
- S. Overland
- L. Jahr
- Johan Jahr
- Gunnar Dahle
- Rasmus Groettum
- Ole Carstensen
- Peter M. Olsen

- Halvor Nordby
- Anders Ness
- Halvor Haasarud
- H. Paulsen
- Even E. Dahl
- Ellert Ellertsen
- E. Jensen
- Lars Humble
- Carl Frandsen Rue
- G. Storaasli
- M. Nordness
- M. Hegland
- Hans Frandsen
- O. Thorud
- Bjørn Endru
- Østen Engebretsen
- Dreng Lundeberg
- Jørgen Andersen
- Aanund Berland

The first minister to visit this community was Pastor U. V. Koren from Washington Prairie near Decorah, Iowa. His name will always be remembered because of his unselfish service to his parishioners. As one of the area's first pastors, he traveled most of the time. He was truly a home missionary—preaching, baptizing, visiting the sick, comforting the sorrowing and dying, and officiating at funerals.

He first visited southern Minnesota in 1854. Whether he at this time visited the town of Norway or Highland Prairie is not definitely known, as a fire in 1870 destroyed Pastor Koren's parsonage. Consequently, his books and all records were lost. But from 1855 on, Highland Prairie has records showing that services were conducted from time to time.

The first pastor to be called to serve this and associated congregations was N. E. Jensen. Jensen had been ordained in Norway. He and his young wife arrived here in the fall of 1859. Since there was no parsonage at that time, they lived part-time in Rushford, and for a while made their home with the Halvor Nordby family.

On 15 June 1855, the first children were baptized at Highland Prairie:
- Ola, son of Ole Johanneson and wife Gunhild Fransdatter
- Christian, son of Carl Olsen and wife Christie
- Elen Marie (Mrs. Albert Lia), daughter of Harald Olsen and wife Bergit Fransdatter
- Ola Christian (Ole K. Wold), son of Ole Jørgensen and wife Olava Johannesdatter
- Olaf (Ole Dahle), son of Gunnar Gunnarsen and wife Gunhild Halvorsdatter
- Albert (Albert Lia), son of Han Gunnarsen and wife Aasta Anundsdatter
- Karen, daughter of Herman Knudsen and wife Ingeborg Olsdatter
- Betsy, daughter of Anders Haldorsen and wife Marit Gunnarsdatter
- Ola, son of Mikkel Kittelsen and wife Tarand Anundsdatter

In 1859, the first marriages recorded were:
- Svend Aslaksen and Signe Anundsdatter
- Halvor Kittelsen and Ingeborg Olsdatter
- Johan Carlsen and Sunnive Sørensdatter
- Hans H. Nordby and Guro Johannesdatter

Highland Church

In July of 1855, John Johnson Rodebakken arrived in this area. He was born in Norway in 1827 and came to Illinois in 1849. He moved from there to Holt Township in 1855 with his brother-in-law, John Ellefson.

Other early settlers included the following families:
- Knud Olson
- Hans Gunvalson and wife, Ingeborg Tostensdatter Nøbben
- Ole Rue
- Nils Evenson (also known as Neils Evensen, Nelson Evans or Nels Evans) and wife Gunhild Tostensdatter Nøbben
- Knud Knudson
- Abraham Jensson
- Andres Nepstad
- Ingebrette Larson

- Jens A. Highland
- Cornelius Strand
- Thore Quam
- Hans Olson
- Dreng Lundeberg
- Thore Johnson
- Knud Lerol
- Helmick Helland
- Thore Erickson

In 1856, the first white child, a son of J. J. Rodebakken, was born in the township.

On 15 February 1858, the Highland Evangelical Lutheran Church was organized at the home of Peder Pederson. Its original name was "Highland Prairie Norske Evangeliske Luthers Kirke." According to church records, the first child to be baptized there, on 3 January 1858, was Jonnas Pederson, 3 January 1858. Pastor Scheie performed the ceremony.

Elstad Lutheran Church, between Highland and Amherst

When these first colonists arrived in Fillmore County in the early 1850s, land was still available for them to build their first primitive homes. The early settlers around Amherst were no exception to this rule. When the settlers began to pour in, there were no railroads in the county and only a very few trading points.

According to the *Centennial History of Elstad Lutheran Church*:

"The first Norwegian settlers came here in 1852 when Knud Knudson and family established their home on the land where Amherst Village was to be located. The family came from Hallingdal in Norway, which is a district from which no settlers came to this community for several years. But no matter where later arrivals came from in Norway, they would find the Knudson home open to them with all the hospitable accommodations it could provide." *[Knud Knudson Sævre, great-great-grandfather to Deb Nelson Gourley, arrived in 1853 –Gourley]*

In 1853 the following families settled in this locality:

- David Dunham
- Halvor Peterson
- Gulbrand Holt
- Torger Lunde
- Anders Tollefson Lunde

David Dunham took land south of Highland, while Holt settled farther north in the township that was later named after him. The Lunde families settled to the west in what is now Preston Township.

A large number of settlers came in 1854, many of whom were either relatives or friends of the families who arrived the previous year. This group included the following families:

- Lars Elstad
- Peder Stenshoel
- Anders T. Ask
- Knud Lerol
- Thomas Lerol
- Thomas Ask
- Ole Blagstvedt
- Hans Dammen
- Mons Blagstvedt
- Hans Gunvalson
- Lars Flattum
- Jon Gullickson
- Anders Nepstad
- Johan Sæthre
- Osmund Johnson
- Simon Soine
- Martin S. Anderson
- Lars Trulson Ask

The year 1855 brought additional families. These included:

- Halvor Laastuen
- Lage Vesteren
- Bore Feiring
- Hendrik Dammen
- Peder Sørenson
- John Carlson
- Ole Pederson
- Christian Dunham
- Gubrand Dunham

In 1856 and 1857 the following families came:

- Ole Rustad
- Iver Rustad
- Anders Baalerud
- Ole Storhov

- Anders Evenson
- Truls Soland
- Nels Stubberud
- Peder Rosheim

This marks the last year in which settlers came here in any sizable groups. All the suitable land had been pre-empted by that time because of the influx of settlers of other nationalities. (Minnesota became a state in 1858).

Harmony

Looking at it from the viewpoint of a farmer, Harmony is no doubt as beautiful a place as one will find in Minnesota. Nice groves of trees may be found here and there, and even a few streams, while the quality of the land for farming is tops.

Tallak Brokken, who originated in Setesdal, discovered this country. He arrived in June 1854, together with seven other *Sætersdøler* who came up from Rock River in Wisconsin. En route they stopped to consult with Even Ellertson, already settled on the Iowa-Minnesota state line. Four of these men settled near Harmony, including:
- Tallak Brokken
- Arne Sigurdson Kirkelie
- Sven Sigurdson Kirkelie
- Torger Drengson Høftø

Two more in this group of seven, Eyvind Besteland and Knut Kviste, went west to York Township, where

Udsigt fra Faleide

they founded a big *Sætersdøler* colony. The other two, the brothers John H. Homme and Knut H. Espetvedt, went north to Arendahl, where they were the first in that area.

Tallak Brokken is widely known both in Norway and the U.S. as the richest man among *Sætersdøler*. When he arrived in 1854, he had only $150, which he used to purchase 120 acres of land. For many years he had to borrow money at 48 percent interest from that usurious man Easton in Chatfield *[southeast of Rochester, Minnesota –Rosholt]*. But with patience and wisdom, he acquired a fortune. Now he pays $2,000 in taxes and owns 6,000 acres of land.

If thrift is a virtue, then Brokken is to be admired. The most prominent house in Harmony is his, and a U.S. coin is to him a holy jewel to be regarded with devotion and not as a frivolous token.

Only one other *Sætersdøler*, Charles Kjøgjei (Charles Harstad), came to Harmony, an area known as a strong Telemark community. A few days later, a party of *Tinndøler* came up from Muskego, driving oxen and wagons. They included:
• Erik Solseth, Tinn
• Herbjørn Ingolfsland, Tinn
• Johannes Sauali, Tinn
• Ellis Thoen, Tinn
• Johannes Thoen, Tinn

In July 1854, John Jacobson Einong and Austin Øvrebakke (Austin Eastman) arrived. That same year, two *Tinndøler* settled in Canton Township, east of Harmony. One was Gjermund J. Kasen, one of the most distinguished Tinn emigrants in America and full of old memories, juicy as grapes, about the pioneer times in Muskego and in Minnesota.

That fall, another big party of *Telemarkinger* came up from Sun Prairie in Dane County (Wisconsin), including the families of:
• Ole Scrabek, Siljord (Seljord)
• Kittil Fjortoft, Siljord (Seljord)
• Gunder Thoe, Siljord (Seljord)
• Torger Felland, Vinje
• Asle Flatastøl, Vinje
• Ole Flatastøl, Vinje

Ole Scrabek was an especially capable and friendly man, and both Americans and Norwegians considered him to be the most prominent in the settlement.

Andrew Tollefson, Torger Peterson and Ole Munson, all from Hedmark, reached Preston Township as early as 1853; since that time, many more from Hedmark have joined them.

Greenfield Prairie and Greenfield Church

The congregation at Harmony is called Greenfield, a name that harkens back to the time when a small rat-hole of saloons once stood where the church was later built. A Tinn emigrant by the name of Knut Peterson Husevold settled here in 1855, platted a village and started in business, full of high hopes. But something happened, and the village gradually disappeared. Later, Husevold went north to become the first Norwegian settler in Stevens County. He presently (1908) serves as postmaster in Cyrus *[10 miles west of Starbuck, Minnesota –Rosholt]*.

Some of the first settlers to arrive at Greenfield Prairie were the following:
• J. E. Sauerlie
• Johannes Thoe
• Erick Solseth
• Herbjørn N. Ingulfsland

Although these early colonists were preoccupied with building log cabins, breaking virgin soil and making a living, they also remembered God. Church work was begun on the Greenfield Prairie in 1856. The word of God, and the early sacraments, were provided to these pioneers by the Reverends N. E. S. Jenson, P. A. Rasmussen and U. V. Koren.

Before they had a church building, they gathered for services in homes, or in a little red schoolhouse a half mile east of the old Greenfield Church near Harmony. On 10 December 1864, the first recorded meeting of the Greenfield congregation was held. The first pastor called to serve this congregation was Rev. Tobias Larsen.

In 1856, Knut Husevold donated an acre of land for the Greenfield Cemetery.

Following are 85 names of Greenfield's charter members, the original founders of the congregation:
- Ole S. Eriksen Solseth
- Herbjørn Nilsen Ingulfsland
- Dreng Evenson Kirkelie
- John Thompson Krosso
- Johannes Elefson Sauerlie
- Arne A. Aaberg
- John Jacobson Einong
- Ole Olsen Skrabek
- Halvor Svennungsen Bostrak
- Tallak Brokken
- Erik Eriksen Solseth Jr.
- Svend E. Solseth
- Erik Eriksen Solseth Sr.
- Thorgrim Drengson Rege
- Kittil A. Harstad
- Gjermund Johnson Kasen
- Gregar Herbjørnsen Bøen
- Torger Halvorsen Rollag
- Nils Knutsen Gaasedelen
- Tosten Ellefson Kvammen
- Helge Halvorsen Rollag
- Herbjørn Olsen Vaae
- O. H. Oppegaard
- Anders J. Boxrud
- Aslag Nubson
- Hans S. Johnson
- Østen Maland
- Thomas Thompson Krosso
- Hellik Morem
- Nels Johnsen Boxrud
- Nils Nilsen Morem
- Gunulf J. Bruflodt
- John Nilsen Boxrud
- E. G. Johnson
- Nils Bøen
- Gunulf Johnson Qvile
- Lars Larsen Hegland
- Arne Arnesen
- Ole Pedersen
- John Sevalsen
- John Johnson Kasen
- Johannes Olsen Thoe
- Ole Østensen Bomaagen
- Arne Evensen Kirkelie
- Even B. Haugum
- Gullek A. Maland
- Herman Knudsen Hemmestvedt
- Harvey Gregersen Bøen
- Kittil Alfson Veseth
- Ole Olsen Traim
- Even Wilsen Neshaug
- Ole J. Kasen
- Ole J. Morem
- Ole Olsen Flatastøl
- Thomas Wilson Traim
- Ola Kittelsen
- Tallak Larsen
- Peder Mathisen Rakkestad
- Andreas P. Helgeland
- Nels H. Gausta
- Ole Christiansen
- Nils N. Ingulfsland
- Svend E. Kirkelie
- Kittil Fjostuft
- Gunder Thoe
- Torger T. Felland
- Asle Olsen Flatastøl
- Østen N. Ingulfsland
- Tollef A. Harstad
- Thomas H. Vindleik
- Erik Matsen Staur
- Johannes Jensen Auren
- Knut Arnesen
- Thor E. Kirkelie
- Aanon Torgerson Omlie
- Jørgen Kittelsen Bjørgo
- Kristian Olsen
- Svennung O. Haugerud
- Julius Markestad

When the original parish became too large to be served by one pastor and one church, plans were made for new parishes. The Union Prairie Church withdrew from the Greenfield Parish in 1879 to unite with Bethlehem congregation at Lanesboro and with the Whalan Church at Whalan, Minnesota. The Root Prairie congregation withdrew to unite with North Prairie congregation. Saterdal joined with a church in Cresco, Iowa, and later with the Bloomfield congregation

Et Pas i Uladalen i Jotunheimen med Semmeltind

near Ostrander, Minnesota. Henrytown, a daughter congregation of Greenfield, organized in 1870; it is located northeast of Harmony. Fremont, another daughter, organized in 1896.

Stringtown (Strung-out-town), Amherst
Supplemented by Deb Nelson Gourley

Northeast from Harmony lies the Henrytown neighborhood. A Halling by the name of Knut Knutson (Knud Knudson Sævre) was the first man in Amherst Township, and he settled in Stringtown (old name for Amherst) in 1853. But no more *Hallinger* came to join him.

[Knud Knudson Sævre and his wife, Gunhild Guttormsdatter Syversrud Myhre, were great-great-grandparents to Deb Nelson Gourley. Deb's family still owns and operates the original Knudson site, making it one of the oldest Norwegian farms of continuous family ownership in the state of Minnesota.]

Two sons, Carl Gustav Knudson and Mikkel Knudson, were born to Knud and Gunhild and baptized at Luther Valley, Rock County, Wisconsin. In May 1853, the family came west with Pastor Clausen's wagon train caravan bound for St. Ansgar, Iowa, but broke away from the group and went north into Minnesota.

Among Gunhild's family members who arrived in 1857 to Stringtown were her mother, (then age 65), stepfather, and two half-sisters as follows:
• Astri Herbrandsdatter Børtnes Syversrud
• Tosten Larson Ursdalen Nøbben
• Gunhild Tostensdatter Nøbben (married Nels Evenson Lian from Tunhovd, Numedal
• Ingeborg Tostensdatter Nøbben (married Hans Gunvalson from Aadalen)

Gunhild's full brother, Jens Guttormson Syversrud Kolsrud (Jens Guttormson Nøbben) immigrated in 1846, the same year as Knud Knudson Sævre. However, no further information is known about Jens.

The village of Amherst and Amherst Township were organized in 1858. Amherst was one of the early and wealthy villages of Fillmore County. The dark loam mixed with clay soil and its generally rolling prairie with timber made the land valuable.

The early names of Amherst—Strung-out-town and Stringtown—were indicative of its early growth. The name Stringtown came from the fact that all the settlers built their houses along the road in the ravine where the village is located. Ethan P. Eddy gave Amherst its name in honor of his wife, Julia Onstine, who was born in Amherst, Ohio.

Hurrakroken (Hurrah-Corners)

Another settlement with a strange name is Hurrah-Corners, which is located near Harmony. Here is how it came by its name: Often, on their way home, the settlers, their pockets empty and their heads stoned, were in the habit of racing their horses down across the bottomlands yelling, "Hurrah!" Thus the name, "Hurrah-Corners."

Rushford, North Prairie and Lanesboro

When one travels up through the Root River Valley on the railroad from La Crosse, Wisconsin, to Fountain, Minnesota, some nice farmlands may be seen here and there, but the terrain is hilly and swampy as well. West of Rushford, however, there lies a nice plain with fertile soil.

A party of *Numedøler* came in June 1853 from Rock Prairie including:
• Peter Peterson Haslerud
• Hellik Glaim
• Erik T. Lien
• Ole Berland

Oliver Wilson, a youth from Hjartdal in Telemark, was also along.

These men were experienced land-lookers who had lived in America for some time and had bypassed considerable good land before they were entirely satisfied.

The same Arthur Bow, mentioned earlier as a nuisance in Spring Grove, was also squatting on the valley here. He wanted several hundred dollars for every quarter section before he would give up his assumed rights. He emphasized this demand by showing how good he was with a handgun.

But Hellik Glaim, one of the most daredevil and quick-witted types to ever leave Norway, soon had Bow under control. Before the Yankee troll could say Jack Robinson, Glaim was sitting on his chest, refusing to release him before he swallowed his words and permitted everyone to take the land they wanted. Then Glaim let him up, promising him that if he ever showed his face around again, he would never get away before he had swallowed his own revolver. Hellik Glaim later became a pioneer in Yellow Medicine County, Minnesota.

In the spring of 1854, the first *Sogninger* began to fill up that part of Fillmore County that lies north of Root River—Rushford and Lanesboro. It is now one of the largest Sogn centers in the U.S., with a population of nearly 3,000. Members of this first *Sogninger* party included:
• Knut Knutson Bedle (Knut Knutson Bell), with three sons: Knut Knutson, Tollev Knutson and Ragnvald Knutson
• Ragnval Knutson Stondall
• Christian O. Bratrud
• Tore O. Bratrud
• Ole O. Bratrud
All were originally from Urland (Aurland) in Sogn, and all had lived for a time around Koshkonong.

This first *Sogninger* party settled a short distance east of Lanesboro and began housekeeping in an abandoned Indian village of 40 houses constructed of elm bark bound together with willow. Some of these houses were quite large, up to 40 by 60 feet. The bark on the houses was later found useful by the pioneers when they began building their own homes.

Not far from here lay another Indian village of 60 braves with their families. These people went into the homes of the pioneers, took what they wanted and even insulted the daughters of some Irish families in the neighborhood. The Irishmen and the *Sogninger* took council together, assembled a force of nearly 20 men and marched over to the Indians, who were advised in no uncertain terms that unless they removed by not less than two days' journey within the hour, there would be war. The Indians replied with disdain but went inside for a council. Frightened by the determined attitude of the whites, they decided to leave, the last ever to live in Root River Valley.

The following year, 1855, more people from Urland (Aurland) in Sogn arrived in Root River Valley. They included:
• Anders Olson Ulvestad
• Anders Olson Lødal
• Lars Olson Lødal
• Hans Augunson Høigje
• Anders Erikson

All came by way of the Norway Grove colony in Dane County (Wisconsin) and settled on North Prairie, north of the town of Peterson. Lars Ulvestad later wrote letters home, which influenced many more people to join him.

The fall of 1855 saw the arrival of the following from Sogn fylke:
• Svend Thompson
• Lars Thompson
• Christian Johnson
• Nils A. Gullickson
• Harold Olson
• Tore Knudsen Jutland

Among the first from Norway to reach Rushford (circa 1855) were the brothers Even Reishus and Sondre Reishus. Originally from Flatdal in Telemark, they were the first to emigrate from this community to the U.S. in 1843.

Joining the settlement in 1857 were Arne Boyum, Ole Boyum and Syvert Boyum, who later became some of North Prairie's leaders and its most wealthy men. The Boyum family is from Balestrad in Sogn; Arne Boyum was a lay pastor who, in 1856, had visited North Prairie as a mission worker for the Ellingean *[Elling Eielsen –Rosholt]* Lutheran Synod.

In 1858 a rather large congregation was organized here, which called Arne Boyum as its pastor. He was then ordained and has now (1908) worked in the ministry for 50 years. In 1876 he was elected president of the Hauge Synod *[the former Eielsen Lutheran Synod –Rosholt]*.

In 1861, the North Prairie congregation built an 18-by-34-foot frame church, the first Norwegian church completed in Minnesota. The annual meeting of the Hauge Synod was held here the same year.

The first immigrant from Sogn into Rushford—where there are now many—was John Iverson from Vik, who settled here in 1855. He was a master shoemaker, widely known in this district. His son, state auditor Samuel G. Iverson, is prominent in Minnesota politics (1908).

Lanesboro, the county's second largest town and a completely Norwegian center, was not platted before 1868. Charles Johnson from Hedmark owned the ground where the town now lies.

In 1868, some strangers began to build a big hotel of stone in the middle of Johnson's wheat field, for which he was awarded $50 in damages. About the same time, an enterprising editor, under the shade of an oak tree, was getting out the first edition of a newspaper for the village. Under another tree sat a Yankee selling raw whiskey in a tin cup.

Now (1908) the village has a population of 1,300, the majority of whom are Norsemen. One of these is Samuel Nelson, the oldest businessman in town and one of its leading citizens. He is a state senator, a church warden and a man to trust.

Pastor U. V. Koren, who made periodic visits to the Norwegian colonies in this area, organized a number of congregations in 1855, including Spring Grove and Highland.

North Prairie Lutheran Church

Like that of many of the Lutheran congregations in Fillmore County, the history of North Prairie congregation began before Minnesota became a state. In 1803, the Louisiana Purchase gave the United States possession of all the land formerly owned by France, west of the Mississippi River, extending from Canada to the Gulf of Mexico and west as far as the Rocky Mountains.

Missouri was the first state formed in the Louisiana Territory (1812). In 1838, the Territory of Iowa was created. Most of the southern part of Minnesota was included in the Territory of Iowa. In 1846, Iowa became a state and its present boundaries were established.

By an Act of Congress, 3 March 1849, the Territory of Minnesota was created, and President Zachary Taylor appointed Alexander Ramsey as the first governor. By a treaty with the Sioux Indians, negotiated at Mendota and dated 5 August 1851, the Indian land included in the Minnesota Territory was ceded to the United States. This treaty was finally approved by the Senate and proclaimed by President Millard Fillmore on 24 February 1853.

Fillmore County, created by the Minnesota Territorial Legislature, 5 March 1853, included all of Winona and Houston counties and a part of Olmsted County. Winona and Houston counties were created out of the much larger Fillmore County on 23 February 1854. The present lines of Fillmore County were fixed when the legislature created Olmsted County on 20 February 1855.

North Prairie congregation is located in both Fillmore and Winona counties. In Fillmore County, the county offices were first located in Chatfield in 1853, but were moved to Carimona in

1855. On the first Monday in April 1856, an election was held, and by popular vote, the permanent county seat was relocated to Preston. For two years beginning 1 August 1854, a U.S. Land Office was located in Brownsville, Houston County. It was moved to Chatfield on 12 June 1856. On the 11th day of May 1858, Minnesota became a state and was admitted into the Union.

A few white settlers had moved into Fillmore County, near Newburg, in 1851, "...but there was no general movement of emigrants into this territory until 1853, nor did the tidal wave strike heavily until 1854. But from that time until 1857, there was scarcely an ebb in the tide, but a constant flow into and through this county to points further west." –*History of Fillmore County, 1912 edition*

The North Prairie community received the following settlers in 1853 from Rock Prairie, Wisconsin:
• Peter Peterson Haslerud, Numedal
• Hellik Glaim, Numedal
• Erik T. Lien, Numedal
• Ole Berland, Numedal
  Other settlers included:
• Oliver Wilson (1853)
• Aslak Anderson (1854)
• Halvor Sinnes (1854)
• Knut Knutson Bedle (Knut Knutson Bell), and his three sons; Knut Knutson, Tollev Knutson and Ragnvald Knutson (1854)

Others who came from Urland (Aurland), Sogn, by way of the Koshkonong settlement in Wisconsin in 1854, included:
• Ragnvald Knutson Stondal
• Christian Bratrud
• Tore Bratrud
• Ole O. Bratrud

The spring of 1855 saw many more of the sturdy Vikings settling in Houston County:
• Osmund Rollefson
• Andrew Olson Olnestad
• Andrew Olson Lodahl
• Hans Augundson Hogie
• Knud Torvildsen
• Halvor Olson Wraalstad
• Christian Thoresen
• Christian Johnson
• Anders Erickson
• Svend Thompson
• Lars Thompson
• Anders Olsen Ulvestad
• Nels A. Gullickson
• Harold Olson
• Tore Knutsen Jutland
• Even Reishus

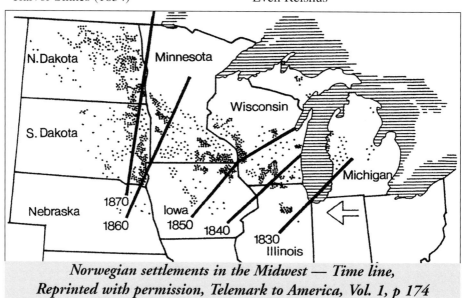

Norwegian settlements in the Midwest — Time line, Reprinted with permission, Telemark to America, Vol. 1, p 174

- Sondre Reishus
- Lars Pedersen Helme
- Tore Pedersen Helme
- Guldbrand Aaberg
- Hans Hansen

Coming into the community in 1856 were:
- Peter Berg
- Sigur Berg
- K. O. Aarthun
- Peder Einarsen
- Ole Tollefsen
- Egil Guttormsen
- Ola Thompson
- John Gilbertsen Tinglestad
- Isaac Jackson

North Prairie congregation was organized on 4 May 1858; work for the congregation began in 1856. The church records show that on 1 September 1856, Pastor U. V. Koren was on North Prairie, conducting services and baptizing children at two different homes.

In Carrolton Township at the home of K. O. Aarthun, the following were baptized:
- Ola, child of Lars Olsen and wife Auguna
- Kirsti, child of Hans Augnundsen and wife Mette
- Torkild, child of Erik Torkelsen and wife Ingri
- Peder, child of Ragnvald Stondalen and wife Marte
- Anna, child of Sigurd Sigurdsen and wife Sigri
- Einar, child of Peder Einarsen and wife Ingeborg

The following were baptized at the home of Isaac Jacobson Jackson in Arendahl Township:
- Guro, child of Isaac Jackson and wife Karen Jacobson
- Kittel, child of Ole Tollefson and wife Aslaug
- Inger Karine, child of Halvor Wraalstad and wife Inger Olson
- Anne Marie, child of Egil Guttormsen and wife Marta
- Halvor Lauritz, child of Knud Halvorson and wife Gunlaug
- Thormod Andreas, child of Ala Thompson and wife Sofie
- Johan, child of Knud Torvildsen and wife Sigri
- Torvald, child of Christian Thoresen and wife Anna

Newcomers in 1857 included:
- Marcus Olson Ulvestad
- Halvor Olsen
- Marcus Olsen Olnestad
- Erik E. Torsnes
- Albert Anderson
- Harold Olsen

Most of the men brought their families with them. Some lived in dugouts, others in shacks made from bark. Hardships were many. Brownsville, La Crosse and Winona were the nearest markets. 1857 was a particularly severe year. The winter was severe; panic hit the entire country and emigration almost came to a standstill.

Trials of pioneer life

The first generation occupying the land, which went through the trials and tribulations of pioneer life, has now passed on. The new generation lacks both the knowledge and imagination to grasp the actual conditions of life as it was lived by the pioneers. It will be of interest, then, to follow an interview I (Holand) had with Rasmus Spande, one of the first to arrive on Stavanger Prairie in June 1854:

"I was born on Finn Island north of Stavanger and came to Fox River settlement in company with neighbors from our community in Norway. Land around Fox River was already too dear to buy, and it was hard even to find work.

"There was at this time considerable talk about Iowa, but as some of my neighbors had gone to Minnesota the year before, I decided to follow. Where this place Minnesota was or whether it was as large as a church parish or a continent I had no idea. But we started off, and were kept looking from railroad to ferry, and from ferry to steamboat.

"The callousness shown us poor

immigrants on this trip was unbelievable. In fact, we treat our pigs much better than the way we were treated. With some justification, perhaps, we were looked upon as untamed animals because we could only say 'ha' and 'ja' and stare stupidly ahead whenever we were spoken to.

"The first winter we lived with my brother-in-law, Tore Faae, and later we found a 40 of land and built a house. There were three of us, and the work went rapidly. The first day we felled some trees and skidded the logs together; the second day we raised a house, and the third day we moved in. The building was 12 feet square, the walls of round aspen logs and the floor of split and hewed timbers. The roof was also of split logs covered with a sheathing of clapboards and turf. The clapboards were about a quarter of an inch thick, split from oak logs with a special axe. I had never handled a broad-axe and wedge before, but soon got used to it.

"In addition, doors, tables, chairs, beds and other household furniture were made of split oak and planed with a broad-axe. For door hinges we used twigs with knots in them, and there was not a nail in the building. *[Wooden pegs were inserted into holes made with an auger. –Rosholt]*

"The first 10 years I did not have an overcoat, overshoes or underclothes, just a blouse and overalls. What else could we do? We were desperately poor and our neighbors almost in the same fix. There was no country store where we could buy on credit, and the little I made working in the logging woods was hardly enough for food and interest on our debt.

"The first winter I split 2,700 rails at 50 cents a hundred. I was small, not very strong and unaccustomed to this kind of labor. For lunch at noon, all I had was a dry piece of bread, frozen stiff, which I chipped off with an axe.

"The worst were the long trips to Winona, the nearest marketplace where one could buy what there was. It was 40 miles from our place. Making the trip dressed in thin clothing and driving the slow-moving oxen in wintertime over impassable roads was the farthest thing from comfort.

"One time, I recall, Tore Faae and I were on the road when a big snowstorm overtook us. I had just my blouse and overalls on and froze something awful. And there was no house to be seen for miles.

"Finally, around 9 o'clock that night, we came to the house of a German and went inside to ask if we could stay. The German said 'no.' Tore Faae then became angry and sat down, saying that he would not leave, as he was completely exhausted, and that to go back into the storm was to invite death.

"The German then went to the wood box, picked up a big stick of wood and held it over Tore's head, shouting, 'Will you go now?'

"There were six or seven men in the shanty, so we had to leave again to face the darkness and the snowstorm.

"The snow was getting so deep that we had to walk ahead of the oxen and tramp down a track. We continued in this manner until 11 o'clock and had gone only two miles when we came to the house of a German pastor. He received us in a most friendly manner, awakened his wife to give us food and made everything as comfortable as possible for us. I will never forget that man.

"When I think of those long, freezing trips to town, the tiring work in the woods, the loneliness, our pressing needs, the ignorance and all the trials we had to live through, I have to ask myself which was the better bargain—to be here or back among the poor but at least comfortable people of Norway."

South of Spring Grove, a man by the name of Banning had built a gristmill on a local river. This was an undertaking that filled the uninitiated Indians with reverence. To judge by all accounts, this must have been quite an affair. Worst of all, the rig was so ingenious that it took three or four men to watch it or it would jam. The biggest difficulty was to get the grain to run into the spout slowly enough, for if an entire handful was thrown in at a time, the mill stopped dead.

Knut Bergo relates that he saw his grain go into the grinder but nothing came out. A search was made and it was found that a mouse, which sat below the mill funnel, was eating the grain and throwing the husks away.

But this was still better than going all the way to Dorchester or Decorah with a sack upon one's back, which he had done several times and been away from home a week at a time.

In winter the millpond froze, and then there was no alternative but to grind some grain in the coffee grinder or pound it with a mortar.

The old-timers remember the winter of 1857 as the worst ever experienced in this part of the state. About three feet of snow fell, followed by a hard crust on top. Then the wolves had Christmas dinner, as the deer fell through the crust while the wolves ran lightly over the top. The pioneers killed hundreds of deer with clubs as the creatures stood helplessly in the deep crust and the hunter glided easily over on skis.

For most of the winter, it was impossible to use horses. Embrik Melbraaten made a sort of snowshoe for the feet of his horse, and after the horse got accustomed to the shoes, he managed quite well. The horse was called upon often, especially for funerals. A light sleigh was fashioned on which the coffin was laid, while the mourners followed the procession on skis, the pastor in the lead.

Loan sharks prey on pioneers

But worse than natural disasters, long trips to town, hard times and hard work were the visits from the usurious moneylender. Hard work was the lot of life, lonesomeness, hunger and need expected, and misfortune and misery ever to be endured. But the interest on the mortgage was something else again, with 20-, 40-, 60- and even up to 75-percent interest rates.

It is general knowledge that the majority of the pioneers were virtually penniless when they came into the wilderness. They could buy as much land as they wanted from the government for a dollar and a quarter per acre. This was, of course, very cheap. Besides, they were given a whole year's respite in making their payments.

But during the first years when they were preparing the land for agricultural production, they had little or nothing that could be converted into ready cash. There were no banks in the vicinity where they could apply for a loan, and if they traveled far enough to find a bank, they were so far from home that they could not get a loan because nobody knew them.

It was an unavoidable necessity to have enough money to pay for the land, as well as for buying the essential farm implements, oxen, and other necessities. They were, therefore, compelled to seek the nearest loan shark, who was lying in wait for a victim.

Such a man was Lars Dommerud, who for a long time operated in Winneshiek, Houston and Fillmore counties. He came to America as early as 1843, and since he was an outrageously miserly person, he saved up a heap of money.

He was among the first settlers who came to Winneshiek County near the southern border of Minnesota. At that time there was only a territorial government, and he could demand as high a usury as he pleased. The general rate was about 40 percent, but he sometimes demanded as much as 75 percent from the pioneers who were in a serious financial pinch.

For many years he had everything his own way. But in 1858, when Minnesota was admitted into the Union as a state, this glorious state of affairs came to an end. The legal rate of interest was limited to 12 percent.

But Dommerud knew what to do. He attended every auction he heard about and bought up a great deal of junk. When someone came to him for a loan, Dommerud would show him his collection of antiquated articles, old furniture, dilapadated vehicles and rotted sets of harness. If the indigent borrower was willing to buy any of the junk at many times its actual worth, Dommerud would let him have about three-quarters of the requested sum of cash and subtract the remainder as the buying price for old junk.

To close the deal, the needy borrower would sign a note for the total amount at the highest rate of interest. In addition, he would have to pay $10 or $15 to Dommerud as a bonus.

Harassing the loan shark – When Dommerud, the loan shark, came to the Highland Prairie Church to collect interest payments, he noticed that some boys had written on his wagon, with chalk: "Beware of Death, Judgmint Day, the Devil, and Dommerud."

35
Setesdal, western Fillmore County, southeastern Minnesota
(Source: De Norske Settlementers Historie, by Hjalmar Rued Holand, translated by Malcolm Rosholt, 1908, pp. 379–382)

In the western part of Fillmore County, one comes upon the Root River's narrow valleys, hidden among deep-wooded slopes. These slopes reach to the top of sterile ridge-backs. Around Rushford and Houston, they rise to 500 feet above the uncertain bottomlands, where they merge with small valleys into a gentle, rolling prairie.

While the people in the eastern part of the county have their greatest difficulty with floods that threaten to wash out the topsoil on the slopes every time it rains, people in the west of Fillmore and adjoining Mower County have their greatest trouble finding drainage.

Nevertheless, some 3,000 Norwegians live here, in a settlement that starts at Lime Springs on the Iowa-Minnesota line and extends northwest eight miles past Grand Meadow in Mower County. The settlement, about four miles wide and 35 miles long, is divided into three sections, the southern part of which is called Setesdal *[after a valley in southern Norway –Rosholt]*.

The Setesdal community, which actually lies in York Township of Fillmore County, is of interest because it is the oldest in which *Sætersdøler* assembled in any significant numbers.

The movement of emigration from this region in Norway began quite early. It actually started in the spring of 1843 with the departure of Tollef Gunnolfsen Huset and family from Bygland, Augun Berge and Kjøgei Harstad from Valle, and Tollef Knudsen from Hyllestad. These four men had all settled first in Muskego and later moved west.

There were quite a few Setesdal people on Rock River in Jefferson County (Wisconsin) in the 1840s, but when the movement into Minnesota began in 1854, the Jefferson County settlement was completely overshadowed by the one in York Township of Fillmore County.

In the next 20 years, several thousand *Sætersdøler* moved into Fillmore County, most of them eventually winding up in the Red River Valley near Grand Forks, North Dakota. But it was the Setesdal settlement in York Township that became the scene for that Norwegian-American story, *Fra begge Sider of Havet (From Both Sides of the Ocean) [written by Tellef Grundysen –Rosholt]*, based on actual events presumed to have occurred here.

The first to settle in this American-made Setesdal were Knut O. Kviste and Even K. Besteland, who arrived from Rock River in Wisconsin together with six others, who took land in the east of Fillmore County. The third man to settle in Setesdal was Ole Kittelson from Siljord (Seljord) in Telemark.

A little later in the summer, the following came from Setesdal:
- Osmund Olson Trydal
- Frank Olson Trydal
- "Big" Ole Thistelson Hofto
- "Little" Ole Thistelson Hofto
- Torge Torgeson Bakka
- John Thorson

Ole Arneson Lien, one of the most prominent among the early pioneers, arrived in 1856.

"Little" Ole Hofto was the most outstanding among all the old pioneers. A resolute man who had gone to

California to dig for gold, he returned with $6,000. He used his money to take a leading role among his fellow citizens in Fillmore County. Despite his diminutive size, he was a fighter who could take care of himself in the rough and tumble times when fights were common in the settlement.

Things were especially lively on the long and difficult trips to town. For the first 14 years, it was necessary to drive all the way to McGregor, 75 miles distant. When the pioneers reached "the Pocket City," or "Hell City," as it was also called, the natural tendencies of the Setesdal people often got the upper hand. A whole load of wheat—the fruit of a season's work—could be squandered on a big binge. Then one had to borrow hay for the oxen in order to get home. And there, in contrition and duress, they had to struggle through till the next harvest.

Invasion of the chinch bugs

With the arrival of the railroad in Lime Springs in 1868, the long trips to town were a thing of the past. But just about the same time another miserable aspect of life arose, much worse than the first—namely, the invasion of the chinch bug. For a number of years in the 1870s, the fields were dominated by this pest, which nearly drove the helpless pioneers to distraction.

In the morning when people drove to church, the fields of grain could be standing ripe for the harvest, and folks could be heard congratulating each other that this year, at all events, there would be enough to live on. But by evening the grain was black with crawling insects, and by the following morning the straw lay this way and that, robbed of its sap—the worst example of devastation a farmer would ever see.

What was more, the pioneers were already in debt up to their ears for seed, food and other necessities.

Meanwhile, Tobias Larson, the pastor in Setesdal and surrounding congregations during those years, was lenient in money matters. But one year the situation was almost too much for this long-suffering man to endure—when only $10 came in from the entire congregation. The chinch bug had taken everything.

Pastor U. V. Koren had organized a congregation here as early as 1855.

Many strange stories could be told about the first years in this Setesdal community. Year after year big parties of *Sætersdøler* arrived directly from their homes in Norway. The change from the confining valleys of the mother country, its philosophy and environment, to the vast, unfilled spaces of America was so sudden that the transition could be both humorous and tragic.

An innocent little incident, at least, probably explains why the designation "Norwegian Indians" was often applied to our people here.

The first summer when two newcomers from Norway arrived in Fillmore County, they were employed in clearing land on the farm of a nearby American. When they came into the house to have supper, they sat a few minutes waiting for the farmer's wife to finish her preparations.

In the middle of the floor stood a jar of pickled apples. The two men glared at it for a moment, wondering what sort of mush this could be. Finally, with the woman's back turned, one of them stuck his finger in the jar and tasted of it. The taste was so inviting that he forgot all appearances and grabbed the jar with one hand and, using the other hand as a fork, scooped up a big portion on his plate and ate hand to mouth.

The other sat watching this, bug-eyed, and finally asked, "What is it? Does it taste good?"

"Try it yourself," was all the answer he got from his busy table partner, whereupon both of them dove into the jar with their clumsy hands.

The farmer's wife stared at this a moment, speechless, and then picked up the jar and poured the contents into the pig-swill barrel, exclaiming, "They are what I would call 'Norwegian-Indians!'"

36

Bloomfield Settlement, Fillmore and Mower Counties, southeastern Minnesota

(Source: De Norske Settlementers Historie, by Hjalmar Rued Holand, translated by Malcolm Rosholt, 1908, pp. 383–386)

Toward the northwest of Fillmore County, a Setesdal community thrusts up to Bloomfield settlement, the largest, most beautiful and most prosperous of the three communities referred to in the previous chapter.

Bloomfield settlement lies around the village of Ostrander (Minnesota). The population is, for the most part, from Tinn in Telemark, with lesser numbers from Hurdal in Norway.

O. P. Hadland, a son of one of the first settlers, has written, at my request, something about the history of the settlement, which follows:

"The first settlers of Norwegian origin who came to Bloomfield were the following:
- Brothers Ole Helliksen Krokan and Mathias Helliksen Krokan
- Ole Herbjørnson Øien
- Peder O. Hadland
- Herbjørn G. Bøen
- Ole O. Halling
- Guro, a widow (related to the Mathias Helliksen family)
- Sidsil, a widow (related to the Mathias Helliksen family)

Erik Solseth and Østen Ingolfsland were also along with this party, but they took land around Harmony (Minnesota) instead.

"These people, with the exception of Ole Halling, were from Tinn, and had lived some years in Muskego. Driven either by the promise of greater riches to be found in the little known Minnesota Territory or by the Viking spirit, which still animates our people, these early settlers left to find land and build themselves homes in the 'Wild West.'

"Under the leadership of Ole Helliksen, who had lived in America for 15 years and had more experience and money than the rest, the party left their homes around Muskego in June 1854.

"It took two weeks to reach the place of Gjermund Hitterdal (Gjermund Johnson), who lived five miles east of the present city of Decorah, Iowa. Here the caravan stopped for a couple of weeks. But little thought was given to settling down here, as the land around Decorah was already occupied. So it was necessary to go farther west.

"Meanwhile, Peder Hadland, Ole Herbjørnson Øien and Herbjørn G. Bøen made a trip to see an acquaintance on Turkey River. But they did not like the land around there. They went on to Burr Oak, but a terrible rainstorm the first night forced them to seek shelter at Torger Luraas's place on Big Canoe. From here they crossed Looking Glass Prairie to Lenora, and then followed two Americans who had claims to sell on Highland Prairie.

Ole Helliksen and some others in the party took a team of horses and went farther west to the newly platted village of Frankford in Mower County (Minnesota). Here they got an American to lead them to some unoccupied tracts of land on Bear Creek. This is what they were looking for, as there they found wood, water and prairie. They paid the American $5 for his services and returned to their party on Washington Prairie near Decorah. *[If Hadland is quoted correctly it seems that he was confused in the sequence of events and in the role of the participants –Rosholt]*

"On 1 July 1854, they started off again with their families and movable goods, and on 4 July reached Bear Creek. But here they encountered deep disappointment.

"Three days earlier, a party of Valdres people—Ole Finhart and Ole O. Hovda among them—had arrived ahead of them and taken the tract of land the others had their eyes on. For a price, the same Yankee had shown the Valdres people this land, and now they refused to give it up.

"On 6 July most of the Muskego people then returned to Spring Valley, where they again set up their wagons. Ole Helliksen and some others went off in the face of an easterly wind bringing rain, and cut through the woodlands along Root River. When they returned in the evening, Mathias Helliksen had also returned from Bear Creek, saying that he would rather live in 'Lapland' than Bear Creek.

"The next day they drove south again. In the woods they found some logs skidded together and a shanty on the land that Ole Halling later occupied. When they emerged from the woods on the south side of the river, Mathias Helliksen yelled, 'Here is my pasture!'

"And when they went a little farther on, Ole stopped and said, 'Yes, this is where I'm going to build my house.' And this he did the very next day. They had found the place that Fate had probably meant for them.

"Mathias returned to 'Lapland' to fetch his wagon. While he was away, four Yankees arrived, all armed. One approached the Norwegian party and asked which one had taken his claim. Herbjørn Bøen admitted he had. The Americans politely asked him if he would go away, and Herbjørn said he would.

"After some discussion, the Americans said they would be willing to sell their claims for $160 in gold. Ole Helliksen bought two 40s for $80; Mathias and Ole Halling bought two 40s for the same price. For $15, Peder Hadland and Bøen purchased the right to some land that the Yankees said belonged to their friends.

"In order to make the deal legal, the man had to go to John Batman, who was secretary of the 'Club Law

Det Indre af en Bondestue i Telemarken

Index

Norway Map and Statistics	C2
Arne Brekke Translation Tips	C3
Maps Before 1918 and After 1918	C4-C5
NAF Veibok Maps and Shields	C6-C31
1901 Settlement Map	C32

Maps & Shields

Kommuner og fylker	C6
Østfold	C7
Akershus og Oslo	C8
Hedmark	C9
Oppland	C10
Buskerud	C11
Vestfold	C12
Telemark	C13
Aust-Agder	C14
Vest-Agder	C15
Rogaland	C16-C17
Hordaland	C18-C19
Sogn og Fjordane	C20-C21
Møre og Romsdal	C22-C23
Sør-Trøndelag	C24-C25
Nord-Trøndelag	C26-C27
Nordland	C28-C29
Troms	C30
Finnmark	C31

Norway

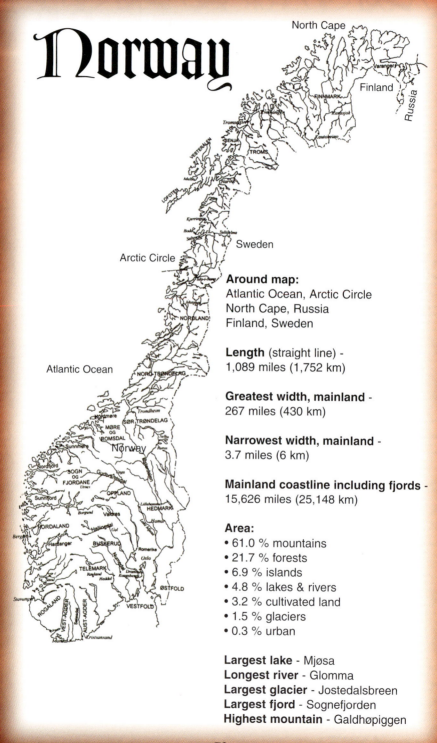

Around map:
Atlantic Ocean, Arctic Circle
North Cape, Russia
Finland, Sweden

Length (straight line) -
1,089 miles (1,752 km)

Greatest width, mainland -
267 miles (430 km)

Narrowest width, mainland -
3.7 miles (6 km)

Mainland coastline including fjords -
15,626 miles (25,148 km)

Area:
- 61.0 % mountains
- 21.7 % forests
- 6.9 % islands
- 4.8 % lakes & rivers
- 3.2 % cultivated land
- 1.5 % glaciers
- 0.3 % urban

Largest lake - Mjøsa
Longest river - Glomma
Largest glacier - Jostedalsbreen
Largest fjord - Sognefjorden
Highest mountain - Galdhøpiggen

Translation tips of Norwegian geographical terms and political designations

By Arne Brekke, Ph. D., Place Name Research, University of Chicago, 1963
Field: Comparative Germanic/Indo-European linguistics

Over the years, there has been considerable confusion when it comes to the translation of Norwegian geographical terms, especially the political designations known as *fylke* and *kommune*.

It has been common to use the word county for both *fylke* and *kommune*, although it is not a good translation for either. It is best to use the Norwegian word *fylke* for district, and the Norwegian word *kommune* for municipality.

As of 1 January 2005, Norway had 18 *fylker* (plural) or administrative districts; 433 *kommuner* (plural) or municipalities; and one *bykommune* (Oslo). Example: Bergen is considered a *kommune* (municipality) within Hordaland *fylke* (district).

Norway contains 88 places with more than 200 inhabitants. These places are called *byer*, or towns. Places with fewer than 200 inhabitants are called *tettsteder*, or population centers.

A *fylke* in Norway is a much larger and more significant political unit than a county in an American state. The standard Norwegian-English dictionaries have been the culprits here!

Following are additional suggestions for American-English equivalents of Norwegian geographical terms:

• *Dal* would usually translate valley, but when it includes the adjacent areas, such as Hallingdal, Gudbrandsdal or Valdres, one can talk about the Hallingdal, Gudbrandsdal and Valdres areas.

• An area within a *kommune* served by an individual church, called a *sokn* or *sogn* in Norwegian, should be translated as parish.

• A *bygd* is usually referred to as a rural settlement.

• Fjord names are normally not translated, but compound fjord-name elements are usually spelled separately in English, as in "Oslo Fjord," the "Sogne Fjord," etc. Sometimes, when the other name element is obvious and meaningful, it can be translated as in *Sørfjorden* (South Fjord).

• Areas including several *fylker*, such as Østlandet, Sørlandet, Vestlandet, Midt-Norge and Nord-Norge, are best referred to as regions.

Norwegian fylke (district) names

Before 1918, the proper term for Norway's major administrative districts was *amt* or *amter*. After 1918, they were referred to as *fylke* or *fylker*. There are 18 *fylker* (districts) and one *bykommune* (Oslo). These districts are further divided into 433 *kommuner* (municipalities).

In 1908, when the first edition of *De Norske Settlementers Historie* was published, the old *amt* names were still in use. This can be confusing to anyone searching a modern map to find places of origin listed in the book. Therefore, both versions of the names of Norway's major districts from both before and after 1918 have been included to aid the reader.

before 1918

Before 1918 (Amt)
Akershus
Bergen (1)
Bratsberg
Buskerud
Vardøhus
Hedemarken
Jarlsberg and Larvik
Kristians/Oplandenes
Lister and Mandal
Nedenes/Agdenes
Nordland
Nordre Bergenhus
Nordre Trondhjem
Romsdalen
Smaalenene
Søndre Bergenhus
Søndre Trondhjem
Stavanger
Tromsø
Kristiania (3)

after 1918

After 1918 (Fylke)
Akershus
Bergen (2)
Telemark
Buskerud
Finnmark
Hedmark
Vestfold
Oppland
Vest-Agder
Aust-Agder
Nordland
Sogn og Fjordane
Nord-Trøndelag
Møre and Romsdal
Østfold
Hordaland
Sør-Trøndelag
Rogaland
Troms
Oslo (4) - capital city/district

(1) Bergen was included in Søndre Bergenhus.
(2) The city of Bergen in 1972 was merged into a *kommune* (municipality) within Hordaland and is no longer listed as a *fylke*.
(3) Kristiania (Oslo) was formerly included in Akershus.
(4) Oslo as of 1 January 2005 is often listed as a separate *fylke* or as a *bykommune*.

Used by permission of Origins Genealogy Bookstore, Janesville, WI, publisher of *Norwegian Research Guide*.

Norske fylker og kommuner

Innbyggertall: 4 552 252
Areal: 323 758 km^2
Hovedstad: Oslo

TEGNFORKLARING
Det er 18 fylker og 433 kommuner i Norge.

← Kommunens/fylkets våpen

Aremark ← Kommunens navn
1 458 innb. ← Kommunens innbyggertall
321 km^2 ← Kommunens areal
Aremark ← Kommunens adm.senter

● ← Kommunens adm.senter
□ ← Fylkets adm.senter

©NAF – Norwegian Automobile Association – www.naf.no

Østfold

255 122 innb.
4 183 km²
Sarpsborg

18 kommuner

Aremark	Askim	Eidsberg	Fredrikstad	Halden	Hobøl	Hvaler	Marker
1 458 innb.	13 876 innb.	9 968 innb.	69 288 innb.	27 438 innb.	4 469 innb.	3 617 innb.	3 408 innb.
321 km²	69 km²	236 km²	290 km²	641 km²	141 km²	88 km²	413 km²
Aremark	Askim	Mysen	Fredrikstad	Halden	Hobøl	Skjærhalden	Ørje

Moss	Rakkestad	Rygge	Rømskog	Råde	Sarpsborg	Skiptvet	Spydeberg
27 534 innb.	7 217 innb.	13 775 innb.	658 innb.	6 380 innb.	49 044 innb.	3 327 innb.	4 672 innb.
63 km²	433 km²	74 km²	183 km²	119 km²	407 km²	102 km²	142 km²
Moss	Rakkestad	Dilling	Rømskog	Råde	Sarpsborg	Skiptvet	Spydeberg

Trøgstad	Våler
4 991 innb.	4 002 innb.
205 km²	257 km²
Trøgstad	Våler

Akershus

483 283 innb.
4 917 km²
Oslo

22 kommuner

Oslo

517 401 innb.
454 km²
Oslo

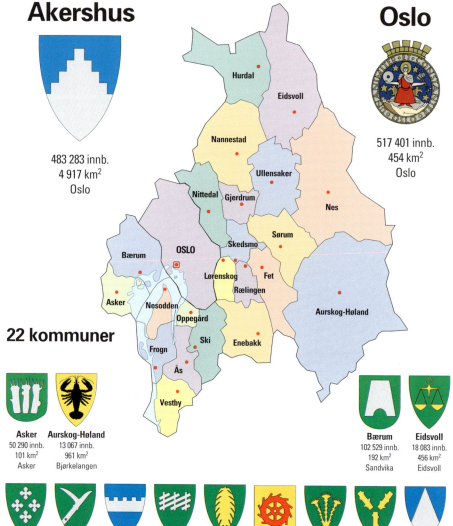

Asker
50 290 innb.
101 km²
Asker

Aurskog-Høland
13 067 innb.
961 km²
Bjørkelangen

Bærum
102 529 innb.
192 km²
Sandvika

Eidsvoll
18 083 innb.
456 km²
Eidsvoll

Enebakk
9 111 innb.
232 km²
Kirkebygda

Fet
9 361 innb.
176 km²
Fetsund

Frogn
13 116 innb.
87 km²
Drøbak

Gjerdrum
4 877 innb.
83 km²
Ask

Hurdal
2 664 innb.
285 km²
Hurdal

Lørenskog
30 220 innb.
71 km²
Lørenskog

Nannestad
9 751 innb.
341 km²
Nannestad

Nes
17 765 innb.
639 km²
Årnes

Nesodden
15 943 innb.
60 km²
Nesoddtangen

Nittedal
19 300 innb.
187 km²
Nittedal

Oppegård
23 243 innb.
37 km²
Kolbotn

Rælingen
14 679 innb.
71 km²
Fjerdingby

Skedsmo
40 676 innb.
77 km²
Lillestrøm

Ski
26 155 innb.
166 km²
Ski

Sørum
12 571 innb.
207 km²
Sørumsand

Ullensaker
22 931 innb.
252 km²
Jessheim

Vestby
12 724 innb.
134 km²
Vestby

Ås
14 227 innb.
103 km²
Ås

Hedmark

188 281 innb.
27 388 km²
Hamar

22 kommuner

Alvdal
2 422 innb.
944 km²
Alvdal

Eidskog
6 421 innb.
641 km²
Skotterud

Elverum
18 638 innb.
1 229 km²
Elverum

Engerdal
1 512 innb.
2 195 km²
Engerdal

Folldal
1 764 innb.
1 275 km²
Folldal

Grue
5 395 innb.
839 km²
Kirkenær

Hamar
27 120 innb.
351 km²
Hamar

Kongsvinger
17 348 innb.
1 038 km²
Kongsvinger

Løten
7 317 innb.
370 km²
Løten

Nord-Odal
5 050 innb.
508 km²
Sagstua

Os
2 134 innb.
1 039 km²
Os

Rendalen
2 193 innb.
3 178 km²
Øvre Rendal

Ringsaker
31 830 innb.
1 280 km²
Brumunddal

Stange
18 137 innb.
725 km²
Stange

Stor-Elvdal
2 888 innb.
2 167 km²
Koppang

Sør-Odal
7 538 innb.
517 km²
Skarnes

Tolga
1 796 innb.
1 122 km²
Tolga

Trysil
7 025 innb.
3 016 km²
Trysil

Tynset
5 423 innb.
1 870 km²
Tynset

Våler
3 964 innb.
705 km²
Våler

Åmot
4 389 innb.
1 339 km²
Rena

Åsnes
7 977 innb.
1 041 km²
Flisa

Oppland

183 582 innb.
25 191 km²
Lillehammer

26 kommuner

Dovre	**Etnedal**	**Gausdal**	**Gjøvik**
2 883 innb.	1 427 innb.	6 189 innb.	27 349 innb.
1 366 km²	459 km²	1 190 km²	673 km²
Dovre	Etnedal	Segalstad bru	Gjøvik

Gran	**Jevnaker**	**Lesja**	**Lillehammer**	**Lom**
13 085 innb.	6 299 innb.	2 219 innb.	24 946 innb.	2 481 innb.
758 km²	225 km²	2 257 km²	477 km²	1 945 km²
Jaren	Jevnaker	Lesja	Lillehammer	Lom

Lunner	**Nord-Aurdal**	**Nord-Fron**	**Nordre Land**	**Ringebu**	**Sel**	**Skjåk**	**Søndre Land**	**Sør-Aurdal**
8 461 innb.	6 567 innb.	5 890 innb.	6 878 innb.	4 644 innb.	6 102 innb.	2 399 innb.	6 127 innb.	3 326 innb.
292 km²	908 km²	1 145 km²	955 km²	1 250 km²	909 km²	2 079 km²	729 km²	1 109 km²
Roa	Fagernes	Vinstra	Dokka	Ringebu	Otta	Bismo	Hov	Bagn

Sør-Fron	**Vang**	**Vestre Slidre**	**Vestre Toten**	**Vågå**	**Østre-Toten**	**Øyer**	**Øystre Slidre**
3 335 innb.	1 636 innb.	2 282 innb.	12 627 innb.	3 801 innb.	14 649 innb.	4 891 innb.	3 089 innb.
733 km²	1 504 km²	465 km²	257 km²	1 349 km²	554 km²	640 km²	964 km²
Hundorp	Grindaheim	Slidre	Raufoss	Vågåmo	Lena	Tingberg	Heggenes

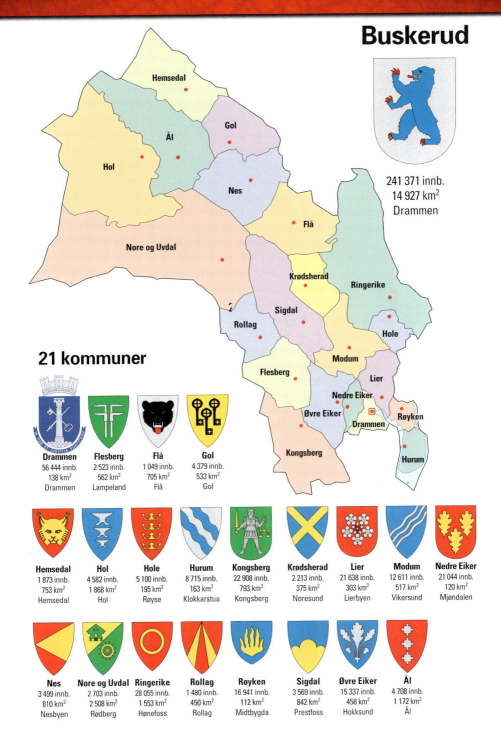

Vestfold

218 171 innb.
2 216 km²
Tønsberg

14 kommuner

Andebu	**Hof**	**Holmestrand**	**Horten**	**Lardal**	**Larvik**	**Nøtterøy**	**Re**	**Sande**
4 899 innb.	3 040 innb.	9 486 innb.	24 557 innb.	2 406 innb.	40 877 innb.	19 927 innb.	8 111 innb.	7 554 innb.
186 km²	164 km²	86 km²	69 km²	278 km²	530 km²	59 km²	225 km²	178 km²
Andebu	Hof	Holmestrand	Horten	Svarstad	Larvik	Borgheim	Revetal	Sande

Sandefjord	**Stokke**	**Svelvik**	**Tjøme**	**Tønsberg**
40 696 innb.	9 985 innb.	6 436 innb.	4 541 innb.	35 656 innb.
122 km²	118 km²	58 km²	38 km²	106 km²
Sandefjord	Stokke	Svelvik	Tjøme	Tønsberg

Telemark

165 855 innb.
15 315 km²
Skien

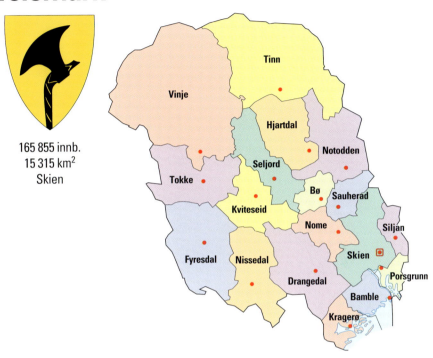

18 kommuner

Bamble	Bø	Drangedal	Fyresdal	Hjartdal	Kragerø	Kviteseid	Nissedal	Nome
14 170 innb.	5 220 innb.	4 184 innb.	1 310 innb.	1 616 innb.	10 559 innb.	2 647 innb.	1 445 innb.	6 579 innb.
300 km²	266 km²	1 062 km²	1 277 km²	798 km²	307 km²	709 km²	902 km²	434 km²
Langesund	Bø	Prestestranda	Fyresdal	Sauland	Kragerø	Kviteseid	Treungen	Ulefoss

Notodden	Porsgrunn	Sauherad	Seljord	Siljan	Skien	Tinn	Tokke	Vinje
12 402 innb.	33 204 innb.	4 363 innb.	2 921 innb.	2 343 innb.	50 272 innb.	6 354 innb.	2 454 innb.	3 812 innb.
915 km²	161 km²	316 km²	711 km²	216 km²	779 km²	2 063 km²	980 km²	3 117 km²
Notodden	Porsgrunn	Akkerhaugen	Seljord	Siljan	Skien	Rjukan	Dalen	Ytre Vinje

Aust-Agder

103 195 innb.
9 212 km²
Arendal

15 kommuner

Arendal	**Birkenes**	**Bygland**	**Bykle**	**Evje og Hornnes**	**Froland**	**Gjerstad**	**Grimstad**
39 502 innb.	4 343 innb.	1 296 innb.	848 innb.	3 327 innb.	4 708 innb.	2 511 innb.	18 549 innb.
272 km²	675 km²	1 331 km²	1 461 km²	561 km²	642 km²	323 km²	304 km²
Arendal	Birkeland	Bygland	Bykle	Evje	Osedalen	Gjerstad	Grimstad

Iveland	**Lillesand**	**Risør**	**Tvedestrand**	**Valle**	**Vegårshei**	**Åmli**
1 131 innb.	8 982 innb.	6 988 innb.	5 918 innb.	1 422 innb.	1 840 innb.	1 830 innb.
261 km²	185 km²	191 km²	217 km²	1 289 km²	356 km²	1 143 km²
Iveland	Lillesand	Risør	Tvedestrand	Valle	Myra	Åmli

Vest-Agder

159 219 innb.
7 281 km²
Kristiansand

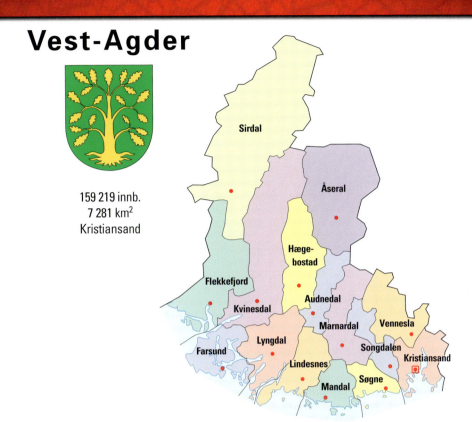

15 kommuner

Audnedal
1 562 innb.
254 km²
Konsmo

Farsund
9 578 innb.
269 km²
Farsund

Flekkefjord
8 871 innb.
539 km²
Flekkefjord

Hægebostad
1 622 innb.
460 km²
Birkeland

Kristiansand
74 590 innb.
276 km²
Kristiansand

Kvinesdal
5 578 innb.
970 km²
Kvinesdal

Lindesnes
4 468 innb.
316 km²
Vigeland

Lyngdal
7 163 innb.
391 km²
Lyngdal

Mandal
13 662 innb.
221 km²
Mandal

Marnardal
2 203 innb.
397 km²
Marnardal

Sirdal
1 786 innb.
1 547 km²
Tonstad

Songdalen
5 517 innb.
217 km²
Nodeland

Søgne
9 367 innb.
148 km²
Søgne

Vennesla
12 346 innb.
386 km²
Vennesla

Åseral
906 innb.
888 km²
Åseral

Rogaland

385 020 innb.
9 326 km²
Stavanger

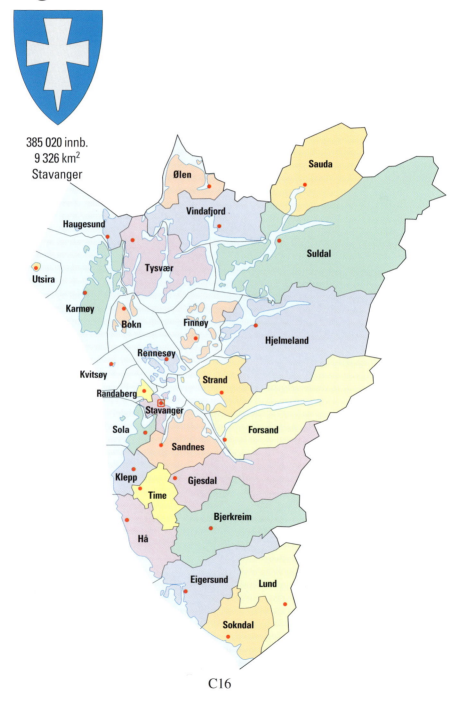

C16

27 kommuner

Bjerkreim
2 480 innb.
660 km²
Vikeså

Bokn
765 innb.
48 km²
Føresvik

Eigersund
13 350 innb.
430 km²
Egersund

Finnøy
2 806 innb.
106 km²
Judaberg

Forsand
1 076 innb.
773 km²
Forsand

Gjesdal
9 137 innb.
609 km²
Ålgård

Haugesund
31 013 innb.
72 km²
Haugesund

Hjelmeland
2 708 innb.
1 092 km²
Hjelmeland

Hå
14 417 innb.
255 km²
Varhaug

Karmøy
37 199 innb.
228 km²
Kopervik

Klepp
14 135 innb.
115 km²
Kleppe

Kvitsøy
519 innb.
6 km²
Sandeid

Lund
3 097 innb.
414 km²
Moi

Randaberg
8 998 innb.
25 km²
Randaberg

Rennesøy
3 261 innb.
65 km²
Vikevåg

Sandnes
55 729 innb.
303 km²
Sandnes

Sauda
4 915 innb.
513 km²
Sauda

Sokndal
3 294 innb.
294 km²
Hauge

Sola
19 538 innb.
69 km²
Sola

Stavanger
111 007 innb.
70 km²
Stavanger

Strand
10 298 innb.
215 km²
Jørpeland

Suldal
3 923 innb.
1 728 km²
Sand

Time
13 909 innb.
182 km²
Bryne

Tysvær
9 092 innb.
419 km²
Aksdal

Utsira
224 innb.
6 km²
Utsira

Vindafjord
4 776 innb.
444 km²
Sandeid

Ølen
3 354 innb.
185 km²
Ølen

Hordaland

441 660 innb.
15 449 km²
Bergen

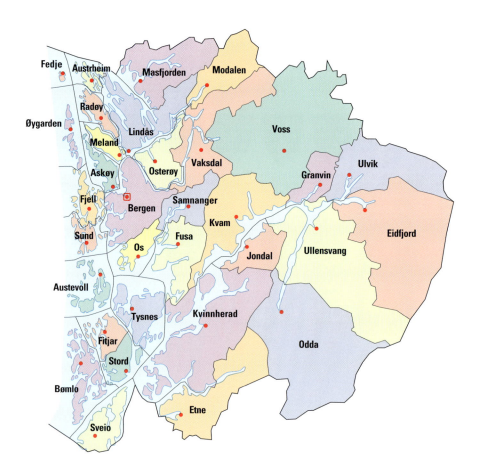

33 kommuner

Askøy	**Austevoll**	**Austrheim**	**Bergen**	**Bømlo**	**Eidfjord**	**Etne**	**Fedje**	**Fitjar**
21 018 innb.	4 439 innb.	2 519 innb.	235 423 innb.	10 867 innb.	915 innb.	3 960 innb.	672 innb.	2 892 innb.
100 km²	114 km²	56 km²	465 km²	247 km²	1 502 km²	708 km²	9 km²	145 km²
Kleppestø	Storebø	Mastrevik	Bergen	Bremnes	Eidfjord	Etne	Fedje	Fitjar

Fjell	**Fusa**	**Granvin**	**Jondal**	**Kvam**	**Kvinnherad**	**Lindås**	**Masfjorden**	**Meland**
19 294 innb.	3 751 innb.	1 037 innb.	1 071 innb.	8 467 innb.	13 157 innb.	12 721 innb.	1 738 innb.	5 704 innb.
147 km²	379 km²	212 km²	208 km²	616 km²	1 136 km²	474 km²	558 km²	91 km²
Straume	Eikelandsosen	Granvin	Jondal	Norheimsund	Rosendal	Isdalstø	Masfjordnes	Frekhaug

Modalen	**Odda**	**Os**	**Osterøy**	**Radøy**	**Samnanger**	**Stord**	**Sund**	**Sveio**
346 innb.	7 513 innb.	14 328 innb.	7 140 innb.	4 649 innb.	2 340 innb.	16 310 innb.	5 345 innb.	4 666 innb.
385 km²	1 648 km²	140 km²	254 km²	111 km²	265 km²	144 km²	99 km²	247 km²
Modalen	Odda	Os	Lonevåg	Manger	Tysse	Leirvik	Skogsskiftet	Sveio

Tysnes	**Ullensvang**	**Ulvik**	**Vaksdal**	**Voss**	**Øygarden**
2 821 innb.	3 539 innb.	1 171 innb.	4 151 innb.	13 821 innb.	3 875 innb.
255 km²	1 393 km²	722 km²	738 km²	1 816 km²	66 km²
Uggdalseidet	Kinsarvik	Ulvik	Dalekvam	Voss	Tjeldstø

Sogn og Fjordane

107 274 innb.
18 619 km²
Hermansverk

26 kommuner

Askvoll
3 314 innb.
322 km²
Askvoll

Aurland
1 781 innb.
1 489 km²
Aurland

Balestrand
1 505 innb.
430 km²
Balestrand

Bremanger
4 077 innb.
831 km²
Svelgen

Eid
5 762 innb.
468 km²
Nordfjordeid

Fjaler
2 927 innb.
418 km²
Dale

Flora
11 392 innb.
693 km²
Florø

Førde
10 906 innb.
590 km²
Førde

Gaular
2 797 innb.
579 km²
Sande

Gloppen
5 739 innb.
1 022 km²
Sandane

Gulen
2 450 innb.
596 km²
Eivindvik

Hornindal
1 195 innb.
191 km²
Hornindal

Hyllestad
1 537 innb.
259 km²
Hyllestad

Høyanger
4 579 innb.
907 km²
Høyanger

Jølster
2 974 innb.
664 km²
Skei

Leikanger
2 193 innb.
185 km²
Leikanger

Luster
4 926 innb.
2 702 km²
Gaupne

Lærdal
2 180 innb.
1 341 km²
Lærdal

Naustdal
2 731 innb.
369 km²
Naustdal

Selje
3 046 innb.
236 km²
Selje

Sogndal
6 680 innb.
745 km²
Sogndal

Solund
904 innb.
228 km²
Hardbakke

Stryn
6 768 innb.
1 382 km²
Stryn

Vik
2 901 innb.
828 km²
Vik

Vågsøy
6 349 innb.
166 km²
Måløy

Årdal
5 661 innb.
979 km²
Årdalstangen

Møre og Romsdal

244 309 innb.
15 104 km²
Molde

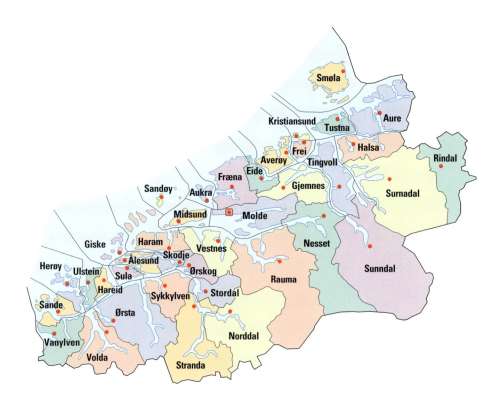

38 kommuner

Aukra
3 038 innb.
59 km²
Aukra

Aure
2 671 innb.
503 km²
Aure

Averøy
5 462 innb.
174 km²
Bruhagen

Eide
3 235 innb.
153 km²
Eide

Frei
5 256 innb.
65 km²
Rensvik

Fræna
8 937 innb.
368 km²
Elnesvågen

Giske
6 495 innb.
40 km²
Valderøy

Gjemnes
2 657 innb.
382 km²
Batnfjordsøra

Halsa
1 756 innb.
304 km²
Vågland

Haram
8 819 innb.
257 km²
Brattvåg

Hareid
4 730 innb.
82 km²
Hareid

Herøy
8 355 innb.
121 km²
Fosnavåg

Kristiansund
17 112 innb.
22 km²
Kristiansund

Midsund
1 959 innb.
94 km²
Midsund

Molde
23 955 innb.
362 km²
Molde

Nesset
3 244 innb.
1049 km²
Eidsvåg

Norddal
1 899 innb.
941 km²
Valldal

Rauma
7 312 innb.
1 501 km²
Åndalsnes

Rindal
2 115 innb.
641 km²
Rindal

Sande
2 599 innb.
94 km²
Larsnes

Sandøy
1 295 innb.
20 km²
Harøy

Skodje
3 590 innb.
120 km²
Skodje

Smøla
2 266 innb.
275 km²
Nordvika

Stordal
994 innb.
249 km²
Stordal

Stranda
4 705 innb.
867 km²
Stranda

Sula
7 304 innb.
59 km²
Langevåg

Sunndal
7 405 innb.
1 712 km²
Sunndalsøra

Surnadal
6 208 innb.
1 366 km²
Surnadal

Sykkylven
7 424 innb.
337 km²
Sykkylven

Tingvoll
3 146 innb.
337 km²
Tingvoll

Tustna
1 009 innb.
140 km²
Gullstein

Ulstein
6 721 innb.
97 km²
Ulsteinvik

Vanylven
3 820 innb.
381 km²
Fiskåbygd

Vestnes
6 442 innb.
354 km²
Vestnes

Volda
8 335 innb.
548 km²
Volda

Ørskog
2 075 innb.
130 km²
Sjøholt

Ørsta
10 269 innb.
803 km²
Ørsta

Ålesund
39 695 innb.
98 km²
Ålesund

Sør-Trøndelag

268 188 innb.
18 832 km²
Trondheim

25 kommuner

Agdenes	**Bjugn**	**Frøya**	**Hemne**	**Hitra**	**Holtålen**	**Klæbu**	**Malvik**	**Meldal**
1 808 innb.	4 655 innb.	4 146 innb.	4 312 innb.	4 048 innb.	2 177 innb.	5 188 innb.	11 735 innb.	3 994 innb.
318 km²	382 km²	231 km²	659 km²	680 km²	1 209 km²	185 km²	172 km²	633 km²
Selbekken	Botngård	Sistranda	Kyrksæterøra	Fillan	Ålen	Klæbu	Hommelvik	Meldal

Melhus	**Midtre Gauldal**	**Oppdal**	**Orkdal**	**Osen**	**Rennebu**	**Rissa**	**Roan**	**Røros**
13 579 innb.	5 824 innb.	6 441 innb.	10 388 innb.	1 097 innb.	2 660 innb.	6 382 innb.	1 089 innb.	5 599 innb.
696 km²	1 861 km²	2 273 km²	593 km²	386 km²	936 km²	621 km²	373 km²	1 956 km²
Melhus	Støren	Oppdal	Orkanger	Steinsdalen	Berkåk	Rissa	Roan	Røros

Selbu	**Skaun**	**Snillfjord**	**Trondheim**	**Tydal**	**Ørland**	**Åfjord**
3 973 innb.	6 003 innb.	1 029 innb.	152 699 innb.	907 innb.	5 119 innb.	3 336 innb.
1 235 km²	224 km²	508 km²	342 km²	1 331 km²	71 km²	955 km²
Selbu	Børsa	Krokstadøra	Trondheim	Tydal	Brekstad	Årnes

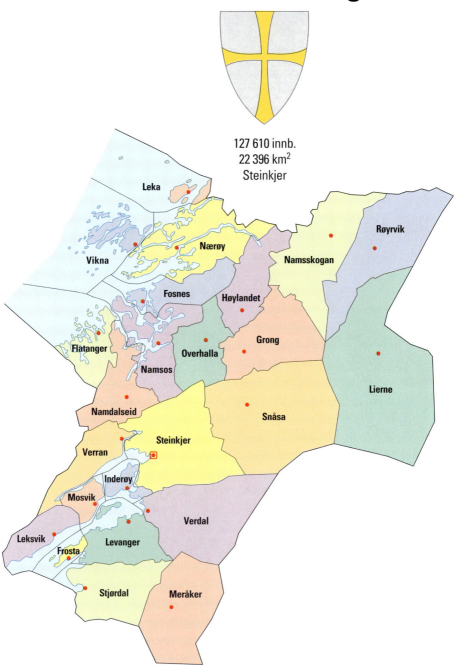

24 kommuner

Flatanger
1 244 innb.
458 km²
Lauvsnes

Fosnes
762 innb.
546 km²
Dun

Frosta
2 474 innb.
76 km²
Frosta

Grong
2 530 innb.
1 140 km²
Grong

Høylandet
1 275 innb.
756 km²
Høylandet

Inderøy
5 870 innb.
146 km²
Straumen

Leka
672 innb.
108 km²
Leka

Leksvik
3 510 innb.
431km²
Leksvik

Levanger
17 700 innb.
656 km²
Levanger

Lierne
1 552 innb.
2 972 km²
Nordli

Meråker
2 556 innb.
1 273 km²
Meråker

Mosvik
895 innb.
219 km²
Mosvik

Namdalseid
1 799 innb.
769 km²
Namdalseid

Namsos
12 380 innb.
775 km²
Namsos

Namsskogan
966 innb.
1 416 km²
Namsskogan

Nærøy
5 269 innb.
1 065 km²
Kolvereid

Overhalla
3 606 innb.
730 km²
Overhalla

Røyrvik
547 innb.
1 587 km²
Limingen

Snåsa
2 312 innb.
2 329 km²
Snåsa

Steinkjer
20 417 innb.
1 563 km²
Steinkjer

Stjørdal
18 940 innb.
923 km²
Stjørdal

Verdal
13 697 innb.
1 548 km²
Verdal

Verran
2 679 innb.
602 km²
Malm

Vikna
3 958 innb.
310 km²
Rørvik

Nordland

236 950 innb.
38 463 km²
Bodø

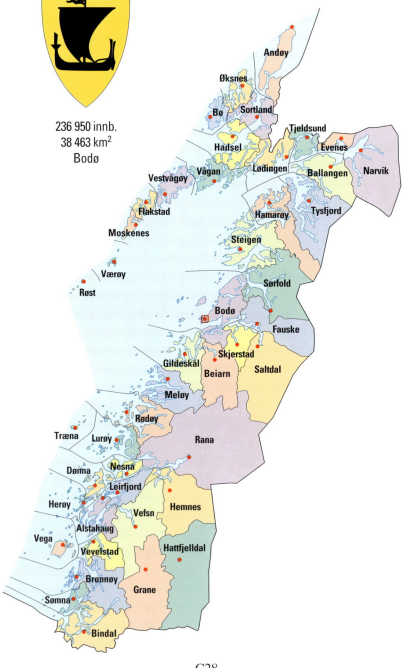

45 kommuner

Alstahaug	Andøy	Ballangen	Beiarn	Bindal	Bodø	Brønnøy	Bø	Dønna
7 445 innb.	5 477 innb.	2 680 innb.	1 221 innb.	1 822 innb.	42 186 innb.	7 519 innb.	3 100 innb.	1 541 innb.
215 km²	659 km²	930 km²	1 226 km²	1 262 km²	921 km²	1 040 km²	248 km²	193 km²
Sandnessjøen	Andenes	Ballangen	Moldjord	Terråk	Bodø	Brønnøysund	Straumsjøen	Solfjellsjøen

Evenes	Fauske	Flakstad	Gildeskål	Grane	Hadsel	Hamarøy	Hattfjelldal	Hemnes
1 494 innb.	9 528 innb.	1 527 innb.	2 220 innb.	1 542 innb.	8 051 innb.	1 926 innb.	1 569 innb.	4 551 innb.
252 km²	1 208 km²	180 km²	664 km²	2 017 km²	566 km²	1 038 km²	2 683 km²	1 594 km²
Bogen	Fauske	Ramberg	Inndyr	Trofors	Stokmarknes	Oppeid	Hattfjelldal	Korgen

Herøy	Leirfjord	Lurøy	Lødingen	Meløy	Moskenes	Narvik	Nesna	Rana
1 793 innb.	2 214 innb.	2 016 innb.	2 382 innb.	6 845 innb.	1 248 innb.	18 470 innb.	1 838 innb.	25 313 innb.
62 km²	444 km²	262 km²	531 km²	871 km²	120 km²	2 030 km²	202 km²	4 464 km²
Silvalen	Leirfjord	Lurøy	Lødingen	Ørnes	Reine	Narvik	Nesna	Mo

Rødøy	Røst	Saltdal	Skjerstad	Sortland	Steigen	Sømna	Sørfold	Tjeldsund
1 462 innb.	641 innb.	4 834 innb.	1 061 innb.	9 476 innb.	2 875 innb.	2 100 innb.	2 228 innb.	1 444 innb.
706 km²	11 km²	2 213 km²	465 km²	713 km²	1 013 km²	193 km²	1 654 km²	317 km²
Vågaholmen	Røstlandet	Rognan	Misvær	Sortland	Leinesfjord	Vik	Straumen	Hol

Træna	Tysfjord	Vefsn	Vega	Vestvågøy	Vevelstad	Værøy	Vågan	Øksnes
464 innb.	2 241 innb.	13 456 innb.	1 391 innb.	10 751 innb.	538 innb.	769 innb.	9 036 innb.	4 665 innb.
15 km²	1 463 km²	1 894 km²	159 km²	422 km²	530 km²	18 km²	477 km²	317 km²
Træna	Kjøpsvik	Mosjøen	Gladstad	Leknes	Forvik	Sørland	Svolvær	Myre

Troms

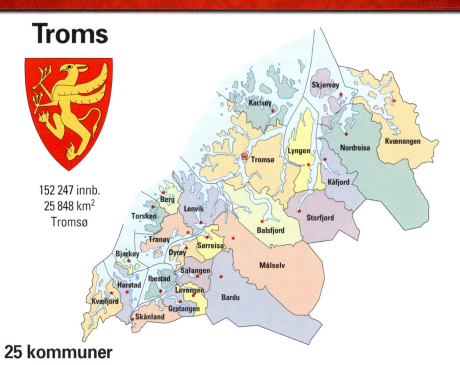

152 247 innb.
25 848 km²
Tromsø

25 kommuner

Balsfjord
5 638 innb.
1 494 km²
Storsteinnes

Bardu
3 841 innb.
2 698 km²
Setermoen

Berg
1 042 innb.
288 km²
Skaland

Bjarkøy
533 innb.
75 km²
Nergårdshamn

Dyrøy
1 317 innb.
290 km²
Brøstadbotn

Gratangen
1 302 innb.
313 km²
Årstein

Harstad
23 161 innb.
364 km²
Harstad

Ibestad
1 689 innb.
242 km²
Hamnvik

Karlsøy
2 463 innb.
1 040 km²
Hansnes

Kvæfjord
3 102 innb.
522 km²
Borkenes

Kvænangen
1 418 innb.
2 110 km²
Burfjord

Kåfjord
Gáivuotna
2 359 innb.
997 km²
Olderdalen

Lavangen
1 069 innb.
304 km²
Tennevoll

Lenvik
11 049 innb.
895 km²
Finnsnes

Lyngen
3 176 innb.
810 km²
Lyngseidet

Målselv
6 845 innb.
3 322 km²
Moen

Nordreisa
4 726 innb.
3 435 km²
Storslett

Salangen
2 260 innb.
457 km²
Sjøvegan

Skjervøy
3 021 innb.
473 km²
Skjervøy

Skånland
3 040 innb.
494 km²
Evenskjer

Storfjord
1 879 innb.
1 538 km²
Oteren

Sørreisa
3 312 innb.
361 km²
Sørreisa

Torsken
1 119 innb.
246 km²
Gryllefjord

Tranøy
1 704 innb.
523 km²
Vangsvik

Tromsø
61 182 innb.
2 558 km²
Tromsø

Finnmark

73 514 innb.
48 637 km²
Vadsø

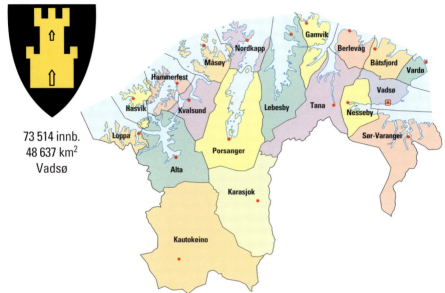

19 kommuner

Alta	Berlevåg	Båtsfjord	Gamvik	Hammerfest	Hasvik	Karasjok Karasjoga	Kautokeino Guovdageaidnu	Kvalsund
17 359 innb.	1 193 innb.	2 404 innb.	1 205 innb.	9 076 innb.	1 107 innb.	2 844 innb.	3 022 innb.	1 097 innb.
3 845 km²	1 120 km²	1 434 km²	1 414 km²	848 km²	559 km²	5 464 km²	9 704 km²	1 844 km²
Elvebakken	Berlevåg	Båtsfjord	Mehamn	Hammerfest	Breivikbotn	Karasjok	Kautokeino	Kvalsund

Lebesby	Loppa	Måsøy	Nesseby	Nordkapp	Porsanger Porsangu	Sør-Varanger	Tana	Vadsø
1 500 innb.	1 329 innb.	1 425 innb.	929 innb.	3 497 innb.	4 294 innb.	9 547 innb.	3 068 innb.	6 122 innb.
3 459 km²	691 km²	1 136 km²	1 442 km²	924 km²	3 967 km²	3 967 km²	4 055 km²	1 259 km²
Kjøllefjord	Øksfjord	Havøysund	Varangerbotn	Honningsvåg	4 873 km² Lakselv	Kirkenes	Tanabru	Vadsø

Vardø
2 496 innb.
601 km²
Vardø

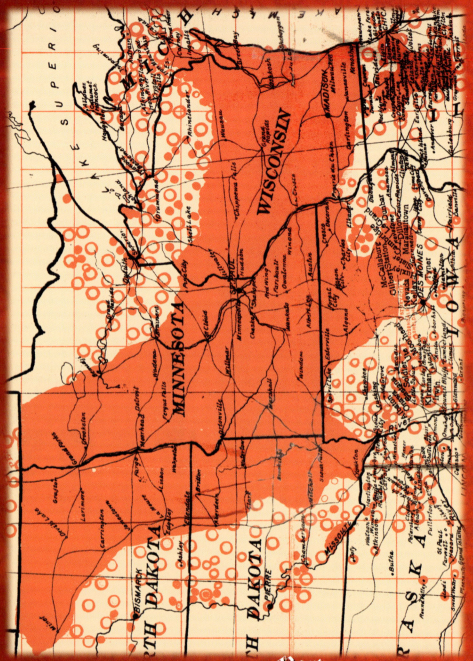

Association.' Batman was in favor of driving the Norwegians out entirely, but the Yankees now had the money in their pockets and were satisfied with the arrangement.

"The Club Law, or the organization operating under the name of the Club Law, was the only thing that counted in those days. For mutual protection against claim jumpers, people organized themselves in every community, the members pledging to help each other through thick and thin. In many places the Club Law was abused to keep later settlers away or to squeeze money out of them.

"The first man from Hurdal to emigrate to the U.S. was Thorstein Søgaarden, who came to Muskego in 1843. One of his descendants still lives in Bloomfield. In the fall of 1856, H. C. Gullickson, Ole O. Østrud and Gudbrand H. Østrud arrived at Bloomfield from Muskego (Wisconsin), where they had spent two years.

"In 1857, the following arrived, with their families from Hurdal:
- Lars Norgaarden
- Lars Gullickson
- Andreas Østrud
- Paul Peterson
- Kristen Lundby

In 1861, another party arrived from the same place, including:
- Hans Østrud
- Nils Ronbun
- Erik Tangen
- Petter Sæthre
- Martin Anderson
- Hans Thoreson
- Andreas Rustan

Most of them were heads of families.

"Many of these first settlers now rest in Bloomfield cemetery. The few still living can look back on a long and useful life. Instead of wild woods and prairie, there are now well-cultivated farms, and the small log huts have given place to handsome dwellings.

"But it would be well for future generations with all their 'comforts' to preserve the simplicity and hospitality that were found among these first pioneers."

Early church groups

Pastor U. V. Koren organized the first congregation here in 1858. *[Norsk Lutherske Mehigheter, p. 442, lists Bloomfield Norwegian Evangelical Lutheran church, located two and a half miles southeast of Ostrander in Fillmore County, giving 1858 as the date of organization. But it does not mention Koren. –Rosholt]*

But the man who carried on the first church work here was a candidate in theology named A. E. Frederikson *[spelled A. E. Friedrichsen in the above-named source –Rosholt]*, one of the most peculiar young divines ever to come to America. He first served a couple of years in Texas, but when he could not convince any of the Norwegian Synod pastors to ordain and accept him, he resigned and became one of the first settlers in Freeborn County, Minnesota.

Using his sod hut near Albert Lea as his headquarters, he traveled about visiting the Norwegian settlers, baptizing children and preaching. He was not fussy about the kind of payment he got so long as he was paid well. In fact, he preferred hides, meat, tallow, small pigs, wool or socks. As for himself, he went about dressed in coarse buckskin pants and was therefore known as the "Buckskin Pants Preacher."

When he had accumulated a load of donations that only nature could provide, he went off to Winona, where he exchanged them for hard coins. He loaned this money out on "safe" mortgages at remarkable rates of interest. He continued in business for many years.

[Norsk Lutherske Menigheter lists A. E. Friedrichsen as a pastor at Bloomfield in 1858-59, which conflicts with Holand's version as "unordained." But it is not entirely certain that Norsk Lutherske Menigheter is correct in referring to him as a pastor. –Rosholt]

Romsdalen i Nærheden af Horgheim

37

Bear Creek Settlement, Mower County, southeastern Minnesota

(Source: De Norske Settlementers Historie, by Hjalmar Rued Holand, translated by Malcolm Rosholt, 1908, pp. 387–389)

Bear Creek, or "Lapland," as the *Tinndøler* scornfully called it, lies in Mower County north of the present village of Grand Meadow, Minnesota. Here the settlement is made up entirely of Valdres people or those from Aurdal. As mentioned in the previous chapter, it was founded at the same time as Bloomfield.

Fourteen families from Dane County, Wisconsin, arrived here on 1 July 1854, under the leadership of Ole O. Finhart. They took claims along Little Bear Creek. Finhart had read about the tracts of land on upper Root River. In order to make an investigation, he organized a party that included:

From Sør-Aurdal
- Ole O. Finhart
- Syver Olson Skalshaugen
- Erland Olson Skalshaugen
- Ole Simonson Jobraaten
- Ole O. Hovda
- Hans Anderson Gamlemoen
- Anders Anderson Lybek
- Amund Johnson Lindelien
- Nils Syverson Moen
- Ole O. Syverud, Etnedal
- Amund Johnson Klostøl, Etnedal

From Nord-Aurdal
- Knud Nilsen Haugestuen
- Ole Nilsen Haugestuen
- Ole Julson, Vestre Slidre

As the Valdres people came in considerable force, the *Tinndøler* had to yield. But this was in a sense a victory for the people from Tinn, because the terrain on Bear Creek was not to be compared with Bloomfield's fertile acres. The Bear Creek land is too flat for real productivity. As a result, the people here have not done as well as the people around Bloomfield. In fact, most of Mower County is bare, bleak and wet.

A troublesome wedding trip

The first white child born in this county, 2 November 1854, was a daughter of Nils Syverson Moen. The following summer, the parents could not rest until they had the child baptized. Ole Finhart had also won the heart of Kari Hovda, who had said "yes." So they joined the Moens in their search for a pastor.

The nearest one was Clausen at St. Ansgar, a good 50 miles over the blazing hot and roadless plains. Ole Finhart had made the same journey the winter before to help an exhausted old American reach his son and nearly lost his life fighting the big snowdrifts and biting winds.

During the night the two couples who were en route to find the pastor slept in a haystack, which was the only sign of civilization on the entire route. They reached Clausen's people on Cedar River the following evening.

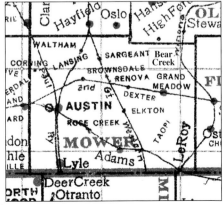

Here the two women remained on the riverbank while the men went to find the pastor.

Elen now got busy preparing Kari to look her best as a bride, and the child had to be washed for the baptismal ceremony. But in these hopes they were disappointed. Clausen was out on one of his missionary errands, and no one knew when he would return. But Ole was not going to be put off. He took his bride in hand and traveled 75 miles to the northeast in Fillmore County, where he found a settler who was also a justice of the peace. Here they were married, even if it had to be without the seal of the church.

At Bear Creek stands the first and oldest house in the county, built in 1854 by Ole Simenson Jobraaten. The first winter four families lived here, and the first white child born in the county was born here. The congregation was organized here, and the building also served for a time as the first schoolhouse. The house was roofed with bark, and the openings between the logs were stuffed with hay, which the cattle were fond of nibbling.

A strict pastor

Pastor C. L. Clausen organized Bear Creek congregation in July 1856 and served it as occasion warranted. The first resident pastor was Lauritz Steen, who must have been quite a character. He is still remembered, even though it is nearly 50 years since he left.

Steen was manifestly a man of hellfire and brimstone who believed more in discipline than in loving admonition. He was too much for most members, and all but nine families went over to the Methodists. After a highly charged last-hour meeting in which Steen placed the entire settlement under the ban of the church, he moved to Dakota

Lapper i Tromsødalen [Sami]

Territory. But people later got together again in one congregation and sent their former disciplinarian both money and friendly greetings.

Nearly 1,000 *Valdriser* live in this area. *[Norsk Lutherske Menigheter, p. 450, lists Steen as pastor at Bear Creek church from 1861 to 1869. –Rosholt]*

From Dane County to Bear Creek

According to the book *A Brief History of the Bear Creek Community*, written by Lars G. Hanson (1915), the first Norse settlers into Mower County, Minnesota, came to America on assorted sailing vessels. All landed at either New York or Quebec after seven to 12 weeks on the Atlantic. All were from Valdres in southwest Oppland fylke. They settled first in Dane County, Wisconsin, some arriving there before 1850.

The starting point for these 14 families (numbering 36 individuals) seeking new homes in Mower County was Spring Dale, Wisconsin. Traveling in two wagon trains, they arrived at Bear Creek on 1 July 1854. Members of this first party of colonists included:

From Sør-Aurdal
• Ole Olsen Finhart, Bang
• Ole Simonson Jobraaten, wife Liv and children, Simon Olson, Beret Olsdatter and Syver Olson, Begnedal
• Ole Olsen Hovda, wife Kari Bøen and children, Syver Hovda, Hermand Hovda, Arne Hovda, Engebret Hovda and Guri Hovda, Reinli
• Amund Johnson Lindelien and wife Marit, Bang, and child, Beret Lindelien
• Anders A. Lybeck, wife Sigri and child, Kari Lybeck, Bang
• Syver Olsen Skalshaugen, Bang
• Erland Olsen Skalshaugen, Bang
• Nils Syversen Moen, Bang, and wife Elen, Lands
• Ole Olsen Sjurud (Ole Olsen Syverud), Sør-Etnedal *[great-great-grandfather to Jo Ann Winistorfer]*, second wife Magdalena Trondsdatter Dokken, Reinli, and children, Anne Olsen *[great-grandmother to Jo Ann Winistorfer]* and Trond Olsen *[Note: Ole Olsen Sjurud's first wife, Anne Marie Hougseie, died at sea on the trip to America in 1852. She was the mother of Anne Olsen, born in 1847.]*
• Hans Andersen Gamlemoen, Begnedal, and wife Ragnhild Berg, Etnedal
• Amund Johnson Klastølen and wife Anne, Etnedal

From Nord-Aurdal
• Ole Julsen, Vestre Slidre
• Fiancee of Ole Julsen (engagement dissolved)
• Knud Nilsen Haugerstuen (Knud Nilsen Haugestuen)

Lappevugge [Sami]

Lappehytte [Sami]

[Note that Ole Nilsen Haugestuen is not listed in this account, while he is listed in Holand's version. These first Norwegians to settle in Mower County are also listed in Nordmændene i Amerika: deres Historie og Rekord, by Martin Ulvestad, published by Tryst in Minneapolis, Minnesota, in 1913. Ulvestad's account also lists Ole Nilsen Haugestuen among the first settlers.]

The book *Early History of Mower County*, by R. N. Paden, published in

Fjeldlapper [Sami]

1876, tells how the settlement got its name: "Ole Syvrud *[Ole Sjurud, Ole Syverud]* was an ingenious man, a gunsmith. Soon after their arrival, Syvrud killed a bear, hence the name Bear Creek." This same Ole, this time listed as Ole Severrud, is referred to in a later (1884) *History of Mower County* as Fiddler Ole.

The 1915 Bear Creek history book continues with more details of their journey to Mower County: "The colonists moved in two separate bodies, all in tented wagons drawn by oxen ... They passed through Blue Mounds and Dodgeville, crossing the Mississippi River at Prairie du Chien. They and their teams and cattle were taken over the Mississippi River on a ferry drawn across by horses in a treading power. They landed at McGregor, Iowa, and proceeded in a northwesterly direction. ..."

The lands chosen by these settlers were located in the townships of Racine, Grand Meadow and Frankfort. Except for a few quarter sections claimed by land speculators under soldier warrants, all was government land. In a few days, all those entitled to pre-empt public land had selected their homesteads.

The book goes on: "It must be understood that the first great necessity for all the settlers or homesteaders was to build shelters for themselves to live in and some kind of hovels for their domestic animals. It was also necessary to get as many acres of ground broken the first summer as possible to enable them to grow something for food the next year.

"The settlers brought their steers together and put four, five or six pairs together in a string. This string they called 'breaking teams.' In this way each and all got a patch of an acre or a few acres broke."

According to the 1915 history, the first settlers were "very much like a large family," with "little or no friction" when it came to such things as selecting claims. "This colony was a competent collection of skilled mechanics as well as farmers. Many of them were carpenters; several blacksmiths, one an artistic turner, a couple of wagon makers, three shoemakers and tanners, several stone masons and plasterers, and every man could hew and fit a log into the wall of a log house."

More people came to Bear Creek in the following years:

From Sør-Aurdal
• Halvor Olsen Klastølen and wife Johanna, Etnedal (1855)
• Kjersti Olsdatter Klastølen, Etnedal (1855)
• Gulik Erlandsen Bruflat (Gulik Erlandsen Dalen), Etnedal, and wife Kari Syversdatter Kirkeberg Moen, Bang (1856)
• Erland Bruflat, Etnedal (1856)
• Jonas Nelsen Berg, Etnedal, wife Marit Halvorsdatter Milevandet, Bang, and children, Ragnhild Berg and Kirstin Berg (1856)
• John Amundsen Lindelien, Hedalen, wife Beret Knudsdatter, Bang, and children, Thora Lindelien, Ole Lindelien, Gulik Lindelien and Gunhild Lindelien (1856)
• Amund Finhart, Bang (1858)
• Sigrid Finhart, Bang (1858)
• Ole Sørflaten, wife Olia and child, Ole, Bang (1858)
• Anders Halvorsen Milevandet and wife Olia Finhart, Bang (1858)
• Gutorm Hansen Modalen, wife Kjersti and children, Else Modalen, Lars Modalen, Beret Modalen, Hans Modalen, Kari Modalen, Christi Modalen, Gunhild Maria Modalen and Anne Christine Modalen, Begnedal (1861)
• Engebret Sorben, wife Kari and children, Ole Sorben, Beret Sorben and Anton Sorben, Bang (1861)
• Ole Jorgens, Reinli (1861)
• Knud Knudsen Østegaarden and children, Knud Knudsen Jr., Ingeborg Knudsdatter and Sigri Knudsdatter, Reinli (1861)

Reisende i Lapland [Sami]

- Syver Skaran, wife Marit and children, Reinli (1861)
- Jørgen Olsen Hellingen, wife Secil Hagen, Reinli, and children, Eilif, Siri, Sigrid and Halvor (1863) *[This family also had two older children—Ingrid and Ole. They later adopted the surname Jorgens.]*

From Nord-Aurdal
- Christen Tuff, Vestre Slidre, and wife Anna, Lier (1855)
- Nils Nelsen Haugerstuen and wife Anne (1855)
- Halvor Johannesen Vig (Halvor Johannesen Week), wife Jorand, Haugerstuen, and children, Johannes Week, Siri Week, Ragnhild Week and Kari Week (1856)
- Ole Lunde (1856)
- Nils Lunde (1856)
- Peder Huset (1856)
- Gulbrand Renna (1856)
- Anders Torhaug (1856)
- Helge Johnson Ødegaarden and wife Barbra (1857)
- Trond Arneson (1861)
- Engebret Nelsen Haugerstuen, wife Aaste and children, Nels Haugerstuen, Haldor Haugerstuen, Erik Haugerstuen and Siri Haugerstuen (1862)

From other areas
- Ole Frøland (Ole Florand), Telemark, wife Martha, and child, Ragnhild, Oxnaberg, Voss (1856)
- Anna Oxnaberg, Voss (1856)
- Torgeir Oxnaberg, Voss (1856)
- Hans Simonson, wife Olia and son, Simon, Aadalen (1861)
- Ragnhild Guliksbraaten, Næs, Aadalen (1861)
- Anna Thorina Guliksbraaten, Næs, Aadalen (1861)
- Erik Suversen Øymoen, wife Maria and children, Ragnhild and Simon, Aadalen (1861)

Place of origin in Norway not given
- Aslak Knudsen Aamot (1855)
- Martha Syversdatter (1861)
- Erik Eriksen Haugen (1861)
- Anne Bøen, wife of Trond Bøen, and children, Syver Bøen, Ole Bøen, Beret Bøen and Dortia Bøen (1861)
- Jens Brager, wife Kari, and children, Ole Brager, Hans Brager and Oliana Brager (1861)
- Arne T. Bøen (1862)
- John Week Sr., wife Ingeborg and child, Johanns Week Jr. (1862)
- Nils Juelson 1862)
- Ole Baker (1862)
- Ole Juelsen and wife Ragnhild (1862)
- Erick Eriksen Tveit and wife Astri (1862)

Church activities

In June of 1856, Pastor C. L. Clausen held the first official church service in a log house owned by Ole Simonson Jobraaten. The following six children were baptized (parent's name listed in parentheses):
- Gunhild Syversen (Nils Syversen)
- Marit Syversen (Nils Syversen)
- Ole Finhart (Ole Finhart)
- Joseph Tuff (Christen Tuff)
- Anne Hansen (Hans Andersen Gamlemoen)
- Engebret Lindelien (Amund Lindelien)

The first person to be buried in the original Bear Creek Cemetery was Anders Torhaug. He died of overexertion while chasing a pair of runaway steers. The second death was that of Erland Bruflat, father of Gulik Erlandson Dalen.

Before this settlement had the services of a permanent pastor, it received irregular visits from Pastor Jensen, preacher at Highland in Fillmore County, Minnesota. Pastor Fredricksen, the *Skinfeld* (sheepskin) preacher *[referred to as the "Buckskin Pants Preacher" elsewhere in this book]*, also ministered to Bear Creek people.

In May 1858, Rev. A. C. Preus came to nearby Rock Dell, inviting the Bear Creek people to visit his church. Most all the settlers went to Rock Dell, where many of their children were baptized and eight were confirmed. The girls in this confirmation class included:
- Beret Simonsen
- Siri Week

- Ragnhild Week
- Guri Hovda
- Gunhild Johnson

Early in the summer of 1861, Pastor Jensen, who temporarily served as minister at St. Olaf, Rock Dell and Bear Creek, confirmed the following Bear Creek youngsters at Rock Dell (parent's name in parentheses):
- Syver Simonsen (Ole Simonsen)
- Kari Week (Halvor Week)
- Ragnhild Tuff (Beret Tuff, widow)
- Anne Sjuru (Anne Sjurud, Anne Syverud, Anne Olson) (Ole Sjurud)
- Kari Nelsen (Jonas Nelsen)

In 1861, Pastor I. Steen came in answer to the call sent by St. Olaf Parish of Rock Dell and by Bear Creek. *[See Holand's description of Steen earlier in this chapter.]*

The present Bear Creek Lutheran Church, built in the years 1869 and 1870, stands today as a monument to these early settlers.

Fra Søndmøre: Geirangerfjorden

38
Little Turkey and Crane Creek Settlements, Chickasaw County, northeastern Iowa
(Source: De Norske Settlementers Historie, by Hjalmar Rued Holand, translated by Malcolm Rosholt, 1908, pp. 390–394)

In Chickasaw County, Iowa, which nearly hooks up with the larger Winneshiek County settlement a few miles to the east, lies a small community of about 1,200 Norwegians divided into two independent churches.

At Turkey River, the eastern (and the oldest and smallest) congregation, nearly all the people are from Nedre-Telemark, while in Crane Creek the people are nearly all from Sogn.

One of the pastors who served here, I. G. Rugland *[1903-09 –Rosholt]*, has written an article on the history of the settlements, which follows in part:

"The first settlers in this district known as 'Little Turkey' arrived in the summer of 1854 and included the following families, all formerly with Pastor H. A. Stub's congregation in Muskego:
• Ole G. Vaala
• John Landsverk
• John Svennungson Bølaager
• Knut Kultan (Knut Kulton)
• Kittel Haugen
• Ole Tostenson
• Jermund Kittelson
• Aslag Thorvildson

"Church work was begun here by Pastor C. L. Clausen in the summer of 1854, at which time Birgit Thorvildson and Gunild Haugen (now Mrs. John Treider) were baptized. On 26 November 1856, Pastor U. V. Koren held services at the house of Gregor Vaala, where 24 people took communion and one child, Anton Søringen, a son of Anders Olson Søringen and H. Eli, was baptized.

The ministerial records show that on 12 May 1857, services were again held by Koren, and the following children were baptized:
• Ole Andreas Sivertson, son of Sivert Olson and wife Gjøri Ingebrigtsdatter (Sivert Olson is a brother of Pastor O. Estrem.)
• Eli Anderson, a child of Anders Olson and wife Eli Olsdatter
• Johan Jeremias, a son of Jermund Kittelson and wife Johanna Olsdatter

"On 1 June 1858, a letter of call was sent to Pastor Koren and signed by the following members:
• John Svennungson
• Sivert Olson
• Tobias Jacobson
• John Sall
• Ole Torstenson
• Anders Olson
• Kittil Olson
• Svennung Svennungson
• Tollev Olson
• Ole Kittilson
• John Johnson
• Gregor Olson
• Kittil Kittilson
• Alf Olson
• Knud Olson
• Anna Larsdatter (widow)
• Aslag Thorvildson
• Ragnild Jonsdatter (widow)
• Anders Larson
• Johanna Olsdatter (widow)

"Of those who may be recognized as the original incorporators of the congregation, only two are living (1908)—namely, Gregor Olson Vaala and the widow Johanna Olsdatter (Mrs. Johanna Halvorson). Both are today honorary members of the congregation.

"1 June 1854, is also recognized as the anniversary of our 50th jubilee, which we are celebrating today. But in a document written by Pastor J. C. T. Moses (1869-89) and placed in the cornerstone of the church on 15 August 1875, and again replaced in the cornerstone of the present church on 24 June 1904, we learn the following:

   " 'This place where we live is called Little Turkey River settlement, lying in Utica Township, Chickasaw County, Iowa. Those who settled the land and organized this congregation were:
• John Johnson Landsverk, Øvre Telemark
• Tollef Olson Haugen, Øvre Telemark
• Aslak Thorvildson, Øvre Telemark
• Knud Olson Kulton, Øvre Telemark
• Kittel Kittelson Stordobu, Øvre Telemark
• Halvor Eivindson, Øvre Telemark
• Ole Torstenson, Øvre Telemark
• John Svennungson Bølaager, Nedre Telemark
• Gregor Olson Vaala, Nedre Telemark
• Alf Olson Vaala, Nedre Telemark
• Knud Torstenson Einang, Slidre, Valdres

"The congregation was organized in the spring of 1857 by the above-mentioned men and a few others.

"On the basis of this report, the 50th anniversary could have been observed a year earlier.

"Together with the Crane Creek congregation (which was organized about 1870 as a part of the same call with the Little Turkey congregation), there is a congregation in the village of Cresco in Orleans Township, Winnishiek County, that, with the exception of the years from 1878 to 1880, was served by the Little Turkey and Crane Creek pastor until 1895.

"Little Turkey congregation built its first church of logs in the early 1860s. This served until December 1875, when a frame structure replaced it at a cost of $4,000. On 8 July 1903, the church was struck by lightning and burned. On 26 June 1904, the church in which we are assembled today was dedicated. Completely equipped, it cost more than $6,000.

"On Sunday, 14 July 1867, the first confirmation service was held in this (Little Turkey) congregation. Before this time, the confirmands met at Washington Prairie congregation and were confirmed in that church. Among the first class of 13 confirmands were Mrs. Knut K. Stensland and Miss Emma Munson, both members of Little Turkey congregation, and Anders Robinson, a member of Crane Creek congregation. All are with us here today.

"The first couple to be married in Little Turkey church, 2 September 1866, was Christofer J. Natvig and Kristina Hoffland. Mr. Natvig, a widower, is with us today.

"The ministerial records show that Martha, Aslag Nilson's wife, died in the summer of 1855, the first in the congregation to pass on. The word 'burned' appears as a notation in the entry on her death. It is said that she and her husband and three small children were living in a 'hay-shanty.'

"We must remember that in those times people did not have ovens as we find them now in all homes around Little Turkey, but had to lay up some brick work or other facility on the earthen floor, where the family cooked its meals and heated the room. We can easily imagine how difficult it was to prevent fires with this kind of heating.

"One day when Aslag Nilson was away from the shanty, a fire started. The mother saved the three children but was herself so badly burned that she died soon after. There was no doctor to alleviate the pain, no pastor to comfort the mourners at the grave."

Crane Creek, a name not entirely clear in the above article, forms the west part of the settlement that was founded along Crane Creek's watercourse.

I Kirken

The soil here is quite sandy and the settlement developed some years after Turkey River, as there were no Scandinavians here until 1862.

In that year, 10 families arrived from Koshkonong. These people had taken land around the later-known Yankton, South Dakota, but were forced to flee for their lives in the face of the Sioux Indian uprising. In their retreat, they had to cross the length of Iowa, which was then practically uninhabited.

They remained at Crane Creek where, owing to the light soil, they found a big tract of unoccupied land somewhat to the east and decided to settle down. Their names are as follows:
• Ole Anderson Mjølvær, Justedal in Sogn
• Thor Halvorson Faaberg, Justedal in Sogn
• Søren Torbjørnson Faaberg, Justedal in Sogn
• Hans Olson Nigard, Justedal in Sogn
• Otto Olson Nigard, Justedal in Sogn
• Kristian Olson Steinbakken, Justedal in Sogn
• Mikkel Monson Rønnei, Lyster (Luster)
• Halvor Nilsen Lysne, Lærdal
• Jetmund Knudsen Bjerke, Lærdal
• Helge Mathieson, Hardanger
• Mikkel Skare, Hardanger

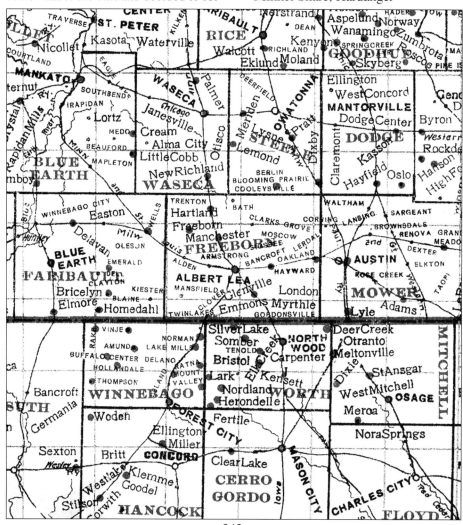

39

Clausen's Big Colony, Iowa and Minnesota border

(Source: De Norske Settlementers Historie, by Hjalmar Rued Holand, translated by Malcolm Rosholt, 1908, pp. 395–401)

One of the largest connecting Norse settlements in the U.S. lies on both sides of the state line between Iowa and Minnesota, about 120 miles west of the Mississippi River. This takes in Mitchell and Winnebago counties in Iowa, and Freeborn, Mower, Faribault and Waseca counties in Minnesota. Here, no fewer than 40,000 Norwegians, most of them farmers, live in well-built homes.

Among the more prominent Norwegian centers in this territory may be mentioned Albert Lea, Lake Mills, Northwood, Lyle, St. Ansgar, Blooming Prairie, New Richland, Bricelyn and Forest City (Iowa). The land here is as rich as any land in America, and the farmers are especially known for their dairy productions

The man to whom all these thousands of Norwegian farmers owe a vote of thanks for their present good fortune is none other than Pastor C. L. Clausen. Although born in Denmark, he has worked most of his life among Norwegians, who therefore have adopted him as one of their own.

He was the first pastor to be called by any Norwegian congregation in America, at Muskego in 1843, the same year he arrived in the U.S. At Muskego he took the lead, both in body and in spirit, in building the first Norwegian church in America. *[Holand probably errs. The first Norwegian church to be actually completed and dedicated was located at east Koshkonong in Dane County –Rosholt]*

Later, together with others, he published the first Norwegian church paper in America, a paper that still continues under the name of *Evangelisk Luthersk Kirketidende*. It may also be mentioned that he was the first president of both the Norske Synod and the Wisconsin Conference.

From this, it may be seen that Clausen's name is closely associated with our countrymen's development in America. But above all, he is best remembered as the founder in 1853 of the foremost Norwegian settlement in America.

Pastor Clausen's explorations

In the late 1840s, Clausen was serving as pastor at Rock Prairie (Luther Valley), Wisconsin, which at that time was one of the two most common destinations for newcomers to America. Hundreds were arriving here every year, and it disturbed Clausen deeply to see the desperate situation these people were in when they came and could not find the free land they had expected to find. Unacquainted with conditions in the U.S., it was easy for them to believe that if they could only reach Rock Prairie they would find the answer to their dreams.

In an effort to find a solution to this problem, Clausen made an extensive journey in 1849 through northern and western Wisconsin. In Pierce and St. Croix counties he located some of the best land to be found in the northern part of the state.

But this was not sufficient to meet the needs. Therefore, in 1851, Clausen made a trip through Iowa, which was then on the ascendancy. It was also on this trip, while visiting Washington Prairie, that he held the first worship services ever conducted by any Norwegian-speaking pastor in Iowa.

As the outcome of this trip was not entirely satisfactory to him, in 1852 Clausen left Rock Prairie once again on a longer tour through northern Iowa and into southern Minnesota, all the way north to St. Paul. It was on this tour, accompanied by Gulbrand G. Myhra, after several weeks of roaming around that Clausen discovered the beautiful terrain where the center of St. Ansgar now lies, and which he the following year chose as his future home.

The two men, Clausen and Myhra, were on their way back from St. Paul and had reached Mitchell County in Iowa. They have spent a couple of days circling around Freeborn County's swamps and were pleasantly surprised when they came upon the gently rolling landscape around Deer Creek *[which lies in Mitchell County near the state line of Iowa –Rosholt]*. Finding so many deer in the area, Clausen gave it the name "Deer Creek," which it has since been called.

When the two men reached the fine tracts of land along Cedar River, where St. Ansgar is now situated, they were completely won over to its rustic beauty. Clausen took a claim for himself on the riverbank (where later part of St. Ansgar was built) and also picked out some excellent pieces of land for his friends in Rock Prairie.

Clausen's report in Emigranten

On his return to Rock Prairie, Clausen wrote an account of his journey to the editor of *Emigranten* in which he justifiably praised the Cedar River territory. This article created quite a sensation and greatly hastened the movement of newcomers into Iowa.

As this article caused thousands to move to Iowa and the adjoining counties of southern Minnesota instead of into northern Wisconsin, it will be repeated here in full as published by *Emigranten* on 1 October 1852 *[an article apparently rewritten by the editor from Clausen's letter –Rosholt]*:

Bondekvinder fra Hardanger

"Pastor Clausen first visited the place near Turkey River called 'The Big Timber of Turkey,' a wooded stretch of land of about 20 square miles with excellent timber, mostly oak. This is no doubt a big advantage. There is plenty of water here but not suitable for raising hay. And one more point, which must not be omitted, some 16 to 18 claims have already been entered on the forest tracts.

"At the upper end of Iowa River there may be found oak openings of which some are quite good, although there is not much forest here. In wet years, the prairie is bound to be somewhat raw, as there are many underground springs that make for soggy farming. A farmer would do best here raising cattle, as the meadows provide good grass and there is plenty of water.

"At Wapsipinicon River, Howard County (Iowa), they found large forests, especially along the river. The land is overall raw and filled with springs. The grass growth is lush, but the soil is by no means meant for cultivation.

"The best land Clausen found, however, was along Cedar River. Here the prairie is good, dry and slightly rolling.

"On the prairie, the soil consists of a foot and a half of deep black humus and a little mixed clay. The grass growth is so high that if it were standing up, it would hide both horse and wagon. Here there is no marshy land to be found, but the meadows grow a choice, leafy grass. At several places, springs may be found with excellent water.

"The river itself is about as large as the Fox at Rochester in Racine County (Wisconsin), and the water is nice and clear; the bed of the river is stony, and the rapids are fast. There are plenty of fish but scarcely any trout. Wild game abounds, including some elk. All the land around is still unoccupied except four or five claims that were taken while Clausen was there, and the same is true of land along the rivers in southern Minnesota. For all these reasons, there is ample opportunity for a large settlement that could stretch along both sides of the river some 30 miles.

"On the claim that Clausen entered, there is a good site for a mill. And as it lies in the center of Mitchell County, there is every reason to believe that, in time, the county seat will be located here. The place lies 84 miles, as the crow flies, west of the Mississippi. But in order to reach it, one must go by way of McGregor Landing, which makes it about 100 miles distant.

"It should be borne in mind that the journey will be expensive, and that it will be costly to live at first, owing to the fact that one has to travel so far to the nearest market. Taking these factors into consideration, it would be unwise for people who have no means to venture forth, and it is especially important to have cattle at the start. Pastor Clausen believes that emphasis should be placed on cattle-raising and the growing of grain sufficient for household needs.

"The land is not yet surveyed nor on the market, but it is said that surveyors will begin early next year, which, if

Norsk Bondepige fra Hardanger

true, will perhaps make the land available for purchase soon. And for those who have the desire to make the journey, there is no time to lose. They must leave this fall, or at any rate early next spring, to take out claims.

"And besides, the Americans have had their eyes opened to the many advantages of the region, and already many new settlers have arrived in Floyd County, which lies to the south. The general rule is to take a claim on 80 acres, half prairie, half wooded, but if one cannot manage to buy that much, naturally he should take less in order to give others a chance.

"This description is not meant to coax anyone to blindly take off on the journey. Pastor Clausen has described both the good and the bad about the place, and everyone must naturally see it for himself. But we must repeat that there is not much time to lose for a person looking for land before it falls into the hands of speculators.

"Clausen will leave in a few days for Iowa to get things in order and will move his family, God willing, in spring."

Fantoft Kirke

40

St. Ansgar and surroundings, Mitchell County, northern Iowa

(Source: De Norske Settlementers Historie, by Hjalmar Rued Holand, translated by Malcolm Rosholt, 1908, pp. 402–411)

In the article quoted in the previous chapter, Pastor Clausen stated that he would leave "in a few days" to go to Cedar River "to get things in order." This he did in September 1852, accompanied by several men for whom he had already made entries on land, namely:
- Mikkel T. Rust, Hallingdal
- Hans Halvorson Smedsrud, Land
- Ole Hansen Haugerud, Ringerike
- Levor Olsen Lindelien, Aadal

The last named had no claim reserved for himself. He therefore left the party at Cedar River on a roundabout tour that brought him to Rock Creek, about 10 miles south of St. Ansgar. Here he took a claim. As his judgment in choice of land was highly regarded by others, the effect of his decision eventually brought thousands of others from his native place in Norway to the same area, where a large Lutheran congregation was organized.

While he was making his tour of Rock River Creek, Lindelien discovered a haystack that an earlier settler had raked together. When Lindelien returned to Pastor C. L. Clausen, he told him about the haystack. As Clausen needed hay for his horses, he went there and took a load. But lest there be any misunderstanding, he wrote his name and address on a piece of wood and laid it in the haystack. Not long after, the owner came to Clausen and was paid for the hay in an exchange of warm friendship.

After six weeks, during which time everyone was busy on Cedar River building log shanties, all returned to Rock Prairie (Luther Valley) in Wisconsin. Throughout the following winter, there were long discussions about the risks involved in going to Iowa. Clausen's report in *Emigranten* had been read by thousands, and all who were already satisfied with their Wisconsin farms were anxious to get a piece of the action in that grand and glorious territory out in Iowa that was bound to supersede anything on Rock Prairie.

But to begin with, one had to consider the distance—nearly 300 miles. And for another, there was the matter of travel expenses and capital to build with before one could expect to harvest anything. These considerations forced everyone to take a second look.

Largest Norwegian emigration group

Finally, after Clausen promised to move out there and be their pastor, 40 men and their families agreed to join him.

The caravan left Rock Prairie in the middle of May 1853—the largest party of Norwegian land-lookers ever to embark on an expedition of this kind. The men in the party included the following:

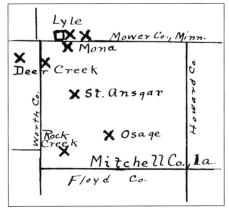

- Mikkel Tollefson Rust, Hallingdal
- Tollef Tollefson Rust, Hallingdal
- Gulbrand O. Mellem, Hallingdal
- Jacob Asleson Hognerud, Hallingdal
- Assor Knutson Gulbrandsgaard, Hallingdal
- Erik Helgeson Espedokken, Hallingdal
- Hans O. Rust, Hallingdal
- Ole Cølbjornson Livdahl, Hallingdal
- Halvor Thoreson Sagabraaten, Hallingdal
- Erik Thoreson Sagabraaten, Hallingdal
- Mikkel T. Golberg, Hallingdal
- Ole Olson Grovo, Hallingdal
- Tollef Olson Grovo, Hallingdal
- Ole Erikson Sando, Hallingdal
- Ole C. Braaten, Hallingdal
- Levor Kvarve (Levor Quarve), Hallingdal
- Jørgen Kvarve (Jørgen Quarve), Hallingdal
- Knut Knutson, Nes in Hallingdal
- Gulbrand G. Myhra, Numedal
- Hellik Bensen Brekke, Numedal
- Torkel Reierson, Numedal
- Gullik H. Blakkestad, Numedal
- Peter Gunderson, Numedal
- Thor Olson Auvesaker, Vraadal in Telemark
- Peter Rasmussen, Kristiania (Oslo)
- Hans Halvorson Smedsrud, Land
- Johannes Johnson Rue, Ringerike
- Ole Hanson Haugerud, Ringerike
- Ole Olson, Ringerike
- Asle Larson, Sigdal
- Lars Asleson, Sigdal
- Ole Torgerson Fagerbakken, Sigdal
- Ole Haroldson Ulen, Aadal
- Levor Olson Lindelien, Aadal
- Helge Johnson Røningsand, Aadal
- Helge H. Røningsand, Aadal
- Syver Johnson, Aadal
- Erik O. Støveren, Aadal
- Nils Syverson Turtnes, Valdres
- Gulbrand H. Nilsen, Valdres
- John Knutson Lee, Valdres
- Ole Knutson Lee, Valdres
- Carl Meyer, from Denmark

All of these men were from Rock Prairie, Wisconsin, with the following exceptions: The Valdres people came via Spring Prairie, Auvesaker came via Koshkonong, and Støveren joined the party in Calmar (Iowa).

In order to cut down on expenses, Clausen purchased, on behalf of the members of the party, no fewer than 44 wagons in Milwaukee for $48 each. But neither Clausen nor his heirs ever got much in return on this loan. *[A footnote by Holand: "Pastor Clausen had been newly married to a widow formerly married to an American of means, and therefore had the money to make this purchase."]*

Included in the caravan were about 300 head of cattle, but remarkably enough, not one pig. With the exception of Clausen's horse-drawn rig, oxen pulled all the wagons. Owing to some church business he had to attend to at the last minute, Clausen was prevented from leaving with the main party but followed a few days later.

Dissatisfied scouts

The spring of 1853 had been extremely wet and all the small creeks in the northeastern part of Iowa were in flood stage. As a result, the caravan often had to stop and build bridges.

Owing to the frequent delays, three men—Knut Knutson, Levor Quarve and Jørgen Quarve—went ahead on foot to see how their new home looked. They had no idea it was so far out in the wilderness. *[Knut Knutson (Knud Knudson Sævre) was the great-great-grandfather to Deb Nelson Gourley. Knud Knudson and his family were the first settlers to Strung-Out-Town (Stringtown) in Amherst Township, Fillmore County.]*

And as they had to pass through Howard County and a big part of Mitchell County, both of which were suffering from heavy rains, the trio returned to the caravan, deeply disappointed, and took their wagons out. To continue farther west, they said, would never do.

People could boast all they wanted to about the famous Cedar River County, but not for them, thank you! It was so outlandishly far away from any place of decency, and the land itself, no matter how good, was surrounded by marshes 50 miles wide and would never be cultivated in the next several hundred years. People on Cedar River would have to live like men in a wilderness, without law and order, and subject always to Indian attack.

The decision of the three men not to continue caused a considerable stir in the camp, and many were afraid they were heading straight for doomsday. But Gulbrand Myhra and Levor Olson, who had seen the land under more favorable conditions, declared that the whole thing was due to the heavy rains and that this would change soon enough.

They finally got nearly everyone calmed down, but the three dissatisfied ones and some others, whose names are not recorded, could not be convinced.

They predicted certain ruin for their dim-witted fellow travelers and thereupon went north to Spring Grove *[and Stringtown]* (Minnesota), where they settled on the highest ridges they could find.

Owing to misfortune and delays at the ferry point in McGregor, the caravan split up so that half the wagons did not reach Cedar River until two or three days later. This unexpected delay had most unfortunate consequences. It went this way:

In the second section of the caravan were Hans H. Smedsrud and Ole H. Haugerud, who had been at Cedar River the fall before and built shanties on their claims. When they arrived, they learned to their amazement that Gulbrand H. Nilsen, John Lee and Ole Lee from Valdres, who had arrived in the first section, had been out to Deer Creek, occupied their houses and taken their

Norsk Bondegaard

claims. A terrible quarrel followed, but as the land had not been surveyed, no one really had a legal right to it. The Valdres men maintained their position by first rights.

Many times Pastor Clausen waded across Cedar River to mediate, but nothing helped, and Smedsrud and Haugerud had to go elsewhere. The bitterness created by this pre-emptory seizure lasted for many years in the settlement.

Pastor Clausen's first task was to get the land formally surveyed. This he did in such a manner that each man got a piece of land along the river, which included some standing timber as well as prairie. As the nearest post office was 10 miles away, he got an office opened in the center of the community and gave the future city the blessed name of St. Ansgar, after one of Christendom's pioneer missionaries to the Scandinavian countries (801-854 A.D.). The city was platted on 120 acres of his land.

Pastor Clausen's church, mill

Shortly after the caravans arrived, Clausen began teaching school in his own house. On the last Sunday in June 1853, two weeks after his arrival, the first worship services were held, and regular services were conducted thereafter. The congregation was formally organized 4 December 1853, with Clausen as resident pastor.

Although the three congregations that called Pastor Koren were organized in 1852, St. Ansgar congregation was the first west of the Mississippi to be served on a regular basis. It was six months ahead of the others in this respect.

The same year he came, Clausen began to build a gristmill on his land along the river. This mill was a blessing to the pioneer because anyone who could leave his own work for a few days could find employment at the mill at one dollar a day. *[This is rather doubtful. Wages for common labor in the early 1850s were around 50 cents a day. –Rosholt]*

In order to spare expenses and time, Clausen's horses and wagon were constantly being used to bring in big loads of flour and meat, which were sold to people of the colony at lowest prices.

In 1854, Clausen opened a land office in association with Jørgen Ziiølner (Jørgen Sollner), a student from the University of Oslo and later a businessman in Austin (Minnesota). But in this enterprise, both lost money—especially Clausen. There was a constant stream of hard-up newcomers coming to him with their complaints, and Clausen, who could never say "no," gave them credit. In a few weeks many of these people moved on, leaving their accounts unpaid.

There were, in addition, many expenses with the mill and many headaches. The first dam on the river washed out, and the Dane, Carl Meyer, who was in charge of repairing and maintenance, was unable to keep it in good repair. The following spring the dam went out again.

A little later, while repair work was in progress, some Virginians arrived on the scene intent on getting control of the mill. They amused themselves by standing on shore and shooting over the heads of the poor Norwegians who were working in the river under a blazing June sun. The Virginians hated Meyer, who was supposed to be "boss" and who gave the Virginians curt replies to their questions.

Sollner recalls that one day Meyer completely disappeared, and all enquiries regarding him were fruitless. People thought he might have been murdered. But a couple of days later, when Clausen and Sollner were out driving, they found an elk horn on the road. When they picked it up, they found written on the underside: "The Virginia devils are after me, but I am hidden in the big oak tree on the hill."

Sure enough, they found poor Meyer in the top of the tree, sitting there like a wingless crow, scared to death and hungry.

Arriving at St. Ansgar in September 1853 were the following:
• Christopher Hanson, Lillehammer
• Simon Hanson, Lillehammer
• Thomas Osmundson, Hallingdal
• Peter Golberg, Hallingdal
• Torstein Reierson, Numedal
• Lars Reierson, Numedal
• Elling Meyer, Aadal
• John H. Røningsand, Aadal
• Ole H. Røningsand, Aadal
• Tore Thompson Mørk

The three from Aadal settled on Rock Creek, where Elling Meyer became the first schoolteacher in the county. Tore T. Mørk was the first to move north to Otranto in the neighborhood of Lyle village. He was a well-versed and judicious man whose advice was sought by many. Incidentally, he had a pig that he sold to some hungry Americans for $50. With this money he purchased a 40 of land, where he later cultivated corn and fattened an unbelievable number of hogs.

Later, the price of pork in McGregor dropped to a cent and a half a pound and the price of wheat in proportion. In fact, a load of wheat often brought just enough to buy a barrel of whiskey, which in those days was considered nearly an indispensable medium of exchange.

In 1854 about a hundred families arrived in St. Ansgar, although comparatively few of these people remained permanently. Those who did were:
• Assor Grøth, Hallingdal
• Ole O. Blakstad, Hallingdal
• Narve Cølbjornson, Hallingdal
• Anders Olson, Hallingdal
• Lars Nilsen Skaftedahl, Hardanger
• Nils Johnson, Hardanger
• Ingebret Knutson, Hardanger
• Peter Nilsen Børsheim, Hardanger
• Lars H. Røningsand, Aadal
• Lars Nilsen Odden, Aadal
• Knut Tollefson, Kristiania (Oslo)
• Erick Amundson, Kristiania (Oslo)
• Trond O. Steile, Valdres
• Thomas Thomassen, i Døtten, Valdres

[the expression i Døtten is not clear –Rosholt]
• Nils H. Nilsen, Valdres
• Halvor Anderson Lysaker, Drammen
• Hellik Benson, Numedal
• Hellik Blakstad, Numedal

Assor Grøth was one of the eight hefty Grøth brothers who settled in Clayton County (Iowa) in 1852. Now only one remains, but their many descendants make up an especially well-liked and distinguished family. Assor Grøth had many fine talents and will long be remembered. Interestingly, when he first came here, he brought along a sow. This became the progenitor of future generations of pigs for northwest Iowa and helped make Mitchell and Worth counties famous for pork production.

In the years after 1852, a steady stream of immigrants arrived at or passed through St. Ansgar, the majority going on to unsettled lands farther away. Later these people returned to be married by Clausen, to have their children baptized, or to have some lumber sawed or grain ground. Hundreds of old pioneers in the distant counties remember, with deep appreciation, the many kindnesses shown them by the *Hallinger* in St. Ansgar who offered them food and lodging while they were passing through.

Mikkel Rust's hotel

One of the most delightful stopping places was at old Mikkel Tollefson Rust's place (he was the father of Tollef Tollefson) who, next to Clausen and Gulbrand Myhra, must be considered St. Ansgar's most respected man. His house became a regular hotel, with 15 to 20 travelers often being given lodgings.

Finally, against his will, he was forced to make a charge. For supper, lodging and breakfast, he got the big sum of 25 cents! *[Holand apparently did not realize that common labor wages were 50 cents per day. At Scandinavia, Wisconsin, Thomas Knoph often lodged travelers overnight for 25 cents, which included supper and breakfast. –Rosholt]*

The food at Rust's place was nothing elaborate—mostly venison and cabbage. It was often difficult to find sleeping accommodations for everyone, but a wagon box that rested on the ceiling joists provided a cozy bed for many on a frosty night.

Pastor Clausen was the spiritual and secular leader of the settlement, a common-sense friend to everyone and guide in all mundane arrangements. Not only was he a pastor, he also served as doctor, teacher, lawyer and businessman. The first person that an eager youth, filled with plans for the future, went to for advice was Clausen, and the first man the weary oldster called for on his deathbed was Clausen.

Clausen found time to build essential business establishments at home, and he found time to carry the gospel. He also served as one of the first county commissioners, as a justice of the peace and as state superintendent of schools. In 1856 he became the first Scandinavian representative in the Iowa state legislature. And when the Civil War broke out, he went off to war as a chaplain, but he became ill and had to resign his commission.

As a result of his wise leadership, the affairs of the settlement went ahead with rapid strides. Although it lay more than a hundred miles from the nearest marketplace, the material progress was so rapid that St. Ansgar now stands in the forefront among Norwegian settlements in America.

Odda

41
Six Mile Grove and Adams, Mower County, southern Minnesota
(Source: De Norske Settlementers Historie, by Hjalmar Rued Holand, translated by Malcolm Rosholt, 1908, pp. 412–417)

St. Ansgar, the settlement founded by Pastor Clausen, stretches north beyond the river *[presumably Cedar River –Rosholt]* to Lyle in Mower County, Minnesota. There it bands to the east and continues northeasterly some 25 miles, through Six Mile Grove and Adams.

With the exception of the forest in the neighborhood of Lyle (that goes by the name of Six Mile Grove) and some small wood plots around the village of Adams, the landscape was naked and flat, without any variation whatsoever—a well of loneliness and playground of the storms. In addition, the land was quite waterlogged, with excessive clay or "gumbo" topsoil.

Today these treeless spaces are divided into section-large squares with a muddy ditch around each square that looks like a road. In the corner of each square there is a tiny square planted to bristling willow trees. And within these rows of trees Norwegians now live.

First Norwegian farmer in Mower

Thov Olson Uvesaker was the first Norwegian to settle in Mower County and also became its first farmer. He came with Clausen's big caravan to St. Ansgar in 1853, the only *Telemarking* (from Vraadal) in the entire party. Whether he was afraid that one *Telemarking* could not live in peace among so many *Hallinger*, or whether he just could not make up his mind about the superior terrain along Cedar River will remain unanswered. Suffice it to say that he stayed only two years.

In the spring of 1854, he moved about 15 miles north to Six Mile Grove, or four miles east of where the village of Lyle was later platted. He found quite a large grove of trees, ample for the kitchen stove and building materials. A creek also ran through the land.

A few weeks later, Auvesaker heard that several other *Telemarkinger* had arrived at St. Ansgar. He then made a trip there and convinced the newcomers to accompany him back to Minnesota. These men included:
• Ole Sampson Bjørndalen, Siljord (Seljord)
• Hans Swenson Tvingli, Siljord (Seljord)
• Sven Jørgenson Trasimot, Siljord (Seljord)
• Trond Richardson Kleppo, Laurdal
• Aslak O. Flaten, Laurdal
• Torjus O. Flaten, Laurdal

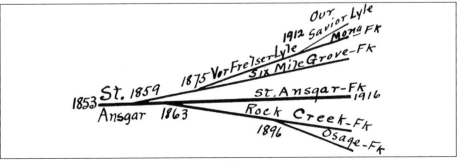

- Martin Hanson, Toten
- Peter Martin, Toten
- Anders Anderson Bytte, Toten
- Ole Quale, Valders
- Knut Quale, Valders

The first three came up from Long Prairie (Illinois) and the others from Koshkonong. A considerable number of *Telemarkinger* also settled around there later on.

Gunder Halvorson Stabbestad, later the most distinguished citizen in the community, sought out this future settlement in 1854 by taking a claim here. He was a cheerful and friendly person, popular with people and ready with a helping hand to everyone. If anyone needed wood for the kitchen stove, he drove to Stabbestad's, where the wood was free, with a free drink to boot.

Targe Guttormson Lee from Kviteseid in Telemark, father of pastors O. T. Lee and G. T. Lee, was another well-known pioneer. Even as Stabbestad was known for his Norwegian hospitality and helpfulness, Guttormson was known for his stubborn insistence on what he considered the pure doctrine of the church. When the congregation split with the Norwegian Synod over the question of slavery, Guttormson stood by the old synod, called a pastor and organized a congregation from among the members of his own family.

For a time, conditions in the settlement were so bad that many regretted they had come to settle. A number of Germans who had settled along the north edge of the tree groves were reduced to starvation and had to leave. But the *Telemarkinger* were tougher and survived.

As the distance to market was far, and as prices for farm produce before the Civil War were low, trips to market were few and far between, and never once to grind grain. Gunder Stabbestad and Halvor Volstad (from Drangedal) drove a heaping load of wheat to market, hoping it would bring enough to buy provisions to carry them through the winter. When they reached McGregor, the price of wheat was so low that, after paying their hotel expenses, they had just enough for a barrel of salt. This they sawed in two, and on the way home, each man sat on his own half-barrel of salt.

It was important, then, to be content under the most modest conditions, grinding one's grain in the coffee grinder and trusting to God.

Ole Bjørndalen's stump mill

Grinding the grain in the coffee grinder was one of the most tedious procedures imaginable, and many elderly women say their arms still ache from this everlasting turning of the handle. Every day, early and late, the coffee grinder was in action. The wife of Hans Swenson kept a record one winter and estimated that she personally ground not less than six bushels of corn and four bushels of wheat. It was then that Ole Bjørndalen, like an angel of light, came forward with his invention.

As Ole was a bachelor and had to do the chores both inside and outside the house, he had long pondered what he could do to lighten the burden of preparing a dish of porridge. Finally he got a bright idea: He carved out the top of a big stump to resemble a sort of mortar a couple of feet across the top. The grain was poured into this and given a thorough pounding with a long wood pestle operated on a hoist. He then cooked the crushed grain in lye to separate the hull from the grain. It rasped a bit in one's throat, but hunger is a good cook.

The new invention went so brilliantly that the womenfolk began to flock to Ole Bjørndalen from far and near with stockings and sacks filled with grain. The stamp mill did the job in a jiffy, and the women went home happy in the thought that a new age was at hand.

However, johnnycake and hominy were not the only fare on the dinner menu. There was wild game and quite often a delicate venison steak. Deer, elk, rabbits and wild fowl took refuge in the tree groves in bad weather and were easy to harvest. Christopher Svenson was not more than 9 years old when he clobbered a deer with an axe, killing it on the spot.

Indians discover "saleratus"

Owing to the profusion of wildlife, Six Mile Grove was a favorite hunting ground of the Sioux Indians, their camp lying directly over the hill from Thrond Kleppo. The two tribes (white and red) got along famously. The little red papooses gabbled in Indian and the little whites spoke Telemark dialect, and between them they developed a jargon that answered all the needs for playing games.

The Indian women were not very efficient in preparing food. Aside from their half-burned meat, the most important staple in their diet was a sort of "hoecake." This was prepared by burying a grain mash in the ashes of the fire where it turned into a clump, heavy as lead.

But when Mrs. Kleppo not only permitted them to bake this mash in her oven but also introduced the women to the secret of using "saleratus" (baking soda), they could scarcely contain their pleasure and went off to town at once to lay in a supply of saleratus. This they mixed with their grain mash in big quantities and baked it, devouring the whole with ecstasy.

After that, nothing was too good for the Kleppo family. The Indians brought them venison quarters, thick woolen blankets for the beds, embroidered moccasins for the children and the most striking colored calico that could be found for Mrs. Kleppo.

Out in the Kleppo yard stands a tree that is possibly the largest in the entire northwest, an elm 35 feet in circumference. The great top of this tree provides shade for half an acre, and under it Pastor Clausen conducted the first meetings of the congregation. Here, too, Pastors Preus and Ottesen preached *[probably A. C. Preus and Jacob Aall Ottesen –Rosholt]*. The tree is still in good condition (1908).

Adams settlers

Between Six Mile Grove and Adams lies a naked prairie nearly 15 miles long, which was not settled for some time. But the groves of trees around Adams attracted the Norwegian settlers shortly after the *Telemarkinger* came to Six Mile Grove. Today, nearly all the people around Adams are *Sogninger*, with some scattered *Striler [from north and west of Bergen and not a complimentary designation –Rosholt]* and Valdres people.

The Valdres people were first. The founder of the colony was Tideman Knutson Objør, who came in June 1855 accompanied by his brothers, Halvor Knutson Objør, Erik Knutson Objør and Arne Knutson Objør. They had moved from Koshkonong with the intention of going to Six Mile Grove, where some of their acquaintances from Koshkonong had gone the year before. But as the land around Adams lies higher and drier and is better provided with wood, they decided to stay here.

Tideman Objør was well satisfied with the place. He wrote to his friends in Koshkonong, and six weeks later a party arrived that included:
- Ragnvald Olson, Sogn
- Ole Johnson Holstad, Sogn
- Johannes Olson, Sogn
- Stephen Olson, Sogn
- Stephen Christenson, Sogn
- Johan Olson Hesjedalen with his sons, Johannes Johnson and Ole H. Johnson from Strileland near Bergen

Ragnvald Olson was deeply interested in getting Norwegians to settle here and influenced many to come from Sogn.

A deadly blizzard

Although considered to be among the founders of the settlement, Stephen Olson and Stephen Christenson were not to see the fruits of their labor in the new land. As nothing was harvested the first year, they left the 8 December for Six Mile Grove to buy food. On the way they ran into a terrible snowstorm, lost their bearings and drove around until they froze to death. The next day the oxen returned home, one with a hat hanging on its horns.

This naked, storm-filled prairie claimed many lives before it was conquered and built up by the Norwegians.

Now it is part of a connecting settlement between Adams and Six Mile Grove and farther to the south all the way to St. Ansgar and Osage. These two settlements, which have endured both poor years and harsh conditions, trace their origin to Pastor Clausen's colonization efforts at St. Ansgar.

Congregation under the mighty elm

42

Worth and Winnebago Counties, northern Iowa

(Source: De Norske Settlementers Historie, by Hjalmar Rued Holand, translated by Malcolm Rosholt, 1908, pp. 418–429)

The Norwegians were the first settlers throughout northern Iowa and southern Minnesota, which takes in the finest part of the entire Upper Midwest. Stray hunters and speculators had hurried across the open spaces earlier, but our countrymen were the ones whose prairie schooners made the first tracks across the primeval, rolling landscape. One county after the other was first developed by the Norwegians.

The sons of Norway were also the first to settle in Worth County, Iowa, and until Gulbrand Mellem came here, not a white man had lived here since the beginning of time. Mellem was a member of Pastor Clausen's big party, which reached Mitchell County in 1853. Despite the excellent land to be found along Cedar River, he was not entirely satisfied and soon went farther west, accompanied by four other land-lookers:
• Ole Colbjørnsen Livdahl (Mellem's brother-in-law)
• Ole T. Fagerbakken
• Asle Larson
• Lars Asleson

About 20 miles west of Clausen's place, they found what they were looking for. Mellem took a quarter section, on which he built a roomy log cabin. This quarter section now takes in the south half of the village of Northwood (Iowa).

Ole Livdahl went a few miles to the north and became the first white man to settle in Freeborn County, Minnesota. He built the first house there, which is still standing (1908). The other members spread out between the first two, but soon felt that life was too bleak to

be living this far from people. All three returned to St. Ansgar that summer, and eventually Ole Livdahl followed them.

For a year, Mellem was alone in Worth County. To the north, west and south for hundreds of miles, there was not a single white man. Eighteen miles to the east across the plains, his old friends from Hallingdal were building a new life. Over at St. Ansgar there were people and friends going to parties and singing church hymns. But here, where he raised his log cabin, only some sad-looking Indians stared in suspicion at this man who had forced his way into their hunting grounds.

Certainly it must have been a gloomy prospect, but Mellem was not one of those whose teeth begin to chatter when night falls. Calm and composed, he and his young wife let a year slip by before they found any reason to visit the main settlement at St. Ansgar. The purpose of this mission was to have their child, Ole Mellem—the first white child born in Worth County—baptized.

Gulbrand Mellem and the Indians

At this time there was considerable restlessness among the Indians, and it looked for a time as though there might be an uprising. The cause for this uneasiness stemmed from an incident in which some trappers had stolen a pair of horses from the Indians. The latter, deeply resenting this incursion, were looking for the thieves, convinced that all white men were in league with them. A couple of men were actually killed in the general uproar over this incident.

One day a band of Indians came to Mellem and demanded that he produce the horse thieves, as the Indians had heard they were hiding at his place. Mellem told the Indians he had no knowledge whatsoever of their whereabouts. The Indians grabbed him and went to the barn to punish him together with the thieves, if they could be found there.

But when there were none to be found, the Indians took their tomahawks and danced around Mellem, gesturing fiercely. He was not going to be bluffed. He stood with arms folded without batting an eye, whereupon the Indians threw aside their weapons and were all smiles, slapping him on the shoulder and assuring him in their tongue that they knew he was a "good white man."

Later, they often stopped to get a drop of milk or a pipe of tobacco and carried on in great style, talking about the wind and weather, hunting, the glories of the past and decline of the present.

In the spring of 1854, Mellem got his first neighbors, a party from Rock Prairie (Luther Valley, Wisconsin) who had first thought of settling at St. Ansgar but did not like it there. These people included:
- Simon Rustad, Kristiania (Oslo), born in Faaberg
- Kristian A. Aanrud, Gudbrandsdal
- Ole Olson (Ole Smith), Kristiania (Oslo)
- Andreas Peter Nilsen, Sweden

The last named was not destined to live long. He was digging a cellar for a house on a site not far from Mellem's place but became ill and died suddenly. His neighbors took his wagon box and used it for a coffin, burying him in the same hole intended for a cellar. After Simon Rustad read the funeral rites as found in the church hymnary, the men covered the wagon box with the soil around the cellar hole. Although every soul in the county was present, there were not many in attendance on this very sad occasion.

Shell Rock, Silver Lake, Bristol and Elm Creek colonies

The above-named party was all that came to Worth County in 1854, but in 1855 quite a few more arrived, mostly Scandinavians, including:
- Abraham Christopherson, Siljord (Seljord)
- Ole Lie, Siljord (Seljord)
- Ole Aslakson Lysbæk, Siljord (Seljord)
- Knut Johnson Dalseid, Hardanger

- Syver Johnson Haugerud, Land
- Ole Hove, Vik in Sogn
- Aslak Lien, Hallingdal
- Johannes Syverson Mørk, Hallingdal
- Tosten O. Groe, Hallingdal
- Ole Fluto, Hallingdal
- Amund Langeberg, Hallingdal
- Lars Nilsen, Næs in Romerike (near Oslo)

Most of these men settled at Shell Rock, which was the name of the community in Gulbrand Mellem's neighborhood near Northwood. In 1855, these newcomers began spreading out across the county. Tosten Groe and Syver Haugerud went to the west and were the first to take land at Silver Lake; Aslak Lien settled at Bristol, and Lars Nilsen went north into Freeborn County, Minnesota.

Amund Langeberg and Ole Fluto went down to Elk Creek, where they founded the big colony of people from Hallingdal. Amund Langeberg bought 14 40s of land for his friends in Rock Prairie (Wisconsin), and these people came out the following year.

In 1856, another substantial party of newcomers arrived.

Those going to Elk Creek were:
- Ole P. Langeberg, Hallingdal
- Amund Helgeson, Hallingdal
- Endre Henrikson, Hallingdal

Those going to Bristol were:
- Knut H. Trøstem, Hallingdal
- Ole Mehus, Hallingdal
- Ingebret Trilhus, Hallingdal

Those going to Silver Lake were:
- Lars Løberg, Solør
- Theo. K. Hundeby, Solør
- Gunnerius Hundeby, Solør
- Østen O. Jordspek, Hallingdal

Those going to Shell Rock were:
- Aslak Gullikson, Vik in Sogn
- John O. Hove, Vik in Sogn
- Erik O. Fosse, Vik in Sogn
- Halvor H. Brekke, Siljord (Seljord)
- Hans Kaldal, Siljord (Seljord)
- Gunder J. Sanda, Siljord (Seljord)
- Elling E. Svensrud, Romerike
- Iver Dahl, Valdres

The same year saw the arrival of the first white men in Winnebago County (Iowa), which bounds Worth County on the west and runs north to the Minnesota state line. These men had moved up from Jefferson Prairie (Wisconsin) and included:
- Helge G. Emmons, Eggedal
- Hans J. Knudsen, Eggedal
- Erik Erikson Braaten, Eggedal
- Henrik Larson, Eggedal
- Narve F. Grønhovd, Eggedal
- Stengrim N. Jellum, Eggedal
- Gunbjørn Nilsen, Eggedal
- Ole Terum, Urland (Aurland) in Sogn
- Nils Bergersen, Stavanger
- Lars Nilsen Wilberg, Kristiania (Oslo)
- Kolbein Larson Graue, Voss

They had heard about the land from Rustad and Mellem and were the first to push into the silent plains of Winnebago County. Emmons, Braaten, Bergersen and Jellum settled north of the state line in Freeborn County.

Lime Creek settlement

The others moved farther south along Lime Creek, after which the settlement is named. This was a thriving little settlement, which for a time lay the farthest away of all Norwegian communities. The closest marketplace was 150 miles away at McGregor, but people's requirements were small and their hopes high. They had nearly forgotten the existence of money, but so much the greater was mutual helpfulness and family solidarity.

When they began building, they organized bees and went from one place to the next to raise houses. The houses were not pretentious affairs, taking only half a day to build and consisting of some crooked logs and a roof covered with sod.

Left to their own devices, they did not forget their catechism but organized themselves into a congregation. This took place in 1857, while they were on a barn-raising bee at Ole Terum's farm. Helge Emmons suggested that the community should organize. In appreciation for this, he was elected trustee.

The following year it was learned that Pastor H. A. Preus was in the area, and the trustee left on official business, driving a yoke of oxen, to bring back the pastor. Preus, who was traveling some miles north of Albert Lea, was inclined to be a bit put off because he was not asked to ride in something a little more fancy than an ox wagon. But Emmons said, "You'll have to take what we have."

The two men finally reached the community, and Preus bestowed the proper seal and blessing on the newly organized congregation.

Pastor C. L. Clausen, meanwhile, had already founded the Shell Rock and Silver Lake congregations in 1857.

In 1857 the following settlers arrived in Winnebago County, settling on Lime Creek:
- Even Neset, Borgund in Sogn
- Peder Gjermo, Voss
- Hellik K. Helle, Numedal
- Peter Larson Wollager, Sogn
- Nils N. Lofthus

After this, there were no new arrivals for many years, and it was not until after the Civil War that the migration to this area was resumed.

Lake Mills colony

At this time the first *Nissedøler*, T. O. Brekke, Jørgen Johnson Kleven and Kittil Gunderson, arrived to found the big Nissedal colony south of Lake Mills. Tarald Thompson and Johannes Uvaas, two *Tinndøler*, arrived in the colony in 1865. Knut Johnson Fie, a distinguished gentleman from Nissedal, came in 1869.

The reason this remaining land in Worth and Winnebago counties was not occupied by the settlers earlier was the heavy forest that had to be cleared before cultivation could begin. Many

Krokkleven i Nærheden af Kristiania

therefore bypassed this land in favor of the plains farther west. But after the war it was hurriedly occupied, and these two counties now have a Norwegian population of more than 15,000. Waldorf College, established later, is now a promising academy.

Among other pioneers who came in the 1850s were the families of Gulbrand Mellem's brother-in-law, who were encouraged to come and join him. Of all the old-timers in this area, the steady, cheerful Mellem was the best known and most popular. He had 13 children, and the family has many descendants across the land.

The two sides of Simon Rustad

A name commonly mentioned in the same breath with Mellem is that of Simon Rustad. Even as his whiskers were half white and half black, so there were two sides to his character—to the utter amazement of many people. Usually he was quiet and unassuming. But he could, when occasion demanded, become edgy and ready to raise his fists.

Although both boastful and modest, he could get on his feet and deliver a thoughtful speech. He was especially well informed about this country's history and constitution. At the annual meetings of the church, he was a well-known figure who often jumped up on his chair and held forth at great length on matters before the meeting. After the meeting he could be just as good-natured, neither bragging nor sulking, whatever the outcome.

Amund Langeberg, respected pioneer

Among other prominent pioneers, one must certainly name Amund Langeberg. Who in Worth or Winnebago counties has not heard about this bullheaded, hard-nosed but witty old character? And can anyone forget his wife, Ingeborg, who has carried nearly the entire new generation of Elk Creek to the baptismal font?

Amund, with his sister, who also was called Ingeborg, reached Minneapolis as early as 1850 before there was even a plat here. The few people who were there lived about eight miles north in the present village of Fridley. Amund remained here a few months, but his sister continued to live there, and later in Minneapolis, until her death—the first Norwegian in a city where there are now about 45,000 (1908).

Amund Langeberg was a man highly respected both for his resourcefulness and sense of authority. People came a long way to seek his advice. If he was in good humor and flattered, he was helpful and gave advice that was sound and to the point. But if he was feeling contrary, he could be extremely hotheaded, not to mention unreliable. He had luck with him from the beginning, accumulating considerable property and buying up every farm around for most of his eight sons, who he lorded over like some grand old patriarch.

Like nearly all of the other early pioneers, he was at one time a boozer. Once, on the way home from town, he badly froze both hands and feet. The doctor was called and said it would be necessary to cut off both hands. Amund argued that it would be enough if the fingers were amputated, but the doctor insisted on his own diagnosis. Amund became angry, gave the doctor a piece of his mind and told him to clear out.

The patient then took a homemade saw—made from the spring of a clock—and cold-bloodedly sawed off his fingers, then reached down and just as assiduously cut off his toes. *[One wonders why he did not cut off the toes first. –Rosholt]*

When the doctor later met Langeberg and saw the stump of the thumb, which was all that was left on one hand, he said, jokingly: "Hummh! You don't have much left after all, do you?"

But Langeberg stuck the thumb in the doctor's face and said, "Your weight in gold could not match the value of this to me."

Later, Langeberg became, at intervals, a strong temperance speaker who, with mouth and hands, revealed the perils of whiskey to the young generation. But his luck seemed to have changed together with his former habits. Things went badly for him as well as for his sons. He lost his old confidence and finally became quite ill. He made out his will, sent farewells to old friends and lay down to die.

Suddenly a change came over him, and he determined to live yet a while longer. He became well in a hurry, whereupon he and his sons sold out, kit and caboodle, and moved to Becker County *[Detroit Lakes, Minnesota –Rosholt]*. Here they all took farms, and the Langeberg clan once again rose to power and prosperity.

"Lucky" Ole Sanden

Ole Evenson Sanden was another noted pioneer of Worth County. He was usually called "Lucky" Ole Sanden because no matter how things went, luck always smiled on his undertakings. If he plowed early and got his grain in on the double while others waited, it was certain to be an early frost that year. If he delayed and others hurried to get their crops in, it was bound to be a dry and unseasonable year.

The year 1877 was the best for wheat in these parts, and also the last. The following year was a tragic one for wheat, but Ole Sanden had his entire farm planted in corn, and this swarmed with small pigs across the entire half section of land. Prices for pigs went up to 7 cents a pound, and while other people went from farm to farm to borrow money, Ole Sanden hauled pigs all winter.

Ole was also a real estate broker who operated from his farm, but if anyone came to do business, he first had to go out into the pigpen to find Ole.

"Business, did you say? Well, I guess so." First he went into the house to find the key to the moneybag.

"Shoes?" Why, these he had in the attic of the wagon shed.

"Kerosene?" In the cellar.
"Nails?" In the granary.
"Plows?" In the barn.

By the time a man finally got through with his business, he had traveled through the wagon shed, barn, granary, storehouse and pigpen and perhaps some other places as well.

If business was slack, Ole filled the wagon box and drove around to his customers. Downhearted? Never!

On Sunday Ole went to church, grazing his herd of cattle along the road en route. If it was a festival day, he always got there late. If he had no business to attend to on Sunday, he took his hammer and a can of staples to look after the fencing. He had to be doing something all the time. If there was a meeting of the congregation, he always took a load of pigs along to town at the same time.

Many well-to-do farmers in the Upper Midwest will remember this lucky Ole Sanden because there were many newcomers who spent a term or two working in Ole Sanden's flesh heap. There was an unshakable conviction with Ole that the correct place for a newcomer to understand American conditions was around his manure pile. Here, year after year, he put a new batch.

But he was a good master to work for; he was reasonable and fair in his pay, and food was served five times a day, like only lords could eat.

Ole's sister Kari was married to Gjermund Engen (Gjermund Grosvult), a relative of Gulbrand Mellem. "Gjermund's Kari," as she was always called, was a strong-willed woman. She could drive the breaking plow and load pigs better than most men.

In fact, nothing fazed her, no matter what.

"Oh, do you know Kari, that lively gal? She can bake, weave and spin. Handy as a man, even on the haystack. She can haul loads over hills, make horseshoes or sleds as good as new and still fashion her own clothes, too!"

43
Freeborn and Waseca Counties, southern Minnesota
(Source: De Norske Settlementers Historie, by Hjalmar Rued Holand, translated by Malcolm Rosholt, 1908, pp. 430-441)

The first white man to settle in Freeborn County, as mentioned earlier, was Ole Colbjørnson Livdahl. He came west with Pastor Clausen's big party in June 1853 and later settled in the southeast corner of Freeborn County, near the present village of Gordonsville. This may have been around 4 July 1853.

Today (1908) the county has a Norwegian population of more than 9,000, or about half the total population, most of them concentrated north of Albert Lea. From here they stretch into Waseca and Steele counties, where there are now more than 3,000 Vikings. As this is somewhat of a connecting settlement with common beginnings, the different sections will be treated under one heading.

Ole Livdahl arrived considerably earlier than the others and for a couple of years continued to be the only white man in several counties (as they are now constituted). Spring and fall followed one another and time passed, but Freeborn County and the open spaces of the Upper Midwest were still superfluous for mankind's needs.

But in 1855—which must be considered the birthday of the county—determined parties of farming people from Norway, unbeknownst to one another, cautiously approached this undisturbed frontier of America. And after many great trials and disappointments, they gradually achieved success and helped to make the county a proud and enterprising part of the world.

The next party of land-seekers included five Norwegians from Rock Run in Illinois. In the spring of 1855, under the leadership of the well-known Klemet Stabek, they took land in the area where the city of Albert Lea now stands. Stabek himself occupied a piece of land south of Fountain Lake, which now takes in the center of the city.

This party then returned to Rock Run to bring back their families. As they had many things to attend to before they got ready to return to Minnesota, they did not reach Freeborn County again before late fall of 1855.

By then they were too late, as a man from Pennsylvania—George S. Ruble—had discovered the waterpower site at Albert Lea and pre-empted Stabek's claim with the intention of platting a village. As he had 20 men and workers with him, he was ready to build a mill at once. Just the sight of that formidable Ruble and the awful looking creatures around him was enough to warn Stabek and his party not to make any fuss about it and leave. *[A footnote by Holand: "One of the five who were first to reach Albert Lea was Halvor K. Wrolstad, who still lives in Six Mile Grove near Lyle, Minnesota, where he was actually one of the first to settle. One of George Ruble's workmen was Charles Kittilson from Eggedal in Norway. Kittilson operated a saloon for a time, served in the Civil War where he advanced in rank to lieutenant and after his discharge became county treasurer and in 1879 was elected state treasurer of Minnesota."]*

Bancroft and people from Sogn
A short distance north of Albert Lea, other land-seekers had arrived ahead of George Ruble, especially in

Bancroft Township, where the influx into Freeborn County, including the Norwegians, began in earnest.

In the summer of 1855 the following people of Norway arrived, although not all in the same party:
• Lars Mikkelsen Trugstad, Nannestad in Ringerike
• Christopher Mikkelsen Trugstad, Nannestad in Ringerike
• Charley Peterson, Hakadal
• Charles Olson, Hakadal
• Martin Hanson, Hadeland
• Anders Olson, Aardal
• Ole Hove (Ole Haave), Vik in Sogn

Only Lars Mikkelsen was married, and these seven men, one woman and their cattle lived together for a time in a barn where the Bancroft Dairy now stands.

Glasses on the trail

But it was the people from Sogn in Norway who left their peculiar stamp upon the Norwegian population of Freeborn County. In the next party of pioneers, we come to the progenitors of this strong stock. And here it is also interesting to note that the finding of a pair of glasses was the main reason for the Norwegian settlement of Freeborn County.

The above-mentioned Ole Hove, father of professor Elling O. Hove, spent a few weeks in Clausen's colony at St. Ansgar. But as the best land had already been taken, he drove at random to the northwest, looking for land. Some miles beyond St. Ansgar, he lost a pair of glasses he had acquired at Long Prairie in Illinois. He finally reached Mikkelsen's barn in Freeborn County.

Two days after Hove lost his glasses; a party of land-lookers from Long Prairie came upon the trail left by Hove. There were nine families in the group, including Guttorm Bottolfson Espeseth and Jon Hermundson from Vik, and the others from Telemark and Hardanger. All had intended to go to Worth County in Iowa, where they had acquaintances.

Somewhere along the road, one of the wagons struck an object on the ground. On this stoneless, flat prairie, anything unusual like this is noticed, and so the people stopped to investigate—only to find a pair of glasses! This was certainly something to come upon way out here on the prairie!

But Guri Bottolfson knew the answer: "What do you know if these aren't Ole Hove's glasses," she exclaimed. "Where do you suppose he can be?"

But the skepticism of the *Telemarkinger* prompted one of them to ask, "How do you know for sure these are Hove's glasses?"

"I ought to know," Guri protested, "because I was with him when he got them. Let's follow the wagon tracks and I'll bet we soon find Ole Hove."

The *Telemarkinger* refused to listen to this. They were determined to go on to Worth County and were not going to be put off their course by some foolishness about a pair of glasses, which could just as well have belonged to Old Erik himself for all they knew. *["Old Erik" is a slang expression in Old Norse for the devil. –Rosholt]*

It was finally decided that the *Telemarkinger* would take their own road to Worth County and the *Sogninger* would take the new track north to Freeborn County, where they in fact found Ole Hove, owner of the glasses.

Later, Ole Hove, afraid of Indian trouble, moved south to Worth County in Iowa, becoming one of the pioneers there. Guttorm Boffolfson and Jon Hermundson settled in Freeborn County three miles north of Albert Lea. They in turn wrote to their friends in Long Prairie, and in time an important segment of emigrants, originally from Sogn and/or Vik kommune, reached Freeborn County.

Now there are close to 3,000 *Sogninger* in addition to 300 or 400 who live north across the town line in Steele County around the village of

Ellendale. All of these *Sogninger* and many other Norsemen have to thank Guttorm Bottolfson, Endre Bottolfson and Jon Hermundson for their presence in Freeborn County.

Lars Mikkelsen and Christopher Mikkelsen from Ringerike also had an important influence on the movement of immigrants to Freeborn County, as there are a couple of thousand people from Ringerike scattered around the county. The first, who came in 1856, included:
• Gulbrand Bagaasen, Ringerike
• Ole Narveson Melby, Ringerike
• Christopher Narveson Melby, Ringerike

The following came in the summer of 1856:
• Peder Lunde, Aadal
• Endre Gulbrandson, Aadal

They drove west all the way to Spirit Lake in Iowa through several uninhabited counties before they turned back and found land near Hayward east of Albert Lea, Minnesota, and became the first in Hayward Township. Both of these families are descendants of the big Lunde clan in Aadal, of which family records (1908) list 1,153 living members, 572 living in America.

Red Oak Grove (Blooming Prairie)

A few miles northeast of the *Sogninger*, across some broad marshes, lies Red Oak Grove, or Blooming Prairie, as it is now called. This is the name of a large and rich colony of some 1,300 *Hallinger* whose farmlands extend north into Steele County and northeast into Mower and Dodge counties.

This settlement also traces its genesis to Clausen's colony at St. Ansgar. When a group of *Hallinger* in Primrose, Dane County, Wisconsin, learned that there was a Halling colony near St. Ansgar, they decided in 1855 to move to Iowa. The men in this group included:
• Christen E. Rukke, Hallingdal
• Knut E. Rukke, Hallingdal
• Nils Iverson Wenaas, Hallingdal
• Guttorm Halsteinson, Hallingdal
• Tore Peterson Bergo, Hallingdal
• Anderson Melhøv, Hallingdal
• Guttorm Olson Engen, Hallingdal
• Tosten Olson, Sogn

But when they reached Mitchell County they found the good land taken. Thus they went north along Cedar River for nearly 50 miles until they reached the northeast corner of Freeborn County, where they found both wood and prairie land.

In 1856, the former Primrose people were joined by:
• Tollef Sommerhaugen and his son, Ole Tollefson
• Christen Johnson Rukke, Hallingdal
• Helge Olson Oterdokken, Hallingdal
• Jens Amundson Børdalen, Hallingdal
• Knut Bjørnson Bakken, Hallingdal
• Syver Bjørnson Bakken, Hallingdal
• Bjørn Bjørnson Bakken (Bennett Benson), Hallindal
• Ole Throndsen, Hallingdal
• Erik Eriksen Børsness, Sogn

Later on, no one but *Hallinger* moved into the area, making it the most prominent Halling settlement in the U.S.

Helge Oterdokken, best known among the *Hallinger*, is remembered as a clever man with a knife, as practiced in the old school of fighters. He had a clergymen's certificate in good standing for axe handling, and 13 stab wounds.

Old-timers also remember the wild man from Hallingdal, Tosten Dengerud, who was defeated by Helge Oterdokken with a broad-axe blow to his back side. These are epic characters and fighters who achieved the same fame in Hallingdal as the heroic exploits of Achilles in Greece. Both of these former champs eventually came to the U.S.—Oterdokken to Blooming Prairie and Dengerud to Zumbrota. The latter also served in the Civil War.

Oterdokken led a fast life after he immigrated to Minnesota but eventually became a strong temperance man and farmer. He had exceptional talents, and his many genial traits are still remembered.

Manchester and Hartland

Two *Telemarkinger*, Ole K. Morreim from Tinn and Hans Kjønaas from Bø were first to reach Manchester in 1856, after living a year and a half in Goodhue County near Zumbrota. They had good land in Goodhue County and were near to market, but youthful impatience and wanderlust drove them a hundred miles farther west.

Two parties of newcomers also arrived in the summer of 1856 and settled a bit farther west in Freeborn County. One group included:
- Stener Mikkelson, Telemark
- Gunder Thygeson, Telemark
- Rollef Thygeson, Telemark
- Ole Kleppe, Telemark
- Nils Vangen, Voss

Three weeks later came the following:
- Ole Fossum, Telemark
- Per Fossum, Telemark
- Anders Libæk, Krødsherad
- Thor Anderson, Sigdal
- Ole Slette, Sigdal
- Halvor Slette, Sigdal
- Ole Kittelson, Sigdal

They had all lived temporarily at Jefferson Prairie (Wisconsin) and St. Ansgar.

New Richland and Ellendale

The first Norwegians to reach the upper Le Sueur River in Waseca County in 1856 were from Rock Prairie. They were:
- Anton Sampson Kongsgaarden, Sandsvær
- Even O. Strenge, Sandsvær
- Halvor T. Bakstevold, Sandsvær
- Hans H. Sunde, Sandsvær
- Ole K. Hagen, Hallingdal
- Vebjørn Anderson, Hallingdal
- Halvor Thoreson Haugerud, Hallingdal
- K. O. Rotegaard, Hallingdal
- Christen Knutson, Hallingdal
- Nils K. Kopstad, Eker
- August Møller, Skien

They left Rock Prairie on 6 May and arrived in Waseca County on 10 June, bringing 12 yoke of oxen and wagons, 80 head of cattle and $600 in gold.

The following came the next year:
- Anders N. Berg, Sandsvær
- Torkel T. Lund, Sandsvær
- Ole Halvorson, Sandsvær
- Ole. H. Sunde, Sandsvær
- Per O. Rotegaard, Hallingdal
- Ole J. Høgaas, Numedal.

This part of the settlement, which now numbers nearly 2,000, is about evenly divided between *Sandsværinger* and *Hallinger*, the former probably in the majority. Emigration from Sandsvær actually began in 1842, with the departure of Halvor Tubbehaatvedt and Ellev Anderson Berg (who was also called *Skræder*, meaning "tailor"). These men first went to Muskego and later to Rock Prairie before moving to Minnesota. The largest settlement of people from Sandsvær in the U.S. is now situated around New Richland.

East of New Richland around Ellendale is a thriving branch of *Sogninger*, although only one-tenth the size of the colony near Albert Lea, but determined and able to defend and uphold their old Sogn dialects. Anfin Anfinson Seim, Ole Anfinson Seim and Halvor Hougen, all from Aardal, were the first to settle here.

Famine and floods

The pioneers in this area faced tremendous odds in the first five or six years. Although 50 years have passed, these years have not dimmed the memories of adversities and helplessness, need and loneliness. Indeed, the pioneers have many different memories, noble, pathetic and comic, but mainly of hunger and worry.

The first summer it was common for everyone to help each other in "bees" and to get a few acres of the tough sod plowed. People then sowed flint corn and waited for a rich harvest. But it was all for nothing, because earth and sky swarmed with gophers and blackbirds that ruled the fields, day and night.

The men who had guns walked up and down the fields and shot at the birds. Those without guns ran through the fields hollering at the top of their voices, drumming on tin pans. A stranger coming upon this scene would think people had gone mad. But when fall came, the blackbirds were the victors, and the pioneer had nothing to show for all his work.

The following year was just as bad, and many people were beginning to starve to death. Flour was $11 a barrel. Furthermore, a man had to drive 100 miles to get it. Many had to endure this, and for nourishment lived mainly on fish and wild roots. The question was: Which of the roots were poisonous? People tried them first on the local idiot and stood around waiting to see what would happen. Would he live? Of course, there was no danger; he downed the food and begged for more.

Worst was to listen to the children who cried for food and could not be satisfied. Instead of bread, they got hazelnuts. Many a well-to-do farmer in Freeborn County can remember the time when he longed for a slice of moldy bread as a delicacy, and his mouth watered at the thought of a drip of bacon.

There was considerable malaria in Freeborn County in those first years. On one day a man could be in bed shuddering with cold; the next day he was running a high fever. This reoccurred once a month. As for help from a doctor, there was none.

In 1858 the big swarms of thieving birds left and the crops looked good. But another bitter battle lay in the offing: In the latter part of July and early August, heavy rains completely destroyed the crops. The rain poured down so that the fields resembled lakes. Big trees were torn from their roots; fences, vegetables and houses floated away. The destruction was unbelievable. People took refuge on the high points of the land, speechless and bewildered, their hopes for a better life dashed. That winter, there was not much milk, either, because many cattle died of starvation for lack of fodder.

At this point many a tortured and famished settler lost all hope and left this land whose plagues seemed to be as many and as heavy-handed as the ancient Egyptians once had to face.

The Buckskin Pants Preacher

The first "pastor" in this and surrounding counties of southern Minnesota was A. S. Fredricksen [*Norsk Lutherske Menighets, p. 442, mentions an A. E. Friedrichsen as having served Bloomfield congregation in Fillmore County in 1858-59. The authors of the book refer to him as among the pastors, but this is probably an error, as a biography of Norwegian Synod pastors appearing in Festskrift, published in 1903, fails to include this name. But people were not always particular in pioneer times whether a man was ordained or not, so long as he could stand up and preach. –Rosholt*]

Many people have almost forgotten the name Fredricksen because this is not the name people associated with him. Instead, he was known as *Skindbrokpræsten [the Buckskin Pants Preacher –Rosholt]*. Actually, he was never a pastor, but a former student who had once studied theology in Oslo. There, it is said, he was some kind of dandy and deeply in love with himself.

For good and sound reasons, which are now forgotten, he was assisted in getting passage on a ship sailing to America in 1855. On the trip over, he was encouraged by some Texas-bound immigrants to act as their chaplain. This he did in his own manner and with so much unction that he decided to make a career of it among his countrymen in the open spaces of the West. He received some sort of a call from his Texas friends to serve as their pastor for two years.

Meanwhile, Fredricksen was anxious to be ordained and sought out several pastors to assist him. He especially

Hornelen

appealed to Pastor U. V. Koren in Decorah, Iowa, but failed miserably. Koren refused to recommend him, especially for the ministry. He left in anger and decided to work among the people out on the prairie, eventually to gather them into a synod of his own.

For two or three years he continued his mission endeavors all the way from Fillmore County in the east to Brown in the west. He lived in a sod hut near the Freeborn congregation's church, a piece of land still referred to as the "preacher's land" because of him.

As collections were small among the sod hut dwellers, Fredricksen found it necessary on occasion to take a ball of wool or a hide as a fee for a baptismal service. In time he acquired a whole load of these commodities and then drove to Winona to dispose of them. Here, contrary to expectations, he got paid so well that he always asked to be paid in sheepskin blankets and other such items. Thousands of people saw the preacher thus attired, driving around with horse and wagon, collecting hides, balls of wool, socks, wooden spoons and hauling his merchandise to Winona for more profits. These profits were easy to take.

While he traveled around dispensing the gift of grace, he also invested considerable sums as a pawnbroker, but far from interest-free, as it is said he collected up to 40 percent on his loans. When Koren once brought this to his attention and asked if he had ever taken more than 40 percent, he replied, unabashed, "Yes, I've even gotten 60 percent."

Despite the fact that the Buckskin Pants Preacher was the first in some places and helped to organize many congregations, he was never called to ordination. The trouble was that his manner of preaching was a bit too coarse, even for these hard-bitten settlers ordinarily not too fussy in this respect. A sample of his preaching cannot be repeated, as it would not pass in polite company. Moreover, the old pioneers did not think it was proper for one who would be pastor to stare every time a woman walked into church.

If he was impossible as a pastor in the pulpit, he was even more hopeless as a considerate pastor in his rounds of the pioneer shanties. He spared no one his visits and always expected bed and board, in which people found little spiritual comfort.

In the late evening, when his hosts, in humility and pious expectations, sat down for devotions, the would-be pastor sat stiff and starched and soon began to yawn, saying, "No, I want to go to bed, I've eaten too much porridge."

This was the substance of his communication, and there was certainly not much spiritual refreshment in this. Thus, the Buckskin Pants Preacher was seldom a welcome guest when he drove into the yard.

As people in these times drove oxen and the barn doors were proportionally lower, they tried to excuse themselves in an effort to discourage the man by saying that the barn door was too low for his horses. But this did not faze Fredericksen.

"Ah, poof," he would say, "that's nothing. My horses can walk on their knees." He thereupon commanded his horses to their knees, and in they went as the farmer watched, absolutely flabbergasted.

When he was no longer wanted as a pastor on the prairie, Fredricksen moved up to French Creek in Trempealeau County (Wisconsin), where he took a piece of land and remained for a time.

Several of the women who lived nearby can tell about his remarkable domestic arrangements. Sometimes he got one to mend for him, and when the clothes were brought back to him, he often served them *brændnedslethe*, which is all he ever had to drink. This tasted a bit strong for the women, especially as it was brewed from an herb that grew on the sunny side of everyone's necessary but unmentionable little house. *[Oivind Hovde of Luther College and Harold P. Anderson, Rosholt, both recall that a medicinal tea was brewed from the common nettle. It was considered good for ague, rheumatism and other ailments. –Rosholt]*

Pastor Ole Paulson, in his *Erindringer (Memories)*, gives a good description of a meeting he once had with the Buckskin Pants Preacher:

"A short distance out of Prairie du Chien, an unsightly looking tramp boarded the train carrying a common flour sack. When the conductor asked for his ticket, he had none.

" 'Where are you headed for?'

" 'Clinton.'

"The conductor gave the price of the ticket. The tramp began to dig in his many pockets, found a few pennies here and there but for all his digging could not raise the fare. The conductor gave him a hard look and passed on.

"The next day, as we were assembled in church for services, an elegantly dressed man walked in, plush hat and cane in hand. I thought I had seen him before but for the moment could not recall where. Sure enough, it was the tramp of yesterday. But who in the world was he? None other than the widely known Herr Pastor Fredricksen. He came to the meeting hoping to be accepted into the ministry, but he knocked on all the church doors without gaining entrance."

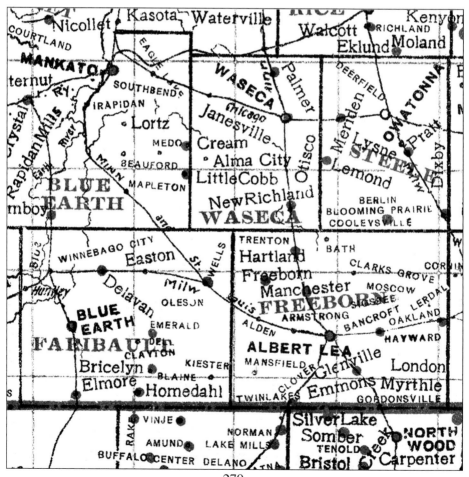

44
Faribault County, southern Minnesota
(Source: De Norske Settlementers Historie, by Hjalmar Rued Holand, translated by Malcolm Rosholt, 1908, pp. 446–450)

On 11 June 1857, the first Norwegians, all from Sogn, reached Faribault County. They included:
- Ole Nilsen Hauge, Lærdal
- Ole Nilsen Hundere, Lærdal
- Knut Johnson Skrenes, Lekanger
- Gjæst Anderson Esse, Lekanger
- Jens Tue, Lekanger
- Jens La, Hafslo
- Henrik Larson, Hafslo
- Henry L. Rønnei, Lyster (Luster)

These men had never seen each other before they reached Iowa, where they happened to meet on the road west of McGregor. They arrived in Faribault County shortly after the Indian massacre at Spirit Lake. Nearly all the settlers in the county were gathered in a newly built hotel located on the future site of Blue Earth, only a day's journey southwest to Spirit Lake, where Inkpaduta (Indian chief) and his band of renegades were still menacing the neighborhood. Most of the *Sogninger* in this party took land in Section 36 of Emerald Township.

At the time, it seemed quite daring for these Norwegians to leave for such an isolated area as Emerald Township. Although they were aware of Inkpaduta's depredations at Spirit Lake, they were young and carefree, afraid of nothing and anxious to test their dreams against the future.

As they traveled behind some hills and joked about their future, they nearly scared the daylights out of two Yankee-Americans who had settled in the neighborhood. Hearing the Norwegians in the distance, they took them for a band of Indians. Without waiting to see for certain, they fled to Blue Earth to report that the Indians were in the vicinity. They escaped, they said, but had been so near that they could hear their high-pitched chants of victory and talk of scalping and burning. The Indians had, no doubt, surprised and killed an unsuspecting party of newcomers because their oxen were pulling wagons loaded with loot. This account, which created considerable excitement, heralded the arrival of the first *Sogninger* to Faribault County.

Now there are four townships in the county populated mainly by *Sogninger*, while the county as a whole has a population of about 4,000 Norwegians. Not many newcomers came to Faribault County until after the Civil War (1865). Among those who did were the following, listed here with their dates of arrival:
- Ole Legreid, Aardal (1858)
- Hans Urness, Hafslo (1858)
- Erik Amundson, Balestrand (1858)
- Eivind Skatte, Toten (1860)
- Gullik Ulriksen, Toten (1860)
- Christopher Anderson, Toten (1860)

The latter three came by way of Koshkonong.

Gullik Peterson from Lærdalsøren, a well-known man and father to Pastor N. G. Peterson, came to Faribault County in 1862, although he was actually among the first to reach Oakland in Freeborn County in 1857. He was a big, strong man, and once served as a skipper on a square-rigger sailing ship.

Peterson was a friendly man but easily angered, and when his temper got the upper hand, it was better to avoid him. Once when he was being teased by "Jens-on-the-School Land," he grabbed the would-be joker and threw him through the wall of a blacksmith shop. He then went out, picked him up and threw him into a wagon of a passing driver and said, "Take this — home!" *["Jens" was probably someone living in the school section of the township, the sale of which was used for school purposes. –Rosholt]*

One of the first men from eastern Norway to reach Faribault County was Anders Hanson from Hadeland, a gifted man who stood high in the esteem of his community. He was the father of Dr. Otto Hanson of Forest City, Iowa.

Pastor Arne Boyum, riding a horse, also visited the district on one of his first mission tours. But it was C. L. Clausen who organized a congregation here in 1859. *[Boyum served as pastor in Arendal, Fillmore County, from 1858 to 1896. From 1876 to 1887 he was president of the Hauge Synod –Rosholt]*

Long trip to the mill

Ole Nilsen Hauge of Forest City is one of the few living members among the original founders of the Faribault settlement. Although quite advanced in years, he is still (1908) of sound mind and has a remarkable fund of stories.

He tells us that in the first six years of wheat growing, the farmers harvested nothing but straw owing to the depredations of the blackbirds. It made no difference what kind of devices were used to scare or trap them, and no matter how many cowbells were rung or shots fired; it all came to nothing when harvest time came around. The seventh year he got 50 bushels of wheat on a 14-acre field. He planned to have part of this wheat ground into flour.

First he drove some 30 miles to Albert Lea where he heard there was a gristmill, only to learn that it was a sawmill. He continued another 25 miles to Austin, but the little "corn-cracker" mill there had been moved to an unknown location. From here he drove 20 miles south to St. Ansgar, but again, only a sawmill was operating there. Finally he got to Mitchell, eight miles farther, where there was a gristmill. But he then had to wait five days before his turn came. He was away from home for 18 days.

It is no wonder that flour was so expensive. In those days, a barrel of flour cost $10 in Mankato, and salt was seven cents a pound.

Indian panic

As the majority of Norwegians did not reach Faribault County until after the Indian war, they were spared the terrors of 1862. The county, so to speak, was situated on the periphery of civilization and therefore was open to Indian attack. When the news came on 22 August (1862) that the Indians were on the warpath, people became panicky. Without delay they hitched up their oxen and took off to the east, leaving ripened crops, cattle in the pasture and vacant homes.

Ole Nilsen, young and daring, decided not to leave until he actually saw the Indians coming. But he admits that he stood guard on a hill two days and nights watching the main road below, where a steady stream of refugees was moving east.

For 48 hours the exodus continued, some people cursing and some praying, some yelling or crying, all the while lashing their oxen forward. And then just as suddenly the movement stopped and all was quiet.

Everyone not already gone lay behind either dead or taken prisoner by the Indians. As all his neighbors had fled, Ole Nilsen was the only one left.

Ole decided finally to walk west to Blue Earth to learn the latest news. On the 16-mile stretch cross-country he did not meet a soul. When he arrived in the village, he found that all except four or five young bachelors who were watching from behind a log bunker had abandoned it.

The Indians actually did reconnoiter in Faribault County. But when they found it deserted, they wasted no more time and attacked outposts farther north.

45
McGregor, Clayton County, northeastern Iowa
(Source: De Norske Settlementers Historie, by Hjalmar Rued Holand, translated by Malcolm Rosholt, 1908, pp. 451-457)

In the northeast corner of Iowa, at the mouth of a narrow valley, lies the village of McGregor. A relaxing place for people with tired nerves, it lies quite secure in the embrace of big tree-clad ridges. Cattle graze peacefully in the village streets, and the mighty Mississippi flows nearby, vast and silent.

For 50 years this dreamy little village was the main marketplace for the pioneers, and it would be difficult to find a place quite like it anywhere. Its grass-covered streets were a beehive of activity as people came and went from sizeable areas of two states, emblazoning McGregor's name across hundreds of miles of the western frontier.

The town was for many years the port of entry between East and West. The railroad terminated on the east bank of the Mississippi after passing through Wisconsin, while to the south ran the flat-bottom steamboats to St. Louis and also to the Gulf of Mexico. To the west lay the great open spaces, Indian hunting grounds and the lush plains that for thousands of years had waited upon the white man's arrival.

There lay McGregor, on the boundary between the civilized world and the wilderness, trading place for buyer and seller, civilization's last chance, with a nexus of trails leading in all directions. From the east over the ferry came the new settlers with their wagons, their oxen and cattle, their heavily loaded prairie schooners and their sacks of wheat or corn seed. One long immigrant party after the other passed through, patiently and hopefully. A year later they were apt to be back again, coming from the west with a big load of wheat.

Meanwhile, they had been out and taken land, built homes, plowed the turf, and harrowed and dressed the black earth to sow their precious seeds. And through the long spring and summer days they had gone about their work with a feeling of exultation mixed with dread, praying to the heavens for a cool rain or for sunshine. And when the wheat stood thick and yellow, they cut it by hand, threshed it with the oxen and cleaned the chaff with the help of the wind.

The roads leading to McGregor came in from the south and north, far and near, joining at the military road east of Calmar, Iowa. From the valleys of Oneota, Turkey River and Wapsipinicon they came; from Big Canoe's hills and Spring Grove's heights, from Root River's narrow ravines and from Harmony's rich plains, from Bloomfield's gentle terrain and St. Ansgar's delightful frontier, from Freeborn and Faribault's big marshes and endless plains and hills. All headed for McGregor, the main trading post of the western marches.

A trip to McGregor

When the day came for a settler to start out for McGregor, it was a festive occasion. For many weeks he had waited for the day when he would haul that first load of wheat. There were scores of small things he wanted for the farm as well as for the house—such as coffee, sugar, syrup and salt, which had to be purchased before winter arrived.

Time and again through the long days and months when he had rested on the scythe handle, he had wondered what was going on back there in the big world. He had no newspaper to read, only the hymnbook and father's old *Huspostil* [book of sermons for laymen –Rosholt].

Once he had acquired from a visiting pastor an old copy of *Emigranten*, the only Norwegian paper published. This he had read so many times he had practically memorized it. But now he was finally on his way to McGregor, where there would be people, traffic and newspapers, gossip, and wheeling and dealing. This was a city of the world, and you better believe it!

Finally the departure date was at hand—a date not so easily agreed upon when normally six to eight men with their ox teams and wagons went together. Perhaps they lived 75, even 150, miles out on the frontier. In any case, they were never without danger of

Geirangerfjorden

Indian attack. Whatever, it was more fun to be traveling together. A good supply of provisions was taken along, as there was no thought of staying at a hotel for the three to six nights. A man could just as easily sleep under the wagon box.

Everything was quiet and rather deserted as each man left his place long before daylight to join the others. Finally, after several days of driving, they reached the military road east of Calmer, where they met more wagons of wheat and people. It paid to use one's ears, because here the stream of traffic divided into two unbroken strings of wagons. The one with heavy loads and deep thoughts of prices was heading east; the other, with small packages, kitchenware and loud jokes originating in the hot air of the saloons, was heading west.

Pocket City's many temptations

Because McGregor had only one main road leading into town, which ran downhill along a narrow gap, it was often called the "Pocket City."

Downtown, there were two double scales where all farm produce was weighed. Although four loads could be weighed at the same time, the traffic could not be accommodated as fast as the wagons arrived, especially in the fall when hundreds would line up for several miles over the hill, waiting to be weighed.

Walking among these wagons of wheat came the many buyers to dicker with the farmers to "sell in round numbers." Things were moving so slowly with the weighing, they said, that it would be all night and the next day before their turn came. Better to sell for an estimated poundage, and then they could go directly down to the warehouse on the river.

Day after day the cunning buyers tramped up and down among the wagons, shedding crocodile tears over the uncertainty of prices and the endless delays the farmers had to put up with. And day after day the farmers stood by their loads, patient and persevering.

When the wheat was finally weighed and paid for, the fun began. Into the nearest saloon for a glass or two on the deal and after that, there was no end of important matters to be attended to. There was horse and bull trading, socializing, wrestling and what not, and everything had to be concluded and sealed with a couple shots at the bar.

Everyone felt himself inspired by an uncaged gaiety. Later on, a fellow got real chummy with some of the fine chaps around and exchanged views on the awful conditions out on the "claim." Pretty soon someone suggests a game of cards, and a guy certainly has to take a fling at this, too. Before long, the whole night is gone, burned up in an irresistible convulsion of wild abandon nurtured in the bones by six months of self-denial on the wild frontier.

When the settler wakes up in the morning, it is often with a headache and a premonition that something terrible has happened. And when he counts his money, reality dawns on him. Stone broke! He has blown half a year's crop in one night of living it up.

There stands the empty wagon box, screaming accusations at the bounder when he thinks of all the things he had promised to bring back to his wife and family. He hurriedly harnesses the oxen and clears out of town like a criminal, before he is recognized by any of his neighbors.

Up over the hills stands a long line of wagons, moving slowly homeward. He thinks the passengers are staring holes into him and his empty wagon, reading his innermost thoughts.

"Look at that guy," their glances say. "Not so much as a sack of flour to take home with him! Gone are the fruits of six months of hard labor in a one-night binge. He will pay for his boozing with his family's tears and sadly chew his cud for several months to come."

Waiting at home in the sod hut are

Mother and little Anne. They have talked so many times about all the new things Father is going to bring them. Little Anne has kept a lookout for a couple of days. And now she can at last see that he is actually coming.

Now both Mother and Anne are standing at the door, waiting to welcome

Springdansen

Father home. But it is odd how empty the wagon looks! And when he finally drives up, dark and stern, without a greeting, both understand what has happened. And little Anne, with her rag doll for company, goes behind the house to cry. Father had made a solemn promise that he would get a new…

Inside the hut, Mother broods. She is tired and worn out. What are they going to do now? The flour barrel is low. There is nothing to do now but grind corn in the mortar. The shoe situation is even worse. Little Anne and the other small ones cannot go barefooted any longer with winter approaching.

And as she worries about her needs and the hopelessness of things around her, it occurs to her that McGregor is not the big trading and shopping center it is alleged to be. To her, it is a monster from hell that sucks up, dragon-like, all they earn.

But not all trips to town are terminated as gloomily as this one. Over at one of the neighbors' places, the husband has returned home—and what a celebration this is!

While Grandpa unharnesses the oxen, Father, Mother, Grandmother and all the children help to bring in the precious packages father has brought home. Grandmother is almost reduced to tears when she is handed a thick, warm dress. And there is a big package of goodies for everyone to share, plus a wondrous almanac and picture cards for one and all.

For Mother, he has bought a whole set of spanking new knives and forks, which will really be something compared to the wooden utensils and sheath knife used up to now. Now it will be possible to invite the Ladies' Aid Society. And a matchless oilcloth for the table designed with a picture of the whole world—would you believe it!

In addition, he has bought sheeting and pillow shams. These last articles, as well as the new tablecloth, Mother puts away in the chest. These things will be brought out when the pastor comes a-visiting.

Now Mother has to get busy and bake pancakes, taking care that everyone gets a taste of the new syrup without exhausting the supply at one meal. And while the mountains of pancakes disappear like icicles on St. Hans Day, Father has to tell about all the remarkable things he saw at McGregor—about the big steamboats on the Mississippi that sucked up a thousand wagonloads of wheat and glided downriver, light as a feather. And about all the terrible fighting on the streets. And the amazing circus where a bear stood on two legs and danced the *Springdans [a dance with a high spring, once common in Norway –Rosholt]*. And where an elephant with a long snout could write its own name if only someone would give it a chew of tobacco.

Out in the yard, Grandfather putters with the lumber to be unloaded from the wagon. God willing, now there would be a double floor in the house. There has always been such a draught in the floor when the wind blew from the southwest.

And in the cozy bed corner lie the small boys who mumble to themselves about ways that they can help Father so that next time he will take them along to town. Sleep, and its half-brother, dreams, finally steal over the tired eyelids and conjure the most vivid pictures of that town of all wonders—McGregor.

Today (1908), McGregor lies quiet and peaceful in its narrow little valley. The small, old log houses, cracked and moss-grown, sink silently together in common with memories of its one-time greatness. In the street, where the dust was once tracked by thousands of oxen hooves, contented cows now pasture. The big tree-covered ridges still stand above the village, and the tree leaves fall softly downward, some into the mighty Mississippi River moving by silently and grandly.

Parti af Nordfjord

46
Stavanger and Hordaland colony, Story, Hamilton and Hardin Counties, central Iowa
(Source: De Norske Settlementers Historie, by Hjalmar Rued Holand, translated by Malcolm Rosholt, 1908, pp. 458–467)

In the 1840s and 1850s, old Fox River in Illinois was the main rendezvous every year for hundreds of emigrants from Stavanger, Hordaland and Hardanger. For them it was a sort of port of entry to America. Here they remained a short time and worked for others, and then moved west to build their own homes.

Among these early emigrants from Norway, mention must be made of the Sheldal brothers, all sons of a bailiff in Norway, and all schoolteachers:
- Lars Sheldal
- Rasmus Sheldal
- Erik Sheldal
- Halder Sheldal
- Osmund Sheldal

The brothers immigrated to the U.S. in 1846 and became leading figures among their fellow newcomers in Illinois and Iowa.

Torkel Henryson from Etne in Hordaland must also be mentioned and today (1908) occupies a worthy position among his countrymen around Story City, Iowa.

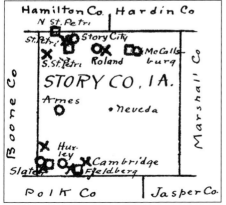

In 1847, at the suggestion of the Sheldal brothers and in company with Lars Sheldal, Henryson organized an emigrant party of 165 people, took over a ship called the *Kong Sverre* in Bergen and brought it safely to New York. *[Holand in the above uses the expression "leiede et Skib," which can mean to lead or guide, direct or even rent. It seems too much to believe that Henryson could act as a captain or navigator unless he had been at sea himself. –Rosholt]*

Erik Nilson's advice: Go to Iowa!

Erik Nilsen, one of the leading men in the Lisbon and Fox River colonies of Illinois in the 1850s, was the first person to leave from Sigdal in Norway. Although he was one of the few persons from the east of Norway in this big settlement of West Coast people, he was by no means an isolated figure. The pioneers around Iowa and Illinois recall with deep affection his cheerful personality and willingness to help others.

He was an informed, experienced person and fairly well off, but he lost money more than once because of his willingness to help his unfortunate countrymen. But he was not discouraged, and never was there a need too great or his house too crowded that he did not find room for one more homesick and hungry immigrant.

Wise in giving advice and quick to help,
He was a leader among men.
In church and community affairs,
He was a heroic figure.

As one group after another of Stavanger and Hordaland people poured into the prairie around Lisbon, hard times developed. Prices of land went up, and hundreds of poor and confused immigrants went without work, deeply despondent. In Norway they had heard that, in America:

The colonists swim
In tea, coffee, milk and cream
Meat and wheat are daily fare, and
Every man rocks in the cradle of fortune.

Now they found out that conditions in the U.S. could be just as hard as in Norway, or even more so. They became embittered at the thought that they had let empty promises tempt them to leave their fathers' farms. At least they had it good living at home. What more could they ask?

Then Erik Nilsen told them about Iowa's wide-open spaces.

"There, across the Mississippi River, lies a land as rich as Egypt. There are rolling plains, with here and there a river or forest. The highlands are as fertile as the Mount of Olives, and the lower lands as fat as the herbage geese thrive on. And the land is so vast that a man could lay the whole of Norway with both Buskerud and Hordaland and Finmark, lengthwise and crosswise, and still have room for a fenced-in mountain pasture. Go there and find your own land, as there are practically no settlers yet."

This was advice to sink one's teeth into. It was discussed at endless bull sessions, for in the beginning it was hard to reach a decision.

Go to Iowa! What an impossible idea! Did not the lawless American desert begin on the other side of the Mississippi, where one found only cactus, rattlesnakes and volcanic mountains? This was only tempting Providence. Better to return home to Norway.

But others insisted that the desert could not be so big as all that. Did it not begin on the other side of the great Missouri River, where the water ran cold and muddy with silt that the desert blew in? Furthermore, Erik Nilsen knew all this, for had he not been all the way to California?

The situation took a new turn after an unexpected visit by Nils Olson Næs, a lay preacher who had been in northeastern Iowa. He reported there was an overabundance of both wood lots and prairie, which could be bought from the government at $1.25 per acre. After lengthy debate, the people agreed to send four men to cruise the land and give them the authority to buy a tract suitable for farming.

The Hauge Synod church people took no part in this. Elling Eielsen, who did not wish to see his big congregation on Fox River divided by migration farther west, declared that such uncertain searching after temporal things was only a throwback to the old heathen Viking blood.

He advised people not to tempt Heaven by going forth into the wilderness where they would be separated from merciful communion with the faithful and would come to harm by suffering the loss of their childhood faith. Victims of the delights of the flesh and mammon's desires, they would end up delivered to the devil who roams about like a roaring lion, devouring any who get in the way.

The four land-lookers sent out included:
• Osmund Sheldal
• Ole Fatland
• Ole Upland
• Osmund Johnson

Sheldal later became the new settlement's pastor and served here for many years. The quartet left on its mission 24 September 1854.

In those days, the road to California ran straight across Iowa from Davenport to Omaha, Nebraska. In those days it was strewn with litter from the forced marches of the gold hunters. On the advice of Erik Nilsen, the party followed this road, driving a light spring wagon until coming to Story County in Iowa. Here the men found an oversupply of good land. They took what they wanted and then went to the government land office at Des Moines, where they got their papers in order. Four weeks after leaving Illinois, they were back in Lisbon.

Great were the expectations, then, when people heard that the four scouts were all going back to Iowa; in one day they seemed to tower over the heads of every man in the area. A meeting was called with the cool and collected Osmund Sheldal as spokesman.

"We have accomplished our mission," he said. "We found a land that surpasses our highest expectations in beauty and fertility. There are smooth, sun-kissed hills, but no stones; rich, broad pastures, but no floods. There is good water and fine forest groves along the streams. It is truly a land, which, like Caleb's Canaan, is flowing with milk and honey. The land lays quiet and peaceful, waiting for us.

"Brothers, this is the land Heaven has prepared for us. We came from Norway's mountain nooks where we had to break ground in stones and on sharp mountain slopes, between flood and landslides, and where our pastures lay in the shadows of glaciers. Now we can stretch our limbs in a comfortable walk with plow and sickle, and the fat loam will richly reward our labor. And we've got the papers on our land from the government assuring our rights to it until the end of time."

Ole Fatland and Ole Upland fully agreed with this. Osmund Johnson was a bit doubtful, and though he did not wish to detract from the truth of what Sheldal said, he was nevertheless convinced that the land under no circumstances would be built up that far west in all time to come. Indeed, it was 300 English miles from Lisbon and would take not less than 400 or 500 years to develop.

Meanwhile, there would be no railroad, and it would be some time before any sort of authority and order could be established. No, he was not about to leave.

A new Palestine

The winter passed quickly with all sorts of hopeful preparations. Among other things, those going to Iowa decided to form a church congregation. As a symbol of their high hopes, the congregation called itself *Palestine*. Ole Anfinson was chosen pastor, Erik Sheldal, sexton, and K. A. Bauge, parochial schoolteacher.

The following people joined the congregation and also made the journey to Iowa:
- Ole Anfinson
- K. A. Bauge
- Severt Gravdahl
- Ole Hauge
- Ole Heggen
- Christian Heggen
- Barney Hill
- Torger Olson
- Osmund Sheldal
- Lars Tesdahl
- Guro Shaw
- Ole Upland
- Knut Ersland
- Ole Fatland
- Torbjørn Hauge
- Salve Heggen
- Engebret Heggen
- Axel Larsen
- Erik Sheldal
- John Severson
- Ivar Tvedt
- Wier Weeks

There is only one other instance—the Moravian church at Ephraim, Wisconsin—in the history of Norwegian emigration when an entire congregation, with pastor in the lead, moved to settle a new land. It is also one of the biggest parties of immigrants to go forth together to break the new land.

Finally 17 May 1855, dawned—the day set for departure. Ready to leave, the immigrants all assembled on Holdeman's Prairie, about midway between Lisbon and Fox River. The party consisted of 106 persons and 25 oxen and horse teams, in addition to cattle. With many good wishes from the big crowd of well-wishers, the teamsters started to move their wagons.

As everything went smoothly, people had time to think and dream of the future. The children particularly considered this a glorious adventure, chasing cattle ahead and day after day seeing new scenery. On three Sundays the caravan rested and held worship services in the open. On 7 June it arrived at its destination.

How different in character was this party of Norwegians compared to the gold-diggers, adventurers and others who had gone ahead of them. They did not come to establish new kingdoms like the Mormons, or to dig for gold, or with force and intrigue to gain political power. Their aim was to establish peaceful communities and build roads, to till the soil and get the wilderness to bloom.

In the forefront rode the pastor who, with Bible in hand, pointed from the present to the eternal. Their swords were hoes, their spears sickles. Obviously, their chests were empty of fine clothes, gold finery and weapons. But the little seed that these pioneers brought with them has now grown to acreage big enough to feed millions.

Every year Iowa's harvest represents double the value of all the world-famous gold and silver mines, while the annual corn harvest alone would easily pay the public debt of half a dozen European states.

This was the beginning of the so-called "southern settlement" that lies around Cambridge and Slater, Iowa. Today, around 3,000 people of Norse descent live here, prosperous and comfortable.

Haugeans settle Story, Hamilton and Hardin counties

The main settlement of Norwegians in this part of the state lies about 25 miles farther north in the so-called "northern settlement," which begins east of Roland and stretches quite a distance west of Jewell Junction, taking in most of Story, Hamilton and Hardin counties. Around here there are more than 9,000 Norsemen. Their beginning is as follows:

When the Hauge church people around Lisbon heard about the fine land in Iowa and how easy it was to get it, they decided, despite Elling Eielson's advice, to try their fortune. But just to make sure of everything, they chose eight men to cruise the county in advance. These men were as follows:
• Jonas Duea
• Mons Grove
• Jacob E. Aske
• John N. Tarvestad
• Paul Thompson
• Lars Sheldal
• Ole Eino
• John Mehuus

This group set off in the spring of 1855, not far behind the big party under Osmund Sheldal, and found excellent land on the prairie where the village of Roland is now situated.

It has always been something of a mystery why these Hauge people did not follow the first party into the southern part of Story County, where their countrymen from Lisbon had settled. The quality of the soil is of the same richness and there were open spaces still unoccupied. Had this happened, there would have been one connecting settlement instead of two.

The reason, however, is not hard to find. The first party consisted of Norwegian Synod people, while the second was made up of Hauge people. Prompted by the same sincere love that separated Lot and Abraham, and with thoughts of future church peace, they settled 25 miles apart.

A big party, primarily Hauge people, now prepared to leave Illinois for Roland the following year. However, two men had already decided to leave that same fall—namely, Lars Sheldal and Thor Hegland. To them goes the honor of having been the first Norwegians in this big colony, which now stretches 25 miles long and 20 miles wide and is inhabited entirely by Norwegians.

The party of immigrants that went to Iowa the next year included the following men and their families:
- Jacob E. Aske
- Rasmus E. Aske
- Jonas Duea
- A. B. Jacobson
- Lars Næss
- Mikkel E. Aske
- Sjur Brictson
- Lars Hegland
- Jacob Meling
- Bertha Næss
- Hans Pederson
- Erik Sheldal
- Torkel Opstveit
- Hans Tveidt
- John N. Tarvestad,
- Ole Rasmussen
- Rasmus Sheldal
- Erik Søkten
- Hover Thompson
- Rasmus Tungesvig

There were 24 wagons and a couple hundred head of cattle in the caravan.

Hard times

While they had found good land at a reasonable price, their troubles were not over. That very first winter, which will not easily be forgotten, was one of the worst that historians can recall. As most of the new settlers had not built proper houses, they suffered terribly from the cold. The heavy snows made it nearly impossible to move about, and many a poor soul feared that he had strayed into the North Pole. Throughout the entire winter, it was necessary to melt snow for drinking water, both for people and livestock. And when all cups and kettles stood with half-melted snow, there was not much heat in the living room.

On one occasion, several of the settlers that winter decided to go to Marshalltown, a distance of 45 miles. To be wrapped up in warm bearskins and driving spirited horses is certainly not such a bad way to travel, even if the snow and weather are a bit sharp. But at this time there were not many fur pelts in the entire settlement. One had to make the best of it by wrapping up in all the old rags and scarves that could be spared and depend for the rest on body heat.

Unacquainted with the countryside as they were, the men took the wrong road, and when night came, they had to bed down on the open prairie. The cold was penetrating—a northwest wind to boot—and the night pitch dark. The men scraped a hole in the snow down to the ground and stood there all night tramping back and forth to keep warm and awake. To keep busy, they even tore off the sacks on the load, changed the harnesses and messed around hour after hour until the first streaks of dawn appeared, but morning was really an unkind joke.

In the next several years before the Civil War, these pioneers experienced hard times, a period our country has never seen the like of, before or since. Marengo, a distance of 110 miles, was the nearest railroad station, but it was scarcely worth the effort to haul produce.

Pork was a cent a pound, butter 4 cents a pound, and a man had to trade 10 dozen eggs for one spool of thread. Calico was 25 cents a yard and sheeting material 75 cents a yard.

Slettafossen

47
Norway Settlement, Benton County, and Calamus Settlement, Clinton County, eastern Iowa

(Source: De Norske Settlementers Historie, by Hjalmar Rued Holand, translated by Malcolm Rosholt, 1908, pp. 468–469)

While the people of Rock Prairie (Luther Valley) and Koshkonong tended to move northwesterly into Wisconsin and thence into Minnesota, the stream of migration from Fox River in Illinois was somewhat due west.

Through central and northwest Iowa, there are a series of important settlements that, nearly without exception, are inhabited by people from around Stavanger in Norway.

In addition to the extensive settlement in Story and Hamilton counties, there are two other Stavanger communities in Iowa. Founded before the Civil War, they are Norway in Benton County, and Calamus (or Kvindherred) in Clinton County, which lies on the Mississippi. A distance of 70 miles separates the two towns of Norway and Calamus. They lie in eastern Iowa on a direct line between Fox River settlement in Illinois and Story County, Iowa.

The area was actually built up by people who had decided to move to Story County. Finding it was too far west, they instead settled in the first attractive place they came to after crossing the Mississippi.

Norway settlement now (1908) has a Norwegian population of about 1,000, and Calamus about 500. One Lutheran pastor serves the two locations. In Norway settlement, there is also an important Quaker congregation, which was organized before the others.

Benton/Stearns County settlers

The first two Norwegian settlers in Benton County were Lars Øiesø and Askaut Nag, both from Stavanger, who settled here in 1854. The founder of the colony, however, is generally considered to be Jonas P. Norland from Strand in Sogn, who came here shortly after the first two arrived in 1854.

That same summer of 1854, other arrivals included:
• Osmund Tutland
• Elling Myrah Ellingsen
• Sara Darnell (a widow, daughter of Anders Nordvig, who had reached Chicago as early as 1836; her sister was the mother of Victor Lawson, the most

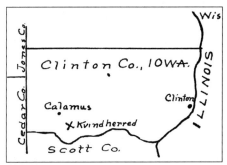

outstanding businessman among Norwegians in the U.S.)

As it was 100 miles to Davenport, the nearest marketplace on the Mississippi, Jonas Norland grew tired of his pioneer experience in Benton County and decided to move to St. Cloud, Minnesota, where some of his acquaintances had settled. They included:
• Ole Tow
• Ole Weland
• Kristofer Alsvig

A man named Ole Bergeson settled at St. Cloud in 1852, the first white landowner in Stearns County.

Norland, however, did not get any farther than Pastor Clausen's new settlement in Mitchell County, where he remained for two years. At that time, Ole Bergeson came down from St. Cloud and, accompanied by Norland, returned to Fox River in Illinois.

Thereafter, in 1859, Norland and many others went back again to Benton County, which from then on had a rapid growth. Among those who came to the county at this time were the following:
• Jørgen Dyrland
• Erik Dyrland
• Govert Dyrland
• Ole Dyrland (four brothers)
• Lars Strand
• Lars Tow
• Andrew Tow
• John Tvedt

Norway settlement

The *History of Benton County* states that the village of Norway got its name from Asbjørn Tuttle. When the railroad was built through here in 1863, he gave five acres of land to the builders on condition that the station be called "Norway."

Pastor N. Amlund organized the first Lutheran congregation in 1867 in the town of Norway (Benton County). *[Norsk Lutherske Menigheter, p. 375, states that Amlund served Benton congregation 1865-66 –Rosholt]*

Calamus settlement

John D. Johnson Døsland from Kvindherred, the first Norwegian male in Clinton County, arrived in 1853 and lived alone for five years. Then came:
• Hans Christenson, Kvindherred
• John Christenson, Kvindherred
• Lars Olson, Kvindherred
• Anders Olson, Kvindherred
• Herlaug Pederson, Kvindherred
• Sten H. Nerhus, Kvindherred

The Kvindherred church congregation in south Clinton County was organized by Pastor P. A. Rasmussen in 1861, and continued to have the majority membership in the parish that included both Norway and Calamus. *[Rasmussen served in 1861-62 and was followed by N. Amlund in 1863-66. –Rosholt]*

De syv Søstre

48
Lykkensborg Village, Hennepin County, Minnesota
(Source: De Norske Settlementers Historie, by Hjalmar Rued Holand, translated by Malcolm Rosholt, 1908, pp. 470–476)

The first man with family to emigrate from Solør in Grue kommune, Hedmark fylke (1850) was Paul Olsen Vaalberg, father of old Pastor Ole Paulson in Blanchardville, Wisconsin.

Before he left Norway, Vaalberg read an old but detailed letter in possession of the district judge, which the latter had received from his half-brother in the U.S.—the widely known Ole Rynning. Rynning's forceful presentation of conditions in America helped Vaalberg decide to leave, so it is clear that Rynning's writings influenced the movement of emigration from Solør.

The Vaalberg family first lived in Muskego. But as the land here was dear (expensive), they moved in 1852 to the newly discovered Washington Prairie settlement near Decorah, Iowa. That same year, Ole Paulson moved to Ridgeway (west of Decorah), where he was among the first to purchase land.

Soon afterward, one of Paulson's sisters found employment at the home of Doctor Foster in Hastings, Minnesota *[probably Dr. Thomas Foste –Rosholt]*. This doctor was interested in colonizing the fertile plains around Hastings, and preferred to establish a Norwegian settlement.

The sister wrote to her brother in Ridgeway. And together with Ole Hendrikson, another Solør man, Paulson made the trip to the Hastings region. He disliked it so much that one day when a steamboat came by en route to St. Paul, he and Hendrikson jumped on board.

First look at Lykkensborg
It was a beautiful spring day in 1854 when the two Oles from Solør walked off the ship in St. Paul. With fewer than 2,000 people, this village was at this time the terminal point of civilization. West of the Twin Cities, there were no colonies, and no whites until one came to Mormon country in Utah.

People had only a vague conception of the country between these points—probably Indians, buffaloes, mountains and deserts. The few who had heard of the Red River Valley believed this was a land still in the Ice Age, inhabited by wolves and polar bears.

The nearest railway track was 300 miles away in the opposite direction. All communications with the outer world went via the Mississippi's notorious steamboats, and Jim Hill, the future railroad empire builder, was at this time only a hopeful stevedore along the St. Paul waterfront.

As the two Oles stood on the busy dock and talked, a man came by, stopped and looked at them, and finally said in Norwegian, "How do you do. I hear from your talk you are Norwegians."

"Ja."

"It's fun to meet a countryman," the stranger said. "I am now the first Scandinavian west of the river, perhaps in all of Minnesota. My name is Axel Jørgensen, and I'm from Fredrickshald. I have platted a village called Lykkensborg, located a short distance up the Minnesota River in the finest place in the territory. If you are looking for good land, then this is just the place. Aren't you looking for land?"

[The name "Lykkensborg" in English would mean something like "Palace of Happiness." –Rosholt]

"Yes, that we are."

"Then it was lucky we met here," Jorgensen assured them, and began to talk a blue streak.

"Lykkensborg is an uncommonly thriving place with the best farmland one can find. You see, I was just out there and took a claim before the Yankees snapped it up. It will not be long before St. Paul will have to hustle to keep Lykkensborg from becoming the capital. Come along with me and I'll show you."

"Well, it does sound worthwhile."

"I'm running a hotel myself and have the beginnings of an iron foundry. In addition, I'm operating a ferry between here and Lykkensborg. If you do not care to bother about farming, then there are opportunities to go into just about any kind of business you like. In such a village a little of everything is needed. And if nothing else, it's possible to make six to eight dollars a day just picking cranberries. Now if you want to go along with me, I'll provide free passage on a boat."

"Okay, then."

They felt they had fallen headfirst into a gold mine.

After Jørgensen finished with some purchases, the men went on board his boat. The newcomers were somewhat disappointed, though. Without any clear notion what this "boat" was, they had imagined it to be a small steamer. But this was not even a sailboat—just a flat scow without oars, propelled forward with the aid of oak sapling poles.

When Jørgensen explained that the main exports from Lykkensborg still consisted of wood, the newcomers were able to comprehend the nature of the vessel. They expressed their thanks by taking a hand with the poles, which Jørgensen was quite willing to let them do.

This was an invitation that soon turned to anger. It was hard work to push the scow against the current, filled with deadheads of timber and hidden sandbars. It was only supposed to be 30 miles, and the men kept looking and looking for this proud place called Lykkensborg. On both banks of the river there were only lonely hills and brush.

Finally, after three days of labor with the lead-heavy scow, Jørgensen exclaimed, "Here we are!"

"Where?"

"Lykkensborg." He pointed to a small hut on the hillside.

"Where's the town? You said there was a place here."

"Well, this is the beginning."

"What about the iron foundry?"

"It's there," he said, pointing to the hut, its lower side standing on high poles. Underneath the overhang a person could see a small affair resembling a blacksmith shop.

"But the hotel?"

"That's above."

On the wall of the hut there appeared in big letters: "Luckensborg Hotel." Other than that, there was not a sign of a house or people anywhere.

The two newcomers were, without a doubt, disappointed. But they were young, and after the village's patron saint rambled on with big talk and a little shot of whiskey welcoming them to the "future big city of Lykkensborg," they finally had to laugh at their own misplaced hopes.

So the men went forth to look over the land, but by now they were quite

288

suspicious. But Jorgensen assured them that better land could not be found in Goshen.

After their big expectations, all the land looked bad to them, and they wandered far and wide before they found anything satisfactory. Finally, about four miles from Lykkensborg and just a few miles from beautiful Lake Minnetonka, they found a piece of fairly nice land. Paulson marked this for himself and returned to St. Paul, where he entered several claims for his family and friends.

As to Axel Jørgensen (Anders Jørgensen), there is not much more to add. According to Pastor Paulson, who knew him for many years, he was one of the first Norwegians to establish a home and own property in Minnesota, arriving in Carver County in 1851 and platting the village of Lykkensborg. He later changed the name to "Carver," which is now (1908) a village of 600 inhabitants. Later he moved to Wright County, married a Swedish widow and died around 1898.

When Paulson first came here, Jørgensen had a hired man named Kleven from Nord-Tron in Norway. He made entry on some land in the neighborhood and became an intimate friend of Paulson's.

Lykkensborg colony

Later in the summer, Paulson and his friends prepared to leave Winneshiek County in Iowa and take up their new land in Minnesota. The party included Paulson, his parents, sisters and brothers, along with Østen Gunnøvson Svadde and Gunnøv Østenson Svadde from Tinn in Telemark. The group acquired a *kubberulle* (a low wagon) and oxen, loaded up their bedding and other household necessities, and were ready to move out 150 miles into the wilderness.

This was the very beginning of Minnesota's history. Down on the Iowa line in the southeast corner of Minnesota, a half dozen Norwegians had settled a year earlier. But from Norwegian Ridge, as it was called, to St. Paul, there lived only one white man—a long-bearded Frenchman who had settled on the Zumbro River. In St. Paul there perhaps were some Norwegians in the sawmills, but none that could be considered permanent colonists.

On one stretch of the road, the Paulson party followed a track across the plains left by a man who had driven some cattle to St Paul. Then, like all cow trails, the track disappeared and they drove at random in a northwesterly direction.

It was a fairytale sort of trip across the best farmland that can be found in the Upper Midwest. But at this time there was not a soul to be seen—here and there a white grouse or partridge, and far off on the horizon probably a herd of deer staring at them. Now and then, from the top of a ridge, they could see Indians moving silently down a valley, one after the other.

Along the banks of Zumbro River sat an old Frenchman who begged them to settle down here, a place where one could find all the good things of Paradise, he assured them, except neighbors.

While it was charming and tempting, the party went on without stopping. Nor did anyone stop when the travelers came to the later known Kenyon and the delightful Goodhue County, where a couple of years later one of the biggest and richest colonies of Norwegians was to be founded. There, wheat production would exceed anything the world had ever seen.

They could have had their choice of the best farms in the county, but as they were headed for other places, they thought it expedient to go on.

They rambled ahead, down through Cannon River Valley's sharp chasms, past the strange towers of Castle Rocks, and over Dakota County's sand hills until they reached Lykkensborg. After all the excellent country they had crossed, the general aspect here was disappointing.

However, the party remained here and formed the beginning of the first Norwegian colony west of St. Paul. Now (1908) there are more than 600,000 Norwegians west of St. Paul and several times that many from other ethnic groups. Nearly all the farmers are well situated. All this has happened in 50 years, and the first settler is still of sound mind and a capable worker.

The settlement of Minnesota represents a movement of immigration without equal. People talk about the remarkable growth of Chicago, but this cannot hold a candle to the rapidity with which the Midwest was settled, where Scandinavians have taken the leading role.

Among the first to settle here, in addition to the above-mentioned, were the following:
• Lars Erikson
• Syver Olson
• Hans Blaker
• Carl Sørenson

John Paulson (brother of Pastor Paulson) was also among the first to settle here. A soldier during the Civil War, he attained the rank of major.

As the colony lay close to the Mississippi River and not far from St. Paul, it experienced a rapid growth. A congregation was organized here as early as 1856.

49
St. Peter area and Nicollet County, Minnesota
(Source: De Norske Settlementers Historie, by Hjalmar Rued Holand, translated by Malcolm Rosholt, 1908, pp. 477–480)

Forty miles up the Minnesota River from St. Paul lay St. Peter *[actually more than 75 miles southwest of Minneapolis –Rosholt]*, one of Minnesota's most beautiful cities.

Unlike most other towns that have grown up without much tradition or individuality to set them apart, St. Peter has a stamp of its own, a certain individualism combined with a sense of the past that lingers in one's mind long after leaving the place.

For one thing, it has an exceptional location at the head of a bend on the Minnesota River. The high ridges here are well away from the riverbanks and leave a gentle, sloping flat overlooking the river. Toward the east, the ridges are crowned with big trees. Toward the west, where the Gustavus Adolphus College buildings tower, the ridges are bare and fortress-like, even as they were in the terror-filled days of 1862, when they served as a natural defense works against the attacks of the Sioux.

Toward the north are the ruins of Traverse des Sioux, the old Indian trading post *[American Fur Company –Rosholt]*, and to the south lies the big stone quarry at Kasota, which has made this name famous.

The first Norwegian to settle here and in the surrounding county is still (1908) living in comfort: Matthias G. Evenson, now of St. Paul, originally from Biri in Oppland fylke. He left there in 1849, reaching St. Paul in 1852.

In the spring of 1853, together with his brother Peder G. Evenson, he went up the Minnesota River to the place where St. Peter was later platted. Also in this party was the later-known Captain A. K. Skaro, who was to fall in a battle near Nashville, Tennessee, during the Civil War.

A tragic event

In this early period, the area around St. Peter was called "Eagle Bend." The territory was entirely inhabited by Indians and mixed-bloods, and the outlook seemed so unpromising for the three men that they wondered whether they should not turn around and go back—when a tragic event gave their plans a new direction.

The summer before, an American, James Howard, had taken a claim on the place that is now part of the St. Peter residential district. According to the law, he was permitted to be away from his pre-emption claim six months at a time. On this occasion, he had gone east to visit his family in New York State.

About the same time as the Evenson brothers and Skaro approached Eagle Bend, Howard returned from the east and found that his claim had been "jumped" by three brothers named Kingsley. In his attempt to drive them away, Howard was fatally wounded from a shot fired by one of the Kingsleys.

All three brothers were overpowered and locked up in a log shanty jail at Traverse des Sioux, which at this time was an important trading center. During the night they were forcibly removed by a band of Indians and punished. They were taken to the river edge, tarred and feathered, forced to run the gauntlet and afterward, bound hand and foot and set adrift on the river in a canoe. They were never seen again in these parts.

While the Indians were punishing the Kingsley brothers, James Howard was approaching death at the trading post, where Evenson nursed and consoled him as well as he could. Howard's last wish to his three newly found friends was that they should provide him with a Christian burial, and as compensation, he turned over his claim to them for any expense connected with the funeral.

It was in this manner that Evenson became one of the three original owners of the land where the village was to be founded, and the builder of the first house in the soon-to-bloom little country village inhabited by Evenson and his two associates.

The first summer in the settlement, the three men quarried stones for a big warehouse being built by General Henry Sibley in Traverse des Sioux. The stones were floated down stream on a scow. Soon settlers began to move in, and by the winter of 1856-57, it

Trondhjems Domkirke

looked like the three comrades were on their way to becoming rich.

Political shenanigans

There was at this time considerable agitation in favor of moving the capital from St. Paul to St. Peter, and prices of building lots were climbing higher and higher. For the quarter section that the late James Howard turned over to them, Evenson and Skaro were offered $40,000 by Territorial Governor Willis A. Gorman, but they turned it down.

On 18 February 1857, a bill for the removal of the capital from St. Paul to St. Peter was introduced in the territorial legislature. At this point Joe Rolette, the representative from Pembina (in what is now northeast North Dakota), absconded with the still unsigned bill, and dreams of riches and glory disappeared as suddenly as they had risen.

Norseland and Scandia Grove
Supplemented by Gene Estensen, historian, Telelaget of America

In the meantime, many other Norwegians were arriving in Nicollet County, nearly all going a few miles northwest from St. Peter to Norseland and Scandia Grove, where the soil is richer. The first among these were:
- Swen Swenson Rudning, Hallingdal (father to the former diplomatic envoy, Laurits Swenson)
- John Tollefson, Toten
- Tosten Østensen Bøen (Tosten Estensen), Tinn in Telemark
- Ole Østensen Bøen (Ole Estensen), Tinn in Telemark

Ole and his brother Tosten served with the Scandinavian Guard of Nicollet County during the Sioux Uprising of 1862. Ole Østensen and his wife Astrid Johnsdatter left Tinn, Telemark, for America in 1851. A baby daughter, Aase, arrived with them in New York but died at an unknown place on 1 October 1851. A second child, Jon, was born in a railroad shanty near Galena, Illinois. After working their way west, a journey of five years, Ole and Astrid arrived at Norseland at St. Peter in the spring of 1856. A son, Østen Olsen Bøen (Austin Estensen) was born a couple of weeks later.

Ole Norman, Brynhild Norman and Carl Larson, all three from Voss, came shortly thereafter. Quite a few *Sætersdøler* also settled here, the first being Gunder Nerison and S. Torgerson.

Pastor Lauritz Larson organized a congregation in 1858. Thomas Johnson, a native of Slidre in Valdres, became its first resident pastor in 1863. He carried on missionary work and organized congregations far and wide in central Minnesota. For a time he served the following congregations:
• St. Peter and Swan Lake in Nicollet County
• Linden and Bergen in Brown County
• Carver in Carver County
• Upper and Lower Watonwan in Watonwan County
• Ness in Meeker County
• Crow River in Stearns County
• Norway Lake in Kandiyohi County
• Lake Johanna, Chippewa and White Bear in Pope County
• Homes City in Douglas County
• Vinje in Otter Tail County
He continued to serve Nicollet County until his death in 1905.

The settlers in Nicollet County were very much exposed to the terrors of the Indian war in 1862. The heaviest engagement in the war took place at New Ulm, the nearest town. Many of the pioneers were killed and others fled. But the Norwegian and Swedish settlers in Nicollet County were a bloodthirsty lot, and more than a hundred volunteered to engage the Indians.

Special commendations went to the Norwegian Captain A. K. Skaro and the Swedish Captain Gustav Stark for their capable services. Matthias G. Evenson was a sergeant and took part in many engagements. He also served with the military detachment that hanged 38 Indian rebels at Mankato.

Here in Nicollet County, the Swedes became the predominant ethnic group. There are now (1908) only 1,500 Norwegians in the county, of which a third live in St. Peter.

50
Christiania Settlement, Dakota, Scott and Rice Counties, Minnesota
(Source: De Norske Settlementers Historie, by Hjalmar Rued Holand, translated by Malcolm Rosholt, 1908, pp. 481–482)

The nearest settlement to Minneapolis, the geographic center of the Norwegian population in the U.S., is the settlement at Christiania, which lies 30 miles south of the city in adjoining areas of Dakota, Scott and Rice counties.

The founders of this settlement, who all reached Chub Lake in Dakota County on 18 July 1854, included:
• Peter Sampson, Voss
• Magnus Peterson (Peter Sampson's son), Voss
• Ole Thoreson, Hallingdal
• Ole Olson, Hallingdal
• Johannes Jacobson, Vinje in Telemark

Arriving in 1855 were the following:
• Peter Thompson, Valdres
• Thorstein Knutson, Valdres
• Ole Thoreson, Eidsvold
• Stephen Thoreson, Eidsvold
• Juul Knutson, Eidsvold
• Christian Anderson, Eidsvold
• Eland Levorson, Eidsvold
• Peter Ruh, Eidsvold (father of Pastor M. P. Ruh)

First emigrants from Eidsvold
Ole Olson Bækken, who arrived in Muskego in 1851, was the first man to emigrate from Eidsvold. In 1853, Lars Christenson Elstad left Eidsvold and came to Fillmore County.

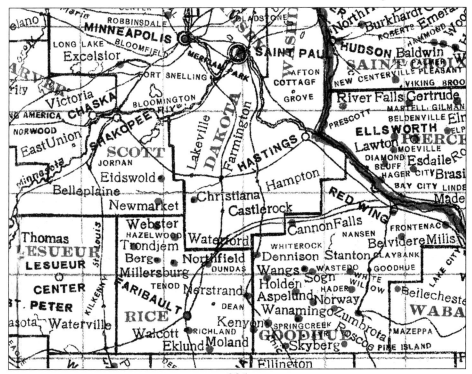

In 1855, Peter Ruh and family reached Dakota County, Minnesota.

"When he came here, everything seemed to be a wilderness except for Indians and reindeer. When there was talk about opening a post office, he suggested 'Christiania,' which has now been augmented by Eidsvold (and Trondheim)." *[Holand gives no source for this quotation, nor does it seem possible that even a newcomer could have mistaken a reindeer for the common white-tailed deer of Minnesota. –Rosholt]*

Owing to its proximity to St. Paul, the influx of people to the Christiania settlement was rapid, and a congregation called Christiania was organized here as early as 1857 *[a Norwegian Synod church, then located several miles southwest of Farmington –Rosholt].*

Indian panic

In the Sioux uprising of 1862, people fleeing from the west overran the settlement. The panic in the settlement itself was also great, and many went back into Wisconsin. Others held themselves ready for months on end, their chests and bundles packed.

Halvor Torgerson, originally from Telemark, makes the following observation:

"In 1862, when the Indian war broke out, it was not safe in Christiania settlement, either. In order to meet any emergency, the settlers agreed on a point of assembly—John Jacobson's place. On one occasion, Ouver Olson and Torger Juvland were in charge of a group of refugees, mostly women and children.

"Believing that the Indians were approaching, Olson commanded, 'Get down, everyone!' All threw themselves headfirst, thinking that death was near.

"In a while, Torger Juvland, the cooler of the two commanders, peeked to see where the Indians were. When he saw none, he shouted. 'Now you can get up. It was nothing but the tail end of a deer Ouver saw!'

"This created considerable amusement among the frightened Rømnings people."

[A footnote by Holand says this quotation is from Martin Ulvestad's Nordmændene i Amerika, p. 89. It agrees with the source. –Rosholt]

Tromsø

51
Big Goodhue County colony, Minnesota
(Source: De Norske Settlementers Historie, by Hjalmar Rued Holand, translated by Malcolm Rosholt, 1908, pp. 483–497)

Beautiful and rich as a farmer's dream of paradise lies the Norwegian colony in Goodhue County. Its plains are as magnificent as Moses' vision of the Promised Land. If it does not actually flow with milk and honey, then it is the nearest thing to it. About 10,000 Norwegians live here in the southwest part of Goodhue and adjoining sections of Rice and Dodge counties.

It is an uncommon thing to be considered the biggest and richest Norwegian colony in America. This colony is not the largest by any means, and what riches there are can still not quite measure up to Koshkonong.

The Norwegian farmers hereabouts are estimated to be worth between $16 million and $20 million, but it would take more than that to surpass Koshkonong's tobacco kings. But Goodhue County has a bigger share of wealth than nearly any other place in the Upper Midwest, as there are conditions here for future prosperity other than land use.

It is about 50 years since the prosperity and productivity of the county had its beginning. One still finds elderly people here who clearly remember their birthplace in Norway, and who witnessed and were part of the pioneer development. Such an experience, one would think, would give a person a larger outlook on the world. But it is seldom one finds any evidence of this. People have been burdened by the small details of daily living, and the great epic qualities of this pioneer period have glided past them, unheralded and unsung.

First Goodhue County settlers

Matthias Petersen Ringdahl from Faaberg, the first Norwegian to settle in

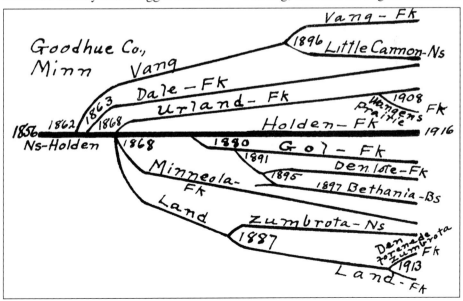

Goodhue County, came to Red Wing in 1851. The village consisted of three or four houses. He remained there a year before going on to St. Paul, where he also spent a year. In 1853 he returned to Goodhue County, which has been his home ever since.

Out in the summer of 1854, the traders in Red Wing heard from some nearby Indians that white people had settled 30 miles from Red Wing up the Zumbro River. Ringdahl and a Swede named Nilsen were sent to find these people and advise them that they could buy provisions and also market their produce in Red Wing.

After wandering about a couple of days, Ringdahl found the people he was looking for. Great was his surprise when he learned that they were not only civilized whites, but actually some Norwegians he had not seen for a year or more. He brought good news to them, because they did not know of any marketplace closer than Decorah, Iowa, a hundred miles away.

Ringdahl liked it so well here that the next spring he took a piece of land in the vicinity of the present Zumbrota River and later became a prosperous farmer.

Following are the names of the Norwegians Ringdahl met on his trip:
• Henrik Nelson Talla, Lyster (Luster), Sogn
• Tøge Nelson Talla, Lyster (Luster), Sogn
• Mrs. Jens Ottun (sister of Henrik and Tøge)
• Mrs. Nils K. Fenne (another sister of Henrik and Tøge)
• Tosten A. Aaby and family, Sigdal in Buskerud
• Wm. Rønningen, Telemark
• Nils Gulbrandsen, Telemark

All had arrived in the same party from Dodgeville, Wisconsin, a few weeks earlier.

Henrik Talla had been to California, where he had some bad luck. In the end, he managed to save a little money. Tøge, his brother, was also a proven Viking and gold-digger in Australia. They met again in Dodgeville, where they organized the immigrant party to look for better land in Minnesota.

With six loaded wagons, they took off along the old military road to Prairie du Chien. After crossing the Mississippi, they continued across Iowa and into the Minnesota prairies.

Tosten Aaby became sick after the journey began and had to lie in an overloaded but springless wagon that bumped and shook him unmercifully. What a relief it was every time the caravan rested; he was even secretly elated when an axle broke or something else held them up for a day or two.

Finally, on 12 June 1854, after three weeks of roving about, the immigrants arrived at a place on the north branch of Zumbro River, where they found an exceptionally beautiful tract of land. There were wide flats with black soil, grown to heavy wild hay, a spirited little river, big groves of trees and suitable openings between the trees. Toward the south there was not a tree to be seen—only a vast plain as far as the eye could see, wild hay waving easily in the last rays of the afternoon sun. Everyone in the caravan stood transfixed by the scene before him.

Then Tøge Talla shouted, "I've lived in three different parts of the world, and I've roamed through many lands, but I've never seen a more beautiful sight than this. Goodbye to foreign yokes and tiresome journeys without home or comfort. Here I'll live, and here I shall die!"

The Club Law

Henrik Talla and Tøge Talla had traveled so much among strangers that their inborn humanity had given away to selfishness. As the discoverers of this excellent tract, they were not satisfied with taking the best 40s for themselves, but took possession of the land for several miles around. They did this, ostensibly, in the name of friends and relatives who they said would soon be arriving from Wisconsin. But, of course, this was just a pretext.

The Talla brothers did next to nothing to encourage more immigrants. Their purpose was to acquire squatter's rights that they could later sell to new settlers at high prices. This was a common practice among the Irish and mixed-bloods, but seldom among Norwegians.

To make things worse, Talla's old friend and traveling companion, Tosten Aaby, was not permitted to settle in the neighborhood and had to go three miles farther on before he got permission to claim any land.

The first thing the Talla boys did was to locate all the section corners and quarter stakes for several miles around and inscribe their names on them. This worked as expected: When one or another tired land-looker came by, he found the name "Talla" or "Nelson" on the stake and assumed from this that the land had been occupied.

This land grab by the Talla brothers created a situation between them and the Tosten Aaby families that was less than happy. The latter felt quite isolated in their new surroundings. Day after day they waited for people to move in, but thanks to the vigilance of the Talla boys, no one was permitted to get any closer.

One day in the summer, Aaby's wife was awakened by the sound of a strange cowbell. She sat up in bed and listened. Never in her life had she heard the likes of such a delightful sound from a cowbell! New people, no doubt, had moved in after all! She prepared breakfast in a jiffy and then went off with the children to find the cow and its owner.

The wild hay was heavy and wet from the morning dew, but this did not deter her. Finally, she caught sight of some cows grazing peacefully on a slope as if they were completely at home here. The children became so happy to see the cattle that they jumped and danced, and tears ran down the cheeks of the mother.

The newly arrived party included:

- Ole Oakland, Øvre-Telemark
- Amund Oakland, Øvre-Telemark
- Andreas Bonhus, Øvre-Telemark
- Hans Ovaldson, Øvre-Telemark
- Gunder Hestemyr, Øvre-Telemark
- Haldor Johnson, Bergen
- John Strømme, Bergen
- Andreas Hesjedalen, Bergen
- Kolbein Ektveidt, Bergen

They had arrived from Koshkonong in a roundabout way and thus accidentally avoided a confrontation with the Talla brothers. They proceeded to locate some good farms, and their descendants still live here in good circumstances.

Arriving around the same time, from Primrose, Wisconsin, were:
- Erik Gunhus, Snarheim near Drammen
- Halvor Ødegaarden, Gol, Hallingdal
- Østen Haukestad, Gol, Hallingdal

The latter two men later founded a *Hallinger* colony in Kenyon, Minnesota.

By this time, Henrik and Tøge Talla realized that it would be extremely difficult to keep people away from their conquered territory by themselves. Remembering that in unity there is strength, they went to the other newcomers to make a proposition.

The Tallas told them that the land laws in Minnesota were different from those in Wisconsin, and convinced them that every man could take and occupy as much land as he wanted to, if he only said the land was being held for relatives. It was suggested, therefore, that they should all band together to defend each other should anyone try to deprive them of their land.

Yes, indeed, this was not bad information—if it could only be depended upon. But the *Telemarkinger* had their doubts. Those pesky peasants from around Bergen enthusiastically supported the idea and decided to join the confederation. And Andreas Bonhus finally gave in, too.

Henrik Talla, who liked to see everything done in an orderly manner,

Den naturlige Tunnel gjennem Torghætten

As Henrik himself had never been initiated into the secrets of writing, Bonhus offered to push the pen. With his face in deep thought and with great solemnity, Henrik began to outline the resolutions, which were adopted one by one. He resurrected some judicial phrases he had picked up in his travels and which he quoted in the document as often as possible. Bonhus, who struggled hard to record the resolutions, found the legal terminology a bit difficult; it is said that, as he wrote, the sweat dripped from his face.

When the law was ready, it was signed by the Talla boys and others, including, in part:
• Wm. Rønningen (Henrik's hired man)
• Andreas Bonhus
• John Strømme
• Andreas Hesjadalen
• Mrs. Jens Ottun (in her husband's name)

suggested that a set of by-laws be drawn up so that everyone could sign the pact and not withdraw without being laughed at the rest of his days. This idea was also accepted.

Thereupon Tøge Talla brought forth a big oak club, on which all solemnly declared that they would stand together in word and deed, uphold

Torghætten fra Østsiden

the law (the Club Law) and used the club against anyone who tried to oppose them or encroach on their domain.

Everyone thereupon proceeded to occupy all the land he saw around. It was not long before these land pirates had occupied the best land in most of two townships.

Thousands of dead laws are produced each year and are now buried, but not so with the famous Club Law. For more than a year it was in force, to the great satisfaction of its authors. Although more newcomers were continually arriving, none tried to settle in the vicinity. The Bergen peasants formed a fierce border guard to the east, while the Talla brothers swung the club to the south, thus preventing any trespassing on the fertile plains.

Big Svend challenges Club Law

But one day late in the summer of 1855, an immigrant party of 30 wagons was seen slowly making its way northward directly across the big plains south of the Talla farms. It was about 15 to 20 miles from one branch of the Zumbro River to the other—a long day's march for the slow-moving oxen to go without water across the blazing hot plain.

As nightfall came, the newcomers finally saw signs of a river, and farther off they saw two farms comfortably situated, each in its own grove of trees. Happy that the day was coming to an end and happy that they should find white people again, they hurried the cattle onward in the direction of the two farms.

Not far from the buildings, the newcomers had begun to unhitch their wagons when two men came up. One carried a big club on his shoulders.

The other said, "Good day."

"Good day! Have we also run into Norwegians?"

"Yes, but what do you want here?" one asked harshly.

The newcomers looked at each other, bewildered. This did not sound like a very nice welcome.

A big, broad-shouldered man among the newcomers then stepped forward and said, "Good day! My name is Svend Nordgaarden. I'm a *Telemarking*, and so are nearly all the others. It looks like we have finally arrived at the right place, for here there are neighbors and an abundance of good land. Who are you?"

"My name is Tøge Talla, and this is my brother Henrik. But if you are looking for land, it is best you go on. The land is all taken here."

"Is that so," said Svend. "That's too bad. But we'll have to unpack for the night. Have you got an awl you can loan us? Shoe leather does not last as long in this grass."

"No, we have nothing to loan, and you'd better pack up and leave right now, because we don't want any strangers lying about the house at night."

"We're not going any farther tonight, even if Old Erik himself says so. We're not wandering around in the dark for anyone, period."

And Svend turned to the oxen to begin unhitching.

Henrik and Tøge mumbled together for a time and then went home.

The next morning Svend (or Big Svend, as he was always called, because of his giant strength) and his party went to the north in search for land. But every quarter-section post they came to had the name Nelson on it.

Toward mid-morning, they approached nice woodland, and Big Svend said: "Now, I don't care whether the next stake has the name Nelson on it or Jorgen-the-Hat-Maker. I'm not going farther than into that grove of trees there."

So said, so done. The rest of the party also stopped and began to cruise the land on foot. This was half a mile south from where the Holden parsonage presently stands.

There were no other people around. But next morning, as Big Svend and

Et Vandfald i det nordlige Sverige

some of his friends were cutting down trees to build a house, they saw seven or eight men with their women approaching. Tøge Talla, a brave fellow, came with a club over his shoulders. Some of the others carried sticks in hand.

"Now, look at that, will you," said Big Svend. "Now we're going to have some fun."

At this point, one of his companions came forward with a gun and said, "Do you want to borrow this, Svend? It's loaded."

"No," Svend replied. "We must not be too hard on them. Oak against oak is enough," whereupon he picked up a dry oak branch lying on the ground. "But listen," he continued. "You can do something for me after all. Walk back into the woods and turn around while keeping an eye on these gypsies. When you see that we are in the middle of the dispute and ready to rush at each other, fire your gun into the air. But be careful you don't shoot a hole through your own hat!"

It was not long before the attackers came forward, and in no uncertain terms made clear that if Svend and his people did not leave this instant, death would be their lot. From the expression on his face, Big Svend was obviously no less determined to stay, and he and Tøge faced each other, clubs ready.

At that instant, a shot was heard back of Tøge. Surprised by this interruption, he turned to see what it was. In the same instant, Big Svend swung his club across Tøge's neck so that Tøge fell like one dead, his club dancing over the ground.

Thereupon Big Svend turned to Henrik and gave him one so hard the oak cracked. Henrik's sister now came running up with Tøge's club, at the same time that the other peasants began pounding Big Svend with their sticks. This went on while the womenfolk screamed and children howled, but it did little good.

With one thrust, Svend got from under the pack and grabbed the club from Henrik's sister. Now he resembled a *Telemarking* gone berserk. Although all alone now, he was more than a master for them, and soon the fallen warriors lay about. Those who could still use their feet bolted across the prairie as if the Evil One were after them.

Big Svend's victory was complete and far-reaching. Of course, there was a big stir in Red Wing, where the case was brought before the county judge. But as the Club Law folks did not have a foot to stand on legally, they also lost their case here.

The Club Law's confederacy of terror was broken forever. Big Svend held the battlefield, and people came and took land wherever they wanted, without interference. The ill-tempered peasants no longer maintained a watch on the east, and Tøge and Henrik sat quietly by while all sorts of Philistines moved in from the south to settle around them.

[In the above account, Holand refers to the people on the east as Striler, which I have translated merely as "peasants." Haugen's dictionary defines "strill" as a derogative term for an inhabitant of the Norwegian coast, especially north and west of Bergen. –Rosholt]

But as things happen in old history books, so it also happened here on the open spaces of the Midwest.

From being the gentle guardian and defender of the law, Big Svend himself became a self-opinionated local despot whom no one dared to oppose. The tricks he had learned from the Talla boys he began to apply himself, and he occupied several nice pieces of land in this manner.

A man from Valdres, generally known under the name of Wilhelm the Shoemaker, settled on one of these 40s. He had not yet finished his house before Svend learned about it. Mad as a dog, he went and found the shoemaker.

"What are you doing on my land,

you miserable creature?" he shouted. "Out with you, and pull down that lousy house, too."

With that he grabbed the Shoemaker, threw him to the roof and would not let him come down before he promised to take the house down with him.

Big Svend versus "Halvor-the-Devil"

Big Svend Nordgaarden was not only physically strong, but also had an uncommonly smart head on him. If he had only been able to resist the bottle, he would certainly have amounted to something among his countrymen. But in Red Wing, his friends were always ready to buy him a drink to get him started on his long-winded stories. The result of all this carousing and boasting made him arrogant. One still hears stories about the tricks he played and the wild fights he got into in Red Wing.

As he was inclined by nature to mix up in all sorts of disputes, it is said that he cost the county thousands of dollars with his lawsuits. Remarkably enough, he had luck with him, and this made him completely reckless.

Finally, he trusted to Lady Luck once too often and suffered such a resounding defeat that he had to leave the county an impoverished man. It went this way:

By some intricate transaction, Big Svend became half-owner in a threshing rig with a man by the name of Halvor Johnson at Kenyon. There were some peculiar circumstances about the case. Svend did not like the new arrangement and wanted Halvor to withdraw from the partnership. This Halvor refused to do.

In a fit of anger, Svend came with a couple of friends to make a citizen's arrest. With a bottle of whiskey to fortify themselves, and with Halvor in the back of the wagon box, they drove around the community to show him off.

Every time they met anyone on the road, Svend shouted, "Hey, men! Come here and take a look at Halvor-the-Devil!" Whereupon he tore off Halvor's hat.

The latter was conveyed to Faribault, where by some conniving, the fun-makers managed to have Halvor jailed. But while Halvor sat in jail, he borrowed some law books. And when the case came to court, he defended himself so well that Svend suffered a bad defeat and had to mortgage his entire farm to pay the costs.

Therefore, Halvor won such fame for his legal learning and cunning that he thereafter was in big demand as the community lawyer. Anyone with a complex judicial knot to unravel always went first to *Halvor-Fanden* (Halvor-the-Devil), as he was always called.

Losing his case in court was too much for Big Svend's pride. He sold what little he had left and moved to Yellow Medicine County where he, too, became a lawyer. Here it was not long before he, with his cleverness and wild stories, painted his name in big letters across the county.

He later moved to Cooperstown, North Dakota, where, with old age's chilly blood creeping upon him and discretion won in scores of engagements, he died some years ago.

While Big Svend became arrogant by his earlier victories, his old opponent Henrik Talla became quiet and reasonable in defeat. After the foregoing battle at Holden parsonage, Talla relinquished all authority over the settlement and became more of a help than a hindrance to incoming settlers.

He worked hard, and when other people were driving out to their fields in the morning, he was already swinging a sledgehammer, making plow points and other repairs that people needed. By wise management of his excellent farm, he finally became one of the richest men in Goodhue County.

As the years went by, Henrik Talla became more and more outgoing and friendly. And when he died, he had one of the biggest funerals in Goodhue County.

Ole Bakko and the grindstone

Henrik Talla's brother, Tøge, had an irascible disposition and never achieved the esteem of his brother. He had made some money in Australia and became rather overbearing, even among his less fortunate neighbors.

One of the first years, he had loaned some money to Ole Bakko, a good-natured but powerful *Halling* who lived west of Kenyon. Times were hard, and Bakko finally saw no way out of his predicament than to sell his oxen. When he was away at Cannon Falls a big snowstorm came up, preventing Ole from returning home at once.

Meanwhile, Tøge had come to the farm for his money. When he did not find Ole at home, he began to scold Ole's wife, who was alone with a child on her lap. When Ole returned home, he found his wife crying. Learning what had happened, Ole, fighting mad, went off to pay the loan.

When he reached Tøge's house, he played it cool, walked in and laid the money on the table. But as he was leaving, his anger got the better of him.

In the lean-to off the kitchen stood a grindstone. Ole picked it up and threw it against the strong homemade door, knocking it off its hinges like a feather. As the door tumbled down, it hit Tøge, who fell against the kitchen stove, tumbling that over, too. There everything lay in a heap—the man, the stove, the door, kitchen utensils and grindstone.

"Stay where you are or I'll knock the daylights out of you," Ole commanded. "And if I ever see you on the road again, bring your funeral shirt with you!"

Ole J. Bakko and the brothers Knut Finseth, Anders Finseth and Herbrand Finseth came to Goodhue County in 1853. They were among the first of 700 *Hallinger* who now live around Kenyon.

Ole Bakko's son, Per, now a champion fighter, was once stolen by the Indians. But his mother did not think of herself. As soon as she missed the boy, she ran after the thieves and tore the boy from their hands and brought him home.

She did not dare tell Ole about this until later, for had he heard of it, he would have taken on the whole Sioux nation.

Bakko's brother-in-law, A. K. Finseth, was for many years the leading man in the settlement. He served as a state senator, a member of the church council, a presidential elector and other high posts.

Settlers from many places in Norway

In addition to *Sogninger*, *Telemarkinger* and *Hallinger*, there are many other localities from Norway represented. West of Zumbrota there is a big colony of *Landinger*, and north of the *Hallinger* there are about a thousand *Valdriser*, foremost in agriculture and church struggle.

The following came in 1855:
- John Hamre
- Holien brothers
- Nils Lien
- Anders Remmen
- Gudmund Norsving
- Endre Haugen

[Note from translator Rosholt: In Holand's third edition of De Norske Settlementers Historie, brought out in 1909, he adds more material to this paragraph, which is cited in a special page in the back of the book. He writes:

"In addition to those who came in 1855 and settled north of Kenyon were:
- Kittil H. Tunnesgaard, Hallingdal
- Finkel Thorson, Valdres
- Peder Givre, Valdres
- Thomas Nilson, Valdres
- Nils Heen, Valdres
- Erik A. Ødegaard, Sogn
- Ole O. Næseth, Sogn
- Iver Kvamme, Sogn
- Nils A. Dalsbotten, Sogn

"Those arriving in 1856 were:
- Engebret A. Hougen, Sogn
- Ole B. Broin, Sogn

"The Goodhue County colony of

Norwegians also reaches into Rice County, which was settled early. The following people all came here in 1855:
- Syver Vesledal, Hallingdal
- Elef Briskemyren, Hallingdal
- O. H. Sire, Hallingdal
- Ole Kaalsrud, Hallingdal
- Truls Kaalsrud, Hallingdal
- Fingar Kaalsrud, Hallingdal
- Ole Roningen, Hallingdal
- Hans Sagedalen, Hallingdal
- John Gjelle, Hallingdal
- Østen Holen, Hallingdal
- Halvor Braaten, Hallingdal
- John Hellerud, Hallingdal
- Andres Hellerud, Hallingdal
- Hans Stenbaken, Hallingdal
- Truls Vold, Hallingdal
- Truls Snedkerpladsen, Hallingdal
- Syver Vold, Hallingdal
- Einar Bonde, Valdres
- Iver Lockrem, Valdres
- Engebret Egge, Valdres
- Johanes Isdalen, Sogn
- Erick Engeseth, Sogn
- Ingebret Engeseth, Sogn
- Sjur Engeseth, Sogn

"Also arriving in 1855 were:
- Osmund Osmundson, Stavanger
- John Vespe, Stavanger
- Halvor Kvi, Hallingdal
- Truls Kvi, Hallingdal

Nearly all of these people moved up from Spring Grove, Minnesota."
Now to return to Holand's 1908 first edition. –Rosholt]

Fra Sogn: Laxevarf

Holden church, Pastor Muus

This entire area was at this time included in the Holden congregation organized by Pastor H. A. Stub in 1856.

Nils O. Brandt, the itinerant pioneer pastor who laid the groundwork for most church work (Lutheran) in the upper Mississippi Valley, was actually the first here, coming around 1 July 1855, after a trip up the Zumbro River and a night's rest in a hay stack under the open sky.

By the following evening he had reached Henrik Talla, where he also spent the night. It rained while he was here, and he recalls that the house was so leaky that he became dripping wet, even though he moved his bed from one place to the other half the night.

On this tour, Brandt officiated at the marriage of Tøge Talla—the first marriage ceremony held in the county. He also held several worship services. In 1857, Pastor Munch *[probably Johan Storm Munch –Rosholt]*, as well as pastor and later professor Lauritz Larsen, visited the settlement in Goodhue County. Larsen preached six days in succession before big audiences, and many people followed him from place to place. In one week in June he baptized 100 children, 33 of them at a service held in the neighborhood of Nerstrand.

There is one person more closely associated with the history of Goodhue County than any other—namely, Bernt Julius Muus. Originally from Snaasen in Trondheim, he became pastor at Holden in 1859 and for 40 years remained the spiritual leader of the county.

He was endowed by nature with a zealous disposition, which never swerved from its course—no matter how immovable the apathy of the people to whom he preached or how large the obstacles placed in his path. He left an impression on the settlement that will not soon be forgotten, nor the anecdotes people still tell about him.

Although nearly everyone in his big congregation had their differences with him over reprimands for human failings, they are now forgotten, and the entire church body looks back in admiration on the man.

And, one by one, as death approached for these pioneers—even for those who had moved away—they wanted to be buried at Holden cemetery where they had sat and listened to Muus's soul-filled sermons.

Although Pastor Muus took a stand on the side of the Anti-Missourians (the United Lutheran Church Synod) in the church struggle of the 1880s, he regarded

Henningsvær

the doctrine on predestination strictly a theological question—one that should be studied within the institutions of higher learning and not used as a reason for church schisms. He therefore never actually left the ranks of the old Norwegian Synod, although he was expelled from it in 1898.

That his old friends and co-workers should misjudge his own efforts for peace and harmony so much that they would expel him from their religious community left a wound on his heart from which he never recovered, and he died two years later.

Pastor Muus was a typical Lutheran of the old school, quite thoughtless in his condemnation of all that deflected from the pure doctrine *["renelære," a combined word heard often in the struggle over predestination in the 1880s and 1890s, but a word not included in either the Haugen or Larson dictionaries –Rosholt]*.

Kristoffer Janson relates that, once when he was visiting Muus and they were sitting down to dinner, Muus folded his hands and merely repeated the first line of the common table prayer, "In Jesus name we come to eat . . ." but did not go farther, as he did not wish to include the expression of "thanks to God," which he thought would offend this rank heretic. *[Janson was a Norwegian immigrant, later pastor, who came to accept the Unitarian faith. –Rosholt]*

Pastor Muus was one of the biggest men we have had among us, a powerful force for the awakening of the people and for leading them forward. He was a fire on the American prairie, or, as Per Strømme once said, a twinkle in his eye: "It is well-known that Muus is a head taller than all the people of Minnesota."

Goodhue County deserves a special niche in our history because the Norwegian settlement here bore the heaviest share in the development of two of our leading schools. After having been one of the best contributors to Luther College for years, a number of Goodhue County men, together with Muus, took the lead in laying the groundwork for the building of St. Olaf School in 1874, which later became St. Olaf College.

Four years later, a Goodhue County man, Hans Markussen Sande, who mortgaged his farm to raise the necessary funds, purchased the Red Wing Seminary property.

Among all the rich and fruitful communities that have made the name of Minnesota known the world over, there is none that can measure up to the Norwegian colony in Goodhue County. Big and stately stand the farms, ringed by big shade trees planted by the first pioneers. Inside the average farm home, there is comfort and well being, with rural refinement and old traditions of parental achievement.

The future beckons brightly to their happy children.

Hiterdals Kirke

52
East and West St. Olaf colonies, Olmsted County, Minnesota
(Source: De Norske Settlementers Historie, by Hjalmar Rued Holand, translated by Malcolm Rosholt, 1908, pp. 498–501)

The year 1854 is one of the most meaningful in the history of Norwegian immigration, for in that year more settlements were actually founded in the U.S. than at any other time before or after.

Bold Norwegian pioneers went out that year and occupied the best lands throughout southeastern Minnesota. Here, isolated and distant from one another, they founded small colonies, which in a few years became important communities that spread across southern Minnesota.

Fillmore County's hills and Mower County's plains were settled by Norwegians that year, as well as Freeborn, Steele, Nicollet, Carver and Dakota counties. Goodhue County's beautiful acres were occupied at the same time that other Norsemen reached Rock Dell in Olmsted County.

Rock Dell settlement covers the southwest of Olmsted County and the southeast of Dodge County. Some 3,000 Norwegians inhabit it, although considerably mixed in origin. However, there are quite a few from Hallingdal.

Three immigrant parties
Three different immigrant parties reached Olmsted County in 1854. The first included the following:
• Ole Golberg, Hallingdal
• Tollef Golberg, Hallingdal
• Nils N. Giere, Hallingdal
• Thrond Sæther, Sigdal
• Guttorm Olson Fraagot, Sigdal
• Ole Amundsen, Numedal

In the second party, which arrived nearly at the same time, were the following:

• Even Halvorson Holtan, Kviteseid
• Knut O. Holtan, Kviteseid
• Hans Holtan, Sandøkedal
• Syvert Nilsen, Land
• Nils Feseth, Bamble

In the third party, which arrived on 24 June 1854, were:
• Kristoffer Tvedt, Gjerestad
• Torbjørn Tvedt, Gjerestad
• Ole Veggar, Andebø near Tønsberg
• Abraham Veggar, Andebø near Tønsberg
• Kristen Hellikson, Andebø near Tønsberg
• Jacob Dahlen, Andebø near Tønsberg
• Johannes A. Aasved, Trondheim
• Aron Anderson, Trondheim

This last group settled farthest north in the settlement on what is still called the "Veggar Prairie." All three parties moved up from Koshkonong in Wisconsin.

No one can remember whether anyone arrived in 1855, but the following year several came who played an

important role in the affairs of the Rock Dell settlement. Those who arrived in 1856 were as follows:
• Magne Bystølen, Voss, and Nils Gilderhus, Voss, two of the original founders of Koshkonong
• Jacob K. Thoe, an outstanding figure from Voss
• Ole S. Sættre, Voss, father of Pastor Sættre *[probably Thorbjørn Andreas Sættre –Rosholt]*
• Andrew Seeverts (Anders Syverson), Ole S. Sættre's brother, Voss

Amund Giere, father of Pastor Nils O. Giere, is also a pioneer of 1856.

Ole Sættre was the biggest man in the community, standing seven feet tall.

Nedre Indgang til Borgund Kirke

But he was a prominent man in other respects besides his long body. He was a well-read and cultured person whose advice was sought by many.

As he subscribed to the first English newspaper (Norwegian papers had not yet reached this far west), his house was often filled with attentive listeners when he read to them about events in the outside world.

Grandfather Satran's wanderings

The parents of Ole Sættre (Ole Satran) were among the first settlers on Koshkonong, and his son, Pastor Sættre, recalls a delightful story about his father's arrival at this distant settlement in the Midwest:

"Early in the year of 1840, when the brothers Ole Satran and Sjur Satran left Voss to go to America, old Grandfather Satran was in good circumstances after he sold his farm. In America, Ole and Sjur Satran first worked for a time in Chicago, then a small village. Two of their children who died here were buried in the church cemetery, which is now part of Lincoln Park.

"When the Satran brothers heard about the new settlement in Koshkonong, they decided to move there. They purchased a yoke of oxen, farm tools and implements and started north across the prairies of Illinois. At Koshkonong they took land and established themselves, as others had already done.

"As with so many people in those days, the Satrans could read but not write. As a result, they had not written anyone in Norway of their present address. Not hearing from his boys, old Grandfather Satran became impatient and one fine day got enough money together for a ticket to America and left Norway.

"He followed the stream of immigrants and, after a difficult journey, reached Milwaukee, a stranger in a strange land. He tried to use both the dialects of Voss and Bergen, but no one understood him when he asked about his sons. Some, who realized he was Norwegian, pointed westward, as they knew there was a settlement of Norwegians out in that direction somewhere.

"The old man went off on foot and eventually reached Muskego, where he again asked about his sons. Knut Langeland, who was the best-informed man in the settlement, knew nothing about them but had heard that a new settlement had been established to the west at a place called Koshkonong. He could only point to the west, and as the old-timer was afraid to miss the direction, he took off at once. Neither swamps nor brush could stop him.

"And then one fine day, while one of the wives of the sons sat and gazed through the window, she caught sight of a lonely figure off in the hills. It was quite a surprise to her when she finally recognized the nearly 80-year-old grandparent, Magnus Satran. He had made a beeline for his son's house without any guide other than instinct.

"Yes, sir, this was indeed a surprise party in the new settler's hut." *[Holand cites Waldemar Ager, prohibitionist and editor of Reform, as the authority for this statement. –Rosholt]*

In the fall of 1856, C. L. Clausen and A. C. Preus organized St. Olaf congregation at Rock Dell. But as times were hard, things moved slowly toward getting a church built or calling a resident pastor.

The panic of 1857

In 1857, a financial panic struck the nation, the most severe the country had ever experienced. The years previous to 1857 were characterized by great speculation and easy money. Land speculators were everywhere, platting villages on hills and marshes and selling lots in these paper towns at big prices. New railroad lines were surveyed and widely advertised in every valley, and fictitious business enterprises were transacted overall. It was the great American *Age of Humbug.*

As a result of all this speculation, moneymen began to tighten up on their credit and refused to loan even on good security. The result was runs on banks that forced them to close, and this brought business life to a standstill.

Across the entire nation, east, west, north and south, the dark night of despair descended over the people like a pestilence. Thousands of men who were considered rich became beggars, and tens of thousands of working people went about hungry and hopeless.

The panic was felt in the distant settlements, making it impossible for the simplest improvements to be made.

Klokketaarn ved Borgund Kirke

Borgund Kirke

53

Main community of Gudbrandsdøler in America, Brown and Watonwan Counties, southwestern Minnesota

(Source: De Norske Settlementers Historie, by Hjalmar Rued Holand, translated by Malcolm Rosholt, 1908, pp. 507–518)

The first Norwegian immigrants looked with suspicion on the great treeless plains of the Upper Midwest. They were unaccustomed to a terrain like this and believed there was something wrong with the soil, since no trees grew here. Furthermore, people feared that it would be altogether too cold in winter where there were no trees.

As it was also difficult to find water and timber for building purposes, these fertile prairies were shunned like a desert. Instead, the first Norwegian immigrants sought out small tree groves and sites along the marshes to build their homes.

But it was not long before the Yankees realized that these judgments of the plains country were false. The Norwegians too, little by little, began to move out on the prairie.

In the settlement which is here described, we have the first where all concern for trees was disregarded, and where we see the majority of Norwegian settlers boldly building their homes out on the open plain without protection of trees.

Mt. Pisqua and the Jesuits

The entire southwest of Minnesota is a monotonous, high-lying plain, nearly as flat as the Red River Valley and just about as lacking in trees. There are many marshes, but few hills.

The highest of these knolls lies in the southeast corner of Brown County, half a mile from the little village of Hanska. On the one side lie two beautiful lakes ringed by trees, and on the other side the view is wide open for a mile. This elevation is called Mt. Pisqua or Pisgah. In this name we have the only remembrance of the Jesuit missionaries who at one time more than a century ago traveled among the plains Indians. Here we have a subject that, if correctly handled, could be made into a stirring adventure story.

Long before hunters and land-lookers found their way to these far-off lands, these zealous Jesuits had forsaken the comforts of civilization and association of friends to bring the gospel to the Indians.

On this high spot at Mt. Pisqua probably stood their humble hut, from whence they sent up prayers to God for the conversion of the heathen. On this

same spot they may have stood and looked across the land that the Lord had given to them for His glorification. From here they set out on their long journeys to seek out, here and there, a soul who might accept the gospel.

Now the Jesuits and their devoted missionary labors are forgotten, and Mt. Pisqua in Brown County is one of the few places that preserve a silent memory of their work of mercy.

But Mt. Pisqua in times past was also a holy place for the Indians, for it was here that they brought their chiefs, even from distant places, to be buried. When a church was built on Mt. Pisqua, many of the Indian mounds were smoothed over to make place for the foundation work, and the excavators found the remains of several Indians sitting on stones in a circle (the position of chiefs in burial.)

Gudbrandsdøler settlements: Linden, Hanska, Butternut Valley, Madelia, Rosendal, St. James, Long Lake and Odin

It was here, at the foot of Mt. Pisqua and vicinity that the widespread settlement, which takes in the south of Brown County and nearly all of Watonwan County, had its beginning. This settlement now numbers around 6,500 Norsemen.

The majority of these people are from Øvre-Gudbrandsdal, from communities such as Vaage (Vaagaa), Lesje and Lom. The settlement is so extensive that there is no single entity. Instead, it divides into the following branches: Linden, Hanska, Butternut Valley, Madelia, Rosendal, St. James, Long Lake and Odin.

In 1856, the movement of immigrants to Minnesota's eastern counties had barely begun, and the whole of western Wisconsin lay practically deserted. It must therefore be considered more than commonly bold for a party of pioneers to travel 200 to 300 miles farther than anyone else to build their homes in western Minnesota. But this happened.

In the summer of 1856, 14 men with cattle left Rock Prairie in Wisconsin and eventually reached Mt. Pisqua in Minnesota. Most of them were *Hallinger*. Among these, Ole Næss had the most experience and personal property. He was therefore some sort of a leader.

But on reaching Mt. Pisqua, the party fell into disagreement. Ole Næss and several *Hallinger* wanted to continue on, while the others wanted to stay. Those who wanted to remain included the following:
- Peder Thormundson, Stavanger
- Gunder Paulson, Stavanger
- Jens Harbø, Stavanger
- Tosten Levik, Stavanger
- Endre Levik, Stavanger
- Palmer Olson, Aadal
- Helge Palmerson, Aadal
- Thore Olson Kirkebø, Hallingdal

Only Kirkebø was married, and he took land at the foot of Mt. Pisqua, while the others found nice farms in the vicinity of Linden Township of Brown County.

This party of immigrants was influenced into coming here by an article that appeared in *Emigranten*, the only Norwegian newspaper in the U.S. at the time.

In 1855, two men from Oslo, Paul Eckstorm and Theodor Brown, had followed the Minnesota River upstream until they reached South Bend, a hopeful little village that had been platted about three miles west of where Mankato is presently located, 20 miles east of Mt. Pisqua. Here the two men started a business, and Eckstorm wrote to *Emigranten* about the fertile land in the vicinity. As his article influenced many to come here, Eckstorm must be remembered as the actual founder of the settlement.

As to Ole Næss and his companions, it can be reported that they went 75 miles farther north and settled in the neighborhood of the present Litchfield in Meeker County, where they founded what was to become the largest Norwegian settlement in the U.S.

"Thore Olson Kirkebø, the most widely known among the early pioneers here, was a man who had a good reputation around Linden. He had been a peddler in his youth, and was possessed by the *Hallinger's* natural cunning and leader in all sorts of fun escapades.

"If the activities went a bit beyond the strict definition of the law, such as incidents in which an Irishman or two might have been victimized, Thore Olson Kirkebø was always ready to take the credit—because he was proud of 'presenting myself,' as he called it.

"But this was only an occasional outpouring of inborn sociability. He was at the same time fearless, friendly and zealous of one's honor, and competent in everything he undertook. He was equally Norwegian both in his good points and his faults." *[Holand fails to give the source of this quotation. –Rosholt]*

Among the first settlers in Linden Township, Tosten Levik, was no doubt the one person who did most to establish order and organize the pioneers. He was in the forefront when the congregation was organized and in the building of a church. He served as sexton, and as Justice of the Peace, he officiated at weddings where he added a religious touch to the ceremony by having a hymn sung and using an English ritual.

Later, when he moved to the neighboring village of Madelia, he occasionally returned on days like Good Friday, Ascension Day and the second day of Easter to see that people were observing these days in accord with Norse custom. If they were not, he was there to put them on the right path of virtue.

Notto Jensen from Evje in Setesdal was another who arrived here in 1856. He came by way of Rock River in Jefferson County, Wisconsin, where he had remained for a time before moving to Pierce County in western Wisconsin.

In Minnesota, he went into the south of Watonwan County, where he became the first Norseman to settle in Rosendal east of St. James.

Endre Levik was a schoolteacher at Rock Prairie, Wisconsin, and returned there in the autumn to fulfill his teaching contract. The following spring (1857), he returned to western Minnesota, bringing with him the following:
• "Big" Knut H. Helling, Hallingdal
• "Little" Knut H. Helling, Hallingdal
• Anders Grøtte, Hallingdal
• Iver Nilsen, Hallingdal
• Ole Sørbølle, Hallingdal
• Thor Thorson Omserud, Valdres
• Ole Thorson Omserud, Valdres
• Torgrim Torgrimson, Valdres
• Anders Olson, Skien
• Anders Lundberg, Hurdal
• Hans Johnson Berdal, Feios in Sogn

Notto Jensen's new settlement at Rosendal attracted many neighbors in 1857. The following from Rock River (all from Kragerø) joined him that year and settled around him:
• Halvor Barland
• Nils Thorson
• Jens Thorson
• Thomas Thorson
• Jacob Taraldson
• Knut Ørvig
• Ole Jørgensen

The following from Øier settled Butternut Valley, east of Linden, in 1857:
• Knut Strøm
• Anders Strøm
• Even Pederson
• Paul Olson Sletjord

That year also marked the arrival of the first people from Øvre-Gudbrandsdal; their compatriots now make up the majority of the population.

In 1857, arrivals at Linden included the brothers Hans Sørlien, Amund Sørlien, Lars Sørlien and Johannes Sørlien, the first to leave from Lom in Norway.

Tosten Levik, who often wrote for *Emigranten*, also described for the paper the Indian attack on Spirit Lake. This halted the stream of migration until after the Civil War ended.

The economic circumstances at the time also did little to encourage people to this area. The nearest railway town was at Prairie du Chien, 300 miles away. St. Paul, an unimportant village 120 to 150 miles to the northeast, was the nearest marketplace. Flour could be purchased locally but cost $18 a ton; calico cloth cost 50 cents a yard.

Little was harvested owing to the plague of blackbirds, gophers and other pests, and prices on what little that could be sold were minimal. Prairie fires were frequent, and the settlers never left their huts without fear of finding them in ashes when they came home.

Furthermore, most of the settlers felt the need of something to sustain their spiritual lives. Not once in many years had they assembled on a Sunday for meditation. The settlement lay entirely too far out even for the indefatigable pioneer pastor to reach it.

Now and then Buckskin Pants Fredrickson visited the settlement when he was out buying fur pelts and, in passing, baptized some children. But as to this man's ministerial functions, the less said, the better.

Nils Rukke, originally from Hallingdal, who arrived in 1859, later became county treasurer and had many interesting experiences as a town promoter in North Dakota. Herman Matson, Mads Boxrud and Ole Boxrud, all from Toten, arrived at the same time as Rukke. The Toten people are, after the *Gudbrandsdøler*, the most numerous in the settlement.

Indian War of 1862

Herman Madsen recalls that many of them went around warning the people of the Indian uprising and giving them a chance to flee. His brother-in-law, Mads Boxrud, was killed by the Indians while out hunting.

Gjerom Patterson (Jerome Patterson) from Bergen was one of the pioneers who came before the Civil War. He had barely settled down a short distance west of Madelia in 1862 when the Indian War broke out. Two of his teen-age sons were killed, while his wife, daughter and a third son were taken captive.

The wife was a cripple, and the Indians became tired of dragging her with them. One day around noon she was bound to a tree, whereupon the Indians, with demonic glee, began to use her for target practice. One sighted in on her arms, another her eyes and the third on her heart until the old body fell in a heap.

Meanwhile, her husband, hiding in the grass nearby, witnessed the gruesome murder of his wife, unable to come to her assistance. The daughter and son were freed after two years of captivity.

Meanwhile, the movement of immigrants into Long Lake and Odin, south of St. James, got under way. The first to arrive was Hans J. Berdahl from Sogn, who moved over from Rosendal to Long Lake in 1858.

A little later in the same summer came the following:
• Johan Roland, Gausdal
• Simon Roland, Gausdal
• Ole Nilsen Viger, Aadal
• Ole Palmeson, Aadal
• Gulbrand Palmeson, Aadal
• Gabriel Ellingson, Stavanger
• Iver Johnson, Stavanger
• Rasmus Danielson, Stavanger
• John Petterson, Telemark
• Salve Torgerson, Telemark
• Lars Langemyr, Telemark

Of these, Ole and Gulbrand Palmeson; Gabriel Ellingson, a step-son of Simon Roland; and a Norwegian soldier were killed by the Indians while out on a hunting trip a short distance from St. James.

A detachment of troops then arrived and built fortifications on the Watonwan River. While the troops were stationed there, a Norwegian, whose name is forgotten, went to their camp and asked if two soldiers would stay with his family overnight while he went to town on an errand.

Two Norwegian soldiers—Ole Eriksen from Odalen and Mons Hansen from Nannestad—were then quartered in the house while the owner left. Early the next morning, a group of Indians stole up to the house and shot both the wife and Eriksen, whom they could see through the windows, whereupon Mons Hansen ran out of the house pointing a gun at the Indians, who fled.

Soldiers then went out to bring in the scattered settlers to safety, but were already too late, as 15 families had been killed during the night. This was in the vicinity of the present St. James.

After this attack, those still in the area fled, and the land lay deserted until 1866. Only two of the original settlers at Long Lake and Odin—Hans J. Berdahl and Rasmus Danielson—came back.

During the Indian uprising from 1862-64, Brown and Watonwan counties became the central arena of hostilities, and many pioneers were killed there. All of Cottonwood Valley was plundered and burned, and at Leavenworth alone lay 60 dead, scalped persons. Among these were many Norwegian.

The hardest fighting took place around New Ulm, some eight miles from Linden. Here, around 2,000 fleeing settlers had taken refuge and were encircled by 650 Indians for days. Only 200 of the whites had weapons. For a time it looked as if the Indians would be victorious. House after house was captured and torched until 150 stood in flames. Tired, starving settlers were squeezed together in 30 small houses.

The situation was desperate. The sharp bangs of the rifles, the whistle of the bullets, the Indians' screams, the wounded moaning, the little children crying, and the sparking fires that rose on all sides in the dark, were enough to shake even the strongest heart.

For safety reasons, many women and children hid in a cellar under one of the houses. Down there was a barrel of gunpowder. A widow of one of the murdered settlers sat beside it, ready to put fire to it and blow up the house and everyone in it as soon as she heard the victory call of the Indians upstairs. Better to end it that way than to take a chance on the life the Indians would give them.

After two days of very hard fighting, the Indians withdrew. This was a Godsend, as the settlers could not have held out one day more. The dead were hurriedly buried in one grave; the wounded were loaded on 150 wagons, and the 2,000 worn-out settlers went east to Mankato.

Many Norwegians were along in these dreadful days in New Ulm, but their names are forgotten. Fourteen pioneers in Cottonwood Valley escaped to New Ulm and later went up the valley to look for their friends. But they found only the dead and homes in ashes. On the way back they ran into an Indian ambush, and 10 of the pioneers were killed. The names of these 10 appear on the big monument in New Ulm, four of them Norsemen— namely, Ole Olson, Nils Olson, Thore Olson and John Thompson. The Olsons were from Urness in Sogn.

Although this terrible battle took place only eight or 10 miles from the Norwegian settlement in Linden, there were not many here who fled. This was no doubt the only settlement in western Minnesota that was not made a desert by the flight of the refugees.

The reason for this is in part due to the security the settlers felt by the presence of 30 soldiers stationed in a poorly built fort nearby (Fort Hill), on the banks of Lake Hanska. Ole Synsteby now (1908) owns the ground on which the fort stood. But it was a false security, as the fort did not have the strength to make any sort of a stand against several hundred Indians, had they decided to come.

Kristian Rud and his pig

While the Indian War involved the most frightful and tragic incidents, it also happened now and then that something comical arose that the old people can still laugh about. The following is one story still remembered:

"A man by the name of Kristian Rud fled from his home on the outskirts of the settlement one day when the Indians approached. In a few days he returned, but found his house and barns burned and everything carried off except a small pig. This he butchered and hauled to New Ulm, which at the

Parti af Mjøsen samt Ruiner af Hamars gamle Kloster

moment was filled with troops.

"But discipline had broken down a bit, and just for the hell of it, some of the troops were raiding one saloon after the other. While the farmer Rud was away from his wagon for a moment, the troops discovered the dressed pig and took it.

"Rud went to the commanding officer and complained. The officer went with him to the troop encampment, where some soldiers were at that moment bringing in the stolen pig. The officer explained the history of the pig, and the soldiers swore they would never rob a poor settler, and they carried the pig back to the wagon amidst considerable joking.

"But it was not long before another unit among the drunken soldiers discovered the pig in the wagon and carried it back to their camp for a barbecue. Then they heard about the destitute farmer and brought the pig back to the wagon, only to have still another party of soldiers do the same thing.

"How many times the pig was stolen no one knows, but it is said that it was being carried one way or the other all night.

"But to make a long story short, Kristian Rud retained possession of his pig."

More immigrants arrive

The immigrants began moving into Brown and Watonwan counties again in 1867. In that year, Ole Jørgenson from Lesje was the first among the Norwegians to arrive. A shrewd businessman, he later became one of Brown County's most prominent citizens.

The year 1867 also marks the time when emigrants from Vaage (Vaagaa) began to move into Brown County—among them:
- Ole Pladsen
- Anders Kjølstad
- Einar Smedsmo
- Knut Steen
- John Steen
- Iver Sandbuløkken
- "Big" Ole Sandbuløkken
- "Little" Ole Sandbuløkken

About the same time, parties of immigrants also reached Albion, Long Lake and Odin.

Ole Jørgenson was for many years the sexton in the local Lutheran congregation. For pay, he was entitled one bushel of oats from each member.

When Serumgaard *[no first name given – Rosholt]*, his "tax collector," went from farm to farm to pick up the oats, he came upon a rube named Torger Olson, originally from around Bergen. Torger plainly saw no reason at all for this tax on behalf of the sexton and said: "If I want any singing done, I'll sing myself. Then I won't have to pay for it, either."

Olaus Solberg, father of the editor O. F. Solberg, was also an old pioneer in this settlement who had seen some interesting things in his time.

He came to this country in 1852, and for a period he served as manager of Ole Bull's big colony at Oleana, Pennsylvania. When the colony broke up, Solberg was among the first to reach Freeborn County in Minnesota, where he was commissioned a 2nd lieutenant in the Army. He then moved to Watonwan County, where the Indians drove him out. Later, he settled in Blue Earth County near a Gudbrandsdal settlement.

Norwegian Unitarian Church

This settlement, especially around Hanska, is of special interest as the only place in the U.S. where one can find a Norwegian rural congregation of the Unitarian faith.

This came about following a dispute over the location of the first Lutheran church to be built here. The minority in the congregation wanted to have the church on Mt. Pisqua. When this was voted down, the minority members established their own congregation and built a church where they wanted it.

Among other things, Kristoffer

Janson was invited to give some lectures, and his preaching aroused so much interest that he was called to be the congregation's pastor under the Unitarian confession. Janson served here for 15 years, living in the summertime in a small house on Mt. Pisqua, where he fussed with gardening and other useless affairs.

While the church was under construction in 1883, it was torn off its foundation by a tornado. Pieces of lumber flew hundreds of feet into the air, although 16 men at work around the building were unharmed.

Now, a nice church stands on the hill, together with a beautiful parsonage and grounds. The congregation has about 60 families and is in sound financial condition. The young peoples' league is perhaps the only one in the U.S. that owns its own premises. In Hanska, it has a large building, 40 by 72 feet, with library facilities, a gymnasium, guest room and auditorium. The congregation also operates a land office—actually, a cooperative—that has a turnover of about $70,000 annually.

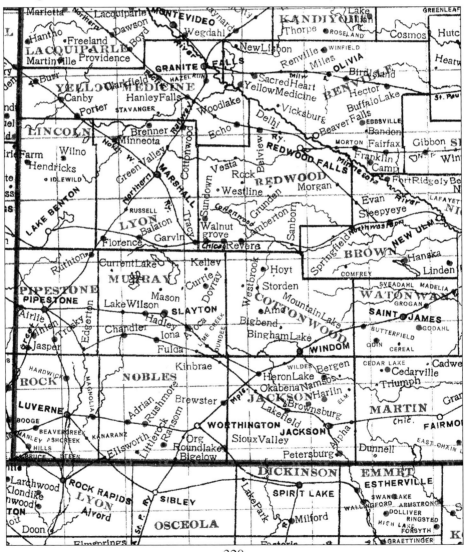

54
Jackson County and the 24 August 1862 Belmont Massacre, southwestern Minnesota

(Sources: De Norske Settlementers Historie, by Hjalmar Rued Holand, translated by Malcolm Rosholt, 1908, pp. 519–521
and
Astri, My Astri: Norwegian Heritage Stories by Deb Nelson Gourley, 2004, 2005, pp. 15-32, 231-236)

Quite long from north to south, another settlement begins that takes in the greater part of eastern Jackson County. It runs along the Des Moines River from Windom in Minnesota to Estherville in Iowa, a distance of approximately 40 miles. About 4,500 Norwegians, mostly from Sør-Trøndelag and Nord-Østerdalen in Norway, live in this tree-decked valley and on the adjoining prairie opening.

Anders Olson Slaabakken, from Tolgen (Tolga), Østerdalen, was the first Norwegian in the Des Moines valley, coming here via Spring Prairie, Wisconsin, and Houston, Minnesota, in 1858. Only the year before, this same territory was laid waste by Chief Inkpaduta and his Indians.

Legend tells that the Slaabakken farm name in Norway originated when the Swedes would travel by sled to the coast of Norway for supplies. Spring came unusually early one year, and a thaw forced them to leave their sleds on a certain hill and continue their journey without them. The Swedes never returned for the sleds, so they were left there to rot. The hill became known as Slaabakken, meaning "Sled Hill," and thus the name of the farm.

It would be considered quite rash for a man to settle in such an outlying place. But Anders Slaabakken, later known as Anders Belmont, plodded ahead several days' journey from his nearest neighbor and built a house. He also brought about the later migration of his countrymen to this area.

1859 or 1860 arrivals

The primary immigration began in 1859 or 1860, when a party of families arrived from Big Canoe in Winneshiek County, Iowa. Some settled a few miles north of the present city of Jackson; the others followed the river south, crossing the state line into Emmet County, Iowa. They included:
• Børre Olson (Burre Olson Ramlo), Holtaalen, Sør-Trøndelag; wife Guri Estensdatter Nysetvold
• Ole Børreson
• Jonas Børreson
• Hans Johanson Lien, Røros, Sør-Trøndelag; wife Gjertrud Børresdatter, Holtaalen, Sør-Trøndelag and family
• Ole Pederson Eide (Ole Pederson Evavold), Røros; wife Berit Erelien Olson and son Ole
• Knut Mestad (Knut Haldorson Ro), Evanger; wife Brita Mestad (Brita Andersdatter Røte), Store Røte, Voss
• Ole Olson Fyre (Ole Olson Førde), Evanger, Voss; wife (Mrs. Fyre) Kari Nilsdatter Horvei, Evanger, Voss, and stepchildren/children: Ole (the older, went by Ole F. Forde), Ole (the younger), Martha, Anna, Guro and Niels
• Bottolf Peterson Brugjeld (Botolv Pederson Bruhjell), Leikanger, Sogn; wife Kari Larsdatter Hovde–settled in Estherville
• Niels Pederson Brugjeld (Niels Pederson Bruhjell); wife Britha

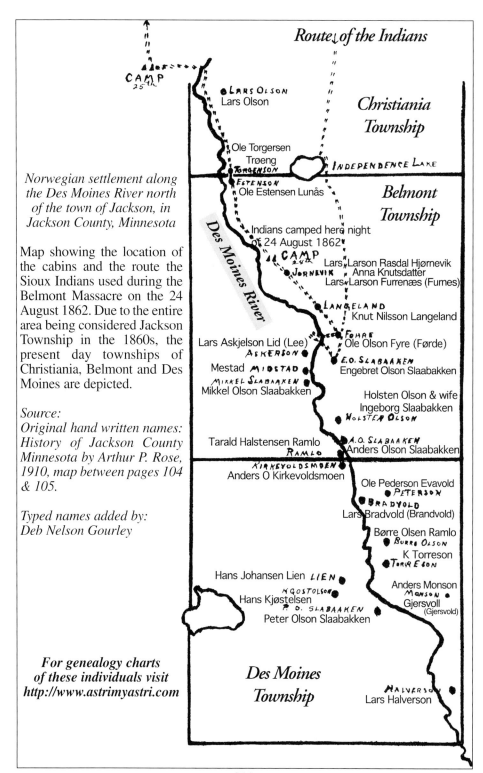

Olsdatter Erikson Rauboti, Mundal, Leikanger, Sogn–settled in Estherville
• Matthias Aasved (F. Mathias Asved) and family–settled in Estherville
• Lars Paulson Trøos (Lars Paulson Troo), Hallingdal; wife Guri Sjurgurdsdatter Sundbrei, Aal, Hallingdal–settled in Estherville
• Ole Fladland (Ole Knudson Fladeland), Fyresdal, Telemark; wife Turi Larsdatter Paulson–settled in Estherville. Ole died in the Civil War; Turi then married Tosten O. Berg
• Ole Ranum and family, Valdres–settled in Estherville
• Lars Brandvold (Lars Bradvold) and family
• Lars Larson Furrenæs (Lars Larson Furnes), Askøy, Strilelandet/Bergens Stift *(and wife Anna Knutsdatter?)*
• Tarald Halstenson Ramlo (Tarald Ramlo), Holtaalen, Sør-Trøndelag; wife Marit Halvorsdatter Stene and family

The prairie was treeless and uninviting, but the settlers liked the area because the tree-covered hills along the Des Moines River were sheltered and the soil extremely fertile. Thus these early arrivals sent word to their family and friends in Winneshiek County to join them, and many did, including:

1860 or 1861 arrivals
• Kirsti Helgesdatter Eide Slaabakken, Tolga, Østerdalen–immigrated as a widow with her Slaabakken children
• Engebret Olson Slaabakken
• John Olson Slaabakken
• Tollef Olson Slaabakken
• Mikkel Olson Slaabakken
• Peter Olson Slaabakken
• Simon Olson Slaabakken
• Lars Askjelson Lid (Lars Askjelson Lee), wife Ingebjørg Olsdatter Fyre (sister to Ole Olson Fyre), Evanger, Voss, and family
• Torrild Nielsen; wife Anna Svendsdatter–settled in Estherville
• John Svendson Ramlo (John Swenson), Holtaalen, Sør-Trøndelag; wife Kari Hansdatter Megard and family

The Norwegian settlers who arrived in the early 1860s understood and spoke very little English. Their interests were centered in their homes, and they had few dealings with the outside world. They had settled on the exposed frontier, almost in the heart of the Indian country, yet they knew nothing of the Indian customs or Indian warfare.

1861 wagon train arrivals
In 1861, the following arrived via wagon train:
• Jakob Nilsson Ekse, Evanger, Voss; wife Ragnhild Knutsdatter Langeland–before returning to Big Canoe in spring 1862, Ragnhild was baptism sponsor for the orphan Johannes Larson
• Johannes Knutson Ekse, Evanger, Voss; wife Brytteva Jonsdatter Mestad (Mrs. Ekse), Evanger, widow of Johannes's brother, Nils Knutson Ekse. Became stepfather to her five children, who later took the last name Mestad: Britha, Knut, Nils Storre, John, and Nils Vesle
• Lars Larson Rasdal Hjørnevik, Evanger, Voss *(and wife Anna Knutsdatter?)*
• Knud Nilsson Langeland, Evanger, Voss; wife Anna Knutsdatter Bjørgo, Evanger, and children: Anna, Martha, Aagaata, Julia, Nicolai Johan, and Knud
• Ole Estensen Lunaas (Ole Estensen Lunaashaug), Tynset; wife Anne Pedersdatter Kinndøl, children Esten and Ingeborg
• Ole Torgersen (possibly Ola Torgersen Trøeng), Tolga, Østerdalen; wife Kari, children: Sarah, Martin and Theander
• Anders Monson Gjersvoll (Anders Monson Gjersvold, Andrew Monson), Holtaalen, Sør-Trøndelag; wife Berit Johnsdatter and children: John, Mons, Dorothy, Mary and Anna
• Lars Halverson and family
• Anders Olson Kirkevoldsmoen (Anders Olson Kirkvold) and family
• Hans Kjøstelsen (Hans Chesterson); wife Marit Syversdatter and family
• Holsten Olson (Halsten Olson); wife Ingeborg Olsdatter Slaabakken and family

- Lars Olson and family
- K. Torreson (possibly Kolbein Torrison) and family

The movement of immigrants was halted for several years because of the Civil War. Nearly all able-bodied men were absent, fighting their adopted country's Civil War battles. However, this left the frontier settlement vulnerable to attack.

Fra Romsdalen: Troldtinderne

Great Sioux Uprising of 1862

The Indian war, which broke out in 1862, crushed the newly blooming settlement. The Indians laid a heavy hand on this small colony.

There were several causes for the Sioux Indian uprising. The Sioux land had been reduced to one-half its size by a treaty, in return for promised monetary and material compensation. Problems arose due to the high concentration of the Indians, a food shortage and exorbitant prices.

Unsympathetic Indian agents, with ample supplies and food, refused to give food to the Indians until their annuity money had arrived from Washington, D.C. The Indians had given up their hunting grounds, deeded their lands, and now were near starvation.

Frustrated and provoked by years of broken treaty promises, government lies and forced cultural change, the previously peaceful Sioux began a spontaneous bloody revolt in which more than 800 settlers and soldiers were slain in less than one week during August 1862.

More than 40,000 people fled their homes, depopulating 23 southwestern Minnesota counties. The tragic episode marked the outbreak of a series of Indian wars that did not end until nearly 30 years later at the Battle of Wounded Knee in South Dakota.

The 24 August 1862 Belmont Massacre in Jackson County was a part of the Great Sioux Uprising. Thirteen Belmont settlers were murdered in cold blood by a band of about 50 Indians, who went swiftly from cabin to cabin.

Holand's account in question

The book *History of Jackson County, 1910*, suggests that Holand's Belmont Massacre account, as it appears in *De Norske Settlementers Historie*, pp. 519–521, and in *Norwegians in America: The Last Migration*, pp. 173-176, is misleading.

The Jackson County history, published two years after Holand's *De Norske Settlementers Historie* (1910 vs. 1908, respectively), states: "For some reason, no authentic account of the Belmont Massacre has heretofore been written, and there is a wonderful lack of general knowledge of the details of the terrible affair. There are differences of authority even as to the date of the massacre in Jackson County.

"The inaccuracies of the printed accounts of the affair are shown in **bold** in the following extract from *Norwegian Settlers (Settlement) History*, published in the Norwegian language in 1908 by J. M. Holland, A. M., of Ephraim, Wisconsin *[note errors in Holand's name]*:

"On Sunday morning, 24 August 1862, before any preacher ever found his way to this wilderness, the new settlers, after having an abundant harvest, felt thankful and happy to God and **gathered for a prayer meeting in Mrs. Holsten Olson's house**.

"She had a sweet voice and had just finished a hymn when the door flew open and a half-grown boy, the son of Ole Forde (Ole Fyre), entered, dripping with sweat and blood. 'Hurry up! Hurry up!' he screamed, gasping for breath. 'The Indians are coming!'

"They were so astonished and frightened that they rushed to the door to escape, but ***they were too late. The Indians had surrounded the cabin.***

"Then followed a hopeless fight with bare fists against the Indians' bright tomahawks and bullets. The women's praying for mercy was mixed with the Indians' yells of exultation over their victory. The women were compelled to stand while the Indians took the children by their heels and crushed their skulls against the trees."

Actually, the home chosen for the meeting was that of Taral Ramlo, located south of where the massacre took place, NOT at Holsten Olson's house. This was not merely a worship service; this meeting had been called by Holsten Olson to discuss a dispute between two religious factions.

No fighting or killing took place at

the Ramlo place. The terrible bloodbath that claimed 13 lives actually took place to the north of the Ramlo farm, near and at the farms of the Langelands and the Fyres.

Because of conflicting reports, we have chosen to include the following eyewitness accounts, one a letter written a year after the event. Although based on memories, we believe the following first-hand stories may present a more accurate picture of what actually happened on that terrible day of 24 August 1862.

The Belmont Massacre, as witnessed by Nils Storre Mestad—part 1

Nils Storre Mestad, the older of the two brothers named Nils, was age 7 at the time of the massacre. He was among those hiding in a cellar when the massacre occurred overhead. A relative of Nils's, Kermit Mestad from Decorah, Iowa, gave the hand-written account to Deb Nelson Gourley. Nils was age 66 when the account appeared in the *Mason City Globe Gazette* on 26 March 1921. Gourley has identified and added the Norwegian names below in brackets:

"To my father's *[Johannes Ekse, stepfather]* homestead *[Ole Olson Fyre homestead—History of Jackson County, 1910]* on a Thursday in August 1862 came nine neighboring families, expecting an outbreak of the hostile Sioux. With the exception of one family, they left at dawn on the following Sunday *[24 August 1862]* to care for their stock.

"Shortly after they had gone, we became aware of a commotion among the cattle in a nearby lot. An old team of oxen was in a panic, horned heads held high and distended nostrils sniffing ominously in the direction of the wind.

"As Mother *[Brytteva Mestad]* stepped to the door to investigate, an Indian peered cautiously from behind a stump. Surmising that he had been observed, the savage arose to his feet and came boldly toward the house. His companions soon joined him as they leaped from behind the trees and quickly surrounded the house.

"A large chest in the dooryard (yard) attracted them. Shooting away the lock of the chest, they helped themselves to a small supply of tobacco and several gallons of liquor.

"There were nine loaded rifles in the house at the time, and Father made ready to protect his family and property; but Mother implored him not to use the guns, fearing that resistance would mean the death of us all. Mother and the other woman *[actually, two women, Mrs. Fyre and Anna Knutsdatter]*, together with the 10 [11] children, were hurried to the cellar beneath the cabin floor. Father and an 11-year-old boy *[the oldest of the two Fyre brothers, both of whom were named Ole Olson]* remained above to guard the doors.

"When admittance was refused them, three Indians leaped against the door, tearing the leather hinges from the jamb and breaking away the wooden latch. As they rushed inside, the boy ran through the opposite door and escaped to the woods; but Father was seized by the bloodthirsty trio and dragged outside. He was then taken a short distance from the house and, while two of them held him by his arms, the third savage shot him through the back with a carbine (a short-barreled rifle). *[Lars Larson Furrenæs, Lars Larson Rasdal Hjørnevik, and Ole Olson Fyre (the father) were shot. –History of Jackson County, 1910]*

Account of Ole Olson Fyre (older Ole brother)—part 1

According to *History of Jackson County, 1910*, one of the first acts of the savages was to search the wagons, which were loaded with provisions that had been brought from Mankato the day before.

Ole Olson Fyre, the older boy who was standing guard inside, bolted out the door and ran down a trail that led to a spring. An Indian saw him and fired; the bullet tore away the tip of the boy's right elbow. The boy then hid in some brush. Just as he was about to be discovered, the Indians at the cabin found a jug of whiskey. Their love of firewater saved Ole's life.

The older Ole boy ran to notify the other settlers of their danger. He headed for the home of Taral Ramlo, where a group of settlers were gathered for worship services. This meeting had been called by Holsten Olson in an attempt to consolidate two religious factions in the settlement. Holsten was the leader of one faction and Burre Olson of the other. (Burre did not attend, as he was holding a meeting at his house at the same time.)

At Ramlo's, the congregation was just beginning a hymn when the older Fyre boy burst in with the news that the Indians were murdering the settlers on the east side of the river. The bloody condition of the boy added to the alarm, and all was confusion. Fortunately, the Ramlo place, located on the southwest quarter of Section 34 on the west side of the river, escaped the awful carnage, as the Indians did not go farther south than Section 22.

Meanwhile, west of the Ole Fyre home, the Indians came upon Knut Mestad and his wife Brita and murdered them. *According to History of Jackson County, 1910,* these unfortunate people lived on the west side of the river, and were on their way to Ole Fyre's when they were ambushed on the trail.

Nils Storre Mestad—part 2

"At the report of the firearms, a 2-year-old child *[Johannes Larson; see "orphan child" writeup toward end of this chapter]* began to scream and cry. Knowing that the noise would betray the hiding place of her friends, the mother *[Anna Knutsdatter]* took her child and went to the room above. The infant continued to cry, and the noble woman walked from the room out into the yard.

"She was fired upon by the now drunken marauders, and at the seventh shot fell to her knees. The bloody work was finished at the chopping block with the axe in the hands of the same assassins that had taken Father's life. When the Indians staggered out of sight, the orphan baby crawled to its mother and cried itself to sleep at her side."

The next account is found on pp. 175-176 of *Norwegians in America: The Last Migration* by Hjalmar Rued Holand, translated by Helmer M. Blegen:

"The following day (25 August), all the survivors met at the post office in Jackson. Here it was resolved to move south to Estherville and warn the settlers there. Late that day, all set out on foot and succeeded, under the cover of darkness, in reaching Estherville, 20 miles away, early in the morning of the following day (26 August). They were given quarters in the schoolhouse.

"Exhausted from their long walk, they found a momentary release from their fatigue, sorrow and wretchedness in sleep on the floor of the schoolhouse.

"They did not rest there very long. Already that same day (26 August), a company of the neighborhood's men organized to march north again, and they left on the following day (27 August). First, they arranged to quarter all the women and children in the schoolhouse and in the two small houses, which constituted the entire town.

"Packed tightly together, they spent a whole week here. It was terribly crowded at night, but during daylight everybody, young and old, was busy with the construction of a log palisade around the three buildings, as a protection against attack.

"The men had gone north of Jackson to the Belmont settlement. Here they found 12 dead and two wounded. *[The wounded included two 11-year-old boys—Ole Olson Fyre (the older of the two brothers named Ole) and Anders E. Olson Slaabakken. The count does not include the two wounded Langeland children, one of whom died during the family's flight to Iowa. –Gourley]*

Ole Olson Fyre—part 2

History of Jackson County, 1910, tells the following story about one of the surviving children:

"Close to the Fyre home, Mikkel Olson Slaabakken was killed and his nephew Anders E. Olson Slaabakken, the 11-year-old son of Engebret Olson Slaabakken, was seriously wounded and left for dead. The Engebret Olson Slaabakken home was half a mile south of the Fyre home, and also in Section 22.

"About the time the attack was begun, Mikkel and his nephew started from that place for the home of Ole Fyre. They heard the firing but thought nothing of it, as they supposed the neighbors were shooting blackbirds. They soon became aware of the seriousness of their condition.

"The Indians were stationed along the trails in the timber, and the unfortunate white men were soon discovered. The savages fired, and the white men set out on a run through the timber. Mikkel was hit at the first fire and exclaimed: 'I am wounded and cannot run any farther.' Immediately he was hit again and killed instantly.

"A bullet from the first volley passed through the hat brim of the boy, and a moment later another one inflicted a slight scalp wound, plowing a furrow through his hair. Anders was not stunned or badly hurt, but he was so scared that he fell and lay with his face to the ground. The savages came up and one of them plunged a knife into his left side and, as the victim described the event in after years, 'twisted it around before he pulled it out.'

"The Indians left him for dead, and Anders lost consciousness. When he came to his senses, he crawled to his father's home. There was no one there; the Indians had visited the place and taken everything in the line of provisions. The wounded boy made his way to the log stable and hid in a manger, where he remained three days with nothing to eat except two raw eggs.

"When the cows came home at night, he tried to milk them, but they would not allow him to approach them on account of the blood on his clothes.

"From the time of the attack on Sunday until Wednesday, Anders remained in the manger, when he was found by a rescuing party and taken to Estherville, where he slowly recovered form his wounds."

"When the Jackson settlers returned from their rescue mission, they found that their houses and grain stacks had been burned and their cattle driven off. They also heard that the nearest town of any importance, New Ulm, had suffered two severe attacks, during which the entire town had been burned, and that all the people of the town had fled to other places for protection.

"Now that they had lost everything—homes, food supplies and cattle—they resolved to move back east to Winneshiek County, Iowa.

"The Estherville people did not move away. They still had their homes, and they would defend them as long as it was possible. After a week of difficult existence in their wretched fortress in town, in a hysterical and unbearable concentration in too-restricted quarters, the Norwegians of the group moved back to their homes and stayed there.

"But for a long time life was filled with fear and anxiety. Every time they looked out over the prairie, they thought they could see something suspicious moving out there, and then they feared that a new attack was imminent.

"Often at night, they would awaken and hear the wind howling about the houses. And, breathless, they would lie there waiting to hear the wild war whoops of the Indians."

[After the Belmont Massacre, many of the Slaabakkens moved back to Jackson County. Active in their community, they helped tell the story of what happened that bloody day of 24 August 1862. As for Anders Olson Slaabakken, he, too, returned to Jackson County.

After his father's death, he became the owner of the Belmont farm. Anders died on 26 September 1885. –Gourley]

Nils Storre Mestad's account continues: "An hour elapsed before we ventured from the cellar. The sleeping child *[Johannes Larson]* had just been carried in when a girl *[Martha Langeland]*, half crazed with fright, came screaming from the woods.

Langeland account

The following account was given to Deb Nelson Gourley by Tom Atkins, a descendant of Julia Langeland:

"Knud Langeland, his wife Anna Langeland and their six children resided in Belmont Township. On Sunday morning, 24 August, Knud discovered that his cattle had broken out of the rail pen. He went to search for them, which took hours before he found them. Although he heard shots at a distance, Knud knew his two oldest daughters had gone into the cornfield to chase off blackbirds.

"While in the cornfield, Anna Langeland (age 9) and Martha Langeland (age 8) heard their mother scream. They ran to the edge of the field and saw Indians by the house. Daughter Anna ran to the house, where she was shot by Indians, who also shot her mother, Anna. Martha instead turned and ran farther into the cornfield to hide and then make her way to the Ole Fyre cabin.

"Meanwhile, after Knud Langeland found and chased his cattle to the pen,

Et Overfald af Indianere

he walked into his house and saw a frightful sight. Six dear ones lay on the floor, four of whom were dead. Knud thought he saw life in two of the children, Julia (age 3) and a younger boy.

"Knud took them up in his arms and hurried to the timber by the Des Moines River. He crossed the river, walked over the prairie and continued without food or drink until he arrived at Spirit Lake, Iowa.

"On that 26-mile walk, Knud's wounded boy died, but Julia was revived. Julia and her little brother had been grabbed at the feet and their heads bashed on a chopping block that stood near them. *[The Indians did not typically waste bullets on the children.]*

"Martha remained in the cornfield until she walked into a neighbor's field where two women and some children, who came from hiding in a cellar, saw her. The small group proceeded toward Estherville, Iowa."

Nils Storre Mestad's—part 3

"Bewildered by the tragedy that had just occurred, unnerved by the fearful sight in the front yard and utterly weighed down by the responsibility now confronting her, Mother was as helpless as the frightened brood under her care. What hope was left; how to continue with 10 *[11]* little children, all under 12, was too much for the half-demented mind to grasp.

"The initiative was taken by the children themselves. At the first sound of the war whoop of the returning Sioux,

Midnatssolen

we ran to the cornfield and scattered like quail between the rows, followed by Mother *[and Mrs. Fyre]* and a girl *[Martha Langeland]* of mature years *[actually only 8 years old]*.

"We remained hidden until night. When darkness came, we started on our flight. Mother knew that somewhere to the south was a frontier town, and in that direction we laid our course. Through the tangled underbrush of the wilderness and fallen trees and across damp, boggy forest swamps we crept slowly on. We knew not at what moment a lusty savage might appear in our path.

"At times we saw the lurid light of burning cabins fired by the Indians and heard their savage yells of death and victory as we stole along through the ghostly gloom. Every step was a death peril, and when morning came (25 August), we had covered scarcely five miles.

"At dawn we hid again in a field of corn. Half naked, hungry and utterly exhausted, the children began to cry for food and water. There were springs near the river, but we dared not venture that way, for we knew the red man's haunts lay along the watercourse.

"When our cries became too piteous, Mother (both women) tore a sleeve from her dress and with it mopped up the dew on the grass and leaves of the corn into a little tin pan that a child had carried with her all the way. The drops of water were thus gathered one by one, and before the sun had dissipated the morning dew, our thirst was in a measure appeased."

"Subsisting on the soft, green, uncooked corn and drinking the morning dew for three days and three nights, we continued our plight from our plundered homes."

"On Wednesday morning, we were discovered by a small detachment of U.S. Cavalry sent out to gather in survivors of the massacre. On their approaching the edge of a prairie opening, we darted into the underbrush like hunted fowl, thinking they were Indians. After a time, we were rounded up and soon realized that it was a rescue party of whites and not a capture by the red foe.

"In due time, we were placed in great Army wagons and taken overland at government expense back to our former homes in Winneshiek County, Iowa. It was a long, long trip through central *[southern]* Minnesota and across the prairies of *[northern]* Iowa, but the soldiers were kind and fed us well on their course fare of beans, corn, bread and milk. Mother was paid $400 by the federal government to reimburse her for improvements on the abandoned homestead."

Ole Olson Fyre—part 3

The journey of Nils Storre Mestad's mother, Brytteva Mestad, Mrs. Fyre and the children (including Nils) is further described by Ole F. Forde (Ole Olson Fyre) in an account found in the files of the *Historical Data Project*, Bismarck, North Dakota:

"Four of the children were not big enough to walk. A younger boy (the younger of the two Ole Olson brothers), age 9, transported two of the children while the other two women each carried one.

"To carry these two children, he would take one in his arms, run ahead some 25 to 50 rods (425 to 825 feet), put the child down, and then run back and get the other child.

"The boy, Ole (older of the two Ole Olson brothers), who had been given up for dead, joined the group a week after the massacre."

Massacre memories of Mons Monson

The following, from the *Biography of Andrew Monson and Beret Monson*, was given to Deb Nelson Gourley by LaVerna Moothart, author of *Norway to Montana: Monson-Thompson Levang, 2002*. The Monson family moved from Allamakee County, Iowa, to Jackson County in June 1861:

"On 24 August 1862, a German, fleeing from New Ulm, brought the news to the settlers that the Indians were on the warpath and had attacked New Ulm, destroying considerable property, killing people and coming south. The settlers gathered at different cabins at night, which seemed to give better protection, and returned to their homes in the morning.

"In the evening of 25 August 1862, some of the settlers saw smoke to the north, and they knew it was smoke from an Indian bonfire. Several of the settlers went to the home of Mr. Thomas in Jackson, which afforded better protection.

"Our oxen were feeding about three-quarters of a mile from our house. B. Burreson, who was visiting with Father *[Andrew Monson]* when we came home, went after the oxen and hooked them to the wagon. We loaded Father *[who was disabled]* into it and started for the Thomas place, a mile south of where we lived.

"In a short time, some of the people living to the north of us also began to arrive. Some were on foot and some with ox teams. It was agreed that we should stay here at the Thomas home and fight the Indians.

"Mr. Thomas had a big house and barn. Jim Farmer and the Thomas boys had three guns, two bars of lead and some powder. Some of the men made bullets, and some cut portholes in the house and barn. The younger boys were sent out in the cornfields to gather in corn for food.

"About sundown, some of the men backed out and would not stay, so we all started for the place that is now Estherville, Iowa, 20 miles south of the town of Jackson. There were about a dozen families living there.

"We then sent a man on horseback to Spirit Lake, Iowa, to notify the 20 soldiers who were stationed there. The soldiers arrived on Tuesday (26 August) morning, took our men with them and started for Jackson County. On the following Monday, 1 September, we all started out for the vicinity of Decorah, Iowa."

1863 letter describes massacre (written by Ole Estensen Lunaas)

Karl Jakob Skarstein discovered the following account by Ole Estensen Lunaas at the Norwegian-American Historical Association (NAHA), St. Olaf College, Northfield, Minnesota, and gave a copy to Deb Nelson Gourley. The letter (a portion of which is printed here) was originally written to Ole Estensen's relatives in Norway on 18 December 1863, a little over one year after the massacre. J. A. Renolen transcribed the text from Old German to Norwegian in 1936; James Skurdall translated the account to English in 2005 and made the following remarks in brackets.

"18 December 1863
Hesper, Iowa

"To E. Embresen Lunaavug, my good friend and relative! *[A footnote reads (in translation): "This should no doubt be written as E. Embresen Lunaashaug."]*

"I received your welcome letter dated 12 March. Thank you ever so much. We were pleased to see that you have been doing well and enjoying good health. We can say the same for ourselves, as we have had good health up to now.

"We have been through some hardships, of course, since I last wrote to you. Then I was in Jackson County. We did not make the move out of necessity, but rather because we hoped to acquire government land. Indeed, we found as fine land as we could have wished for, and not yet inhabited.

"Then last summer we had to leave because of the Indians, who had begun to murder white settlers and plunder their farms. We feared the Southerners were the cause of it all.

"We received word on the 22nd of August that they *[the Indians]* had begun to murder settlers, but it was 60 English (nine Norwegian) miles from where we lived. We and the neighbors decided to gather at one place to defend ourselves.

"On the 23rd we loaded our most important possessions onto wagons and planned to meet half a Norwegian mile from where I lived. But we took some time rounding up the cattle, so it was late, and after we had gone a ways, some of the animals ran back. As it was already dark, we decided to return home until the following morning.

"Besides myself, our group consisted of Ole Torgersen and the Tolgens (Tolga) family from Hodalen (Holtaalen). The latter stayed at my place for the night, but Ole continued on to his own farm.

"Before our departure the next morning (24 August), while the women were preparing breakfast, I took my rifle and went down to the river. It flowed approximately 400 feet from the house and was always full of wild geese and ducks.

"As soon as I reached the river, I heard five gunshots fired in such quick succession that I could scarcely count them, and with such force that the earth shook. They came from the direction of my house. I returned immediately to see if the shots had been fired near my house, but no one had heard anything. I ordered them to prepare to leave at once and told them I would go over to Ole Torgersen's.

"Then I went to the barn to feed the pigs, and as I opened the barn door I heard four gunshots from the same direction. I immediately sensed that something was wrong. As we were about to leave, we spotted four persons on the other side of the river, standing completely still. They were Indian scouts.

"When we arrived at Ole Torgersen's, he told us he had also seen someone, but having heard nothing more, he assumed it was some of our neighbors who had gone to check on us.

I expressed my doubt, for they had seen me, and had they been neighbors, they would have signaled to me in some way.

"Ole believed the shots I had heard had been fired by soldiers. We were waiting for a detachment to arrive. But they...*[this is a translation of a transcription of the original letter made in 1936 by J. A. Renolen, who was unable to decipher the entire text]*...so that I was inclined to believe it. We dared not leave. The direction in which we intended to travel was the very direction from which I had heard the gunshots, and there was no other route to take.

"We remained at Ole's until after 5 in the afternoon (24 August), and then I asked everyone to follow me home. This we did, as it was but a short distance between the farms. Then I proposed that Ole and I should look after the animals, and perhaps we would spot some of the neighbors.

"We had not gone far before we caught sight of two persons at least 1,200 feet from us. We signaled to them as we approached each other. When finally only the river separated us, we recognized them as two Indians. They fled, and we returned home in all haste. Everyone spent the night in my house. No one ventured out. Only two of us could offer appreciable resistance. The women were frightened to death and incapable of helping.

"The next morning (25 August), everything was calm. But as I sat on the doorstep around noon, the dogs suddenly began barking in an unusual manner. I stood up at once and saw five of the redskins near the house, moving in close formation.

"I ran in and grabbed my rifle, and when I turned toward the door, I saw that little Ingeborg *[Ingeborg Estensen]* and Martin *[Martin Torgersen]*, the son of Ole Torgersen, were standing close to the entrance. I dropped my rifle and fetched them in, but in the meantime, the redskins circled around to the back of the house. We had no chance to let them know how many rifles we had *[this sentence seems to have posed a problem for the transcriber].*

"They *[Indians]* crawled back a few yards to find cover, then began firing at both windows and continued for two hours. As Ole and I kept watch, ready to return fire, a bullet missed my

En Indianerlejr ved Fort Snelling, Minnesota

head by barely an inch. We feared they might storm the house, but they would have turned pale before reaching the inside, for we had weapons enough. When they began shooting, all fear seemed to vanish.

"Finally, they left *[the person transcribing had a problem here]* my house and continued on to Ole Torgersen's place, where they destroyed everything. They murdered 12 *[13]* of our closest neighbors on the 24th of August—five men *[six men]*, three women and four children, all from Voss in Norway with the exception of one, Mikkel Olson Slaabakken, Tolgen (Tolga).

"We remained in my house until 26 August, when soldiers arrived. We took livestock and household goods with us, but the crops had to be left behind. Worst of all was the hay, which later burned. We later resettled here *[Hesper, Iowa]*, and since then I have been farming leased land close to our first farm. ..."

The letter continues with a description of the land in Iowa, weather and economic conditions, and urges the Norwegian recipient of the letter to emigrate to the U.S.

The letter is signed thus:
"Yours most gratefully, Ole Estensen Lunaas (and) Anne Pedersdatter"

[Ole Estensen Lunaas/Ole Estensen Lunaashaug was born 15 March 1834, Tynset. His parents were Esten Oleson, born 1792, Vingelen, and Ingeborg Embretsdatter Lonaas, born 1801, Tynset. Ole's wife was Anne Pedersdatter Kinndøl, born 14 Jan 1831, Tynset. Sources: Tynset Bygdebok II: (p. 234, Haugen Gn98-bn20), (p. 250, Lonaasen Østre Gn98-bn33), (p. 385, Kinndøl Nørdre Gn117-bn1 –Gourley]

Fate of the survivors

When it was all over, the surviving panic-stricken Norwegians fled back, mainly to Winneshiek County, Iowa, and Houston County, Minnesota, leaving their homes to be plundered and destroyed by the Indians.

The Slaabakken family, which later took the name Olson, returned in a little caravan of ox teams for the purpose of taking care of the cattle, which were reported to be roaming about without food. On their return trip, they prepared to camp for the night in Jackson.

While the men were gone for water, a terrific prairie fire swept down from the northeast and enveloped the campers. As a result of this tragedy, Holsten Olson was burned so badly he was permanently disfigured, and Mrs. Engebret Olson Slaabakken and her baby died as a result of their burns.

By the time the Norwegian settlers returned, nearly all trace of the earlier settlement had disappeared. Cattle were gone, pioneer cabins burned either by Indians or prairie fires, and the cultivated acres had returned to Nature's harsh care.

One group of pioneers found that their hogs, which had been left behind, were roaming the woods in a wild state. For several years the hunting of wild swine furnished sport for the settlers.

An account from *Historie om Udvandringen fra Voss og Vossingerne i Amerika*, 1930, pp. 643, 417 and 418, further tells the fate of the two Ole brothers and the Langeland family:

"Ole Olson (Fyre), the older Ole brother, was treated by a doctor in Spirit Lake, but the doctor wanted to amputate the arm. This the mother would not allow. After this, he was treated by Dr. Billington of Decorah, Iowa, and he recovered.

"In 1873, he entered matrimony with Betsie Nilsdatter Gilderhus, daughter of Koshkonong's first pioneer, Nils Sjurson Gilderhus. First, they claimed a homestead, but sold this; Ole has worked for the Great Northern Railway since. He lives in Wyndmere, North Dakota, and had seven children: Martha, Ragnild, Nellie, Albert, Seward, Oscar and Albin.

"Ole Olson the younger, who was in the cellar during the massacre, was one of the first pioneers in Sogn, Nelson

Ashley Park Monument located in Jackson, Minnesota
• • • • •

"Erected by the State of Minnesota in the year 1909, to the memory of the pioneer settlers of Jackson County, whose names are inscribed below, massacred by the Sioux Indians in 1857 and 1862":

28 March 1857 massacre:
• William Wood
• Joshua Stewart
• George Wood
• Willie Thomas
• Two children of Joshua Stewart

24 August 1862 massacre:
• Ole Fohre (Ole Olson Fyre)
• Mikkel Olson (Mikkel Olson Slaabakken)
• Johanes Axe (Johannes Knutson Ekse)
• Knud Middssad (Knut Haldorson Ro Mestad) and wife Brita Andersdatter Røte Mestad)
• Brita Langeland (Anna Knutsdatter Bjørgo Langeland, the mother)
• Aagaata Langeland (Aagaata Knutsdatter Langeland, child)
• Anna Langeland (Anna Knutsdatter Langeland, child)
• Nickolai Langeland (Nicolai Johan Langeland, child)
• Knud Langeland (Knut Knutson Langeland, child)
• Lars Gjornevik and wife (Lars Larson Rasdal Hjørnevik, and Anna Knutsdatter** *[unknown whether she is the wife of Lars Hjørnevik or Lars Furrenæs]*)
• Lars Furness (Lars Larson Furrenæs/Lars Larson Furnes)

24 August 1862 wounded children who survived:
• Ole Olson Fyre (Ole F. Forde), the older Olson brother—age 11
• Anders Engebretson Slaabakken (Anders E. Olson)—age 11
• Julia Langeland—age 3

County, North Dakota. He held the position of county assessor.

"Knud Langeland lived in Big Canoe, Winneshiek County, Iowa, with his two surviving daughters until 1870 *[1872]*, when he again moved west. He lived the rest of his life with his daughter Julia Langeland, the one he had carried to Spirit Lake. *[Julia was survived by one daughter, Josephine Langeland Franz.]*

"Daughter Martha married George Peter Sivertson *[from Tøttdal in Fosnes]* and lived in the Westbrook, Cottonwood County with their six children *[Knute, John, Petra, Agita Julianna (Gertie), Anna, and Mabel]*."

Monument honors the dead

A monument located in Ashley Park, Jackson, Minnesota (left), commemorates those who died in both the 1857 and 1862 Indian massacres. In addition to those killed in 1862, three wounded children survived.

Johannes Larson, Belmont Massacre orphan
• • • • •

After Brytteva Mestad and Mrs. Fyre rescued the newly orphaned baby, Johannes Larson *[great-great-grandfather to Deb Nelson Gourley]*, the child was taken to Black Hammer Township, Houston County, Minnesota. Lars Nilsson Ekse (first cousin to Johannes Knutson Ekse) and his wife, Anne Eriksdatter Berdal, raised the orphan child.

But who were the actual parents of the baby? We know that his mother, Anna Knutsdatter, was murdered on 24 August 1862, sacrificing her own life to keep those hiding in the cellar safe from detection by the rampaging Indians.

The orphan's parents are believed to be one of the following two couples:
• Lars Larson Furrenæs (Furnes) and possibly Anna Knutsdatter Langeland, Evanger
• Lars Larson Rasdal Hjørnevik and possibly Anna Knutsdatter Rjodo Rio, Voss

On 26 September 1861, eight baptisms were performed at Jackson County, Minnesota. Only a few days later, on 30 September 1861, three more baptisms were held to the south in Estherville, Emmet County, Iowa.

One of the children listed as being baptized in Jackson County was Johannes Larson (#523—see chart on page 336). The records show a January 1861 birth with the parents being listed as Lars Larson and Anna Knutsdatter.

It is believed that two Lars Larsons and only one Anna Knutsdatter (unknown last name) lived on the same site, NW1/4, Section 16, Belmont Township. All three of the adults were killed in the Belmont Massacre, leaving the orphan child, Johannes Larson.

Two of the four baptism sponsors of Johannes Larson were relatives:
• Ragnild Knutsdatter Langeland Ekse (sister to Anna Knutsdatter Langeland)
• Knud Langeland (second cousin to Lars Larson Rasdal Hjørnevik) and Knud's wife, Anna
• Ole Olson Fyre

In 1882, at age 21, Johannes Larson married a niece to Lars Nilsson Ekse, Ingeborg Nielsdatter Ekse, in Houston County. Ingeborg was the daughter of Nils Nilsson Ekse and Kari Hermundsdatter Nese.

Johannes farmed near Black Hammer and was a rattlesnake hunter. Although bitten three times, he died of natural causes at age 47.

Early baptisms performed at home

The following information was supplied by Ruth Hackett, genealogy researcher, Estherville, Iowa:

When the Lars Paulson Troo (Lars Paulson Trøos) and Niels Peterson Brugjeld families arrived at the village of Estherville, Iowa, on 23 June 1860, there was no minister.

Passing through St. Ansgar on their way to Emmet County, Lars talked with Pastor C. L. Clausen and invited him to come to the new settlement to which they were heading.

When a son was born to Lars (see #525 in box), the child was baptized at home *(hjemmedøpt)* by one P. M. Osfwed (Osswed). The infant son of Niels (see #526) was baptized at home by his father.

When Clausen came in September, he rebaptized the children as well as performing a marriage of a young couple and a confirmation. He did not return to Estherville until two years later; there were few visits from ordained ministers in those early years. Meanwhile, families gathered in homes for devotions and Sunday school, and baptisms were done at home; children were rebaptized when a pastor could be located.

Eleven 1861 home baptism records from the Jackson County, Minnesota, and Estherville, Emmet County, Iowa, Norwegian pioneer immigrant settlements were recorded in the First Lutheran Church, St Ansgar, Iowa, by Rev. C. L. Clausen on page 122, # 517 – # 527. They were discovered by Deb Nelson Gourley and her mother, Char (Knudson) Nelson. *[Note: Last names were not included in the original baptismal records; they have been added to the chart purely for identification purposes]*

Other sources for this chapter:
• *Historie om Udvandringen fra Voss*, 1930, by K. A. Rene, translated by Stanley J. Nuland, M.D, pp. 641-644
• *History of Jackson County*, 1910, by Arthur P. Rose, Chapter VII: The Norwegian Settlement 1860-1862 and Chapter VIII: The Belmont Massacre 1862, pp. 93-109
• *Krigen mot Siouxene - Nordmenn mot Indianere*, 2005, by Karl Jakob Skarstein, pp. 105-117
• *Nordmændene i Amerika*, Volume 1, 1907, by Martin Ulvestad, pp. 99-100
• Research assistance by Margit Bakke, Viggo Fosse, Ruth Hackett, Blaine Hedberg, Gunnar Hjørnevik, Knut Hjørnevik, Anita Særvold Johannessen, Jean Marthaler, Char Nelson, Karl Jakob Skarstein and Jo Ann B. Winistorfer

*Eleven 1861 home baptism records from Jackson County, Minnesota, and Estherville, Emmet County, Iowa

517 – **Ingeborg Anne**, born 25 Feb. 1861, Jackson County, Minnesota. Hjemmedøpt av Børre Olsen Ramlo, rebaptized 26 Sept. 1861. Parents: Tarald Halstensen Ramlo and Marit Halvorsdatter Stene. Sponsors: Anders Olsen and wife, John Svendsen Ramlo and wife Kari Hansdatter Megard

518 – **Beritre Marie**, born 4 Aug. 1861, Jackson County, Minnesota. Hjemmedøpt av Børre Olsen Ramlo, rebaptized 26 Sept. 1861. Parents: John Svendsen Ramlo and Kari Hansdatter Megard. Sponsors: Ole Pedersen and wife, Hans Johnsen and wife

519 – **Børre**, born 20 Dec. 1860, Jackson County, Minnesota. Hjemmedøpt av Ole Pedersen, rebaptized 26 Sept. 1861. Parents: Hans Johannesen Lien and Gjertrud Børresdatter. Sponsors: Børre Olsen Ramlo and wife, Christen Torrisen and wife

520 – **Knud**, born 26 Juli 1861, Jackson County, Minnesota. Baptized 26 Sept. 1861. Parents: Knud Nielsen Langeland and Anna Knutsdatter Bjørgo. Sponsors: Ole Olsen Fyre and wife Kari Nielsdatter Horvei, Lars Larson *[Furrenæs or Hjørnevik?]* and wife Anna Knutsdatter

521 – **Niels**, born 15 Apr. 1861, Jackson County, Minnesota. Hjemmedøpt av Barnet's Fader, rebaptized 26 Sept. 1861. Parents: Ole Olsen Fyre and Kari Nielsdatter Horvei. Sponsors: Knud Nielsen Langeland, Lars Askjelsen Lid Lee and wife Ingebjørg Olsdatter Fyre, Kari Nielsdatter Horvei

522 – **Anne**, born 28 Aug. 1861, Jackson County, Minnesota. Hjemmedøpt av Børre Olsen Ramlo, rebaptized 26 Sept. 1861. Parents: Anders Monsen and Berit Johnsdatter. Sponsors: Børre Olsen Ramlo and wife Guri Estensdatter Nysetvold, Arne Sjursen and Anna Ingebrigtsdatter

523 – **Johannes** *[Belmont Massacre orphan]* born 14 or 24 Jan. 1861, Jackson County, Minnesota. Hjemmedøpt av Børre Olsen Ramlo, rebaptized 26 Sept. 1861. Parents: Lars Larson *[Furrenæs or Hjørnevik?]* and Anna Knutsdatter. Sponsors: Ole Olsen Fyre, Knud Nielsen Langeland and wife Anna Knutsdatter Bjørgo, Ragnild Knudsdatter Langeland, wife of Jacob Nielsen Ekse

524 – **Petrea**, born 9 Mai 1861, Jackson County, Minnesota. Hjemmedøpt av Ingebrigt Olsen Slaabakken, rebaptized 26 Sept. 1861. Parents: John Olsen and Anna Pedersdatter. Sponsors: Ingebright Olsen Slaabakken and wife, Anders Olsen and Barnet's Moder

525 – **Svend Edward**, born 12 Jan. 1861, Estherville, Emmet County, Iowa. Hjemmedøpt av P. M. Osfwed (Osswed), rebaptized 30 Sept. 1861. Parents: Lars Paulsen Troo and Guri Syvertsdatter Sundbrei. Sponsors: P. M. Osfwed (Osswed), Ole Knutsen, Birgith Olsdatter and Barnet's Moder

526 – **Peder**, born 22 Feb. 1861, Estherville, Emmet County, Iowa. Hjemmedøpt av Barnet's Fader, rebaptized 30 Sept. 1861. Parents: Niels Pedersen Brugjeld and Britha Olsdatter Erikson Rauboti. Sponsors: Ole Ingebrigtsen, Torrild Nielsen, Haldis Olsdatter and Barnet's Moder

527 – **Niels**, born 6 Juni 1861, Estherville, Emmet County, Iowa. Hjemmedøpt av Salve Slouge Pladsen, rebaptized 30 Sept. 1861. Parents: Torrild Nielsen and Anna Svendsdatter. Sponsors: Lars Paulsen Troo, Helge Olsen, Hanne Pedersdatter and Barnet's Moder

Norsk translation: (Fad = Fader = Father); (Mod = Moder = Mother); (Barn = Child); (Hjemmedøpt av = Baptized at home by); (Barnet's Fader = Child's father) (Barnet's Moder = Child's mother)

55

Largest Norwegian Settlement in America, central Minnesota

(Source: De Norske Settlementers Historie, by Hjalmar Rued Holand, translated by Malcolm Rosholt, 1908, pp. 532–537)

Running directly through the middle of Minnesota from Mankato to St. Cloud, north to south, stood a huge forest, which was named the "Big Woods." It was about 100 miles long and from 10 to 14 miles east to west. For many years it served as something of a wall blocking immigration to the west.

Northwest of this line of trees lies the widely known and extensive Lake Park region of Minnesota. From a farmer's point of view, this region is a series of rolling prairies covered with a black and fertile soil, interspersed by several thousand lakes of all shapes and sizes.

100,000 Norwegians

In this charming territory, the Norwegians have their principal place in America. Nearly all of the many lakes are surrounded by Norwegian homes, and nearly the whole of Lake Park region is owned and populated by no less than 100,000 Norsemen who cleared the land and built their homes.

This contiguous settlement reaches from Litchfield and Willmar in Minnesota to McHenry and Osnabrock in North Dakota *[east of Minot –Rosholt]*. Norwegians own nine out of 10 farms through this general area. No less than 10 large connecting counties are so overwhelmingly populated by Norwegians that local government is almost entirely in their hands. The many Norwegian places names are a witness to their presence.

When Norman County, Minnesota, was organized, for example, a man from Telemark christened it, and county government was almost entirely in the hands of *Telemarkinger*. [But no one would guess that the name Norman in this instance came from Nordman, meaning man from the north. –Rosholt]

When the settlers of Pope County decided to establish county government, a man from Sogn sat on a stump and officiated as president of the assembly. A man from Setesdal sat on a log with a board over his knee to act as recording secretary. And a man from Valdres served as speaker, while sober delegates who once hailed from Gudbrandsdal and Nord-Trøndelag and Sør-Trøndelag carried on the business of the meeting.

In the beginning, justice was administered out of Willmar, where a typical case might involve a Dane as prosecuting attorney, a Norwegian as defense counsel, a Norwegian as clerk of court and a Norwegian judge.

Often, one of the parties could not make himself clear in English (which, for the most part, seemed to be an unnecessary language in these circumstances). But the law was written in English and enforced in English. And even if someone had to be called to act as interpreter, the proceedings were carried on in English.

Ole Næss and his settlement

The first Norwegian to find his way west of the "Big Woods" was Ole Halvorson Næss from Hallingdal. He became the founder of the biggest and most handsome of all Norwegian settlements. He was accompanied by the following:

• Henrik Halvorsen Thoen, Hallingdal

- Ole Halvorsen Thoen, Hallingdal
- Kittil Haraldson Rauk, Hallingdal
- Nils Hanson Golberg, Hallingdal
- Gunder Olson, Hallingdal
- Amund Nilsen Fosen, Eker

This party of immigrants came up from Rock Prairie in Wisconsin in July 1856 and settled near the future city of Litchfield.

It was 400 miles from Rock Prairie to Litchfield, and the last half of the distance ran through a stretch of land that was then still open to settlers. But Ole Næss was quite fussy in the choice of his future home and was not satisfied until he had reached the delightful surroundings of Meeker County *[west of Minneapolis about 60 miles –Rosholt]*.

Red River caravans

Until Ole Næss and his companions found their way through the "Big Woods" and arrived at Parkland's fascinating plains, no white man had ever settled here permanently.

No doubt fur buyers for the Hudson Bay Company had crossed this region. Twenty years earlier, a regular freight service had been maintained through here from Fort Snelling to a lonely trading post 400 miles north in Canada.

The Red River caravans, as they were known, wound around Parkland's lakes on the early marches out of Snelling. These caravans consisted of 30 to 60 high-wheeled carts with wooden axles, which creaked and squeaked without grease.

Coming down from Canada, the carts were loaded with hides and pelts, while on the homeward trip they carried clothing and finery for the Indians, food for the working people and whiskey for everyone. Often in these early years, the new settlers were frightened in the middle of the night when they heard creaking carts and shouts of men, which naturally sounded twice as loud and frightening in the dark.

Norwegians first to till the soil

Stray hunters and townsite speculators could have been here first. But until Ole Næss and his comrades set plow in the ground, no white men had tilled the soil of the Lake Park region.

These *Hallinger* were very satisfied with their new surroundings. The following year, Ole Næss wrote an article for *Emigranten* that created considerable interest. As a result, many more courageous pioneers followed him and founded new colonies nearby.

For a few years, the influx of immigrants was halted by the Indian wars that left the entire region a wasteland and cost nearly a thousand lives, many of them Norwegian.

The dates of Parkland's real beginning are the years 1865-66. The Civil War was at an end, and tried and tested combat veterans of the war now began to look to the wilderness for a place to begin life anew. These men had felt the sting of bullets and tortures of imprisonment, and now they would have a chance to taste the hardships of the frontier and the wiles of the Indians. So many old soldiers were among the first settlers on Parkland that a list of their names would sound like a roll call of the 15th Regiment of Volunteers.

Farther and farther out into the frontier they went, stubbornly unafraid, beating a track for later generations to follow.

56
Norway Lake and surroundings, Kandiyohi County, central Minnesota
(Source: De Norske Settlementers Historie, by Hjalmar Rued Holand, translated by Malcolm Rosholt, 1908, pp. 538–565)

Among all of Parkland's distinguished pioneers, none are better known than the brothers Anders Railson Glesne (Anders Railson) and Even Railson Glesne (Even Railson) of Norway Lake, Kandiyohi County, Minnesota. Their mature personalities, extensive activities and hospitality have put them in a class with the old Viking chiefs of Norway. The two brothers, especially Even, are considered to be the county's Norwegian founders.

Kandiyohi's first Norwegians

Even Railson was not the first Norseman to visit this beautiful county, as he himself has admitted. Lars Endresen Rosseland and Syver Endresen Rosseland from Vikør in Hardanger were first. They settled on Solomon Lake, six or seven miles north of Willmar, on 12 August 1857. Three years later, Indians killed Lars Endresen.

Lars was married to the heroic Guri Rosseland. Syver Endreson Rosseland and Guri's brother, Amund A. Rosseland, were the first to leave from Vikør for the U.S. in 1837. *[A footnote by Holand: "Amund A. Rosseland was in the first party of Norwegians to visit Koshkonong, in 1840, but he did not wish to stay there. He settled temporarily on Jefferson Prairie but left in 1843, moving through the entire length of Columbia County's fruitful acres to find a home on some yellow sand hills west of the Wisconsin River, halfway between Baraboo and Wisconsin Dells."]*

Berger Thorson and Nils Olson Alvik, Hardanger people, arrived in Kandiyohi County a week after the Endresons. Thorson took a claim on the south side of Foot Lake, where the city of Willmar was later built. Indians killed him three years later.

[Holand says the Indians killed Thorson in the Indianerkrigen, which could mean the Indian war that began in 1862, or in earlier raids. Thus the expression "three years later" presumably refers to three years after 1857, which would be circa 1860. –Rosholt]

Meanwhile, Nils Olson Alvik went to Alexandria, Minnesota, in 1860, where he became the first Norseman in Douglas County. These four men—the two Endresons plus Thorson and Alvik—all moved to western Minnesota from the small colony founded by Amund Rosseland near Wisconsin Dells.

In the years following, many people from Hardanger joined the settlement around Willmar. Several Lutheran congregations there are made up, for the most part, of Hardanger people, especially from Vikør.

Among other early arrivals to Willmar may be mentioned Asbjørn Erikson (Oskar Erikson) from Rykken, who came in July 1859, and Lars Larson Rosseland, who came in 1860. Lars had scarcely got his nice log house ready when the Indian wars began and he had to flee. While he was away, someone even stole his house.

Even Railson's race

It was in the latter part of the summer of 1858 that Even Railson first visited Kandiyohi County. Born on the Glesne farm in Krødsherad, Sigdal, on 27 December 1830, he came to the U.S. in 1850 and settled at Jordan on the out-

skirts of Wiota in Lafayette County, Wisconsin.

Later, Railson came to read the rosy reports about the Lake Park region of Minnesota, which Ole Næss had written for *Emigranten* in 1857. Together with Ole Walhovd, Anders Walhovd and Emil Falk, three *Landinger*, Railson decided to visit the region.

The quartet traveled on foot 400 miles and finally reached the place of Ole Næss in Meeker County. Tired and irritable after the long journey, they did not find the land to their liking.

"Okay, then," said Ole Næss, "why not go to Eagle Lake?"

The newcomers took his advice. After 30 miles of wandering around, they came to a lake where three Swedish families had settled. The four men had had nothing to eat on the way and were both tired and hungry.

But here they ran into another problem: the Swedish families were out of provisions, and the menfolk had gone off to Carver (80 miles east) to replenish their supplies.

At this point the *Landinger* wanted to return to where they came from, as they were afraid of starving to death. But Railson managed to contrive a fish-hook, and with this he caught several northern pike in the lake. The fish were baked in coals. Thus fortified, the men went on.

Despite feeling tired and down-at-heel, they were captivated by the scene they viewed from the top of Dovre's high hill. So they returned to the Swedish families to ask whether the land to the north had been taken. The answer was "no." On this visit, one of the women went so far as to give the men a biscuit from her vanishing supply.

Feeling better, they went off again, this time a long 15 miles to Norway Lake. There were many small marshes to go around and creeks to wade across. Suddenly, they stepped into quicksand. All escaped with their lives, although soaked through.

It was therefore a pathetic-looking group of men who continued to struggle forward in the blazing sun. Their wet clothing stuck to their bodies, the high grass tired them, their shoes were wearing through, their toes bleeding, their faces swollen from mosquito bites, and they were nearly losing their minds for lack of food.

How much more sensible, they thought, if they had stayed home and cut grain in Lafayette County's dependable ridges instead of frittering away a whole summer in this manner.

Finally, the wanderers reached the spot where Norway Lake's church now stands, and here they saw the beautiful peninsula that juts into the lake. It was smooth and nearly flat, fairly well wooded, with a lake on three sides. None had ever seen anything more attractive, and each coveted it.

As it was clearly not big enough for more than one farm, an argument arose over who had the first claim. One insisted that he had seen it first, another that he had spoken first, the third that he was the oldest and therefore had first choice.

In order to settle the matter, it was agreed that the contestants would run a race, winner-take-all. A big oak that still stands on the peninsula was marked as the goal. Railson knew in his own mind that he was the fastest runner and therefore could, in his high-mindedness, hold back a bit. But this nearly cost him the farm.

After the others began spurting, he realized for the first time that Emil Falk was both knock-kneed and pigeon-toed, and the sight of these strange-looking feet running like two sticks was so funny he nearly died laughing. But he got control of himself in time and, with all his youthful vigor, threw himself into the race and reached the oak tree first.

This peninsula on Norway Lake is so fertile, so easy to work and has such pleasant surroundings that many people regard it as the finest of all Minnesota farmland.

The four men now returned to the place of Ole Næss, where they also met Andrew Railson. After a couple of weeks' rest and a supply of food, Even and Andrew Railson went back to Norway Lake, while the suspicious *Landinger* returned to Lafayette County.

A dangerous crossing

Norway Lake had no name at the time and was christened by the Railson brothers. As they wanted to cross the lake from Even's peninsula to the opposite shore where Anders entered a claim, they rolled a couple of dry logs into the water, sat astride and tried to paddle with their hands.

This went well for a time, but soon the wind came up, and despite their best efforts, they were driven farther and farther into the lake. The choppy waves also threatened to break up their log boom, and they had to lie on their stomachs with hands and feet lengthwise to hold it on even keel.

Late in the afternoon, when they had nearly reached land, the wind changed and drove them out again. This continued late into the night, by which time they were chilled to the bone, soaked and hungry as wolves. They felt that the lake that day had been so thoroughly surveyed by Norwegian seamen that it should be called Norway Lake. The two brothers legalized their claim on this tour and returned to Wisconsin.

Big White Chief

In August 1858, Andrew Railson moved to Minnesota to become the first white man to settle in the region around Norway Lake. Three weeks after him came Thomas Osmundson (a *Haring*), John T. Totland and Helge T. Totland. The Totlands were the first among the many people to leave from Finaas north of Haugesund, later colonizing to the north of Norway Lake.

Another member of this party was Johannes Iverson, originally from Hurdal in Norway, who, like the others, came to Minnesota via Rock Prairie in Wisconsin. However, the above-mentioned men were not the only ones to come in 1858.

Meanwhile, Even Railson did not return to Norway Lake before 1859. At that time he brought along a cow, a colt and a yoke of oxen that were pulling a breaking plow mounted on a pair of iron wheels. He drove this strange-looking contraption 400 miles from the Jordan colony on the Wisconsin River near the Dells. He gave a widow a ride on the plow as far as Paint Creek in Iowa, about half the distance to Norway Lake.

In later years, Even Railson was to be known as one of the most distinguished as well as picturesque personalities in Kandiyohi County. A giant in size and possessed of an authoritative, slightly swaggering appearance, he impressed both whites and Indians—the latter referring to him as Big White Chief.

He was widely known in other parts of Minnesota and Dakota, where he engaged in horse trading and threshing operations. He also raised many fine trotting horses and took part several times with varying success on the racetracks of Paris, London and Antwerp.

On one of his several return visits to Norway, he drove past the king, who, with regal pace, was traveling far too slow for this big-shot farmer from Minnesota. Railson, you might know, took considerable pride in recalling this incident.

Some early settlers

Mainly as a result of his influence and reports on Norway Lake's charming attractions, quite a few people moved to this distant territory as early as 1859. Arriving that year were:
- Christoffer H. Engen, Land
- Erik G. Kapperud, Land
- Haavald Haavaldson, Land
- Ole Halvorson, Gausdal
- Johannes Halvorson, Gausdal
- Amund Johnson Dale, Gausdal

- Lewis Johnson Dale, Gausdal
- Johannes Peterson Grindheim, Finaas
- Nils Peterson Grindheim, Finaas
- Lars Olson, Finaas
- Olaf O. Haugan, Biri, Oppland

Haugan settled a mile south of the Hardanger settlement. *[A footnote by Holand: "The two brothers, Johannes and Nils Peterson Grindheim were the first to immigrate to the U.S. from Finaas."]*

When Even Railson actually settled permanently in Kandiyohi County in 1860, a year after he had brought the breaking plow from Wisconsin, he brought back with him the following:
- Even O. Glesne, Sigdal
- Ole Knudson Storbraaten, Sigdal

Also arriving that year were:
- Even G. Borgen, Numedal
- Gunder Swenson, Numedal
- Matthias Johnson, Haugesund
- Anfin Thompson, Haugesund
- Torres Thomassen Tyse, Haugesund

The last three mentioned settled in Colfax Township of Kandiyohi County.

A beginning was also made in 1860 of a Gausdal settlement in Burbank Township and in the adjoining townships of Stearns County to the northeast.

George G. Johnson from the Gausdal community of Waupaca County (Wisconsin) was the first to arrive here and is looked upon as the father of this part of the county since he encouraged many other *Gausdøler* to follow him.

There were, however, some *Telemarkinger* there before him. Jørgen Postmyhr with sons Halvor Jørgenson Postmyhr, Thor Jørgenson Postmyhr and Ole Jørgenson Postmyhr from Tørdal, in addition to Jørgen's son-in-law, Torkel J. Nygaard (Torkel J. Newgard) from Finaas, settled on the Stearns County line next to Kandiyohi County as early as 1859.

[The movement of the Postmyhrs and Newgards (originally Nygaard) from Scandinavia in Waupaca County was not undertaken by all members of the family in the same year, but it appears that all had reached the Minnesota colony by 1859. Postmyhr was one of the pioneers of Scandinavia Township. He kept a charge account for groceries and liquor purchased at the log cabin store of Thomas Knoph in 1852-54, a copy of which was sent to the Wisconsin Historical Society Archives. –Rosholt]

Georgeville on the Soo Line Railroad is named after Jørgen Postmyhr. *[The name Jørgen in Norwegian is usually translated into English as George. –Rosholt]* His son-in-law, Torkel, was widely known as an ox tamer.

In 1860 the Postmyhr family circle was augmented by the arrival of the following:
- Jørgen O. Bergan, Tørdal
- Levor Nerison Quie, Drangedal
- Østen A. Quie, Drangedal
- Ole Reine, Finaas

[Among these, Nerison and Reine settled first in Scandinavia Township, as noted in the tax rolls of 1856, and it is quite likely that Bergan and Quie were also from Waupaca or Portage county. –Rosholt]

This was about all that came before the Indian uprising. When the Civil War broke out, there was constant demand for manpower and there were few men to spare for "breaking the land."

Indian Uprising

Up to 20 August 1862, the pioneers of Kandiyohi County had no reason to fear the Indians. This charming territory, so well provided by nature with fish and game, was no doubt a favorite place to camp for the Indians as well. Mt. Tom, north of Norway Lake, was known as an old council ground.

Meanwhile, the Indians wandered among the pioneer families, seeking small favors, friendly in their attitude. These Indians had not yet offended any whites, although they often recounted battles fought in times past that the Sioux lords of the prairies had with the Chippewa, lords of the forest to the east.

Then, suddenly, without warning the storm broke, and this peaceful territory, where no one suspected danger, became the stage for murder and fire, disgrace, bewildering flight and all the attendant miseries that an Indian war, or any other war, brings.

It was on a beautiful summer day, Wednesday, 20 August 1862. The tough prairie turf had been tilled several times and now gave promise of a bountiful harvest. A few miles west of Norway Lake on the boundary of Swift County lived some Swedish families who were gathered at the house of a neighbor, Andreas Lundberg, to listen to an itinerant pastor named Jackson. Suddenly a boy rushed in to report that the Indians were at his home mistreating his brothers and sisters.

Nearly everyone at the meeting began to look to his weapons. But Pastor Jackson advised against this and told them there would be no danger. This was a fatal mistake, and only one of the men, Andreas Lundberg, picked up his gun and took a short cut to the house ahead of the others.

When he reached a spot where he could see the house, a terrible sight met his eyes. The Indians were after his four sons. One of the boys, who had preceded his father to the house, was badly wounded and in desperation, had run back to a rail fence, which his father was at the moment approaching. As the boy was about to climb the fence, the Indians shot him, cut his throat and tore off his clothes. The father was frozen to the spot, terror-stricken. But in his extreme confusion he gave a heart-piercing cry.

Now the Indians discovered the father and were about to take after him when a wagonload of people driving an ox team arrived from the religious meeting. The Indians then turned their attention to the new arrivals and Lundberg escaped. In the wagon were Daniel Broberg and Sven Johnson with his wife and two children, plus a boy, P. Broberg, later a businessman in New London, Minnesota.

When his party reached the house, they hid in the cellar and the Indians quickly surrounded the house, shooting through the windows, breaking down the door and smashing furniture. A clock on the wall was torn down and stamped on, but as luck would have it, the invaders failed to discover the trap door leading to the cellar.

Mrs. Broberg was in the same wagon with the others but had jumped off with a child in her arms and ran into a marsh. Here two Indians confronted her and amused themselves by poking their knives into the child while it lay in her arms. She defended herself as well as she could, but shortly a tomahawk cleaved the child's head and then a blow to the head killed her.

Meanwhile, Lundberg rushed back to his house to save the members of his family who were still alive. He got them into a hiding place in a marsh while he, together with an old man named Swenson, ran ahead to warn Ole Knudsen, who lived three miles to the east of the Norway Lake colony.

En route, they were sighted by some young Indians and took refuge in a marsh hole. The Indians danced around and peppered them with bullets, which fortunately went wide of their mark.

The guns carried by Lundberg and Swenson had now become waterlogged and could not be used. Annoyed by the poor marksmanship of the Indians and made foolhardy by his sorrow, old Lundberg stood up and shouted, "You shoot like fools! I will show you how to shoot."

Faced by much opposition, the Indian youths ran out of rifle range and hid behind their tepees, peeking now here, now there.

The two pioneers in the marsh hole emerged quite calmly and resumed their trip to Knudsen's, followed at a respectable distance by the Indians.

Finally the Indians caught sight of some other refugees, which permitted Lundberg to go and warn others in the widely separated homes.

Through Lundberg's efforts, a meeting of refugees was held that night at the house of Ole Knudsen, where it was decided that everyone should travel farther east to the farm of Even Railson. All arrived safely and, together with Railson, the party took refuge on a small island in Norway Lake. The passage to the island was made in a dugout canoe of basswood, which could scarcely take more than two people at a time.

Nearly the entire colony now assembled on the island, but when a roll call was held, Lundberg's wife and daughter and some others were missing.

Although the night was dark and rainy and the country around swarming with Indians, six men decided to return to land and look for the missing people. When they reached old Knudsen's log shanty, it was pitch dark, the rain still pouring down, thundering and lightning. Some of the rescuers now wanted to give up the search, but Railson, Knudsen and Lundberg insisted they continue despite the darkness.

Finally they found five people hidden in some high marsh hay—but not Mrs. Lundberg. The rescued were taken to Knudsen's shanty and rushed the next morning to the safety of the island.

The following day a larger party of refugees left the island to look for missing people. They broke up into two groups and agreed to meet in Knudsen's woods. Although they had some small skirmishes with the Indians, no one was killed. But they found no one.

An accident was narrowly averted when the two search parties, mistaking the other for Indians, opened fire. However, some provisions had been picked up and brought back to the island, to the relief of the women and children, who had not eaten since the day began.

The next morning the men again went ashore, about 10 miles to the west, this time to bury the dead and to rescue those perhaps still alive. This time they found old Lundberg, who had been wounded by the Indians and left for dead. He managed to get to his feet but was extremely weak from lack of blood.

After returning him to the island, the men went to the place where the murders had been committed. Here lay the mutilated bodies of friends and

Siolefosen

neighbors, some inside the hut, others out on the ground.

Broberg's two sons, one 16 and the other 17 years old, lay in a grove of trees nearby. The one was holding a hammer in his hand, and near the other lay a bloody knife. Both had been struck in the head with a tomahawk, and both had their throats cut. A 6-year old boy who apparently had tried to run away lay with his head smashed in.

The clothing was torn from some of the dead, and on others the clothing had been burned. A child was badly mutilated, nose cut off and forehead crushed. The mother lay at the child's side. She had apparently fought off the attackers as long as she could. Thirteen dead were found here. There was no time for ceremony, and the dead were buried in one grave after lying three days in the burning sun.

After the burial, Andreas Lundberg brought out a bottle of wine to toast the participants in the funeral rites, saying, "Drink, this was to have been a toast to the wedding of my boy who now lies in that hole."

A search was now made for Mrs. Lundberg, the only one still missing. But when nothing further could be learned of her whereabouts, the party returned to the island. In their absence, a woman and child had reached the island. Her home was three miles to the south, where the Indians had killed her husband, Johannes Syverson, while he was out in the field cutting hay.

The Indians had intended to take her captive, as well as her 16-year old daughter, but while they were trying to get the girl to mount a horse, the mother fled into nearby woods. The girl fought the efforts of the Indians so vigorously that the horse became frightened, threw her to the ground and galloped off. As the Indians ran to retrieve their horse, the girl also ran into the woods.

The mother, with the youngest child, then went to Norway Lake, as mentioned earlier, while her teen-age daughter returned to the house during the night to rescue her four brothers and sisters. She managed to get them away from the house, but then she lost her way on the prairie in the dark. Early the following morning, she came to a house belonging to Svend Borgen. Here the children found a little milk to drink and were eventually rescued.

For the refugees on the island, further delays were bound to be hazardous, as the food supply was running out. People were quietly rowed to shore. And early one morning, the oxen were hitched up, and everyone prepared to move to the east.

But they were not yet finished with the Indians. Before leaving, Thomas Osmundsen and his father-in-law, Svend Borgen, wanted to return to Borgen's house to pick up some things. As they were approaching the house, half a dozen Indians charged out of the woods and began shooting. The two men called for help and when a reply came from the people on the lakeshore, the Indians became frightened and rode off.

The men waiting at the lake pursued the Indians for a short distance but turned back for fear that the women and children would be attacked in their absence.

Shortly after this incident a new direction was given to events—this time ended in rejoicing. A big group of people was seen approaching from the west, some on horseback, some driving teams. At first the hard-pressed refugees thought there was more trouble brewing, but this time it was help on the way. The village of Paynesville and surrounding district had sent out an expedition to bring assistance to their fellow human beings at Norway Lake.

While traveling from Paynesville to Norway Lake, these rescuers discovered the five children of Johannes Iverson, whose father had already been killed. Seeing the rescue party and thinking they, too, were Indians, the children ran off like wild deer, and speedy efforts had to be made to bring them back. The children were then reunited with their mother at Norway Lake.

The men from Paynesville also told Lundberg that his wife was alive. She had arrived at Paynesville together with Even O. Glesne, Lars Iverson and their families, who had joined Erik Kapperud and two men whose horses had been stolen by the Indians near Ole Knudsen's farm. This last group had gone east from Norway Lake, traveling through the woods and marsh areas.

The main body of refugees and their rescuers now took the road east to Paynesville, where they arrived in the evening. There was no end to the joy when Lundberg was reunited with his wife, as both had given up hope of ever seeing each other again.

Refugee caravan

The refugees remained in Paynesville three weeks, hoping to return to their homes. But when the Indians continued to rove about in big bands, shooting people and animals, the Norway Lake people decided to continue east to older settlements.

Meanwhile, some men arrived from St. Cloud and advised the refugees not to go east, as they had heard it would be difficult to find food supplies. On the other hand, if they would return to their homes, they would be supplied with both weapons and ammunition—indeed, even military assistance. It would be rather pointless, it was said, to go any farther east, as they would under no circumstances be permitted to cross on the Mississippi River ferry.

The eloquence of the St. Cloud men was futile. The refugee caravan moved east, and was joined en route by other farmers, all frightened to death.

The caravan, now made up of both Yankees and Norwegians, did not stop until it reached St. Cloud. But here, efforts were made by local inhabitants to hinder them from crossing the Mississippi. There was no bridge at the time, and the ferryboat was chained and locked.

One morning the homeless people again asked the operator to use his ferry, but he replied that no Scandinavians could use his boat. Thereupon, the Scandinavians and others drove their cattle down to the river. T. Osmundson sat on the back of an ox and reached the other side without incident. The others followed suit, and before evening, all the oxen had swum the river.

Next on the program was to break loose the ferry. The owners tried to prevent this but withdrew when the refugees declared they would rather risk a fight with the officers of the law in St. Cloud than go back and fight the Indians.

On 20 August, the same day that the pioneers of Norway Lake were under attack, other Indians to the south and east of the county began to kill and molest unsuspecting settlers.

One of the first was Berger Thorson at Willmar, who was killed by a blow from a tomahawk while out working. The Indians then went to Olaf O. Haugan, the nearest neighbor to the north, and killed him, together with his wife and son. Haugan's body was found in a hay field, where he apparently had attempted to stop the blood flow from his wound by letting the hay soak up the blood.

Toward evening, the same Indians appeared at the house of Oskar Erikson. *[A footnote by Holand: "This place is now known as the Gunderson farm and lies at the point where the road to Eagle Lake church crosses Eagle Lake creek."]* A man by the name of S. R. Foote had learned of the killing and had warned several neighbors, who, together with Foote, assembled at Erikson's house.

When the Indians approached and found Foote there, they acted in a friendly manner and protested inno-

Parti fra Smaaland [Sweden]

cence to any evil intentions, because they knew that Foote was an experienced hunter and a dead shot with a gun. They rested in the neighborhood and several times during the evening sent one of their braves to the white men to borrow different things. Their real purpose, of course, was to learn how many whites there were and whether or not they were armed.

In addition to Foote and Erikson, there were also two Swedes in the house—one named Swanson, who had a family, and the other known as Swede Charley.

In the morning, the Indians sent word to the house that they would like some potatoes and a kettle to cook in. Foote replied that they could have the kettle, but they would have to dig the potatoes themselves.

Swede Charley protested this inhospitality and said it could only lead to hostility from the Indians. He offered to go out and dig the potatoes for them. Foote warned him not to, but he grabbed a hoe and went just the same.

Slightly uncertain just what he should do, Foote also met an Indian who stood by a rail fence, smiling in an easy manner. Not until he looked into the eyes of this Indian did Foote realize that he had made a serious mistake, and he ran for all his might back toward the house.

But the Indians, their guns ready, were hiding in their tepee and shot Foote in the back so that he fell. This fall saved him from more bullets when another Indian hiding behind the house got off a couple of shots at him that went wide of their mark.

Foote was unable to raise himself, but his wife ran out and pulled him inside. He was not giving up that easy. He grabbed one of his rifles and sneaked up to a window, took a shot and felled one of the Indians. Then, with blood from his wound trailing him, he crawled to the other side of the house, knocked out some caulking between the logs and shot another Indian warrior.

Meanwhile, Swede Charley had gone out to dig for potatoes. At the moment he bent over to pick up the first potatoes for his red hosts, a shot rang out and he fell over dead, one hand on the hoe and the other holding a potato.

For several hours, a furious engagement continued between Foote and Erikson in the house and the Indians who had moved into a nearby woods. Several Indians were killed, but both Erikson and Foote were so badly wounded they could scarcely move. Lest the Indians learn of this, the womenfolk continued to shoot.

Swanson was a useless coward who sat in the corner and whined, urging that they should open the door and give themselves up. But Mrs. Foote warned him that if he got near the door, she would shoot him dead on the spot!

Eventually the Indians got tired of this siege, which had cost them several men, and they left. As soon as they were far enough away, Swanson took his family and left the hut.

Of his fate, it may be related that two days later, when he and his family were about to escape from this bloody land, they met a party of men thought to be Indians but who were actually a rescue party. Overcome by fear, Swanson led his family into Indian country and was never seen again.

The others remained in the house during the night. The next morning, which was Friday, the women, at Foote's urging, prepared to leave. He and Erikson did not have long to live anyhow, he said, and they should therefore not expose the children to more danger by remaining longer.

With sad farewells, Mrs. Erikson and her three children, and Mrs. Foote and her four boys, started to leave the house but repeatedly came back, as it seemed unbearable to leave their men suffering in their hour of death. But at the insistence of the men, they finally left and, after further hardships, were finally rescued.

Stillness now hung over the little hut, broken now and then by a moan of dying men. Before the women left, Erikson was raised to his feet, the blood dripping to the floor. The day was very warm. Attracted by the blood, mosquitoes swarmed in to plague the wounded men, who were unable to move. When would the end come?

Guri Rosseland's heroic struggles

When the Indians gave up the fight at Erikson's house on that Thursday afternoon, they went a few miles west to the place of Erikson's father-in-law, Lars Endresen Rosseland, who lived on the north side of Salomon Lake.

Straight across the lake from him lay a favorite camping ground of the Indians. Living this close to Rosseland's place, the Indians often visited him. So when six or eight armed warriors marched into his house and sat down, there was no cause for alarm, as they had done this many times before.

They asked for a bowl of milk, but when Rosseland kindly extended a bowl to the nearest Indian, the latter jumped up and shot the old man dead.

His oldest son, Endre, was returning home from the field and, not knowing what had taken place, fell in a hail of bullets a short distance from the house. His wife was killed at the same time, and a brother, Ole, badly wounded in the shoulder.

With remarkable presence of mind for a boy of 14, Ole played dead so convincingly that the Indians paid no more attention to him except to give him a couple of blows to his head with the butt of a rifle.

During this time Mrs. Lars Rosseland (Guri Rosseland) and a small daughter, Anna Rosseland, lay hidden in another cellar away from the house. She had just started to leave the cellar door when she saw her husband shot. At the same time one of the Indians sent a shot after her but missed.

In her alarm, she fell backward down the cellar stairs, dragging her child with her. Here they remained until the Indians left. Two of the Rosseland daughters, Brita Rosseland and Guri Rosseland, were taken away as captives.

When Guri Rosseland emerged from the cellar to find her family either dead or carried off, she decided to warn her son-in-law, Oskar Erikson. She lingered only long enough to lay a pillow under the head of her dead husband (Ole had meanwhile fainted) and went off with her little Anna. But in her haste and because it was dark, she took the wrong road and wandered about half the night. Finally, she had to lie down and rest under the open sky.

The next day she started out again and arrived back at her own house with the quiet dead. Here, amidst sorrow, she was overjoyed to find her son Ole, wounded in the shoulder but at that moment picking up some food to take along on the road to find his relatives.

The Indians had either killed or chased away nearly all the cattle. But Guri managed to round up one of her own and captured another out on pasture. They were two young oxen, strange to each other and not yet broken to a yoke. But Guri struggled with them until she got them hitched to a sleigh. The wagon box had been loaned out, and in this way the family drove off to Oskar Erikson's place. They approached the house carefully. And while Guri and little Anna held the sleigh some distance back, Ole crawled up to the house where it was easy to see that the Indians had cleared out, kit and caboodle *(gjort rent bord)*. The cattle were gone, and the haystack was still burning. Ole then thought he heard the sound of voices. Thinking they were Indians, he hurried back to his mother.

The family then drove around to find other neighbors, but the Indians had raided everywhere. Log houses were deserted or burned, and here and there lay the mutilated bodies of old neighbors. The once-blooming settlement was like a wasteland without a living thing other than the wild Indians and Guri and her children. They therefore returned and spent the next night in their own house with the dead.

Early the next morning, the second day of the bloodbath, Guri hitched up the oxen to the sleigh and loaded bed clothing and family necessities. Ole was badly wounded and could not be of much help; he later died of his wounds.

The family returned to Oskar Erikson's house, without hope, but only to exchange the sleigh for a wagon that had been seen there. This time they were able to get into the house and here found Foote and Erikson approaching their ends to life.

Now we discover another side of Guri's heroic nature. Although the territory was swarming with Indians, she was not deterred in the least. Without whimpering, she went to work bathing and changing bandages on the wounded men, bringing in water and cooking food. After all preparations had been made, she carried them out to the wagon box, which she had made comfortable with fresh marsh hay and blankets.

It was particularly difficult to get Foote on the wagon, as he weighed more than 200 pounds and, like Erikson, was completely helpless in his personal needs. Guri picked up some other things and put them in the wagon, as she knew they would be needed on the way. The group then left for Forest City (northeast of Litchfield, Minnesota), where she had visited earlier.

The journey across the prairie took two days, and as the refugees passed by pioneer shanties, here and there they saw only dead bodies. Guri did not sleep a wink all this time, maintaining a constant watch for the Indians, rifle at the ready. She was the last to leave this blood-drenched land.

Guri's arrival in Forest City created another sensation. That one old woman had survived four days among hostile Indians, caring for sick and wounded and finding her way south, was an achievement that gave the newly organized volunteer garrison at Forest City courage to stand up and fight the Redskins.

Her own joy on reaching Forest City was doubled when she learned that her two daughters—the ones who had been carried off by the Indians—were also in the city. They had, on the first night of captivity, escaped from their guards but were chased and recaptured, only to escape again in some tall grass. They wandered around several days, keeping alive on berries and milk from stray cows. A rescue party finally brought them back to the city. *[A footnote by Holand: "Under the sponsorship of Senator L. O. Thorpe, a historical marker was raised in 1907 in honor of the heroic Guri Rosseland. It stands in the churchyard of Vikor congregation north of Willmar. She was born in Vikør 26 March 1813, and died on the family farm near Solomon Lake 20 June 1881. Her son-in-law, Oskar Erikson, was then living on the farm."]*

This account only deals with the Norwegian phase of the Indian wars. But there were hundreds of Swedish settlers and Indians who went through the same experiences. All of these people, together with the Norwegians, left Kandiyohi County and scattered among the older settlements in southern Minnesota and Wisconsin, where it became difficult for them to find work or enough to feed their families.

Out on the prairies stood their rich grain harvest, stacked but unthrashed. Their dearly loved pioneer homes stood empty or in ashes. Their cattle, pigs and chickens wandered about on the silent countryside, where only a band of victorious Indians could be seen galloping across the plains.

Aftermath

For three years Kandiyohi County lay deserted, but in 1865 the exiles began to return. The first to arrive was Andrew Railson.

[A footnote by Holand: "Just as Andrew Railson was the first to settle in this region, he was also first in the esteem of his fellow citizens. He served in several commissions of public trust, among them as a representative to the state legislature for several terms. He was also a member of the state senate for one term, and was instrumental in bringing a post office to Norway Lake. He still (1908) lives on his beautiful farm overlooking the lake, a rare type of pioneer, cultivated in his tastes, easy-going and democratic in his personal relationships."]

The same year, 1865, many others returned to the county, and the influx of new settlers also speeded up. Among the latter immigrants, there were many *Hallinger* who now make up the majority ethnic element in the district.

Other newcomers settled in the northwest of the county and into the adjoining townships of Stearns County to the northeast. Here, north to Belgrade and Brooten, the *Hallinger* are also numerous. In 1865, the first to arrive, all coming from Spring Grove, Minnesota, included:
• Elling Sagadalen
• Erik Ruud
• Ole O. Liabraaten
• Kittel N. Strande
• Hans P. Heieie
• Nils O. Strandmoen

Still another *Halling* to arrive was Kittel Halvorson, a man who later achieved the honor of serving as a member of the U.S. Congress. *[Martin Ulvestad says Halvorson, born in Tuddal, Telemark, was elected to Congress in 1890 and served one term. See Nordmaendene i Amerika, p. 390 –Rosholt]*

In the early days of Norway Lake, there were quite a few who emigrated from Nannestad north of Oslo. There is still a congregation by that name here. Among the first of these people to arrive in 1866 was old Mother Holter, who came from the Nannestad settlement in Fillmore County, accompanied by her 10 fatherless children.

Mother Holter was unusually tough and managed to steer her big family through all pioneer difficulties. The family is now quite numerous, and among the descendants may be mentioned Karl Holter, publisher of *Undommens Ven*, and Pastor Christian Holter in Kenyon, editor of *Budbæreren*.

The Norway Lake settlement extends west into the northeast corner of Swift County. This is the end of Parkland region. It is here that the lonely and mellow prairie takes its beginning, although it is a bit stony.

None of the Norwegian immigrants settled here until after the arrival of the following in 1866:
• Tosten Quamme, Valdres
• Ole Søndrol, Valdres
• Henrik H. Sagadalen

The first two were the founders of a colony of about 300 *Valdriser*, mostly from Vang, who now live on what is known as "Valdres Prairie."

East of New London *[a few miles north of Willmar –Rosholt]* lies a colony of *Nordlændinger [loosely, northern Norway –Rosholt]* of about 500, the largest colony of these people in one place in the U.S. The first among these to arrive (in 1866) were:
• Ole. C. Christianson
• Styrk Larson
• R. Emerson
• B. C. Benson

Most of the people in the district are from Ranen in Helgeland.

Church wars

Norway Lake is a widely known place. Its importance to the history of Scandinavian settlement in the U.S. must be considered second only to such famous names in immigrant annals as Fox River, Koshkonong, Washington Prairie and Goodhue County. Although it lies far from any railroad, it is a meeting place for old memories, and the goddess of fate has spun many human-interest stories by the shores of this beautiful lake.

The landscape is charming, and the people in the area are the most prosperous of any between Minneapolis and Otter Tail County. It is also an important center for church affairs, as there are no fewer than four congregations called "Norway Lake Congregation," in addition to the church actually located near the lake.

In church affairs, Norway Lake is something of a saga, which, for sad memories, is almost as bad as the Indian wars. The church, which should be the home of the dove of peace, has nearly always been a center of religious strife among Norwegians. But in Norway Lake, this controversy degenerated into such acrimony that it can only be hoped it is an isolated phenomenon.

How many clandestine meetings, filled with intrigue and fabrication, have people held here in their homes? And how many terms of abuse and acts of violence were part of congregational meetings? Here, padlocks and crowbars became common in church life; here, the president of the synod was denied entry to the church; and here, the people had the audacity to throw out their pastor.

Ridicule and petty remarks flew in all directions, hateful character assassination was exchanged in the newspaper, and visiting committees formed to bring peace to Norway Lake held one quarrelsome investigation after the other.

In the early development of the local church, there was nothing to suggest the peculiarly bitter struggles that were to follow. The first pastor to visit here was Thomas Johnson, who came in 1867 and baptized 44 children in three days. A congregation was organized, and John C. Moses was called as resident pastor in 1868.

Misunderstanding quickly arose, and Moses resigned the next year. Lars Markhus then became the pastor, and while there was much with which to contend, he served for 15 years.

But it was during his time that the fateful struggle over predestination arose, which tore through most congregations of the former Norwegian Synod like a storm, rupturing old friendships and neighborhood relationships.

The majority in the congregation at Norway Lake joined with the Anti-Missourian Brotherhood (later the United Lutheran Church) and denied the minority, who refused to go along with this, the use of the church. And just to prove this was no empty injunction, they put padlocks on the doors.

In spite of this, the minority, accompanied by an old synod pastor, arrived at the church armed with a heavy crowbar, broke the detestable locks to smithereens and occupied the building.

The majority group then became angry and sent for a lawyer, none other than the famous John Arctander. Under his leadership, a fairly large body of men trooped into the church and told the opposition to clear out. When this was refused, Pastor Markhus, despite all protestations, was carried out of the church. *[This probably occurred not long before Markhus died, in 1885. –Rosholt]*

While Markhus was being carried out, Arctander protested.

"Oh, come on. Carry me a little farther," begged Markhus.

"No, set him down here," ordered Arctander.

The minority party in the church did not make any further open attempts to acquire the church, but after this incident, there was no peace for the majority party, either.

The bitterness of the controversy that developed in the congregation overshadowed anything previously seen. Officials of the congregation were constantly being changed. Pastor E. H. Midtbøe was denied the right to speak at a meeting. It went so far that when it was announced that Gjermund Hoyme, president of the United Synod, was going to visit the congregation, he was locked out of the church. *[As Hoyme* was elected president of the United Synod in 1890, his visit to Norway Lake probably took place before he was actually president. –Rosholt] Sarcastic letters and uncomplimentary pictures were sent to the resident pastor. For a time, there was complete anarchy in the affairs of the congregation.

[At this point in the text, Holand reprints a poem about the struggle in the Norway Lake church, written by pastor Rolf Fjelstad, who served the congregation briefly after Markhus died. The poem recounts the tragic loss of Christian ethics among the members of the East Norway Lake congregation. In a footnote, Holand advises the reader that further information about the struggle in this church may be found in a small pamphlet called "Concerning the Church Struggle at Norway Lake," written by Gabriel Stene in 1903. Holand calls it a "literary gem." He also refers to the Norwegian Synod's annual report of 1886, pages 100-101, the newspaper Skandinaven for January 1903, and annual reports of the United Lutheran Synod. The fact that attention is called to the Norway Lake affair in the annual report of the old Norwegian Synod (de Norske Synode) in 1886 suggests that the split in the church between the two factions developed earlier here than in most congregations of the Norwegian Synode. –Rosholt]

Parti af Ulvik

57

The Indian war of 1862-65

(Source: De Norske Settlementers Historie, by Hjalmar Rued Holand, translated by Malcolm Rosholt, 1908, portions of pp. 566-583; where necessary, paragraphs have been rearranged for continuity)
and
(Source: Den Siste Folkevandring Sagastubber fra Nybyggerlivet i Amerika, by Hjalmar Rued Holand, 1930; Norwegians in America: The Last Migration, by Hjalmar Rued Holand, translated by Helmer M. Blegen, 1978, pp. 167-176)

The saddest memories in America's history are those in connection with the displacement and maltreatment of the Indians. Only two centuries ago, the Indians were the proud possessors of the world's most fertile continent. They were as great and strong as were few other people. Happy in their enjoyment of nature's abundance, they had a past filled with proud remembrances.

But the white man came with his greed for gold and his inscrutable cunning. And he employed sly, sweet persuasiveness to entice the Indian to give him his land. When this did not work, the white man made use of powder and bullets. But the most effective of all was his delightful, poisonous whiskey.

Before the white man came, the Indian knew nothing about intoxicating liquor. His drink was the pure water from heaven—and then he was strong. But beguiled by the white man's firewater, the Indian was made dull and dispirited, indifferent to his tribe's greatness, and his sole aspiration became to acquire more whiskey and more money with which to buy it.

With the white man, he signed one worthless treaty after the other in which he gave up vast expanses of his fair land—millions of acres for a few paltry thousands of dollars. One by one, these treaties were broken by the white man, whose only thought was to conquer the country and who often regarded the payment as a mere gift. There are scores of these treaties on the books of the government in Washington that, up to the very recent years (1908), were not kept by the white man.

It was a couple of these treaties that were broken by the government that caused the Indian War of 1862-65. It is estimated that about 600 to 800 new settlers lost their lives in this war, in addition to many soldiers. There were several hundred Norwegians in each of these two classifications.

One of the greatest of all Indian tribes was the Sioux, who reigned over the land between the Mississippi River and Montana. They were a virile and bold people, tempered by suffering and patient in adversity and trials. They were high-minded and loyal toward their friends, but they were cunning and crafty and capable of diabolical cruelty when they felt themselves to be victims of fraudulence and deceit. Like the Israelites of an ancient day, they demanded an eye for an eye and a tooth for a tooth.

Broken promises

In 1851, two treaties were signed whereby the Sioux turned over 30 million acres of excellent farmland in Minnesota, Iowa and Dakota to the government of the United States. According to this agreement, the

Sisseton and Wahpeton tribes were to receive a sum of $1,665,000. Of this amount, they were to be given $275,000 in cash upon moving to a reservation along the upper Minnesota River. A sum of $30,000 was to be used for plowing the land, building schools, mills and the like. The remaining sum of $1,360,000 was to be invested for 50 years at 5 percent rate of interest. This interest, amounting to $68,000, would be paid annually. At the end of the 50-year period, the principal, $1,360,000, would revert to the government.

The Medewayankton and Wapakota (Mdewakanton and Wahpekute) tribes were to receive $220,000 when they moved to the reservation, $30,000 in work on the land, and $58,000 annually for 50 years. In exchange for these promises, the Indians gave up their rights to 30 million acres of land, an area almost six times as large as all of Denmark.

Since a time before the memory of man, this enormous territory had been the hunting grounds of the Sioux. They had held it and defended it against many enemy attacks. But the white man came to their powwow campfire and smoked the pipe of peace with them. He wanted to buy this land, and he offered them money—amounts of money that seemed to them so great as to be beyond measure. With this money they could buy food and they need not be dependent on hunting, which was uncertain. One by one, the chiefs came forward to the table on which the treaty was spread out, touched the pen and said, *"Washta"*—good.

But during these same days, the chiefs signed another paper, with dire consequences. Here and there throughout the vast land, bold traders had built stores where they traded with the Indians. To these so-called Indian trading posts, the red men brought their furs and, in return, received ammunition, clothing, groceries and other necessities.

The majority of these traders were conscienceless scoundrels who never lost an opportunity to cheat the unwary and trusting red men. With the help of a few drinks, they fooled the Indians into buying far more than they could afford to pay for. In this way the Indians were constantly in debt to the trader and had to exert themselves to the utmost to bring in great piles of furs in order to keep up their credit at the store.

Now that the tribes were about to receive enormous sums of money from the government, the traders saw a fine opportunity to get rich very quickly. They drew up a document in which the Indians admitted to a debt of specified

Hammerfest Havn

amounts and authorized the government to pay the trader out of the money they were entitled to receive.

These were not small sums, either, that were listed. They ran from $10,000 up to $100,000. And in the aggregate, they amounted to precisely the sum that the Indians were supposed to receive from the U.S. government in cash money.

As soon as a chief came up to the table to sign the contract with the government, he was pulled aside to a second table, where the infamous certificate of debt lay ready to receive his signature. No explanation was made to him about the contents. And the Indian, who thought this a part of the government contract, obediently placed his mark on this paper also, for he was utterly inexperienced in such affairs and, in good faith, trusted the white man.

The Indians then returned home, happy as children at the thought of very soon getting a lot of cash with which to buy many things. But two whole years later, when the money finally arrived, the Indians discovered to their consternation that they had been deceived. The money was paid out to the traders, and the Indians received not a penny.

Delegations were sent to St. Paul and to Washington to protest this matter. The Indians admitted that they owed money to the traders, but they insisted that the amounts were insignificant, and they demanded the right to pay them themselves. But the government's cocky agents, who received their rake-off percentages from the traders, could not be bothered with such trifling matters. The Indians had admitted their debts, and that was that.

One would expect the Indians to seek revenge among the traders, but this was not done. The proud, free spirits of the plains had now become so dependent upon the traders that they, who had got along so well by themselves in former times, could not now manage without the traders, even though they hated them to the core.

Year after year passed like this. The traders were always very clever in inventing new schemes whereby they could, with a semblance of legal justice, lay hands on the interest money that was paid out every summer. This was not difficult to do, for they bribed the petty officials who performed the local details of the contract. When the Indians, at payment time, gathered at the agency, they were sadly disappointed. About all they were given was the grievous vexation of seeing nearly all of their money given to the traders.

"Let them eat grass!"

The year 1861 was an unlucky year for the Indians. There was a total crop failure, which made it a difficult problem to survive the winter. With the coming of spring 1862, the trader got in his fresh supply of provisions, and now the Indians tried to buy some of the things they needed most, but they were not granted any credit before their money came in.

The payments were usually made in June, and hundreds of Indians were at the agency to receive their payments. But June passed, then July was over, and yet no money arrived. Time and again, the Indians came to the agency or to the mission and begged for help.

A portion of the payment consisted of foodstuffs, and the agency was a storing place for enormous supplies that belonged to the Indians. The government agent refused to distribute these wares until the money came in, for it had been a custom of longstanding to make the distributions at the same time. And as a hidebound bureaucrat, he could not, of course, adjust himself to circumstances.

Embittered because they had to go hungry day after day when the agency was full of wares belonging to them, the Indians finally stormed into the warehouse by force to take what was rightfully theirs. But just at that moment, a large troop of soldiers arrived with cannon. They were immediately stationed at the door, and the plundering stopped. *[There were two Indian agencies in the valley, 30 miles apart. The event above occurred at the Upper, or Yellow Medicine, Agency. However, things would soon erupt at the Redwood, or Lower, Agency. —Winistorfer]*

Thus, time went on, with the Indians in the most wretched of situations. It seemed to them that the government agent and the traders were in collaboration to starve them to death.

In early August, several hundred Indians, with Chief Little Crow (a Mdewankanton chief) as their leader, went to the Redwood Agency and asked the agent to use his influence with the traders (there were four of them there) so that they would let them buy food.

"We have waited a long time," said the chief. "The money is ours, but we do not get it. We have no food, but here are these traders who have a surplus of food in their stores. We ask of you, the government's agent, make arrangements with the traders so that we can get some food from them. If you do not do something, we shall have to use our own ways to keep from starving to death. When people are starving, they help themselves."

Frightened by this veiled threat, the agent turned to the traders and asked them what they were going to do about it. They conferred together, and one of them said, "Whatever Myrick does, we shall do."

The agent turned to Nathan Myrick, and with the most heartless contempt, Myrick said, "If the Indians are hungry, let them eat grass. It is none of my concern."

When the Indians heard about this brutal rejection of their request, they broke out in bitter cries of despair, but the chief commanded them to be silent, and then he led them all away.

Several other chiefs were now summoned to come to a council meeting, and in all quiet secrecy these chiefs began to lay plans for a war. They had reached a point where this seemed to be the only alternative. They had been deceived and they had been made to look ridiculous. Better a death on the warpath than to endure further humiliation. They had given the whites a choice; now let the war determine the outcome.

[There are many accounts of this war, written from many points of view, and they differ widely in their treatment of details. –Blegen]

The uprising begins
(From Rosholt's translation:)

On Sunday, 17 August 1862, six Indians came to Robinson Jones's house (near Acton, Minnesota). He had a store and a guest house about 10 miles west of Litchfield in Meeker County.

Jones did not care much for the Indians and had cheated them before. When he refused them whiskey, a quarrel started. He then went over to his neighbor, Howard Baker, but the Indians followed. For a while they acted friendly and even encouraged the whites to play a game of fast shooting, to see who could fire their rifles the fastest. This way they had the whites empty their rifles. Then they suddenly turned on them, and a regular butchering followed. Five white men were killed.

These men lived on the outskirts of a Norwegian settlement, but no Norwegians were attacked (up to this point). The Indians rode hastily off to Redwood, a distance of 60 miles, where their head chief, Little Crow, lived.

Little Crow was a smart and fearless, glory-happy Indian. Even so, he had always been against revolt. The Indians who had done the killing woke Little Crow in the middle of the night. While sitting in bed, he listened to their story of the murder in Meeker County. These Indians asked Little Crow to lead them and declare regular war, because the whites could certainly ask a hard punishment for their dead.

Now the time was right to hit the first blow. At first, Little Crow held back. But after intense requests about protecting his people's honor and their rights, he decided to break all agreements and let the war begin.

With this decision, Little Crow became the leader who, without the least amount of sympathy, would suddenly and fearlessly overtake his victims.

That same night (17 August), several small groups of Indians were sent out to surprise the new settlers spread out in different parts of Kandiyohi, Renville, Redwood, Cottonwood, Murray and other counties where white people had settled. These were the Indians who suddenly brought death, fear and imprisonment to thousands of unsuspecting settlers who lived all over the wide terrain.

In the meantime, the main group of Indians gathered at the Redwood Agency where Little Crow lived. At 7 o'clock the next morning (Monday, 18 August), the white men at the agency were attacked and killed. One of the first fatalities was the trader Nathan Myrick. When his body was found, his mouth was stuffed with grass. The Indians had given him a little of the food that he had recommended for *them*.

First battle with U.S. troops

Chief Little Crow collected his troops near the reservation agency and immediately launched a series of battles in which the casualties were extremely high in proportion to the number of men involved.

The government had several forts in this widely extended territory, but since the garrisons were rather small, they were not in a position to meet the Indians on equal terms. These troops fought valiantly against a much larger force.

A speed messenger was sent to Fort Ridgely 12 miles away to report the attack (on the Redwood Agency). At 2 in the afternoon (18 August), a group of 44 soldiers arrived at the agency under the command of Captain Marsh. Missionary Hinman met him on his way to the fort and advised the captain to hold back and return to the fort. But the captain, very brave, would not listen to the pastor's words and declared he could "beat up all the Indians."

When he came to the ferry dock, he lined up his men so they could be seen from all sides. In the bushes lay 300 to 400 Indians, all taking aim at the lined-up soldiers. Almost half of the soldiers were dead or wounded by the first blast, some with as many as 20 bullets in their bodies. Captain Marsh, not wounded, assembled what was left of his men and started back toward Fort Ridgely.

Now followed a terrible retreat, with hundreds of bullets fired at the soldiers from every wooded area, and hand-to-hand combat with 20 Indians to each soldier. The Indians had taken all their clothes off. With their war paint and their horrible war cry, it was like fighting devils.

Just a few tired men escaped. Among the fallen soldiers were two Norwegians, Christian Jorgenson and Ole Svendson (wounded).

That same day, the long-awaited money arrived (at Fort Ridgely). There was an amount of $71,000 in gold coins, but by the time it arrived, about a hundred white men had already fallen dead on the field of battle. If the money had arrived one day sooner, there would surely have been no Indian uprising. But because of the bureaucratic routine so firmly established in all higher offices of the capital city, the payment was several months behind schedule. As a result, 600 to 800 innocent people had to sacrifice their lives for the sins of an inept government bureaucracy.

Battle for New Ulm and Fort Ridgely

The next day (19 August), Little Crow attacked New Ulm 46 miles down river. The Indians believed it would be an easy takeover. But the Germans who lived there had found out

Romsdalshornet

about it and were prepared to put up a good fight. Little Crow was in a hurry to attack Fort Ridgely, so he left New Ulm for the time being.

Fort Ridgely was an important military base on the Indian border. The Indians wanted to take over the fort. With the fort in their hands, nothing would stop their forward march to Fort Snelling and the counties to the east. Fort Ridgely consisted of a number of log buildings and one stone building surrounding an open place.

Since no trouble was expected, Lieutenant Sheehan, with about 60 men, was ordered to Fort Ripley, 200 miles to the north. On the evening of 18 August, these troops had made camp in a wooded area between New Auburn and Glencoe. Suddenly a man rode into camp and gave Sheehan orders from Captain Marsh to turn back immediately, since the Indians were raising hell around him.

Lieutenant Sheehan did not hesitate. Even though his men had just camped after a long day's march, he and his soldiers broke camp immediately and marched through the night. At 9 the next morning (19 August), after riding 42 miles, they reached the fort.

The next day (20 August), Little Crow attacked the fort. To begin with, he had around 500 warriors, which he later increased to 1,500. By now, many settlers had fled to the fort from all directions, so around 180 men with weapons and some 300 women and children had gathered there.

For three desperate days, there was a continuous fight. The Indians used all their cunning and showed the total depth of their courage. They fired burning arrows, sneaked up through the tall grass toward the fort from all directions, made some desperate storm attacks and went completely berserk.

But Lieutenant Sheehan showed himself to be a quick-thinking commander, always ready to meet the attacks. He also had a couple of cannons that he put to good use against the warriors.

Once in a while the fire silenced among the tired warriors, and the white men could hear Little Crow encouraging his warriors to take courage and make one finishing attack. With glowing words, he begged, coaxed and ordered his warriors to take the fort or die trying.

Since he had so many men, he sent new groups out time after time. These groups stormed the fort by shooting bullets through the buildings, but at last they had to give up because of the sure rifles and the fire-spewing cannons.

After regular attacks of this kind, in which a large number were killed, the Indians gave up, and the battle was over. As fast as he could, Little Crow gathered up his dead and wounded, broke camp and retreated. During the silence that followed, the cries of the squaws were heard. Their song of sadness over the dead lifted over the valley, mixing with the hysterical women's and children's cries from within the stone building. The moment was too grave for joy to take hold of the whites. Even though the danger was over, no one felt much like yelling victory calls.

The situation inside the stone building, where so many women and children were locked in, was horrible. The thundering cannons, the dreadful war screams, the bleeding men and the burning buildings brought forth a fear and hysteria that overtook most. Nine children were born during the siege; just two of these lived. The misery was indescribable.

Many of these women courageously stood by their men in those fearful days. When the ammunition was running low and the small arms ammo out, Lieutenant Sheehan put them to work opening bullet-round cardboard containers to retrieve the gunpowder inside in order to make more cartridges.

The projectiles were made of thin iron string used for making nails. These were cut into small pieces. In addition, they pulled the Indians' bullets from the wooden walls and used them with good results against their old owners.

On a monument at Fort Ridgely are cut the names of these brave women. Among them is one Norwegian woman, Julia Peterson. The heroic protectors of the fort named on the monument are the following Norwegians, all of them members of the 5th Minnesota regiment:
• Ole Svendson
• Ole G. Wall
• Halvor Ellefson
• Martin Ellingson
• Andrew Gulbranson
• Peter Rissen
• Andrew Peterson

Upset over their defeat at Fort Ridgely, Little Crow turned again to New Ulm. With 650 trained warriors, he fiercely attacked the city on 23 August. Meanwhile, around 2,000 refugees had taken shelter in the city. Out of these, Colonel Chas E. Flandreau had organized a troop of 250 respectable men.

For a while it looked as if the Indians would win. The city consisted of 150 houses, and one after the other fell into the hands of the Indians, who torched the city. New Ulm became an ocean of flames, and only 30 houses were left. At this time it looked bad for the brave protectors.

Because the situation was so hopelessly desperate, not only from Indian bullets but also from fire and famine, a group of about 100 men resolved to attempt one last excursion. Shoulder to shoulder, like crazed berserks, they rushed the Indians in such a frenzied assault that the superstitious redskins believed they were not fighting mortal men but evil spirits. Terrified, they flung their weapons and fled beyond range of the rifles.

Then the settlers loaded their women and children and their wounded on 153 wagons, and the 2,000 destitute people made their way to Mankato, 30 miles farther east. They made a pitiful procession of miserable creatures. At Mankato, they were met by government troops.

On the memorial statue honoring the fallen in New Ulm are also the names of nine scouts who were overtaken, killed and scalped outside the city. Among these were four Norwegians:
• Ole Olson
• Nils Olson
• Thor Olson
• John Thompson

No one can, at this date, tell where they came from in Norway, but their modest names are inscribed on the soldiers' monument in New Ulm.

Battle at Birch Coulee

For a few days nothing was heard from the Indians. Then on 31 August, a group of 150 men was sent up the valley from Fort Ridgely to spy out the area and to bury the bodies of any murdered whites that they might encounter. They found many bodies but not any sighting of Indians.

The next day (1 September) they marched through a beautiful meadow, where all signs of violence had ceased. The weather was delightful. In their good mood and happy tone due to some extra whiskey, the soldiers forgot they were in enemy territory and walked around as if on a picnic.

That night they made camp at a place called Birch Coulee, 16 miles from Fort Ridgely. The place they chose, without any regard to danger, was in the middle of an open field, with a few wooded groves close by. Here they lay down to sleep without the least fear of any Indians.

Just before dawn (2 September), an ear-stopping rifle burst suddenly awakened them. The surprised soldiers jumped up. All around the woods and hillside, the field below and air above seemed to be crawling with howling Sioux. The soldiers started to line up, but they finally came to their senses when Captain Anderson hollered: "Lie down, you Dumbheads! Lie down and fire!"

The field gave absolutely no cover at all from the frenzied Indians, who easily fired at the exposed soldiers. Just three shovels could be found, so the soldiers tried using bayonets and pocketknives to dig holes in the ground for shelters. The nonstop fire from the Indians gave them no time for this, and one man after the other fell, dead or wounded. Their 90 horses were killed during the first hour.

Lieutenant Sheehan, who had so bravely protected the fort, watched for a chance, then ran straight through the Indians to get help from the fort. A group of 240 men was sent immediately, but the Indians, 500 strong, prevented the connection. More troops had to come from the fort, and finally General Sibley arrived with 400 men, his total garrison.

At this time, the men at Birch Coulee had been lying there for 48 hours without food or drink. As soon as anyone lifted an arm to reach for food from the provision wagon, he was drilled through by hundreds of bullets.

The soldiers' ammunition had almost run out. Most of them lay in dark despair, saving one last bullet so as to at least take one Indian along through death's door. Twenty-three men were killed and 60 wounded. Several Norwegians took part in this desperate fight.

Battle at Wood Lake

The war continued, with varying success. Then came the battle at Wood Lake in Yellow Medicine County, where there is now a large Norwegian settlement. This was the first battle in which the government had sufficient troops at its command.

Until now, the Indians had thought that the government had all its soldiers and cannons tied up on the battlefields of the Southern states (fighting the Civil War, 1861-65). To meet this overwhelming strength on the government's side was a stunning surprise to the Indians.

Little Crow had sent many of his warriors north (northwest) to the Red River Valley to overtake Fort Abercrombie (on the Red River, bordering present-day Minnesota and North Dakota). There, they met more resistance than they had expected. While Little Crow waited for these troops to return, he negotiated with other Indian tribes to join him.

The Chippewa Indians, even though they and the Sioux were enemies, decided to unite with Little Crow's band in a joint endeavor. But Little Crow met unexpected opposition from two of the Sioux tribes. These were the Sissetons and Wahpetons, who had only taken a small part in the war and wanted to surrender. In spite of Little Crow's and the other chiefs' fiery speeches, they saw the war as completely hopeless. Their refusal was a letdown to the warring party.

On 19 September, General Sibley, with 2,000 men, set out to try his strength against the Indians. He went right at the Indians who were still negotiating with their brothers. The Red River warriors had not returned, and the Chippewa Indians were still not ready.

Thus Little Crow had just 500 warriors. But with any luck, he thought he might fire up the (other bands of) Indians. So he made a very quick attack on Sibley's army.

The battle (23 September) took place by Wood Lake on a piece of land that now (1908) belongs to G. D. Homme. The field soon became very bloody. The overwhelming number of white men and their cannons proved too much for the Indians, and they had to withdraw.

Camp Release

The situation was hopeless for the Indians, and a peace negotiation started. At Camp Release, across the river from Montevideo, Minnesota, the negotiations ended on 26 September. The Sioux people gave up all their belongings. Women, children and several hundred prisoners (around 1,500 Indians) surrendered to General Sibley. Little Crow and his supporters had managed to escape.

After having endured the most unspeakable sufferings and indignities, a total of 200 white girls and adult women were released. About one-half of these were Norwegians and Swedes whom the Indians had taken prisoner on pioneer farms. In his report, General Sibley included the following account about this:

"Out of the tents came more than 200 girls and adult women, the majority of whom were so scanty in dress that it barely served to conceal their nakedness. Many of them had on nothing but a single, often tattered, piece of cloth, while merciful squaws had supplied others with some worn-out and wretched garments fit only for temporary protection. Imagination balks at presenting a picture of a more poorly clad and sorrier group of civilized creatures than this.

"A few of them walked with an expression in their stiffly staring eyes and on their numb faces as if this mental suffering had driven them into imbecility. Others fell into despair at the thought of what had happened to them, and they felt themselves to be forever ruined. A few sat motionless, staring stiffly into space, and others broke into convulsive fits of wailing and weeping.

"Most of the pitiful creatures rushed wildly to the place where I was standing with my officers. They pressed about us with implorations not to let the red devils take them again into their power. I did my best to calm them by repeatedly assuring them that they were now free again and with friends, and that their horrible sufferings were now at an end.

"Many became hysterical and fell into convulsions. They laughed and cried at the same time, as if they could not bring themselves to believe that they were now in the custody of liberators. The most attractive of the girls had been given to select warriors. The rest of them, in their helplessness, were turned over to the wild masses for their enjoyment. The brutality of the bestial violence and rape to which they were subjected is revolting to imagine and impossible to describe."

White man's justice prevails

General Sibley ordered an immediate court-martial, and 303 Indians were sentenced to die by hanging.

When the news of this verdict reached the Eastern states, the people there, who had never experienced the savagery of the Indians, rose up in indignation at the thought of such a mass execution. President Lincoln was subjected to much pressure, and all but 38 of the convicted Indians were pardoned.

On a cold winter day, 26 December 1862, in Mankato, Minnesota, the 38 dusky, defiant figures mounted the scaffold together. With nooses around their necks, they turned their eyes toward their homes in the West and sang in deep, throaty tones their lugubrious death dirge. Hand in hand on the scaffold, as the large trap door was sprung, all 38 made their entry together into eternity.

The man who offered his services as executioner was one of the unlucky new settlers at Lake Chetec, who had seen his daughter shamed and his wife mutilated and tortured to death by the Indians.

More hostilities follow

The authorities believed that this execution marked the end of the uprising, and they sent jubilant telegrams to all sections of the country to announce the news of this quick and successful conclusion to the hostilities. Many of the settlers, accordingly, returned to their ruined homes.

But in the spring of 1863, new bands of Indians were back on the warpath. Pressing toward the eastern counties in Minnesota, they killed many people. In Brown and Watonwan counties, several Norwegians were either killed or taken prisoner.

General Sibley, with 3,000 troops and many cannons, was once again sent out to punish the red warriors. He followed them through all of Dakota and had some violent confrontations with them. This operation extended throughout the whole summer, and the Indians suffered one defeat after another. They were (eventually) dispersed and laid down their weapons .

Many Norwegians took part in this expedition. One was Ole Paulson, who served as captain and later as pastor in the Free Church. All told, around 600 Norwegians took part in this war from time to time.

Aftermath

This was the worst Indian revolt in this country's history. In some battles the white people were attacked by larger groups of red warriors than at any other time. Some 1,500 whites were killed and over 300 taken prisoner.

Of those killed, not many fell in battle. Most were settlers attacked without warning. Among these were many Norwegians, because they were the most fearless and dared to go out on the newly built border. Small groups of Indians would come out to their homes, acting in a friendly manner as if everything were fine. They sat down and were served what little the settlers could offer.

Vøringfossen

Then on a given signal, the war axe came up, the bullets were fired, and their hosts fell down. *[Here follows an account of the atrocities suffered by the settlers, which we've chosen to omit. –Winistorfer]* Weakened women, carrying their little children, wandered around 20, 30 and 50 miles until they found a safe place. They were often wounded, sick and practically naked. Many died from hunger and the injuries they received during that terrible time.

The ones lucky enough to be warned, fled, head over heel, leaving behind everything for which they had worked so hard. Thousands, mad with fear, rushed down toward the older settlements, swinging the whip continuously over the backs of the worn oxen, crying, pleading, praying and swearing.

The panic spread east to the Mississippi River and even into Iowa and Wisconsin. Counties as far as 200 to 300 miles away from the blood bath could feel its fear. In Fillmore and Allamakee counties, stories went around of huge flocks of wild Indians just a few miles away, and many fled in fear. In Winneshiek County, people were extremely fearful, and Decorah was full of refugees. A dirt cellar on a hillside not far from Decorah was used as a fortress, and people made bullets all night.

At Washington Prairie stood Pastor Koren's horses, stomping on a hollow wood floor. The noise had almost created a panic, because it was taken to be the drumbeat of marching Indians.

Like an "end-of-the-world" curse, the Indians simultaneously had arrived at hundreds of different places, sweeping the country clean of the hated palefaces. The settlers fled, and the land was deserted for three years.

Far away in the eastern settlement, starving and sad refugees thought about their rich harvest now rotting in the stacks, their children crying for milk, and their ownerless cattle roaming the prairie. As they took shelter in dirt cellars and outhouses, they thought about their cozy homes, now in ashes.

An impartial historical judgment will admit that the Indians had good legal reason for taking up arms, but the unfortunate feature of the sad situation was that their revenge did not strike the guilty ones. Instead of hurting the thieving traders, the crooked agents and the bungling bureaucrats, their revenge was taken out on the innocent pioneers who had settled on Indian lands. It was the honest, hard-working and peaceful settlers who had to suffer for the sins of others.

If the Sisseton and Wahpeton Indians had not refused to join Little Crow's warring bands (thus hindering the Chippewa Indians from joining with Little Crow), the fight would have taken a different course. It could have spread death and destruction over several more states and further depleted the already low resistance of the people in the country.

Among the Sioux Indians, as among all other human beings, there were some individuals who were scoundrels and cowards. It was a few of these who had calculated that it was easier and safer to plunder the widely separated pioneer settlers than to confront the trained government troops in battle. These Indians, the worst dregs of mankind and the rabble of the tribe, were the ones who so suddenly and savagely murdered the whites. In about a week, they had swarmed over a score of counties and killed 600 to 800 settlers. *[Many Indians and mixed-bloods (including some who had become farmers) did not take part in the uprising. Some became victims themselves; some even helped protect the settlers and whites at the agencies. –Winistorfer]*

For about one month, the Indians had the upper hand. From the names on the monuments in the military cemeteries, it is obvious that a considerable number of Norwegians were members of the troops that fought in these engagements.

58

The first large prairie settlement

(Source: Den Siste Folkevandring Sagastubber fra Nybyggerlivet i Amerika, by Hjalmar Rued Holand, 1930; Norwegians in America: The Last Migration, by Hjalmar Rued Holand, translated by Helmer M. Blegen, 1978, pp. 177–186)

One of the biggest concentrations of Norwegians in America, outside of the large cities, exists in western Minnesota on the two sides of the Minnesota River. This widely extended but densely populated settlement stretches across almost all of Lac qui Parle and Yellow Medicine counties and over the contiguous counties along the Milwaukee Railway. This region includes the Minneapolis and St. Louis railroads, and all the land between these two railroads. From Delhi to Louisburg, the settlement is about 70 miles long and, in a couple of places, 50 miles wide. This region is divided into 72 Norwegian congregations, with a collective membership of about 24,000. The total Norwegian population is more than 30,000.

The land is primarily a high, open prairie. On the steep hills along the Minnesota River's great valley, there are some woods, and small belts of trees grow along the smaller watercourses. Most of the big farms, however, are built on the open prairie, where there was not a single tree until the pioneers planted their little groves around the buildings.

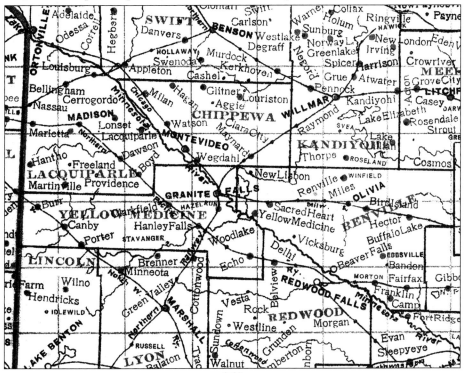

Land of Canaan

Like the land of Canaan in all its glory is this settlement when its rolling prairie is covered with billowing, yellow fields of wheat. It is like the land of Canaan in other respects, also, for it is divided among many tribes, each with its own special dialect and characteristics. In the eastern part, there are people in great numbers from Valdres, Numedal, Nordfjord and Setesdal. Farther west are even more from Stavanger and Trondheim, and in the extreme western end are *Striler*, *Telemarkinger* and another colony of *Valdriser*.

This whole immense settlement can be traced back to two men. In the manner of Caleb and Joshua in ancient days, they set out to spy out the country where the Canaanites (the Indians) had reigned with the greatest cruelty and power. Admittedly, a few earlier Norwegian pioneers had preceded them, but all of these had fallen under the frenzied rage of the Indians, and today their names are not known.

This settlement lies around and inside the former Sioux Reservation, where the war began in 1862 and where some of the toughest battles were fought. The battlefields of Wood Lake, Birch Coulee and Camp Release are wholly within the boundaries of the settlement and are now owned by Norwegian people.

The Indian War lasted three years. During this time, there were practically no new pioneers bold enough to settle here when this war was raging, for none could tell what the outcome might be. Among the first, who at last in 1865 ventured into this western area to see land, were two Norwegians who became the founders of the great settlement in the valley of the Minnesota River. These men were Hellik Glaim and Torstein Rosgaard, both of them from Opdal in Numedal.

On their way west, these men frequently saw the ashes of cabins burned by the Indians and the skeletons of unburied pioneers and their Indian enemies, who only a short time previously had been engaged in their deadly fight against each other. Who could be sure that these sly redskins would not appear again on these plains?

But, these two *Numedøler* were not men who could be frightened when they saw dead bones, for they were unusually resolute and experienced fellows. Hellik Glaim, in particular, was a remarkable man whose unusual boldness, strength and quick resourcefulness made him the central figure of many a traditional legend still current in all the Numedal settlements. He was one of the first to emigrate from his district. He settled on Rock Prairie as early as the year 1841. There are many anecdotes about his many pranks, shared in earlier chapters.

In 1850, Hellik Glaim became one of the earliest settlers in Iowa, where he helped to establish the big Numedal settlement in Clayton County. In 1853 he went with some other *Numedøler* to Root River in Fillmore County, Minnesota, to a place where Rushford was later built. These were the first Norwegians in this valley, where several thousands of Norwegians now reside.

Land swindler "bites the bullet"

In that part of Minnesota, there was at the time an extremely sly Yankee by the name of Arthur Bow, who was a big annoyance to the land-seekers. He used to keep an eye on anyone looking for some good land. If anybody happened to find a satisfactory piece of land, he would inform him that he had already filed a pre-emption claim on this particular plot. If he was asked to give up his claim to it, he would be glad to do so for a consideration, let us say, $25 to $50. Being a large, husky man who was a little too free with the revolver at his hip, there were many who paid him in order to keep the peace.

The Yankee tried this swindle on Hellik Glaim and his friends, too. But here he met his match. In a twinkling, Hellik Glaim had grabbed the Yankee's revolver, and before the swindler knew what was happening, he found himself on his back, with Glaim sitting on his chest.

One by one, Glaim fed him the cartridges from the revolver and forced the Yankee to swallow them. When the last cartridge was swallowed, he was turned loose with the warning that if he dared to show his face in this district again, he would be made to swallow the revolver as well.

Go west, young men…

In 1865, Hellik Glaim had lived in Rushford for 12 years, and now he thought it about time to go out to seek new adventures. Fillmore County was now completely settled, and hundreds of newcomers had arrived who did not know where they could find any land that suited them. Glaim wanted to help these newcomers, so with a companion of his childhood days, Torstein Rosgaard, he went west to look for good land. There was not yet any railroad in the western part of Minnesota, but Rosgaard had a prairie schooner.

They covered a distance of between 400 and 500 miles before they found any land that looked good enough. Then they reached the upper part of the Minnesota River Valley, where the land was broad and fair, and very rich soil stretched far and wide, with wooded ridges of hills on both sides.

Besides, in the course of the ages, the river had dug itself down to a level where huge red granite cliffs lay bare, with fine trees growing in all the crevices branching out from the bottom of the valley for miles. All this combined to produce an especially secure and comfortable impression.

The spot chosen by the first settler, Rosgaard, lies about 10 miles southeast of the present town of Granite Falls. Hellik Glaim was not entirely satisfied with this area, so he went on to a location 20 miles farther west, where he took up land. Then he trudged back to Rushford to sell his farm and fetch his possessions.

Because Glaim was the best-known and most experienced of all the pioneers in all of Fillmore County, his decision to move was the cause for a great deal of talk and discussion throughout the winter months, and many resolved to go along.

Among these was a group of *Numedøler* who did not wait for Glaim. Early in the spring of 1866, they started out, with Tov Kolien as their leader. Tov had worked for the government as a driver to deliver supplies to a number of Indian forts and thus was very familiar with the road to Fort Ridgely, located only 30 days from their destination. They arrived at the fort, and left their horses and wagons there because they feared they might meet Indians.

Starting out from the fort on foot, they shortly lost their way and did not know where to go. They had consumed their provisions and tried in vain to still the qualms of hunger and thirst by chewing on the long grass. The tall, stiff grass made walking difficult, and the prairie was terribly big. Fearing that it was all over for them and that they might never be rescued, they dragged themselves on like this for a couple of days.

Then one day toward evening, they caught sight of a man carrying a gun. They dragged themselves to him and found Torstein Rosgaard, who was out hunting. He had been living there all alone for almost a year, depending on his gun and fishing pole for his support.

He brought them to his cabin and gave them food. The next day he led them to the top of a high granite cliff, from which they had a clear view for miles up the valley and down the land through which the Minnesota River winds its way. Sitting there, each chose the site for building his future home, beginning with the eldest. There was plenty of land for all of them, nice fertile soil, wooded hillsides and excellent access to water. This was how a large

El Capitan i Yosemite-Dalen [California]

settlement of *Numedøler* had its origin, as both sides of the river became built up.

Blackbirds devour first crop

Without money and often without implements and cattle, these resolute pioneers attacked the wilderness in western Minnesota. They were filled with hope, for the landscape was matchless in the eyes of these people accustomed to the rocks and mountains of their homeland in Norway. Here they saw level expanses of bottomless, black loam, woods, water, rain and sunshine. This must be a Goshen to live in, they thought. They bought oxen by borrowing money at exorbitant rates of interest. Often, they made their own plows out of wood. With untiring effort, they undertook to break the tough sod.

The year they arrived, 1866, the price of wheat had risen to $3 a bushel, and many were confident that it would never be lower.

"Just wait until the fields are yellow with ripening wheat; then there will be prosperity," they thought.

The next summer they had a hundred acres seeded to wheat, and everybody was happy. As the wheat ripened, millions of blackbirds came and attacked the fields. People realized that something must be done to save the grain. They shot off all available firearms. The swarm of birds rose a little, but immediately came down on the wheat again.

The people raced up and down the fields, shouting, howling and screaming. This scared up the flocks, but in a moment the birds again alit to continue the feast. The settlers pounded on tin pails, rang cowbells and made all the noise they possibly could. They exhausted their strength in a never-ending attempt to drive away the birds, but to no avail. When autumn arrived, they harvested a grand total of one bushel of wheat from the hundred acres.

Since they had depended upon this wheat to furnish them with flour, and since they had no money with which to buy any flour, the food supply was very meager that winter. The majority struggled through the winter on a diet of kohlrabi.

When spring arrived, they had no food and no money. Many were obliged to leave their farms and seek temporary employment someplace or other so that they might keep their families from starving to death. With the husband away, the wife labored with the clumsy, slow-moving oxen to get patches planted to provide some provisions for the winter.

That summer the blackbirds were not quite so bad, because there were countless new fields for them to divide among themselves. By means of a united and persistent effort with noisemaking devices such as tin cans and shrieks and cries by young and old during the days when the wheat was ripening, the most active harvested a very good crop. But that year the price fell to 35 to 50 cents a bushel. It was not of great significance anyway, for it took many years before a railroad came so near that they could bring their wheat to market or ship any of their products.

From harvest to market

As there was not yet any threshing machine in the settlement, the wheat had to be separated from its straw by means of a flail, or tramped out by oxen and then cleaned with the aid of a shovel and the wind. The work had to wait until the fall plowing was finished, and it required the greater part of the winter to get it done. For this reason, they accumulated so many pieces of ice in the wheat that it was almost impossible to grind it into flour.

Tov Kolien tells that when he was ready, he loaded up a big amount and took it to the mill. Now there would be an end to the flour famine in the neighborhood, he thought. When the miller saw the wheat, he said that it would be impossible to grind. He did not know if he could give him one sack of flour for the entire load.

Finally, the miller took pity on the

man and promised him a little flour. But Tov did not get it at that time. He had to make a long and laborious trip later in order to pick up the little dab of flour.

For those living on the north side of the river, the trips to Redwood Falls to get their wheat ground were really a hardship. They had to cross the river, which at times was so large that they could only cross it by boat. Then they would take only a few sacks of wheat at a time in the boat. When all the wheat had been transported to the other side, they would take the wagon apart and transport it, piece by piece, in several trips across. The last job was to drive the oxen into the water and make them swim across the river. When they got the oxen on the other side, they would then have the trouble of putting it all together again.

Ole Enestvedt relates: "Once, we had freighted everything to the other side except five sacks of wheat and the rear half of the wagon. We laid the sacks in the bottom of the boat, and then placed the half wagon across the boat so that the wheels were in the water on both sides.

"When we got out in the current, the wheels began to turn like the paddlewheels on a steamboat. The current somehow got too much control over one wheel and tipped the whole business into the river. We clambered to the upset hull and managed, after some difficulty, to reach the shore. We were also successful in fishing out the rear wheel, but the sacks of wheat were never seen again."

Bout with a blizzard

The newcomers far to the east in Fillmore County knew nothing about these problems, however, and they kept on coming without interruption to the West in order to acquire a home and some land for themselves and families. The first to arrive chose the land along the small watercourses where the low places were heavily wooded. This gave them a fine shelter against the harsh winds.

But these protecting, wooded areas were relatively small, and the latecomers had to build their houses out on the naked, open prairie, where there wasn't a tree to be seen so far as the eye could see. There was nothing wrong with the soil, but because of its lack of trees, this 1,000-mile stretch of hay meadow is more exposed to the ravages of wind and weather than any other place in the United States.

The cold is not too impossible to endure when it is without wind. But when the air moves at the rate of 60 miles per hour, there is no house, no wall, no bearskin coat that can keep it out.

To protect their homes, the farmers on these naked plains have planted a dense windbreak of quickly growing trees around their buildings. These are effective in shutting out much of the storm, but they have the disadvantage that they also shut off the view of the magnificent expanses. It took many years before these trees were large enough to make an effective windbreak.

In the meantime, life for the pioneer was so uncomfortable that no bumper crop could compensate for the hardships. Hundreds of living beings, both human and animal, have succumbed and paid with their lives. There are reports of many a man losing his bearings on the short trip between the house and the barn when the blizzard raging about him made it impossible to see anything in front of him.

On one occasion during the early years, the settlers were having a meeting of the Sharon congregation, a few miles north of Granite Falls. It was on 13 January 1873, before they had their own church built. The weather was mild, and no less than 43 men had gathered in the home of a pioneer who had one of the biggest houses in the settlement. It was 16 by 18 feet in size, but when all these men got inside, there was very little space for each of them.

They finished their business during the course of the afternoon and got up to start for their respective homes. Just at that time, they noticed a black, lowering cloud moving swiftly toward them from the north. This looked ominous. All of a sudden, they felt an icy rush of air, followed immediately by a snowstorm so dense and dark that one could not see anything an arm's length away from him. They were caught in the worst blizzard of the 1870s' decade. For two whole days and nights, the storm howled and hissed without let-up, with a violence that even these pioneers, who had already defied the harshest powers of nature for several years, had not believed possible.

Meanwhile, the entire company sat imprisoned in this small cabin. I say sat, but that is an error. There was not room for all of them to sit. The room was no larger than an ordinary kitchen and contained not only the kitchen range, but also a bed, a table and other furniture. Some of the men were squatting side by side along the walls. But most of them had to stand in a cluster, with now and then an opportunity to change places with someone who was squatting on the floor. The air turned so foul that it became hard to breathe.

The first night and day passed tolerably well in spite of the lack of sleep. Everyone hoped the morning would bring improvement in the weather and suffered calmly the imprisonment. But when the second day dawned with no abatement in the whining and howling blizzard, the confinement became very depressing.

Pastor Ericksen suggested that they sing some hymns to pass the time. After a few attempts, they gave it up. It was impossible for them to sing after they had stood for 20 hours, anxiously wondering how their families were getting along at home. Some of them had open and rickety barns that offered little protection against this kind of weather. Others worried that their wives and children might try to take care of the animals in the barn and, very likely lose their bearings and perish in the blizzard.

Even if they stayed indoors, a family would be in danger, for the woodpile was quite a distance from the house.

The thought of all these dangers to their loved ones was so unsettling that, time and again, one or another of the men would open the door to see if he could rush to the rescue of people at home. But he never stayed outside for long. As soon as he stepped out, he was overwhelmed by the savagery of the blizzard, which assailed him like a thousand hard lashes from a whip. Snow filled his eyes, his nose and his mouth. The whirling, swirling snow, so white and yet so blinding and choking that he could not see one step ahead of him, confused him so that he lost all sense of orientation. It was with utmost difficulty that the man was able to get back inside the sheltering door again.

Soon, the woodbox was empty. The woodpile was only 40 feet from the house, but how could anyone get to it? One man had come to this meeting from quite a distance, and he had come driving in a new, freshly painted wagon that he had left by the wall, just outside the cabin door. He proposed that they break the wagon up in small enough pieces to burn in the stove. No one was willing to consent to this.

Finally, they agreed to make a living chain from the cabin door to the woodpile. While one man kept a firm grip on the wall, six or seven others linked hands and reached the woodpile. Then they dug out sticks of wood from the snowdrift and passed each chunk, hand over hand, back to the inside of the cabin, where they split it on the floor.

It was worse to feed the crowd, but even this was managed somehow. The supply of cooked food was quickly exhausted by the 43 men. Fortunately, there was a good supply of flour in the cabin. There was also a small iron pot, and by cooking a mush made of flour and water from morning to evening and from evening to morning, they were able to give each man a little mush. And

Mirror Lake i Yosemite-Dalen [California]

when they had made the round of all 43, the first man had had ample time to appreciate another saucerful.

The third morning arrived with the same frenzy of storm. It seemed that the world was already destroyed, and all that remained of the cosmos was this company of men in this cabin. Gloomy thoughts tormented each man. Was this God's way of punishing him for leaving his father and mother in the Old Country? There were many deep sighs, and many a man silently prayed for himself and for his dear ones.

By the afternoon it seemed as if the storm were slacking down a bit. Before long, they could almost see the barn through the lighter blasts of snow. Then they clearly saw the barn and other buildings, half buried under the snow. They did not tarry very long after this. Each man fought his way through deep drifts in the direction of his home, rejoicing that this fateful congregation session had at last ended.

Hardships of pioneer life

Up to the time that this settlement was founded, the Norwegian pioneers had been rather fortunate in that they had been able to establish their homes and colonies in places well sheltered within the protective environment of forest growth. Even the open country, as they called the larger prairie patches, was very favorable and possibly better, as it had no trees to clear off before plowing. There were a few isolated settlers out on the open prairie, but not until after the Civil War ended were there any extensive Norwegian settlements out on the naked prairie. This one, on both sides of the Minnesota River, was the first of the large prairie settlements.

The pioneers were bitterly reminded that their choice involved hardships. Not only were their small houses frigidly cold in winter, and not very comfortable at best, but summer days did not offer many advantages.

Where the wooded areas were full of a variety of game that helped substantially to enrich the pioneers' food supply, there was very little out on the prairie fit to put in a pot on the stove. The rich, productive soil did not bring speedy returns, either, for they had to wait so long for railroads.

1873-77: Grasshopper years

The year 1873 is remembered as the year of the devastating financial panic. It was impossible to borrow money. For many years the people lived a wretched life of seemingly hopeless battle against a whole series of plagues and troubles. They fought the mosquitoes, blackbirds, storms, starvation, cold and heat—an endless battle against odds such as impossibly high interest rates and other burdens.

But they had never experienced anything so heartbreaking as the grasshopper years of 1873 to 1877. The mosquitoes were atrocious bloodsuckers, but they, at least, did not devour the grain. The blackbirds, to be sure, did eat grain, but they rarely took all. They usually left a little for the farmer.

Grasshoppers had no sympathy at all. They wiped the table clean. They devoured anything that was green, no matter whether big or small. They ate the grass of the field and left not a leaf on the trees. When the grasshoppers had finished, they left the pioneer stripped—literally and figuratively. He had mortgaged his property to the limit to get through his first years of preparation, and now he was reduced to accepting alms from people far away. The grasshopper plague was so great a disaster that it cannot be fully described here in merely a few sentences. (Read more on the grasshopper plague in the next chapter.)

Religious division on the prairie

In the face of so many setbacks and disasters—a continual succession of disappointments, the settlement made very slow material progress. It took a long time before the pioneers could acquire good homes and build their churches.

And yet they did not completely lack a certain measure of spiritual and intellectual cultural life. From time to time they were visited by itinerant preachers, both laymen and clergy. They had very few books, but some newspapers found their way to the settlement, and these were read and loaned to others until they were worn to shreds.

According to an old superstition brought with them from their old childhood home, these pioneers looked upon all worldly troubles as a divine punishment for sins. Many of these early settlers had no end of troubles, and this may explain why so many of them developed an unusually narrow and pietistic view of Christianity. Both the Haugeans and the Ellingianers found among these long-suffering pioneers a very fertile field for their activities.

Some of the first preachers were also somewhat unfortunate in their choices of themes for their preaching. Instead of bringing to these depressed and discouraged people a practical and cheerful message of hope that might encourage them toward a collaboration in a spirit of love and friendship, they preferred to present an interpretation based on obscure doctrinal problems "so that our people may know what our synod believes and teaches concerning this point."

Thus a bitter dissension developed on the question of justification. The people became so passionately worked up in discussing this abstract question that they forgot all about their own needs, and it split the first congregation up into two bitter factions.

Shortly afterward, a preacher came to clarify the synod's position on the matter of owning slaves. There were no slaves in this settlement, unless you counted several exhausted mothers. Even though slavery had been abolished all over the country, the debate on this question became so heated that the factions found it impossible to sit in the same church together, and the result was a new split.

Things were quiet for a time, but then a new spiritual epidemic, the question of election, infected the settlement. Has God preordained certain human individuals to hell? This was, in its simplest form, the way many ordinary laymen formulated the disputed question. Old friendships broke up. Families divided, relatives forgot their blood ties, and new congregations broke up into factions.

When one hears about how wrought up the people became over purely theological questions, one now feels compelled to laugh. But this was certainly no laughing matter at the time. There was a tragic side to this: People forgot Christianity and became Pharisees.

However, there was one more church fight that had so few elements of dignity and so much of the comic in it that one may, if one feels like it, laugh at it with impunity. Out on the prairie, there was one congregation that held on to a tendency that today is almost extinct. The characteristic feature of their tenet was that they ascribed no importance to faith, but placed supreme stress and emphasis on grief and melancholy as the proof of a true Christian living. Woe unto him who sang and was joyful! He was a lost soul.

In harmony with such an attitude, they put undue significance into externalities, such as dress. He who went around in the shabbiest clothing and habitually had a sour-faced expression had almost fulfilled the law, especially if he mortally hated all forms of clerical garb, gowns and canonicals. This congregation and its minister were for years mutually satisfying in their relationship. The preacher dressed in homespun of an intermediate hue, and the parishioners' outfits were of skins, with no color at all.

Now it came to pass that the preacher, a layman from Norway, was delivering a sermon about the rich man and Lazarus. In the course of his exposition, he happened to state, perhaps unconsciously prompted by his thought of the hated clerical gown, that the rich man was dressed in *black* clothing and fine linen. After church the congregation, as usual, lingered a while to exchange greetings and conversation.

"Well, Per," said Ole, "what did you think of today's sermon?"

"Oh," sighed Per, "if we could only live as it admonishes us to do."

"Yes, but what do you say about the way the preacher misrepresents the Scriptures?"

"Misrepresents the Scriptures!" exclaimed Per, horrified. "Gee, you don't say he has done that, do you?" Per, obviously had dozed off a little during the sermon.

"Why, of course he did!" Ole assured him earnestly. "In the Scriptures it is expressly stated that the rich man was garbed in purple, but the preacher said he was dressed in black. Wouldn't you call that a distortion of the word of God?"

This was, indeed, a serious accusation, and people became very busy discussing the seriousness of an offense like this—a preacher publicly, from his pulpit, perverting the Holy Writ.

Finally, the preacher also became aware of this discussion. The next time there was a church service, he took the congregation severely to task for having made such a big issue of an unimportant word. It was rather the lesson and the truth of the parable that should be taken to heart, not the empty letters of a word. Whether the rich man was dressed in black or in red was not an essential part of the lesson.

But then the storm erupted in full fury.

"Aha, so that is the kind of a man you are!" exclaimed Ole and his fellow parishioners. "Instead of humbly acknowledging your sin, you stand there puffed up in your pride and tell us the words in the Scriptures are of no significance. Don't you know that it is written: 'It is easier for heaven and earth to pass than one tittle of these, my words'? And here you fling away one of these words, worth more than all the earth—throw it away and tell us that it means nothing?

"It is surely some preacher we have! You, who pretend to be a clergyman, had better think about what Luther said. He said that whoredom and murder were less reprehensible than the great sin of perverting the word of God. But since you do not respect the Scriptures, I suppose you do not have any respect for Luther, either."

Not very long afterward, a sack of flour disappeared in the settlement, and many wondered who the thief could be. Then someone hinted that a man so hardened that he could stand in the pulpit and pervert the word of God would also very likely be capable of stealing a sack of flour.

This, too, at last reached the ear of the preacher, and he moved away. Soon thereafter, he died of grief.

Torstein Rosgaard's later years

Torstein Rosgaard, the first one to take up land in this settlement, did not remain for long. One day, at the beginning of the 1870s, he set fire to a piece of dry prairie lowland in order to lessen the risk of a prairie fire. In doing this, he was unfortunate in that he burned up a couple of haystacks belonging to his neighbors. They became very angry and made a big fuss about it. Since Rosgaard disliked being on bad terms with his neighbors, and being single and without any bonds to hold him there, he suddenly returned to Numedal in Norway.

No one heard anything about him for 40 years. Then, one evening in 1911, the Chicago police found an old tramp sitting on a curb. They took the old man to a police station and put him in a cell. The next morning, they discovered that the supposed tramp had $10,000 in cash and papers of value on his person.

It was Torstein Rosgaard in his 81st year.

Skar i Næheden af Eide

59

The grasshopper plague

(Source: Den Siste Folkevandring Sagastubber fra Nybyggerlivet i Amerika, by Hjalmar Rued Holand, 1930; Norwegians in America: The Last Migration, by Hjalmar Rued Holand, translated by Helmer M. Blegen, 1978, pp. 187–190)

It is quite likely that if the emigrants had known in advance how much struggle, reversal and disappointment they had in store for them in America, not many of them would have left their homes in Norway to come here.

The great majority of them found their sphere of activity in this new and primitive land that was completely lacking in all the well-ordered sociological elements to which they were accustomed. Everything had to be created and organized from the bottom up.

Even the climate was so different from what they were used to. To begin with, it was extremely disagreeable for them. It was their lot to encounter a great diversity of hardships before they, by constant exertion, succeeded in subduing the wilderness and organizing a new society.

Invasion of the grasshoppers

The worst of the plagues was the scourge of grasshopper invasions. These were so overwhelming and so destructive that even the most buoyant of the old pioneers shudder at the memory of those bitter years when they seemed to have been forgotten and abandoned by both God and men.

Fortunately, this invasion did not descend upon the entire territory of Norwegian settlements in America but was limited to the west-central areas of Minnesota and to South Dakota, where the Norwegians had made their homes only a few years before.

The book of Exodus contains the famous account of the many plagues that Jehovah, through Moses, inflicted upon the Egyptians in order to persuade Pharaoh to let the Israelites go. Pharaoh remained stubbornly defiant.

Then Moses threatened him with a plague so terrible that it made Pharaoh quake in his boots. This was the locust plague. Pharaoh knew, as well as did his people, what it meant to be ravaged by this scourge. They knew from experience that in their path would follow famine, lawlessness and despair.

The pioneers in western Minnesota, however, had little or no knowledge of the ravaging devastation these small creatures could cause. Unlike Pharaoh and his people, they were not rich and powerful rulers in an ancient realm. They were merely plain pioneer farmers and not at all wealthy.

The grasshopper invasions the pioneers experienced were even worse than those that terrified the haughty Pharaoh into humility born out of fear. For their scourge lasted several years.

The grasshoppers have their permanent hatchery on the broad, rain-free plains immediately east of the Rocky Mountains. Sometimes these plains have an overpopulation of grasshoppers. When this occurs, suddenly billions of them take flight and head eastward, without stopping, for hundreds of miles.

It was one of these swarms that the pioneers of western Minnesota saw on 12 June 1873. The swarm was so thick it obscured the sight of the sun, even though it was a bright, clear day.

The curiosity of the pioneers changed from amazement to disgust in a few minutes. For the insects alit not only on the fields but on everything—walls, fences and machinery—and fouled every inch with nauseating excrement. The ruts of the roads were so filled with the vile insects that a wagon wheel, crushing them by the thousands, made a distinctly audible squishing sound.

Grasshoppers were everywhere! When the farmer was milking a cow, the milk pail became black with grasshoppers that leaped into the pail and drowned. They penetrated the houses, got into the food and gnawed holes in the clothing. The air was alive with their buzzing, and the walls were covered with them.

The first summer, some of the farmers in the district were spared the infestation, for there were sometimes several miles between the swarms. One neighbor might lose almost his entire crop, while his neighbor suffered no loss at all.

But these hoppers laid billions of eggs, and the following summer the entire southwest half of the state of Minnesota became prey to the greedy insects. On every straw was a row of them, incessantly eating. Watching this, a farmer would see one straw after the other break and fall silently to the ground.

Something must be done, but what to do?

At first they tried to scare away the insects by making noise. They beat on tin pails and cans, rang bells and used other noisemakers that had been partly successful in scaring off the swarms of blackbirds. But the hoppers must have been deaf, for they paid no mind to this terrible racket.

Then they tried something else: They got some long ropes and stretched them across a field. The people then pulled them along, back and forth, over the field, sweeping the insects off the straws and to the ground. Some people thought this helped, and they ran back and forth for weeks with their ropes.

Others were of the opinion that the grasshoppers sat just as thickly on their way back with the rope as they had at the start, so they tried other means. They dug deep ditches with vertical sides at the end of the field and swept thousands of grasshoppers into these ditches, from which the insects seemed to have some difficulty in hopping out.

One man invented a device called a "hopper-dozer," which was used by many. It resembled a large dustpan, 10 to 12 feet wide, smeared all over with coal tar and pulled over a field. Millions of insects were caught, sticking to the tar. They were then scraped off and buried in a trench.

Others gave up these efforts and gathered for prayer meetings, where they groaned and wept. Some called meetings at which they adopted long, wordy resolutions to be submitted to the government. These usually began with the words: "Whereas it has pleased God to punish us…"

Finally, there were many who became bored with hopper-dozers and prayer meetings and turned to a protracted binge in order to forget their problems and privations.

All attempts seemed futile. When autumn arrived, the hoppers had made a clean sweep. Some farmers harvested a few bushels; others got not a kernel of grain. On some of the farms, even the pastures were as black as though they had been plowed, and the cattle had to be sold—yes, even the chickens were sold—for lack of feed.

That fall the farmers plowed deep, thinking to bury the grasshoppers. Where there was anything left on the fields to burn, they set fires in hopes of cremating the insects. Then came a heavy frost; and since there was no snow, they hoped that the eggs would freeze and that the grubs would be killed. But later in the winter, when they thawed out frozen chunks of soil inside the house, they soon saw hundreds of tiny insects hopping about. Deep plowing, fire and frost had not hurt them in the least.

That winter there were many lay preachers in action. They delivered thundering doomsday sermons to the tortured people. The scourge of the grasshoppers had been sent to them as a punishment for their sins. "Repent, and seek the Lord, so that He will not destroy you as He destroyed Pharaoh and his people in the Red Sea" was the tenor of all these sermons.

And the people bent under the whiplashes and prayed humbly to the Lord that He would have mercy on them and avert this frightful scourge that was threatening them with famine.

Spring came, and people planted their seed in fear and trembling. But there were many who had achieved a buoyancy and hopefulness through prayer and reading the Scriptures that gave them the assurance that the Lord does not let a sparrow fall to earth unless it be His will. They were now also assured that God would not forget them, because they had bowed themselves to His will.

They had borrowed every dollar they could on their pioneer homes. They had broken the sod, plowed large areas and bought much seed in hopes that a bumper crop this year would compensate their loss.

Alas, this hope was not to be realized. As spring advanced and the grass grew green, the grasshoppers hatched and buzzed around by the millions. They devoured the grass as quickly as it grew. On many of the farms, they did not leave enough fodder to support the oxen and the last cow.

Eventually, the bitter hour arrived when the pioneer realized that he must leave his place to save his life, and the farmer went elsewhere. The payment was due on his land. Neither money nor credit was to be had. The bin was bare, the flour sack was empty, there was no milk for the children, and his trusty oxen were nothing but hides on a skeleton.

Hoping against hope for some unexpected miracle to occur, he postponed the day of departure, but that only brought the inescapable day of doom a little closer. The day would come when he would be reduced to begging his neighbor for bread to survive. So, with an unspoken farewell, he took his wife and children away, retreating across the prairie in defeat and despair.

There were others who stuck it out because they had enough of everything to get through the winter without begging for alms. Financial aid began to trickle in from Wisconsin.

The fourth spring arrived—and so did the grasshoppers. That spring, many farmers did not put seed into the ground, some because they had no seed to plant and others because they thought it would be stupid to waste the seed. They walked about in a dull, semi-stupor of despair, brooding about how long it would be before they, like many of their neighbors, would be forced to give it all up and go back to their more prosperous countrymen farther east and humbly beg them for help.

A miracle takes place

Toward the end of June 1877, a miracle took place. As usual, people were sighing and staring sadly at the ruined landscape all around. The grass of the earth and the foliage of the trees had all been devoured. It looked as if nature's creative powers to rejuvenate had been shut off.

Then, the miracle!

Suddenly, a strong buzzing began to sound on every side. As if in obedience to a command, the grasshopper hordes arose, and in one big, dense cloud, mounted heavenward until they darkened the sun, and then moved eastward. Not one live grasshopper remained on the ground.

It must have been a miracle. How could this black pestilential cloud, several hundred miles in diameter, mobilize and assemble with such military discipline and dispatch and vanish into the blue?

The sailors on the Great Lakes later reported that Lake Superior was covered with a blanket of grasshoppers, and seamen told of sailing for hours on the Atlantic Ocean through a layer of floating insect corpses.

The grasshoppers had departed, but they did not take with them the mortgages, the debts and the postponed improvements. These remained to preserve for years in pioneer minds the memory of the grasshopper visitation.

On almost all the farms, implements and machinery were lacking. The farmer had bought them on time. After repeated failure to meet the payments, he had to surrender possession of them to the county sheriff, upon orders from the farm implement dealers to foreclose.

A historical curiosity of this period was the collection of repossessed farm equipment that might be spread over several acres in every one of the harried counties. The local sheriff had been assembling the collection over a period of years. From time to time, these implements were auctioned off to pay the debts. But in all cases, the auctioneer heard only one bid—that of the dealer, for the pioneer was too broke to make any bids.

There was considerable variation in the damage done by the grasshoppers. Not all years were equally bad, nor were all areas equally ravaged. For example, the year 1875 saw less damage than either 1874 or 1876. It has been estimated that the farmers in southwestern Minnesota, during the four years of the plague, suffered an aggregate loss amounting to about $10 million. On the majority of the farms, every last horse, cow, and bit of machinery had been mortgaged to the limit. It took many years before the farmers were able to pay off their debts in full.

The news of the devastating grasshopper scourge was carried and spread to Norway through letters and newspapers. The immigration statistics reveal that the report of the catastrophic phenomenon deterred many Norwegians from leaving their country to seek new careers in the United States.

During the nine years immediately following the Civil War, the annual average of the total Norwegian migration to America was 14,000 for the years 1866 to 1874. This average dropped to only 4,000 annually from 1875 to 1878.

Nordkap

60

The Land of a Thousand Lakes

(Source: Den Siste Folkevandring Sagastubber fra Nybyggerlivet i Amerika, by Hjalmar Rued Holand, 1930; Norwegians in America: The Last Migration, by Hjalmar Rued Holand, translated by Helmer M. Blegen, 1978, pp. 191–196)

There was a time long, long ago when Manitou, the good creator of the red man, walked about on earth. As he was looking at his creation to see how his children were getting along, he noticed that his red sons at the feet of the Rocky Mountains were languishing. Only rarely did the refreshing rains fall from the heavens, so the grass withered and the deer were seen no more. The few lakes remaining held only bitter, salty waters; and it was a long, long walk to the cool, fresh springs.

Then Manitou took up an old water bag that he had not used since he created the world, and he carried it to the big inland sea that people now call Lake Superior. This lake is filled with the world's purest and tastiest water, issuing from the thousand eternal springs. There, he filled his water bag to bring water to his thirsty children in the Far West.

But the water bag was old and fragile, and once in a while big drops leaked out and fell to the ground. These became shiny lakes, twinkling pearls on the broad bosom of Minnesota.

When Manitou got as far as the high land that people call Otter Tail County, the bag burst, thus forming hundreds of delightful lakes. The water, clear and cold, flowed out of these lakes and gathered into big rivers. One river flows east and one flows west. One river flows north to the darkness of the sea of ice, and another river flows south to the steamy sea where the palm trees grow.

Then Manitou noticed that he had come to the middle point of the world, the ancient Paradise from which rivers flow in different directions. This, one can still read in the books of the palefaces.

And Manitou looked, and he saw that the place on which he stood was very beautiful, and so he said: "Why should I carry water to my children in the Far West, where only the cactus and the rattlesnake thrive? My sons are young and strong. Let them come here where there is much game, billowing plains and great woods, where there are lakes with many, many fish, and a very beautiful land."

And Manitou opened wide his mouth and called with a powerful voice. The red children of the Far West heard his call, and they came, and they found great joy when they beheld the beauty of the land.

Norwegians rule in Otter Tail County

Otter Tail County is a mighty county. It is about as large in area as the state of Delaware, which has a governor, senators, state graft and corruption, and obscenity.

These last things are not found here, for it is the *Norwegian* who here reigns with wisdom and power.

The county has a population of about 47,000, of which nearly half are Norwegian in origin. The southern and western parts of the county are especially fertile, and here the Norwegians are in uncontested control. With the exception of Polk County, Minnesota, no other county in the U.S. has a greater Norwegian population.

Otter Tail County's Norwegian history goes back to the year 1867. Down in the southeast corner of Minnesota, about where the little town of Mabel is located, there were, in 1866, many *Trønderne* and others who wanted to go west to look for land. In the vicinity of Mabel, the land was already too high in price for them to buy.

Being inexperienced in the matter of land-seeking, they agreed among themselves to send out a couple of capable and experienced men to discover a region that offered the best possibilities for the founding of a new colony and had promise for the future. A dozen men chipped in $5 each, and they selected Nils Wollan and Ole Aasved, both from Stod near Trondheim.

Nils Wollan was a very knowledgeable man of a certain particular nature that bordered on the traditional *Trønderne* stubbornness. Ole Aasved was also an intelligent man of long experience in America. He had been here since 1850 and was the actual leader of emigration from the Trondheim district. They were, thus, two fine fellows—strong, daring and persevering. They were just what was required to undertake such a difficult and risky journey.

The two men headed toward the north and west and examined the land in an area 300 miles long, until they reached Fort Pomme de Terre, an old frontier fort in the northeast corner of Grant County. From here they set their course straight southward through a half-score of still quite unoccupied counties in western Minnesota. They slept outside at night, waded or swam across great rivers and lived on what their rifles could provide them.

They continued onward across the naked wastes of Iowa, where all they saw was an occasional pioneer shanty, until they reached the village of Des Moines in southern Iowa. From there they headed northeast, traversed the whole state of Iowa and returned to Mabel. They had been gone about two months and had made the whole distance of 1,100 miles on foot.

When they were to deliver their report on their travels, a large audience was present to hear what Nils Wollan and Ole Aasved had to say. Their account was followed by a long discussion.

The final outcome of all these activities was that a group of 18 men, almost all of them *Trønderne*, decided to accompany Nils Wollan to northwestern Minnesota, while three men went with Ole Aasved to southern Iowa. Another company of nine men, mostly *Sogninger*, resolved to follow Wollan, but they traveled in a separate expedition.

At the end of May 1867, Wollan and his company started out with many wagons, oxen, cows, pigs, chickens, household goods and many other things. It was a large and substantial caravan that hereby set out to push the milestone of civilization's frontier a hundred miles farther out into the wilderness.

The old-timers remembered the summer of 1867 as the rainiest summer in history. One rainstorm came directly after the other. The level plains turned into lakes, and every low place and swampy depression became a deep lake. Tiny brooks grew to the proportions of mighty rivers, and the larger watercourses became rushing floods. The few bridges were washed away, and the wheels of wagons sank, deeply and heavily, into the water-soaked ground.

This was the kind of weather and road conditions that the company experienced on its trek to its unknown destination, 300 miles away. Many times it seemed a hopeless undertaking to attempt a crossing over the foaming stretches of lowlands; but a man from Østerdal, Ole Lillemoen, soon earned recognition for being the most skillful and competent navigator of the company. He proved to be so resourceful that he could master the most difficult of situations.

At the Zumbro River, the current was extremely strong and broad. Here they removed the wagon boxes and ran chains through the eye, or loop, at the end of the bolsters of the wagons. Then they placed the boxes back on the wagons so that they rested higher on the vehicle than before.

Having secured the strong chains to keep the wagon box firm, they placed the women and children on top of the piles of bedding and pillows in the wagon box. Then they hitched 16 oxen to each wagon and drove them into the stream. The drivers, clinging to the horns of the oxen, waded and swam beside them to guide them across.

Each unit was composed of a long string of oxen pulling a wagon on which sat, precariously perched on high, the women and children. The wagons reeled from side to side, but as soon as the lead oxen felt their feet touch the ground, the strong-legged animals easily pulled the wagon safely up on land. Then the 16 oxen were unhitched and driven back to the other side, and the same process was repeated until all the wagons were safely brought to the opposite shore.

From here the caravan resumed its journey to St. Paul, Minneapolis and St. Cloud. Now they were entering the mysterious unknown of the wild territory, and here all that they saw were Indians and sometimes a solitary hunter.

They drove across the counties of Stearns, Pope, Douglas and Grant, at that time unpopulated, quiet and empty. They saw many places that seemed very beautiful and promising, but there was always someone who found one objection or other, since there were so many kinds of personalities in this large group.

An air of Old Testament noble grandeur prevailed about these pathfinders who were so boldly moving toward a land of promise so far out in the unknown remoteness. It must have been like this when Abraham and his people in the dawn of history walked far to the west to find new land.

It was not only need that urged them onward. Essentially, it was the burning flame of a creative urge deep within their being, the strongest and best motivating power that all human creatures carry inside them, whether conscious of it or not.

They had cattle, large and small, plows, tools, seeds for planting and many children. Now they were advancing, undaunted, defying all opposition and eager to work hard in order to build a new kingdom.

When they eventually reached Pomme de Terre, the fort at the most northern point visited by Nils Wollan on his voyage of discovery, he and several others did not want to go any farther. With a few other *Trønderne* men, Wollan went back to Pope County, where they laid the foundation for the big *Trønderne* colony north of Starbuck. Gradually, eight of the Wollan brothers settled here and, in time, became the progenitors of a populous tribe of Wollans in the county.

The other half of the large company went on north to Otter Tail County. Here they also found, only a couple of hours from Pomme de Terre, a fascinatingly beautiful and fertile stretch of country.

They settled east and west of Dalton, a town named after Ole Dahl. This town is in St. Olaf Township, which is not surpassed by any township in the state in fertility or beauty of the surroundings.

Blue Mounds Township

The following information comes from Blue Mounds Historical Society documents and from the book *Builders of Pope County* by Daisy Ellen Hughes (1930):

The first to settle Pope County's Blue Mounds Township in 1867 were Rasmus Olsen Signalness, his wife, Bergitte Stolsdoken Signalness, and their family.

Rasmus was born at Ophem-Lien, Nord Torpe, Buskerud fylke. Bergitte was born on Blegtved farm near Gol, Hallingdal, Buskerud fylke. They were married at Gol. Rasmus and Bergitte lived on Signaldalen, Nordland, before coming to the U.S. in 1862.

For the next five years, the family lived in Dane County and then at Colfax, Dunn County, Wisconsin. They moved to their homestead in Blue Mounds Township, Minnesota, in 1867.

The following 11 children were

Norsk Brudefærd

born to Rasmus and Bergitte :
Ole Signalness, Olaus Signalness, Thore Signalness, Gustav Signalness, Anton Signalness, Marie Signalness, Gurine Signalness, Rasmus Signalness, Bertin Signalness, Caroline Signalness and Ole Martin Signalness.

Their first winter in Minnesota, Rasmus and Bergitte lived in a dugout near a creek among the trees. They had an Indian family for neighbors, and the Indians taught Rasmus and his family how to survive in the wilderness.

In 1868 and 1869, the following settled in Blue Mounds Township:
• Peter E. Barsness
• Engebret Thompson
• Thomas E. Thompson
• Ole Skaarden
• Peter Svendsrud
• Ole Haugen
• Svend Olson Kaus
• Ole Hagestuen
• Isaac Engebretson
• Andrew L. Brevig
• Cornelius Berg
• Hans Johnshoy

Times were tough for the new settlers in those early years. Luckily, their cows provided them with milk, while the surrounding woods and lakes contained an abundance of wild game and fish. For cash, they turned to trapping, while others worked in the pineries in northern Minnesota. Their oxen furnished them with power and transportation. When these new families needed caulking for their log homes, the Signalness family burned limestone to create lime, an ingredient in plaster.

The nearest market was at St. Cloud, about 90 miles away from the Signalness farm. Olaus would sometimes travel on skies or by oxen to get supplies. From this point he would transport supplies to Fort Abercrombie in northern Dakota Territory.

Once, when he delivered his merchandise, he was cheated on his payment. A large man with a temper, he soon made it clear he was a man to respect. He got his money!

In 1873, Olaus traveled to Benson, Minnesota, to visit some acquaintances. While there, a snowstorm hit. Despite warnings from his friends, Olaus started for home, about 20 miles away. The storm intensified, making travel all but impossible. Olaus found an abandoned shelter for his oxen, but the roof soon caved in from the weight of the snow, forcing them to move on.

While crossing a river north of Benson, the rig broke through the ice, dumping the box off the sleigh runners. Olaus finally managed to get the box back on the runners. He then crawled into the box, letting the oxen have their heads. The oxen followed the snow-packed yet familiar trail, halting when they came to the place of a family acquaintance named Benson. There, Olaus and his team took shelter until the storm let up.

Besides being a farmer, Rasmus held the following positions in Starbuck: assessor, supervisor, school clerk and postmaster. The fine oak log home he built for his family—the oldest house in Pope County—stood for a hundred years. Part of the land was later donated by a grandson to present-day Glacial Ridge Park near Starbuck.

Few towns with Norwegian names

Although the Norwegian pioneers were the first to set a plow in the ground in almost every region they settled in Minnesota and Dakota, there are, nevertheless, only a few place names to commemorate their conquest.

The chief explanation for this is that these old pioneers were a rather modest lot. They even thought it a presumption to burden the English language with such strange names as Torger and Lars, so they humbly allowed themselves to be addressed as Tom and Louis. It was, therefore, an unthinkable monstrosity to impose upon an American landscape the name reminiscent of Norway.

Even when Norwegians almost

exclusively populated a township, they waited until some quick-tongued Yankee proposed that the township be named York or Utica in honor of his birthplace. This pliant yielding was a natural consequence of the many years of subjugation to which the Norwegian *husmann* class had been subjected in the social classification of Norway's population.

However, this general criticism does not apply to Otter Tail County, for in this county there are many Norwegian names: Aastad, Aurdal, Dalton, Folden, Henning, Norman, Nidaros, Norwegian Grove, Oscar, St. Olaf, Sverre, Sverdrup, Stod, Tordenskjold, Trondheim and Weggeland.

It was a *Valdris* by the name of Ole Jørgensen who was enterprising enough to get most of these monuments to his countrymen placed on the map. He established his home at Wall Lake, east of Fergus Falls, in 1868. In 1869 he was elected to the office of county auditor. This gave him considerable standing and the opportunity to place Norwegian names on many parts of the county.

Two Norwegian centers

From the beginning, Otter Tail County had two focal centers, or points of departure, from which the Norwegian settlers spread out on its extensive areas. The first and the largest of these was the *Trønderne* settlement in the southern part of the county, the origin of which has been briefly mentioned. The second settlement was Norwegian Grove in the northwest corner of the county. It was started the year after, in 1868, and soon spread over several townships until there now are 12 Norwegian congregations in this part of the county.

From there the Norwegian communities continue without interruption for more than a hundred miles up through the counties of Becker, Clay, Norman and Polk.

To get to Norwegian Grove, when one does not travel by automobile, one changes trains in Fergus Falls. From here there is a small branch line about 20 miles north through a beautiful countryside up to Pelican Rapids.

All around lie Norwegian settlements in every direction, but especially toward the west. Five or six miles away is the old Norwegian Grove, a patch of woods several miles across. Inside these woods is a nice little lake about three miles long called St. Olaf Lake, because there was an Ole living at either end of the lake.

The first settlers built their homes around this grove. Before them, they had the rich billowing prairie and, behind the houses, the protection of the woods. A short distance inside was the lake, with an abundance of fish in it. What more ideal a setting could one desire? To the old pioneers who had come from a rocky and soil-stingy home, this must have seemed like a paradise.

The old pioneers were not blind to the glory, both practical and poetic, that spread out before them when they looked out upon the virgin plain of meadowland on which they had chosen sites for homesteads. Many of them have told of the great lift to the soul they experienced when admiring this Canaan.

It took several years before the pioneers enjoyed any returns from their lands. They lived more like hunters than like agriculturists. They lived so far from any market that it was impossible for them to sell their products.

When they first came here, in 1867, there was no railroad nearer than St. Cloud, 150 miles away. The Great Northern Railway, which now cuts through Otter Tail County, was not built until 12 years later.

Even after the railway came to them, it took a long time for the farmer to realize any profits. The freight rates were so high, as was the cost of the elevators, that the hard-working pioneer had nothing left for himself after so much labor.

The first railway companies, which built their roads under extremely difficult economic conditions, were constantly short of funds, and they took advantage of every possible way to make some money. Their first, and most important, step was to bribe the legislators. For many years, this was a public scandal. By this means, the railroads became free agents and could rob the pioneers as much as they desired.

Muskrat money

The main source of income was, therefore, not wheat or butter, as it is today. It was the muskrat. It was very plentiful, and its skin was used as currency and cash. With a dozen skins, the pioneer would trudge to the trading post, 15 to 20 miles away. Here he would barter the skins in exchange for his indispensable coffee, tobacco and syrup. He often gave some of the skins to the pastor for lack of any other medium of exchange.

In the beginning, many of the first pioneers worked for the government as drivers of the oxcarts carrying provisions. In this capacity, they fared far and wide over the unpopulated plains of the Dakotas. They obtained several span of oxen and hauled heavy loads of supplies. From St. Cloud they would sometimes drive a train of six or seven wagons in tandem, loaded with provisions for the forts. They would bring supplies to the lonely forts, here and there in the wilderness, that were established to control the Indians.

Some of these forts had names that became well known: Fort Gary, Fort Wadsworth, Fort Abercrombie, Fort Totten, Fort Ransom, Fort Winnipeg, the Black Hills and others.

At each of these lonely outposts was a garrison of American troops that wistfully looked forward to the coming of these Norwegian drivers, who brought them news from the outside world and fresh provisions. Sometimes they had to wait a long time, for the drivers were exposed to the risk of many kinds of dangers and accidents on their routes.

The worst and most frequent of these were the prairie fires. When the broad expanses of tall, thick grass were on fire and the flames were driven speedily forward by a strong wind, the drivers often had a desperate battle to save their lives. If their freight was made up of a large supply of powder for the soldiers and the prairie fire threatened to catch up with them, their only recourse was to unhitch the oxen with all possible dispatch and run for their lives.

But, on the whole, they were a cheerful and merry lot who soon learned to accept the prairie's risks and dangers with laughter and to enjoy the adventures of trying to outwit the prairie's practical jokes. When they made camp for the night, the sound of accordion and fiddle music cast a homelike quality over the lonely bivouac in the vast emptiness of space.

Battling mosquitoes

One of the most disagreeable pests to torment the pioneer for many years was the mosquito. There were many lakes and swamps to serve as perfect breeding places for unbelievable multitudes of these insects.

In the course of the ages, nature had finally endowed the red-skinned Indians with a protective feature against this enemy, for there seemed to be a scent emanating from the Indians' skin that kept the insects at a distance.

But here arrived these thin-skinned palefaces to offer a feast of most delicious savor. Mosquitoes came from near and far by the millions to enjoy the banquet.

When a pioneer was about to mow the hay, he had to wear a net to cover his head and face. And even then he had to slap, sweep, puff and blow as hard as he could.

The cattle were frantic and rolled on the ground like horses. At milking time, it was necessary to build a ring of smudges around the cows. But in spite of the smoke, the mosquitoes would fall into the milk pail in sufficient numbers to make a dark covering of dead insects on the surface of the milk.

In the evening, a huge bonfire of twigs, branches and rubbish would be lighted. In the morning there would be a ring, five feet deep, of dead mosquitoes around it. Some of the new settlers could not stand it. The little mosquito was powerful enough to drive a pioneer to flee southward.

Farms, churches dot landscape

Otter Tail County, with its thousands of ever-fresh lakes, has an idyllic landscape. Lakes are there in all sizes, from the tiniest duck pond to small seas where the waves can roll for a half score miles before striking the shore.

The circle of fine, stately farm homes in this area are reminiscent of Swedish author Selma Lagerløf's descriptions of Løfvensjø in Vermland. Only the ancient traditions are lacking There is no recounting of the tale of Gøsta Berling's riding to wild adventures at the head of his 12 cavaliers, nor of any love story about the fair Ingeborg and her Frithiof. There are no memorial monoliths to commemorate the tragic duels of proud knights or the eternal sleep of weary, heroic warriors.

Who can say that the shades and spirits of such ancient heroes do not hover over these waters? It is quite possible that if the Indians had had their poet, their Homer, we might then read, even here, about individuals who could rival those of the half-barbaric Grecian antiquity in heroism and nobility and in great exploits.

But even if this place lacks the magical veil of romanticism that clings to every Norwegian rock and promontory in sacred peace, it nevertheless possesses mementos that give testimony of a better and truer type of struggle and triumph.

Five thousand splendid Norwegian homes, with their cultivated fields and green meadows, tell the story of the pioneer's triumphant battle and conquest of the primordial wilderness. Fifty Norwegian churches testify to his hope in a realm above.

From hill to hill, church spires greet one another across intervening space and their bells ring out, deep-voiced and melodiously: "Glory to God on high! And on earth, peace, good will toward men!"

Bræen Svartisen ved Melfjorden

61

When law and order came to Grant County, Minnesota

(Source: Den Siste Folkevandring Sagastubber fra Nybyggerlivet i Amerika, by Hjalmar Rued Holand, 1930; Norwegians in America: The Last Migration, by Hjalmar Rued Holand, translated by Helmer M. Blegen, 1978, pp. 197–200)

Before the year 1873, there was no government in Grant County, Minnesota. Until then, every individual was a law unto himself, and he lived as he pleased.

If hungry, he shot a deer in midsummer, as there was no county judge to levy on him a fine. When he felt like selling whiskey, there was no license to buy. Should he prefer to drink it up himself, he ran no risk of being arrested for intoxication in public.

There were no schools, no taxes, and no churches or roads. Folks lived in a state of innocence, for it is written that where there is no law, there is no sin, either.

But now all this was going to come to an end. Now Grant County was about to get a government and political candidates, taxes and social order.

In 1871, Grant County was organized by the state legislature as a separate county, and its boundaries were established. The governor also appointed three commissioners to take over and run the county. The three he appointed were Knut Melby, Søren Frogner and Henry Sanford. The first two of these were Norwegians. But the county was still so thinly populated that the three potentates found no opportunity to exercise their power and dignity.

Two years later, the population had increased considerably, and after having their appointments confirmed by a popular vote, they took steps to bring order to the various affairs of the county.

Battle for the county seat

On 12 April 1873, the commissioners met at a place in the northeast corner of the county called Pomme de Terre, named for an Indian fort that had stood near there years earlier. A Yankee with high hopes had laid out a town here (on paper). A proposed railway was staked out through the city, and there was also a little water-power for a mill.

In the expectation that a new St. Paul would spring up and flourish here, one of the Yankee's friends by the name of Timothy Heald had erected a huge store building, which was as yet practically vacant. Almost the only cultural nourishment the inhabitants enjoyed for many years was the enthusiastic description by Timothy Heald on the subject of the future opportunities this place offered.

Here, in this vast and capacious building, the three authoritative gentlemen held their meeting. Their first and most important item on the agenda was to determine the location of the county seat. This was a difficult decision, for there were already two embryonic villages in the county, and, each one was determined to become the county seat. One was the already mentioned Pomme de Terre.

Although the large store building, almost empty, constituted the total municipality, it was at least large enough to furnish sleeping quarters for the county's total population, if needed.

A railroad was also a prospect, and many of the leading men of the county were in favor of this place as their county seat. Knut Melby, who lived in this part of the county, had sworn that he would vote for it.

In the opposite corner of the county was the town of Herman. The railroad had come to Herman two years previously. Herman was already the marketplace for the whole county and had several business places in operation.

Søren Frogner, the first settler in this part of the county, was in business there. He had been elected commissioner in order to ensure the choice of Herman as the county seat.

Henry Sanford was a young Yankee bachelor and hunter who lived a few miles south of Pomme de Terre, on the shore of Elbow Lake. This place had neither waterfalls nor railroad and had never even thought of becoming a town.

After a lively discussion, Sanford took Frogner aside and explained to him that there was not the slightest chance that Herman could be chosen as county seat. So the main thing now was to prevent Pomme de Terre from being picked. Since they had become deadlocked and were making no progress at all, why not choose a third spot?

"Where would that be?" Frogner asked, there being no other towns in the county.

No, there were not, admitted Sanford, and that was why he was going to propose that the quarter section next to his on the north side by Elbow Lake should be the place.

He explained that if they could get Pomme de Terre out of the contest, it would put an end to its chances of becoming a town. This would make Herman the only town in the county, and then it would easily be possible to consider moving the county seat to Herman.

This motion was passed, with Melby voting against it. The commissioners then appointed a full slate of county and district officers. Fortunately, there were enough male citizens in the county to fill all the positions.

Officially, Elbow Lake was now the county seat, but there was no town there for another 13 years, nor were the official county records transferred to this place until many years later. The reason for this was that there was not a single cabin or shack on the place to hold the records.

To be sure, a Halling by the name of Knut Laastuen had filed on the land designated to be the county seat, and his prairie schooner stood on the precise spot that had been specified as the site for a proposed courthouse. But, like most *Hallinger*, he had a wagonful of children and could not, therefore, use the wagon as a courthouse.

For this reason, Henry Sanford's little log cabin was, for more than five years, used as a courthouse. That is to say, the county commissioners met there to transact their official business.

Outside of the official sessions, each commissioner had his office in his own home, log cabin or dugout.

When it was necessary to have a document registered, one had to go to Ole Larson at Pelican Lake.

For any business with the county treasurer, one had to go to Elk Lake, where Ole Olson had custody of the county's valuable papers, which he kept in an unlocked chest under his bed.

If it was the county auditor, R. I. Talbot, with whom one wanted to confer, it was often necessary to travel over the entire county to find him. If one succeeded in catching up with him, one found that Talbot had his pockets crammed with county accounts and other papers relating to the office.

In order to put an end to all this confusion, a small shed was erected on Knut Laastuen's land in 1878 and used as the official courthouse.

The population of the south part of the county had been waiting a long time for the opportunity to move the county seat to Herman. This town had gradually grown to become a sizable town, whereas Elbow Lake was still just a place on the ground.

In 1881 they persuaded the state legislature to adopt a resolution to move the county seat from Elbow Lake to Herman, provided that the voters of the county at the next election ratified this resolution.

Now a very lively campaign followed to ensure votes against the move. It turned out to be primarily a contest between the Norwegians on one side against the Yankees and Swedes on the other.

The northeastern part of the county (the part in favor of Elbow Lake) was much more densely populated than the southwestern corner. Thus the Norwegians felt confident of the victory to such a degree that many of them, as usual, failed to cast their ballots. It was, therefore, with great amazement that they heard Herman had won with 439 votes, with Elbow Lake receiving 369 votes.

The governor signed the document to authorize the transfer, which thereby made it a law, and the various officials immediately moved their things to Herman, where the townspeople built a courthouse.

County seat case goes to court

When the Norwegians had recovered somewhat from their vexation, they began to wonder if everything had gone on decently and in legal order. Timothy Heald, the sage of Pomme de

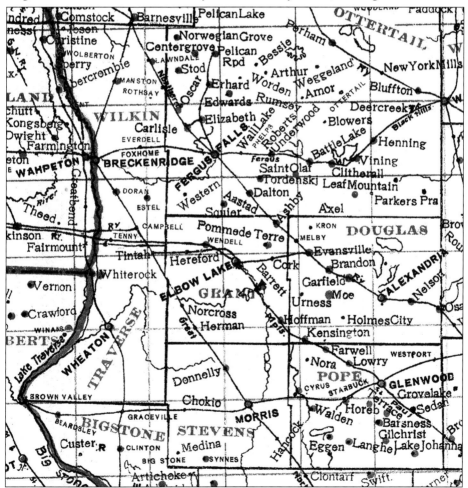

Terre, agitated in favor of appealing the case to the courts, and the future senator, Knute Nelson, was to represent them as their lawyer.

Knute Nelson hired a detective to sniff into the case, and he found out many strange facts. Among other items, he was able to ascertain that the town of Erdahl, where every vote had been cast in favor of Elbow Lake, was left out entirely in the totaling up of the votes. He also discovered that in the southern part of the county they had not only *permitted* but even *persuaded* many non-eligible individuals to vote.

Nelson finally established that, just before the election, the town of Herman had imported a big crowd of Italian laborers from St. Paul to work on the town's streets. These Italians remained in Herman just long enough to vote. Then they were shipped back to St. Paul.

After a thorough examination of the list of voters, a recount was held. It was found that a substantial majority had voted in favor of Elbow Lake. Knute Nelson laid all these facts before the court, and the judge announced his verdict: Elbow Lake had won the election.

When the news of this outcome reached Grant County, there was great rejoicing in the northern part of the county. Those who had any liquor to sell did a thriving business, and the public was aroused. They awakened from the dullness of their everyday routine and discovered that it was fun to be alive.

Vigilantes rescue records

The leaders were not satisfied with this alone. They agreed that these crooks, the "Hermanites," were such a band of outright scoundrels and depraved rogues that they would not easily relinquish possession of the county records without a struggle, now that they had them in their hands. If they were given a little time, they would find a way to prolong the strife by a whole string of legal postponements and delays. The only thing to do now was to catch the Philistines off guard and carry the county property away by force.

Accordingly, a company of brave and daring berserks got together and moved across the 20-mile stretch of prairie in 15 crowded wagonloads of determined men. The procession made its way under cover of darkness, rumbling through the lonely villages with ear-splitting cries and racket.

The sleeping settlers woke up, terror-stricken. What was this? Were the Indians on the warpath again? An empty bottle or two crashed against a wall, and the procession vanished in the darkness, leaving the pioneer and his wife in fear and wonderment at this mysterious disturbance of their peace.

In the morning, when the people of Herman saw the town invaded by such a noisy and formidable power of belligerency, all thought of resistance evaporated—if there had been any such thought.

The courthouse janitor had been captured in his bed and threatened with being skinned alive, and then drawn and quartered, if he did not immediately open the doors to the county's treasured archives. Humbly, he found his keys. And soon protocols, record books, bottles of ink, safes and other inventory were piled into the wagons from the north.

With a fresh supply of drinks, blaring bugles and vocal noise never before heard in this town, the victors hurried back where they came from.

A few years later a railroad was built through Elbow Lake, and from then on the town made rapid growth. It is now the largest town in the county and very well built up.

The new courthouse, completed in 1906, is a particularly attractive and imposing structure. It was constructed of brown sandstone and is one of the best in the state. It stands on a rise of ground at the head of the town's main street, precisely on the spot where Knut Laastuen's pioneer cabin stood in the early days when they agreed this was to be the county seat.

62

When Dakota was settled

(Source: Den Siste Folkevandring Sagastubber fra Nybyggerlivet i Amerika, by Hjalmar Rued Holand, 1930; Norwegians in America: The Last Migration, by Hjalmar Rued Holand, translated by Helmer M. Blegen, 1978, pp. 201–214)

In proportion to its population, Hallingdal is perhaps the district in Norway that can claim the record for sending the greatest number of emigrants to the U.S. In addition to the thousands of individual *Hallinger* scattered throughout the Norwegian settlements and elsewhere, we can find at least 30 large congregations where the membership is mainly *Hallinger*.

Apparently there are three times as many *Hallinger* in America as in Norway. The first *Halling* in America was Hermo Nilsen Tufte, who came from Aal in Buskerud fylke in 1841 to settle on the Yorkville Prairie near Muskego, Wisconsin. This marked the beginning of a rapid emigration of *Hallinger* to the north-central states of our country, and they are to be found among the earliest pioneer settlers.

This is the case in South Dakota, too. During the late 1850s, rumors of the fabulous wonders of the Dakotas reached the Wisconsin settlements. These reports claimed that Dakota had the finest soil to be found anywhere. At this time, the entire western half of Iowa was yet to be settled. Several million acres of Iowa's unsurpassably fertile land were waiting for pioneers to come and settle there, but these attractive acres were ignored and passed over.

Several large companies of adventurous Norwegian frontiersmen crossed the entire state of Iowa and trekked several hundred miles to reach what was then called the Missouri Bottoms, for Dakota had not yet acquired its name.

This vast region had not been surveyed and was neither a state nor even a territory. It was merely a great wilderness located north of Nebraska. The Missouri River flowed between these two stretches of land, and it was only the north side of this river, the Missouri Bottoms, that constituted the Mecca toward which the people were heading.

Between the years 1857 and 1859, no less than 40 land-seekers had collected on the south shore. Immigrants from Voss made up the majority of this group, but there were also several from Hallingdal. Their intention was to cross over to the north side of the Missouri, where the best land was to be found.

However, the group hesitated. There were certain difficulties to be resolved first. Not only were there many Indians on the north side, but it was also uncertain who owned this land, the Indians or the American government.

Squatters first to arrive

The following insertion is from Holand's Den Norske Settlementers Historie, translated by Rosholt:

The township squatter was usually the first outrider in civilization's groping hand toward the big open spaces of the West. Two and three hundred miles ahead of the first settlers, these business-like Yankee fortune hunters explored the most suitable places for future villages and cities.

Often as not, they had little or no idea of a good spot for a place or the platting of it; nevertheless, by making wild claims they managed to sell their worthless lots and made themselves some money. But often they made intelligent choices, and the cities they platted later became cities.

In many cases, the government had not acquired the land in question from the Indians, but the speculators took no notice. Without stopping to ask questions about the legality of their actions, they went recklessly ahead and laid out their towns.

The township squatter was also the first to reach Dakota. In May 1857 a group of adventurers, later organized under the name of "The Dakota Land Company," approached the Sioux River. Following it northwesterly, they reached the present Brookings County, where they laid out the villages of Medary and Flandreau. Farther down the river they came to an excellent waterfall, and here they laid out the future city of Sioux Falls.

Among this group was a man called Ole Olson. As this was a favorite camping ground for the Indians and the land still in their legal possession, trouble soon arose between the Indians and the settlers, and the whites were driven off. Later, Olson and a couple of other men returned, but the Indians killed one and the other fled. Only Olson remained and waited through the winter of 1857-58 for relief and provisions. But when none came, he also left for Sioux Falls.

This expedition by Olson and his friends became the cause of hostilities with the Indians, which involved not less than 5,000 federal troops. As usual, the Indians drew the short end of the stick and had to give up nearly all their land east of the Missouri River.

First Norwegian settlers

Although Olson went off disappointed in his mission (after having lived through constant danger for years), there were many of his countrymen in the neighborhood who were waiting for an agreement to be made with the Indians in order for them to advance into that mysterious land of Dakota Territory. These, however, were not speculators—but the first of the tillers of the soil that have made the name Dakota famous throughout the nation.

Blegen's translation continues:

Between the years 1857 and 1859, no less than 40 land-seekers had collected on the Nebraska side of the Missouri and "cast avid looks of longing over the river to the heavily wooded and the flat fertile meadows on the Dakota side." Most of this group was from Voss, Norway. They included:
- Halvor Brynjildson
- Ole Bottolfson Sivlesøen
- Erik Bottolfson Sivlesøen
- Erick O. Selland
- Ole O. Selland
- Anders O. Selland
- Erik J. Lunde
- Ingebret Sølhaugen
- John O. Førde
- Bendit Olson Sivlesøen
- Ole Stalheim
- Erik Stalheim
- Mons Stalheim
- Mikkel L. Rokne
- Bottolf Lunde
- Brynjild Ure
- Erik Ure
- Bottolf Jordahl
- Christen Jordahl
- Brynjild Bjerness
- Ole Sampson Opheim
- Kolbein O. Opheim
- Holger Endreson
- Elling Sande
- Aslak Iverson Lekve
- Thomas Thompson Alsager
- Syver Vinje
- Nils E. Egge
- Christen Larson Lunde
- Peder Enerson
- Peder Tveite
- Ole Lewison
- Mikkel Bøe
- Frantz Skiaker
- Johan Aalseth
- Christian Brude
- Matthias Minne

The second group to arrive, in 1859, had formerly settled in Winneshiek County, Iowa. They included:

- Ole Olson Gjeitli (Ole Olson Jetley), Voss
- Syvert Myhren, Hallingdal
- Halvor Svendsen, Hallingdal
- Lars Anderson Torblaa, Ulvik, Hardanger
- Elling Olson Engum, Sogn
- Anders Fosen, Skjold, Stavanger

Dakota, at last!

On 8 August 1859, two of the men decided to wait no longer. The summer was soon over. Ole Olson Gjeitli from Voss and Halvor Svendsen from Hallingdal constructed a raft, on which they boldly crossed over to the other side. They started to build their permanent homesteads on land approximate nine miles east of the spot where the town of Vermillion was later to be established in Clay County.

These two men were the very first white farmers to set up a permanent abode in all of what would eventually become the states of North and South Dakota.

[A community of white men, their Indian wives and mixed-blood (Métis) offspring thrived in the Pembina area of extreme northeastern North Dakota as early as 1802. However, they made their living by hunting and trapping or as trading-post employees, not as farmers. –Winistorfer]

The remainder of the group waited until the river froze over. Then they followed by crossing on the ice.

The following spring, on 2 March 1860, a son was born to the Ole Gjeitlis. The boy was also given the name of Ole. Thus Ole Olson Gjeitli was the first child born of white parents in South Dakota. He later played a prominent part in politics, including service as a state senator. Not until 1861, the year following Ole's birth, was Dakota organized as a territory.

[About this same time, three other settlements were founded in this general area—Bergen, The Lake and James River (or Bangen). According to Holand, "These colonies later spread to the north and west, and there are now (1908) more than 5,000 emigrants from Norway in the area." –Rosholt]

Blegen's translation continues:

In 1860, the following crossed the Missouri and settled in Clay County (in what is now South Dakota). They had abandoned their land near Spirit Lake, Iowa, because a large swarm of blackbirds ate them out. This group included:
- Lars Syverson
- Amund Hanson Eide
- Andreas Peterson
- Ole Syverson Sølhaugen
- Ole Olson Sølhaugen
- Ellend Borlaug
- Nils Remme
- Knut Vik
- Lasse Bothun
- Bjørn Larson
- Thor Halvorson
- Hans Olson

The same year, Kjeld Rønne, Christopher Lassesen Haave and Lars Johanson Ruud arrived from Gausdal and Trondheim, Sør-Trøndelag. They settled about 30 miles farther east, where they founded the Elk Point settlement in Union County, South Dakota.

There were also a few others in the group that left Spirit Lake, but they moved north to Jackson in Jackson County, Minnesota, where two years later they were killed by Indians.

The Missouri Bottoms, where the first Norwegians in Dakota settled, extend for several hundred miles and are from 12 to 15 miles wide. The soil is exceedingly fertile.

But the settlers soon discovered that their land was subject to frequent flooding. Often, water would cover the entire valley. When the river rose above its banks, the powerful current would sweep away houses, barns, cattle and all movable property.

The river would frequently shift and cut a new channel as the swift current eroded the black soil. The greedy water sometimes required only a few days to devour the greater portion of a

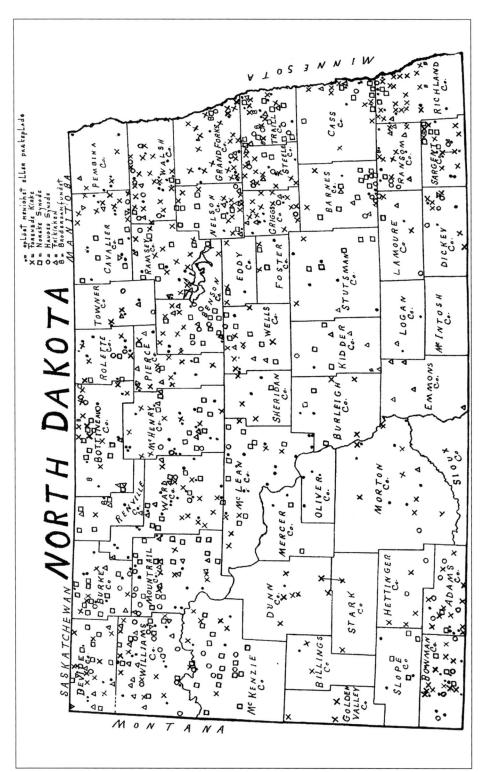

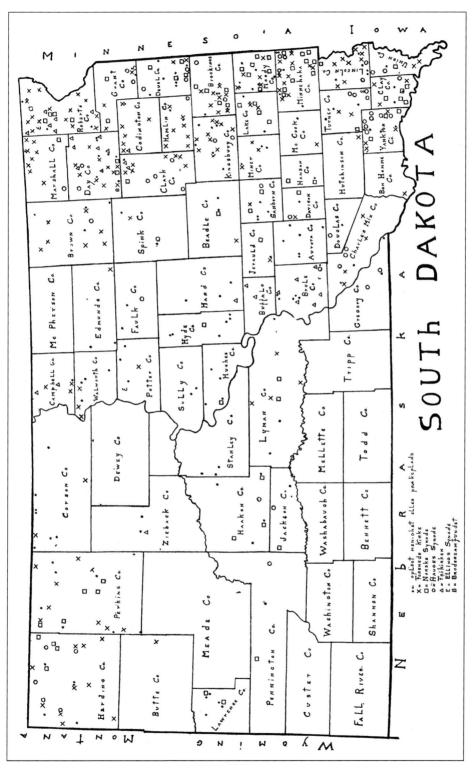

quarter section of farmland. Or, a farmer might find that his farm in Dakota had been expanded with the deposit of a substantial slice of Nebraska's fat and fertile loam.

Before long, the settlers learned that by choosing the most elevated places on their farms for building sites, they could diminish considerably the risk of being flooded out.

Indians good neighbors

The Indians promptly sold this part of the country to the U. S. government, but they did not move off the land. They continued to live there. And as before, they roamed in large bands up the river and down as they hunted and fished and also frequently traded with the white settlers.

These Indians were a friendly people who associated so much with the Norwegians that the latter picked up much of the Indian language. They acquired the habit of mixing Sioux words and expressions into their Norwegian speech in the same manner that their descendants later spoke a mixture of Norwegian and English.

Ole Sampson, a Vossing of extraordinary size and strength, was one of the first three county commissioners. The Indians, accordingly, considered him to be the Big Chief of the whites and showed him great respect and deference. They sometimes came to his house and performed a dance in his honor.

These Indian dances can be fascinatingly interesting provided the performers are skilled, but this was rather an exception than a rule. The dancer bent his body forward very low, made a succession of short hops and swayed from side to side.

Four or five Indians who beat out the rhythm on a drum provided the music. One of them sang, in a hoarse and monotone voice, a song that most often seemed to be concerned with the subject of food. The following lines from an Indian song became very popular among the boys of the Norwegian settlement:

Juta ota washte-do,
Juta voniche sitje-do.
(Much food—good. No food—much bad)

Late one evening, a squaw, accompanied by several children, came running from a nearby Indian camp to Ole Sampson and begged him to protect them. It seems that her husband, a medicine man, had become drunk and had chased them out of the house.

Sampson welcomed the refugees, asked them in, and closed the door. He gave a shirt and a pair of overalls to a 14-year-old boy, who had fled stark naked.

No sooner had the group achieved a degree of calmness when suddenly the door was violently pushed open and the enraged medicine man, tearing the door off its hinges, stormed into the room. This apparition frightened the squaw so badly that she jumped into Ole Sampson's bed with him.

Ole, wearing nothing but a shirt, leaped out of bed, grabbed the Indian by the neck, gave him a few violent shakes and hurled him out through the door. Strange as it may seem, this action promptly restored peace and good will among all the parties concerned.

The year 1862 saw the outbreak of the great Indian War, but these Indians of the Yankton tribe took no part in the hostilities. Even though the settlers were completely surrounded on all sides by a large number of Indians and were at their mercy, not one of the Norwegian settlers was disturbed in any way.

[Following the uprising, at least 18 Norwegians from this area enlisted in Company A, Dakota Cavalry, under General Alfred Sully, in a prolonged campaign to subdue the Sioux Indians. –Rosholt]

Blegen's translation continues:

This Indian war, together with the frequent floods, resulted in the total cessation of migration to this region until 1867 and 1868.

Dakota's first Norwegian pastor

Pastor Abraham Jacobson was the first Norwegian clergyman to visit Dakota, where he conducted a number of church services in 1861. He also gathered most of the settlers into an organized congregation, but this fell apart after he left.

In 1864, the Reverend Jens Ivarsen Krohn arrived here, after making a missionary journey into Kansas. During his sojourn, a permanent congregation was organized and given the all-inclusive name of "The First Norwegian Evangelical Lutheran Congregation of Dakota Territory." This congregation included all Norwegians within a 60-mile area who wanted to join.

Through the church council, a call was sent to the Reverend Emil Gustav Andreas Christensen to come and serve as pastor. He accepted the call and came to Clay County in August of the year 1867, thus becoming the first pastor to serve a congregation in southern Dakota territory.

There was nothing glamorous or pompous about Pastor Christensen's entry into Dakota. Under a scorching August sun, the oxen made slow progress pulling the cart, the wheels of which were cross-sections of a large log. The face of Mrs. Christensen was one large blister. And besides, two of the children were ill with whooping cough.

Course grass stood six to seven feet deep over the entire Missouri and Sioux bottoms, resembling a veritable forest. At night, one was lost in a thick fog: The air, filled with myriads of ravenous mosquitoes, hummed like a beehive. The mosquitoes seemed as large as queen bees.

Mrs. Christensen was at that time 21 years of age. She was by nature endowed with a cheerful and optimistic disposition, a perfect mate for the zealous pioneer with whom she had been joined in the intimate bonds of matrimony. And if ever there was a time when a stout-hearted, indomitable spirit was needed, this was it.

The pastor's company left Sioux City (Iowa) at 1 p.m. and reached Brule Creek at 4 o'clock the following afternoon. That same evening, Pastor Christensen was called upon to conduct a marriage service. The couple had been waiting in the cabin of Christopher Lassesen Haave as soon as they heard a rumor that the pastor was coming. That very same day also saw the return of hordes of grasshoppers. And that is how the Reverend Christensen made his entry into Dakota in August of 1867.

When Christensen arrived, the Dakota settlers were disconcerted and nonplussed. They had not been prepared to see him bringing a wife and children! What to do!

They did, however, give the pastor credit for having sufficient faith in Dakota to bring along a family, no matter how this new discovery upset all their plans for lodging the pastor in the settlement. They had arranged that he was to have a room or office in Iver Iverson's house (later occupied by Mikkel Mikkelsen), and he would get his meals at Ole Gjeitli's place. But this was something else!

They solved the problem of a parsonage by cleaning out an old log cabin that had served as a shelter for wagons and machinery. This cabin was located in the woods near Thorbjørn Thompson's residence. The cabin was almost lost to sight in tall grass and weeds, but among the very few buildings available, this one was by far the roomiest of all.

Lumber was not to be had. Until this house could be made fit for occupation by the pastor and his family, they were given temporary quarters at Aslak Iverson's. The congregation had in advance taken up a collection for the pastor, but the $50 they had collected went to pay for an old cookstove that the pastor had bargained for down at Brule Creek and had hauled home himself.

With a bag of flour, some sour milk,

and also some eggs and other groceries from Syver Myhren, the young wife cheerfully and gratefully set about her first housekeeping. She managed very well until the flour was all used up. From then on, she had to get along with corn, which the Christensens for some time ground with their coffee grinder.

At the Missouri River Bottoms

For a while, there was no flour to be bought in Vermillion, and the settlers had such a limited supply for themselves that the preacher's wife refrained from mentioning this lack in the parsonage. Since the nearest flour mills were in Pankow, Nebraska, and at the Floyd River in Iowa, it was no easy matter to obtain any flour. Otherwise, she knew that the pioneers would have shared their last pound of flour with her. But, after all, why whimper and whine?

Not very long afterward, the wife of Christen Jordahl became ill, and the loving husband made a vow that if his wife recovered her health, he would give a cow as a gift to the first poor man he met. Everything turned out very well, and Christen was prevailed upon to donate the cow to the preacher. And so it went, on and on.

The pioneers were reduced to privation by the ravages of the grasshopper hordes, and yet they took care of their minister's family to the utmost of their ability. At the same time, one must also admire the minister and his wife for cheerfully renouncing all creature comforts to obey the call that was for Pastor Christensen the lodestar of his life: preaching the word of God and administering the sacraments among the Norwegian pioneers in the Midwest.

Pastor Christensen was an enthusiastic and well-endowed clergyman who accomplished a great work in Dakota and Nebraska. For years, he rode his old horse, Jim, bareback through many counties and founded a large number of new congregations. Both he and his wife originally came from Ephraim, Wisconsin, where he had had a home in the woods.

Canton's beginnings

Near the southeast corner of South Dakota and northeast of these settlements on the Missouri Bottoms is located an attractive little town called Canton. It has a population of about 2,000 (in 1908). Canton has become a highly desirable place of refuge for prosperous elderly farmers who have built fine homes in town, where they enjoy a comfortable and leisurely retirement.

They have one of the largest and most imposing church structures to be seen outside of great cities. In addition, they have here a large institution of higher education—Augustana Normal School, where their children can acquire an excellent education. Located about two miles south of town, they also have the Beloit Orphans' Home, the biggest children's home in Norwegian-America. As an example of steady, intelligent Norwegian enterprise and progress, Canton and its vicinity is as fine as any Norwegian town in America.

Canton lies on the west and north banks of the Big Sioux River, which meanders among a series of low, wooded hills. Surrounding the town are many large Norwegian congregations, primarily on the Dakota side but also in Iowa.

The founder of this community was a *Halling* with rich experience, broad vision and ample means. His name was Halvor Nilsen (Halvor Nelson). He came from the *gaard* (farm) Espeseth in Gol, Hallingdal, in the year 1846 with his parents, brothers and sisters.

This family of nine arrived in Milwaukee with total capital of one dollar, and there was no one to meet them when they arrived. Their destination was Rock Prairie (Luther Valley), the American Mecca of the Hallingdal immigrants.

Leaving their baggage at the station, they set out with much confidence and little else. They carried some sandwiches and a few coffee beans as provisions. Dressed in their colorful Hallingdal mountain garb, they walked the 85 miles to their destination. Now and then the youngest children had to be carried, but eventually they arrived at Rock Prairie.

In 1849 Halvor Nilsen started west to look for land. In Clayton County in eastern Iowa, he found what he was looking for, and here he founded a sizable settlement of Norwegians from Hallingdal and Hadeland.

Shortly thereafter, rumors of the discovery of gold in California swept like wildfire through the settlement. Halvor Nilsen and two of his brothers became infected with the gold fever and joined the gold rush to the West.

Many of these adventurers perished before reaching their destination, and of those who made it alive to California, not very many found any gold. Halvor Nilsen was one of the lucky few, for he came back with enough wealth to establish himself as a big-scale farmer in Clayton County.

In the course of the next few years, an increasing number of *Hallinger* arrived in Clayton County, and many of them found employment on Nilsen's 700-acre farm. Many others came to this affable and understanding man to seek counsel or assistance.

Before long, all the desirable land in Clayton County was taken up, and new arrivals had to go farther west to seek homesteads. Consequently, Halvor Nilsen himself decided in 1867 to pull up stakes and look for a suitable location where he might start a large Norwegian settlement farther west. He explored all of western Minnesota as well as the adjoining areas of Iowa and Dakota.

Big Sioux Falls

At long last, he discovered the superb tracts along the Big Sioux River in the vicinity of the future town site of Canton, South Dakota. Here he found the finest and most fertile soil he had ever encountered in his wide travels.

Here was deep, rich loam covering an endless vista of prairie landscape, gently rolling yet flat enough to permit a man to plow all day long in a straight line without encountering a natural obstacle. The Big Sioux River, winding through the middle of this fertile valley, leaped over many a cataract and waterfall; here was power to turn millstones. A broad, green belt of dense woods on both sides of the river would furnish timber for sawmills.

Now he had found the perfect location on which he could place his countrymen in new homes. In his mind's eye, he saw great Norwegian communities arise in this glorious but uninhabited region, communities in which cities, churches and schools would appear and flourish.

Jubilant over finding such an excellent place to which he could lead his inexperienced countrymen, Halvor Nilsen bought from the government 5,373 acres along the river. For several reasons, he preferred the east side (the Iowa side) of the river.

The group, under Halvor Nilsen's leadership, started out from Clayton County in the spring of 1868. The group consisted of more than 30 families, the majority of which were from Hallingdal and Hadeland.

With their many cattle and much personal property, the group could not travel swiftly. It took them more than three weeks to travel the distance of 300 miles. The youngsters chased the cattle, picked flowers and thought the journey was a delightful experience. The grownups found the trip quite boring, but there were several good fiddlers in the group who helped make the evenings lively with many a *springdans* and *Hallingdans*.

On the last half of their journey, they crossed over land that looked so good to them that they said to Halvor, "Here is as good a soil as anyone could desire. Why go any farther?"

But Halvor insisted that they continue onward and said, "Just wait till you get to the Big Sioux River! This land is nothing but gumbo, a sticky watertight mud."

Finally, they arrived at the place where Canton was later to be built. Here they found that Halvor's enthusiastic descriptions were not exaggerated. Never had they seen a more attractive and fertile area. This surpassed their wildest dreams!

Happy at having found the setting for developing their future careers, they scattered in every direction to pick out the sites for their homesteads. Almost all of them filed on land on the Dakota side, because a recent prairie fire on the Iowa side had destroyed the grasslands so necessary for grazing.

Each family lived temporarily in its own wagon on its respective quarter section until the new arrivals had time to build sod houses.

Halvor's first act was to invite everybody to a Fourth of July celebration. The orations were to be delivered by a couple of Yankees who had already taken up land in the neighborhood.

The Sioux Falls

Halvor contributed a fat sheep to be barbecued whole. Hope and enthusiasm mounted sky-high as the settlers discussed the opportunities in this, their new homeland, 300 miles from the nearest railroad.

Here in this remote wilderness, these Dakota pioneers now began, with perseverence and thrift, to build a new society. They were, however, somewhat more fortunate than most of the pioneers in their situation, because Halvor Nilsen was for all of them a powerful friend in need. He lost no time in building a dam and erecting a sawmill and other useful structures. Any person in search of employment could find it here.

However, the pioneers had other things to do besides working for Halvor. They had to cut hay for fodder, break the prairie sod, and build houses for themselves and their families.

At all times it was customary to work as a group and to cooperate in each settler's project. Some plowed up the turf in thin slices; others cut these into workable lengths with a spade. The pieces of sod were hauled to the building site, where they were used to build the walls by laying the strips of sod and making them even and level by sprinkling dirt between the layers, as needed. Each layer was pounded firm by means of a heavy club.

The ridgepole and beams were laid in the forked end of vertical uprights, and then a number of more or less straight rails were laid from the ridgepole down to serve as the basis for a roof, which was made of thick layers of coarse slough grass and covered with turf and dirt. The same process was employed in building shelters for both man and beast.

When the job was skillfully done, such a sod house offered a comfortable protection against the cold. But the biggest problem was the roof. It was almost impossible to make it watertight. In rainy weather, the leaking roof sometimes made the floor just as sloppy as the ground outside.

A peculiarity of these sod houses was that they seemed to make an ideal breeding place for fleas to multiply and flourish. One of the settlers collected a whole bottle of fleas and sent it to his relatives in Wisconsin in order to show them what a robust race of fleas the Dakota prairies nurtured.

The first summer, the pioneers arrived too late to harvest any crops that year. Consequently, the food supply in some homes was nearly depleted before the winter was over.

Halvor Nilsen had heard a rumor to the effect that the government was planning to discontinue the fort in Sioux Falls, which had been maintained to protect the settlers from Indian attacks. Halvor went to Sioux Falls and found that a huge supply of salt pork was for sale. He bought the entire stock and divided it among the settlers so that each family received one-fourth barrel of the meat. This came like manna from heaven, for it helped the pioneers to survive until spring brought fresh grass for the cows to produce milk again.

That summer brought the first harvest of wheat, which the settlers cut by hand, threshing out the grain with the help of oxen. A hard, dry place on a hill was leveled and swept. Then they laid the sheaves in a big circle. The neighbors brought their oxen and hitched them in tandem by means of chains, one span behind the other. The oxen were driven round and round over the ring of sheaves until the grain was separated from the straw.

Sioux City, now a large city, was then an insignificant trading post on the Missouri River. However, it could offer some kind of market for the wheat, since at irregular intervals a small river steamboat would arrive, and it could carry the wheat south to Omaha.

It took almost an entire week to make the trip to Sioux City. Those making the journey brought with them a generous supply of provisions and a sheepskin quilt so that they could sleep in or under the wagon. An indispensable item was a good spade to use in scraping the gumbo off the wheels, which at times became so large that they could not revolve. The more experienced pioneers also took with them a sturdy jackscrew in order to lift the wagons out of the deep, frozen ruts in case they met another wagon. If one did not have a jack, it might become necessary to unload the entire cargo before the wagon could be lifted out of the ruts.

Winter of the big snow

Wintertime was a season of horror and terror on these open, windswept prairies until the groves planted around the houses reached sufficient size to furnish some protection against the cold wind. As far as the cold wind was concerned, the sod huts were, to be sure, good protection. But in most of these, the customary fuel—thick, twisted bands of hay—burned so quickly that the task of keeping a fire going was enormous.

To be caught outside during a winter storm was a frightful experience on the open prairie, where there was nothing to break the force and fury of the wind. The worst winter of all was that of 1880-81. It is still spoken of as the "winter of the big snow."

As early as 14 October, there came a very heavy fall of snow that remained until it began to thaw in the month of April 1881. All of North and South Dakota and the western part of Minnesota lay buried under several feet of snow.

The everlasting wind continued to heap up massive drifts around the huts of the pioneers until, in some places, there was no visible sign of them. The surface of these huge drifts eventually froze into a thick crust of ice, but this crust was not strong enough to bear the weight of horses and oxen. The animals broke through the crust and ran the risk of suffering serious cuts and bruises.

The roads were, of course, impassable. One ingenious mail carrier made a large sled to which he attached skis and a mast. Hoisting sail, he was then conveyed with dizzying velocity over the icy wastes.

Between buildings, the snow lay in a thickness of several yards. It was a problem to get in and out through low doorways. In many places, the settlers dug a tunnel between the house and barn and could do their chores cozily. A path made on top of the snow soon drifted over, but after persistent tramping by man and beast, the path would be packed so firmly that by exercising extreme caution one could manage to go from one building to another. Except on skis, a person would be completely helpless outside of these paths, for there lay loose snow full fathoms deep, which sucked like quicksand any intruder.

When the snow reached a depth of eight to 10 feet, it was customary to clear an area in front of the door and then cut steps to reach the surface. These steps were soon worn down. Always being slippery, they were the cause of frequent accidents, especially to visitors who were not familiar with these insidious stairways. It happened, occasionally, that a visitor would not enter a house by first rapping on the door. He might slip on the icy steps and, like an avalanche, come crashing through the door and come to rest on his back in the middle of the room.

A certain old maid, who did not savor the idea of being knocked unconscious each time she wanted to exit or enter, rejected the plan of cutting steps in the snowbank. Instead, she took a bottomless barrel and made of it a means of egress all winter. And that was not easy, for her hut was buried under eight feet of snow.

The winter of 1880-81 seemed never to end. It was a long period of many privations and unremitting toil. Each individual had to manage with the provisions available in the house and

barn, and these were most meager at best. For months, it was impossible to take a trip to town.

The worst of all was the lack of bread. The usual supply of flour did not suffice. Then it became necessary to bring out the coffee mill and try to grind some wheat. The result was a small supply of crushed kernels that they boiled in water and afterward stamped and pounded to a sort of mush. It was nourishing, but a poor substitute for bread.

The small towns had much difficulty in finding adequate fuel. Finally, they started to burn pieces of furniture, telegraph poles, railroad ties and even the railroad station buildings. Since there was not a single train in motion for several months, these articles were not missed for some time.

Spring arrived eventually, and by 16 April all the snow had disappeared. The winter blockade had lasted six months. But to many of the unprepared, starving and sorely beset pioneers, it seemed more like six years.

That spring, every watercourse in the low-lying areas was flooded. The Missouri River rose so high that many buildings, never before endangered by risk of inundation, were swept away by the raging waters.

The house near Vermillion—that of a well-known Vossing, Hans J. Hamre—was carried 15 miles downstream with 10 persons in it. Meanwhile, Hamre was busy up on the roof of the house, where he succeeded in nailing together a boat, using the floorboards of the attic. With the aid of his makeshift boat, he succeeded in saving the entire group.

Conflict in the congregation

Almost all the settlers around Canton had come from a well-organized Norwegian Synod congregation, which was served by the very capable clergyman, the Rev. U. V. Koren. They felt, as a matter of course, that the proper thing to do was to organize a congregation here in their new location, also.

However, just at this time they learned that a synod leader, Prof. Laur. Larsen (Peter Laurentius), had issued a public statement to the effect it was not sinful to own slaves, provided that they were not mistreated. *[The slavery question became one of the causes of dissension and schism among the early Norwegian Lutherans in America. –Blegen]*

To the Norwegians of the northern states, the idea of slavery was offensive and unacceptable. Several thousands of them had fought on the Union side in the War between the States and were firm believers in the abolition of slavery. For this reason, many of the Norwegian Lutherans refused to become members of the Norwegian Synod. They therefore organized a congregation in their new settlement that became affiliated with the Augustana Synod.

When it had been in existence for a few years, this Canton congregation acquired a pastor who soon became well known in the Lutheran Church. This man's name was Ole E. Hofstad, who had come as a young lay preacher from Trondheim, Norway.

Hofstad had very little formal schooling, but he was endowed by nature with a remarkable talent for public speaking and a gift for illuminating his ideas with the most original and peculiar illustrations. He had a fine singing voice, and he was a zealous student of the Scriptures. And in all his activities, he manifested a burning zeal that drove him to make personal contact with every individual he encountered.

When he had finished his sermon, he would stand by the church door, where he grasped the hand of each worshipper and had a different remark for each individual. To one he would say: "Have you found peace with God?" And to another: "If you were to die tonight, do you feel prepared to meet your Judge?"

To the people who had been accustomed to the formality of the synod clergy, it was something new to find a preacher manifesting a burning evangelical enthusiasm and making such intimate, personal remarks to individuals.

It made a very profound impression on the parishioners. But there were those who found it offensive, and they withdrew, scoffing and ridiculing such behavior. However, there were more who maintained that Hofstad was the greatest preacher since John the Baptist.

Everyone admired Hofstad's singing voice. People in Luverne can still recall being awakened early one morning in pioneer days to the resounding notes of a Norwegian hymn. The sound seemed to be coming right down from the sky. Dressing hurriedly, they rushed outside to investigate. Soon they caught sight of a man standing atop the highest hill and greeting the rising sun—with song. This man was Preacher Hofstad. On a missionary journey to the Luverne community, he chose this way to let people for miles around know that he had arrived.

Hofstad was a man of feeling, and it was understandable that his powerful and passionate enthusiasm could lead him to make ill-considered and rash statements and to commit imprudencies. He was a combination of Salvation Army revivalist and petty pope who could foment violent disagreements among the members of his congregation.

Eventually, a merger of three church bodies formed the Canton congregation. In 1890, the United Norwegian Lutheran Church in America was organized, and both the Canton and Bethlehem congregations became affiliated with it. But, in spite of the fact that they now were fellow members of the same church body, each congregation for another 12 years continued to have its own pastor.

After a time, the people began to realize the absurdity of employing two pastors where one would be enough, and they voted to merge the two churches. Reverend Hofstad resigned, and the Rev. P. H. Tetlie of the former synod congregation was called to serve the merged church.

Now the question arose: Which of the two church buildings was to be used? A compromise was made to the effect that services were to be held on alternate Sundays in each of the two churches.

It soon became apparent that this plan was not going to be successful in bringing about a genuine union. To get rid of the ticklish problem concerning the choice of buildings, it was agreed that the two structures should be joined and made into one by moving them together and removing the separating walls.

This was done, and for a long time this hybrid constituted the strangest-looking house of God imaginable. One half of the edifice had a very tall and slender steeple, whereas the other half had a sturdy, squat bell tower. The pulpit was placed precisely on the line of junction.

The problem of union was not yet solved, for on Sundays the worshipers came and seated themselves, as before, in their own customary places in their respective church pews. Finally, it became clear to the good citizens of Canton that they must have a completely new church. They razed the two old churches and erected an imposing new building of red quartzite.

It was not long before this magnificent church, equipped with all its modern facilities, attracted the loyalty and love of its members. Now they began to feel that it was their very own temple of worship, which had absolutely nothing to do with former differences and disagreements. And now peace came to Canton.

The legacy of Halvor Nilsen

Halvor Nilsen, the doughty founder of the settlement, continued his career as the community's foremost mentor and broad-visioned philanthropist until the day of his death at an advanced age. On his property, he had established a small town that the neighbors called Nelsonville. But Nilsen, in all modesty, succeeded in having the name changed to Beloit in commemoration of his first American home: Beloit, Wisconsin.

Here in Beloit, Iowa, a sawmill, a gristmill, a blacksmith shop, a grocery store, a real estate office and other conveniences had made their appearance.

On Nilsen's initiative and especially through his financial aid, Augustana College in Marshall, Wisconsin, was moved to Beloit, Iowa. When the first railroad was constructed through this region, the station—for reasons of topographical features—was placed two miles from Beloit on the Dakota side, where Canton is now located.

Augustana College was moved to new buildings in Canton in 1884. Not the man to let the former Augustana buildings remain unused, Halvor Nilsen transformed them into a home for children. This is the origin of Beloit Orphanage, to which Halvor donated 1,000 acres of land. It gave the orphanage such a fine support that, before long, Beloit Orphanage became the largest children's home in all of Norwegian-America.

Det Indre af et norsk Bondehus

63

The Red River Valley, western Minnesota

(Source: Den Siste Folkevandring Sagastubber fra Nybyggerlivet i Amerika, by Hjalmar Rued Holand, 1930; Norwegians in America: The Last Migration, by Hjalmar Rued Holand, translated by Helmer M. Blegen, 1978, pp. 215-222)

A valley is ordinarily thought to be a relatively deep and narrow depression between two ranges of higher land. This definition does not apply to the Red River Valley, however. It is a perfect plain and so broad that the eye cannot see across it. This plain is so level that from its sides to the middle and from its upper end to its lower end, there is a drop of only one foot in every 5,000 feet. It is like a motionless sea of congealed earth.

Down its very middle runs a deep and crooked little channel (the Red River), whose general direction is straight north. There it finds its outlet, which sometimes in the springtime is quite inadequate. The river has innumerable branches.

There was a time, ages ago, when there was a great inland sea where the Red River Valley now lies. In outline, it was similar to Lake Michigan, but very much larger. As a matter of fact, it was merely an arm or bay of a much larger lake to the north of it.

This huge lake was created when an immense sheet of ice several thousand feet thick and thousands of miles long came pushing down from the Arctic Ocean. As an impenetrable wall, this glacier lay there and closed off all natural flow of water to the north. When the glacier finally began to melt and withdraw northward, a lake formed at its foot. This water found its outlet through the Minnesota River, where its mighty current cut broad furrows into the bed of granite.

The lake (Lake Agassiz) lay as barren as the Dead Sea. When the wind raced over its broad surface, there was no sail for it to fill with its breath. The storms shrieked and whined, and huge billows rolled along in greenish-white water lanes, thundered against the shores, leveled the bottom and rolled giant boulders forward. Now these stones, worn to roundness, lie heaped up in deep layers along the former strands as mementos of a vanished sea.

After many thousands of years, there occurred a new and violent natural transformation. The enormous glacier to the north finally melted away, and these immense masses of water that had set their ultimate course for the Gulf of Mexico found a new outlet in the opposite direction and began to stream into Hudson Bay.

Today, between the equator and the Arctic Ocean lie two tiny lakes on a continental divide: Lake Traverse and Big Stone Lake (both located on the border between Minnesota and South Dakota). They are reminders of the time when great and mighty waves roared at this place on our prairies.

The waves had done their work very well indeed. Now the sea bottom lay as level and even as the surface of the water above would have been on a still summer day that had not a breath of breeze. The earth was deep—very deep—and collected the riches of the fertilized remains of millions of rotting fish.

Now it was time for the wind to perform a new work: It spread seeds over the steaming young land, inch by inch, foot by foot. Soon the green grass germinated and grew strong and stiff, until at last the whole vast former sea bottom was carpeted in green.

Big herds of antelope and buffalo came up from the south, including mature and sensible cow bison and frolicsome young heifers. Lusty young bachelor-bison gave the venerable and dignified old buffalo bull, who was their leader and guide, grave concern. They nibbled a luscious tuft of grass here, another there, and in their good time paid for it with a rich deposit on the plain. They had come to a good place. They tested their brawn in exuberant duels of strength, and they chewed their cud in contented surrender to the will of an indulgent Mother Nature.

But look! From far distant places come Indians on their fleet horses. They howl the jubilant shouts of a hunter's joy at success in the chase. They shoot their arrows, and they ride in crazy circles around the nonplussed herd.

In close and compact clumps, the defenseless beasts huddle for mutual protection. Only the big leader maintains an intrepid and challenging stance against the strange enemy. Several sharp arrows penetrate his hide, and in an insane frenzy he attacks. Riddled with a hundred arrows, his bright eyes turn to glass, and the giant falls. But the dizzying round does not stop until the hunter has dropped one after the other and, at last, is the supreme master of the field.

There are new changes coming, and new times and races. Far in the eastern lands, people are trampling on each other in order to find a place in the sun. More and more mouths are trying to bite less and less bread.

Bread! Bread! Bread!

The glib-mouthed spout eloquently of state aid, and the well-to-do preach a gospel of industry and economizing. But the boldest and most resolute say their farewells to their forefathers' graves and dauntlessly set out for new skies under which to seek fame and fortune.

Norwegian newspaperman promotes the Red River Valley

In 1924 the unveiling of a bronze tablet occurred in St. Paul, Minnesota. It bore a suitable inscription to commemorate Paul Hjelm Hansen, "the discoverer of the Red River Valley and its first spokesman."

In 1810, Hansen was born in Bergen, Norway, and later became an editor and journalist in Fredrikshald and Christiania. He was already a mature man—too old to seek his fortune in a foreign land—when he went to America in 1867.

Hansen was against emigration and made this trip at the request of *Selskapet for Folkeoplysningens Fremme* (The Society for the Promotion of Public Education), which wanted an accurate report about America in order to agitate against the emigration that was growing at an alarming rate.

But when Hansen had been in America for a year or two, he obtained a completely different view of emigration from the one he had when he came here. He became the editor of *Fædrelandet og Emigranten (The Fatherland and the Emigrant) [a merger of two of the earliest Norwegian newspapers in the U.S. –Blegen]*. And before long, he was writing about America as the great place of refuge for the oppressed people of Norway.

In 1869, the Bureau of Immigration of Minnesota decided to make a definite attempt to colonize the great unpopulated expanses of the northern and western parts of the state. The state especially favored Norwegian and Swedish immigrants. Accordingly, Paul Hjelm Hansen was requested to visit the Red River Valley—at state expense—and to publish his reports on it in the Norwegian press.

Hansen accepted the offer, and that same year he made an extensive journey of exploration throughout the valley in a wagon drawn by oxen. The trip took him two or three months. Afterward, he wrote a long series of articles for *Nordisk Folkeblad (The Norwegian Popular Journal)*. These articles were the cause of a great emigration.

In one of his articles, he wrote these effective words: "My travels through this region (the Red River Valley) have been for me a source of both satisfaction and joy, for I have become convinced of one thing that I consider of primary significance.

"The goal of the poor immigrant in this country is obviously economic gain. But the road leading to the achievement of this goal demands so much courage and perseverance, so much physical and spiritual effort, and involves such a degree of privation and suffering, that the man who succeeds in reaching his goal has become a better and more capable person than he would have become had he remained in the Old Country.

"It is, by and large, a joy and satisfaction for me that when I return to Norway, I shall be in a position to testify on the basis of firsthand experience that my countrymen in America, with relatively few exceptions, have improved their economic conditions while they have at the same time developed into better, more capable and more intelligent human beings."

Already, two years previous to Paul Hjelm Hansen's visit, several hundred Norwegians had gazed upon the Red River Valley's endless expanse. Several large companies arrived there in 1867 and 1868. They did not, however, build their homes down in the valley proper, but on higher land east of it. They found what they considered to be a more attractive landscape there.

The soil was fertile enough, even though it was not quite so good as in the Red River Valley. Furthermore, it was much more desirable to live where there were large wooded areas and lakes that offered good fishing opportunities.

It was not until all the best land in the fine Park Region was occupied that people began to move out over the open prairie, where the groves were small and far apart and where drainage was a problem. This began in 1870, but was so rapid that by 1880 the entire Red River Valley was taken up, with the exception of the less desirable and treeless spots.

The pioneers who came to the Red River Valley in the 1870s were the most fortunate of all the new settlers in America. Not only did they acquire an immensely fertile land, but it was perfectly flat and easy to cultivate.

They did not have to wait many years for railroads, for the land was so level that the railroad builder was spared all the time and expense of building a level roadbed. As a result, the railroads followed on the heels of the land-seekers. This made it possible for them to ship their grain immediately.

They escaped the ravages of cholera and other infectious epidemics that took such a heavy toll of lives in settlements farther east. Nor were the grasshoppers and similar scourges as bad here.

Some harsh realities

In spite of all its many virtues, the Red River Valley was, nevertheless, not paradise when the first settlers came to it. The first 10 years or so, the settlers feared they had tempted fate too much.

There were, especially, four great evils that they had not anticipated that took a long time to overcome: the disastrous spring floods, the horrible blizzards in wintertime, the overpowering loneliness on the prairie all the year, and the sudden and terrifying assault of the prairie fire.

The valley is so flat and its numerous small watercourses are so shallow that merely a small rise in the water level will put the whole valley into a state of flood.

During the first years, flooding was almost a regular annual phenomenon. The level valley would be inundated as far as the eye could see. The steamships that plied between Fargo and Winnipeg could, in the 1870s, take excursions for miles over the plains where all signs of life seemed to have been extinguished. Many a settler picked up and left permanently *because* of this.

However, except in the very lowest parts of the valley, this is now a rare occurrence. The bottom of the valley has been steadily rising since the glacier retreated, and this has created an improved outlet for the water northward.

The notorious North Dakota blizzards were especially formidable in this valley, where they encountered less resistance than in any other region in the nation. These affected primarily the later settlers, who built their homes out on the open, exposed prairie. The first pioneers had built their homes in the small groves along the watercourses and were much better sheltered.

But far worse was the crushing burden of loneliness on the prairie. For the people reared in the cozy Norwegian valleys with the sheltering protection of wooded slopes all about them, their radical transplantation to the awesome emptiness of the treeless, level prairie was a trauma.

At home they had become accustomed to a refreshing multiformity in Nature's display of her rich resources of beauty. The boundaries of their district were precise and obvious. But on the prairie all they had was a boundless monotony, the harsh, restless wind, the scorching sun and the naked horizon, devoid of any possible place in which to hide and find repose and peace.

There is no rest to be found on the prairie. It engenders, in the majority, a sense of feverish restlessness. In the weak and unstable, this ends in a depression that sometimes leads to insanity. The Dakota prairie is no place for weaklings, and many Norwegians have succumbed under the pressing weight of the cruel vastness and have ended their days in an asylum. But most of the old pioneers were not weaklings.

Even though all experienced, at the outset, that peculiar anxiety created by the prairie, this unrest soon evolved into a furious zeal to work. And when, eventually, the fruits of that work began to appear, they gradually, in the course of time, became reconciled with the prairie, even as the sailor and the sea.

Soon the pioneer found himself in love with the prairie. Here all roads are open and all the fields are flat. All that is needed here is the strength and will to work. This, the pioneer had.

Pioneer's greatest fear: prairie fire

Most to be feared was the prairie fire. In spring and fall, the prairie fire lay in ambush, ready to pounce upon the settler. During these two seasons, he knew no moment of peaceful unconcern by day or night, except on the days when rainfall made the fire impotent.

Perhaps he had managed to build up a fine, spacious home and had granaries bulging with wheat, soon to be sold in order to make a payment on the note or mortgage. But in every direction, he saw the prairie covered with a cloak of grass, dry as tinder. One tiny spark far off in the distance was enough to make the whole, broad valley burst into a moving ocean of flame that would consume his houses and crops in one greedy flash.

The prairie fire always moves forward in the form of one or more wedge-shaped units, like the blade of a snowplow. The point races quickly ahead, its velocity conforming to that of the wind. Throwing gigantic tongues of flame into the long, dry grass, the prairie fire gallops forward in the manner of a spirited warhorse.

The sides burn more slowly outward and are not so difficult to extinguish. But until the spearhead of the fire is quenched, the danger is not diminished.

As a protection against prairie fires, it was the usual practice to plow a circle of furrows around the house and another larger circle around the first one in such a way that there was a distance of a few yards between them. It was fairly safe to burn off the grass between these circles of furrows. This would make a fire break, causing the advancing fire to detour, if the wind was not too strong.

When the wind was quite powerful, it would cause tufts of burning grass to whirl aloft and then drop like a torch, far ahead. Then a new fire would be started where each tuft fell.

A prairie fire was such a serious thing that all the people came together to collaborate in fighting it and to limit its ravages, as far as humanly possible. The most experienced of the pioneers

Plowing the firebreak

became the commander, and under his quick and definite leadership, everyone did his part in a fine spirit of teamwork.

There was little use in attacking the point of the fire. They started from the rear by putting out the fire on the sides. Armed with brooms, old pieces of clothing, spades and whatnot, they beat out the flames and started backfires. In this way, it was possible to confine the fire to a narrow strip.

Often the wind increased in velocity, and the fire advanced in spite of all they did to restrain it. Then fire fighters might become confused from smoke and fear. Each one would, in desperation, beat and slap at the flames, gasping for air in the hot smoke, puffing and grunting with exertion. Burned and exhausted, they would fall to the ground and watch as stacks of grain, fences, houses, granaries—everything—burst into flame, while the triumphant red tip of the prairie fire's tongue licked furiously onward and beyond.

For many years, the fear of prairie fires was the pioneer's nightmare. At night he peered through his windows with uneasy eyes to check any possible sign of the ominous flicker of a flame. In the daytime, especially when he had to leave his place temporarily, he was haunted by vivid premonitions of finding his house in flames upon his return. Fall and spring, year after year—such was the prairie's lot.

Golden age for Norwegian farmers

All these difficulties and sufferings did not seem to dampen the pioneers' joy in work. They resolutely continued to work with the same restless eagerness, a characteristic that is especially pronounced in America's north-central regions, where the climate seems to charge the people with an inexhaustible energy. Here in the Red River Valley, and in North Dakota as a whole, the people were more than amply repaid for their efforts with tremendous bumper crops of wheat.

It was the report of these matchless expanses and their huge crops of wheat that brought about the rapid rise in the rate of emigration from Norway, which began in 1880. During the next decade, this great folk-migration reached its peak, for more than 200,000 emigrated from Norway to America.

These years were also the golden age for the Norwegian farmers in America. The crops were excellent, and the rapid development of the country made a demand for all produce, resulting in prices that were consistently very good. There was no other place in the U.S. where wheat could be raised so

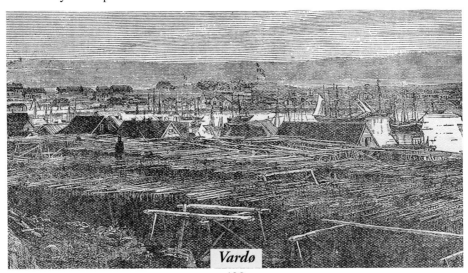

Vardø

cheaply as on the flat Red River Valley, especially in the 1880s, when wages were very low for farm laborers.

On almost every farm, there were poor newcomer boys who were glad to work for small pay in order to get the money to pay for their tickets to America, for which they still were in debt. Frequently, they worked on farms for board and room for a year or so to pay for their tickets. After that, they had to continue to work as farm laborers until they had saved up enough to start out on their own, by going farther west to file on homesteads.

As a result of this fortunate combination of circumstances, many of the Red River Valley pioneers became very wealthy. Some of them used their money to buy up all the adjoining farms, until they had to stop because they had reached the border of the land belonging to another farmer who was doing the same as they. Some of these farms constituted two thousand acres.

Others preferred to live well and, especially, drink well. There were many of them. They raced their fine, sleek horses on the roads and gave many elaborate parties with much good food and a great deal of drink. They played the old Norwegian card games of *knak* and *femkort*, with big piles of money on the table.

It was the tempting lure of the Red River Valley's golden wheat that made North Dakota a Norwegian state. Through the 1880s and 1890s, there was a prolonged race between the railroads and the Norwegian land-seekers all the way across the length of North Dakota until they reached the rainless fields of Montana. Then the stream of land-seekers swerved north into Canada, and is still continuing (1908).

Religion comes to the Valley

The Red River Valley had many pastors who, with remarkable perseverance, traveled all over the bleak expanses to bring the consolation and encouragement of Christianity to the widely scattered pioneers. The first of these was Bjug Harstad from Setesdal, and even today there remains an aura of saintliness over his persevering activity.

He had a favorite expression that became a slogan for the younger clergymen who came later: "How glorious it is to wear oneself out in the Lord's service!"

But old Harstad seems to be everlastingly durable, for he is alive, vigorous and robust today (1908? 1930?). Harstad has seen the Red River Valley and North Dakota transformed from an uninhabited hunting ground to a rich and well-developed modern land.

Another durable and ageless pioneer preacher is the Rev. Bernhard L. Hagboe from Romsdal. He came to the Red River Valley with the first pioneers and has constantly worked among them. He seems to be in his element when he is battling the wilderness.

Wherever a small flock of pioneers found a nest in northwestern Minnesota or northern Dakota, it was not long before they saw Pastor Hagboe come to them to talk with them on the greatest things in life. He walked or rode horseback over the trackless wastes, shared the pioneers' food in their sod huts, slept in straw stacks, was pursued by prairie fires, whipped by storms, and associated with Indians.

No comfortable parish in an old, well-established settlement tempted him in the least. As the new land-seekers moved westward, he moved with them. He was ever an ecclesiastical outpost on the outer fringe of the frontier.

A pioneer at Shelly (Minnesota) relates that when Hagboe visited him, the Marsh River was so swollen that Hagboe had to swim across. He held his watch between his teeth and tied his clothes into a bundle that he bound to his neck. Since he had not a little to carry, he had to make two trips across the river.

Although the pioneers were a generous lot, there was so little money among them during the first years that they did not have any cash to pay the preacher's salary. He had to be satisfied to accept gifts in nature.

One day Hagboe came driving into Crookston in an old buggy pulled by one long-legged bronco and another with very short legs and with very long hair. When he was asked where he came from, he told them he had been out collecting his salary.

"How did it go?"

"Quite well, thank you. I got all this."

And he pointed to the back of the buggy. There lay a half bushel of potatoes, three carrots and a head of cabbage.

The Prairie

(From De Norske Settlementers Historie, by Hjalmar Rued Holand, pp. 502-503. The following is an excerpt from a chapter in Holand's book entitled "The Prairie," translated by Helmer M. Blegen and printed in Norwegians in America: The Last Migration. The final four paragraphs printed here are excerpts from the same chapter, as translated by Malcolm Rosholt)

• • • • •

Deep within the heart of America lies the prairie, vast, endless, incomprehensible. For unless one has lived or roamed about on the prairie, one cannot comprehend it—it is unlike all other natural phenomena, and it affects minds in its own peculiar heavy and corrosive way, as if it were brooding a deep secret.

All large things are imposing, and the prairie is immensely large. It extends from horizon to horizon in all its vast monotony. For hundreds and hundreds of miles, only two things are to be seen: sky and prairie.

There is no mountain to arrest the eye, no valley to refresh the landscape, no forest whispering of cool, shady retreats—only a scrubby growth along its tiny streams. All other vistas of Nature's topography are forced back with brutal force, leaving only two concepts: sky and prairie.

That is why the prairie is impressive, overwhelming, crushing in its effect. Because of its monotonous, constraining vistas, it makes the beholder lose his feeling of lightness and liveliness, his sense of soaring fantasy. He begins to feel oppressed, confined and small, crushed into the earth's surface, an inconsequential insect.

No place on earth does one get a greater impression of the overpowering might of the unseen, and nowhere else inspires such a feeling of personal, paltry insignificance. It is, therefore, not strange that the end is sometimes religious fanaticism. The wide, open spaces of the prairie are home to many a wild sect, and the Canadian prairie is the paradise of fanatical visionaries.

Since the beginning of time, Nature has strived here to produce the most fertile ground on earth. Year after year it has been decked with glorious hay and flowers, bowing to the dancing winds in this heartland of America, only to sacrifice itself in purposeful waste as a fertilizer for the grain to be raised by future generations.

Without stones or stumps, the prairie lies flat and luxuriant, covered with a layer of black earth several feet deep, bulging with food for the world's millions. This is the pride of agriculture, the nation's food bank and fortress against hunger.

No fewer than 600,000 Norwegians live on the prairies of the Northwest (today's Midwest) across immense spaces, in settlements as large as several adjoining counties.

It was fortunate, indeed, for the mountain dwellers from Norway's stony land to get this great share of America's—and the world's—best agricultural land.

ACKNOWLEDGMENTS . . . AND A BOATLOAD OF THANKS

Behind every book there is a long list of people whose names may not appear prominently in the book, but without whom the project would never have been completed. This book is no exception. We wish to acknowledge the many who helped turn *History of the Norwegian Settlements* from dream to reality. They include:

- **Mei-fei (Rosholt) Elrick and husband David Elrick**, for giving permission to publish the translation by Malcolm Rosholt (Mei-Fei's father) of Hjalmar Rued Holand's book, thus fulfilling one of Malcolm's final wishes
- **Helga Onan**, who typed Holand's manuscript into a Publisher program
- **Evelyn Ostraat Wierenga**, who edited and owns the copyright to *Norwegians in America: The Last Migration* (1978), translated by Helmer M. Blegen, for allowing publication of Blegen's translation
- **Edna Rude**, for translating Chapter 1 (The Vinland Expeditions)
- **Arnold Ness**, who promoted the publishing of this translation and did scanning work
- **Kristi Karels**, who helped transfer the manuscript from Publisher to Microsoft Word
- **Barbara Olson** (Holand's granddaughter) and husband David, for their encouragement
- **Steinar Opstad**, Ph. D., for his suggestions as well as his back-cover review
- **Walter F. Mondale**, for his back-cover review
- **Rev. Jens Dale**, for his back-cover review

• • • • •

• 32-page colored map section sources
—**Arne Brekke**, Ph. D., for his information on Norwegian geographic terms
—**Origins Genealogical Book Store**, Janesville, Wisconsin, publisher of *Norwegian Research Guide*
—**NAF (copyright) – Norwegian Automobile Association – www.naf.no** – 18 *fylke* (district) and 433 *kommune* (municipality) maps
—*Kart over de Forenede Stater og Norge i Amerika*, by Martin Ulvestad, Norge i Amerika Publishing Co., Minneapolis, Minnesota, 1901: Upper Midwest settlement map

We are grateful to the following historians and genealogists for their research assistance:
- **Blaine Hedberg**, Vesterheim Genealogical Center, for checking names and places throughout the book
- **Dee Grimsrud**, Wisconsin State Historical Association, for providing assistance and material to Malcolm Rosholt
- **Scott F. Wolter** and **Richard Nielsen**, photographs of the Kensington Rune Stone, Chapter 1 (The Vinland Expeditions)
- **Georgia Rosendahl**, Chapter 34 (Spring Grove and Wilmington, Houston County)
- **Gordon Eddy**, Chapter 34 (Black Hammer, Houston County)
- **Jim Skree**, Chapter 34 (Houston and Badger Valley)
- **Gene Estensen**, Chapter 49 (Norseland and Scandia Grove, Nicollet County)
- **Karl Jakob Skarstein**, Chapter 54 (Belmont Massacre, Jackson County)
- **Kaye Nelson**, Chapter 60 (Blue Mounds Township, Pope County)

Additional thanks go to those who provided research assistance to Deb Nelson Gourley in supplementing Chapter 54 (Belmont Massacre, Jackson County):
- **Tom Atkins, Margit Bakke, Viggo Fosse, Ruth Hackett, Gunnar Hjørnevik, Knut Hjørnevik, Anita Særvold Johannessen, Jean Marthaler, Kermit Mestad, LaVerna Moothart and Char Nelson**

Translation assistance for Chapter 54 was provided by:
- **Stanley J. Nuland and James Skurdall**

• • • • •

We express our appreciation to the following for their helpful comments and suggestions along the way…
- **Darrel Johnson, Alice Stangeland Kirn, Doris Lynne, Margaret "Peggy" Miller, Elaine Nordlie, Barbara Olson and Jorand Olson**

…and to those mentioned below for their technical assistance and advice:
- **Chris Shelton**, cover design and colored section layout
- **Erik Anundsen**, Anundsen Publishing Company, Decorah, Iowa, printing and distribution

• • • • •

And finally, we gratefully acknowledge the following sources for the maps and illustrations used to enhance the book:

—**Hand-written maps** used in chapters: *Norsk Lutherske Menigheter i Amerika, 1843-1916*, by Pastor O. M. Norlie, Augsburg Publishing House, Minneapolis, Minnesota, 1918: County and state maps used in chapters

—**Canal map** (Chapter 4), courtesy of Lorna Anderson

—**Printed maps** used throughout the book and on the front cover: *Kart over de Forenede Stater og Norge i Amerika*, by Martin Ulvestad, Norge i Amerika Publishing Co., Minneapolis, Minnesota, 1901

—**Traverse des Sioux map** (Chapter 34): Nicollet County Historical Society

—**Norwegian settlements in the Midwest** time-line map: Telelaget of America

—**Illustrations by Elsie Hotvedt Thorson**, reproduced in *Norwegians in America: The Last Migration*, published by The Center for Western Studies, Augustana College, Sioux Falls, South Dakota, 1978; illustrations courtesy of Evelyn Ostraat Wierenga, editor

—**Lithographs** on pp. 14, 26 and 38, courtesy of Deb Nelson Gourley

—**Lithographs** from *De Hjem vi Forlod og De Hjem vi Fandt*, John Anderson Publishing Co., Chicago, Illinois, 1892: courtesy of Lorna Anderson

—**Lithographs** from *Solskin i Hjemmet: Ung og Gammel*, Review & Herald Publishing Co., 1890: courtesy of Jean Marthaler

HISTORY OF THE PROJECT

Building a book is a long, labor-intensive project. In the case of *History of the Norwegian Settlements*, the process really began about 1895, when Hjalmar Rued Holand first started collecting pioneer stories for his 1908 *De Norske Settlementers Historie*, one of two books by Holand featured in this edition.

Holand's book was originally written in Dano-Norwegian and printed in Gothic script, making it difficult for modern-day readers on both sides of the ocean to understand. A translation was sorely needed to make the century-old book's contents accessible to later generations.

Years before the book went into production, a lot of research, travel, phone calls, letters and detective work went into the project. Besides the pre-production work listed below, advice and help came from many volunteers, librarians, archivists, genealogy specialists and historians along the way. In all, many years of combined efforts have been invested in this project, in addition to Holand's 13 years of collecting data for the original book.

• • • • •

Following is a chronology of the steps leading up to production of this book:
• 1978—The Center for Western Studies, Augustana College, Sioux Falls, South Dakota, publishes *Norwegians in America: The Last Migration*, Helmer Blegen's translation of Holand's 1930 book *Den Siste Folkevandring Sagastubber fra Nybyggerlivet i Amerika* (portions of which appear in this new book), edited by Evelyn Ostraat Wierenga.
• 1979—Correspondence between Helmer Blegen and Lorna Anderson ensues regarding his translation of Holand's 1908 book (Blegen completed the translation, but it was misplaced after his death in 1982 and never located).
• 1986—Malcolm Rosholt finishes his translation of Holand's *De Norske Settlementers Historie*, putting rough drafts of the manuscript in several Norwegian-American libraries and genealogy centers.
• 1986-90—Lorna photocopies Rosholt's manuscript and presents it to several Norwegian-American bygdelags, including Telelag; she charts and summarizes the Norwegian settlement history from the translation for a book she co-wrote with Jan Frye called *Norway to America: Genealogy and Settlement History Guide*. The charted history is also included in the Telelag book, *Telemark to America Emigration, Volume 1*.
• 2003—Arnold Ness, past-president of Telelaget of America, urges publishing the translation. Lorna contacts the centers that have the translated manuscript; none are interested in publishing. Through Jerry Rosholt, Malcolm's cousin, Lorna makes contact with Malcolm Rosholt (then in his mid-90s). Malcolm agrees to have his translation published. He hires Helga Onan to type his manuscript into a word-processing program. Malcolm dies in February 2005 before his translation can be published. His daughter, Mei-Fei Elrick, along with her husband, David, is determined to fulfill her father's dying wish to get his translation into print.
• 2005—After Rosholt's death, Lorna works with Mei-Fei regarding printing of the translation. Lorna works on pre-production, assisted by her daughter, Kristi Karels, who helps transfer the text to a Microsoft Word document. Deb Nelson Gourley of Astri My Astri Publishing is selected to design, layout and publish the book. Jo Ann B. Winistorfer comes on board as editor. Lorna communicates with and assists in getting permission from Mei-Fei Elrick and Evelyn Ostraat Wierenga for Deb Nelson Gourley of Astri My Astri Publishing, Waukon, Iowa, to copyright, publish and market the book. Production on the book begins in mid-October.

—Lorna Anderson, pre-production coordinator

Biographies
Major Contributors

Hjalmar Rued Holand: Heritage was his mission

Historian, author and archaeological researcher Hjalmar Rued Holand, was born 20 October 1872 in the parish of Høland near Oslo, Norway, to Johan Olsen Fagermøen and Maren Olsen Rued. Upon his mother's death in 1883, Holand, age 11, immigrated to the United States with his sister Helen, living with his brother, Anders, in Chicago. After their father's immigration, the family moved to Wisconsin. Holand received a bachelor's degree, and later (1899) a master's degree, from the University of Wisconsin.

While still a student in Madison, Holand traveled to Door County, and was so enchanted by the area surrounding Ephraim, Wisconsin, that he purchased 57 acres there. Shortly after his marriage on 13 June 1900, he and his wife, Lillian Theresa Ingesoll, moved to Eagle Cliff, the name they gave to their homestead. To earn a living during those early years of marriage and raising a family, Holand traveled the Midwest selling books and maps in wholesale quantities for advertising purposes. Later, he devoted his time to growing fruit, as well as to lecturing and writing.

Holand served as archivist and historian of a Norwegian cultural society. This position prompted him to travel, without reimbursement, across the Midwest, collecting the history of the first Norwegian-American colonists. Along with statistical material, he gathered the memories and anecdotes of these Norse pioneers, preserving them for future generations through his writings.

His first widely published book was *De Norske Settlementers Historie* (1908), written in Norwegian, the language of his readers. Based on research and on interviews with hundreds of first-generation Norse settlers, the book recounts the settlement of the Norwegians in the Upper Midwest. This monumental task took Holand 13 years to complete. The book was reprinted in 1909 and 1912.

Among his other works, Holand penned the following: *History of Door County*, Wisconsin, two volumes (1917); *Old Peninsula Days 1925*, eight editions; *Coon Prairie 1928*, two editions; *Norwegians in America: The Last Migration* (1930); and *Wisconsin's Belgium Community* (1931).

One of Holand's most intriguing (and controversial) obsessions arose from his interest in the Kensington Rune Stone. Despite critics who claimed the stone was a hoax, Holand became convinced that the runic inscription chiseled into the 230-pound stone was authentic. His faith in the rune stone led him to write five books on the subject, along with numerous articles for a variety of publications.

Holand and his wife moved to another farm after their beloved Eagle Cliff was purchased as part of Peninsula Park near Ephraim. Sadly, in 1934, a fire destroyed the family's new home and, along with it, many of Holand's books, manuscripts and memorabilia from his childhood home in Norway.

In 1957, King Olav V of Norway presented Holand with the prestigious St. Olaf's Medal, honoring him for his many contributions. In his later years, Holand served as curator of the Wisconsin State Historical Society. The same year (at age 84) he published his autobiography, *My First Eighty Years*. Hjalmar Holand died 6 August 1963 at age 90.

Malcolm L. Rosholt: Translation brings stories to new generations

Malcolm L. Rosholt was born 28 September 1907 in Rosholt, Wisconsin, to John Milton and Lillian Anderson Rosholt. He attended grade school and two years of high school in Rosholt, graduating from Emerson High School in Stevens Point, Wisconsin. He enrolled in Spokane College and later attended St. Olaf College in Northfield, Minnesota.

After graduation, he went to Shanghai, China, where he worked as a journalist on The China Press. On 26 March 1933, he married Margaret Njaa in Northwood, North Dakota. Her father, Sven Njaa, a Lutheran pastor, performed the ceremony. They settled in Shanghai and lived there for five years, where Malcolm worked at the newspaper while Margaret taught English. A daughter, Renee Mei-fei, was born in 1936. They left China in 1937, returning to the United States. He lectured for several years, moving to San Francisco in 1941 where he worked for the China News Service.

During World War II, he was commissioned as 1st lieutenant in the Army Air Force and returned to China. His knowledge of the country qualified him to serve as a liaison officer in the field with the Chinese Armies. He was discharged in December 1945 with the rank of major. Moving back to Wisconsin after the war, Malcolm wrote more than two dozen books, some on local history and others on his experiences in China and the war. In 2004 (at age 96) he published his autobiography, *Rainbow around the Moon*.

Malcolm Rosholt died on 20 February 2005 at 97 years of age. At the time of his death, he had four grandsons and five great-grandchildren. His daughter, Mei-fei, and her husband, David Elrick, live in Ontario, Canada. Mei-fei Elrick assisted with preparing the manuscript of her father's translation of Hjalmar Rued Holand's *De Norske Settlementers Historie*.

• • • • •

Helmer M. Blegen: *A master of languages*

Helmer M. Blegen, professor and archivist emeritus of Augustana College, Sioux Falls, South Dakota, was born on 8 March 1898 at Churchs Ferry, North Dakota, to Norwegian immigrant Hans O. Blegen, Faaberg, Gudbrandsdal, and his third wife, Marit Erickson Berild.

Upon graduation from St. Olaf College in Northfield, Minnesota, Blegen taught at colleges in Illinois and Iowa. He spent three years in advanced studies at the University of Minnesota while teaching German and French at Augsburg College. In the early 1930s, he studied languages at the University of Paris and at the Berlitz school of languages at Florence, Italy.

Blegen married Ann Rytterager in 1939. From 1927 to 1968, he served as professor of French, Spanish and Norwegian, and as chairman of the Humanities Division at Augustana College in Sioux Falls. From 1968 to 1970, he was named official archivist at Augustana. In 1978, the Center for Western Studies, Augustana College, published *Norwegians in America: The Last Migration*, Blegen's translation of Holand's 1930 book, *Den Siste Folkevandring Sagastubber fra Nybyggerlivet i America*.

A highly respected lecturer and translator, Blegen earned listings in *Who's Who*. Among his many honors was the St. Olaf Medal, conferred upon him in 1954 by King Haakon VII of Norway. Helmer M. Blegen died in June of 1980. He leaves a rich legacy for future scholars of Norwegian history.

Deb Nelson Gourley: author and publisher

Deb Nelson Gourley was born 1 April 1954 in Fillmore County, Minnesota, to Sylvan and Charlotte (Knudson) Nelson. She was raised on a 150-year-old Norwegian ancestral farm in Amherst, near Canton in southeastern Minnesota. Deb received her Bachelor of Science and Master of Science degrees from the University of Minnesota and worked on staff for both the University of Minnesota and University of Wisconsin. Inspiration for her *Astri, My Astri: Norwegian Heritage Stories* bilingual English-Norwegian book were her 27 Norwegian ancestors who began emigrating as early as 1845 from Hallingdal, Numedal, Telemark, Voss, Sogn, Valdres and Selbu near Trondheim. During the 1840s and 1850s they first settled in Luther Valley and Koshkonong, Wisconsin, moving onward to Norwegian settlements in Fillmore, Houston and Jackson counties in Minnesota and Winneshiek County in Iowa. Deb is sole owner of Astri My Astri Publishing in Waukon, Iowa. She has two sons, Alex and Ben Huntrods.

• • • • •

Jo Ann B. Winistorfer: author and editor

Jo Ann B. Winistorfer has been seriously tracing her roots since 1984. Three-fourths of her roots stretch into Hallingdal, Valdres and Ringerike. Her earliest immigrant ancestor, from Etnedal, Sør-Aurdal, was among the first group of Norse settlers into the Bear Creek region of Mower County, Minnesota. Retired associate editor of *North Dakota Living* magazine, Jo Ann does free-lance writing and editing projects through Win Editorial Services, her at-home business. She edits the *Scandinavian Heritage News*, a quarterly publication of the Scandinavian Heritage Association in Minot. In 1999, she co-authored a book called *Tracing Your Dakota Roots: A Guide to Genealogical Research in the Dakotas*. The book won two awards in 2000, including a National Federation of Press Women award. Daughter of Virgil and Alvina (Temanson) Luyben, Jo Ann was born in 1939 and raised in Bismarck, North Dakota. She and her husband, Nick, now "homestead" on 160 acres just west of Pick City, where they raise Angus cattle. Their herd of grandkids now stands at seven; in addition, they have three great-grandchildren.

• • • • •

Lorna Anderson: genealogist and writer

Lorna (Erickson) Anderson, whose roots are in Telemark and Gudbrandsdal, was born in 1941 to Orvin and Marion (Klefstad) Erickson. After graduating from the University of Minnesota, she taught home economics for four years, owned fabric and sewing machine businesses for 20 years, and spent 15 years in home health care. In 1964, she married Glen Anderson, who served in the Minnesota legislature for 18 years. The couple farmed near Louisburg, Minnesota. Lorna, whose pioneer ancestors settled in Highland Prairie, Fillmore County, has researched and assisted in writing a number of books related to genealogy, including Telelag of America publications and regional and family histories. For years before the *History of the Norwegian Settlements* became a reality, Lorna gathered materials, worked with translator Malcolm Rosholt's family and coordinated pre-production efforts. Lorna owns a home-based business called Norway Innovation, Perham, Minnesota. She and Glen have four children and eight grandchildren.

Index

By Deb Nelson Gourley
(Note: "aa" and "æ" indexed with "a" and "ø" indexed with "o")
Searchable at http://www.astrimyastri.com

A
A. A. Scheie 202, 203
A. B. Jacobson 283
A. Byholt 210
A. C. Preus 96, 237, 255, 311
A. E. Frederikson 229
A. E. Friedrichsen 229, 268
A. E. Lien 73
A. J. Lee 73
A. K. Finseth 305
A. K. Sagen 74
A. K. Skaro 291, 294
A. L. Kittilsby 180
A. M. Teigen 74
A. Mikkelson 101
A. Mortenson 42
A. O. Throndrud 90
A. S. Fredricksen 268
A. Trovatten 74
Aagaata Knutsdatter Langeland 336
Aagaata Langeland 336
Aamund Eriksen 198
Aamund M. Sanden 199
Aanon Torgerson Omlie 215
Aanund Aanundson 201
Aanund Berland 211
Aanund Gjermundson Veum 200
Aanund M. Sanden 199
Aanund Mikkelson Sanden 200
Aanund Veum 199
Aasta Anundsdatter 211
Abbott Nikolaus 3
Able Anderson 73
Abraham Aanundson 119
Abraham Christensen 201
Abraham Christopherson 258
Abraham Hanson 173
Abraham Jacobson 188, 403
Abraham Jensson 211
Abraham Olson 172, 173
Abraham Olson Rustad 172
Abraham Oneson 119
Abraham Veggar 309
Adne Engen 61
Agnes Larson 146
Ala Thompson 221
Albert Anderson 221
Albert Kittelson 73
Albert Lia 211
Albert Nash 140
Albert Olson 73, 200
Albert Ousel 200
Alexander O. Norman 68
Alexander Ramsey 167, 219
Alexander VI 2
Alf Olson 239, 240
Alfred B. Olson 73
Alfred Sully 402
Amund A. Rosseland 78, 341
Amund Anderson Hornefjeld 67
Amund Arneson 184
Amund Drotning 68
Amund Eidsmo 93
Amund Finhart 235
Amund Giere 310
Amund Gulbrandsen Lunde 196
Amund Hanson Eide 399
Amund Helgeson 37, 259
Amund Helgeson Maakestad 37
Amund Holt 104
Amund Johnson 164
Amund Johnson Dale 344
Amund Johnson Klastølen 233
Amund Johnson Klostøl 231
Amund Johnson Lindelien 231, 233
Amund Langeberg 167, 259, 261
Amund Lindelien 237
Amund Mikkelson 105
Amund Mortenson 99
Amund Nilsen Fosen 340
Amund O. Eidsmoe 94
Amund Oakland 299
Amund Olson Haaheim 154
Amund Pederson 185

Amund Rosseland 67, 77, 341
Amund Salveson 109
Amund Sørlien 315
Amund Torgerson 163
Amund Torson Barskor 201
Amund Veum 199
Ananias Olsen Hemri 199
Anders A. Lybæk 233
Anders A. Potterud 103
Anders Amundsen 104, 109
Anders Amundsen Holt 104
Anders Anderson 32
Anders Anderson Bytte 254
Anders Anderson Lybek 231
Anders Aubol 109
Anders Baalerud 212
Anders Baardsen 145
Anders Bakke 144
Anders Belmont 321
Anders Bersei 184
Anders Bottolfson 139
Anders C. Qual 109
Anders Call 139
Anders Christiansen Stensrud 195
Anders Daae 43
Anders E. Olson 327, 328, 336
Anders E. Olson Slaabakken 327, 328
Anders Engebretson Slaabakken 336
Anders Engen 60
Anders Erickson 220
Anders Erikson 218
Anders Evenson 213
Anders Fauske 163
Anders Finseth 305
Anders Fosen 399
Anders Gaarsrud 88
Anders Gilbertson 151
Anders Grini 110
Anders Grøtte 315
Anders Gulbrandsen Ellestad 202
Anders Haldorsen 211
Anders Halvorsen Milevandet 235
Anders Halvorson 207
Anders Hanson 119, 124, 272
Anders Hanson Omli 119
Anders Hauge 178
Anders Himle 130
Anders Holm 130
Anders Isaksen 109
Anders J. Boxrud 215
Anders Johannesen 110

Anders Johanson Tømmerstigen 68
Anders Jørgensen 289
Anders Kilen 139
Anders Kjølstad 319
Anders Langeteig 78
Anders Larson 39, 239
Anders Larson Flage 39
Anders Libæk 266
Anders Lundberg 315
Anders Lundsæteren 60
Anders Midtbøen 60
Anders Midtbøn 60
Anders Mikelsen 134
Anders Mikkelson 91
Anders Monsen 338
Anders Monson Gjersvold 323
Anders Monson Gjersvoll 323
Anders N. Berg 266
Anders Nepstad 212
Anders Ness 211
Anders Nilsen 39, 125
Anders Nilsen Hjelland 39
Anders Nilsen Kjos 195
Anders Nordvig 285
Anders Nyflødt 99
Anders O. Øien 109
Anders O. Selland 398
Anders Olsen 338
Anders Olsen Ulvestad 220
Anders Olson 108, 139, 185, 239, 251, 264, 286, 315
Anders Olson Aabol 108
Anders Olson Hestehun 139
Anders Olson Kirkevoldsmoen 323
Anders Olson Kirkvold 323
Anders Olson Lødal 218
Anders Olson Slaabakken 321, 328
Anders Olson Søringen 239
Anders Olson Ulvestad 218
Anders Østensen Guberud 196
Anders Østenson Bøen 108
Anders Pedersen Kroshus 195
Anders Pederson 201
Anders Railson 341
Anders Railson Glesne 341
Anders Remmen 305
Anders Robinson 240
Anders Siljord 99
Anders Slaabakken 321
Anders Stangeland 16
Anders Stedje 104

Anders Steensrud 98
Anders Strøm 315
Anders Svartangen 130
Anders Syverson 310
Anders T. Ask 212
Anders T. Knudtsen 109
Anders Thompson Nundal 139
Anders Thompson Sandvik 139
Anders Tollefson Lunde 212
Anders Torhaug 237
Anders Veblen 114
Anders Walhovd 343
Anderson Melhøv 265
Andreas A. Prestemoen 151
Andreas Bjørnsen Vigh 197
Andreas Bjørnsen Viig 197
Andreas Bjørnsen Vik 197
Andreas Bonhus 299, 300
Andreas Ekern 155
Andreas Erstad 60
Andreas Førde 204
Andreas Gulbrandson Ellestad 204
Andreas Halvorsen 109
Andreas Halvorson Haugen 58
Andreas Hermundson Numedal 55
Andreas Hesjadalen 300
Andreas Hesjedalen 299
Andreas Hogden 155
Andreas Holo 73
Andreas Kristensen Ohnstad 197
Andreas Kristensen Onstad 197
Andreas Lundberg 346, 348
Andreas M. Iverson 116
Andreas O. Week 85
Andreas Olson 175
Andreas Østrud 229
Andreas P. Helgeland 215
Andreas Peter Nilsen 258
Andreas Peterson 399
Andreas Prestemoen 152
Andreas Rustan 229
Andreas S. Byholt 209
Andreas Skogen 150
Andreas Sørum 60
Andreas Waller 98
Andres Hellerud 307
Andres Nepstad 211
Andrew Anderson 201
Andrew Gulbranson 364
Andrew Hendrikson 201
Andrew L. Brevig 389

Andrew Larson 104
Andrew Lee 73
Andrew Lomen 179
Andrew Monson 323, 331, 332
Andrew O. Johnson 73
Andrew O. Lomen 178
Andrew Olsen Bye 196
Andrew Olson 73, 155
Andrew Olson Lodahl 220
Andrew Olson Olnestad 220
Andrew P. Johnson 43
Andrew Peterson 364
Andrew Railson 344, 353, 354
Andrew Seeverts 310
Andrew Stangeland 16
Andrew Thompson 95
Andrew Tollefson 214
Andrew Tow 286
Andrew Week 85
Anfin Anfinson 149, 150
Anfin Anfinson Seim 266
Anfin Thompson 345
Anna Eriksdatter Berdahl 199
Anna Ingebrigtsdatter 338
Anna Iverson 203
Anna Knutsdatter 323, 326, 327, 336, 337, 338
Anna Knutsdatter Bjørgo 323, 338
Anna Knutsdatter Bjørgo Langeland 336
Anna Knutsdatter Langeland 336, 337
Anna Knutsdatter Rjodo Rio 336
Anna Langeland 329, 336
Anna Larsdatter 239
Anna Olsdatter Otternes 196
Anna Oxnaberg 237
Anna Pedersdatter 338
Anna Rosseland 352
Anna Svendsdatter 323, 338
Anna Thorina Guliksbraaten 237
Anna Torsdatter 198
Anne Bøen 237
Anne Christine Modalen 235
Anne Eivindsdatter 201
Anne Eriksdatter Berdal 336
Anne Hansen 237
Anne Jacobsdatter Einong 51
Anne Kjøstufsdatter Storaasli 201
Anne Kragness 199
Anne Kristine 100
Anne Krokenes 199

Anne Mari Nilsdatter 60
Anne Marie Hougseie 233
Anne Nilsen Oxhovd 109
Anne Olsen 233
Anne Olson 238
Anne Øverland 208
Anne Pedersdatter 201, 323, 335
Anne Pedersdatter Kinndøl 323
Anne Sæterbraaten 109
Anne Scheie 207
Anne Sjuru 238
Anne Sjurud 238
Anne Syverud 238
Anne Tostenson Ulve 108
Ansin Seim 55
Ansten K. Blækkestad 172
Ansten Knudson 173
Ansten Nattestad 45, 53, 54, 57, 58
Anthony Dahl 163
Anton Amundson 123
Anton Olson 123
Anton Sampson Kongsgaarden 266
Anton Signalness 389
Anton Sorben 235
Anton Søringen 239
Anton Thompson 118, 125
Aren Evenson 149
Arian Tønneson 200
Arne A. Aaberg 215
Arne Arnesen 215
Arne Arneson 85, 154, 184
Arne Arneson Vinje 85
Arne Boyum 218, 219, 272
Arne Evensen Kirkelie 215
Arne Hansen 41
Arne Hoff 90
Arne Hovda 233
Arne Knudson 175
Arne Ottesen Sørheim 157
Arne Røste 91
Arne Rustad 130
Arne Sigurdson Kirkelie 213
Arne Sjursen 338
Arne T. Bøen 237
Aron Anderson 309
Arthur Bow 195, 217, 370
Arthur M. Reeves 3
Arthur P. Rose 322, 337
Asbjørn Erikson 341
Asbjørn Stenehjem 196
Asbjørn Tuttle 286

Askaut Nag 285
Askild Ullensager 60
Aslag Dølven 109
Aslag Nilson 240
Aslag Nubson 215
Aslag Thorvildson 239
Aslak Aae 35
Aslak Anderson 120, 220
Aslak Eyvinson 209
Aslak Gulbrandson 175
Aslak Gullikson 259
Aslak Housker 207
Aslak Iverson 398, 403
Aslak Iverson Lekve 398
Aslak Knudsen Aamot 237
Aslak Lee 90
Aslak Lie 108
Aslak Lien 259
Aslak Moe 98
Aslak O. Flaten 253
Aslak Olsnes 67
Aslak Olson 155
Aslak Simonson Aa 178
Aslak Sølverson 175
Aslak Teisberg 74
Aslak Thorvildson 240
Aslaug Jacobsdatter Einong 51
Asle Endreson Rude 39
Asle Flatastøl 214
Asle Hesla 59
Asle Larson 248, 257
Asle Olsen Flatastøl 215
Asle Svendson 175
Assor Grøth 251
Assor Halsteinson 172
Assor Knutson Gulbrandsgaard 248
Astri Herbrandsdatter Børtnes Syversrud 217
Astrid Johnsdatter 293
Audun Evenson 149
Augun Berge 225
August Dahl 161
August Møller 266
August O. Hengsly 144
Aune Toreson 201
Austin Eastman 214
Austin Estensen 293
Austin Øvrebakke 214
Axel Jørgensen 288, 289
Axel Larsen 281

B

B. Burreson 332
B. C. Benson 354
B. L. Wick 35
Baard Johnson 39
Baard Olsen Qualey 196
Barbo Olson Røvang 108
Barbro Marie Ellingsdatter 197
Barney Hill 281
Bartel Christopherson 207
Beate Larson 201
Bendik Bendixen 104
Bendit Olson Sivlesøen 398
Bendix Ingebretson 73
Bennett Benson 265
Beret Bøen 237
Beret Knudsdatter 235
Beret Lindelien 233
Beret Modalen 235
Beret Monson 331
Beret Olsdatter 233
Beret Simonsen 237
Beret Sorben 235
Beret Tuff 238
Berger Sagerud 130
Berger Thorson 341, 349
Bergit Fransdatter 211
Bergit Fransdatter Rue 208
Bergit Halvorsdatter Haugen 58
Bergit Øverland 208
Bergit, Morgedal 200
Bergitte Stolsdoken Signalness 387
Berit Erelien Olson 321
Berit Johnsdatter 323, 338
Bernhard L. Hagboe 421
Bernt Christianson 201
Bernt Hanson 173
Bernt Jacobson 200
Bernt Julius Muus 307
Bernt Swenson 201
Bersvend Iverson Riseggen 145
Bertha Bakkum 140
Bertha Frøslie 60
Bertha Iverson 203
Bertha Lybæk 60
Bertha Næss 283
Bertha Sørum 60
Bertil Osuldson 172
Bertin Signalness 389
Betsie Nilsdatter Gilderhus 335

Big Svend 301, 303, 304
Big White Chief 344
Bill Schmidt 171
Birgit Thorvildson 239
Birgith Olsdatter 338
Bjorgø Olson 153
Bjørn Anderson Kvelve 67, 68
Bjørn Bakketo 56
Bjørn Bjørnson Bakken 265
Bjørn Brekketo 56
Bjørn Endru 211
Bjørn Hermandson 175
Bjørn Hermundson 174
Bjørn Holland 37, 41
Bjørn Larson 399
Bjørn Olsen Bøen 109
Bjørn Olson Garnaas 204, 205
Bjørn Olson Garness 204, 205
Bjørn Olson Sata 204
Bjørn Spande 207
Bjørn Thorsen Kolsrud 195
Bjørn Tollefson 98
Bjørnstjerne Bjørnson 69, 113
Bjug Harstad 421
Bore Feiring 212
Borre A. Benson Vigh 197
Borre A. Benson Viig 197
Borre A. Benson Vik 197
Børre Hanson 150
Børre Olsen Ramlo 338
Børre Olson 321
Botolf Olson 204
Botolv Botolvsen Berekvam 197
Botolv Botolvsen Berquam 197
Botolv Olsen Hemri 199
Botolv Pederson Bruhjell 321
Bottolf Jordahl 398
Bottolf Lunde 398
Bottolf Olson Øine 184
Bottolf Peterson Brugjeld 321
Boye Amundsen 109
Brede Anderson Holt 172
Brede Bredeson Sander 185
Brede Holt 88
Bretta Underdahl 130
Brita Andersdatter Røte 321
Brita Andersdatter Røte Mestad 336
Brita Ivarsdatter Frondal 197
Brita Langeland 336
Brita Mestad 321
Brita Rosseland 352

Britha Olsdatter Erikson Rauboti 321, 338
Brynhild Norman 294
Brynjild Bjerness 398
Brynjild Ure 398
Brytteva Jonsdatter Mestad 323
Brytteva Mestad 326, 331, 336
Buckskin Pants Fredrickson 316
Buckskin Pants Preacher 229, 237, 268, 269, 270
Buer Bøe 32
Burre Olson 321, 327
Burre Olson Ramlo 321

C

C. C. Lecy 130
C. H. Tollefsrude 59
C. L. Clausen 50, 61, 62, 84, 143, 144, 166, 202, 204, 205, 232, 237, 239, 243, 247, 260, 272, 311, 337
C. R. Mattson 73
California Johnson 139, 140
California Knudsen 87, 199
Carl Christianson 201
Carl Frandsen Rue 211
Carl Franson Rue 209
Carl Gustav Knudson 217
Carl Larsen 175
Carl Larson 294
Carl Meyer 248, 250
Carl Nilson 120
Carl Olsen 211
Carl Olson 145
Carl Solberg 110
Carl Sørenson 290
Caroline Signalness 389
Carsten Tank 116
Charles Harstad 214
Charles Johnson 219
Charles Kittilson 263
Charles Kjøgjei 214
Charles Olson 264
Charley H. Geisness 145
Charley Peterson 264
Chas E. Flandreau 364
Chas. Gustaveson 110
Chas. N. Herreid 73
Chr. Anderson 109
Chr. Halvorson 175
Chr. Larson Ballestad 109

Christ Austin 207
Christen E. Rukke 265
Christen Evenson 61
Christen Johnson Rukke 265
Christen Jordahl 398, 405
Christen Knutson 266
Christen Larson Lunde 398
Christen Nilsen 110
Christen Pederson 104
Christen Puttekaasa 81
Christen Torrisen 338
Christen Tuff 237
Christi Modalen 235
Christian Anderson 295
Christian Bratrud 220
Christian Brokke 200
Christian Brude 398
Christian C. Olson 139
Christian Christopherson 203
Christian Dunham 212
Christian Ekern 150
Christian Evenson 144
Christian Faae 205
Christian Frederik 116
Christian Georgeson 149
Christian Gunvaldsen 144
Christian Heggen 281
Christian Hendrickson 91
Christian Holter 354
Christian Hooverson Nundal 139
Christian Hulberg 149
Christian Iverson 203, 207
Christian Jacobson 201
Christian Johannesen Glasrud 196
Christian Johnson 95, 218, 220
Christian Johnson Aalterud 95
Christian Jorgenson 361
Christian K. Næseth 73
Christian Knudson Aunevik 125
Christian Lunde 60
Christian O. Bratrud 218
Christian Olson 32, 98, 99
Christian Thomasrud 144
Christian Thoresen 220, 221
Christine Nørstelien 60
Christofer J. Natvig 240
Christoffer H. Engen 344
Christoffer Haug 209
Christopher Aamodt 82
Christopher Anderson 271
Christopher Austreim 108

Christopher Eidsmo 93
Christopher Estrem 179
Christopher Hanson 251
Christopher Jerdee 73
Christopher Lassesen Haave 399, 403
Christopher Mikkelsen 265
Christopher Mikkelsen Trugstad 264
Christopher Narveson Melby 265
Christopher Newhouse 53
Christopher Nyhus 53
Christopher Rostad 61
Christopher Svenson 255
Clarence Iverson 207
Claude Dablon 124
Claude Jean Allouez 124
Claus Lauritz Clausen 40, 50
Cleng Peerson 15, 16, 17, 18, 20, 21, 22, 23, 24, 25, 31, 32, 33, 45, 165
Cornelius Berg 389
Cornelius Nilsen 33
Cornelius Nilson Hersdal 16
Cornelius Strand 212

D

Dagny Swan 199
Dan. Johanneson 175
Daniel Boone 207
Daniel Broberg 346
Daniel Rosdal 32
Daniel Stenson Rossadal 16
David Dunham 212
David Johnson 39
Didrich Olson White 139
Didrik Olson Mjøvand 139
Dortea Johnson 201
Dortia Bøen 237
Dreng Evenson Kirkelie 215
Dreng Lundeberg 211, 212
Dyre Halvorsen Lindaas 195

E

E. Embresen Lunaashaug 332
E. Embresen Lunaavug 332
E. G. Johnson 215
E. H. Midtbøe 355
E. J. Ohnstad 73
E. Jensen 211
E. P. Jensen 204
Earl Hanson 169

Ebbe Nilson 120, 121
Ed Charleson 104
Ed Stevens 196
Edvard Olson 73
Egil Guttormsen 221
Einar Bonde 307
Einar Smedsmo 319
Einer Aasen 32
Eivind Johnson 201
Eivind Skatte 271
Elan Peterson 151
Eland Levorson 295
Elef Briskemyren 307
Elen Marie 211
Eli Anderson 239
Eli Olsdatter 239
Elias Cooper 199
Elias Halvorson 110
Elizabeth Olson Faae 203
Ellef Bjørnson 81
Ellef Land 178
Ellef Tollefson 207
Ellend Borlaug 399
Ellert A. Langøen 110
Ellert Ellertsen 211
Ellert Ellertson 209
Ellev Anderson Berg 266
Ellev Charleson 103
Ellev Johnson Kaasa 180
Ellev Kjøstulson 103, 104
Ellev Torgerson 103
Elling Andersen Karlsbraaten 199
Elling Bjertnes 197
Elling E. Svensrud 259
Elling Eielsen 32, 34, 35, 37, 42, 48, 49, 50, 51, 93, 185, 219, 280
Elling Eielson 282
Elling Ellertson 209
Elling Ellingson 184
Elling Erlandsen Snedkerpladsen 195
Elling Foss 184
Elling Hanson 145
Elling Hendricksen Solberg 195
Elling Hendrikson Spillum 49
Elling Knutsen Kieland 195
Elling Meyer 251
Elling Myrah Ellingsen 285
Elling O. Hove 264
Elling Olson Engum 399
Elling Sagadalen 354
Elling Sande 398

Elling Spillum 49
Elling Thygeson 144
Elling Torsen Hauglum 199
Elling Torsen Holum 199
Elling Underdahl 130
Ellis Thoen 214
Else Modalen 235
Embret Skarshaug 172
Embrik Bearson 204
Embrik H. Melbraaten 195
Embrik Melbraaten 223
Emil Christenson 119
Emil Falk 343
Emil Gustav Andreas Christensen 403
Emma Munson 240
Endre Arakerbø 35
Endre Bottolfson 265
Endre Dahl 17, 32
Endre Endreson 39, 175
Endre Endreson Rude 39
Endre Gulbrandson 265
Endre Haugen 305
Endre Henrikson 259
Endre Iverson Røthe 39
Endre Johnson 94, 159
Endre Johnson Lindelien 94
Endre Knutsen Roble 196
Endre Levik 314, 315
Endre Peterson Sandager 178
Endre Stadheim 55
Engebret A. Hougen 305
Engebret Bjørnson Garnaas 204
Engebret Bjørnson Garness 204
Engebret Egge 307
Engebret Gudbrandsen 173
Engebret Gundersen Benson Enderud 195
Engebret Hansen Melbraaten 195
Engebret Haugen 180, 184
Engebret Heggen 281
Engebret Hovda 233
Engebret Knutsen Opheim 195
Engebret Larson 175
Engebret Lindelien 237
Engebret Nelsen Haugerstuen 237
Engebret Olson Slaabakken 323, 328, 335
Engebret Sorben 235
Engebret Thompson 389
Engebret Thorson 62
Engebrigt Larson 75

Eno Bjøno 57
Erick Amundson 251
Erick Engeseth 307
Erick Eriksen Tveit 237
Erick O. Selland 398
Erick Solseth 214
Erik A. Ødegaard 305
Erik Alme 157
Erik Amundson 271
Erik Anderson 178
Erik Bottolfson Sivlesøen 398
Erik Dyrland 286
Erik E. Torsnes 221
Erik Ellefsen Sleen 183, 184
Erik Endreson 39, 178
Erik Endreson Rude 39
Erik Engesæth 75
Erik Eriksen Børsness 265
Erik Eriksen Haugen 237
Erik Eriksen Solseth Jr 215
Erik Eriksen Solseth Sr 215
Erik Erikson 183, 184, 259
Erik Erikson Braaten 259
Erik Erikson Selland 184
Erik G. Kapperud 344
Erik G. Skavlem 53
Erik Gauteson Midtbø 45
Erik Gauteson Midtbøen 45
Erik Gree 154
Erik Gunhus 299
Erik Halvorson Fløse 94
Erik Hatlestad 184
Erik Haugerstuen 237
Erik Helgeson 81
Erik Helgeson Espedokken 248
Erik Henningsen 104
Erik J. Lunde 398
Erik Janson 24
Erik Johanneson 103
Erik Kapperud 349
Erik Kittelson 175
Erik Knutson Objør 255
Erik Kolsrud 59
Erik Matsen Staur 215
Erik Midtbø 34
Erik Midtbøen 34
Erik Nederhaugen 60
Erik Nilsen 179, 279, 280
Erik Nilson 279
Erik O. Fosse 259
Erik O. Støveren 248

Erik Ruud 354
Erik S. Gjellum 73
Erik Sheldal 279, 281, 283
Erik Skavlem 58
Erik Søkten 283
Erik Solseth 214, 227
Erik Stalheim 398
Erik Støveren 180
Erik Suversen Øymoen 237
Erik T. Lien 217, 220
Erik Tanberg 88
Erik Tangen 229
Erik the Red 1, 3
Erik Thoreson Sagabraaten 248
Erik Torkelsen 221
Erik Torvaldson 9
Erik Upsi 3
Erik Ure 398
Erikson Styrmand 17
Erland Bruflat 235, 237
Erland Olsen Skalshaugen 233
Erland Olson Skalshaugen 231
Esten Oleson 335
Ethan P. Eddy 217
Even B. Haugum 215
Even Christianson 144
Even Dahl 169
Even E. Dahl 211
Even Ekeren 155
Even Ellertsen Dahl 169
Even Ellertson 169, 202, 209, 213
Even Erikson 149
Even G. Borgen 345
Even G. Dølalie 209, 210
Even Gullord 135, 136, 139, 140, 141
Even H. Heg 48
Even Halvorson Holtan 309
Even Hanson 150
Even Heg 51, 52
Even Høime 195
Even Jerruldsen 109
Even Johnson Homme 199
Even K. Besteland 225
Even Mahl 130
Even Neset 260
Even O. Glesne 345, 349
Even O. Gullord 135
Even O. Strenge 266
Even Olsen Haugen 195
Even Pederson 315
Even Peterson 136

Even Railson 341, 344, 345, 347
Even Railson Glesne 341
Even Reishus 218, 220
Even Smith Evenson 149
Even Swennestuen 136
Even Thompson 95
Even Wilsen Neshaug 215
Eyvin G. Dølali 209
Eyvind Besteland 213

F

F. Mathias Asved 323
Finbur Hanson 145
Fingal Aslesen Flaten 195
Fingar Kaalsrud 307
Finkel Finkelson 109
Finkel Olsen Røvang 108
Finkel Thorson 305
Frank Olson Trydal 225
Frantz Skiaker 398
Fred P. Brown 73
Frederik Gawog 61
Frederik Goli 88
Frederik III 116
Frederik Peterson 20
Frederik Torkelson 87

G

G. A. Larson 73
G. D. Homme 365
G. G. Krostu 101
G. Gaarder 60, 210
G. Gabrielsen 41
G. J. Klurdal 104
G. Løberg 81
G. M. Johnson 73
G. M. Johnson Lee 73
G. Storaasli 211
G. T. Lee 254
Gabriel Abrahamson 110
Gabriel Ellingson 316
Gabriel Gabrielson 204, 207
Gabriel Sakariason Vatne 119
Gabriel Stene 356
Gaute Gauteson 45
Gellaug Svendson 201
Georg Johnson 17
George Flom 25
George G. Johnson 345

George H. Walker 47
George Olsen 41
George Peter Sivertson 336
George Ruble 263
George S. Ruble 263
George Wood 336
Gerhard Høyme 164
Gerhard Rasmussen 51
Gerhardt Hoyme 179
Germund Høyme 51
Gisle Halland 57
Gitle Danielson 46
Gjæst Anderson Esse 271
Gjermund Engen 262
Gjermund Grosvult 262
Gjermund Haugen 92
Gjermund Hitterdal 227
Gjermund Hoyme 355
Gjermund J. Kasen 214
Gjermund Jackson 92, 93
Gjermund Johnsen Lommen 196
Gjermund Johnson 227
Gjermund Johnson Kaasa 178
Gjermund Johnson Kasen 215
Gjermund Johnson Lommen 194
Gjermund Sunde 66
Gjerom Patterson 316
Gjert G. Hovland 32
Gjertrud Børresdatter 321, 338
Gjøri Ingebrigtsdatter 239
Goro Sanager 195
Govert Dyrland 286
Gregar Herbjørnsen Bøen 215
Gregor Holden 99
Gregor Olson 239, 240
Gregor Olson Vaala 239, 240
Gregor Vaala 239
Gro Johnson Nichols 153
Gro Jonsdatter 45
Gro Jonsdatter Einungbrekke Håkaland 45
Gubrand Dunham 212
Gudbrand Elseberg 90
Gudbrand Gaarder 60
Gudbrand H. Østrud 229
Gudmund Brækken 110
Gudmund Gudmundsen Brekken 108
Gudmund Haugaas 17
Gudmund Haukaas 32, 34
Gudmund Norsving 179, 305
Gudmund O. Quale 110
Gudmund Sandsberg 32
Gulbr. Gulbrandsen 110
Gulbr. Vaarum 110
Gulbrand Andersen Guberud 196
Gulbrand Bagaasen 265
Gulbrand Ekern 155
Gulbrand G. Haslebrek 110
Gulbrand G. Myhra 244, 248
Gulbrand Gulbrandsen Ellestad 202
Gulbrand Gulbrandsen Myhre 53
Gulbrand Gulbrandson Kassenborg 200
Gulbrand H. Nilsen 248, 249
Gulbrand Holt 212
Gulbrand Kassenborg 199
Gulbrand Mellem 257, 258, 259, 261, 262
Gulbrand Michelsen Ruud 195
Gulbrand Myhra 249, 251
Gulbrand Nilsen 155
Gulbrand Nilsen Myhra 195
Gulbrand O. Mellem 248
Gulbrand Palmeson 316
Gulbrand Renna 237
Gulbrand Wold 90
Guldbrand Aaberg 221
Guldbrand H. Sørum 109
Guldbrand Høyme 108
Guldbrand O. Berge 109
Gulik Erlandsen Bruflat 235
Gulik Erlandsen Dalen 235
Gulik Erlandson Dalen 237
Gulik Lindelien 235
Gullek A. Maland 215
Gullick Olson Haugen 204
Gullik Arveson 103
Gullik Gravdahl 59
Gullik H. Blakkestad 248
Gullik Halvorson Skavlem 57
Gullik Iverson 109
Gullik Knudsen Laugen 57
Gullik Laugen 57
Gullik M. Erdall 73
Gullik Olson Gravdahl 57
Gullik Peterson 271
Gullik Springen 57
Gullik Svendsrud 90
Gullik Ulriksen 271
Gunbjørn Nilsen 259
Gundbrand Throndrud 90
Gunder Braatvedt 134

Gunder Evensen 110
Gunder Guelsen Traaen 195
Gunder Halvorsen 61
Gunder Halvorson Stabbestad 254
Gunder Heggeson 153
Gunder Hestemyr 299
Gunder J. Sanda 259
Gunder Johansen 134
Gunder Johnson Braatvedt 134
Gunder Madsen 109, 112
Gunder Nerison 294
Gunder Nichols 153
Gunder Olson 340
Gunder Paulson 314
Gunder Stabbestad 254
Gunder Swenson 345
Gunder T. Mandt 68
Gunder Thoe 214, 215
Gunder Thygeson 266
Gunerius Bjørneby 130
Gunhild Folson 199
Gunhild Fransdatter 211
Gunhild Franson Rue 208
Gunhild Guttormsdatter Syversrud Myhre 217
Gunhild Halvorsdatter 211
Gunhild Johnson 238
Gunhild Lindelien 235
Gunhild Maria Modalen 235
Gunhild Ødegaarden 57
Gunhild Syversen 237
Gunhild Tostensdatter Nøbben 211, 217
Gunild Aamundsdatter Lunde 197
Gunild Haugen 239
Gunleik Olson 153
Gunleik Olson Storlie 153
Gunnar Bjørgusson Homme 82
Gunnar Dahle 210
Gunnar Gunnarsen 211
Gunnar Paulson Blom 209
Gunnerius Hundeby 259
Gunnerius Olson 139, 141
Gunnerius Simonson 149
Gunnøv Østenson Svadde 289
Gunnul Olson Vindeg 66
Gunnul Vindeg 67
Gunnuld Evenson 208
Gunolf Tollefson 91
Gunstein Tollefson Krostu 98, 99
Gunuld Haugen 92

Gunuld Jackson 92
Gunulf J. Bruflodt 215
Gunulf Johnson Qvile 215
Guri Bjørnsdatter Garnaas 204
Guri Bjørnsdatter Garness 204
Guri Bottolfson 264
Guri Estensdatter Nysetvold 321, 338
Guri Hovda 233, 238
Guri Jacobson Haga 203
Guri Rosgaard 130
Guri Rosseland 341, 352, 353
Guri Sjurgurdsdatter Sundbrei 323
Guri Syvertsdatter Sundbrei 338
Gurine Signalness 389
Guro Bjørneby 130
Guro Johannesdatter 211
Guro Øverland 208
Guro Shaw 281
Gustaf Schmidt 40
Gustaf Smith 40
Gustaf Unonius 79
Gustav Reierson 103
Gustav Signalness 389
Gustav Stark 294
Gustav Unonius 40, 41
Gutorm Hansen Modalen 235
Guttorm Anderson 144
Guttorm Boffolfson 264
Guttorm Bottolfson 264, 265
Guttorm Bottolfson Espeseth 264
Guttorm Gutterson 199
Guttorm Guttormson 199, 200
Guttorm Halsteinson 265
Guttorm Iverson 94
Guttorm Olsen Aaotnes 196
Guttorm Olsen Otternes 196
Guttorm Olsen Otterness 196
Guttorm Olson Engen 265
Guttorm Olson Fraagot 309
Guttorm Roen 59
Guul Guttormsen 60
Guul Guttormson 107, 168
Guul Wahl 144, 146

H

H. A. Neperud 140
H. A. Preus 131, 134, 260
H. A. Stub 109, 150, 151, 154, 204, 239, 307
H. Arnston 198

H. C. Gullickson 229
H. Eli 239
H. Halvorsen 41
H. M. Hansen 110
H. N. Neperud 138
H. P. Jacobs 119
H. Paulsen 211
H. S. Stub 84, 140
H. Tollefsrud 60
Haaken Narveson 195
Haakon Knudsen Roble 108
Haakon Nilsen 172
Haakon Olson 209
Haakon Pederson 94
Haavald Haavaldson 344
Haavel Pedersen Johnsrud 196
Hage Olson 91
Halder Sheldal 279
Haldis Olsdatter 338
Haldor Anderson Veblen 108
Haldor Haugerstuen 237
Haldor Johnson 299
Haldor Olsen Viste 110
Haldor Torkelson 154
Halstein Grøth 172
Halstein H. Grøth 173
Halstein Halvorsen Fløse 45
Halstein Halvorson Fløse 94
Halstein Støen 183
Halstein Torrison 39
Halsten H. Støen 184
Halsten Johnson Brakkehaugen 109
Halsten Olson 323
Halvard Hageli 180
Halvor Anderson 120
Halvor Anderson Lysaker 251
Halvor Arveson 103
Halvor B. Hustvedt 73
Halvor Barland 315
Halvor Bergan 184
Halvor Bjoin 75
Halvor Braaten 307
Halvor Brynjildson 398
Halvor Eivindson 240
Halvor Ellefson 175, 364
Halvor Ellefson Jr 175
Halvor Ellefson Sr 175
Halvor Ellefson Turkop 175
Halvor Erickson 208, 210
Halvor Eriksen 210
Halvor Erikson 208

Halvor Førde 184
Halvor Funkelien 68
Halvor Gallog 61
Halvor H. Brekke 259
Halvor H. Peterson Haugen 167, 168
Halvor Haasarud 211
Halvor Halverson Græsdalen 90
Halvor Halvorsen Herrum 144
Halvor Halvorson 58, 81, 173
Halvor Halvorson Groven 178
Halvor Halvorson Haugen 58
Halvor Herrum 146
Halvor Hersgaard 61
Halvor Hougen 266
Halvor Iverson 17
Halvor Johannesen Vig 237
Halvor Johannesen Week 237
Halvor Johnson 304
Halvor Jørgenson Postmyhr 345
Halvor K. Wrolstad 263
Halvor Kittelsen 211
Halvor Kittelson Dumpendahl 209
Halvor Kjørn 61
Halvor Knudson 32
Halvor Knutson Objør 255
Halvor Kravik 68
Halvor Kvi 307
Halvor Laastuen 212
Halvor Larson Lysenstøen 49
Halvor Lauritz 221
Halvor Mikkelson 41
Halvor Modum 49, 178, 179
Halvor Næs 59
Halvor Nelson 46, 405
Halvor Nelson Lohner 46
Halvor Nilsen 32, 171, 172, 242, 405, 406, 408, 413, 414
Halvor Nilsen Espeseth 171
Halvor Nilsen Lohner 51
Halvor Nilsen Lysne 242
Halvor Nordby 211
Halvor Nyhus 130
Halvor O. Storlag 175
Halvor Ødegaarden 299
Halvor Olsen 197, 221, 235
Halvor Olsen Klastølen 235
Halvor Olson Storaasli 200
Halvor Olson Wraalstad 220
Halvor Østenson Luraas 46
Halvor P. Haugen 58
Halvor Paulson 180

Halvor Pederson Haugen 57
Halvor Peterson 144, 212
Halvor Peterson Berge 144
Halvor Ristveit 130
Halvor Rosholt 81
Halvor Ruud 60
Halvor Sinnes 220
Halvor Slette 266
Halvor Steenerson 199
Halvor Stenerson 74
Halvor Sutenje 99
Halvor Svendsen 399
Halvor Svennungsen Bostrak 215
Halvor Svenson 158
Halvor Swenson 130
Halvor T. Bakstevold 266
Halvor T. Herrum 144
Halvor T. Lyngflaat 46
Halvor Thoreson Haugerud 266
Halvor Thoreson Sagabraaten 248
Halvor Torgerson 296
Halvor Tubbehaatvedt 266
Halvor Volstad 254
Halvor Warp 130
Halvor Week 238
Halvor Wraalstad 221
Han Gunnarsen 211
Han Lia 210
Hanne Pedersdatter 338
Hans Aakre 180
Hans Andersen Gamlemoen 233, 237
Hans Anderson Blegen 185
Hans Anderson Fremstad 155
Hans Anderson Gamlemoen 231
Hans Andreas Hoverson 70
Hans Arneson 202, 203, 207
Hans Augnundsen 221
Hans Augundson Hogie 220
Hans Augunson Høigje 218
Hans Barlien 32
Hans Blaker 290
Hans Bøe 32
Hans Brager 237
Hans Brenden 60
Hans C. Tollefsrude 59, 60
Hans Chesterson 323
Hans Christenson 286
Hans Christian Heg 48
Hans Dahle 199
Hans Dalen 138
Hans Dammen 212

Hans Engen Frøslieit 60
Hans Erlandsen Snedkerpladsen 195
Hans Frandsen 211
Hans Franson Rue 208
Hans G. Sørum 109
Hans Gasmann 81
Hans Gassman 27
Hans Gilbertson 151
Hans Gunderson Lia 209
Hans Gunvalson 211, 212, 217
Hans H. Nordby 211
Hans H. Smedsrud 249
Hans H. Sunde 266
Hans Hagemoen 99
Hans Halvorson Smedsrud 247, 248
Hans Hansen 78, 110, 195, 221
Hans Hansen Bakke 195
Hans Hansen Tangen 78
Hans Hanson Loken 201
Hans Hanson Omli 119
Hans Heg 35
Hans Henrikson 173
Hans Holtan 309
Hans Husemoen 59
Hans Isakson Mo 201
Hans Iverson Haugen 143
Hans J. Berdahl 316, 317
Hans J. Hamre 412
Hans J. Knudsen 259
Hans Jacob 98, 99, 100
Hans Jacob Eliason 98, 99
Hans Jacobson Sollien 94
Hans Johannesen Lien 338
Hans Johanson Lien 321
Hans Johnsen 338
Hans Johnshoy 389
Hans Johnson 90
Hans Johnson Berdal 315
Hans Jørgen Bjørnson Garnaas 204
Hans Jørgen Bjørnson Garness 204
Hans K. Larson 136
Hans Kaldal 259
Hans Kankrud 99
Hans Kauserud 130
Hans Kjønaas 266
Hans Kjøstelsen 323
Hans Kjøstulsen 110
Hans Larson 145
Hans Larson Tinderholt 185
Hans Madsen 109
Hans Markussen Sande 308

Hans Modalen 235
Hans N. Neperud 135
Hans Nilsen 138
Hans Nilsen Myhra 195
Hans O. Liebakken 135
Hans O. Rust 248
Hans Øien 130
Hans Olson 184, 185, 200, 212, 242, 399
Hans Olson Dahle 200
Hans Olson Nigard 242
Hans Østrud 229
Hans Ovaldson 299
Hans P. Heieie 354
Hans Paulson Blom 209
Hans Peder Hanson 119
Hans Pederson 185, 283
Hans Røe 81
Hans S. Hilleboe 130
Hans S. Johnson 215
Hans Sagedalen 307
Hans Simonson 237
Hans Smeby 175
Hans Smedsrud 60
Hans Smestuen 155
Hans Sørlien 315
Hans Stadsvolden 60
Hans Stenbaken 307
Hans Stumlie 143
Hans Sveum 60
Hans Swenson 253, 254
Hans Swenson Tvingli 253
Hans Tangen 155
Hans Thomasrud 144
Hans Thoreson 229
Hans Torgerson Dahl 163
Hans Torgrimsen Tveito 195
Hans Tveidt 283
Hans Tveito 51, 52
Hans Uhlen 82
Hans Urness 271
Hans Vælde 32, 202
Hans Værhaug 60
Hans Valder 32, 202, 205, 207
Harald Evenson Gulseth 98
Harald H. Støen 184
Harald Olsen 211
Harald Olson 201
Harald Olson Jordgrav 208
Harold Olsen 221
Harold Olson 218, 220

Harold Olson Rue 208
Harold Ommelstad 59, 60
Harold P. Anderson 270
Harold Thorson 108
Harvey Gregersen Bøen 215
Hegge Anderson Lunden 153
Helene Frøslie 60
Helene Gaarder 60
Helene Klevmoen 60
Helge A. Haugen 43
Helge Asleson Myran 180
Helge Ellingsen Bergsrud 195
Helge Ellingsen Solberg 198
Helge Emmons 259
Helge G. Emmons 259
Helge Gulbrandson 137
Helge Guldbrandsen 109
Helge H. Næs 175
Helge H. Røningsand 248
Helge Halvorsen Rollag 215
Helge Halvorson 175
Helge Hilleson 37
Helge Johnson Ødegaarden 237
Helge Johnson Røningsand 248
Helge L. Ramstad 173
Helge Larson Ramstad 172
Helge Mathieson 46, 95, 96, 242
Helge N. Mørstad 109
Helge Nilsen 185
Helge O. Bjøre 198
Helge Olsen 338
Helge Olson 175
Helge Olson Oterdokken 265
Helge Oterdokken 265
Helge Palmerson 314
Helge Syverson 175
Helge Thompson 48
Hellik B. Brekke 57
Hellik Bensen Brekke 248
Hellik Benson 251
Hellik Blakstad 251
Hellik Glaim 57, 58, 59, 172, 217, 218, 220, 370, 371
Hellik Haugen Stevens 94
Hellik K. Helle 260
Hellik Kjøntvedt 155
Hellik Larson 145
Hellik Morem 215
Hellik Olson Holtan 58
Helmick Helland 212
Hendrik Dammen 212

Hendrik Hendrikson 201
Henrik Christopherson Harwick 17
Henrik Christopherson Hervig 17
Henrik Fadness 184
Henrik Gullord 136
Henrik H. Sagadalen 354
Henrik Halvorsen Thoen 339
Henrik Hanson Estey 120
Henrik Henrikson Fadnes 69
Henrik Johnson 119
Henrik Larson 259, 271
Henrik Nelson Talla 298
Henrik Rime 59
Henrik Sæbbe 32
Henrik Svendsen 154
Henrik Talla 298, 299, 304, 305, 307
Henrik Trøstem 59
Henry Aul Anderson 40
Henry Johnson 73
Henry L. Rønnei 271
Henry Sanford 393, 394
Henry Sibley 292
Henry Sølverson 175
Herbjørn Bøen 228
Herbjørn G. Bøen 227
Herbjørn Ingolfsland 214
Herbjørn N. Ingulfsland 214
Herbjørn Nilsen Ingulfsland 215
Herbjørn Olsen Vaae 215
Herbrand Anstenson 185
Herbrand Finseth 305
Herbrand Pederson 94
Herbrand Præstgaarden 180
Herlaug Pederson 286
Herman Amberg Preus 78
Herman Arakerbø 35
Herman Knudsen 211, 215
Herman Knudsen Hemmestvedt 215
Herman Larson Rønnei 139
Herman Larson Runnice 139
Herman Madsen 316
Herman Matson 316
Herman Olson Norjord 200
Herman Pedersen Dustrud 196
Hermand Hovda 233
Hermo Nilsen Tufte 397
Hermond Nilsen Tufte 49
Hokina Arneson 203
Holger Endreson 398
Holien brothers 305
Hølje Tavane 96

Holsten Olson 323, 325, 327, 335
Hovel Fossum 60
Hovel Jensvold 60
Hovel Smeby 60
Hovel Tollefsrud 60
Hover Evenson 183
Hover Thompson 283
Howard Baker 360

I

I. G. Rugland 239
I. Steen 238
Inge Isaacson 203
Ingebjør Kjøstufsdatter Storaasli 201
Ingebjørg Olsdatter Fyre 323, 338
Ingeborg Embretsdatter Lonaas 335
Ingeborg Estensen 333
Ingeborg Ingebrigtsdatter Gjesme 197
Ingeborg Knudsdatter 235
Ingeborg Leversdatter Langeberg 167
Ingeborg Nielsdatter Ekse 337
Ingeborg Nilsen 166
Ingeborg Olsdatter 211, 323
Ingeborg Olsdatter Slaabakken 323
Ingeborg Ommelstadsæteren 60
Ingeborg Tostensdatter Nøbben 211, 217
Ingebret Bjørneby 130
Ingebret Enerson Bøe 151
Ingebret Engeseth 307
Ingebret Erikson Tveitan 98
Ingebret Homstad 136
Ingebret Johnson 119
Ingebret Knutson 251
Ingebret Ness 139, 140
Ingebret Nilsen Sølland 179
Ingebret Sølhaugen 398
Ingebret Svenson Grøthem 144
Ingebret Torgerson 119
Ingebret Trilhus 259
Ingebret Tveitan 83
Ingebret Vange 55
Ingebrette Larson 211
Ingebright Olsen Slaabakken 338
Ingebrigt Fossum 60
Ingebrigt Grindeland 184
Ingebrigt Olsen Slaabakken 338
Inger Dorotea 201
Inger Gaarder 60
Inger Olson 221

Ingrid Tostensdatter 108
Ingvald Throndsen Doely 196
Inkpaduta 271, 321
Innocent VIII 2
Isaac Engebretson 389
Isaac Holm 130
Isaac Isaacson 203
Isaac Isackson 207
Isaac Jackson 221
Isaac Jacobson Jackson 221
Isaac Rosgaard 130
Isak A. Pederson 110
Isak Ellertson 209
Isak Hansen Findall 110
Isak Isaksen Sætre 110
Isak Larsen 110
Ivar Botolvsen Berekvam 197
Ivar Jonsen Frandle 197
Ivar Jonsen Frondal 197
Ivar Tvedt 281
Iver Aslakson 175
Iver Breaker 89
Iver Dahl 259
Iver Fylie 55
Iver G. Berge 109
Iver Gulbrand 204
Iver Gulbrandsen Ellestad 202
Iver Hagen 184
Iver Ingebretson Hove 55
Iver Iverson 153, 403
Iver J. Klurdal 104
Iver Johnson 316
Iver Knudsen Syse 154
Iver Kvamme 305
Iver Larsen 39
Iver Larson Hove 67
Iver Lawson 39
Iver Lockrem 307
Iver Lund 90
Iver Nilsen 315
Iver O. Berge 109
Iver Øiom 138
Iver Olson 130, 173
Iver Øriansen Torblaa 154
Iver Pedersen Kinneberg 196
Iver Quale 178
Iver Ringestad 180
Iver Risløv 55
Iver Rosgaard 130
Iver Rustad 212
Iver Sandbuløkken 319

Iver Thompson 202, 205
Iver Thompson Bothne 205
Iver Thompson Botne 202
Iver Thorson Aase 89
Iver Torgerson 163
Iver Torkelson 154

J

J. A. Frich 152
J. A. Johnson 73
J. A. Ottesen 71
J. A. Otteson 109
J. A. Renolen 332, 333
J. C. Dundas 69
J. C. Johnson 58
J. C. T. Moses 240
J. C. W. Dietrichson 34, 40
J. E. Olson 73
J. E. Sauerlie 214
J. G. Smith 40, 41
J. H. Johnson 73
J. J. Anderson 73
J. J. Holman 73
J. J. Rodebakken 212
J. K. Rystad 82
J. L. Johnson 73
J. P. Lommen 194
J. R. Reierson 27
J. S. Johnson 60, 62
J. Stensgaard 210
J. W. C. Dietrichson 69
Jacob Abrahamsen 178
Jacob Abrahamson 173, 179
Jacob Alfson 103
Jacob Anderson Slogvig 17
Jacob Asleson Hognerud 248
Jacob Bestul 98
Jacob Dahlen 309
Jacob E. Aske 282, 283
Jacob Elefson 207
Jacob Halversen 109
Jacob Hanson 151, 175
Jacob Hanson Stiga 151
Jacob Jacobson Haga 203, 207
Jacob K. Thoe 310
Jacob Larson 203, 207, 208
Jacob Larson Egrene 207
Jacob Listul 98
Jacob Madsen 109
Jacob Meling 283

Jacob Nielsen Ekse 338
Jacob Olson 175
Jacob Paulson 173
Jacob Rosholt 81, 83, 84, 98, 101
Jacob Slogvig 32
Jacob Taraldson 315
Jacob Thode Brock 55
Jacob Tolefson Rosholt 81
Jacob Tollefsen Rosholt 29
Jacob Tønneson Lavold 153
Jacob Wetleson 68
Jacob Wulff 41
Jakob Nilsson Ekse 323
James Denoon Reymert 49
James Halvorson 109
James Hanson 118
James Howard 291, 292, 293
James Jarvis 103, 104
James Reymert 52, 61
James Rosholt 101
Jean Nicollet 115
Jenny Lind 41
Jens A. Highland 212
Jens Amundson Børdalen 265
Jens Anderson Holt 172
Jens Brager 237
Jens Call 139
Jens Ellingsen Vinjum 196
Jens Ellingsen Winjum 196
Jens Gulbrandsen Myhre 53
Jens Gunderson 110
Jens Guttormson Nøbben 217
Jens Guttormson Syversrud Kolsrud 217
Jens Hanson 209
Jens Harbø 314
Jens Hovland 158
Jens Hundere 103, 104
Jens Ivarsen Krohn 403
Jens J. Hovland 157
Jens J. Torgerson 100
Jens Jensen Gjesme 197
Jens Jensen Jesme 197
Jens Kilen 139
Jens Krohn 40, 41
Jens La 271
Jens O. Boldstad 110
Jens Olsen 39, 40, 41
Jens Olsen Aaotnes 197
Jens Olsen Kaasa 39, 41, 56
Jens Olsen Otternes 197

Jens Olsen Otterness 197
Jens Ottun 298, 300
Jens Syverson 159
Jens Thorson 315
Jens Tue 271
Jeremiah Rusk 140
Jermund Kittelson 239
Jerome Patterson 316
Jerruld Hansen 110
Jetmund Knudsen Bjerke 242
Jette Tobiasdatter 201
Jim Farmer 332
Jim Hill 287
Jo Amundson Herreid 145
Joachim Rosholt 101
Joe Rolette 293
Johan Aalseth 398
Johan Burtness 59
Johan Carlsen 211
Johan Christiansen 109, 110
Johan Ericksen 110
Johan Evenson 144
Johan Frankrige 60
Johan Hole 99
Johan Iverson 99
Johan Jahr 210
Johan Jeremias 239
Johan Larson 39
Johan Lie 82
Johan Løberg 98, 100
Johan Nordbo 32
Johan Olson Hesjedalen 255
Johan Peterson Ringdahl 168
Johan Reiersen 24
Johan Roland 316
Johan Sæthre 212
Johan Smed 60
Johan Stensveen 150
Johan Storm Munch 87, 307
Johanes Axe 336
Johanes Isdalen 307
Johanna Halvorson 239
Johanna Jensdatter Otternes 197
Johanna Olsdatter 239
Johannes A. Aasved 309
Johannes Aakre 180
Johannes Aamodt 99
Johannes Aamundsen Indrelid 197
Johannes Aamundsen Lie 197
Johannes B. Frick 150
Johannes Berg 136

Johannes Botolvsen Berekvam 197
Johannes Botolvsen Berkvam 197
Johannes Brennum 87
Johannes Brenom 60
Johannes Danielson Rosdal 32
Johannes Ekse 326
Johannes Elefson Sauerlie 215
Johannes Eriksen Berdahl 199
Johannes Eriksen Berdal 199
Johannes Erikson 103
Johannes Evenson 180, 185
Johannes Georgeson 149
Johannes Halsteinson 172
Johannes Halvorson 344
Johannes Henriksen 150
Johannes Hogden 155
Johannes Iverson 108, 344, 348
Johannes Iverson Rudi 108
Johannes J. Hønne 149
Johannes J. Thorstad 103
Johannes Jacobson 295
Johannes Jensen Auren 215
Johannes Johannesen 48, 50
Johannes Johnson 95, 248, 255
Johannes Johnson Aalterud 95
Johannes Johnson Rue 248
Johannes Kleiva 56
Johannes Knudsen 109
Johannes Knutson Ekse 323, 336
Johannes Larson 145, 323, 327, 329, 336, 337
Johannes Lie 197
Johannes Nederhaugen 60
Johannes Nichols 153
Johannes Olsen Thoe 215
Johannes Olson 149, 255
Johannes Olson Øverland 208
Johannes Olson Sau 149
Johannes Ommelstadsæteren 60
Johannes Peterson Grindheim 345
Johannes Quale 178
Johannes Sauali 214
Johannes Simonson 185
Johannes Sivesind 184
Johannes Skofstad 48
Johannes Sørlien 315
Johannes Stene 16
Johannes Svendson 109
Johannes Syverson 259, 348
Johannes Syverson Mørk 259
Johannes Thoe 214

Johannes Thoen 214
Johannes Tyttegraff 153
Johannes Uvaas 260
Johannes Week 237
Johanns Week Jr 237
Johans Lybæk 60
John A. Murat 101
John A. Thompson 45
John Amundsen Lindelien 235
John Anderson 40, 41
John Anderson Aksdal 180
John Anderson Bækimellem 150
John Arctander 355
John Batman 228
John Bergum 136
John Brakstad 178
John C. Moses 355
John C. Spooner 71
John Carlson 212
John Christenson 286
John D. Johnson Døsland 286
John E. Homme 199
John Ellefson 211
John Ellingsen Solem 59
John Erickson 204
John Evenson Homme 201
John Evenson Mølee 51
John Følie 55
John Fylie 55
John Gilbertsen Tinglestad 221
John Gjelle 307
John H. Homme 214
John H. Røningsand 251
John Hagemoen 99
John Halverson 150
John Halvorsen 41, 134
John Hamre 305
John Hartvig 98
John Hattle 32
John Hellerud 307
John Hove 55
John Ingebretson Berge 90
John Iverson 201, 219
John J. Abercrombie 163
John Jacobsen Holm 198
John Jacobson 296
John Jacobson Einong 214, 215
John Johnsen Lommen 195
John Johnson 239, 240
John Johnson Kasen 215
John Johnson Landsverk 240

John Johnson Rodebakken 211
John Kaasa 180
John Knudson 185
John Knutson Lee 248
John L. Erdall 73
John Landsværk 37
John Landsverk 239
John Larson Jahr 209
John Larson Stensgaard 209
John Lasseson 109
John Lee 85, 94, 249
John Luraas 94
John M. Nelson 73
John Mattiason Sannes 201
John Mehuus 282
John Mølee 52
John Monsen 201
John N. Johnson 205
John N. Tarvestad 282, 283
John Nilsen Boxrud 215
John Nilson Luraas 46, 67
John O. Førde 398
John O. Gaarder 209
John O. Hove 259
John O. Week 85, 94
John Olsen 338
John Olson 201, 323
John Olson Slaabakken 323
John P. Førde 204
John Paulson 290
John Peterson 94
John Petterson 316
John Reiton 99
John Rendalen 75
John Rosholt 101
John Rud 95
John Sall 239
John Sevalsen 215
John Severson 281
John Smedsand 60
John Smedsrud 87
John Souter 198
John Steen 319
John Steingrimsen Bergrud 195
John Strømme 299, 300
John Svendsen Ramlo 338
John Svendson Ramlo 323
John Svennungson 239, 240
John Svennungson Bølaager 239, 240
John Swenson 323
John T. Totland 344

John Thompson 317, 364
John Thompson Krosso 215
John Thoreson 120
John Thorson 225
John Thun 178
John Tollefsjorden 46
John Tollefson 293
John Torgerson 149
John Torson Lee 201
John Tovson 184
John Treider 239
John Tvedt 286
John Vespe 307
John W. Pixley 47
John Week 85, 94, 237
John Week Sr 237
Jon Gullickson 212
Jon Hermundson 264, 265
Jon J. Børseth 163
Jon Torsteinsson Rue 45
Jonas Børreson 321
Jonas Duea 282, 283
Jonas Gjerdet 60
Jonas Nelsen 235, 238
Jonas Nelsen Berg 235
Jonas Nilsen Ørekvam 134
Jonas Norland 286
Jonas Oscar Backlund 81
Jonas P. Norland 285
Jonnas Pederson 212
Jorand Aanundsdatter Vraa 200
Jorand Gjermundsdatter Storaasli 201
Jorand, Haugerstuen 237
Jørgen Amundson 119
Jørgen Andersen 211
Jørgen Brunsvold 183
Jørgen Buckcreek Lee 139
Jørgen Dyrland 286
Jørgen Georgeson 149
Jørgen Gunderson Bostrok 94
Jørgen Johnson 32, 144
Jørgen Johnson Kleven 260
Jørgen Kittelsen Bjørgo 215
Jørgen Kvarve 248
Jørgen Lommen 180
Jørgen O. Bergan 345
Jørgen O. Brunsvold 184
Jørgen Olsen Hellingen 237
Jørgen Olsen Kaasa 56
Jørgen Pederson 35
Jørgen Postmyhr 345

Jørgen Quarve 248
Jørgen Sande 184
Jørgen Sollner 250
Jørgen Timansen Quarve 195
Jørgen Ziiølner 250
Jorund Halvorson 171
Joseph Thorp 70
Joseph Tuff 237
Josephine Langeland Franz 336
Joshua Stewart 336
Jul Olson Guldhaug 108
Julia Langeland 329, 336
Julia Onstine 217
Julia Peterson 364
Julius Markestad 215
Julius Rosholt 101
Juul Knutson 295
Juul Olson Hoyme 109

K

K. A. Bauge 281
K. A. Rene 337
K. E. Bergh 73
K. K. Hagestad 154
K. K. Snortum 110
K. Lunde 109
K. O. Aarthun 221
K. O. Boldstad 41
K. O. Rotegaard 266
K. Torreson 324
Kamme Knud 35
Karen Jacobson 221
Kari Bjørnsdatter Garnaas 204
Kari Bjørnsdatter Garness 204
Kari Bøen 233
Kari Fransdatter Rue 208
Kari Halvorsdatter 201
Kari Hansdatter Megard 323, 338
Kari Hermundsdatter Nese 199, 337
Kari Hovda 231
Kari Jensdatter Dyrdal Vinjum 197
Kari Johnsdatter Øverland 208
Kari Larsdatter Hovde 321
Kari Lillebæk 60
Kari Lybeck 233
Kari Modalen 235
Kari Nelsen 238
Kari Nielsdatter Horvei 338
Kari Nilsdatter Horvei 321
Kari Nilsen 32, 33

Kari Olsdatter 201
Kari Øverland 208
Kari Øverland Rue 208
Kari Revskil 199
Kari Syversdatter Kirkeberg Moen 235
Kari Week 237, 238
Karl Holter 354
Karl Olson Rue 209
Kirsti Helgesdatter Eide Slaabakken 323
Kirstin Berg 235
Kittel Halvorson 354
Kittel Haugen 239
Kittel Kittelson Stordobu 240
Kittel N. Strande 354
Kittel Newhouse 53
Kittel Nyhus 53
Kittel Olson Jordgrav 209
Kittel Olson Rue 209
Kittil A. Harstad 215
Kittil Alfson Veseth 215
Kittil Fjortoft 214
Kittil Fjostuft 215
Kittil Gunderson 260
Kittil Gunderson Veungen 209
Kittil H. Grøth 173
Kittil H. Tunnesgaard 305
Kittil Halsteinson 172
Kittil Haraldson Rauk 340
Kittil Kittilson 91, 239
Kittil Kittilson Moland 91
Kittil Olson 239
Kittil Tubaas 99
Kjel Bredeson 130
Kjeld Rønne 399
Kjersti Olsdatter Klastølen 235
Kjerstine Tostensdatter 207
Kjøgei Harstad 91, 225
Kjøstil Øiom 136
Kjøstuf Knutson Storaasli 200
Kjøstul Torgerson 103
Klemet Stabæk 54
Klemet Stabek 263
Kleng Pedersen 15
Kleofas Halvorson 59
Knud A. Slogvig 32
Knud Aamundsen Lee 197
Knud Amundsen Lie 197
Knud Amundsen Ytre Lee 197
Knud Anderson 17, 178, 201
Knud Anderson Bakke 178

Knud Anderson Slogvig 17
Knud Anundson Lønnegrav 201
Knud Christophersen Sagedalen 195
Knud Ellingsen Solem 59
Knud G. Opdahl 178
Knud G. Tyribakken 197
Knud Gilbertson 195
Knud Halvorson 221
Knud Helgeson Jøten 109
Knud Helliksen Roe 67
Knud Iverson 173
Knud Johnson Øverland 208
Knud K. Berge 110
Knud Karlsen 41
Knud Knudsen 87, 150, 195, 235
Knud Knudsen Jr 235
Knud Knudsen Kieland 195
Knud Knudsen Østegaarden 235
Knud Knudson 61, 211, 212, 217, 248
Knud Knudson Sævre 212, 217, 248
Knud Langeland 49, 76, 329, 336, 337
Knud Larson Bergan 180
Knud Larson Feeres Eien 109
Knud Lerol 212
Knud Middssad 336
Knud Nielsen Langeland 338
Knud Nilsen Haugerstuen 233
Knud Nilsen Haugestuen 231, 233
Knud O. Oppen 109
Knud Olsen Bergo 195, 196
Knud Olsen Eie 15
Knud Olsen Eik 196
Knud Olsen Ike 196, 197
Knud Olsen Wold 195
Knud Olson 108, 109, 110, 200, 211, 239, 240
Knud Olson Fugelhaug 109
Knud Olson Oppen 108
Knud Olson Sorum 200
Knud Ormson 134
Knud Peerson 35
Knud Person 32
Knud Peterson 34
Knud Rikoldsen 154
Knud Salveson 201
Knud Slogvig 31
Knud Syverson 109
Knud Torstenson Einang 240
Knud Torvildsen 220, 221
Knud Williamson 32
Knut A. Benson Vigh 197

Knut A. Benson Viig 197
Knut A. Benson Vik 197
Knut Alfson 180, 182
Knut Alfson Veseth 180
Knut Amundsen Holt 104
Knut Arnesen 215
Knut Arneson 108, 110
Knut Aslakson Svalestuen 48
Knut B. Rystad 82
Knut Berge 130
Knut Bergo 223
Knut Bjørgo 73
Knut Bjørnson Bakken 265
Knut Bromdalen 94
Knut E. Rukke 265
Knut Eide 16
Knut Ersland 281
Knut Finseth 305
Knut Gudmundson 179
Knut Gudmundson Norsving 179
Knut Guttormsen Tyribakken 195
Knut Guttormson 197
Knut H. Espetvedt 214
Knut H. Helling 315
Knut H. Trøstem 259
Knut Haldorson Ro 321
Knut Haldorson Ro Mestad 336
Knut Hallanger 154
Knut Halvorson 144
Knut Heggeson 153
Knut Henderson 73
Knut Høyme 108
Knut Husevold 215
Knut Hustad 172
Knut Jæger 172, 174
Knut Johnson Dalseid 258
Knut Johnson Fie 260
Knut Johnson Skrenes 271
Knut K. Bjørgo 184
Knut K. Stensland 240
Knut Knutson 61, 161, 217, 218, 220, 248, 336
Knut Knutson Bedle 218, 220
Knut Knutson Bell 218, 220
Knut Knutson Langeland 336
Knut Kultan 239
Knut Kulton 239
Knut Kvedne 108
Knut Kviste 213
Knut Laastuen 394, 396
Knut Langeland 311

Knut Larsen 39
Knut Larson 145
Knut Lawson 39
Knut Luraas 95, 98
Knut Melby 393, 394
Knut Mestad 321, 327
Knut Mikkelson 133
Knut Nelsen Ekse 199
Knut Nelsen Exe 199
Knut Nilson Luraas 46
Knut Nilsson Langeland 323
Knut O. Holtan 309
Knut O. Kviste 225
Knut Ødegaard 108
Knut Olsen Blexrud 195
Knut Olsen Eide 15, 16
Knut Olson Eik 196
Knut Olson Hoff 94
Knut Olson Ike 196
Knut Olson Syverud 90
Knut Ormson 133
Knut Ørvig 315
Knut Pederson 32
Knut Peterson Husevold 214
Knut Quale 254
Knut Sørenson Kvisterud 90
Knut Steen 319
Knut Strøm 315
Knut Syverson Aaberg 108
Knut Thorson Døvre 108
Knut Throndson 179
Knut Tollefson 251
Knut Trøstem 59
Knut Vik 399
Knut Ytrevold 202
Knute Nelson 11, 73, 396
Knute Reindahl 73
Knute Ytrevold 205
Kolbein Ektveidt 299
Kolbein Larson Graue 259
Kolbein O. Opheim 398
Kolbein Sebbø 180
Kolbein Torrison 185, 324
Kristen Bjørneby 130
Kristen Hellikson 309
Kristen Lundby 229
Kristen Puttekaasa 83
Kristen Rønning 130
Kristi Eriksdatter 201
Kristi Evensdatter 201
Kristi Olsdatter Graver 200

Kristian A. Aanrud 258
Kristian Hoff 155
Kristian Laamen 197
Kristian Lamen 197
Kristian Magelssen 205
Kristian Olsen 215
Kristian Olson Steinbakken 242
Kristian Rud 317, 318, 319
Kristina Hoffland 240
Kristine Gulbrandsdatter 201
Kristofer Alsvig 286
Kristoffer Bøland 130
Kristoffer Eriksen 197
Kristoffer Janson 308, 319
Kristoffer Johnson 139
Kristoffer Jorandby 130
Kristoffer Tvedt 309

L

L. Jahr 210
L. L. Hulsæther 73
L. O. Thorpe 353
Lage Vesteren 212
Lars Aasland 180
Lars Amundsen Holt 104
Lars Anderson Songe 103
Lars Anderson Torblaa 399
Lars Askjelsen Lid Lee 338
Lars Askjelson Lee 323
Lars Askjelson Lid 323
Lars Asleson 248, 257
Lars Asmundson Juve 201
Lars Bakken 134
Lars Bradvold 323
Lars Brandvold 323
Lars Brimsø 32, 34
Lars Christenson 139
Lars Christenson Elstad 295
Lars Christopherson 136
Lars Dahle 143
Lars Davidsen Reque 67
Lars Dommerud 223
Lars Dommerude 184
Lars Dugstad 67
Lars Ellendsen Skahjem 197
Lars Ellendsen Skaim 197
Lars Ellendsen Skajem 197
Lars Ellingsen Vinjum 197
Lars Ellingsen Winjum 197
Lars Elstad 212

Lars Embrigtson Grønhovd 172
Lars Endresen 341, 352
Lars Endresen Rosseland 341, 352
Lars Engebretson Grønhovd 173
Lars Eriksen Svartaas 198
Lars Erikson 290
Lars Findreng 197
Lars Flattum 212
Lars Furness 336
Lars Furrenæs 336
Lars G. Hanson 233
Lars Gjornevik 336
Lars Gorden 98
Lars Gullickson 229
Lars H. Jahr 209
Lars H. Røningsand 251
Lars Halverson 90, 172, 323
Lars Halverson Langemyr 90
Lars Hanson 154
Lars Hegland 283
Lars Hilleson 37
Lars Hjørnevik 336
Lars Holm 130
Lars Humble 209, 211
Lars Isaksen 110
Lars Iverson 183, 203, 207, 349
Lars Jenson 55, 94
Lars Jenson Hove 55
Lars Johansen Holo 149
Lars Johanson Holo 68
Lars Johanson Ruud 399
Lars Johnson 55, 202
Lars Johnson Haave 55
Lars Johnson Hove 55
Lars Knudsen 110
Lars Knudson 175
Lars Knutson Jeglum 174
Lars L. Løberg 98
Lars L. Risetter 37
Lars Land 178
Lars Langemyr 316
Lars Larsen 41, 109, 110
Lars Larsen Ballestad 109
Lars Larsen Ekse 199
Lars Larsen Exe 199
Lars Larsen Gulseth 109
Lars Larsen Hegland 215
Lars Larsen Lie 197
Lars Larsen Sannes 109
Lars Larsen Ytre Lie 197
Lars Larson 16, 98, 134, 323, 326, 336, 337, 338, 341
Lars Larson Austeraa 134
Lars Larson Furnes 323, 336
Lars Larson Furrenæs 323, 326, 336
Lars Larson Hasler 98
Lars Larson Rasdal Hjørnevik 323, 326, 336, 337
Lars Larson Rosseland 341
Lars Løberg 259
Lars Markhus 355
Lars Mathieson 109
Lars Medaas 184
Lars Mikkelsen 264, 265
Lars Mikkelsen Trugstad 264
Lars Modalen 235
Lars N. Garen 184
Lars Næss 283
Lars Nilsen 251, 259
Lars Nilsen Odden 251
Lars Nilsen Skaftedahl 251
Lars Nilsen Wilberg 259
Lars Nilsson Ekse 336, 337
Lars Nord Fossum 60
Lars Norgaarden 229
Lars Øiesø 285
Lars Olsen 17, 198, 221
Lars Olsen Blexrud 198
Lars Olsen Helland 17
Lars Olson 17, 37, 55, 144, 218, 286, 324, 345
Lars Olson Espe 37
Lars Olson Helland 17
Lars Olson Hove 55
Lars Olson Lødal 218
Lars Østerhus 180
Lars Paulsen Troo 338
Lars Paulson Troo 323, 337
Lars Paulson Trøos 323, 337
Lars Pedersen Helme 221
Lars Reiersen Halstenrud 195
Lars Reierson 103, 251
Lars Rosseland 352
Lars Røste 57, 59, 60
Lars S. Reque 74
Lars Salvesen 110
Lars Scheie 67, 78
Lars Sevig 209
Lars Sheldal 279, 282, 283
Lars Simundsen Høn 110
Lars Skavlem 57
Lars Sørlien 315

Lars Strand 286
Lars Swennungsen 138
Lars Syverson 399
Lars Tarvestad 205
Lars Tesdahl 281
Lars Thompson 218, 220
Lars Thovson 171
Lars Tollefson Haugen 202
Lars Torgerson 103
Lars Tovson 184
Lars Tow 286
Lars Trulson Ask 202, 212
Lars Ulvestad 218
Lars. C. Tarvestad 202
Lasse Bothun 399
Lasse Olsen 110
Laur. Larsen 412
Lauraus Augondsen 134
Laurits Swenson 293
Laurits Thomasrud 144
Lauritz Larsen 307
Lauritz Larson 146, 294
Lauritz Steen 232
Lavrants Anderson Vraa 200
Leif Erikson 1, 3, 9, 100
Leif Olson Kragness 200
Leif Olson Vraa 200
Leiv Kragness 199
Lemen Lemmonvier 134
Levi Kittelson 73
Levor Anderson Marelien 90
Levor Kvarve 248
Levor Nerison Quie 345
Levor Olsen Lindelien 247
Levor Olson 248, 249
Levor Olson Lindelien 248
Levor Quarve 248
Levor Timansen Quarve 195
Lewis Johnson Dale 345
Little Crow 360, 361, 363, 364, 365, 366, 368
Little John Hove 55
Louis Klinkenberg 125

M

M. Hegland 211
M. Langeland 183
M. N. Johnson 188
M. Nordness 211
M. P. Ruh 295

Mads Boxrud 316
Mads Olsen 110
Mads Rynningen 49
Mads Vefring 184
Magdalena Trondsdatter Dokken 233
Magne B. Bystolen 66
Magne Bystølen 310
Magne Langeland 183, 184
Magnus Anderson 201
Magnus Peterson 295
Magnus Satran 311
Magnus Swenson 138
Malene Torgesdatter 201
Marcus Olsen Olnestad 221
Marcus Olson Ulvestad 221
Marcus Thorson 144
Margit Øygaarden 209
Mari Bjørnsdatter Garnaas 204
Mari Bjørnsdatter Garness 204
Mari Engen 60
Mari Olafsdatter Rue 209
Mari Olsdatter Otternes 197
Mari Pedersdatter 201
Maria Amundsdatter 201
Marie Feen 103
Marie Reiersdatter 201
Marie Signalness 389
Marit Frøslie 60
Marit Gunnarsdatter 211
Marit Halvorsdatter Milevandet 235
Marit Halvorsdatter Stene 323, 338
Marit O. Helle 108
Marit Syversdatter 323
Marit Syversen 237
Martha Botolvsdatter Berekvam Hemri 199
Martha Ivarsdatter Frandle 197
Martha Ivarsdatter Frondal 197
Martha Jonsdatter 16
Martha Knutsdatter 196
Martha Langeland 329, 331
Martha Larsdatter Skajem 197
Martha Larsdatter Skime 197
Martha Larsdatter Ytre Lie 197
Martha Marie Winjum 198
Martha Nelson Sunde 203
Martha Syversdatter 237
Marthe Kauserud 130
Marthea Brendingen 60
Marthias Mikkelson 130
Martin Anderson 229

Martin Bonli 87
Martin Christianson 201
Martin Ellingson 364
Martin Hanson 254, 264
Martin M. Mikkelson 130
Martin Madsen 151, 152
Martin Olson 73
Martin S. Anderson 212
Martin Skardrud 130
Martin Stensgaard 209
Martin Torgersen 333
Martin Ulvestad 234, 296, 337, 354
Martinus Grythe 155
Martinus Scarseth 155
Mary Monroe 205
Mathias Helliksen 227, 228
Mathias Helliksen Krokan 227
Mathias Lia 99
Mathias Lisbakken 138
Matthias Aasved 323
Matthias Evenson 144
Matthias G. Evenson 291, 294
Matthias Johnson 345
Matthias L. Heimo 49
Matthias Minne 398
Matthias Petersen Ringdahl 297
Matthias Peterson Ringdahl 168
Matthias Sletten 143
Michael Bekkelien 110
Michael Johnson 91
Michael Mathison 109
Michael Olson 110
Mikæl Mikælson 109
Mikkel Bøe 398
Mikkel Christensen Onsgard 199
Mikkel E. Aske 283
Mikkel Eidsmo 93
Mikkel Halsteinson Blekkelien 91
Mikkel Johnson 167
Mikkel Kittelsen 211
Mikkel Knudson 217
Mikkel L. Rokne 398
Mikkel Larsen Dal 195
Mikkel Larson 139
Mikkel M. Sinnes 199
Mikkel M. Synnes 199
Mikkel Mikkelsen 403
Mikkel Mikkelson Jordgrav 209
Mikkel Mikkelson Sinnes 200
Mikkel Monson Rønnei 242
Mikkel Olson 323, 328, 335, 336

Mikkel Olson Slaabakken 323, 328, 335, 336
Mikkel Omlie 178
Mikkel Skare 242
Mikkel Solberg 184
Mikkel T. Golberg 248
Mikkel T. Lunde 204
Mikkel T. Rust 247
Mikkel Tollefson Rust 248, 251
Millard Fillmore 219
Mons Adland 49
Mons Anderson 150, 199
Mons Blagstvedt 212
Mons Fladager 194
Mons Grove 282
Mons Hansen 317
Mons Monson 331
Mons Stalheim 398
Morten Kjelsberg 204
Mother Holter 354
Mother Røste 91
Mr. Thomas 332
Mrs. Arveson 103
Mrs. Christensen 403
Mrs. Ekse 323
Mrs. Faae 205
Mrs. Fyre 321, 326, 331, 336
Mrs. Mathieson 96
Mrs. Rud 163, 164
Mrs. Wilhelmsen 127

N

N. A. Giere 73
N. A. Ladd 73
N. A. Qvammen 73
N. Amlund 286
N. C. Amundson 73
N. E. Jensen 211
N. E. S. Jenson 214
N. G. Peterson 271
N. J. Nilsen 110
N. N. Ronning 37
N. O. Giere 73
N. O. Stark 74
Narve Cølbjornson 251
Narve F. Grønhovd 259
Narve Stabek 61
Nathan Boone 207
Nathan Myrick 360, 361
Nathaniel Dane 75

Neils Evensen 211
Nels A. Gullickson 220
Nels Christophersen Tveto 195
Nels Evans 211
Nels Evenson Lian 217
Nels H. Gausta 215
Nels Haugerstuen 237
Nels Holman 73
Nels Johnsen Boxrud 215
Nels Kinnestad 205
Nels Nelson 104
Nels Nessa 205
Nels Stubberud 213
Nelson A. Falk 73
Nelson Evans 211
Neri Asmundson 130
Neri Dalen 91
Neri Syverson 204
Nicholas V 2
Nickolai Langeland 336
Nicolai Johan Langeland 336
Nicolay Andreas Grevstad 43
Niels Bendixen 55
Niels Bjørnson Garnaas 204
Niels Bjørnson Garness 204
Niels Pedersen Brugjeld 338
Niels Pederson Brugjeld 321
Niels Pederson Bruhjell 321
Niels Peterson Brugjeld 337
Niels Torstensen 76
Nils A. Aas 109
Nils A. Dalsbotten 305
Nils A. Gullickson 218
Nils Aasen 60
Nils Anderson Tholdness 98
Nils B. Berge 73
Nils Bergersen 259
Nils Bjørnsen 134
Nils Bjørnson 133
Nils Bøen 215
Nils Bottolfson 175
Nils E. Egge 398
Nils Einarson 91, 92
Nils Ellertson 209
Nils Erikson 125
Nils Evenson 180, 211
Nils Evenson Ramsfjeld 180
Nils Feseth 309
Nils Frøland 32
Nils Gilderhus 310
Nils Gulbrandsen 298

Nils Gullicksen Ristey 195
Nils Gullikson 109
Nils H. Fjeld 108
Nils H. Nilsen 251
Nils Haldorson 154
Nils Halverson 90, 153
Nils Halverson Græsdalen 90
Nils Hanson Fjeld 70
Nils Hanson Golberg 340
Nils Haugen 59
Nils Heen 305
Nils Helgeson Mørstad 108
Nils Henderson 154
Nils Herreid 154
Nils Hulberg 149
Nils Iverson Wenaas 265
Nils Johnson 45, 46, 49, 109, 178, 179, 185, 188, 251
Nils Johnson Kaasa 46, 178
Nils Johnson Nessa 202
Nils Johnson Riis 109
Nils Johnson Rue 45
Nils Juelson 237
Nils K. Fenne 298
Nils K. Kopstad 266
Nils Knudson 204
Nils Knutsen Gaasedelen 215
Nils Knutson Ekse 323
Nils Kristenson 144
Nils Kristoffersen 144
Nils Larsen 66, 109
Nils Larsen Bolstad 66
Nils Lien 305
Nils Lunde 237
Nils Madsen 109
Nils McCusick 167
Nils N. Giere 309
Nils N. Ingulfsland 215
Nils N. Lofthus 260
Nils N. Skogen 91
Nils Nelsen Haugerstuen 237
Nils Nilsen 32, 103, 104, 105, 167, 174, 175
Nils Nilsen Arnesgaard 174
Nils Nilsen Ekse 199
Nils Nilsen Exe 199
Nils Nilsen Haatvedt 103
Nils Nilsen Hersdal 32
Nils Nilsen Jr 32
Nils Nilsen Kinnestad 202
Nils Nilsen Morem 215

Nils Nilson 17, 61, 205
Nils Nilson Hersdal 17
Nils Nilson Kinnestad 205
Nils Nilsson Ekse 337
Nils O. Brandt 80, 84, 140, 146, 150, 154, 173, 175, 183, 184, 307
Nils O. Giere 310
Nils O. Hengsly 144
Nils O. Strandmoen 354
Nils O. Walderdalen 98
Nils Økland 154
Nils Olai Nilsen 41
Nils Olsen Blexrud 195
Nils Olsen Vinjum 199
Nils Olson 57, 92, 93, 280, 317, 341, 364
Nils Olson Alvik 341
Nils Olson Næs 280
Nils Olson Vegli 57
Nils Otto Tank 37, 116, 117, 125
Nils P. Haugen 145
Nils Peterson 139, 140
Nils Peterson Bjørkum 139
Nils Peterson Grindheim 345
Nils Remme 399
Nils Ronbun 229
Nils Røthe 39
Nils Rudi 136
Nils Rukke 316
Nils Salveson Kjær 110
Nils Simonson Aamodt 98
Nils Sjurson Gilderhus 335
Nils Storre Mestad 326, 327, 329, 330, 331
Nils Syversen 233, 237
Nils Syversen Moen 233
Nils Syverson Gilderhus 66
Nils Syverson Moen 231
Nils Syverson Turtnes 248
Nils Thompson 17, 32, 103
Nils Thorson 315
Nils Tollefsjorden 46
Nils Tollefson Rue 174
Nils Torgerson 103
Nils Vangen 266
Nils Voldeng 184
Nils William Olson 81
Nils Wollan 386, 387
Norman Randal 92
Notto Jensen 315

O

O. A. Buslett 83
O. A. Norman 73
O. Aasen 73
O. B. Dahle 49, 90
O. Estrem 239
O. F. Duus 101, 104
O. F. Solberg 319
O. G. Felland 73
O. H. Oppegaard 215
O. H. Sire 307
O. H. Smeby 175
O. J. Hatlestad 61
O. K. Gigstad 110
O. O. Klevjord 73
O. Overland 210
O. P. Fredrikson 185
O. P. Hadland 227
O. T. Lee 254
O. Thorud 211
Odd Himle 67
Odd J. Himle 66, 78
Odd Larson Austeraa 134
Oivind Hovde 270
Ola Christian 211
Ola i Rundtøp 108
Ola Kittelsen 215
Ola Knudson 201
Ola Thompson 221
Ola Torgersen Trøeng 323
Olaf Druetzer 85
Olaf Mandt 73
Olaf O. Haugan 345, 349
Olaf Sanden 199
Olaus Landsværk 37
Olaus Signalness 389
Olaus Solberg 319
Olav Hvite 11
Olav Lee 200
Olav Lie 200
Olav Skree 200
Olav Skrei 200
Olava Johannesdatter 211
Old Knut 32
Old Thrond Steen 184
Ole A. Lomen 178
Ole A. Olson 73
Ole Aagesen Rosaaen 197
Ole Aamundsen Lee 197
Ole Aamundsen Lie 197

Ole Aamundsen Ytre Lie 197
Ole Aasved 386
Ole Aavri 55
Ole Amundsen 104, 309
Ole Amundsen Berg 195
Ole Amundsen Holt 104
Ole Anderson 48, 103, 110
Ole Anderson Lunde 103
Ole Anderson Mjølvær 242
Ole Andreas Sivertson 239
Ole Andreasen 110
Ole Anfinson 266, 281
Ole Anfinson Seim 266
Ole Anundson Jore 200
Ole Anundson Kragnes 201
Ole Arneson Lien 225
Ole Aslakson Graver 200
Ole Aslakson Grover 200
Ole Aslakson Lysbæk 258
Ole Asleson Myran 180, 184
Ole Aubol 109
Ole B. Broin 305
Ole Baker 237
Ole Bakko 305
Ole Bendixen 104
Ole Berdahl 55
Ole Bergesen 168
Ole Bergeson 286
Ole Berland 217, 220
Ole Bjørgulfson Tvedten 201
Ole Bjørndalen 254
Ole Bjørnsen Vinge 198
Ole Bjørnsen Vinje 198
Ole Bjørnson Garnaas 204
Ole Bjørnson Garness 204
Ole Blagstvedt 212
Ole Bøen 237
Ole Bornemann Bull 70
Ole Børreson 321
Ole Botolvsen Berekvam 197
Ole Bottolfson Sivlesøen 398
Ole Boxrud 316
Ole Boyum 218
Ole Brager 237
Ole Brownson 172
Ole Bruden 163
Ole Bull 70, 153, 154, 319
Ole Bye 196
Ole C. Braaten 248
Ole C. Rue 209
Ole Carstensen 210

Ole Christenson 110
Ole Christiansen 195, 215
Ole Christiansen Stensrud 195
Ole Christianson 95
Ole Christianson Gunholt 98
Ole Christophersen Sagedalen 195
Ole Colbjørnsen Livdahl 257
Ole Colbjørnson Livdahl 263
Ole Cølbjornson Livdahl 248
Ole Dahl 387
Ole Dahle 211
Ole Dalen 136
Ole Dyrland 286
Ole E. Hofstad 412
Ole E. Sando 173
Ole E. Stenerodden 195
Ole Eiene 197
Ole Eik 197
Ole Eino 282
Ole Eivindson Dølhus 200
Ole Ellefson 175
Ole Ellingson 154
Ole Embrigtson Grønhovd 172
Ole Engebretson Grønhovd 173
Ole Eriksen 317
Ole Erikson Sando 248
Ole Estensen 293, 323, 332, 335
Ole Estensen Lunaas 323, 332, 335
Ole Estensen Lunaashaug 323, 335
Ole Evenson 109
Ole Evenson Sanden 262
Ole F. Forde 321, 331, 336
Ole F. Ringen 88
Ole Fatland 280, 281
Ole Finhart 228, 231, 237
Ole Fladland 323
Ole Flatastøl 214
Ole Florand 237
Ole Fluto 259
Ole Fohre 336
Ole Forde 325
Ole Fosse 41
Ole Fossum 266
Ole Frøland 237
Ole Fyre 325, 327, 328, 329
Ole G. Storlie 50
Ole G. Vaala 239
Ole G. Wall 364
Ole Gaarder 60
Ole Gilbertson 39
Ole Gilbertson Glopstuen 155

Ole Gjeitli 403
Ole Gjeitlis 399
Ole Gjermundson Tvedt 133
Ole Gjermundson Vraa 200
Ole Golberg 309
Ole Grimsgaard 174, 175
Ole Gudbrandsgutten 195
Ole Gulliksen Jevne 178
Ole Gullord 138
Ole Gunbjørnson 172
Ole Gunderson Lia 209
Ole H. Haugerud 249
Ole H. Johnson 255
Ole H. Røningsand 251
Ole H. Støen 184
Ole H. Thoen 144
Ole H. Tingelstad 173
Ole Haave 264
Ole Hagestuen 389
Ole Halling 227, 228
Ole Halsteinson 172
Ole Halverson Valle 171, 177
Ole Halvorsen Thoen 340
Ole Halvorson 57, 94, 110, 165, 266, 339, 344
Ole Halvorson Fløse 94
Ole Halvorson Næss 339
Ole Halvorson Skree 200
Ole Halvorson Valle 57, 94, 165
Ole Hansen Haugerud 247
Ole Hanson 61, 145, 157, 159, 163, 173, 175
Ole Hanson Haugerud 248
Ole Hanson Lerum 157
Ole Hanson Underdahl 163
Ole Haroldson Ulen 248
Ole Hauge 281
Ole Haugen 389
Ole Heggen 281
Ole Heggeson 153
Ole Hei 59
Ole Helliksen 227, 228
Ole Helliksen Krokan 227
Ole Hellikson Krokan 46
Ole Hendrickson 207
Ole Hendrikson 287
Ole Herbjørnson Øien 227
Ole Herbrandsen 171, 185
Ole Hjelle 90
Ole Hofto 225
Ole Hogensen 48

Ole Hogenson 51
Ole Hovde 183, 184
Ole Hovdelien 60
Ole Hove 259, 264
Ole Hulberg 149
Ole Ingebrigtsen 338
Ole Ingebrigtsen Bjergum 197
Ole Ingebrigtsen Bjørgo 197
Ole Ingebrigtsen Bjørgum 197
Ole Iverson Dale 154
Ole J. Bakko 305
Ole J. Høgaas 266
Ole J. Homstad 49
Ole J. Kasen 215
Ole J. Morem 215
Ole J. Rebne 109
Ole Jacobsen Myhre 198
Ole Jacobson 209
Ole Jenson 201
Ole Jhanson 134
Ole Johanneson 211
Ole Johnsen Svartebraaten 195
Ole Johnson 17, 133, 134
Ole Johnson Holstad 255
Ole Johnson Juve 201
Ole Johnson Lee 200
Ole Johnson Øverland 208, 210
Ole Jone 78
Ole Jorgens 235
Ole Jørgensen 211, 315, 390
Ole Jørgenson 109, 209, 319, 345
Ole Jørgenson Flaten 109
Ole Jørgenson Postmyhr 345
Ole Jørgenson Wold 209
Ole Juelsen 237
Ole Julsen 233
Ole Julson 231
Ole K. Gaarder 175
Ole K. Hagen 266
Ole K. Morreim 266
Ole K. Vangsness 74
Ole K. Wold 211
Ole Kaalsrud 307
Ole Karness 130
Ole Kauserud 130
Ole Kittelson 184, 225, 266
Ole Kittelson Holong 184
Ole Kittelson Kaasa 209
Ole Kittelson Stensrud 209
Ole Kittilson 239
Ole Kittlelson Holong 180

Ole Kjørnes 130
Ole Kleppe 266
Ole Klokkerengen 95
Ole Klungeland 121
Ole Knudsen 149, 150, 346, 347, 349
Ole Knudsen Hoiby 149
Ole Knudsen Ristey 195
Ole Knudson Dyrland 68
Ole Knudson Fladeland 323
Ole Knudson Omodt 200
Ole Knudson Storbraaten 345
Ole Knudson Trovatten 67
Ole Knutsen 338
Ole Knutsen Myhre 196
Ole Knutson 175, 199, 248
Ole Knutson Lee 248
Ole Kolberg 195
Ole Kragness 199
Ole Krokenes 199
Ole Larson 41, 95, 109, 118, 175, 180, 201, 394
Ole Larson Ballestad 109
Ole Larson Bergan 180
Ole Larson Rotnem 175
Ole Lee 90, 249
Ole Legreid 271
Ole Leverson Berge 204
Ole Lewison 398
Ole Lie 258
Ole Lien 99
Ole Lillemoen 386
Ole Lindelien 235
Ole Livdahl 257, 258, 263
Ole Lomen 179
Ole Lund 163, 164
Ole Lunde 237
Ole Madsen 109
Ole Magneson 183, 184
Ole Magneson Sætre 184
Ole Martin Signalness 389
Ole Mehus 259
Ole Mellem 258
Ole Mikkelson Rekaness 209
Ole Moe 98
Ole Moen 145
Ole Monsen Tollefsrud 60
Ole Monson 87
Ole Munson 214
Ole Næss 314, 339, 340, 343, 344
Ole Narveson Melby 265
Ole Nattestad 45, 53

Ole Nichols 153
Ole Nilsen 109, 154, 173, 231, 234, 271, 272, 316
Ole Nilsen Hauge 271, 272
Ole Nilsen Haugestuen 231, 234
Ole Nilsen Hundere 271
Ole Nilsen Skaar 154
Ole Nilsen Viger 316
Ole Norman 294
Ole Nørstelien 60
Ole Nummeland 82
Ole O. Bagli 204
Ole O. Berge 109
Ole O. Blakstad 251
Ole O. Bratrud 218, 220
Ole O. Finhart 231
Ole O. Halling 227
Ole O. Hovda 228, 231
Ole O. Liabraaten 354
Ole O. Næseth 305
Ole O. Oppen 110
Ole O. Østrud 229
Ole O. Rosenwater 139
Ole O. Selland 398
Ole O. Storla 174
Ole O. Storlag 175
Ole O. Syverud 231
Ole O. Tveten 175
Ole Oakland 299
Ole Oleson Moen 108
Ole Olsen 153, 154
Ole Olsen Finhart 233
Ole Olsen Flatastøl 215
Ole Olsen Fyre 338
Ole Olsen Gulbrandsgutten 195
Ole Olsen Hovda 233
Ole Olsen Lee 195
Ole Olsen Qualey 196
Ole Olsen Sjurud 233
Ole Olsen Skrabek 215
Ole Olsen Syverud 233
Ole Olsen Teppen 153, 154
Ole Olsen Traim 215
Ole Olsen Ulen 195
Ole Olson 17, 32, 34, 35, 90, 108, 109, 130, 155, 172, 175, 197, 201, 248, 258, 295, 317, 321, 323, 326, 327, 328, 331, 335, 336, 337, 364, 394, 398, 399
Ole Olson Aabol 108
Ole Olson Bækken 295

Ole Olson Bakken 90
Ole Olson Bergland 201
Ole Olson Brøthovd 109
Ole Olson Førde 321
Ole Olson Fyre 321, 323, 326, 327, 328, 331, 336, 337
Ole Olson Gjeitli 399
Ole Olson Gjerløv 197
Ole Olson Grovo 248
Ole Olson Heier 34
Ole Olson Hetletvedt 17, 32, 35
Ole Olson Jetley 399
Ole Olson Oppen 108
Ole Olson Sølhaugen 399
Ole Olson Studlien 201
Ole Olson Stutlien 201
Ole Olson Wendelbø 197
Ole Olson Wold 172
Ole Olstad 150
Ole Orvedahl 55
Ole Orvold 130
Ole Østensen 215, 293
Ole Østensen Bøen 293
Ole Østensen Bomaagen 215
Ole P. Langeberg 259
Ole P. Selsing 103
Ole P. Tenold 55
Ole Paasaas 130
Ole Palmeson 316
Ole Paulsen 181
Ole Paulsen Wolden 195
Ole Paulson 180, 270, 287, 367
Ole Pedersen 215, 338
Ole Pederson 108, 184, 212, 321
Ole Pederson Eide 321
Ole Pederson Evavold 321
Ole Pederson Helle 108
Ole Pederson Ruen 184
Ole Pladsen 319
Ole Quale 254
Ole Ranum 323
Ole Rasmussen 283
Ole Reierson 103
Ole Reine 345
Ole Rime 59
Ole Roen 59
Ole Roningen 307
Ole Rønnei 139
Ole Rude 175
Ole Rue 211
Ole Rundberg 110

Ole Runnice 139
Ole Rustad 212
Ole Rynning 53, 55, 287
Ole S. Eriksen Solseth 215
Ole S. Olson Gjerløv 197
Ole S. Sættre 310
Ole Sættre 310
Ole Sampson 253, 398, 402
Ole Sampson Bjørndalen 253
Ole Sampson Opheim 398
Ole Sandbuløkken 319
Ole Sande 59
Ole Sanden 262
Ole Satran 310
Ole Scrabek 214
Ole Semb 155
Ole Severrud 235
Ole Shervin 180
Ole Signalness 389
Ole Sigurdson 110
Ole Simenson Jobraaten 232
Ole Simonsen 238
Ole Simonson Jobraaten 231, 233, 237
Ole Sjurud 235, 238
Ole Skaarden 389
Ole Skardrud 130
Ole Slette 266
Ole Smeby 60
Ole Smith 258
Ole Solid 209
Ole Søndo 172
Ole Søndrol 354
Ole Sorben 235
Ole Sørbølle 315
Ole Sørenson 90, 120, 121
Ole Sørenson Kvisterud 90
Ole Sørflaten 235
Ole Stadheim 55
Ole Stadsvolden 60
Ole Stalheim 398
Ole Stølen 130
Ole Storhov 212
Ole Studlien 199
Ole Svendsen 110
Ole Svendson 361, 364
Ole Synsteby 317
Ole Syverson 109, 136
Ole Syverson Lekwold 174
Ole Syverson Sølhaugen 399
Ole Syverud 235
Ole Syvrud 235

Ole T. Fagerbakken 257
Ole T. Kaasa 56
Ole T. Kittilsland 171
Ole T. Lee 73
Ole T. Olson 32
Ole T. Wi 61
Ole Tarjeson Kragness 200
Ole Terum 259
Ole Thistelson Hofto 225
Ole Thoen 144, 146
Ole Thomasen Scotland 196
Ole Thompson 109, 130
Ole Thoreson 109, 295
Ole Thoreson Dovre 109
Ole Thorson Omserud 315
Ole Thorud 145
Ole Throndsen 265
Ole Tistel 55
Ole Tollefsen 221
Ole Tollefsjorden 46
Ole Tollefson 94, 130, 165, 166, 177, 221, 265
Ole Tollefson Kittilsland 94, 165, 177
Ole Tollefson Stølen 130
Ole Torgersen 323, 333, 335
Ole Torgerson 163
Ole Torgerson Dahl 163
Ole Torgerson Fagerbakken 248
Ole Torjussen 110
Ole Torson 184
Ole Torstenson 136, 239, 240
Ole Torstenson Gullord 136
Ole Torstenson Haugen 178
Ole Tostenson 108, 239
Ole Tostenson Bunde 108
Ole Tow 286
Ole Trovatten 77
Ole Upland 280, 281
Ole Valle 166, 171, 172
Ole Vange 55
Ole Veggar 309
Ole Viger 204
Ole Waldeland 152
Ole Walhovd 343
Ole Weland 286
Ole Wensel 209
Ole Wogsland 98
Ole Wrolstad 98
Ole. C. Christianson 354
Ole. H. Sunde 266
Olea Jorandby 130

Olia Finhart 235
Oliana Brager 237
Oliver Thompson 110
Oliver Wilson 217, 220
Omman Hilleson 37
One Eyed Decorah 183
Ørians Torblaa 154
Oskar Erikson 341, 349, 352, 353
Osmund Johnson 212, 280, 281
Osmund Jorgenson 201
Osmund Larson Juve 200
Osmund Larson Weom 200
Osmund Olson Trydal 225
Osmund Osmundson 307
Osmund Rollefson 220
Osmund Sheldal 279, 280, 281, 282
Osmund Tutland 285
Østen A. Quie 345
Østen Andersen Guberud 196
Østen Burtness 167
Østen Engebretsen 211
Østen Eyvinson 209
Østen Flaten 98
Østen Gunnøvson Svadde 289
Østen Haukestad 299
Østen Helgesen Børtnes 197
Østen Helgesen Burtness 197
Østen Holen 307
Østen Ingolfsland 227
Østen Johanneson 175
Østen Johnson Dalen 155
Østen Lundsæteren 60
Østen Maland 215
Østen Møllerflaten 46
Østen N. Ingulfsland 215
Østen O. Jordspek 259
Østen Olsen Bøen 293
Østen Østenson 110
Østen Peterson 175
Osuld Torrison 109, 114
Otto Hanson 272
Otto Olson Nigard 242
Otto Ottesen 73
Ouver Olson 296
Ove Danielson Rosdal 32
Oyen Thompson 16

P

P. A. Rasmussen 35, 37, 93, 214, 286
P. Broberg 346

P. H. Tetlie 413
P. M. Osfwed 337, 338
P. O. Langseth 59
P. Olsen Skaaden 41
Palmer Olson 314
Paul Anderson 41
Paul Brandstad 164
Paul Dagfinson 184
Paul Eckstorm 314
Paul Hansen Rosendahl 195
Paul Hjelm Hansen 416, 417
Paul Jenson Brørby 173
Paul Kittilson Galoger 173
Paul Olsen Vaalberg 287
Paul Olson Sletjord 315
Paul Peterson 229
Paul Skavlem 57
Paul Thompson 282
Peder Asbjørnson 185, 201, 203
Peder Asbjørnson Mehus 185
Peder Christensen Onsgard 199
Peder Einarsen 221
Peder Enerson 398
Peder Erikson 201
Peder Frøland 77
Peder G. Evenson 291
Peder Gaarder 60
Peder Gilbertson Jevne 163
Peder Givre 305
Peder Gjermo 260
Peder Hadland 227, 228
Peder Heggestuen 136
Peder Helgeson 62
Peder Huset 237
Peder Jørgensen 110
Peder K. Hiller 98
Peder Kristensen Ohnstad 197
Peder Kristensen Onstad 197
Peder Langeland 183
Peder Larson 175
Peder Larson Haugen 183
Peder Lunde 265
Peder Mathisen Rakkestad 215
Peder Nilsen Haugen 145
Peder O. Hadland 227
Peder Olson 201
Peder P. Kjær 98
Peder Pederson 207, 212
Peder Rosheim 213
Peder Sampson 182
Peder Sørenson 212

Peder Stenshoel 212
Peder Thormundson 314
Peder Tveite 398
Peder Ulrikson 184
Peer Gynt 25
Peer Strømme 95, 159
Per Anderson Hogden 150, 154
Per Asbjørnson Mehus 35
Per Bakkens 147
Per Bredeson 130
Per Brye 138
Per Davidson 85, 86
Per Davidson Skervheim 85
Per Fossum 266
Per Frøland 77, 78
Per G. Feen 103
Per Granum 143
Per Gunderson Feen 103
Per Haug 130
Per Hovde 144
Per Hove 55
Per J. Unde 85
Per Johnson Aalterud 95
Per Kristensen Ohnstad 197
Per Kristensen Onstad 197
Per Muskego 98
Per O. Brye 138
Per O. Rotegaard 266
Per Olson Moe 78
Per Rølstad 95
Per Røthe 74
Per Strømme 308
Per Ulric 130
Per Unde 55, 56
Peter Asbjørnson Mehus 202
Peter Berg 221
Peter Danielson 81
Peter Dass 69
Peter E. Barsness 389
Peter E. Lee 104
Peter Ekeren 155
Peter Gaarder 59, 166
Peter Golberg 251
Peter Gunderson 248
Peter Halverson Torgenrud 195
Peter Halvorson Haugen 58
Peter Helgeson 172
Peter Hendrickson 73
Peter Holst 41
Peter J. Flaten 109
Peter Jenson 104

Peter Johnsen Lommen 195
Peter Johnson Lommen 194
Peter L. Asbjørnson 202
Peter Larson 129
Peter Larson Wollager 260
Peter Laurentius 412
Peter Lommen 194
Peter Lundesæther 59
Peter M. Olsen 210
Peter Madsen 109
Peter Martin 254
Peter Næss 81
Peter Nilsen Børsheim 251
Peter O. Vinge 198
Peter O. Vinje 198
Peter Olson Slaabakken 323
Peter Peterson 120
Peter Peterson Haslerud 217, 220
Peter Rasmussen 248
Peter Reque 74
Peter Rissen 364
Peter Ruh 295, 296
Peter Sampson 295
Peter Skardrud 130
Peter Svendsrud 389
Peter Thompson 41, 295
Peter Tønneson Lavold 153
Peter Tyttegraff 153
Peter Unseth 136
Peter Wiborg 120, 121
Petronelle Olesdatter 201
Petter Sæthre 229
Porter Olson 35

R

R. B. Anderson 73
R. Emerson 354
R. I. Talbot 394
R. N. Paden 234
Ragnhild Berg 233, 235
Ragnhild Guliksbraaten 237
Ragnhild Knutsdatter Langeland 323
Ragnhild Tuff 238
Ragnhild Week 237, 238
Ragnild Jonsdatter 239
Ragnild Knudsdatter Langeland 338
Ragnild Knutsdatter Langeland Ekse 337
Ragnval Knutson Stondall 218
Ragnvald Knutson 218, 220

Ragnvald Olson 255
Ragnvald Stondalen 221
Randi Jensdatter Otternes 197
Rasmus B. Anderson 68
Rasmus Bækaasen 110
Rasmus Bestul 98
Rasmus Danielson 316, 317
Rasmus E. Aske 283
Rasmus Groettum 210
Rasmus H. Leikaas 110
Rasmus Hanson 119
Rasmus Nilsen 110
Rasmus Olsen Signalness 387
Rasmus Sheldal 279, 283
Rasmus Signalness 389
Rasmus Spande 207, 221
Rasmus Tungesvig 283
Reier Olson 103
Roald Amundsen 25
Robinson Jones 360
Rolf Fjelstad 356
Rollef Thygeson 266

S

S. Hookland 207, 208
S. Midtbøn 60
S. Overland 210
S. R. Foote 349
S. S. Hookland 207
S. S. Reque 74
S. Torgerson 294
Saamund Thorbjørnson Nykus 209
Sæbjørn Pederson Dysterud 90
Sakarias Sakariason Vatne 119
Salomon Juneau 47
Salve Heggen 281
Salve Jørgenson 91
Salve Nilsen 61
Salve Salveson 125
Salve Slouge Pladsen 338
Salve Tønneson Lavold 153
Salve Torgerson 316
Sam Thompson 91
Samson Anderson 207
Samuel G. Iverson 219
Samuel Nelson 219
Samund Thorson Sanden 201
Sara Darnell 285
Sara Larson 17

Sevat Sevatson 173
Sever Halsteinson 172
Severt Gravdahl 281
Sevrena Larson 203
Sherman Haugerud 208
Sidsel Nilsdatter Nubgarden 204
Signe Anundsdatter 211
Sigri Knudsdatter 235
Sigrid Eivindsdatter 201
Sigrid Finhart 235
Sigrid Halvorsdatter Haugen 58
Sigrid Nilsen Majestad 109
Sigrid Sanden 199
Sigrid Torgersdatter 201
Sigtryg Jarl 11
Sigur Berg 221
Sigurd Anderson Skar 200
Sigurd Sigurdsen 221
Simon Aamodt 98
Simon Aanrud 149
Simon Evenson 121
Simon Hanson 251
Simon Iverson 99
Simon Lima 16
Simon Løberg 98
Simon Nilsen 154
Simon Olson 233
Simon Olson Slaabakken 323
Simon Roland 316
Simon Rustad 99, 258, 261
Simon Simonson Aamodt 98
Simon Soine 212
Siri Haugerstuen 237
Siri Week 237
Siver Rishovd 184
Sivert Lund 41
Sivert Olson 239
Sjugul Frankrige 60
Sjur Arneson Bly 37
Sjur Brictson 283
Sjur Engeseth 307
Sjur Grinde 76
Sjur Herreid 154
Sjur Satran 310
Skak Ormsen Hauge 157
Skak Thompson Sandvik 139
Snowshoe Thompson 45, 46, 88, 90
Solomon Juneau 21
Sondre Reishus 218, 221
Sophie Michaelsen 42
Sophus Bugge 2, 7

Søren Bachke 92
Søren Bakke 50
Søren Frogner 393, 394
Søren Halvorsen Herrum 144
Søren Hanson Estey 120
Søren Jerman 139
Søren L. Ballestad 110
Søren Larson Ballestad 112
Søren Olson 59, 166, 171
Søren Olson Sørum 59, 166
Søren Sørum 60
Søren Tollefson Bakke 48, 49
Søren Torbjørnson Faaberg 242
Søren Urberg 119
Søren Wilson 95
Staale Torstenson Haugen 178
Steinar Ellefson 184
Steinar Johnson Øverland 208
Steiner Knutson Meaas 199
Steiner Valle 168
Steingrim Steingrimsen Bergrud 196
Sten H. Nerhus 286
Stener Knudson Meaas 200
Stener Mikkelson 266
Stener Olson 103
Stener Thorson 144
Stengrim N. Jellum 259
Stephen Christenson 255
Stephen Jacobson Nygaard 98
Stephen Kubakke 110
Stephen Olson 93, 107, 108, 109, 110, 255
Stephen Olson Helle 93, 107, 108
Stephen Olson Kubakke Helle 107
Stephen Thoreson 295
Styrk Larson 354
Sunnive Sørensdatter 211
Svein Halsteinson 172
Svein Lothe 39
Sven Enderson Hesla 174
Sven Hanson 94, 168
Sven Johnson 346
Sven Jørgenson Trasimot 253
Sven Nørslien 87
Sven Sigurdson Kirkelie 213
Svend Aslaksen 211
Svend Borgen 348
Svend E. Kirkelie 215
Svend E. Solseth 215
Svend Enderson Hesla 175
Svend Foyn 88

Svend H. Grøth 173
Svend Nordgaarden 301, 304
Svend Olson Bidne 184
Svend Olson Kaus 389
Svend Thompson 218, 220
Svennung Dahle 75
Svennung Halvorsen Herrum 144
Svennung Larson Revskil 201
Svennung O. Haugerud 215
Svennung Svennungson 239
Svien in Lien 91
Swede Charley 351
Swen Swenson Rudning 293
Sylvester Orvold 130
Syver Anderson 150
Syver Bjørnson Bakken 265
Syver Bøen 237
Syver Bøle 109
Syver Brustuen 90
Syver Endresen Rosseland 341
Syver Endreson Rosseland 341
Syver G. Gaarder 60
Syver Gaarder 60
Syver Haugerud 259
Syver Hermandson 175
Syver Hoel 145
Syver Holland 37
Syver Hovda 233
Syver Iverson 153
Syver Johnson 60, 87, 248
Syver Johnson Haugerud 259
Syver Johnson Smed 60, 87
Syver Myhren 404
Syver Nilsen 135, 145
Syver Nilsen Galstad 135
Syver Olsen Skalshaugen 233
Syver Olson 150, 231, 233, 290
Syver Olson Skalshaugen 231
Syver Simonsen 238
Syver Skaran 237
Syver Talla 88
Syver Thompson 145
Syver Vesledal 307
Syver Vinje 398
Syver Vold 307
Syvert Boyum 218
Syvert H. Grøth 173
Syvert Ingebretsen 48
Syvert Myhren 399
Syvert Nilsen 309

T

T. G. Mandt 73
T. H. Tønnesen 145
T. K. Thorvildson 74
T. L. Flom 73
T. O. Brekke 260
T. Osmundson 349
T. Thompson 90
Tallak Brokken 213, 214, 215
Tallak Gunderson 172, 173
Tallak Larsen 215
Tallef Olson 200
Tallef Olson Storaasli 200
Taral Ramlo 325, 327
Tarald Halstensen Ramlo 338
Tarald Halstenson Ramlo 323
Tarald Jørandlien 60
Tarald Ramlo 323
Tarald Thompson 260
Tarand Anundsdatter 211
Targe Guttormson Lee 254
Targe Larson Revskil 200
Targe Olson Kragness 200
Tarje Aslakson Grover 201
Tarje Gunnarson Findreng 200
Tellef Grundysen 225
Theo. K. Hundeby 259
Theo. Nesse 208
Theodor Brown 314
Theodore Blegen 108
Thomas Anderson Grønna 174
Thomas Anderson Veblen 108
Thomas Ask 212
Thomas Barland 32
Thomas Davidson 119
Thomas E. Thompson 389
Thomas Erikson 32
Thomas Foste 287
Thomas H. Vindleik 215
Thomas Herreid 154
Thomas Johnson 194, 294, 355
Thomas Knopf 98
Thomas Knoph 251, 345
Thomas Kopperud 209
Thomas Larson 145
Thomas Lerol 212
Thomas Lie 90
Thomas Madland 16, 32
Thomas Nilson 305
Thomas Olson Helle 108

Thomas Osmundsen 348
Thomas Osmundson 251, 344
Thomas Thomassen 251
Thomas Thompson Alsager 398
Thomas Thompson Krosso 215
Thomas Thorson 315
Thomas Trulson Ask 202
Thomas Warp 130
Thomas Wilson Traim 215
Thor Anderson 266
Thor E. Kirkelie 215
Thor Halvorson 242, 399
Thor Halvorson Faaberg 242
Thor Hegland 283
Thor Heyerdahl 138
Thor Jørgenson Postmyhr 345
Thor Olson 248, 364
Thor Olson Auvesaker 248
Thor Olson Faae 202
Thor Thorson Omserud 315
Thora Ingebrigtsdatter Gjesme 197
Thora Ingebrigtsdatter Jesme 197
Thora Lindelien 235
Thorbjørn Andreas Sættre 310
Thorbjørn Thompson 403
Thore Erickson 212
Thore Faae 203, 205
Thore Helgeson Kirkejord 53
Thore Jensen 195
Thore Johnson 212
Thore Knudsen Hoiby 149
Thore Nelson Sunde 203, 207
Thore Olsen Kaasa 56
Thore Olson 314, 315, 317
Thore Olson Faae 203, 205
Thore Olson Kirkebø 314, 315
Thore Quam 212
Thore Signalness 389
Thore Spaanem 90, 91, 93
Thore Thompson Røisland 88
Thore Thoreson Spaanem 90
Thorfin Karlsevni 10
Thorgrim Drengson Rege 215
Thorkel Dengerud 204
Thormod Andreas 221
Thorstein Helgeson Kirkejord 53
Thorstein Knutson 295
Thorstein Olson Bjaadland 17
Thorstein Søgaarden 229
Thorstein Veblen 108, 114
Thorsten Søgaarden 138

Thos. Anderson 175
Thos. O. Helle 109
Thov Kittilson Svimbil 45
Thov Knutsen Traim 56
Thov Olsen Tveten 196
Thov Olsen Tweeten 196
Thov Olson Uvesaker 253
Thrond H. Engen 180
Thrond Jacobson 175
Thrond Kleppo 255
Thrond Lomen 179
Thrond Sæther 309
Thrond Throndsen Hovde 99
Thundering Bear 68
Tideman Knutson Objør 255
Tideman Objør 255
Timan Burtness 59
Timan Gilbertson 195
Timothy Heald 393, 395
Tobias Henderson 201
Tobias Jacobson 239
Tobias Larsen 215
Tobias Larson 226
Tobias Morbæk 119
Tøge Nelson Talla 298
Tøge Talla 298, 299, 300, 301, 303, 307
Tollef A. Harstad 215
Tollef Amundsen Berg 195
Tollef Arneson 175
Tollef Arneson Sanden 183
Tollef Bakke 50
Tollef Golberg 309
Tollef Gunnolfsen Huset 225
Tollef Gunolfson 91
Tollef Gunsteinson Krostu 99
Tollef Hoganson 199
Tollef Knudsen 225
Tollef Krostu 99
Tollef O. Bakke 48
Tollef Olson Grovo 248
Tollef Olson Haugen 240
Tollef Olson Slaabakken 323
Tollef S. Aa 178
Tollef Sanden 183, 184
Tollef Sanden Arneson 183
Tollef Sommerhaugen 265
Tollef T. Haines 125
Tollef T. Heen 125
Tollef Tollefson 248, 251
Tollef Tollefson Rust 248

Tollef Tollefsrud 59
Tollef Waller 82
Tolleiv Røisland 82
Tollev Helgeson 171
Tollev Knutson 218, 220
Tollev Olson 239
Tone Findreng 199
Tone Olsdatter 200
Tone Olsdatter Storaasli 200
Tønnes Larson Ekeren 139
Torbjørn Halvorsen Herrum 144
Torbjørn Hauge 281
Torbjørn Tvedt 309
Tore Bratrud 220
Tore Faae 222
Tore Gullickson 130
Tore Knudsen Jutland 218
Tore Knutsen Jutland 220
Tore O. Bratrud 218
Tore Pedersen Helme 221
Tore Peterson Bergo 265
Tore Peterson Skotland 178
Tore Skotland 180
Tore Svendsen 145
Tore T. Mørk 251
Tore Thompson Mørk 251
Torfinn Karlsevne 1
Torge Johnson Tvedt 90
Torge Torgeson Bakka 225
Torgeir Luraas 183, 184
Torgeir Oxnaberg 237
Torger A. Torgerson 100
Torger Drengson Høftø 213
Torger Felland 214
Torger Halvorsen Rollag 215
Torger Hanson 130
Torger Ingvaldson Haug 149
Torger Johannesen Tendeland 195
Torger Juvland 296
Torger Kjøstulson Sveningen 103
Torger Kragness 199
Torger Lunde 212
Torger Luraas 227
Torger Olson 163, 164, 281, 319
Torger Østenson Luraas 46
Torger Peterson 214
Torger Sveningen 103
Torger T. Felland 215
Torgrim Torgrimson 315
Torjus Abrahamsen 110
Tørjus Kittilsen Eiken 198

Tørjus Kittilsen Eken 198
Torjus Kjøstulsen 110
Torjus O. Flaten 253
Torkel Aagesen Rosaaen 197
Torkel Aageson 196
Torkel Aageson Rosaaen 196
Torkel Aamundsen Indrelid 197
Torkel Aamundsen Lie 197
Torkel Eiteklep 172
Torkel Gunderson Bergo 154
Torkel Haldorson 154
Torkel Halsteinson 172
Torkel Henryson 279
Torkel J. Newgard 345
Torkel J. Nygaard 345
Torkel Knudson Maakestad 37
Torkel Listul 98
Torkel Nilsen 172
Torkel Opstveit 283
Torkel Peterson Eiteklep 173
Torkel Reierson 248
Torkel T. Lund 266
Torkild Hanson Holla 185
Torkild Husværet 60
Torres Thomassen Tyse 345
Torrild Nielsen 323, 338
Torstein Knudsen 61
Torstein Madsen 151
Torstein Olsson Gollo Rue 45
Torstein Reierson 251
Torstein Rosgaard 370, 371, 379
Torstein Rue 45
Torstein Stabek 61
Torstein Torsteinson Rue 45
Torsten Olson Bjaadland 67
Torsten Unseth 136
Tosten A. Aaby 298
Tosten A. Klomsten 138
Tosten Aaby 298, 299
Tosten Dengerud 265
Tosten Ellefson Kvammen 215
Tosten Estensen 293
Tosten Groe 259
Tosten Gunderson Veungen 209
Tosten Johnsen Lommen 195
Tosten Johnson 194, 197
Tosten Johnson Lommen 197
Tosten K. Rogne 110
Tosten Kaasa 180
Tosten Larson Ursdalen Nøbben 217
Tosten Levik 314, 315

Tosten Næsvig 180
Tosten O. Berg 323
Tosten O. Groe 259
Tosten Olson 32, 265
Tosten Olson Bjaadland 32
Tosten Østensen Bøen 293
Tosten Quamme 354
Tosten T. Ringøen 154
Tosten Thompson 90
Tosten Westby 139
Tov Janson 185
Tov Kolien 371, 373
Trine Eriksdatter Berdahl 199
Trond Arneson 237
Trond Bøen 237
Trond O. Steile 251
Trond Olsen 198, 233
Trond Olsen Hemri 198
Trond Richardson Kleppo 253
Truls Haga 195
Truls Kaalsrud 307
Truls Kvi 307
Truls Snedkerpladsen 307
Truls Soland 213
Truls Swenson 198
Truls Vold 307
Turi Larsdatter Paulson 323
Turi Svinnungsen Tyttegraff 153

U

U. Kolkin 179

U. V. Koren 175, 185, 194, 211, 214, 219, 221, 226, 229, 239, 269, 412
Uldrich Wilhelm Vingaard 55
Ulrik J. Hovrud 109
Ulrik Vilhelm Koren 173, 184, 185, 204
Utley Peterson 139

V

Valentin Valentinsen 197
Vebjørn Anderson 266
Victor Lawson 39, 285

W

Waldemar Ager 311
Wier Weeks 281
Wilhelm Augusta Johanneson 201
Wilhelm the Shoemaker 303
William Arveson 103
William Nelson 73
William Painter 188
William Vilas 71
William Wood 336
Willie Thomas 336
Willis A. Gorman 293
Wm. Rønningen 298, 300

Z

Zachary Taylor 219
Zakarias O. Eggum 130

ORDER FORM
(order form may be photocopied)

History of the Norwegian Settlements:
A translated and expanded version of the
1908 De Norske Settlementers Historie and the
1930 Den Siste Folkevandring Sagastubber fra Nybyggerlivet i Amerika
Written by Hjalmar Rued Holand
Translated by Malcolm Rosholt and Helmer M. Blegen

Order via internet
http://www.astrimyastri.com

OR

Order via postal mail
Made check payable to: Astri My Astri Publishing
Send $39.95 plus $10 shipping and handling in USA
(plus 7% sales tax for Iowa residents only)
&
Mail order form copy and payment directly to the printer:
Anundsen Publishing Company
108 Washington St, PO Box 230
Decorah, IA 52101

Name: _____

Address: _____

City/State/Zip: _____

Phone: _____

E-mail: _____

Amount enclosed: _____